THE ROUGH GUIDE TO

Crete

written and researched by

John Fisher and Geoff Garvey

ROUGH GUIDES

roughguides.com

Contents

OPPOSITE FARMER, AMÁRI VALLEY **PREVIOUS PAGE** FALÁSARNA

Introduction to
Crete

Birthplace of Zeus and cradle of Europe's earliest civilization, Crete is justifiably known as the "Great Island". Fabulous beaches and crystalline seas are just the start of the story; a substantial land in its own right, Crete can also boast enticingly cosmopolitan cities, a host of fascinating historic towns and unspoilt villages, and mountains high enough to keep snow on their peaks well into summer.

Because the island is so big, it is far from dominated by visitors. Indeed, thanks to a flourishing agricultural economy – including some surprisingly good vineyards – Crete is one of the few Greek islands that could probably support itself without tourists. So although tourism is an important part of the economy, traditional life also survives, along with the **hospitality** that forms part of that tradition. There are plenty of visitors, of course, and the populous **north coast** can be as sophisticated as you want it; here you'll find every facility imaginable and, in places, crowds of package tourists determined to exploit them to the full. But in the less-known coastal reaches of the **south** it's still possible to escape the development, while the high mountains and agricultural plains of the interior are barely touched. One of the most rewarding things to do on Crete is to rent a vehicle and head for remoter villages, often just a few kilometres off some heavily beaten track. Here the island's customs, its everyday life, dialects, song, traditional dress and festivals, and above all its welcome to strangers, survive to an extent that's exceptional in modern Europe.

The **mountains**, which dominate the view as you approach Crete, run from one end of the island to the other, and make all but the shortest journey inland an expedition. They are perhaps the island's greatest surprise and biggest reward, providing welcome relief in the heat of summer, giving Crete much of its character, and making the place feel much larger than it really is. Cut through by gorges and studded by caves, they offer fabulous **walking** too, from easy strolls to strenuous climbs, as well as a huge variety of habitats for **wildlife**, including many large birds of prey. For birdwatchers and wildflower spotters, Crete is a rich source of excitement.

ABOVE MINOAN FRESCO

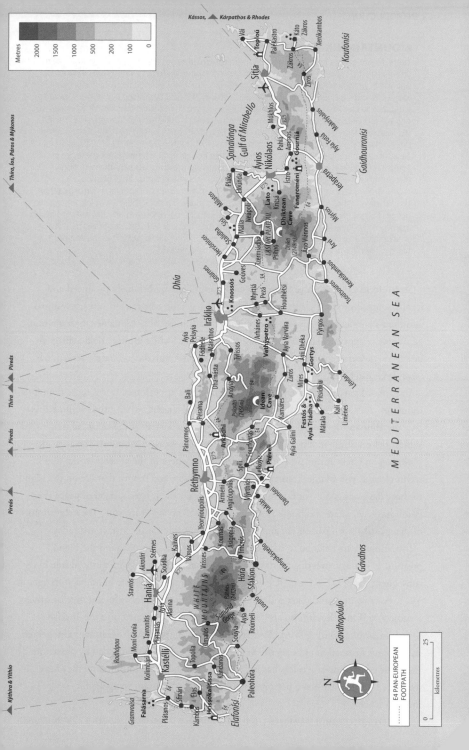

MOUNTAIN HIKING

There are few places in the world where high **mountains** so close to the sea combine with an often perfect climate. This is a paradise for climbers, birdwatchers, botanists and nature lovers, but above all for **walkers** – whether on a brief stroll or a week-long hike. A network of ancient footpaths and shepherds' trails allows you to walk all day and barely see a soul. Yet, should you want to, you can always find a village and Cretan hospitality ensures that almost wherever you end up you will eat well and spend the night in comfort. The daddy of Crete's treks is the **E4**, the long-distance European footpath that traverses the island, taking in many of the highest peaks en route. To walk the entire length takes weeks, but there are plenty of sections that are easily accessible and where you can hike for a few hours. Some of the best of these are in the southwest, where the path splits: one branch following the coast and another winding through the heights of the Lefká Óri; the magnificent Samariá Gorge links the two.

One striking feature of Crete's topography is the sheer number of spectacular **gorges** that slash their way through the mountains. In addition to the Samariá, there are at least fifty more gorges in the Lefká Óri alone, many barely visited at all. On a hot summer's day, heading down a gorge is the ideal hike: you're shaded from the sun's ferocity, with an empty beach and a welcome swim to reward you at the end. Arrange for someone to collect you so you don't have to toil back up, and you have the makings of a perfect day.

Cretan **food** can also prove an unexpected bonus. The traditionally produced and locally sourced produce – sun-ripened fruit and vegetables especially – are exceptional, and there's an increasing awareness of culinary traditions. In fashionable city restaurants, grandma's recipes are being rediscovered to great effect, while in more rustic village or beachside tavernas, the age-old combination of superb ingredients, simply served, has never been forgotten.

An extraordinary **history** plays a large part in Crete's appeal, too. It was more than four thousand years ago that the island's story began to be shaped, when, from around 2000 BC, the **Minoans** developed an advanced and cultured society at the centre of a substantial maritime trading empire: the first real European civilization. The artworks produced on Crete at this time are unsurpassed anywhere in the ancient world, and it seems clear, as you wander through the Minoan palaces and towns, that life on the island in those days was good. For five hundred years, by far the longest period of peace the island has seen, Crete was home to a civilization well ahead of its time. The excavations of the great Minoan palaces are among the island's prime tourist attractions today.

The Minoans are believed to have come originally from Anatolia, and the island's position as strategic **meeting point** between east and west has played a crucial role in its subsequent history. The Greek flag was raised over Crete barely one hundred years ago, in 1913. For two thousand years and more before that the island was fought over by others – subject to Rome, Byzantium and Venice before being subsumed into the Turkish Ottoman empire. During World War II Crete was occupied by the Germans and gained the dubious distinction of being the first place to be successfully invaded by parachute. Each one of these diverse rulers has left some mark, and more importantly they have imprinted on the islanders a personality toughened by constant struggles for independence.

OPPOSITE CLOCKWISE FROM TOP LEFT FORTEZZA, RÉTHYMNO; CRETAN BREAKFAST; PALM BEACH, RÉTHYMNO PROVINCE

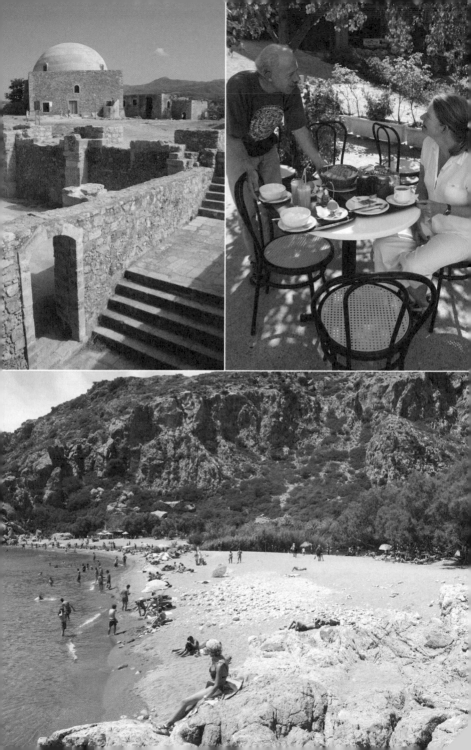

Where to go

Every part of Crete has its loyal devotees who will argue fervently in defence of their favourite spot. On the whole, though, if you want to get away from it all you should head for the ends of the island – west, towards Haniá and the smaller, less well-connected places along the south and west coasts, or east to Sitía. Wherever you're staying, you won't have to go far inland to escape the crowds.

In the centre of the island the sprawling city of **Iráklio** (Heraklion) is home to a magnificent **archeological museum** and lies just a few kilometres from **Knossós**, the greatest of the **Minoan palaces**. You'll find other reminders of history all over Crete, but the best known are mostly here, near the heart of the island; above all **Festós** and **Ayía Triádha** in the south (with Roman **Górtys** to provide contrast) and the palace of **Mália** on the north coast.

As for **beaches**, you'll find great ones almost anywhere on the north coast. From Iráklio to Áyios Nikólaos there's very heavy development, and most package tourists are aiming for the resort hotels in this region. These places can be fun if nightlife and crowds are what you're after – particularly the biggest of them, like **Mália**, **Hersónisos** and **Áyios Nikólaos**. The majority of the island's most luxurious **hotels** and **inclusive resorts** are near Áyios Nikólaos, especially arund **Eloúnda**, overlooking the Gulf of Mirabello. Further east things get quieter: **Sitía** is a place of real character, and beyond it on the east coast are a number of laidback resorts, as well as the beautiful palm beach at **Vái**, a favourite with day-trippers from across the island, and the relatively little-visited Minoan palace of **Zákros**. To the west there's more development around both **Réthymno** and **Haniá**, the most attractive of the island's big towns. Other places at this end of the island tend to be on a smaller scale.

Along the **south coast**, where the mountains frequently drop straight down to the sea, resorts are more scattered. Only a handful of places are really developed – **Ierápetra**, **Ayía Galíni**, **Mátala**, **Paleohóra** – with a few more, like **Plakiás** and **Makriyialós**, on their way. But the lesser-known spots in between, not always easy to get to, are some of the most attractive in Crete.

For many people, unexpected highlights also turn out to be the Island's **Venetian forts** and defensive walls and bastions – dominant at Réthymno, Iráklio and Haniá, magnificent at **Frangokástello**, and found in various stages of ruin all over Crete. The **Byzantine churches** and remote **monasteries** dotted across the island, many containing

A RURAL ISLAND

Despite the rapid growth in the last fifty years of towns like Haniá, Réthymno and particularly Iráklio, Crete remains a land rooted in the **countryside**. Almost everyone seems to have some connection to the land – a smallholding where they grow fresh produce or a village where parents or grandparents still live. The villages, each with its own character and traditions, are the island's pulse, where the pace of the year is determined by the agricultural calendar. Here you can still find everyday life lived as it has been for centuries, where potters spin clay into ewers and jars, weavers make rugs in traditional patterns and farmers cart their olives to the local press.

Author picks

Our authors have explored every corner of Crete in order to uncover the very best it has to offer. Here are some of their favourite things to see and do.

Delightful villages They may not be famous, but they're perfectly picturesque. Don't miss Aspró (p.257), Argiróupolis (p.197), Loutró (p.279) and Kamilári (p.108).

Amazing adventures Bungee jump into a 140m gorge at Arádhena (p.285), windsurf at Koureménos (p.159), or trek down the sensational Samariá Gorge, Europe's longest (p.275).

Fresh from the sea Feasting on fish and crustaceans in sight of the sea is a tip-top Cretan treat. Four of the best places to do it are Caravella (p.311), To Akrogiali (p.297), Taverna Spinalonga (p.131) and Hióna (p.162).

Brilliant beaches Among hundreds of superb beaches standouts include tropical Elafonísi (p.305), the idyllic white-sand Balos Bay (p.298) and the Caribbean-style palm beach at Vái (p.156).

Fantastic forts If castles are your thing Réthymno's Fortezza (p.188), Frangokástello (p.291) and the stirring island forts of Spinalónga (p.130) and Gramvoúsa (p.298) won't disappoint.

Aladdin's caves Crete has thousands of caves, many of which can be explored. The Sendóni (p.207), Melidhóni (p.206) and Dhiktean (p.138) caverns are all well worth a trip.

Intriguing islands The seas surrounding Crete are dotted with dozens of offshore islands and islets. Spinalónga (p.130), Gramvoúsa (p.298), Gaidhouronísi (p.177) and Gávdhos (p.318) all have a unique character.

Mesmerizing museums Iráklio's magnificent Archeological Museum has reopened after a stunning makeover (p.54) but the museums at Haniá (p.240), and Sitía (p.152) are also well worth a visit.

Marvellous views Mátala is famed for its crimson sunsets (p.105), hilltop Mírthios has a fabulous view over the Libyan Sea (p.224) and sunrise seen from the summit of Psilorítis is unforgettable (p.211).

> Our author recommendations don't end here. We've flagged up our favourite places – a perfectly sited hotel, an atmospheric café, a special restaurant – throughout the guide, highlighted with the ★ symbol.

FROM TOP VÁI; BUNGEE JUMPING; FRANGOKÁSTELLO

stunning medieval **wall paintings**, are also unexpected treasures. Smaller Cretan **towns**, supply centres for the island's farmers, are always worth visiting for their vibrant markets, shops and tavernas, whilst Réthymno and Haniá boast atmospheric, cluttered old centres, whose narrow alleys are crammed with relics of the Venetian and Turkish eras.

The mountains and valleys of the interior deserve far more attention than they get, too. Only the **Lasíthi** plateau in the east and the **Samariá Gorge** in the west see really large numbers of visitors, but turn off the main roads almost anywhere and you'll find villages going about their daily agricultural routine, often in the midst of astonishingly beautiful scenery. This is especially true in the west, where the Lefká Óri – the **White Mountains** – dramatically dominate every view, but the **Psilorítis** range in the centre of the island also offers magnificent scenery and mountain villages along with some of the island's finest walking, while the **Sitían** mountains in the east are far less explored.

When to go

The combination of high **mountains** and warm seas, together with a position as far south as any in Europe, makes for an exceptionally long season: you can get a decent tan in Crete right into October and swim at least from April until early November. **Spring** is the prime time to come: in April and May the island is relatively empty of visitors, the weather clear and not overpoweringly hot, and every scene is brightened by a profusion of wildflowers.

By mid-June the rush is beginning. **July** and **August** are not only the hottest, the most crowded and most expensive months, they are also intermittently blighted by fierce winds and accompanying high seas; the south coast is particularly prone to these. In September the crowds gradually begin to thin out, and **autumn** can again be a great time to visit – but now the landscape looks parched and tired, and there's a feeling of things gradually winding down.

Winters are mild, but also vaguely depressing: many places are shut, it can rain sporadically, sometimes for days, and there's far less life in the streets. In the mountains it snows, even to the extent where villages can be cut off; on the south coast it's generally warmer, soothed by a breeze from Africa. You may get a week or more of really fine weather in the middle of winter, but equally you can have sudden viciously cold snaps right through into March.

AVERAGE MONTHLY TEMPERATURES AND RAINFALL (IRÁKLIO)

	Jan	Feb	Mar	Apr	May	Jun	Jul	Aug	Sep	Oct	Nov	Dec
Max °C	15	15	17	20	23	27	29	29	27	24	20	17
Max °F	60	60	63	68	73	81	84	84	81	75	68	63
Min °C	9	9	9	12	15	19	22	22	19	17	13	11
Min °F	48	48	48	54	60	66	72	72	66	63	55	52
Rainfall (mm)	76	48	48	21	10	1	0.5	1	7	30	65	79

OPPOSITE HANIÁ; CHAPEL OF ÁYIOS PANDELEÍMON, RIZINÍA

18

things not to miss

It's not possible to see everything Crete has to offer in one trip – and we don't suggest you try. What follows, in no particular order, is a subjective selection of the island's highlights, including world-famous archeological sites, stunning mountain ranges, lively resorts and great beaches. All highlights have a page reference to take you straight into the Guide, where you can find out more. Coloured numbers refer to chapters in the Guide section.

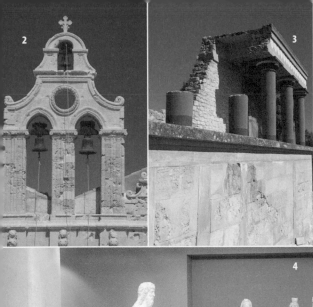

1 LOUTRÓ
Page 279

Accessible only by boat or on foot, this idyllic retreat on the edge of its own bay is the perfect place to get away from it all.

2 MONÍ ARKÁDHI
Page 191

The most celebrated of Crete's numerous monasteries has a fine Venetian church and is an emblem of the island's struggle for independence.

3 KNOSSÓS
Page 63

Crete's biggest attraction, the 3500-year-old Minoan palace is a sprawling maze of royal chambers, grand staircases, storerooms and workshops.

4 ARCHEOLOGICAL MUSEUM, IRÁKLIO
Page 54

The finest collection of Minoan artefacts in the world, with a brand new setting to do them justice.

5 LASÍTHI PLATEAU
Page 135

Traditional village life continues on this fertile mountain plateau, famed for its traditional windmills, where you'll also see a riot of springtime wildflowers.

6 **ELAFONÍSI**
Page 305
Turquoise waters, rose-tinted sands and a shallow, warm lagoon make this coral island-beach one of Crete's most exotic locations.

7 **WINDSURFING**
Page 159
Koureménos Beach is Crete's top windsurfing spot, with constant winds almost year-round.

8 **WILDLIFE**
Page 347
Crete has plenty of spectacular flora and fauna to seek out, from vultures, which can be seen almost everywhere, to rarities like the magnificent lammergeier vulture or fragile mountain orchids.

9 **HIKING**
Pages 6, 27 & 36
Crete's countless walking opportunities include spectacular gorge hikes that take you from the mountains to the sea.

10 **HANIÁ**
Page 237
Wander the streets of Haniá's old town to discover its beautiful harbour and haunting vestiges of a Minoan, Venetian and Ottoman past.

11 **ÁYIOS NIKÓLAOS**
Page 120
With no end of restaurants, bars and clubs, this is one of the island's most vibrant and picturesque towns.

10

11

LEFKÁ ÓRI
Page 237

The Lefká Óri, or White Mountains, snowcapped right through to June, dominate the western end of the island, offering some unbeatable walking, hiking and adventure.

 BEACHES
Page 298

From great swathes of sand at the north coast resorts to tiny pebble coves overshadowed by stunning mountains in the south, Crete has beaches to suit any mood.

 CAVES
Page 206

The awesome Melidhóni Cave is just one of hundreds dotted around the island, many of which can be visited.

 LYRA MUSIC
Page 208

The three-stringed *lyra* is Crete's "national instrument" – no baptism party, wedding feast or celebration is complete without its accompaniment.

 RÉTHYMNO
Page 187

Lose yourself in the old quarter of Réthymno, an elegant town dominated by its Venetian fortress and fine beach.

 THE KAFENÍO
Page 32

Focal point of traditional Cretan life, the *kafenío* is a great place for lively discussions or games of *távli* (backgammon) while downing a coffee, an ouzo or a fiery *raki*.

BYZANTINE FRESCOES
Page 75

Some of the finest Byzantine frescoes in Greece are to be found in Crete's country churches.

15

16

17

18

Itineraries

There are as many potential itineraries as there are visitors to Crete, and you'll no doubt want to create your own to reflect personal interests, whether those be mountain climbing, birdwatching or lying on the beach. The itineraries below should begin to give a flavour of what the island has to offer.

THE GREAT ISLAND

The Grand Tour, taking in the best-known destinations. Allow at least two weeks, taking time off for the beaches and hikes along the way.

❶ Iráklio The inevitable starting point, Crete's capital boasts a world-class archeological museum, and is the easiest base from which to visit the ruins at Knossós. **See p.46**

❷ Áyios Nikólaos Home to the finest of Crete's luxury resort hotels, this is a beautiful town with good restaurants and nightlife. **See p.120**

❸ Sitía Laidback capital of the far east, offering excellent food, subtle charms and an escape from mass tourism. **See p.150**

❹ Zákros A tiny, isolated seaside hamlet with a lovely pebble beach and one of the four great Minoan palaces. **See p.163**

❺ Mátala From hippy hideout in the 1960s to crowded resort today, Mátala and its beachside caves have managed to retain a unique charm. **See p.105**

❻ Réthymno A university city with an enchanting old town, a big sandy beach and beautiful countryside in easy reach. **See p.187**

❼ Haniá The island's second city is for many its most attractive; gateway to the mountains of the west and with plenty of sophisticated charm. **See p.237**

THE EAST: MINOANS, MOUNTAINS AND BEACHES

This itinerary offers a little of everything the east of the island has to offer, with ample opportunities for getting to the beach or hiking into the hills. You could easily do it in four days, or break the journey into day trips from a base almost anywhere in the east.

❶ Knossós The greatest of the Minoan palaces, Knossós lies in the countryside just behind Iráklio. Partly reconstructed and with many of the original frescoes copied, it's an extraordinary sight. **See p.63**

❷ Mália Both the island's most notorious resort and an important Minoan palace, in a glorious seaside setting. Some of Crete's sandiest beaches lie between here and Knossós. **See p.85**

❸ Kárfi An ancient Minoan site on a limestone pinnacle, with spectacular views over the coast and the Lasíthi plateau. Little survives of the site itself, but the journey, the taxing hike up and the chance to visit the plateau afterwards are irresistible. **See p.137**

❹ Spinalónga This island and one-time leper colony can be reached only by boat, with swimming in crystal-clear waters along the way. **See p.130**

❺ Gourniá A unique Minoan town set on the isthmus at Crete's narrowest point, Gourniá

ABOVE OLIVE GROVES NEAR ZÁKROS

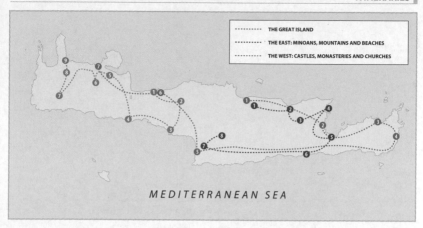

THE GREAT ISLAND

THE EAST: MINOANS, MOUNTAINS AND BEACHES

THE WEST: CASTLES, MONASTERIES AND CHURCHES

MEDITERRANEAN SEA

allows a glimpse of the lives of ordinary Cretans four thousand years ago. See p.143

❺ **Mýrtos** A tranquil, laidback spot on the sunny south coast where there's little to do but lie on the beach, swim, eat and drink. See p.178

❼ **Ayía Triádha** Tiny and enigmatic, Minoan Ayía Triádha has glorious views of both mountains and sea, with easy access to both. It's also very near the major palace at Festós, and the Roman ruins of Górtys. See **p.101**

❽ **Zarós** A wholly traditional village in the shadow of the Psilorítis mountains, Zarós offers some great places to stay and to eat, as well as lovely walks. See p.92

THE WEST: CASTLES, MONASTERIES AND CHURCHES

This itinerary, covering the highlights of the west, takes in some of the region's most famous castles, monasteries and wonderful Byzantine painted churches, many of them located in supremely picturesque locations.

❶ **Fortezza, Réthymno** Sited on a hill, this vast sixteenth-century fortress, the largest ever built by the Venetians, dominates the skyline above the provincial capital. See p.188

❷ **Moní Arkádhi** The island's most important monastery – with a fine Venetian church – is a Cretan shrine to the nineteenth-century independence struggle. See p.191

❸ **Moní Preveli** Near the sea – with a handy beach to swim from – this is another of Crete's great monastic settlements that played a heroic role in World War II. See p.228

❹ **Frangokástello** Almost on the beach, this imposing fourteenth-century Venetian fort was an unsuccessful attempt to subdue the unruly region of Sfakiá. See p.291

❺ **Áyios Nikólaos, Samonas** One of the most beautiful churches on the island, Áyios Nikólaos occupies a dramatic setting and holds some of the most brilliant medieval frescoes ever painted on Crete. See p.255

❻ **Chapel of Metamórphosis Sotírou, Mesklá** Hidden away in a mountain village, this chapel celebrating Christ's transfiguration has superb frescoes dating from the fourteenth century. See p.272

❼ **Áyios Ioánnis, Kándanos** One of four Byzantine churches in this famous village, all with fine frescoes. A dozen others in surrounding villages also have superb paintings. See p.306

❽ **Mihail Arhángelos, Episkopí** With parts dating from the sixth century, the church of the Archangel is possibly the oldest on the island; it also has a unique architecture and tenth-century frescoes. See p.268

❾ **Moní Goniá, Kolimbári** Set by the sea, this seventeenth-century monastery played a stirring role in Crete's wars against the Turks – and has cannonballs lodged in its walls to prove it. See p.267

TOUR BOATS AT SPINALÓNGA ISLAND

Basics

Getting there

By far the easiest way to get to Crete is to fly. The vast majority of visitors are Northern Europeans on package tours that include a direct charter flight. Many of these charter companies sell flight-only tickets on their planes, and there are a limited number of direct scheduled flights too. Overland routes are long, tortuous and expensive, so we've included only the briefest details here.

Even if your starting point is outside Europe the most cost-effective way to reach Crete may well be to get to London – or Amsterdam, Frankfurt or another Northern European hub – and pick up an onward flight from there. The chief disadvantage of direct flights to Crete is a lack of flexibility; most companies have only one or two flights a week. For greater choice, you may have to fly to Athens and take a domestic flight or ferry from there (see p.23).

There are two main **airports**: at **Iráklio** (Heraklion) for the centre and east of the island, and at **Haniá** (Chania) for the west; both have regular charters from across Europe and numerous daily flights from Athens, plus some scheduled international services with budget airlines. **Sitía** in the far east has just a few flights from Athens and regional Greek airports, though that may change.

When **buying flights** it always pays to shop around and bear in mind that many websites don't include charter or budget airlines in their results. Be aware too that a **package deal**, with accommodation included, can sometimes be as cheap as, or even cheaper than, a flight alone: there's no rule that says you have to use your accommodation every night, or even at all.

Flights from the UK and Ireland

The only **direct flights** to Crete are with budget airlines easyJet, Ryanair and Jet2, or with charter airlines. Don't expect them to be cheap though: unless you book far in advance, there are few bargains to be had. **Fares** depend on the season,

with the highest in July, August and during Easter week. But May, June and September are also popular, and since no direct flights operate through the winter (most run from April to mid-October), bargains are rare at any time. In theory, easyJet can fly you from Gatwick to Iráklio for as little as £80 return, but you'll have to move very fast to find fares this low. Realistically you can expect to pay £150–300 return at most times of the year; more if you leave your booking late.

EasyJet (W easyjet.com) flies from Gatwick (daily), Manchester (3 weekly) and Bristol (2 weekly) to Iráklio; and to Haniá four times a week from Gatwick. Jet2 (W jet2.com) has flights to Iráklio from Leeds-Bradford (3 weekly), Glasgow and Manchester (both 2 weekly), East Midlands and Newcastle (once a week each). Ryanair (W ryanair.com) flies to Haniá from Stansted (2 weekly) and Glasgow, Leeds and East Midlands (once a week each).

Most **charter operators** offer very similar flight-only deals, either through their own websites or through package and specialist operators; prices from airports outside London are generally somewhat higher. In summer there are direct charters from most UK regional airports: the biggest operators are Thomas Cook (W flythomascook.com) and Thomson (W thomsonfly.com), each serving numerous regional airports; Avro (W avro.co.uk), with flights from Gatwick, Birmingham, Manchester, East Midlands and Newcastle; and Monarch (W monarch.co.uk), serving Gatwick, Leeds, Manchester and Birmingham.

If you can't find a direct flight, want more flexibility or are travelling out of season, consider travelling **via Athens** (some flights are also routed via Thessaloníki), with a domestic flight or ferry from there to Crete. British Airways (W ba.com) and Aegean (W aegeanair.com) each have daily flights from Heathrow; easyJet can fly you direct from Gatwick, Manchester or Edinburgh. From Athens you will then have to arrange onward transport to Crete (see p.23).

From Dublin there are direct charters to Crete through the summer (rarely less than €400). Aer Lingus (W aerlingus.com) also flies direct to Athens

(April–Sept, 3 weekly) with fares starting at €100 each way, though you can easily pay twice that. At other times of year you'll have to make at least one stop en route to Greece, in London or elsewhere.

Flights from the USA and Canada

Between May and October there are direct **nonstop flights** pretty much daily to Athens from New York JFK with Delta (Ⓦdelta.com) and Hellenic Imperial (Ⓦhellenicairways.com) and from Philadelphia with US Airways (Ⓦusairways.com). Code-sharing airlines can quote through fares with one of the above, or a European partner, from virtually every major US city, connecting at New York, Toronto or a European hub such as London or Frankfurt.

Fares vary greatly; book as far ahead as possible to get the best price. The lowest starting point is around $800 for a restricted, off-season return flight from the east coast, rising to about $1000 for a similar deal in summer; from the west coast, expect to pay ten to twenty percent more. The lower fares are rarely on the most direct flights, so check the routing to avoid lengthy delays or stopovers. Remember too that you may be better off getting a domestic flight to New York or Philadelphia and heading directly to Athens from there, or buying a cheap flight to London (beware of changing airports) or another European city, and travel onward from there.

As with the USA, airfares **from Canada** vary depending on where you start your journey, and whether you take a direct service. Air Canada (Ⓦaircanada.com) flies to Athens out of Toronto, with a stop in Montréal, from once to four times a week depending on the time of year; they're rarely the cheapest option, though. Air Transat (Ⓦairtransat.com) also has seasonal weekly flights from Toronto and Montréal to Athens. Otherwise you'll have to choose among one- or two-stop itineraries on a variety of European carriers, or perhaps Delta via New York. Costs run from Can$900 return in low season from Toronto to more than double that from Vancouver in high season.

For all of the above, a **connecting flight to Crete** will add US$75–150 (Can$80–160), depending on season and airline.

Flights from Australia and New Zealand

There are **no direct flights** from Australia or New Zealand to Greece; you'll have to change planes in Southeast Asia or Europe. Tickets bought direct from the airlines tend to be expensive; travel agents or Australia-based websites generally offer much better deals on fares and have the latest information on limited specials and stopovers. For a simple return fare, you may also have to buy an add-on internal flight to get you to the international departure point.

Fares **from Australia** start from around Aus$1800 return, rising to around Aus$2600 depending on season, routing, validity, number of stopovers, etc. The shortest flights and best fares are generally with airlines like Thai (Ⓦthaiair.com), Singapore (Ⓦsingaporeair.com), Etihad (Ⓦetihadairways.com) and Emirates (Ⓦemirates.com) that can fly you directly to Athens from their Asian or Gulf hubs, though you'll also find offers on Swiss (Ⓦswiss.com), KLM (Ⓦklm.com) and other European carriers. **From New Zealand**, prices are significantly higher: rarely less than NZ$2200, rising to more than NZ$3000 for a more flexible high-season flight.

If Greece is only one stop on a longer journey, you might consider buying a **Round-the-World** (RTW) fare. With luck you might find something for around Aus$2500/NZ$2750, although Greece is rarely included in the cheaper deals, which means you might have to stump up around Aus$3700/NZ$4000 for one of the fully flexible multi-stop fares from One World or the Star Alliance. At that price, you may be better off with a cheaper deal and a separate ticket to Greece once you get to Europe.

Flights from South Africa

There are currently no direct flights from **South Africa** to Greece. Alternative routes to Athens include EgyptAir (Ⓦegyptair.com) via Cairo, Emirates, Etihad or Qatar Airways (Ⓦqatarairways.com) via the Gulf, or just about any of the major European airlines through their domestic hub. Prices start at ZAR6500–7000 for a good low-season deal, rising to double that in high season or if the cheaper seats have gone.

Overland from the UK, Ireland and the rest of Europe

As a result of the economic crisis, all international and some domestic **Greek rail routes** have been **suspended**, and once you reach Crete there are no trains at all. However, that doesn't necessarily mean that you can't travel most of the way to Crete by **train**, provided you have three or four days to spare and accept that it will almost always work out more expensive than flying. Travelling by train offers the chance to stop over on the way; with an InterRail (for European residents only) or Eurail (for all others) pass you could take in Greece as part of a wider rail trip around Europe. The most practical route from Britain crosses France and Italy before embarking on the ferry from Bari or Brindisi to Pátra (see below). Booking well in advance (essential in summer) and going for the cheapest seats on each leg, you can theoretically buy individual tickets for less than £150/€180/$240 each way. Using rail passes will cost you more, but give far more flexibility. For full details, check out the Man in Seat 61 website (ⓦ seat61.com).

Driving to Crete can also be worth considering if you want to explore en route or are going to stay for an extended period. The most popular **route** is again down through France and Italy to catch one of the Adriatic ferries. The much longer alternative through Eastern Europe (Hungary, Romania and Bulgaria) only makes sense if you want to explore the Greek mainland on the way.

Once in **Italy**, regular car and passenger ferries link Venice, Ancona, Bari and Brindisi with Pátra (Patras, at the northwest tip of the Peloponnese). From here you can cut across country to Pireás for daily ferries to Crete, or head down through the Peloponnese to Kalamáta or Yíthio, from where there are a couple of weekly sailings to Kastélli in western Crete.

Flights from Greece to Crete

Flying to Crete **from Greece** doesn't necessarily mean going via Athens, although the vast majority of people do. There are also daily direct flights with Aegean (ⓦ aegeanair.com) and Olympic (ⓦ olympicair.com) from Thessaloníki, and in summer from some of the larger islands, as well as connections from every other regional Greek airport. Local operators Sky Express (ⓦ skyexpress .gr) and Minoan Air (ⓦ minoanair.com) also serve various smaller islands. From Athens, however, Olympic, Aegean and Cyprus Airways (ⓦ cyprusair .com) between them operate at least twelve flights a day to Iráklio in peak season, and six daily to Haniá, while Astra Airlines (ⓦ astra-airlines.gr) flies six days a week to Sitía. Journey time is less than an hour. This may seem plenty of flights, but in summer they can be heavily booked. If time is your main consideration, flying is good value when weighed against a ferry trip: one-way **prices** start from around €75.

Ferries from Greece to Crete

The vast majority of ferry traffic to Crete goes from **Pireás** (the port of Athens), from where there are overnight services every day throughout the year to Iráklio and Haniá, plus daytime services in summer and at other peak periods. There are also four weekly overnight sailings to Réthymno and much slower ferries, once or twice a week, to Kastélli and Sitía.

Much the most useful of the other services is that from the **Peloponnese**. The schedule is somewhat confusing and varies according to the season, but generally there's at least one departure a week from Yíthio and one from Kalamáta to Kastélli.

Ferries are operated by ANEK (ⓦ anek.gr; Iráklio, Haniá and Sitía), Minoan (ⓦ minoan.gr; Iráklio), Cretan Lines (ⓦ cretanlines.gr; Réthymno) and LANE (ⓦ Lane .gr; Kastélli and the Peloponnese route); info for all of them can be found at ⓦ openseas.gr and ⓦ ferries.gr.

Pireás is about an hour from Athens airport by bus (#X96; at least 2 hourly, day and night; €5), or easily reached on the metro from central Athens. A taxi from the airport will cost around €40. You can buy **tickets** online, or from dozens of agencies in Pireás or in central Athens, as well as from booths on the docks near the boats. If you're taking a car or want a cabin it's worth booking ahead, but deck-class tickets are always available on the spot.

These cheapest tickets give you the run of almost the entire boat, excluding the cabins, some reserved seating and the upper class restaurant and bar. Most of the ferries serving Crete are modern and reasonably luxurious, with plenty of café and "pullman seating" areas inside, though often without a huge amount of deck space. If you are travelling deck class, it's worth getting on board reasonably early to claim a good space. Cabins are also available, ranging from four-berth, shared cabins inside (all en suite and perfectly adequate) up to deluxe suites with huge picture windows.

Prices are similar on all the routes: around €35 deck class, €60 for a berth in a basic cabin, and €80–100 per person in a luxurious double, with cars going for €85 and motorbikes for €20.

Agents and operators

Just about every mainstream **tour operator** includes Crete in its portfolio. You'll find far more interesting alternatives, however, through the small **specialist agencies**. As well as traditional village-based accommodation, many of these offer **walking** or **nature holidays** and cater for other special interests such as **yoga** and **art**.

PACKAGE OPERATORS

Hidden Greece UK ☎ 020 8758 4707, ⓦ hidden-greece.co.uk. Specialist agent putting together tailor-made packages to smaller destinations at reasonable prices.

Homeric Tours US ☎ 1800 223 5570, ⓦ homerictours.com. Hotel packages, individual tours, escorted group tours (though none exclusively to Crete), and fly/drive deals. Good source of inexpensive flights.

Inntravel UK ☎ 01653 617001, ⓦ inntravel.co.uk. High-quality packages and tailor-made itineraries and fly-drives; also walking and other special-interest holidays.

Olympic Holidays UK ☎ 0800 093 3322, ⓦ olympicholidays.com. Huge package holiday company specializing in Greece; all standards from cheap and cheerful to five-star, and often a good source of last-minute bargains and cheap flights.

Simply Crete UK ☎ 0871 231 4050, ⓦ www.simplytravel.co.uk. Although part of the vast TUI organization, Simply Crete still manages a personal touch, and has plenty of excellent, upmarket accommodation across the island.

Sun Island Tours Australia ☎ 1300 665 673, ⓦ sunislandtours .com.au. Good choice of hotel-based package holidays.

HISTORY AND GENERAL INTEREST TOURS

Andante Travels UK ☎ 01722 713800, ⓦ andantetravels.com. Minoan archeology tours with expert guides.

Hellenic Adventures US ☎ 1 800 851 6349, ⓦ hellenic adventures.com. Tailor-made itineraries plus small-group tours that include Crete along with other parts of Greece.

True Greece US ☎ 1 800 817 7098, ⓦ truegreece.com. Upmarket escorted travel and custom-made trips including special interests such as cooking.

Astra US ☎ 303 321 5403, ⓦ astragreece.com. Very personal, idiosyncratic, two-week tours led by veteran Hellenophile Thordis Simonsen.

WALKING AND WILDLIFE TOURS

ATG Oxford UK ☎ 01865 315678, ⓦ atg-oxford.co.uk. Pricey but high-standard guided walks in the White Mountains.

Jonathan's Tours ☎ +33 561 046 447, ⓦ jonathanstours.com. Family-run walking holidays with a very experienced guide – English, but based in France.

Naturetrek UK ☎ 01962 733051, ⓦ naturetrek.co.uk. Spring and autumn botanical and birdwatching tours.

Ramblers Holidays UK ☎ 01707 331133, ⓦ ramblersholidays .co.uk. Big, specialist walking-holiday company with a number of options on Crete.

ACTIVITY AND PERSONAL DEVELOPMENT TOURS

Classic Adventures US ☎ 1 800 777 8090, ⓦ classicadventures .com. Twelve-day biking tours.

Cretan Adventures Crete ☎ +30 2810 332772, ⓦ cretan adventures.gr. Biking, hiking, family adventures, and activities including rappel, canyoning and climbing. You'll have to make your own arrangements to get to Crete, though.

Free Spirit Travel UK ☎ 01273 564230, ⓦ freespirituk.com. Yoga and meditation in western Crete, plus some walking holidays.

Freewheeling Adventures Canada & US ☎ 1 800 672 0775, ⓦ freewheeling.ca. Eight-day cycling tours.

Northwest Passage US ☎ 1 800 RECREATE, ⓦ nwpassage.com. Excellent sea-kayaking and hiking "inn-to-inn" tours of Crete, plus art and yoga holidays.

Sportif UK ☎ 01273 844919, ⓦ sportif.travel. Windsurfing packages and instruction in Palékastro.

Yoga Plus UK ☎ 01273 276175, ⓦ yogaplus.co.uk. Ashtanga yoga courses in a remote part of the south.

VILLA AND APARTMENT HOLIDAYS

Cachet Travel UK ☎ 020 8847 8700, ⓦ cachet-travel.co.uk. Attractive range of villas and apartments, plus some boutique hotels.

CV Travel UK ☎ 020 7401 1010, ⓦ cvtravel.co.uk. Upmarket villas, mainly in Eloúnda and Áyios Nikólaos.

Freelance Holidays UK ☎ 01789 297705, ⓦ freelance-holidays .co.uk. Good-value apartment and villa holidays across Crete, mostly in the west.

Greek Islands Club UK ☎ 020 8232 9780, ⓦ gicthevillacollection .com. Upmarket villas with private pools.

Pure Crete UK ☎ 01444 881 402, ⓦ purecrete.com. Characterful converted cottages and farmhouses in western Crete, plus walking, wildlife and other special-interest trips.

Simpson Travel UK ☎ 0845 508 8283, ⓦ simpsontravel.com. Classy villas, upmarket hotels and village hideaways.

Getting around

Crete is, on the whole, pretty easy to get around. The main towns and resorts along the north coast are linked by an excellent road and a fast and frequent bus service. Elsewhere the road network is rapidly being upgraded, and most villages see at least one daily bus. However, if you're keen to escape the crowds and experience some of Crete's remoter beaches and spectacular mountain scenery, you'll need to get off the main roads; for at least some of your time it's worth considering renting some transport or setting out on foot – better still, a combination of the two.

By bus

The only form of public transport on Crete, **buses** cover the island remarkably comprehensively. Modern, fast and efficient services run along the main north coast road every hour or so, though off the major routes standards vary. The ones used primarily by tourists (to Omalós and Hóra Sfakíon for the Samariá Gorge, for example, or to Festós and Mátala) tend also to be modern and convenient. Those that cater mainly for locals are generally older vehicles that run once daily as transport to market or school – into the provincial capital very early in the morning and back out to the village around lunchtime, which means they're of little use for day-trips. There are few places not accessible by bus, though, and if you combine buses with some walking you'll get about extremely cheaply, if not always especially quickly.

Buses on Crete are run by a consortium of companies jointly known as **KTEL**. That this is not one single company is most obvious in Iráklio where there are two separate bus terminals, serving different directions. On the whole, buses to a given village run from the provincial capital – Iráklio, Réthymno and Haniá, or in Lasíthi province from Áyios Nikólaos and Sitía. There are also a number of small-scale services that cross interprovincial borders. Current **timetables** are generally available from bus stations and tourist offices: you can also find timetables and fares on Ⓦ bus-service-crete-ktel.com.

Prices remain reasonable: each hop between the major north coast towns – Iráklio to Réthymno or Áyios Nikólaos, for example, or Réthymno to Haniá – costs around €7 one way.

By taxi or tour bus

Local **taxis** are exceptionally good value, at least as long as the meter is running or you've fixed a price in advance. Much of their business is long-distance, taking people to and from the villages around the main towns (at some city taxi ranks and all major airports, there's a printed list of prices to the most common destinations). If you want to visit somewhere where there's only one bus, or spend some time hiking and get a ride back, it's well worth arranging for a taxi to pick you up: four people together in a taxi will pay little more per person than on the bus.

It's also quite easy to negotiate a day or half-day **sightseeing** by taxi, although this may require some Greek, and over long distances can become expensive. A simpler alternative for a one-off visit is to take a **bus tour**. Travel agents everywhere offer the obvious ones – the Samariá Gorge or Vái beach – and a few offer more adventurous alternatives: some of the best of these are detailed in the Guide.

By car or motorbike

Renting a **car** or **bike** (or bringing your own), will give you a huge amount of extra freedom to explore and to check out mountain villages and isolated beaches. Most people seem to do this for at least part of their stay, and there are numerous operators in every resort, the vast majority of them offering modern, reliable vehicles and competitive rates.

Do take the time, however, to check out any vehicle carefully before driving off. More importantly, take care while driving, as Greece has a very high **accident** rate compared with Northern Europe or North America. This is in part due to the state of the roads and the nature of the countryside: although many minor roads have been upgraded in recent years, they are still mountainous and winding, and you'll frequently pass without warning from a smooth, modern surface to a stretch of potholed track. Signage is also poor in many places, and road traffic rules often ignored. On the main north coast highway – an excellent road for the most part – you're expected to drive with at least two wheels on the hard shoulder to allow faster vehicles to overtake.

Fuel costs are broadly similar to the UK, with regular unleaded (*amólyvdhi*) currently around €1.70 per litre across the country, but often €1.90-plus in more remote areas; diesel is a little cheaper. It's easy to run out after dark or at weekends, especially in the extreme east and west of the island; most rural stations close at 7 or 8pm and some shut at weekends. When touring in these areas it's wise to maintain a full tank, especially when a weekend or national holiday is approaching.

Rules of the road

EU **driving licences** are valid in Crete, and in practice you can rent a vehicle with almost any valid national licence: however, non-EU drivers are legally required to have an International Driving Permit (acquired before leaving home through organizations such as the AAA; Ⓦ aaa.com), and the lack of one could cause problems should you have a run-in with the police. It is compulsory to wear **seat belts**, and for motorcyclists to wear **helmets**, and children under the age of 10 are not allowed to sit in the front seats of cars. There has also been a major crackdown on **drunk driving** in recent years, with random checks and roadblocks especially designed to catch clubbers heading home in the early hours of the morning around major towns and resorts. **Parking** can also be a headache,

SIX SCENIC DRIVES

The Far West A circuit from Kastélli Kissámou, down the west coast and back on the inland roads via Élos offers a bit of everything; stunning coastal vistas, traditional villages, mountains and gorges. See p.301

Omalós The drive from Haniá towards the Samariá Gorge is spectacular, with the option of continuing to the south coast, or circling back. See p.213

Amári valley and Psilorítis Starting from Réthymno, head out past Arkádhi monastery and along the east side of the Amári valley towards Kamáres for glorious mountain scenery. See p.214

Iráklio to Réthymno Take the old road via Anóyia for a complete contrast to the coastal highway, or combine with the Amári route for a total circumnavigation of Crete's highest mountain. See p.78

Lasíthi plateau Beautiful, however you approach it: try a complete circuit, climbing up from the north coast and back through Neápolis. See p.135

The far east Barren and lonely: from Sitía, head east to Vái beach, south through Zákros and Xerókambos, then back on the inland road via Zíros. See p.155

especially in the big towns, where it's rarely obvious where you are and are not allowed to park, or how to pay when you do so.

If you are involved in any kind of **accident** it's illegal to drive away, and you can theoretically be held at a police station for up to 24 hours. If this happens, ring your consulate immediately to get a lawyer, and don't make a statement to anyone who doesn't speak, and write, very good English. **On-the-spot fines** can be issued for minor traffic infringements such as speeding or crossing a central double white line; from around €50 to €200 depending on the gravity of the offence. The address on the ticket will detail the office in the nearest town to which you should go to pay the fine.

Car rental

Car rental starts at around €35 a day or €200 a week in high season for the smallest model, including unlimited mileage, tax and insurance. Outside peak season, prices drop by about 25 percent, especially if you're renting locally. An open-top jeep or a van will cost up to three times as much; jeeps can be fun, but there's little point going for a fancy vehicle – you'll rarely get a chance to drive at great speed, and small cars are an advantage when parking or negotiating narrow village streets.

Many package holidays will include a car, and if not there's a great deal to be said for organizing your rental in advance (especially in high season). If you go for a Cretan company, pick one that is local to where you intend to head or, if you're touring around, one that has offices around the island to ensure that there's help available should you need it.

All agencies will require a blank **credit card** slip as a deposit (destroyed when you return the vehicle

safely); minimum **age requirements** vary from 21 to 25. Be sure to check that full insurance and a **collision damage waiver** is included, and note that damage to tyres and the underside of the vehicle are usually excluded from the insurance, so take care on bumpy dirt roads.

Motorbikes and mopeds

Motorbikes, **mopeds**, **scooters** and **quad bikes** are also widely available to rent in Crete, at prices starting at around €25 a day (€130/week) for a 50cc moped, and €40 a day (€230/week) for a 200cc trail bike. Reputable establishments demand a full motorcycle driving licence for any engine over 80cc, and you will usually have to leave your passport (sometimes a valid credit card is acceptable) as security. For smaller models any driving licence will do.

The smaller bikes and scooters are ideal for pottering around for a day or two, but don't regard them as serious transport: Crete is very mountainous and the mopeds simply won't go up some of the steeper hills, even carrying only one person. Be sure not to run beyond the range of your petrol tank either, as they're not designed for long-distance travel and there are few filling stations outside the towns. For serious exploration, or to venture into the mountains, you really need a motorbike or a more powerful scooter.

Although motorbikes are enormous fun to ride around, you need to take more than usual care: there's an alarming number of **accidents** each year among visitors and locals because basic safety procedures are not followed. It's only too easy to come to grief on a potholed road or steep dirt track, especially at night. You should never rent a bike that you feel you can't handle, and always use a **helmet** (a legal requirement), despite the fact that many locals don't. Quite apart from any injuries, you're likely to be charged a criminally high price for any repairs needed for the bike, so make sure that you are adequately **insured**. Note that some travel insurance policies specifically exclude injuries sustained while riding/driving a rented vehicle.

CAR RENTAL AGENCIES IN CRETE

Alianthos ☎ 28320 32033, ⓦ alianthos-group.com. Cars and bikes, with offices at the airports and across western Crete.

Blue Sea ☎ 2810 221215, ⓦ bluesearentals.com. Cars and bikes in Iráklio and elsewhere.

Clubcars ☎ 28410 25868, ⓦ clubcars.net. Áyios Nikólaos, Iráklio airport and other locations in the east.

Kosmos ☎ 2810 241357, ⓦ cosmos-sa.gr. Iráklio, Réthymno, Haniá, Áyios Nikólaos.

Motor Club ☎ 2810 222408, ⓦ motorclub.gr. Cars and bikes in Iráklio and resort locations.

Walking, cycling and local boats

The idea of **walking** for pleasure is a recent one in Crete, but there are plenty of opportunities for visitors. Choices range from local strolls inland from almost any resort to organized tours through the Samariá Gorge and the challenging E4 trans-European footpath, which crosses the island from west to east. If you have the time and stamina, walking is probably the single best way to see the island. There are suggestions for hikes, from easy strolls to serious climbing, throughout the Guide: check out, too, our list of specialist walking tour operators (see p.24).

Cycling

Cycling isn't greatly popular in Crete – not surprising, perhaps, in view of the mountainous terrain and fierce summer heat. Even so, riding a bike offers an incomparable view of the island and – if you're reasonably fit – guarantees contact with locals whom the average visitor could never meet. **Mountain bikes** can be rented in most resorts of any size, and many of the rental places will offer organized local excursions: there are also some package tours involving group exploration of the island by bike (see p.24). If you're really keen you can also bring your own bike by plane (it's normally free within your ordinary baggage allowance) or by sea if you're coming from Italy or Athens (in which case it should go free on the ferry).

Boats and local ferries

Around the island numerous **local ferry services** run to offshore islets and isolated beaches; these are detailed throughout the Guide. Where there is no ferry service you can often arrange a trip with local fishermen. Asking at the bar in the nearest fishing village will usually turn up someone willing to make the trip – it's always worth trying to knock a bit off the first price quoted. Some adventure travel operators (see p.24) offer tours around the coast by **sea kayak**.

Accommodation

There are vast numbers of beds available for tourists in Crete, and most of the year you can rely on turning up pretty much anywhere and finding something. At Easter and in July and August, however, you can run into problems unless you've booked in advance, especially in the more popular resorts and cities.

The big **hotels** and self-catering complexes in the larger resorts are often pre-booked by package-holiday companies for the whole season. Although

---

ACCOMMODATION PRICES AND SEASONS

There are typically three **seasons** that affect accommodation prices in Crete: October to April (low), May, June and September (mid) and July and August (high) – though Easter and the first two weeks of August may be in a higher category still.

By law, **prices must be displayed** on the back of the door of your room, or over the reception desk. You should never pay more than this, and in practice it is rare to pay as much as the sign says. If you feel you're being overcharged, threaten to make a report to the tourist office or police, who will generally take your side in such cases. Prices are for the room only, except where otherwise indicated; fancier places often include breakfast in the price – where this is the case we mention it in our reviews, but check when booking.

The prices we quote in our accommodation reviews are for the establishment's **cheapest double room in high season** – there may well be other rooms that cost more, and for much of the year you can expect to pay less than our quoted rate.

they may have vacancies if you just turn up, non-package visitors are far more likely to find themselves staying in smaller, simpler places which usually describe themselves simply as **"rooms"**, or as apartments or studios. Standards here can vary from spartan (though invariably clean) to luxurious, but the vast majority are purpose-built blocks where every room is en suite, and where the minimal furnishings are well adapted to the local climate – at least in summer.

Single rooms are rare, and generally poor value – you'll often have to pay the full double-room price or haggle for around a third off; on the other hand, larger groups and **families** can almost always find triple and quadruple rooms, and fancier hotels may have family **suites** (two rooms sharing one bathroom), all of which can be very good value.

Hotels

The tourist police set official **categories** for hotels, which range from L (Luxury) down to E class; all except the top category have to keep within set price limits. C-class hotels and below have only to provide the most rudimentary of continental breakfasts – sometimes optional for an extra charge – while B-class and above will usually offer a buffet breakfast including cheese, cold meats, eggs and cereals.

The letter system is being slowly replaced with a star grading system; L is five-star, E is no-star. Ratings correspond to the facilities available (lifts, dining room, pool etc), a box-ticking exercise that doesn't always reflect the actual quality of the hotel – plenty of D-class hotels, for example, are in practice smarter and more comfortable than nearby C-class outfits.

Rooms and apartments

Many places categorized as apartments or rooms are every bit as comfortable as hotels, and in the lower price ranges are usually more congenial and

better value. At their most basic, **rooms** (*dhomátia* – but usually spotted by a "Rooms for Rent" or *Zimmer Frei* sign) might be literally a room in someone's house, a bare space with a bed and a hook on the back of the door, and washing facilities outside. However, these days almost all are purpose-built, with comfortable en-suite accommodation and balconies – at the fancier end of the scale you'll find studio and apartment complexes with marble floors, pools, bars and children's playgrounds. Many have a variety of rooms at different prices, so if possible always ask to see the room first. Places described as **studios** usually have a small **kitchenette** – a fridge, sink and a couple of hotplates in the room itself – while **apartments** generally have at least one bedroom and separate kitchen/living room.

Rooms proprietors usually ask to keep your **passport**: ostensibly "for the tourist police", but in reality to prevent you leaving with an unpaid bill. Some may be satisfied with just taking down the details, and they'll almost always return the documents once you get to know them. In the larger resorts, though, the only way to keep hold of your passport may be to pay in advance.

Villas and longer-term stays

Although one of the great dreams of Greek travel is finding an idyllic coastal **villa** and renting it for virtually nothing for a whole month, there's no chance at all of your dream coming true in modern Crete. All the best villas are contracted out to agents and let through foreign operators. Even if you do find one empty for a week or two, renting it in Crete usually costs far more than it would have done to arrange through a specialist operator from home (see p.24).

Having said that, if you do arrive and decide you want to drop roots for a while, you can still strike lucky if you don't mind avoiding the coast, and are happy with relatively modest accommodation. Pick an untouristed inland village, get yourself known and ask about; you might still pick up a wonderful

---

HOT WATER AND AIR CONDITIONING

When checking out a room, always ask about the status of hot water and air conditioning. Most modern rooms and apartments have **air conditioning**, but it's frequently an optional extra and you'll be charged an additional €5 or so a night to use it. Just occasionally you may also be asked to pay extra for **hot water**. A more likely problem is that there won't be enough: rooftop **solar heaters** are popular and effective, but shared solar-powered tanks tend to run out of hot water in the post-beach shower crunch around 6–7pm, with no more available until the next day. A water heater, either as a backup or primary source, is more reliable.

deal. Out of season your chances are much better – even in touristy areas, between October and March (sometimes as late as April and May) you can bargain a very good rate, especially for stays of a month or more. Travel agents are another good source of information on what's available locally, and many rooms places have an apartment on the side or know someone with one to rent.

Youth hostels

There are just three official and semi-official **youth hostels** (*xenón neótitas*) left on Crete, all of which must be among the least strictly run in the world. The surviving hostels are in Iráklio, Réthymno and Plakiás; the last two are particularly good. Facilities are basic – you pay around €10 a night for a dormitory bed on which to spread your sleeping bag – but they offer cheap meals, kitchen facilities, a good social life and an excellent grapevine for finding work or travelling companions.

Camping

There are about fifteen official **campsites** in Crete – see Ⓦpanhellenic-camping-union.gr for a list – and on the whole they're not very good, tending to be dominated by camper vans and with very hard earth. Several do have spectacular seafront locations, though. Prices start at around €5 a night per person, but they mount up once you've added a charge for a tent (generally about €3.50 for a two-person model or €5 for something larger), and the same again for a vehicle and for everyone in your group – you're looking at €18–25 a night for two people, tent and vehicle in high season.

Camping outside an official campsite (with or without a tent) is against the law – enforced in most tourist areas and on beaches. Nevertheless, with discretion and sensitivity it can still be done: the police crack down on people camping rough on (and littering) popular mainstream tourist beaches, but there are still places on the south and west coasts where the practice is fairly common.

From May until early September it's warm enough to **sleep out** in just a lightweight sleeping bag (though the nights can be chilly in mountainous zones). A waterproof bag or ground-sheet is useful to keep out the late summer damp, and a foam pad lets you sleep in relative comfort almost anywhere.

Food and drink

Cretans spend a lot of time socializing outside their homes, and sharing a meal is one of the chief ways of doing it. The atmosphere is invariably relaxed and informal, with pretensions and expense-account prices rare outside the fancier hotels. Greeks are not prodigious drinkers – tippling is traditionally meant to accompany food – though there are plenty of bars in the tourist resorts and you can always get a beer, a glass of wine or an ouzo at a café.

The **food** in Crete may be simple, but at its best it is magnificent – vibrantly flavoured with the herbs that scent the countryside. Organic production, local sourcing and foraging for ingredients are not fads or recent developments here, but central to the way people have always eaten; most Cretans have access to a smallholding of some kind, or if not to local markets where the island's superb agricultural produce is sold. In the better tavernas, the bulk of the produce used will be fresh, local and naturally organic. There's a **food and drink glossary** in our Contexts chapter (see p.359).

Breakfast, fast food and snacks

Greeks generally don't eat much in the way of **breakfast**, more often opting for a mid-morning snack (see p.30). Some of the best rooms places will

---

OLIVE OIL AND THE CRETAN DIET

Great claims are made for the **Cretan diet** – comparative studies have shown that the island has (or had) one of the longest-lived and least diseased populations in the world – and any local will be happy to lecture you on the life-enhancing properties of good **olive oil** (plus a little wine or *raki* in moderation). As increasing amounts of meat and dairy produce are added to the everyday diet, the health benefits are falling away, but with plentiful locally produced olive oil, cereals, and sun-ripened vegetables and fruit, this still feels like a very healthy place to eat.

serve up fresh fruit and yoghurt, eggs straight from the hen and home-made breads and pastries; more often, though, "continental" breakfast consists of cardboard-flavoured orange squash, stewed coffee, processed cheese and meats, plus pre-packaged butter, honey and jam (confusingly called *marmeládha*). In the resorts, there are plenty of places offering bacon and eggs too.

Picnics and snacks

Picnic ingredients are easily available at supermarkets, bakeries and greengrocers, most of which open early. Yoghurt, bread, eggs, fruit, cheese, salami, olives and tomatoes are always easy to buy. Note that Greek **cheese** isn't all *féta* (salty white sheep's cheese); tasty local varieties include *mizíthra*, *káskavali*, *kritiko* and *graviéra*, the last – a peppery, mature, full-fat sheep's cheese – is particularly good.

At **bakeries**, you'll find oven-warm flaky pies filled with cheese (*tyrópites*), spinach (*spanakópites*), wild greens or sausage or, better still, stuffed with creamy cheese and sprinkled with icing sugar and cinnamon (*bougátsa*). In the tourist areas many bakeries also cater for northern European palates by turning out croissants, doughnuts and even wholemeal and rye breads.

Ubiquitous **fast-food** snacks include **souvláki** – small kebabs on wooden sticks, which as *píta-souvláki* are served stuffed into a doughy bread (more like Indian naan than pitta bread) along with salad and yoghurt – and, even better, doner-kebab-like **yíros píta**. You'll also find places serving **pizza** (usually excellent at specialist places and awful in tavernas) and **tost** (bland ham-and-cheese toasties).

Seasonal **fruits** are exceptionally inexpensive. Look out for what's on offer in the markets or by the roadside: cherries in spring; melons, watermelons, plums and apricots in summer; pears and apples in autumn; oranges and grapes most of the time. They even grow small bananas in the area around Mália – an endeavour heavily subsidized by the EU.

Tavernas and restaurants

Most Cretan restaurants describe themselves as **tavernas**, though you can also get a meal at an *estiatório* or a *psistariá* as well as in ouzerís and many others. **Estiatória** are very similar to tavernas but tend to be simpler and less expensive, and perhaps more traditionally Greek. **Psistariés** are restaurants that specialize in grilled or spit-roasted meat, usually over charcoal. A **psarótaverna** is a taverna that specializes in fish. **Ouzerís** are bars specializing in ouzo and *mezédhes*; a *rakádhika*, very fashionable these days, is the equivalent, but serving *raki*. They are well worth trying for the marvellous variety of **mezédhes** (small plates of food) they serve, although the most authentic are to be found in the larger towns where there's a local customer base to keep them on their toes. At the better places several plates of *mezédhes* will effectively substitute for a meal (though it may not work out any cheaper if you have a healthy appetite, and *mezédhes* are also served at many tavernas). Wherever you eat, chic appearance is not a good guide to quality; often the most basic place will turn out to be the best, and in swankier restaurants you may well be paying for the linen and stemmed wineglasses.

Sometimes at traditional tavernas and *estiatória* there's no menu and you're taken into the **kitchen** to inspect what's on offer: uncooked cuts of meat and fish, simmering pots of stews or vegetables, trays of baked foods. Even where there is a **menu** (usually in English as well as Greek) it's often a standard printed form that bears little relation to what is actually on offer: again, check the kitchen or display case.

A basic taverna meal with house wine or beer will **cost** around €12–20 per person. Add a better bottle of wine, seafood or more careful cooking, and it could be €20–30 a head; you'll rarely pay more than that. If you're unsure about the **price** of something, ask before ordering since it always seems to turn

---

TAVERNA TIPS AND HOURS

Cretans generally eat late: **lunch** is served at around 2–3pm, **dinner** at 9–11pm. You can eat earlier than this, but you're likely to get indifferent service at a tourist establishment or find yourself eating alone everywhere else. If you find that you can't wait that long, do what the locals do: take an aperitif along with a few *mezédhes*.

The **opening hours** we quote in our reviews throughout the Guide should be taken as indicative rather than set in stone; if you want to sit talking and drinking till the early hours (as many locals do), you'll rarely be thrown out. And if the proprietor has been up till 3am, it's no surprise if he should choose to open a little later than usual the next day.

Prices are supposedly inclusive of all taxes and service, but an extra **tip** of around five percent or simple rounding up of the bill is always welcome.

out more expensive if you wait until after you've eaten. Fish is almost always priced by weight, and is usually very expensive. There's always a small **cover charge** (€0.50–1 per person), which includes the bread you'll inevitably be given.

Greek dishes and Cretan specialities

As Cretan restaurants increasingly adapt themselves to tourists, you'll find that some of the advice below on traditional Greek foods and restaurants no longer applies in the resorts, where you're more likely to get western European-style service (places much patronized by the French, for example, offer fixed-price set menus). On the other hand, the better tavernas have started to recognize the value of their culture and serve more consciously **traditional foods** in traditional ways.

A typical Greek meal consists of appetizers (often in the form of *mezédhes*) and a main meat or fish dish. They may be brought to the table at much the same time as there's no strict concept of courses – if you want the main course later, stagger your ordering. Only the tourist restaurants serve much in the way of dessert, though there's often fresh fruit or yoghurt – the Greek practice is to visit a *zaharoplastío* for pastries, coffee and liqueurs once the main meal is over.

The **main dish** of meat or fish generally comes on its own except for maybe a piece of lemon or half a dozen chips (fries); lamb is usually the best meat, local and excellent, if a little pricier than the alternatives. Check out the kitchen for **oven-baked dishes** (*mayireftá*, such as *moussaká*, macaroni pie, meat or game stews, stuffed tomatoes or peppers, the oily vegetable casseroles called *ladherá*, and oven-baked meat and fish), which are generally delicious and less expensive than straight meat or fish dishes. **Salads and vegetables** are traditionally served as the first course and usually shared. If you ask for salad you'll invariably be brought *horiátiki saláta* – the so-called **Greek salad**, including *féta* cheese: wonderful as it is there are plenty of cheaper alternatives without cheese. Vegetable

TOP 5 VILLAGE TAVERNAS

Miliá Bar-Taverna Miliá. See p.304
Piperia Pefkí. See p.174
Taverna Plateia Mírthios. See p.227
Taverna Vilaeti Áyios Konstantínos. See p.140
Vegera Zarós. See p.94

dishes are often very good in themselves and, if you order a few between several people, can make a satisfying meal.

In season, **fish** is varied and delicious, but in summer visitors get a relatively poor choice as trawling is prohibited from the end of May until the beginning of October. During these warmer months, such few fish as are caught tend to be smaller and dry-tasting. It is also expensive: if the prices on the menu seem phenomenally high, that's generally because they are **per kilo**; but €50 a kilo will still work out at €20 or so a head. Most tavernas will encourage you to go into the kitchen to see what's available and when you've selected your fish they'll weigh it to determine the actual price (don't leave it to the waiter, or you may well get the biggest). Cheaper, tasty alternatives are small **sardine** or whitebait-style fish, eaten whole, fish soups and stews, and **squid**, octopus and shellfish.

Traditional **Cretan specialities** increasingly find their way onto menus too: some of the more common among dozens of typical dishes are snails and rabbit, both often served stewed with onions. Look out too for savoury stuffed pastries. Another speciality you shouldn't miss if you get a chance is *hórta* – the wild greens that grow in abundance on the Cretan hills. These are gathered and boiled to be served up lukewarm (or sometimes cold), dressed with olive oil and vinegar, and can be delicious – or at the very least good for you. Although you can eat them all year round, spring and autumn are the best times, when they grow vigorously in the damper climate.

VEGETARIANS

Although there are scarcely any vegetarian restaurants, **vegetarians** can eat extremely well in Crete. Quite apart from the fact that meals based on eggs, pizza or pasta are available in all the towns and resorts, as are traditional snacks like *tyrópita*, the increased interest in local cuisine, as well as pressure from tourists, has seen far more vegetable dishes appear on local menus. Many *mezédhes* like tzatziki, *dolmádhes* and *yígandes* are naturally meat-free, you'll find excellent salads everywhere, *yémista* (stuffed vegetables) are usually meat-free and there are frequently vegetable baked dishes including ratatouille-like *briam*, *imam bayaldi* (stuffed aubergine/eggplant) and *bouréki* (potato, courgette/zucchini and cheese bake) on the menu.

Cafés and bars

The traditional Cretan coffee shop – the **kafenío** – filled with old men arguing and playing *távli* (backgammon, a national obsession; most places will lend you a set) is still found in every village, though increasingly beleaguered under the onslaught of global mass culture. In the towns and resorts its place has largely been taken over by modern **cafés** and elegant **patisseries** (*zaharoplastía*).

Actual **bars** are rare except in the bigger resorts, but you can get a beer or glass of wine at almost any time in any café or taverna, and the modern cafés that proliferate in the major towns and cities generally become bars by night.

Coffee and kafenía

Traditional Greek **coffee** is what most Westerners would call "Turkish", tiny cups filled with a thick, black, heady concoction. It makes a great start to the day or a pick-me-up later – once you've acquired the taste and learned to leave the grounds behind in the cup. Most Cretans drink it medium-sweet or *métrio*; if you want no sugar at all, ask for *skéto*, while *glykó* is very sweet indeed. If you want Greek coffee, ask for a *kafé ellinikós* – many Cretan *kafenío* proprietors assume foreigners will want ordinary coffee (usually instant), so by choosing it you'll rise greatly in their estimation. *Kafenía* also serve ouzo, brandy, beer, various teas (*tsái*), soft drinks and juices. Some close at siesta time, but many remain open from early in the morning until late at night.

Cappuccino and other coffees, including iced *freddoccino*, are rarely available at *kafenía*, but are of course the staple of more modern cafés. The universal drink of young Greece, however, is **frappé**. This is simply instant coffee powder, ice and water, whizzed to a froth and served with a glass of cold water: but it is infinitely better than that makes it sound, and the quintessential taste of a Greek

summer. Again, you can have it *skéto*, *métrio* or *glikó* and with milk (*me gála*) or without.

Ouzo and raki

In a *kafenío* or ouzerí, the prime time for an **ouzo** is 6–8pm, before dinner and after the afternoon nap. Ouzo, an aniseed-flavoured spirit, is served by the glass or *karafáki* (a 200ml vial or miniature bottle); add water or ice to taste, and watch the clear liquid turn cloudy white. Once, every ouzo was automatically accompanied by a small plate of *mezédhes* on the house: cheese, cucumber, tomato, a few olives, sometimes octopus or a couple of small fish. Nowadays *"ouzomezés"* is often a separate, pricier option, but one well worth going for. **Raki** (see box below), also known in Crete as *tsikoudhiá*, is a burningly strong, flavourless spirit, usually consumed as a *digestif*.

Wine

Wine is the usual accompaniment to a meal in a restaurant or taverna. If you don't specify what you want, you'll be served the **house wine**, traditionally poured cold from the barrel into tin jugs (*kantária*) or carafes in either kilo (litre) or half-kilo measures. Frequently such wine is home-made and a source of great pride: it can be excellent, it's invariably interesting and it's always inexpensive. The home-made stuff is most frequently brownish-pink *kókkino* (red), especially good around Kastélli in the west or Sitía in the east, while *áspro* (white) often has a distinctive sherry-like tang, and again a brownish tinge. If it's not home-made it is likely to be from a wine box or barrel produced by one of the big co-ops, and is almost always perfectly palatable – which is more than can be said for the few bottles of overpriced wine stored on a hot, dusty shelf in the average taverna. If you want to taste the house wine before committing yourself to a *karáfa*, this should never be a problem.

RAKI – A SHOT OF HOSPITALITY

Raki holds a special place in the Cretan heart, and is central to traditional Cretan hospitality. No matter the time of day, if you're invited into a Cretan home you'll be presented with a glass of water, a morsel of cheese or a home-made sweet, and a shot of *raki*, the local firewater. Many tavernas will offer you a shot after your meal, too, though this may be a more commercial (and hangover-inducing) product. Distilled from grape must – the leftovers from winemaking – the real stuff is home-made in hundreds of tiny stills (and a few bigger, communal ones) in villages the length of the island. Each is unique – Cretans pride themselves on being able to detect the most subtle distinctions in taste and quality – all are fiercely potent, and the best have a wonderfully clean yet fiery effect. Accept it if you can; quite apart from the danger of causing offence if you refuse, you'll rarely regret saying yes – and this is a gesture of welcome that still marks Crete out as a uniquely hospitable place.

CRETAN WINE

With the increase in tourism and a new breed of fancier restaurants has come a demand for a more polished product, and Cretan viniculture is developing rapidly; some vineyards even offer tastings (see box, p.69). **Cretan wines** come in many varieties; the hot, dry summers are more suited to producing dry red wines – dark and powerful – than whites. Six grape varieties predominate on the island – *kotsifáli*, *thrapsathíri*, *liátiko*, *mandilariá*, *roméïko* and *vilána* – and there are four appellation wine-growing areas: Pezá, Dafnés, Sitía and Arhánes, the last still using some vineyards cultivated by the Minoans almost four thousand years ago.

Pezá brands like Minos red and white, which you can get everywhere, are palatable if rather boring, although the more mature vintages such as Minos Sant Antonio and Palace VDQS (red and white) are getting much better. The **Arhánes** wine region also produces some pretty good red and white vintages, most notably by a co-operative that sells its wines under the Arhánes brand name. The **Sitian** wines Topiko (medium-dry with a hint of sherry) and Myrtos are both good everyday whites to drink with seafood. In the west, Kissamos red is another good bet. Some of the island's smaller producers also make excellent wines, especially Lyrarakis from the Pezá region, whose *kotsifáli*-and-syrah red, Dafni dry white and Last Supper red are all excellent. Michalakis is another Pezá producer whose Merastri brand is pretty tasty. Dafnés producer Douloufakis is also producing some innovative reds and whites from a variety of grapes. To the west, near Haniá, Manoulakis and Karabitakis are two more small producers turning out wines of high quality.

Retsína is also produced locally, and always available. This resinated wine, which usually comes in half-litre bottles, is an acquired taste, but some varieties are extremely good (particularly those produced by the Central Union of Haniá Wine Producers). It's also exceptionally cheap: a half-litre generally costs less than €1 in the supermarket, much the same as a half-litre of beer.

The media

Greeks are great devourers of newsprint – although few would propose the Greek mass media as a paradigm of objective journalism. Papers are almost uniformly sensational, while state-run TV and radio are often biased in favour of whichever party happens to be in government. Foreign news is easily available in the form of locally printed newspaper editions and TV news channels.

Newspapers

British newspapers are widely available in resorts and the larger towns at a cost of €2–3.50 for dailies, or €4–5 for Sunday editions. Many, including the *Guardian*, *Times*, *Mail* and *Mirror*, have slimmed-down editions printed in Greece which are available the same day; others are likely to be a day old. The *International Herald Tribune*, which has the bonus of including an abridged English edition of the same day's *Kathimerini*, a respected Greek daily, is also sold widely, and in bigger newsagents you'll also be able to find *USA Today* and *Time*.

Radio

Crete's airwaves are cluttered with **local stations**, many of which have plenty of music, often traditional. In resort areas some have news bulletins and tourist information in English. The mountainous nature of much of the island, though, means that any sort of radio reception is tricky: if you're driving around you'll find that you constantly have to retune. The two state-run networks are ER1 (a mix of news, talk and pop music) and ER2 (pop music).

MOVIES

Cretan **cinemas** show the regular major release movies, which in the case of English-language titles will almost always be in English with Greek subtitles. In summer **open-air screens** operate in all the major towns and some of the resorts, and these are absolutely wonderful. You may not hear much, thanks to crackly speakers and locals chatting away throughout, but watching a movie under the stars on a warm night is simply a great experience.

The BBC World Service no longer broadcasts to Europe on short wave, though Voice of America can be picked up in places. Both of these and dozens of others are of course available as internet broadcasts, however, or via satellite TV channels.

Television

Even if your hotel advertises **satellite TV**, the only English-language channels usually included are CNN and BBC World. However, most evenings you'll find English-language films, with subtitles, on at least a couple of the main Greek channels.

Festivals and cultural events

Most of the big Greek popular festivals have a religious origin, so they're observed in accordance with the Greek Orthodox calendar. This means that Easter, for example, can fall as much as three weeks to either side of the Western festival.

On top of the main religious festivals, there are scores of local festivals, or **paniyíria**, celebrating the patron saint of the village church. Some of the more important are listed below; the *paramoní*, or **eve of the festival**, is often as significant as the day itself, and many of the events are actually celebrated on the night before. If you show up on the morning of the date given you may find that you have missed most of the music, dancing and drinking. With some 330-odd possible saints' days you're unlikely to travel for long without stumbling on something. Local tourist offices should be able to fill you in on events in their area.

Easter

Easter is by far the most important festival of the Greek year. It is an excellent time to be in Crete, both for the beautiful and moving religious ceremonies and for the days of feasting and celebration that follow. If you make for a smallish village, you may well find yourself an honorary member for the period of the festival. This is a busy time for Greek tourists as well as international ones, though, so book ahead.

The first great ceremony takes place on **Good Friday** evening as the Descent from the Cross is lamented in church. At dusk, the *Epitáfios*, Christ's funeral bier, lavishly decorated by the women of the parish, leaves the sanctuary and is paraded solemnly through the streets. **Late Saturday** evening sees the climax in a majestic mass to celebrate Christ's triumphant return. At the stroke of midnight all the lights in each crowded church are extinguished and the congregation plunged into the darkness that enveloped Christ as he passed through the underworld. Then there's a faint glimmer of light behind the altar screen before the priest appears, holding aloft a lighted taper and chanting "*Avtó to Fós…*" ("This is the Light of the World"). Stepping down to the level of the parishioners he lights the candles of the nearest worshippers, intoning "*Dévte, lévete Fós*" ("Come, take the Light"). Those at the front of the congregation do the same for their neighbours until the entire church – and the outer courtyard, standing room only for latecomers – is ablaze with burning candles and the miracle reaffirmed. The lighted **candles** are carried home through the streets; they are said to bring good fortune to the house if they arrive still burning.

The lighting of the flames is the signal for celebrations to start, the Lent fast to be broken and, in many Cretan villages, for effigies of Judas to be burned. The traditional greeting, as fireworks and dynamite explode all around you in the street, is *Khristós Anésti* ("Christ is risen"), to which the response is *Alithós Anésti* ("Truly He is risen"). On **Easter Sunday** there's feasting on roast lamb.

The Greek equivalent of **Easter eggs** are hard-boiled eggs (painted red on Holy Thursday), which are baked into twisted, sweet bread-loaves

---

EASTER'S HOLY FLAME – A PAGAN RITE?

The flame from which all the Easter candles are lit has its source at Christ's Tomb in the Church of the Holy Sepulchre in Jerusalem; here the Patriarch of the Greek Orthodox Church celebrates the ceremony of the Holy Fire each Holy Saturday. From Jerusalem the flame is transported on a special flight to Athens, and within hours distributed by land, sea and air to churches throughout Greece and the islands.

These ceremonies around the rebirth of light closely mirror the ancient Greek worship of Persephone, daughter of Demeter, goddess of the earth. In legend, Persephone was banished to the darkness of Hades for the winter, returning joyously to the light of day every spring.

NAME DAYS

In Crete, everyone gets to celebrate their birthday twice. More important, in fact, than your actual birthday, is the "**Name Day**" of the saint that bears your name. Greek ingenuity has stretched the saints' names (or invented new saints) to cover almost everyone, so even pagan Dionysos or Socrates get to celebrate. If your name isn't covered, no problem – your party is on All Saints' Day, eight weeks after Easter.

The big name-day celebrations (Iannis/Ianna on January 7th or Yeoryios on April 23rd for example) can involve thousands of people, and traditional naming conventions guarantee that families get to celebrate together. In most families the eldest boy is still named after his paternal grandfather, and the eldest girl after her grandmother, so all the eldest cousins will share the same name, and the same name day. Any church or chapel bearing the saint's name will mark the event – some smaller chapels will open just for this one day of the year – while if an entire village is named after the saint, you can almost guarantee a festival. To check when your name day falls, see ⓦnamedays.gr.

(*tsourékia*) or distributed on Easter Sunday. People rap their eggs against their friends' eggs, and the owner of the last uncracked egg is considered lucky.

JANUARY

Jan 1: New Year's Day Also celebrated as the Feast of St Basil.

Jan 6: Epiphany Marks the baptism of Jesus and the end of the twelve days of Christmas. Baptismal fonts, lakes, rivers and seas are blessed, especially harbours, where the priest traditionally casts a crucifix into the water, with local youths competing to recover it.

FEBRUARY & MARCH

Carnival (Apokriátika) Festivities span three weeks, climaxing during the seventh weekend before Easter; big in Kalíves, Haniá and Réthymno.

Clean Monday (Kathará Dheftéra) The beginning of Lent, 7 weeks before Easter, is a traditional time to fly kites and to feast on all the things that will be forbidden over the coming weeks.

March 25: Independence Day and the Feast of the Annunciation Both a religious and a national holiday, with military parades and dancing to celebrate the beginning of the revolt against Ottoman rule in 1821, and church services to honour the news given to Mary that she was to become the Mother of Christ. There are special celebrations in Paleohóra.

APRIL

Easter (Páskha) April 20, 2014; April 12, 2015; May 1, 2016; April 16, 2017. Widespread celebration for the most important festival of the year (see opposite); Good Friday and Easter Monday are public holidays.

April 23: Áyios Yeóryios St George, the patron saint of shepherds, is commemorated with big rural celebrations throughout Crete, with much feasting and dancing. There's a major celebration in Asigonía.

MAY

May 1: May Day The great urban holiday – most people make for the countryside to picnic. In the towns, demonstrations by the left claim the day as Labour Day.

May 20–27: Anniversary of the Battle of Crete Celebrated in Haniá and a different local village each year, with veterans' ceremonies, sporting events and folk dancing.

May 21: Áyios Konstandínos The feast of St Constantine who, as emperor, championed Christianity in the Byzantine Empire, and his mother, Ayía Eléni (St Helena), with services and celebrations at churches and monasteries named after the saint, especially Arkádhi; also a very popular name day.

JUNE

Whit Monday (Áyion Pnévma) Seven weeks after Easter, this is both a religious holiday and a secular one marking the start of summer.

June 24: Summer Solstice/John the Baptist Bonfires and widespread celebrations.

Late June: Naval Week Naval celebrations culminating in fireworks – especially big at Soúdha.

JULY & AUGUST

Early July: Réthymno Wine and Food Festival A week of wine tasting and traditional dancing. ⓦrethymnowinefestival.gr

July to mid-Aug: Sitía Kornaria Festival Concerts, dance, theatre and food.

July & Aug: Áyios Nikólaos Lato Festival Cultural and sporting events throughout the summer.

July to mid-Sept: Iráklio Festival A wide variety of cultural events from drama and film to traditional dance and jazz, at scattered sites through most of the summer.

Aug 6: Metamórfosi/Transfiguration Another feast day. Especially celebrated in Voukoliés (Haniá), Máles (Ierápetra) and Zákros.

Aug 12: Áyios Mathéos The feast of St Matthew sees celebrations in Kastélli Kissámou.

Mid-Aug: Sitía Sultana Festival An enjoyable, week-long celebration of the local harvest, with plenty of wine.

Aug 15: Assumption of the Virgin (Apokímisis tís Panayías) A huge holiday throughout Greece, the great feast of the Assumption is a day when people traditionally return to their home village, often creating problems for unsuspecting visitors who find there's no accommodation left. Services in churches begin at dawn, but latecomers usually arrive for the bread, lamb and wine served in the churchyard at the end of the service around lunchtime. Neápoli is a main centre for this feast.

Aug 24: Áyios Eftíhios Celebrated especially in the southwest corner of the island, where many infants are given his name; there are festivities at Kambanós near Soúyia (Haniá).

Aug 24: Áyios Títos The patron saint of Crete is celebrated all across the island and with a big procession in Iráklio.

Aug 29: Áyios Ioánnis A massive name-day pilgrimage to the church of Áyios Ioánnis Giónis on the Rodhopoú peninsula in Haniá.

Late Aug: Kritsá Cretan Wedding A "traditional" wedding laid on for the tourists – quite a spectacle nonetheless.

SEPTEMBER & OCTOBER

Sept 14: Áyios Stavrós/Holy Cross Celebrated with festivities at Tzermiádho and Kalamáfka.

Oct 11: Mihaíl Arhángelos The feast of the archangel is especially popular at Potamiés (Lasíthi).

Mid-Oct: Chestnut Festival Celebrated in Élos and other villages of the southwest where chestnuts are grown.

Oct 28: Óhi Day A national holiday with parades, folk dancing and speeches to commemorate prime minister Metaxas' one-word reply to Mussolini's 1940 ultimatum: Óhi! ("No!").

NOVEMBER & DECEMBER

Nov 7–9: Anniversary of the explosion at the monastery of Arkádhi One of Crete's biggest gatherings.

Dec 6: Áyios Nikólaos The patron saint of seafarers. Many chapels are dedicated to him around the island's coastline, including the one at the resort named after him, where processions and festivities mark the day.

Dec 25 & 26: Christmas It's less all-encompassing than Easter, but Christmas is still an important religious feast, and one that increasingly comes with all the usual commercial trappings: decorations, gifts and alarming outbreaks of plastic Santas on rooftops. Both Christmas Day and Boxing Day are public holidays.

Sports and outdoor activities

Although, not surprisingly, watersports are tremendously popular in Crete, there are perhaps fewer opportunities to take part than you might expect. Away from the coast, it's the mountains that are the great lure, with plenty of hiking options, from gentle strolls to long-distance mountain paths, and above all the great gorge walks, predominantly in the south.

The mountains also offer the opportunity for more strenuous adventure activities.

Watersports

In all the resorts you'll find **waterski** boats that spend most of their time towing people around on bananas or other inflatables, or towing parachutes for **parasailing** (*parapént*). Sometimes there are jet-skis too, but it's rare to find boats or windsurfers to rent. **Windsurfing** is particularly good in the far east, however, with a major centre at Kourémenos Beach (see p.159). **Scuba-diving** is also growing in popularity, largely due to the relaxation of government controls. There are centres where you can learn to dive in all the major north coast resorts, but the best diving is probably off the south coast – especially around Plakiás – and in the far east, where there are fewer facilities. There isn't much life left in the Mediterranean, but these waters have more than most, and they're also exceptionally clear, while the rocky coast offers plenty of caves and hidden nooks to explore.

Hiking, cycling and climbing

There are great **walks** everywhere inland, and many of the best are pointed out throughout the Guide. If you're planning any serious hiking – including any of the various gorges – stout shoes or trainers are essential and **walking boots** with firm ankle support recommended, along with protection against the sun and adequate water supplies. Walking is much better in the spring and autumn than in the fierce heat of midsummer, especially as there will be far more animal and plant life then. Be aware that paths are none too well marked, and even those that start out clear may peter out as you

---

FIVE GREAT GORGE HIKES

Arádhena A challenging and spectacular trek. See p.285

Áyio An easy path through a lonely gorge to a great beach. See p.110

Roúvas An inland gorge, climbing high into the mountains. See p.92

Samariá Always crowded, always extraordinary. See p.275

Zákros, Gorge of the Dead A straightforward walk, rewarded with a Minoan palace and a welcome swim. See p.162

climb into the mountains – always try to get local advice before setting out on anything at all challenging.

In most of the resorts you can rent **mountain bikes**, and many of the rental places lead organized rides, which vary from easy explorations of the countryside to serious rides up proper mountains.

Crete also offers some exciting possibilities for **climbers**: contacts for the local mountaineering clubs (EOS) in Iráklio, Réthymno and Haniá are given in their respective listings or see ⓦ climbincrete.com.

Adventure sports

A handful of adventure operators offer **adrenaline sports** including canyoning, rappel and bungee – the Arádhena gorge (p.285) offers Europe's second-highest **bungee jump** (ⓦ bungy.gr). Climbing and Adrenaline Trekking Plan (ⓦ cycling.gr) offer climbing, canyoning, kayaking, mountain biking in Haniá province.

Believe it or not, it is even possible to **ski** in Crete in winter: there's a tiny ski lift on the Nídha plain above Anóyia, while the *Kalleryi Lodge* in the White Mountains (see p.275) may also open for ski parties. Don't come specially, however. Top spots for **horseriding** are Hersónisos (p.82), Yeoryióupolis (p.260) and Mátala (p.105); operators include ⓦ hersonissos-horse-riding.com, ⓦ horseriding.gr, ⓦ zoraidas-horseriding.com and ⓦ melanouri.com.

Travel essentials

Climate

Among Europe's southernmost spots, Crete has a fabulous climate for holidaymakers, with a season that lasts from March to October. Midsummer can be very hot indeed, but you can always escape to the mountains or into the sea. In spring and autumn the highlands can get very chilly, but the coast remains wonderfully temperate. There's a fuller rundown of the seasons and regional weather in the introduction to this Guide (see p.10).

Costs

The cost of travelling in Greece has dropped markedly since the economic crisis; nonetheless it remains an EU country and member of the euro, and prices in shops and cafés are broadly comparable to other EU countries (including the UK). In general, though, your needs are simple here and public transport, accommodation and taverna meals are among the less inflated items.

Average costs depend very much on where and when you go. The cities and major resorts are usually more expensive, and costs increase substantially in July, August and at Easter. A **budget** of €60/£50/$80 a day will get you a share of a plain double room with bath or shower, breakfast, a picnic or simple taverna lunch, bus ride, museum tickets, a couple of beers and a decent evening meal. You could save a bit on this by camping or staying at hostels and catering for yourself, while for €80–100/£65–80/$100–130 you could upgrade your room, squeeze in a few extra drinks, and share the rental of a motorbike or small car.

Entry charges for archeological sites and museums vary from €2 to around €6 for an important site such as Knossós; entrance to state-run sites and museums is **free** on Sundays and public holidays between November and March.

Most shops have fixed prices, so **bargaining** isn't a regular feature of tourist life. It is worth negotiating over rooms, though, especially off season, or for vehicle rental, especially for longer periods.

Tipping is not essential anywhere, though taxi drivers generally expect it from tourists and most

---

DISCOUNTS AND STUDENT CARDS

State-run sites offer free entry to under-18s, senior citizens, students, teachers and journalists from the EU with proper identification, and substantial reductions for other nationalities; private attractions may also offer reduced prices, especially for children.

Full-time students are eligible for the **International Student ID Card** (ISIC, ⓦ isic.org), which entitles the bearer to special air and ferry fares and discounts at numerous shops and attractions. For Americans there's also a health benefit. You only have to be 26 or younger to qualify for the **International Youth Travel Card**, which costs the same and carries the same benefits – it's not strictly student ID, but will probably work. Teachers qualify for the **International Teacher Identity Card (ITIC)**, offering insurance benefits but limited travel discounts.

As well as the benefits listed above, **senior citizens** are entitled to cut-price fares on some buses, ferries and domestic flights. You'll need to have proof of age to hand.

service staff are very poorly paid. Restaurant bills incorporate a service charge; if you want to tip, rounding up the bill is usually sufficient. If you are offered hospitality by a local they are likely to insist on paying – and offering cash can be seen as offensive. The best solution is to offer to reciprocate, making clear that it's on you next time.

Crime and personal safety

Crete, along with Greece as a whole, remains one of Europe's safest regions, with a low crime rate and a deserved reputation for honesty. If you leave a bag or wallet at a café, you'll most likely find it scrupulously looked after, pending your return. Nonetheless theft and muggings are becoming increasingly common, a trend only likely to be increased by the economic crisis. With this in mind, it's best to lock rooms and cars securely, and to keep your valuables hidden, especially in cities. Civil unrest, in the form of strikes and demonstrations, is also on the increase but while this might inconvenience you, you'd be very unlucky to get caught up in any trouble as a visitor.

In more remote localities **women** may feel slightly uncomfortable travelling alone. The traditional villagers may not understand why you are unaccompanied, and might not welcome your presence in their exclusively male *kafenía* – often the only place where you can get a drink. Travelling with a companion, you're more likely to be treated as a *xéni*, a word meaning both (female) stranger and guest.

Police and potential offences

Though the chances are you'll never meet a member of the national **police force**, the *Ellinikí Astynomía*, Greek cops expect respect: in Crete, on the whole, they're pretty laidback, but they can be harsh if you cross them, and police practice often falls short of northern European norms. If you need to go to the police, always try to do so through the Tourist Police (❶171), who should speak English and are used to dealing with visitors. You are required to **carry suitable ID** on you at all times – either a passport or a driving licence.

The most common causes of a brush with the law are beach **nudity**, **camping** outside authorized sites, **public inebriation** or lewd behaviour. In 2009 a large British stag group dressed as nuns was arrested in Mália and held for several days, having managed to combine extreme drunkenness with a lack of respect to the church. Also avoid taking **photos in forbidden areas** such as airports.

Drug offences are treated as major crimes, particularly since there's a mushrooming local addiction problem. The maximum penalty for "causing the use of drugs by someone under 18", for example, is life imprisonment and an astronomical fine. Foreigners caught in possession of even small amounts of marijuana get long jail sentences if there's evidence that they've been supplying the drug to others.

Electricity

The **electricity** supply – erratic at times, especially during summer peak demand – is 220 volt AC. Plugs are the standard European variety of two round pins and you should pick up an adapter before you leave home, as they can be difficult to find locally. North American appliances (unless they're dual voltage) will also require a transformer.

Entry requirements

UK and all other EU nationals need only a valid passport for entry to Greece, and are not stamped in on arrival or out upon departure (in other words, you can stay as long as you like). US, Australian, New Zealand, Canadian and most non-EU Europeans can stay as tourists for ninety days (cumulative) in any six-month period; make sure your passport is stamped to avoid problems on exit. Your passport must be valid for three months after your arrival date.

Visitors from non-EU countries, unless of Greek descent, are very rarely granted **extensions** to tourist visas. If you overstay you're liable to be deported (at vast expense) or will be hit with a large fine upon departure when you attempt to leave. A full list of Greek embassies and consulates overseas can be found at ⓦmfa.gr.

Gay and lesbian travellers

There are no specifically **gay resorts** on Crete, and few gay holidays offered by tour operators, though a web search will turn up a number of gay-friendly accommodation options.

Homosexuality is legal in Greece over the age of 17, and (male) bisexual behaviour common but rarely admitted; the law code itself, however, still contains pejorative references to passive partners. Greek men are terrible flirts, but cruising them is a semiotic minefield and definitely at your own risk – references in (often obsolete) gay guides to "known" male cruising grounds should be treated sceptically. Out gay Greeks are rare, and out local lesbians rarer still; foreign same-sex couples will generally be regarded with some bemusement but accorded the standard courtesy as foreigners – as long as they refrain from indulging in displays of affection in public, which remain taboo in rural areas.

Health

There are no required **inoculations** for Greece, though it's wise to ensure that you are up to date on tetanus and polio. The main **health risks** faced by visitors involve overexposure to the sun, overindulgence in food and drink, or bites and stings from insects and sea creatures. **Drinking water** is safe pretty much everywhere, though it doesn't always taste great; in the mountains, it often comes straight from the same spring used by the bottling factories. Despite this, almost everyone drinks the bottled stuff instead.

British and other EU nationals are entitled to free medical care upon presentation of a **European Health Insurance Card** (EHIC). This can be applied for, free of charge, by calling ☎0845 606 2030 or online at ⓦwww.ehic.org.uk. The USA, Canada, Australia and New Zealand have no formal healthcare agreements with Greece (other than allowing for free emergency trauma treatment), so insurance is highly recommended.

For serious medical attention you'll find English-speaking **doctors** (mainly private) in all the bigger towns and resorts. There are also hospitals in all the big cities. For an **ambulance**, phone ☎ 166.

Pharmacies, drugs and contraception

For minor complaints, head for the local pharmacy (**farmakío**). Greek pharmacists are highly trained and dispense a number of medicines which elsewhere could only be prescribed by a doctor. In the larger towns and resorts there'll usually be one who speaks good English. Pharmacies are usually closed evenings and Saturday mornings, but all should have a schedule on their door showing the night and weekend duty pharmacists in town. We've listed local pharmacies in our Directory sections throughout the Guide.

If you regularly use any form of **prescription drug**, you should bring along a copy of the prescription, together with the generic name of the drug; this will help you replace it, and avoids problems with customs officials. In this regard, you should be aware that **codeine is banned** in Greece. If you import any you might find yourself in serious trouble, so check labels carefully; it's a major ingredient of Panadeine, Veganin, Solpadeine, Codis and Nurofen Plus, to name just a few.

Contraceptive pills are sold over-the-counter at larger pharmacies, though not necessarily the brands you may be used to; a good pharmacist should come up with a close match. **Condoms** are inexpensive and ubiquitous – just ask for *profylaktiká* (less formally, *plastiká* or *kapótes*) at any pharmacy, sundries store or corner *períptero* (kiosk).

Insurance

Even though EU health care privileges apply in Greece (see opposite), you'd do well to take out **insurance** before travelling to cover against theft, loss, illness or injury. Before paying for a whole new policy it's worth checking whether you are already covered: some all-risks home insurance policies may cover your possessions when overseas, and many private medical schemes offer coverage extensions for abroad. There may be some form of insurance included if you paid for your holiday with a **credit card**, too.

For most, though, it is worth buying **specialist travel insurance**; there are plenty of deals online (it's rarely good value when bought from a travel agent), or consider the offer from Rough Guides (see box below). Most policies exclude so-called **dangerous sports** unless an extra premium is paid: in Crete this could include horseriding, windsurfing, jet-skiing, mountaineering and motorbiking.

If you need to make a **medical claim**, you should keep receipts for medicines and treatment, and in the event you have anything stolen or lost, you

---

ROUGH GUIDES TRAVEL INSURANCE

Rough Guides has teamed up with WorldNomads.com to offer great **travel insurance** deals. Policies are available to residents of more than 150 countries, with cover for a wide range of adventure sports, 24hr emergency assistance, high levels of medical and evacuation cover and a stream of travel safety information. Roughguides.com users can take advantage of their policies online 24/7, from anywhere in the world – even if you're already travelling. And since plans often change when you're on the road, you can extend your policy and even claim online. Roughguides.com users who buy travel insurance with WorldNomads.com can also leave a positive footprint and donate to a community development project. For more information, go to ⓦroughguides.com/shop.

must obtain an **official statement** from the police or the airline that lost your bags. With a rise in the numbers of fraudulent claims, most insurers won't even consider one unless you have a police report.

Internet

In the resorts and bigger towns there's **free wi-fi** in the majority of hotels and rooms places, as well as in many cafés and tavernas. **Internet cafés** are dying out as a result, though you can usually find something (often packed with local kids, gaming online): the most useful are listed throughout the Guide. Rates are around €2–4 per hour.

Living in Crete

Many habitual visitors fall in love with Crete and end up as part- or full-time residents, more likely buying property than renting it, and most probably retired or self-employed rather than working at relatively low Greek wages. EU citizens are entitled to stay indefinitely, and to work in Crete, but this is a highly bureaucratic society where getting a job (at least legally) is fraught with paperwork, as are the everyday needs of getting a phone, power and the like. It's beyond the scope of this book to go into detail, but there's plenty of assistance available locally, above all from the existing expat community who've done it all before. The website Ⓦ livingincrete.net is also an excellent resource.

Work

Work opportunities in Crete are severely limited and, EU membership notwithstanding, **short-term unskilled work** is often badly paid and undocumented. The old standby of work on the harvests is now dominated by immigrants from Albania and Eastern Europe, and appallingly paid even if you can find it.

There's a far better chance of employment in **tourism**, or teaching English. Many bars, tavernas and hotels have seasonal jobs, for which you should turn up early in the season and ask around. Your chances will be better if you can speak more than one language (ideally including Greek!), and if you are female. Men, unless they are trained chefs, find it harder to find any work, even washing up.

On a similar, unofficial level you might be able to work in a **tourist shop**, or (if you've the expertise) helping out at a watersports centre. Perhaps the best type of tourism-related work, however, is that of courier/greeter/group coordinator for a **package holiday company**. Most of these jobs are filled well in advance, but people may leave or fall ill – get yourself known to the reps, locally or on their airport runs, and you may get lucky.

Teaching English is largely a winter job, in the big towns where the language schools are. It's relatively well paid, but almost impossible to get into without a bona fide TEFL certificate.

Mail

Post offices are open Monday to Friday from 7.30am to 2pm, though certain main branches are also open evenings and Saturday mornings. **Airmail letters** take 3–7 days to reach the rest of Europe, 5–12 days to North America, a little longer for Australia and New Zealand. As anywhere, post offices tend to have long queues, so if all you want is a stamp (*grammatósimo*) you're better off buying it when you buy your postcards, or from almost any *periptero* (kiosk) and most minimarkets. Postage for postcards and letters up to 20g is the same for all international destinations, currently €0.75. For about €3 you can use the express service (*katepígonda*), which cuts letter delivery time to two days for the UK and three days for the Americas.

Ordinary **postboxes** are bright yellow, express boxes dark red, but it's best to use those by the door of a post office if possible, since days may pass between collections at others.

Maps

Maps of Crete are easily available all over the island, but you'll almost certainly find a better one at home. Having said that, even the best maps seem to have a number of significant errors. For drivers this is rarely more than a minor irritation, but hikers should take care not to rely solely on a single map and to confirm directions locally wherever possible.

The best maps for **driving and general use** are the Terrain and Road Editions versions; some of the better free car-rental maps are also surprisingly useful – they may be small-scale and covered in adverts, but they tend to be updated regularly, which means that they often show the main roads more accurately than many more professional-looking rivals. The Greek tourist authorities also provide a downloadable map at Ⓦ visitgreece.gr.

If you want more detail, for **hiking** for example, the best maps are from Greek cartographer Anavasi, who cover the island in three GPS-compatible regional 1:100,000 maps and also produce five excellent 1:25,000 hiking maps, three covering areas of the White Mountains, one of Mount Psilorítis, and one of the far east.

Money

Currency in Crete is the euro (€). Euro coins are issued in denominations of 1, 2, 5, 10, 20 and 50 cents and 1 and 2 euros; euro notes come in denominations of 5, 10, 20, 50, 100, 200 and 500 euros. Up-to-date exchange rates can be found on ⓦ xe.com.

Banks and exchange

The airports at Haniá and Iráklio should always have an **exchange desk** operating for passengers on incoming international flights, as well as ATMs – but at peak periods there's often a queue and it's well worth taking some euros to tide you over the first few hours.

Banks are normally open Mon–Thurs 8.30am–2.30pm, Fri 8.30am–2pm, while outside these hours larger hotels and travel agencies can often change money, albeit with hefty commissions. When using a bank, always take your passport with you and be prepared for at least one long queue – often you have to line up once to have the transaction approved and again to pick up the cash. Rates and commissions vary considerably, even between branches of the same bank, so ask first.

ATMs and credit cards

ATMs are plentiful, and can be found in all the resorts and towns of any size, though you shouldn't expect to find them in rural areas or the smaller resorts (especially on the south coast). They're easy to use, with your normal PIN, though you won't normally know what exchange rate you're getting or how much you're being charged. In most cases rates and commission are no worse than the alternatives, often better; you can avoid some of the charges by using a specialist prepaid holiday money card. Using a credit card in an ATM (as opposed to a debit card) is generally more expensive, and you'll be charged interest from the moment you do so.

Major **credit cards** are widely accepted, but only by the more expensive stores, hotels and restaurants: they're useful for renting cars, for example, but no good in the cheaper tavernas or rooms places.

Opening hours and public holidays

It's difficult to generalize about Cretan **opening hours**, which are notoriously erratic. Nonetheless the general pattern is that on Monday, Wednesday and Saturday shops are open 8.30am–2.30pm, and on Tuesday, Thursday and Friday 8.30am–2pm and

---

SHHHH! SIESTA TIME

The hours **between 3 and 5pm**, the midday *mikró ýpno* (**siesta**), are sacrosanct – it's not acceptable to visit people, make phone calls to strangers or cause any sort of loud noise (especially with motorcycles) at this time. Quiet is also legally mandated **between midnight and 8am** in residential areas.

5.30–9pm; offices will generally follow similar hours, but most reopen every evening. In tourist areas, though, stores and offices may stay open right through the day – certainly the most important **archeological sites and museums** do so. As far as possible, opening hours for these are quoted in the text, but they change with exasperating frequency, especially since the economic crisis. If you're planning a special journey try to confirm in advance, or time your visit for the core hours of 9am–2pm; many close on Mondays. **Churches and monasteries** are generally open through the day, though they, too, may well close for an afternoon siesta.

Phones

There's excellent **mobile phone** coverage throughout Crete, and you should be able to pick up a signal just about anywhere. To use your own phone you'll need to call your provider to ensure that you have international roaming switched on (US users should also check that their phone will work in Europe), and you should find out the cost of calls at the same time. International charges are coming down, but they're still very high; remember that you'll be charged for incoming as well as outgoing calls. If you plan to use a phone exten-

---

PUBLIC HOLIDAYS

Jan 1 New Year's Day
Jan 6 Epiphany
Feb/March Clean Monday, 7 weeks before Easter
March 25 Independence Day
April/May Good Friday and Easter Monday (see p.34)
May 1 May Day
May/June Whit Monday, 7 weeks after Easter
Aug 15 Assumption of the Virgin
Oct 28 Óhi Day
Dec 25/26 Christmas Day/Boxing Day

PHONE CODES AND NUMBERS

The international dialling code for Greece is +30. To phone home, dial the country code below, then the area code (minus its initial zero, except for Canada and the US), and then the number.

COUNTRY CODES		USEFUL PHONE NUMBERS	
Australia	❶0061	Ambulance	❶166
New Zealand	❶0064	Fire service	❶199
Republic of Ireland	❶00353	Forest fire reporting	❶191
South Africa	❶0027	Operator (domestic)	❶132
UK	❶0044	Operator (international)	❶139
USA & Canada	❶001	Police/emergency	❶100
		Tourist police	❶171

sively you might well be better off buying a Greek **pay-as-you-go** SIM card (or even an entire phone, starting from around €15); you may have to have your phone unlocked to use this, but most Greek mobile shops can do this for a small fee.

Calling on regular phones is pretty straightforward, and all the resorts and towns of any size will have **call boxes**, invariably sited at the noisiest street corner. These work only with **phonecards** (*tilekártes*), widely available from kiosks and newsagents in various denominations starting at €4. They offer fairly good value even for international calls, especially within Europe. A **calling card** may make international calls cheaper; either one provided by your own operator at home, accessed by a freephone number and charged directly to your domestic account (these are convenient, but rates vary), or a prepaid card which you can buy from many local kiosks and newsagents (compare rates, as different cards offer better value for different countries).

Avoid making calls from your **hotel** room, as a huge surcharge will be slapped on, though you shouldn't be charged to access a free calling card number.

Smoking

Greeks are the heaviest **smokers** in Europe, and although legally you're not allowed to smoke indoors in restaurants, bars or public offices, in practice the law is almost universally disregarded. Effective no-smoking areas are very rare indeed.

Time

Greek **summer time** begins at 2am on the last Sunday in March, when the clocks go forward one hour, and ends at 2am on the last Sunday in October when they go back. This change is not well

publicized locally, and visitors miss planes and ferries every year. Greek time is always 2hr ahead of Britain. For North America, the difference is usually 7hr for Eastern Standard Time and 10hr for Pacific Standard Time – but bear in mind that daylight saving starts 2–3 weeks earlier and ends a week later than in Europe.

Toilets

In **toilets** throughout Crete you're expected to toss paper in a wastebasket, not in the bowl: learn this habit, or you'll block the pipes. There's almost always a sign to remind you, but even if not you should do so, except in the most modern and upmarket hotels. Public toilets are rare except in the towns, usually in parks or squares, often subterranean. Otherwise try a bus station or pay for a coffee somewhere. It's worth carrying toilet paper with you – though it's provided by the attendants at public facilities, there may be none in tavernas or cafés.

Tourist information

The **National Tourist Organization of Greece** (*Ellinikós Organismós Tourismoú*, or EOT; ❿visitgreece.gr) maintains offices in most European capitals, plus major cities in North America and Australia.

On the island, **local tourist offices** in the major towns and many smaller resorts provide an array of maps, timetables and leaflets as well as details of local accommodation, sometimes offering a booking service as well. The economic crisis is taking a heavy toll, though, and most have drastically shortened their hours and reduced staffing; some are likely to close altogether. In their stead, local **travel agencies** are always helpful and many voluntarily act as improvised tourist offices; many of these are listed in the Guide. The **tourist police** may also be helpful: a branch (or often just a single delegate) of the local police, they should have some knowledge of English and deal with complaints about restaurants, taxis, hotels and all things tourist-related; call ☎171 for information and help, and see individual town accounts for local addresses.

Travellers with disabilities

It is all too easy to wax lyrical over the attractions of Crete – the stepped, narrow alleys, the ease of travel by bus and ferry, the thrill of clambering around the great archeological sites. Travellers who use a wheelchair or have limited mobility or vision may not be so impressed. Uneven pavements, steep streets, and lack of facilities in ancient towns will always be an issue. Few of the major archeological sites or museums are at all wheelchair friendly and nor, on the whole, are the towns and resorts.

Having said that, new hotels and apartments, along with modern museums, are subject to **EU legislation** and increasingly take people with disabilities into account in their design. With a little forward planning, it's possible to enjoy an inexpensive and trauma-free holiday in Crete. A quick web search will find a number of organizations that can help, including numerous small specialist agencies. One resort hotel, the *Eria* (☎+30 28210 62790, ⓦeria-resort.gr), in Maleme near Haniá, has been **designed specifically** for disabled visitors and their carers, with facilities including rental of most equipment you might need (from oxygen to hoists), physiotherapy, accessible airport transfers and so on. Inevitably, it's not cheap.

Many other hotels and apartments are accessible, and even mainstream operators and the large package companies now provide information on access, although such advice rarely extends to what happens when you venture beyond the front door.

A **medical certificate** of your fitness to travel, provided by your doctor, is extremely useful; some airlines or insurance companies may insist on it. You should also carry extra supplies of any required **medicines** and a prescription including the generic name in case of emergency. It's probably best to assume that any special equipment, drugs or clothing you may require is unavailable in Crete and will need to be brought with you.

Travelling with children

Children are worshipped and indulged in Crete, arguably to excess – wherever you go, your kids will be welcome. Greek children sleep in the afternoon and stay up late. You'll see plenty of kids at tavernas, joining in with the adult food and conversation.

While there's not much in the way of specifically child-oriented holidays to Crete, many hotels and newer apartment complexes have children's pools and small playgrounds, and most tour operators will be able to book you something suitable. Some of the fancier resort hotels have kids' clubs and activities, while almost all hotels and rooms places have three- and four-bed rooms (or can add a cot to a regular room, at minimal or no extra cost); many have small apartments with fridges and simple cooking facilities, too. There are several water parks along the north coast, and activities like gorge-hiking or boat trips can become real adventures (though don't be overambitious –they can also be really gruelling in the heat). Younger kids may also enjoy the "Happy Train" rides that operate in and around many of the major towns and resorts. Under-18s get **free entry** into state-run museums and archeological sites, and reduced prices at most attractions.

Baby foods and **nappies** (diapers) are readily available and reasonably priced.

Iráklio

MONÍ VRONDÍSI

1

Iráklio

The province of Iráklio sees more tourists than any other in Crete. They come for two simple reasons: the string of big resorts that lies to the east of the city, just an hour or so from the airport, and the great Minoan sites, almost all of which are concentrated in the centre of the island. Knossós, Mália and Festós are in easy reach of almost anywhere in the province, and there are excellent beaches all along the north coast.

Iráklio itself is a big, boisterous city – the fifth largest in Greece. Strident and modern, it's a maelstrom of crowded thoroughfares, building work and dust, and, in high summer, its great sites are packed. Penetrate behind this facade, however, and you can discover a vibrant working city with a myriad of attractive features that do much to temper initial impressions. East of the city, the startling pace of **tourist development** is all too plain to see. In peak season, it can be hard to find a room in this monument to the package tour, and expensive if you do, though some of the resorts, most notably **Mália** and **Hersónisos**, do at least have good beaches and lively nightlife. As a general rule, the further east you go, the better things get: even where the road veers briefly inland, a more appealing Crete – of olive groves, tidy villages and picturesque mountain vistas – reveals itself.

West and south of Iráklio, the beaches are smaller and the coastline is less amenable to hotel builders. To the west, there's just one small, classy resort – in the bay at **Ayía Pelayía** – a few isolated hotels and, in the hills behind, a number of interesting old villages. **Mátala** is the only resort of any size in the south, and a day-trip route takes in the major archeological sites of **Górtys**, **Festós** and **Ayía Triádha**. The rest is traditional farming country; the **Messará plain**, in particular, has always been a vital resource, and its importance is reflected in the number of large and wealthy villages here.

Iráklio city

The best way to arrive in **IRÁKLIO** (Ηράκλειο) is from the sea, the traditional approach and still the one that shows the city in its best light, with Mount Yioúhtas rising behind, the heights of the Psilorítis range to the west and, as you get closer, the great fortress guarding the harbour entrance and the city walls encircling and dominating the oldest part of town.

The reality when you arrive is less romantic: modern ferries are far too large for the old harbour and dock at giant concrete wharves alongside, while on closer inspection what little remains of the **old city** has been heavily restored, often from the bottom up. The slick renovations often look fake, pristine and polished alongside the grime that coats even the most recent buildings – a juxtaposition that seems to neatly sum up much about modern Iráklio. While the city will never be

Highlights

❶ Iráklio Crete's bustling capital boasts great restaurants and cafés, a vibrant market and an impressive harbour fortress as well as an archeological museum with the world's finest collection of Minoan artefacts. **See p.46**

❷ Knossós Crete's major tourist attraction, the world-famous palace of Knossós remains the most impressive of the Minoan sites. **See p.63**

❸ Górtys Capital of Crete in Roman times, this site has plenty of ruins to explore, including the imposing remains of Áyios Títos, the island's first Christian church. **See p.96**

❹ Festós and Mália palaces These two outstanding ancient sites in picturesque locations are superb examples of Minoan architecture. **See p.99 & p.86**

❺ Museum of Cretan Ethnology, Vóri An outstanding folk museum in a mountainous, rural area of great beauty. **See p.103**

❻ Mátala In striking contrast to the brash north coast resorts, Mátala is on a thoroughly human scale, though still with plenty going on late into the night. Nearby are plenty of quieter escapes, and it's in easy reach of many of the major sights. **See p.105**

HIGHLIGHTS ARE MARKED ON THE MAP ON P.48

IRÁKLIO

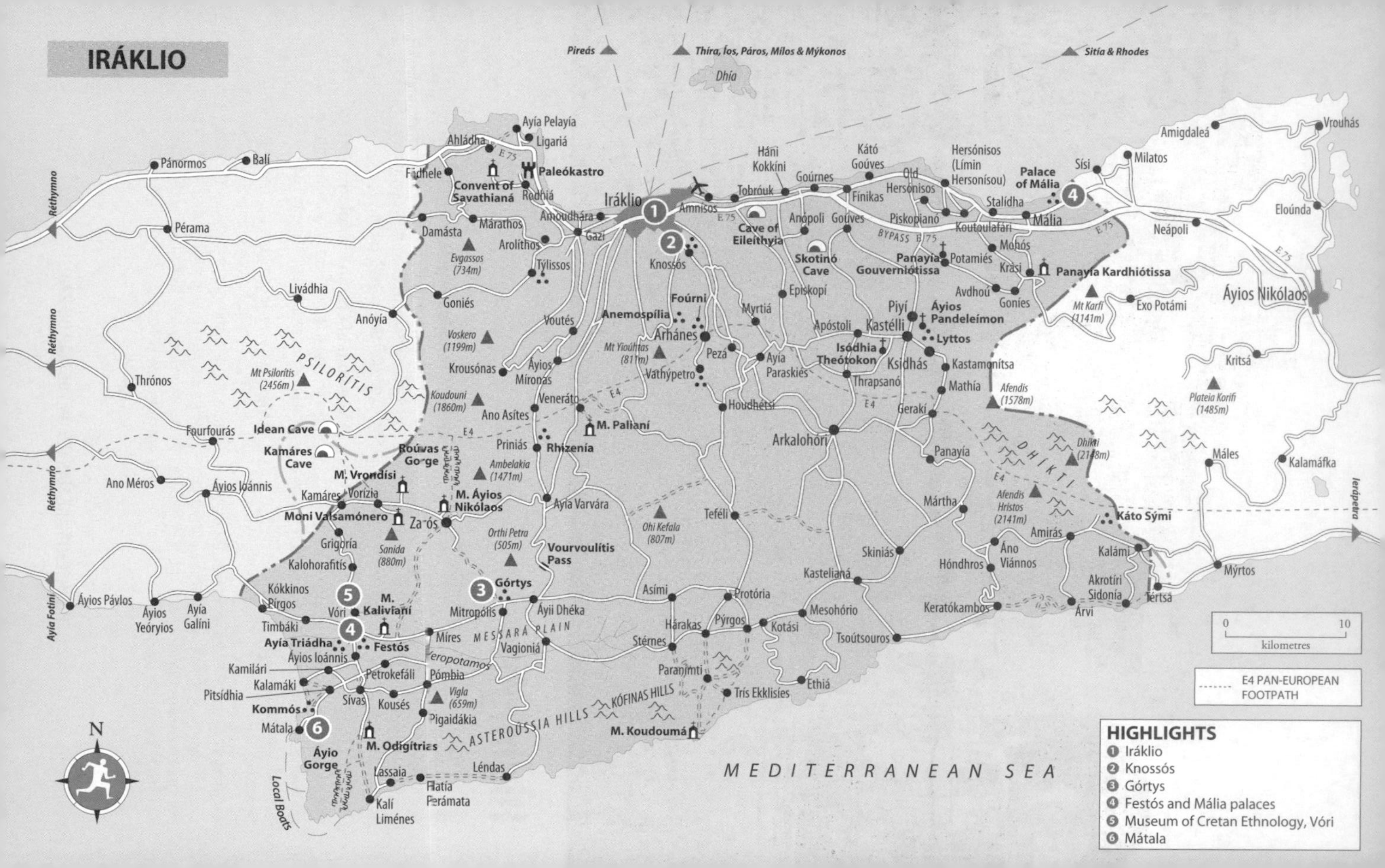

Pireás
Thíra, Íos, Páros, Mílos & Mýkonos
Sitía & Rhodes
Dhía
Ayía Pelayía
Ligariá
Ahládha
Pánormos
Balí
Fódhele
Paleókastro
Convent of Savathianá
Rodhiá
Iráklio
Amnisos
Háni Kokkíni
Tobróuk
Goúrnes
Kátó Goúves
Old Hersónisos
Hersónisos (Límin Hersonísou)
Palace of Mália
Sísi
Milatos
Amigdaleá
Vrouhás
Eloúnda
Neápoli
Réthymno
Pérama
Damásta
Márathos
Amoudhára
Gazi
Cave of Eileithyia
Anópoli
Goúves
Fínikas
Piskopianó
Stalídha
Mália
Koutoulafári
Evgassos (734m)
Arolíthos
Knossós
Skotinó Cave
Panayía Gouverniótissa
Potamiés
Mohós
Krási
Panayía Kardhiótissa
Týlissos
Livádhia
Goniés
Fourni
Anemospília
Myrtiá
Episkopí
Avdhoú
Goníes
Mt Karfí (1141m)
Exo Potámi
Áyios Nikólaos
Anóyia
Voutés
Arhánes
Piyí
Áyios Pandeleímon
Apóstoli
Kastélli
Lyttos
Voskero (1199m)
PSILORÍTIS
Mt Yioúhtas (811m)
Pezá
Ayía Paraskiés
Isódhia Theótokon
Ksidhás
Kastamonítsa
Kritsá
Thrónos
Mt Psiloritis (2456m)
Krousónas
Áyios Míronas
Vathýpetro
Thrapsanó
Mathía
Koudouni (1860m)
Veneráto
Houdhétsi
Afendis (1578m)
Plateia Korifi (1485m)
Ano Asítes
E4
Geraki
Fourfourás
Idean Cave
M. Palianí
Arkalohóri
Kamáres Cave
Roúvas Gorge
Priniás
Rhizenía
Panayía
DHÍKTI
Dhíkti (2148m)
Máles
Kalamáfka
M. Vrondísi
Ambelakia (1471m)
Ano Méros
Áyios Ioánnis
Kamáres
Vorízia
M. Áyios Nikólaos
Ayía Varvára
Afendis Hristos (2141m)
Ierápetra
Moni Valsamónero
Zarós
Orthi Petra (505m)
Ohi Kefala (807m)
Tefeli
Mártha
Káto Sými
Grigoría
Sanida (880m)
Vourvoulítis Pass
Skiniás
Amirás
Áno Viánnos
Hóndhros
Kalámi
Kalohorafitís
Kastelianá
Mýrtos
Kókkinos Pírgos
Górtys
Asími
Protória
Akrotíri Sidonía
Tértsa
Ayía Fotiní
Áyios Pávlos
Áyios Yeóryios
Ayía Galíni
Vóri
M. Kalivianí
Mitropólis
Áyii Dhéka
Mesohório
Keratókambos
Árvi
Timbáki
Ayía Triádha
Festós
Míres
MESSARÁ PLAIN
Hárakas
Pýrgos
Kotási
Tsoútsouros
Áyios Ioánnis
Stérnes
Vagioniá
Yeropotamos
Kamilári
Petrokefáli
Pómbia
Paranjmti
Ethiá
Kalamáki
Pitsídhia
Sívas
Kousés
Vigla (659m)
KÓFINAS HILLS
Trís Ekklisíes
Kommós
Pigaidákia
ASTEROUSSIA HILLS
Mátala
M. Odigítrias
M. Koudoumá
Áyio Gorge
Local Boats
Lassaia
Léndas
Flatía Perámata
Kalí Liménes
MEDITERRANEAN SEA
N
0
10
kilometres
E4 PAN-EUROPEAN FOOTPATH
HIGHLIGHTS
1 Iráklio
2 Knossós
3 Górtys
4 Festós and Mália palaces
5 Museum of Cretan Ethnology, Vóri
6 Mátala

IRÁKLIO ORIENTATION

Virtually everything of interest in Iráklio lies within the old walled city, with the majority of the sights clustered in the northeastern corner. Despite the city's rather cheerless reputation, parts of the old town can be genuinely picturesque, not least the weighty **Venetian defences**: the harbour fortress and the massive walls framing the old quarters. Focal to this area are **Venizélou** and **Eleftherías** squares, and most of the churches and museums – including the **Archeological Museum**, with the world's foremost collection of Minoan antiquities – are just a few minutes' walk from either.

The most vital thoroughfare, pedestrianized **Odhós 25-Avgoústou** (see box, p.53), lined with banks, travel and shipping agencies and car rental outfits, links the harbour with the commercial city centre. West of here, behind Platía Venizélou, is the grandly named **El Greco Park**, which is in reality more of a garden. On the opposite side of 25-Avgoústou are some of the more interesting of Iráklio's older buildings, including the church of **Áyios Títos** and the Venetian Loggia. At its southern end, 25-Avgoústou opens into **Platía Nikifourou Foka**, which forms a junction for central Iráklio's other main arteries: **Kalokerinoú** heads westwards down to the Pórta Haníon and out of the city; straight ahead, Odhós 1821 – a fashionable shopping street – heads southwest; and the adjacent Odhós 1866 is given over to the animated **market** (see p.54).

one of the jewels of the Mediterranean, the ebullient friendliness of its people and an infectious cosmopolitan atmosphere may well tempt you into giving it more than the customary one-night transit.

Brief history

A Roman port, Heraclium, stood hereabouts and the city readopted its name only at the beginning of the twentieth century. Founded by the **Saracens**, who held Crete from 827 to 961, it was originally known as **El Khandak**, after the great ditch that surrounded it, later corrupted by the Venetians to **Candia** – or Candy, as Shakespeare titled it in *Twelfth Night* – a name also applied to the island as a whole. This Venetian capital was, in its day, one of the strongest and most spectacular cities in Europe; a trading centre, a staging-point for the Crusades and, as time wore on, the front line of Christendom. The **Turks** finally conquered the city after 21 years of war, which culminated in a bitter siege from May 1667 to September 1669. Under its new Turkish rulers, the city's importance declined in relation to Haniá's, but it remained a major port and the second city in Crete. It was here, too, that the incident occurred which eventually put an end to Turkish occupation of the island (see box, p.53). Finally united with **Greece**, Iráklio's future prosperity was assured by its central position.

Almost all that you see today dates only from the last sixty years or so, partly because of the heavy bombing the city suffered during World War II, but above all thanks to Crete's booming agriculture, industry and tourism. In 1971, Iráklio regained the official title of island **capital**, and the city is now the wealthiest per head in the whole of Greece. In the boom years the authorities undertook ambitious projects to spruce up and refurbish the city centre, though many of these works have been abruptly put on hold as a result of the economic crisis.

The Harbour

The obvious starting point is the **Harbour**, now home to fishing boats and a pleasure marina but still guarded over by an impressive sixteenth-century **Venetian fortress**, generally known by its Turkish name of **Koúles**, emblazoned with the Lion of St Mark. Though it withstood the 22-year Turkish siege, time has caught up with the underwater foundations and the building has been closed to visitors pending restoration. Even from the outside it is undeniably impressive; sturdy walls protecting

IRÁKLIO CITY

● SHOPS
Eleftheroudakis	3
Iráklio Market	4
Planet International Bookstore	1
Road Editions	2

■ ACCOMMODATION
Atrion	2
Creta Camping	10
Kastro	8
Kronos	1
Lato	4
Lena	3
Megaron	9
Mirabello	6
Olympic	11
Rea	7
Youth Hostel	5

■ BARS, CLUBS & LIVE MUSIC
Central Park	7
Kafenion Fix	9
Iridanós	11
Jailhouse	8
London	1
Mayo	10
To Mílon tis Erídos	12
Pagopíion (Ice Factory)	5
Privilege	3
Rolling Stone Rock Bar	6
Senses Club	2
Take Five	4

● CAFÉS
Hatzaki	16
Kírkor	14
Mare	3
News Café	12
Utopia	11

● RESTAURANTS
Aspro Piáto	6
I Avlí tou Defkaliona	7
Giakoumis	17
Hovoli	19
Ippokampos	1
Katsinas	4
Ta Ladadika	18
Liasti	20
Ligo Krasí, Ligo Thálassa	13
Loukoulos	2
The Mexican	9
O Miltos	5
Pagopíion	10
Peri Orexeos	15
Terzaki	8

> **IRÁKLIO SUMMER FESTIVAL**
>
> The **Iráklio Summer Festival** runs from July to mid-September. Held at venues across the city, mostly open-air, it includes exhibitions, concerts and plays by groups from around the world, some of which are top-notch: details and a brochure listing all the events are available from the tourist office.

a series of chambers in which the defenders must have enjoyed an overwhelming sense of security. The causeway leading to the fort is a favourite place for a stroll and for locals to fish: at night, when the fortress is floodlit, it's a fine place to watch the ferries coming and going.

The Arsenali

On the landward side of the harbour, the vaulted **Arsenali** are marooned in a sea of traffic scooting along the harbour road. Now undergoing a long process of restoration, in their heyday these shipyards were at the water's edge and as many as fifty galleys at a time could be built here, or dragged ashore to be overhauled and repaired.

The city walls

Iráklio's **city walls** were originally thrown up in the fifteenth century, and constantly improved thereafter as Crete became increasingly isolated in the path of Turkish westward expansion: their final shape owes much to Michele Sanmicheli, who arrived here in 1538 having previously designed the fortifications of Padua and Verona. In its day, this was the strongest bastion in the Mediterranean. Though well preserved and restored in parts, the walls are tricky to access. The easiest approach is to follow Odhós Pedhiádhos south from the back of Platía Eleftherías and find your way up one of the dusty tracks that lead to the top of the rampart. With luck and a little scrambling, you can walk all the way around from here, clockwise, to the **Áyios Andréas Bastion** overlooking the sea in the west. To follow the walls in the other direction, simply head west along the coast for a little over 1km from the harbour until you reach this mighty bastion.

There are some curious views as you walk around, often looking down onto the rooftops, but the fabric of the walls themselves is rarely visible – it's simply like walking on a dusty path raised above the level of its surrounds. A word of warning, though: usually completely safe in daytime, the walls tend to attract less desirable types from dusk onwards.

Nikos Kazantzákis' tomb

On the **Martinengo Bastion**, facing south, is the **tomb of Nikos Kazantzákis**, Crete's greatest writer (see p.52). Despite his works being banned for their unorthodox views, Kazantzákis' burial rites were performed at Áyios Mínos Cathedral, although no priests officially escorted his body up here. His simple grave is adorned only with an inscription from his own writings: "I hope for nothing, I fear nothing, I am free". At the weekend, Iráklians gather to pay their respects – and to enjoy a free, grandstand view of the matches played by the city's once proud, but now second-string football team Ergotelis (see p.62) in the stadium below.

City gates

For the most impressive views of the city's defences, stroll out through one of the elaborate gates, the **Pórta Haníon** at the bottom of Kalokerinoú or the **Pórta Kenoúria** at the top of Odhós Evans, and admire them from the outside. Both of these portals date from the second half of the sixteenth century, when the majority of the surviving defences were completed. At the Pórta Kenoúria, the walls are over 40m thick.

1

NIKOS KAZANTZÁKIS

Crete's best-known writer, **Nikos Kazantzákis**, was born in Iráklio in 1883 in the street now named after him. His early life was shadowed by the struggle against the Turks and for union with Greece. Educated in Athens and Paris, Kazantzákis travelled widely throughout his life, working for the Greek government on more than one occasion (serving briefly as Minister for Education in 1945) and for UNESCO, but above all writing. He produced a vast range of works, including philosophical essays, epic poetry, travel books, translations of classics such as Dante's *Divine Comedy* into Greek and, of course, the novels on which his fame in the West mostly rests. **Zorba the Greek** (1946) was his first and most celebrated novel, but his output remained prolific to the end of his life. Particularly relevant to Cretan travels are *Freedom or Death* (1950), set amid the struggle against the Turks, and the autobiographical *Report to Greco*, published posthumously in 1961 (Kazantzákis died in Freiburg, West Germany, in 1957 after contracting hepatitis from an unsterilized vaccination needle during a visit to China).

Kazantzákis is widely accepted as the leading Greek writer of the twentieth century, and Cretans are extremely proud of him, despite the fact that most of his later life was spent abroad, that he was banned from entering Greece for long periods, and that he was excommunicated by the Orthodox Church for his vigorously expressed doubts about Christianity. This last detail gained him more notoriety when his *The Last Temptation of Christ* was filmed by Martin Scorsese, amid much controversy, in 1988. The church was also instrumental in working behind the scenes to deny him the Nobel Prize, which he lost by one vote to Albert Camus in 1957. Many critics now regard his writing as overblown and pretentious, but even they admit that the best parts are where the Cretan in Kazantzákis shows through, in the tremendous gusto and vitality of books like *Zorba* and *Freedom or Death*. Kazantzákis himself was always conscious, and proud, of his Cretan heritage.

The Historical Museum

Sófokli Venizélou 27 • Mon–Sat: May–Oct 9am–5pm; Nov–April 9am–3.30pm • €5 • ⓦ historical-museum.gr

The **Historical Museum** is one of the most dynamic in Iráklio, with frequent events and interesting temporary exhibitions. The fascinating permanent collection – with many interactive displays – helps fill the gap which, for most people, yawns between Knossós and the present day, and since it's always virtually deserted, wandering around is a pleasure.

The ground and first floors

The **ground floor**, if you're working chronologically, is the place to start; it contains sculptures and architectural fragments from the Byzantine, Venetian and Turkish periods. There are some beautiful pieces, especially a fifteenth- or sixteenth-century tiered fountain from a Venetian palace. The **first floor** has religious art, wall paintings and documents from the same periods, plus a reconstruction of a typically domed Cretan church. Here also are two works by **El Greco** – the small *View of Mount Sinai and the Monastery of St Catherine* (painted around 1570) and the even smaller *Baptism of Christ* (1567). Considering the hundreds of canvases by El Greco displayed in the museums of Spain and elsewhere it is sad to note that these are the only works by Crete's greatest painter to be seen on the island of his birth (see p.56 & p.78).

The upper floors

The museum's **upper floors** bring things up to date with reconstructions of the studies of the writer Nikos Kazantzákis and of the Cretan statesman (and Greek prime minister) Emanuel Tsouderos; photos and documents relating to the occupation of Crete by the Germans, plus the odd helmet and parachute harness; and a substantial selection of folk art – particularly textiles. There's also the reconstructed interior of a Cretan farmhouse, and a small **café** with sea-view terrace.

The Priouli fountain and around

1

The Ottoman **fountain of Idomeneus** (mentioned by Kazantzákis in his novel *Kapetan Michalis*), is set into a wall to the rear of the Historical Museum, partly obscured in the evening by diners on the terrace of a nearby taverna. Nearby to the west (close to the junction of Gorgolaini and Dhelimárkou) lies the impressive **Priouli fountain**, built at the very end of the Venetian period during the long siege of the city by Turkish forces. Sited in what was then the old Jewish quarter, the fountain is based on the form of a Greek temple. It used an underground source to supply the city with water after the Turks had destroyed the aqueducts.

Odhós 25-Avgoústou

Pedestrianized **Odhós 25-Avgoústou** heads up from the harbour past or towards many of the city's major attractions. On the left as you climb, the church of **Áyios Títos** commands a lovely little plaza. Originally Byzantine, but wholly rebuilt by the Venetians in the sixteenth century, it was adapted by the Turks as a mosque and rebuilt by them after a major earthquake in 1856. The Orthodox Church renovated the building after the Turkish population left Iráklio, and it was reconsecrated in 1925. A reliquary inside contains the skull of St Titus (see p.333), originally brought here from his tomb in Górtys; his body was never found. In the Middle Ages, the skull was regularly and ceremonially exhibited to the people of Iráklio, but was later taken to Venice, where it stayed from the time of the Turkish invasion until 1966. On August 25 each year, a major procession from the church marks St Titus' Day.

San Marco and around

On the top side of Platía Ayíou Títou, facing 25-Avgoústou, stands the Venetian City Hall with its famous **loggia**, reconstructed after earthquake damage was compounded by the rigours of World War II. Just beyond here on the left, the Venetian-style **San Marco** was the cathedral in the Venetian era (two interesting carved gravestones survive in what was the altar area), and later converted to a mosque, its steps usually crowded with sightseers spilling over from the nearby platía. Neither building has found a permanent role in its refurbished state, but both are generally open to house some kind of exhibition or craft show.

Platía Venizélou

Platía Venizélou (aka Fountain Square or Platía Liontária, Lion Square), formerly the Venetian Piazza San Marco, opens off 25-Avgoústou opposite San Marco church.

STREET OF THE AUGUST MARTYRS

The name of the city's major thoroughfare, in full **Odhós Martírion 25-Avgoústou** (the 25th of August Martyrs), derives from one of the final acts in the ending of Turkish domination of the island at the end of the nineteenth century. In 1898 under the aegis of the great powers of post-Napoleonic Europe (France, Italy, Russia and Britain), an autonomous Cretan state with an Executive Council was formed under Turkish sovereignty, regarded by most Cretans as a prelude to union with Greece. On August 25 a detachment of British soldiers was escorting Council officials along this street from the harbour when they were attacked by a violent mob of Turkish Cretans, smarting at what they saw as the betrayal of their birthright. In the bloody riot that ensued, hundreds of Christian Cretans lost their lives as well as seventeen British soldiers and the British Honorary Consul. This stirred the British to take reprisals and, on the principle of an eye for an eye, they rounded up and hanged seventeen of the Turkish Cretan ringleaders and put many more in prison. Shortly after this, the British navy sailed into the harbour and the city was cleared of Turkish troops. The following November the last Turkish military forces left the island they had controlled for 230 years.

1

Ringed by busy cafés, its focal point is the **Morosini Fountain**, which dates from the final years of Venetian rule and upon its inauguration in 1628 became the city's main source of fresh water. Originally the whole thing was topped by a giant statue of Poseidon, but even without him it's impressive: the lions on guard are two to three hundred years older than the rest of the structure, while the eight basins are decorated with marine themes including dolphins and Tritons.

Odhós 1866: the market

Daily 8am–8pm (though individual stalls vary; some close on Sun, while many take a siesta from around 2–5pm)

Odhós 1866 is packed throughout the day with the stalls and customers of Iráklio's **market**. This is one of the few living reminders of an older city, with an atmosphere reminiscent of an eastern bazaar. There are luscious fruit and vegetables, as well as butchers' and fishmongers' stalls and others selling a bewildering variety of herbs and spices, cheese and yoghurt, leather and plastic goods, CDs, tacky souvenirs, an amazing array of cheap kitchen utensils, pocket knives and just about anything else you might conceivably need.

Platía Kornárou

At the top of the Odhós 1866 market, **Platía Kornárou** makes a pleasantly tranquil contrast. The focal point of the square is a beautiful hexagonal **Turkish pumphouse**, heavily restored, which now houses a café run by the municipality, a meeting place for elderly locals, who converse at the tables under the trees. The small sixteenth-century Venetian drinking fountain beside the café – the **Bembo Fountain** (named after its designer Zuanne Bembo) – was the first to supply the city with running water. It incorporates a headless Roman torso imported from Ierápetra.

Platía Eleftherías

In **Platía Eleftherías** (**Liberty Square**), a line of pricey pavement cafés face a rather uninspiring concourse dotted with gum trees and benches, and skirted by busy roads. Mainly due to its size the square is one of the city's most popular venues for political demonstrations, but most of the time is used by locals for walking, talking and sitting out. There's a small bust of Nikos Kazantzákis and a larger-than-life statue of Eleftherios Venizélos (the leading figure in the struggle for union with Greece), staring out over the harbour from the ramparts and looking remarkably like Lenin. Beyond the statue, you reach the entrance to the **Public Gardens**, as often as not half taken over by a funfair, but otherwise relatively peaceful. On its western flank the square is linked to Platía Venizélou by the pedestrianized alley **Dedhálou**, lined with many of Iráklio's top designer clothing stores.

Above all, however, Platía Eleftherías offers access to the **Archeological Museum**, off its northeast corner.

The Archeological Museum

Xanthoudhídhou 2, entry to annexe at the side, from Hatzidhaki • April–Nov Tues–Sat 8am–8pm, Sun & Mon 9am–4pm; Dec–March Tues–Sun 8am–3pm, Mon noon–5pm; opening hours will change as the refurbishment continues, so call ahead or check with the tourist office (see p.59) for the latest • €4, combined ticket with Knossós €10 • ☎ 2810 279 000

Iráklio's **Archeological Museum** is one of the major reasons to visit the city. The museum houses far and away the most important collection of **Minoan art** and artefacts anywhere in the world, and a visit to Knossós or the other sites will be greatly enhanced if you've been here first. Given the museum's status at the time of writing (see box opposite) it is impossible to know exactly what will be on display, or where, but many of the major exhibits are described below.

IRÁKLIO'S ARCHEOLOGICAL MUSEUM: THE REFURBISHMENT

Iráklio's archeological museum closed in November 2006 for a complete and much-needed **refurbishment**, with a temporary exhibition established at the rear of the building while work took place. The proposed two-year completion date proved hopelessly optimistic – it took four years just to approve the plans, and funds for completion have been held up by the economic crisis – but the first galleries of the new museum opened at the end of 2012 with full reopening pencilled in for 2013; in the meantime, many of the most important items are displayed in the annexe.

1

Prehistory and the early Minoans

The museum begins with the earliest signs of human settlement in Crete, around 6000 BC. The **Vasilikí pottery** here, from an early Minoan site in the east (see p.145), is a foretaste of the more famous **Kamáres ware**, with often elaborate white and red decoration on a dark ground. Examples of this style of pottery from the palace at Festós (p.99) are regarded as the peak of this artistic development – exemplified by a magnificent vase with sculpted white flowers in high relief. The fascinating "**Town Mosaic**" from Knossós consists of a series of glazed plaques depicting multistorey Minoan houses, beautiful pieces that probably fitted together to form a decorative scene. The celebrated **Festós disc**, a circular slab of clay upon which hieroglyphic characters have been inscribed in a spiral pattern, has been the subject of intense academic debate, but remains undeciphered.

The New Palace period

From the New Palace period (1700–1450 BC) the collection features the **Jug of Reeds**, typical of the new styles that replaced the Kámares pottery, and the renowned **bull's head rhyton**, a sacred vessel used in religious ceremonies and found in the Little Palace at Knossós. Also worth looking out for are two representations of the **snake goddess** – both wearing tight-waisted, breast-baring dresses and decorated aprons, each with snakes coiling around their hands – which may equally be priestesses who officiated in the celebration of a snake cult. A **gaming board** from the Corridor of the Draughtsboard at Knossós is beautiful too, made of ivory, blue paste, crystal, and gold and silver leaf, with ivory pieces – a further reminder of the luxurious life which some Minoans at least could enjoy. The "Harvesters Vase" is the finest of the three **vases** from Ayía Triádha (see p.101) depicting with vivid realism a procession returning home from the fields; the harvesters are led by a strangely dressed character with long hair and a big stick, possibly a priest, and accompanied by musicians, one of whom is waving a *sistrum* (a percussion instrument which sounds rather like a maraca).

Among the **jewellery** – gold signet rings, necklaces of gold and beads, and other work demonstrating the subtle granulation typical of Minoan style – is the **pendant of the two bees** from the palace at Mália (see p.86), an intricate work depicting bees storing a golden disc (representing a drop of honey) in a comb. Look out, too, for some fine gold sword hilts and two fabulous **helmets**, one of boar's tusks (reconstructed), the other of bronze with long cheekpieces. And from the final period of the palace culture there's a model of a modest **Minoan dwelling** from Arhánes with small rooms and tiny windows to keep out the bright Cretan sun and fierce winds; the roof terrace above is similar to those seen on village houses throughout Crete today.

Minoan palace frescoes

The most spectacular feature of the old museum and the most likely star attraction of its successor will no doubt be the **Minoan palace frescoes**, among the greatest achievements of Minoan art. Most of those in the collection came originally from Knossós, and date from the New Palace period. Only tiny fragments of actual frescoes survived, but they have been almost miraculously reconstituted, and mounted on backgrounds which

1

continue the design to give as true an impression of the entire fresco as possible. Among the highlights are four large panels from the enormous fresco that led all the way along the Corridor of the Procession at Knossós, the spectacular "**Bull Leaping**" fresco, depicting acrobats performing somersaults over the back of a charging bull, and the famous "**La Parisienne**", a female representation so dubbed for her bright red lips, huge eyes, long hair and fancy dress, almost certainly a priestess or a goddess.

Ayía Triádha sarcophagus

The **Ayía Triádha sarcophagus** is decorated in the same manner as the palace frescoes and, because nothing has been restored or reconstructed, is in some ways even more striking. The only stone sarcophagus to be found in Crete, its unique and elaborate painted-plaster ornamentation has led archeologists to assume that it was made originally for a royal burial and later reused. On one side is a depiction of an animal sacrifice, with a bull already dead on the altar and two goats tied up awaiting their fates. On the other are two scenes, perhaps of relatives making offerings for the safe passage of the deceased. The ends feature a scene of goddesses riding in a chariot drawn by griffins, and of two women in a chariot pulled by goats above a procession of men.

Greek and Roman eras

The first of the new museum galleries to open were devoted to **Classical Greek and Greco-Roman sculpture**. The post-Minoan era in Crete tends to be overlooked given the overwhelming interest in Minoan civilization, but there are some very fine pieces including a magnificent statue of Apollo (or Athena) and a superbly carved second-century AD Roman sarcophagus found at Mália.

Platía Ayías Ekaterínis

Three churches ring the **Platía Ayías Ekaterínis**, a quiet escape from the busy shopping streets close by. The **cathedral of Áyios Minas**, a rather undistinguished nineteenth-century building, is notable mainly for its size and the gaudiness of its decoration. Just in front stands its tiny forerunner; the medieval **church of Áyios Mínas**, whose gilded and elaborately decorated altarpiece contains some interesting icons.

Ayía Ekateríni

The most interesting church on Platía Ayías Ekaterínis, **Ayía Ekateríni**, was part of a monastic school which, up to the end of Venetian rule, was one of the centres of the Cretan Renaissance, a last flourish of Eastern Christian art following the fall of Byzantium. Among the school's students were Vitzentzos Kornaros, author of the Cretan classic *Erotókritos*, and many leading Orthodox theologians; most importantly, however, it served as an art school where Byzantine tradition came face to face with the influences of the Venetian Renaissance. Among the greatest of the pupils was the late sixteenth-century painter **Mihailis Dhamaskinos**, who introduced perspective and depth to Byzantine art, while never straying far from the strict traditions of icon painting. The most famous Cretan painter of them all, **El Greco**, took the opposite course, wholeheartedly embracing Italian styles, to which he brought the influence of his Byzantine training. Although there is little evidence, it's generally accepted that these two – Dhamaskinos and El Greco – were near contemporaries at the school.

The church used to house a **Museum of Religious Art** with the finest collection of **Cretan icons** anywhere, including many of Dhamaskinos' finest works. However, this closed for restoration and appears to have become a victim of the economic crisis, with no sign of reopening and no one sure of the current whereabouts of the icons. In the meantime, you can see two further icons attributed to Dhamaskinos in the fourteenth-century church of **Áyios Mathéos**, a couple of blocks southwest of the cathedral on Odhós Taxiárhou Markopoúlou.

Natural History Museum

Sófokli Venizélou • Mon–Fri 9am–3pm, Sat & Sun 10am–6pm • €6 • ☎ 2810 282 740, Ⓦ nhmc.uoc.gr

Spectacularly housed in a converted power plant overlooking the bay of Dermatás, the **Natural History Museum** examines the ecosystems of the eastern Mediterranean along with Crete's geological evolution, the arrival of man, and the environment as it would have appeared to the Minoans. Exhibits over four floors (with more still to come) display fossils, rocks, minerals and caves, and the flora and fauna of modern Crete. For kids there's the **Discovery Centre** in the basement, a wonderful hands-on interactive natural playground with microscopes and mock-up marine exploration boat. There's plenty on dinosaurs too, including a huge 4.5m-high prehistoric Cretan mammoth, reconstructed from fossil remains; and there's an **earthquake simulator** and a planetarium. An emphasis on respect and care for the environment, and on species endangered by tourism and development, is a welcome reflection of the growing awareness of these issues on the island.

City beaches

When and if Iráklio's cultural pursuits become overwhelming, it's easy to escape the city for a few hours to lie on the **beach**. The simplest course is to head east, beyond the airport, to the municipal beach at **Amnísos** or to the marginally quieter **Tobróuk** beach. Beaches to the west are less prone to aircraft noise but are also more commercialized. Turn to "Getting Around" (see p.58) for details of how to reach them.

Eastern beaches

To the east of the city, past the airport, the old road along the coast runs past a series of sandy strands. A few areas are fenced off as pay beaches with showers, changing rooms and other facilities, but between them are plenty of free spots. **Amnísos** is perhaps the pick here, with tavernas and food stalls immediately behind the beach, and showers and loungers for rent; there's good sand and clean water, too, although the stream of planes coming in to land directly over your head can be wearing. Amnísos itself is a famous name in Minoan archeology, and through a fence you can glimpse the remains of the small settlement here. This was apparently a port for Knossós, from which the Cretan forces engaged in the Trojan War are said to have set sail, and it was in a villa here that the unusual **Fresco of the Lilies** was found – now on display in the Archeological Museum (p.54). In the hills behind is the locked and inaccessible **Cave of Eileíthyia**, which gets a mention in the *Odyssey* as one of Odysseus's stopovers on his way home from Troy.

Just beyond Amnísos, the beach at **Tobróuk** is arguably even better, with more tavernas and drink stalls, slightly fewer people, and relative peace to be found if you walk a little way along the sand.

Western beaches

The beaches to the **west** of the city are less atmospheric and more exposed to the wind and waves than the eastern ones – which makes them popular with local surfers and kitesurfers. Cutting through Iráklio's prosperous western suburbs, you end up on a road which runs through the strip-development of **Amoudhára**, finally ending up at the luxury *Creta Beach* hotel complex, unappealingly sited immediately before the power station and cement works. **Amoudhára Beach** lies on the other side of the many hotels along this road, and getting to it is not always easy; although the beach is open to the public, there are very few access roads.

| ARRIVAL AND DEPARTURE | IRÁKLIO CITY |

BY PLANE

Iráklio airport The airport (Heraklion; ☎ 2810 397 800, Ⓦ heraklion-airport.info) is right on the coast, 4km east of the city. Bus #1 leaves for Platía Eleftherías (every 20min until 11pm; €1.50) from the car park in front of the terminal; buy your ticket at the booth before boarding.

1

There are also plenty of taxis outside, with prices to major destinations posted – it's €10–12 to the centre of town; agree on the fare before taking the cab.

Airlines Aegean (airport office ☎2810 344 324, ⓦaegeanair.com) and Olympic, 25-Avgoústou 27 (☎2810 284 846, ⓦolympicair.com) are the main scheduled airlines with domestic flights to Athens and elsewhere, and international connections via Athens or Thessaloníki; Cyprus Airways, Hariláou Trikoúpi 9 (☎2810 342 776, ⓦcyprusair.com) also fly to Athens and Sky Express (airport office ☎2810 223 500, ⓦskyexpress.gr) and Minoan Air, Vosporoú 1 (☎2810 333 183, ⓦminoanair .com) operate small planes to Athens and the islands. EasyJet, Jet2 and charter airlines have direct flights from the UK in summer.

Domestic destinations Athens (12 daily; 50min); Kíthira (3 weekly, 1hr 30min); Kós (4 weekly; 1hr); Mytilíni (Lésvos, 4 weekly; 1hr 15min); Rhodes (daily; 1hr); Sitía (3 weekly; 30min); Thessaloníki (at least 2 daily; 1hr 15min).

BY FERRY

Ferry wharves From the wharves where the ferries dock, the city rises directly ahead in steep tiers. If you're heading for the centre on foot, for the Archeological Museum or the tourist office, cut straight up the stepped alleys behind the bus station (from where there are buses to the centre) onto Doúkos Bófor and to Platía Eleftherías (about a 15min walk). For accommodation, though, and to get a better idea of the layout of Iráklio's main attractions, it's simpler to follow the main roads: head west along the coast, past the major eastbound bus station and on by the Venetian harbour before cutting left towards the centre on Odhós 25-Avgoústou.

Operators and destinations Minoan Lines, 25-Avgoústou 17 (☎2810 229 602, ⓦminoan.gr) and ANEK/Superfast, Dhimokratías 11 (☎2810 223 067, ⓦanek.gr) have nightly ferries to Athens (9.30/10pm; 8hr 30min); ANEK also operate the *Prevelis*, departing Wed & Sat am to Sitía (3hr), Kássos (6hr), Kárpathos (8hr), Hálki (11hr) and Rhodes (13hr), Sun pm to Añáñ (4hr), Santoríni (6hr), Mílos (10hr) and Pireás (16hr). Hellenic Seaways (ⓦhsw.gr) operate a daily fast catamaran (April–Oct) to Thíra (Santoríni; 2hr), Íos (2hr 40min), Páros (4hr) and Mýkonos (4hr 50min); Seajets (ⓦseajets.gr) also operate daily in summer to Thíra (Santoríni; 2hr 15min).

Agents The local agent for Hellenic Seaways and Seajets is Paleologos Travel, 25-Avgoústou 5 (Mon–Fri 8.30am–9pm, Sat 9am–3pm; ☎2810 346 185, ⓦferries.gr), who have current timetables and can sell tickets for all ferries.

Timetables ⓦopenseas.gr.

BY CAR

Parking Arriving in town by car, the best bet is to head for one of the signposted city-centre car parks (€3–6/day depending on location). One of the best is the large Museum car park on Doúkos Bófor, 70m downhill from the Archeological Museum, which uses space below the city walls and has plenty of shade.

BY BUS

Timetables ⓦbus-service-crete-ktel.com.

Bus Station A On the main road between the ferry dock and the Venetian harbour, Bus Station A serves all the main north coast routes; west to Réthymno and Haniá and east along the coastal highway to Hersónisos, Mália, Áyios Nikólaos and Sitía, as well as southeast to Ierápetra and points en route. There's a left luggage office here (daily 6am–9pm; €2/bag/day).

Destinations Arhánes (15 daily 6.30am–9pm; fewer at weekends; 30min); Ay. Nikólaos (21 daily 6.30am–10.30pm; 1hr 30min); Ay. Pelayía (3 daily 9am, 2.30pm & 5.30pm; 45min); Haniá (16 daily 5.30am–9pm; 3hr); Hersónisos (every 15min 6.30am–11pm; 45min); Ierápetra (8 daily 6.30am–7.15pm; 2hr 30min); Kastélli (6 daily 6.45am–7pm; fewer at weekends; 1hr); Lasíthi plateau (Mon & Fri 1.45pm; 1hr 30min); Mália (every 15min 6.30am–11pm; 1hr); Réthymno (16 daily 5.30am–9pm; 1hr 30min); Sísi (daily 3pm; 1hr 30min); Sitía (5 daily 6.30am–6.45pm; 3hr 15min).

Bus Station B Buses for the southwest (Festós, Mátala and Ayía Galíni) and along the inland roads west (Týlissos, Anóyia and Fódhele) operate out of Bus Station B just outside Pórta Haníon, a 15min walk from the centre down Kalokerinoú or jump on any city bus heading along this street.

Destinations Anóyia (3 daily 9am–2.15pm; 1hr); Ay. Galíni (7 daily 6.30am–4.30pm; 2hr 15min); Festós (6 daily 7.30am–3.30pm; 1hr 30min); Mátala (4 daily 7.30am–3.30pm; 2hr); Míres (11 daily 6.30am–8pm; 1hr 30min).

GETTING AROUND

By bus Only the further-flung sites and beaches really justify taking a bus. For the beaches, head for Platía Eleftherías; westbound bus #6 stops outside the *Capsis Hotel* and heads out through the Pórta Haníon (past Bus Station B); eastbound #7 departs every 15min or so from the tree-shaded stop opposite. Knossós buses start from the city bus stands alongside Bus Station A and pass through Platía Eleftherías; airport buses also pass through the square. It's easier to buy

tickets (€1.50) before you board, from machines in Platía Eleftherías and elsewhere, or from many kiosks.

Bike and car rental 25-Avgoústou is lined with rental companies, but you'll often find better deals on the backstreets nearby; it's always worth asking for discounts. Try Blue Sea, Kosmá Zótou 7, just off the bottom of 25-Avgoústou (☎2810 241 097, ⓦbluesearentals.com). Alianthos, Íkarou 97 and at the airport (☎2810 390 482, alianthos-group.com); Kosmos, 25-Avgoústou 15 (🕿 2810 241 357, ✆ cosmos-sa.gr); Caravel, 25-Avgoústou 39 (🕿 2810 245 345, ✆ caravel.gr), or Ritz in the *Hotel Rea*, Kalimeráki 1 (🕿 2810 223 638, ✆ hotelrea.gr). All offer free delivery to hotels and airport.

Taxis Major taxi stands are in Platía Eleftherías, Platía Kornarou, Odhós Dhikeosýnis by the market and at the bus stations; or call 🕿 2810 210 102 or 🕿 2810 210 168. Prices should be displayed on boards at the taxi stands.

INFORMATION AND TOURS

Tourist office Xanthoudhídhou 1, just below Platía Eleftherías opposite the Archeological Museum (Mon–Fri: May–Sept 9am–5pm; Oct–April 9am–2.30pm; 🕿 2810 246 298, ✆ heraklion.gr). There's a second office at the airport (May–Sept daily 8am–8pm).

Travel agencies 25-Avgoústou is crammed with shipping and general travel agents; Paleologos Travel, 25-Avgoústou 5 (Mon–Fri 8.30am–9pm, Sat 9am–3pm; 🕿 2810 346 185, ✆ ferries.gr) sells tickets for all ferries.

City tours Two rival companies operate hop-on, hop-off bus tours, offering a good overview of the city with stops at all the major sights and museums. The route stays almost entirely outside the walls, so doesn't include the city centre, but they do go out as far as Knossós. In high season they run every 40min or so – the red bus (✆ cretecitytour .com) is more frequent than the green (✆ her-openbus.gr); a 24hr ticket costs €20, though if you hesitate their ubiquitous touts may offer you a better deal.

ACCOMMODATION

Finding a room can be difficult in high season. **Inexpensive places** are mainly concentrated in the streets above the Venetian harbour to the west of Odhós 25-Avgoústou. More **luxurious hotels** mostly lie closer to Platía Eleftherías and near the eastbound bus station. Noise can be a problem wherever you stay; unless stated, all of the following have free wi-fi.

★ **Atrion** Hronáki 9 🕿 2810 246 000, ✆ atrion.gr. This attractive, modern, business-style hotel, with all the comforts that implies – marble bathrooms, minibar, silent a/c – combines luxury with a personal touch and exceptionally friendly welcome. Top-floor suites have stunning views. Breakfast included. **€85**

Kastro Theotokopoúlou 22 🕿 2810 284 185, ✆ kastro -hotel.gr. Very comfy mid-range hotel with a/c rooms, flat-screen TV and modern en-suite bathrooms, handily located on a side street behind El Greco park. Rooms look brand new, though the Olympic theme of the decor has dated badly. Breakfast included. **€60**

Kronos Agarathou 2 🕿 2810 282 240, ✆ kronoshotel .gr. Refurbished in 2011, this friendly two-star hotel is located on a busy street (so there's some traffic noise) by the central seafront. En-suite rooms with a/c, TV, fridge and balcony, some with wonderful sea views (at extra cost). **€55**

★ **Lato** Epimenídhou 15 🕿 2810 228 103, ✆ lato.gr. Stylish boutique hotel in a great central location opposite the Venetian harbour, with luxurious rooms sporting a/c, minibar, TV and fine balcony views over the port (the higher floors have better views). Excellent rooftop bar and restaurant, *Herbs' Garden*, in summer. Breakfast included. **€89**

Lena Lahana 10 🕿 2810 223 280, ✆ lena-hotel.gr. Likeable small hotel with friendly management in a quiet street. Simple en-suite or shared-bath rooms all have a/c, TV and a kettle and mugs. The second floor is airier. Shared bath **€43**, en suite **€55**

Megaron Doúkos Bófor 9 🕿 2810 305 300,

✆ gdmmegaron.gr. Imposing five-star directly above the bus station. Lots of black marble in public areas, and well-equipped a/c balcony rooms (extra for sea views), plus sauna, gym and rooftop pool. It's all a bit soulless, but the rooftop bar (open to all) has spectacular views over the Venetian harbour. Breakfast included. **€150**

Mirabello Theotokopoúlou 20 🕿 2810 285 052, ✆ mirabello-hotel.gr. Slightly old-fashioned, family-run hotel in a peaceful street. Decent balcony rooms, a couple with shared bath, but most en suite with new windows and bathrooms, a/c and TV. Shared bath **€50**, en suite **€55**

Olympic Platía Kornarou 🕿 2810 288 861, ✆ hotel olympic.com. Modern, business-style hotel in a great location. Rooms, with laminated wooden flooring and blonde wood furnishings are quiet and well equipped, with a/c, TV, minibar and strongbox, if a little small. Breakfast included. **€78**

Rea Kalimeráki 1 🕿 2810 223 638, ✆ hotelrea.gr. A good budget option, this friendly, comfortable and clean *pension* is in a quiet area just off Hándhakos street. Some rooms with washbasin, others en suite; there can be some internal noise, and wi-fi doesn't reach all rooms. Shared bath **€35**, en suite **€45**

Youth Hostel Vironos 5 🕿 2810 286 281, ✉ heraklio youthhostel@yahoo.gr. The youth hostel occupies a wonderful old building with high ceilings and tiled or wood floors and you certainly can't complain about the price, though the dorms – single sex, with 8 to 10 bunks – and bathrooms are very basic indeed. Simple private rooms too. Dorms **€10**, rooms **€27**

1

CAMPING

Creta Camping Káto Goúves, 16km east of Iráklio ☏ 28970 41400, ✉ cretacamp@hotmail.com. The surroundings are bleak, but this is a big, well-organized site right on the seafront, with facilities including restaurant, minimarket, wi-fi, beach bar and beach loungers, as well as car rental and organized tours. Decent shady pitches and also tents to rent (€7). Two people plus tent and car **€17.50**

EATING

There's no shortage of excellent places to eat in Iráklio, though **prices** are generally slightly higher than anywhere else on the island. For good quality and reasonably priced food, you need to get away from the more obvious tourist haunts, above all the main squares of Venizélou and Eleftherías (though the former is a great coffee stop). The **market** has plenty of fresh produce, and you can also find **picnic** food at the minimarkets in tourist areas, which are open every day, and at the supermarket on the north side of El Greco Park.

RESTAURANTS

Áspro Piáto Kalokairinoú 10 ☏ 697 27 17 296. Modern *meze* place with tables out on the square beside the Historical Museum. Short menu of good *meze* (*yígandes* €3.50, meatballs €4); you order by ticking the items you want on a paper list. Occasional Cretan music nights. Daily 6pm–1am.

★ **I Avli tou Defkaliona** Kalokairinoú 8 ☏ 28102 44215. Very popular taverna-ouzerí with a great little terrace fronting the Idomeneus fountain, serving up excellent meat and fish dishes (mains €6.50–12). In high summer, you may need to book to ensure an outdoor table. If you despair of getting a table, try *Áspro Piáto* (see above) and others on the square opposite. Daily 5pm–1am.

Giakoumis Fotiou Theodosaki 5 ☏ 2810 284 039. The little alley connecting the market with Odhós Evans is entirely lined with tavernas, catering for market traders and their customers as well as tourists. Established in 1935, *Giakoumis* is very touristy these days, but it claims to be the city's oldest taverna and locals still reckon it serves up some of the best *païdhákia* (lamb chops; €10) on the island – some tribute, given the competition. You can wash them down with the *hyma* (house) wine produced by Lyrarakis, a noted Pezá vineyard (€3.50/0.5l). Mon–Sat 10am–late.

Hovoli Platía Dhaskaloyiánni 3 ☏ 2810 220 320. If all you want is a *yíros* and a beer, or some plain grilled meat, this is the pick of several simple, inexpensive places just off Platía Eleftherías. *Yíros píta* €3, grilled chicken €7. Mon–Sat noon–1am.

★ **Ippokampos** Sófokli Venizélou 3 ☏ 2810 280 240. The first of a row of places with glassed-in, sea-view terraces immediately west of the harbour, *Ippokampos* serves excellent fish at competitive prices (sardines €6.50, red mullet €11). Highly popular with locals, it's often crowded late into the evening, and you may have to queue or turn up earlier than the Greeks eat. Mon–Sat 1pm–midnight.

★ **Katsinas** Marinéli 12, Platía Pireós. A simple, economical and friendly ouzerí/grill serving tasty *mezédhes* and traditional dishes at outdoor tables. Genuinely home-made food, with hand-cut chips, good fish, and earthy *meze* like snails (€5) or wild onion bulbs (€4). Daily 11.30am–1am.

Ta Ladadika Tsikritzí 5 ☏ 2810 346 135. Welcoming little ouzerí in a pedestrianized street with outdoor tables and a cosy interior with monochrome murals of rural scenes. Excellent *mezédhes* – try their *dolmadhákia* (stuffed vine leaves). Daily 9.30am–9.30pm.

Liasti Miliara 7, just off Evans ☏ 2810 343 490. At the end of an alley with a terrace under the trees – in the centre of town yet away from the main hustle and bustle of traffic – this adventurous *mezedhopolío* produces many original dishes at reasonable prices; try the pork hock with honey (€8), the house speciality. There's also indoor dining for the cooler months. Mon–Sat 1pm–1am.

Ligo Krasí, Ligo Thálassa Marinéli at Mitsotáki ☏ 2810 300 501. This small ouzerí is very popular with locals and serves up a good selection of seafood *mezédhes* (seafood *meze* menu for two €39.80; individual dishes around €4), with a small street terrace on a busy corner facing the harbour. Daily 11.30am–1am.

Loukoulos Koraí 5 ☏ 2810 224 435. With a leafy courtyard terrace and an Italian slant to its international menu, this is one of the more elegant tavernas in Iráklio. Not as pricey as it looks (mains around €12, set menu €10–12), though the wine list can bump prices up. Daily 1pm–1am.

The Mexican Hándhakos 71 ☏ 2810 220 334. The red-and-orange ethnic decor creates a warm atmosphere in this restaurant, which serves inexpensive Mexican tacos (€2.50 each), fajitas (€17 for two, with all the trimmings), beers and jugs of sangria. Daily summer 7pm–12.30am, winter 1pm–12.30am.

O Miltos Linoperamata, 5km west of the centre ☏ 2810 821 584. Excellent, friendly and economical fish taverna, one of a cluster owned by three competing brothers, with a terrace overlooking the sea. *Taverna Delfini* and *I Kalouba* are the others, but unlike *O Miltos*, they are open only in the evening. You'll need your own transport or a taxi to get here; they're 1km west of the power station, with its red-and-white chimney stacks, and close to the cement factory – but don't let that put you off. Daily noon–midnight.

Pagopiion Platía Áyios Títos ☎ 2810 346 028. This is the pricier restaurant of Iráklio's most original bar (see below), serving international dishes and modern versions of traditional Greek food; the expansive wine list has bottles from little-known but excellent small vineyards in Crete and on the mainland. *Meze* €5–9, mains €10–20. Daily noon–late.

Peri Orexeos Koraí 10 ☎ 2810 222 679. A popular small taverna that's a good bet for creative Cretan cooking, with generous dishes such as burger stuffed with *féta*, red pepper and olives. Mains from €7; seafood risotto €10. Daily 1pm–midnight.

Terzáki Marinéli 17 ☎ 2810 221 444. This modern, slightly upmarket ouzerí is a favourite among local city-types, and serves *mezédhes*, pasta dishes and mains such as chicken fillet stuffed with spinach and mushrooms, on the outdoor street terrace. *Mezédhes* from €6. Daily noon–midnight.

CAFÉS

Hatzaki Kazáni 5, Platía Ayía Ekateríni ☎ 2810 330 049. The most popular of a group of relaxing, traditional cafés on this quiet square with tables under the trees. Join the locals for a coffee, or something stronger, after a visit to the cathedral. Daily 9am–10pm.

Kirkor Platía Venizélou 29 ☎ 2810 242 705. The cafés on Platía Venizélou that specialize in luscious pastries to accompany a strong mid-morning coffee are an essential visit. *Kirkor* is *the* place to sample authentic *bougátsa* (creamy cheese pie served warm and sprinkled with sugar and cinnamon); also excellent *loukoumadhes* (dough fritters in honey) and *tyrópita*. If you can't get a table, *Fyllo…Sofíes*, next door, is an excellent alternative; both claim to have been founded in 1922. Daily 6am–11pm.

Mare Sófokli Venizélou, opposite the Historical Museum ☎ 2810 241 946. Stylish coffee and drinks bar with a wonderful setting and spectacular glass seafront terrace. Serves a range of snacks, and good cocktails at night. Daily 8am–2am.

News Café Minotaúrou 32 ☎ 2810 241 545. A modern café/bistro on the southwestern side of El Greco Park offering breakfast snacks, omelettes, sandwiches (€3.50–6), burgers (€5), salads and grills, as well as coffee, juices and ice cream. Very busy as a bar at night, too. Daily 9am–2am.

Utopia Hándhakos 51 ☎ 2810 341 321. Locals flock here for the cakes and biscuits, served on fancy cake stands, and above all for the chocolate fondue and chocolate fountains – not cheap, but irresistibly indulgent. At night they also serve more than sixty different beers from all over the world, along with "beer *meze*" (sausages, mainly), but even then, most people are here for the chocolate and cake. Daily 9am–2am.

DRINKING AND NIGHTLIFE

As a university town, Iráklio has plenty of places to let your hair down. Young Cretans tend to be more into sitting and chatting over background music than energetic dancing; consequently large areas of **Koraí** and the surrounding pedestrianized streets are packed with alfresco cafés that transform into bars as the lights dim and the volume ramps up. The bigger **clubs** are generally away from the central zone; they tend to play Western music (and lots of techno) interspersed with Greek pop. Most don't open their doors before 11pm, with the crowds drifting in after 1am and dancing until dawn. For livelier, and earlier, partying head to one of the nearby resorts or look out for posters advertising beach parties in summer. There are good **listings** for all sorts of events online at ⓦ nowheraklion.com.

BARS

Central Park Arkoléondos 19, El Greco Park ☎ 2810 346 501. Big, busy cocktail bar and café with one of the city's most popular terraces for those who want to see and be seen. There's a substantial menu (until midnight) that goes beyond the usual snacks, big screens, and an almost permanent crowd. Daily 8am–2am.

Kafenion Fix Aretoúsas 2 at Meramvélou ☎ 2810 289 023. Traditional café and bar, busiest in the evenings, with tables set out under the trees of an attractive green platía. There's no music, so this is a popular place for a quiet, early drink and great if you want to make yourself heard. Daily 9am–2am.

Iridanós Andróyeo 8, cnr Perdhíkari. Bar-café spread over two floors offering a bit of everything – cool, old-fashioned decor with exposed brick and swirling fans; big-screen sport; free wi-fi; and a constantly changing crowd. Daily 9am–3am.

Jailhouse Ayiostefanitón 19. Friendly rock bar in what turns out inside to be an ancient stone building on two levels; a gathering place for Iráklio's alternative crowd who can hang out here all day until the live music starts next door at *Rolling Stone* (see p.62). Daily 10am–4am.

Mayo Milátou 11, just north of Koraí ☎ 2810 336 000. This extravaganza of a bar with spotlights, screens and music under a big canopy terrace is one of the places to be seen if you're part of Iráklio's student set. Its arrival has spawned a whole new set of bars and cafés along the same street. Daily 9am–3am.

To Mílon tis Eridos Platía Koraí ☎ 2810 241 820. Café-bar that serves everything from twelve types of coffee to cocktails and herbal teas, including *diktamo* (Cretan dittany), a panacea the Cretans have been sipping for thousands of years. Daily 9am–3am.

Pagopiion (Ice Factory) Platía Áyios Títos ☎ 2810 346 028. Stunning bar with arty decor inside Iráklio's former ice factory. Much of the old building has been preserved, including a lift for hauling the ice from the basement

1

freezer and a fascistic call to duty in German Gothic script on one wall – a remnant of Nazi occupation of the factory in World War II. Make sure to visit the toilets, which are in an artistic league of their own. Daily 9am–late.

Take Five Arkoléondos 7, El Greco Park ☎ 2810 226 564. One of the oldest bars in Iráklio, *Take Five* began as a rock bar in the 1980s and is now a slick pavement café with an indoor bar, playing jazzy music; a favourite late-night hangout for a slightly older crowd. Daily 9am–4am.

CLUBS AND LIVE MUSIC

London Makaríou 17 at Venizélou. Dance club that's part of a huge complex including the *Salle de Sports* (see below) and *Baloo* live music venue. The playlist features Greek pop and international chart sounds. 11pm–late.

Privilege Dhoúkos Bofór 7 ☎ 2810 244 850. A glitzy mainstream club close to the centre where you can dance, to house, techno and Greek pop until the sun rises. Entrance €10 including a drink. 11pm–late.

Rolling Stone Rock Bar Ayiostefanitón 19. Rock club attached to the *Jailhouse* bar, with sweaty, late-night live rock and punk bands, and rock DJs – Wednesdays are Greek Rock night. Great atmosphere. Tues–Sat 10.30pm–4am.

Senses Club Papandréou 277, Amoudhára. A lively, summer-only club with a party atmosphere, 5km west of the city, by Amoudhára beach, playing various types of international music including dance & R&B. Good theme nights and special events. Summer daily 9pm–late.

SHOPPING

For **upmarket shops**, especially those selling jewellery, clothes and fabrics, head to Dedhálou, Odhós 1821 and Odhós Evans (east and west of the market respectively) and to Kalokerinoú heading west from here. There's a huge **street market** every Saturday in an open area at Itánou and Leonídhou, southeast of the centre, and a smaller, local one every Tuesday on Irodhótou in the airport suburb of Alikarnassós.

Eleftheroudakis Odhós 1821 10 ☎ 2810 227 500, ⓦ books.gr. Good branch of this Greek bookstore chain, with a decent selection of English titles. Mon, Wed & Sat 9am–2.30pm, Tues, Thurs & Fri 9am–2pm & 5.30–9pm.

Iráklio market Odhós 1866. One of the best markets on the island, good for food as well as for cheap practical goods, leatherware and standard tourist items (see p.54). Daily 8am–8pm (though individual stalls vary; some close on Sun, while many take a siesta from around 2–5pm).

Planet International Bookstore Hándhakos 73 ☎ 2810 289 605. Excellent bookshop, with the best selection of English-language titles and maps. Mon, Wed & Sat 8am–2pm, Tues, Thurs & Fri 9am–2pm & 5.30–8pm.

Road Editions Hándhakos 29 ☎ 2810 344 610. Map specialist with a large selection of maps and guides. Mon, Wed & Sat 8am–2pm, Tues, Thurs & Fri 9am–2pm & 5.30–8pm.

DIRECTORY

Banks The main branches are on 25-Avgoústou, many of them with ATMs; there are more machines at banks along Dhikeosínis.

Football OFI Crete is Iráklio's and Crete's major team playing in the Greek first division. Their matches take place at the Demótikou stadium, Platía Ayía Varvára in the Kamínia district on the west side of town (☎ 2810 283 920). The city's other team, Ergotelis, play at the stadium below the Martinengo Bastion.

Hospitals The closest is the Venizélio Hospital, on the Knossós road south out of town (☎ 2813 408 000); better facilities at the modern University Hospital at Voútes, the island's largest (☎ 2813 402 111).

Internet Many hotels and bars offer free wi-fi. Otherwise try Tunnel, junction of Ayíou Títou & Milátou (9am–3am), Papercut, a comic-book store and gaming place at Hándhakos 30 (9am–1am), or *Salle de Sports*, a cavernous 24hr internet and sports café in the nightlife complex at Makaríou and Venizélou.

Laundry Washsalon, cnr Evgenikoú and Ayiostefanitón (Mon & Wed 9am–6pm, Tues, Thurs & Fri 9am–9pm, Sat 9am–3pm) and Wash Center, Epimenídhou 38, near the *Lato* hotel (Mon–Fri 8.30am–3pm & 5.30–9pm, Sat 8.30am–3pm), both do good service washes.

Left luggage In addition to the left luggage in Bus Station A (see p.58), the youth hostel (see p.59) allows you to leave bags (€5/bag/day to non residents, €3 to residents). Most hotels will look after your bags free for a few days if you've stayed, as will bike rental companies.

Mountaineering and hiking The local EOS is at Dhikeosínis 53 (☎ 2810 227 609, ⓦ eos-her.gr).

Pharmacies Plentiful on the main shopping streets. At least one will be open 24hr on a rota basis; check the list on the door of any pharmacy. There are also traditional herbalists in the market.

Post office Main office in Platía Dhaskaloyiánnis, off Eleftherías (Mon–Fri 8.30am–7pm) with a temporary sub-office in summer in El Greco Park.

Public toilets In El Greco Park, the Public Gardens, Platía Kornárou, Platía Ayía Ekateríni, at the bus stations and at the Archeological Museum (no need to pay entrance charge).

Knossós

…a dancing place
All full of turnings, that was like the admirable maze
For fair hair'd Ariadne made, by cunning Daedalus

Homer, *The Odyssey*

KNOSSÓS (Κνωσός), 5km south of Iráklio on a low, largely artificial hill, was by far the largest of the **Minoan palaces**, thriving more than three and a half thousand years ago at the heart of a highly sophisticated island-wide civilization. Long after Minoan culture had collapsed, a town on this site remained powerful, rivalling Górtys well into the Roman era. Today it is perhaps the most famous – and most visited – of all Crete's tourist attractions. No matter when you come, you won't get the place to yourself, but with luck you will have the opportunity to appreciate individual parts of the palace during the brief lulls between groups. In summer the best time of day to avoid the crowds is in the last couple of hours before closing time, which also has the advantage of being cooler. If you get the opportunity to come back a second time, it will all begin to make a great deal more sense.

Brief history

The discovery and excavation of the palace is among the most amazing tales of modern archeology. Little over a hundred years ago, Knossós was a place thought to have existed only in mythology. **Heinrich Schliemann**, the German excavator of Troy, suspected that a

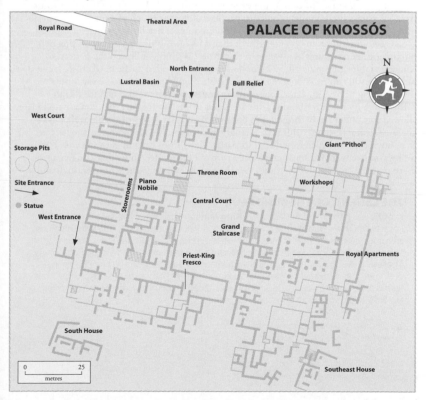

1

major Minoan palace lay under the various tumuli here, but was denied the permission to dig by the local Ottoman authorities. Today's Knossós, whose fame rivals any such site in the world, is primarily associated with **Sir Arthur Evans**, who excavated and liberally "restored" the palace at the turn of the twentieth century. The autocratic control he exerted, his working standards and procedures, and, above all, the restorations he claimed were necessary to preserve the building have been a source of furious controversy among archeologists ever since. It has become clear that much of Evans's upper level, the *Piano Nobile*, is pure conjecture. Even so, his guess as to what the palace might have looked like is certainly as good as anyone else's, and it makes the other sites infinitely more meaningful if you have seen Knossós first. Without the restorations, it would be hard to visualize the ceremonial stairways, strange top-heavy pillars and brightly frescoed walls that distinguish Knossós – and almost impossible to imagine the grandeur of the multistorey palace. To get an idea of the size and complexity of the palace in its original state, take a look at the cutaway drawings on sale outside; they may seem somewhat fantastic, but are probably not too far from reality.

The Palace of Knossós

As soon as you enter the **Palace of Knossós** through its West Court, it is clear how the legends of the labyrinth grew up around it. Even with a map and description, it can be very hard to work out where you are.

The remains you see are mostly those of the **second palace**, rebuilt after the destruction of around 1700 BC (see p.328) and occupied – with increasing Mycenaean influence – through to about 1450 BC. At the time, it was surrounded by a town of considerable size. The palace itself, though, must have looked almost as much of a mess then as it does now – a vast bulk, with more than a thousand rooms on five floors, which had spread across the hill more as an organic growth than a planned building, incorporating or burying earlier structures as it went. In this, Knossós simply followed the pattern of Minoan architecture generally, with extra rooms being added as the need arose. It is a style of building still common on Crete, where finished buildings seem to be outnumbered by those waiting to have an extra floor or room added when need and finance dictate.

The difficulty in understanding the site is not helped by the fact that you are no longer allowed to wander freely through the complex: instead, a series of **timber walkways** channels visitors around. This is particularly true of the Royal Apartments, where access to many rooms is denied or reduced to partial views from behind glass screens. The walkways also make it almost impossible to avoid the guided tours that congregate at every point of significance en route. On the upside, wait anywhere long enough and a

---

THE LEGEND OF THE MINOTAUR

Knossós was the court of the legendary **King Minos**, whose wife Pasiphae, cursed by Poseidon, bore the **Minotaur**, a creature half-bull, half-man (see p.345). The **labyrinth** was constructed by Daedalus to contain the monster, and every nine years (some say every year) seven youths and seven maidens were brought from Athens as human sacrifice, until finally **Theseus** arrived to slay the beast and, with Ariadne's help, escape its lair. Imprisoned in his own maze, Daedalus later constructed the wings that bore him away to safety – and his son **Icarus** to his untimely death. The legend has inspired writers from Homer to Dante, who famously depicts the beast in his vision of Hell:

Into the chasm was that descent: and there
At point of the disparted ridge lay stretch'd
The infamy of Crete, detested brood
Of the feign'd heifer: and at sight of us
It gnaw'd itself, as one with rage distract.

Dante, *Inferno*, Canto XII

free tour will come along – you can always tag onto one of these for a while, catch the patter and then hang back to take in the detail when the crowd has moved on.

The West Court

The **West Court**, across which you approach the palace, was perhaps a marketplace or, at any rate, the scene of public meetings. Across it run slightly raised walkways, leading from the palace's West Entrance to the Theatral Area, and once presumably on to the Royal Road. There are also three large **circular pits**, originally grain silos or perhaps depositories for sacred offerings, but used as rubbish tips by the end of the Minoan era. When these were excavated, remains of early dwellings – visible in the central pit, dating from around 2000 BC and thus preceding the first palace – were revealed. The walls and floor surfaces were found to have been coated with red plaster, and these are among the earliest-known remains on the site.

Following the walkway towards the **West Entrance** nowadays, you arrive at a stones marking the original wall of an earlier incarnation of the palace, then the facade of the palace proper, and beyond that a series of small rooms of which only the foundations survive.

The first frescoes

Anyone entering the palace by the West Entrance in its heyday would have passed through a guardroom and then followed the **Corridor of the Procession**, flanked by frescoes depicting a procession, around towards the south side of the palace; the walkway runs alongside. A brief detour down the stairway near the West Entrance would enable you to view the **South House** (see p.67) before entering the palace proper.

Following the walkway, you come to the reproduction of the **Priest-King Fresco** (which Evans dubbed the Prince of the Lilies, although some scholars are convinced the figure is female or not even a royal personage at all). A revealing glimpse into Evans's mindset comes from an article he wrote in the London *Times* when this fragmentary figure came to light: "…the head is wearing a crown, which terminates in a row of five sloping lilies… That the *fleur-de-lis* of our Edwards and Henrys should find a prototype in prehistoric Greece is a startling revelation". The nearby viewing point offers a chance to look down over the palace. Apparently, a whole series of large and airy frescoed chambers, perhaps reception rooms, once stood here.

The Central Court

The **Central Court**, the heart of the palace, is aligned almost exactly north–south. The courtyard paving covers the oldest remains found on the site, dating back to Neolithic times. In Minoan times high walls would have hemmed the courtyard in on every side, and the atmosphere would have been very different from the open, shadeless space which survives. Some say this was the scene of the famous bull-leaping, but that seems unlikely: although the court measures almost 50m by 25m, it would hardly be spacious enough to accommodate the sort of intricate acrobatics shown in surviving pictures, let alone an audience to watch.

The Throne Room

The entrance to one of Knossós's most atmospheric survivals, the **Throne Room**, is in the northwestern corner of the central courtyard. Here, a worn stone throne sits against the wall of a surprisingly small chamber; along the walls around it are ranged stone benches and, behind, there's a copy of a fresco depicting two griffins. In all probability, this was the seat of a priestess rather than a ruler – there's nothing like it in any other Minoan palace – but it may just have been an innovation wrought by the Mycenaeans, since it appears that this room dates only from the final period of the palace's occupation. You'll spot the Throne Room by the queues of people waiting to press their faces against the glass to view it. Opposite the throne, steps lead down to a

1

lustral basin – a sunken "bath", probably for ritual purification rather than actual bathing, with no drain.

The Piano Nobile

Alongside the Throne Room, a stairway climbs to the first floor and Evans's reconstructed **Piano Nobile**. One of the most interesting features of this part of the palace is the view it offers of the palace storerooms, with their rows of *píthoi* (storage jars). There's an amazing amount of storage space here, in the jars – which would mostly have held oil or wine – and in sections sunk into the ground for other goods. The rooms of the *Piano Nobile* itself are again rather confusing, though you should be able to pick out the Sanctuary Hall from stumps that remain of its six large columns. Opposite this is a small concrete room (complete with roof), which Evans "reconstructed" directly above the Throne Room. It feels entirely out of place; inside, there's a small display on the restoration of the frescoes, and through the other side you get another good view over the Central Court. Returning through this room, you could climb down the very narrow staircase on your right to arrive at the entrance to the corridor of storerooms (fenced off) or head back to the left towards the area where you entered the palace.

The Royal Apartments

On the east side of the central courtyard, the Grand Staircase leads into the **Royal Apartments**, clearly the finest of the rooms at Knossós, though sadly you can't enter any of them. The **staircase** itself is an architectural masterpiece, not only a fitting approach to these sumptuously appointed chambers, but also an integral part of the whole design, its large well allowing light into the lower storeys. Light wells such as these, usually with a courtyard at the bottom, are a common feature of Knossós and a reminder of just how important creature comforts were to the Minoans, and how skilled they were at providing them.

For more evidence of this luxurious lifestyle, you need look no further than the **Queen's Suite**, off the grand **Hall of the Colonnades** at the bottom of the staircase. The main living room is decorated with the celebrated dolphin fresco and with running friezes of flowers and (earlier) spirals. On two sides it opens to courtyards that let in light and air; the smaller one would probably have been planted with flowers. It is easy to imagine the room in use, scattered with cushions and hung with rich drapes, curtains placed between the pillars providing privacy and cool shade in the heat of the day. Guides will describe all this but it is of course almost entirely speculation – and some of it pure con. The dolphin fresco, for example, was found in the courtyard, not the room itself, and would have been viewed from inside or above as a sort of *trompe l'oeil*, like looking out of a glass-bottomed boat. There are many who argue, convincingly, that grand as these rooms are, they are not really large or fine enough to have been royal quarters. Those would more likely have been in the lighter and airier rooms that must have existed in the upper reaches of the palace, while these lower apartments were inhabited by resident nobles or priests.

Whether or not you accept Evans's names and attributions, the rooms remain an impressive example of the sophistication of Minoan architecture. The **Queen's Bathroom**, its clay tub protected behind a low wall (and probably screened by curtains when in use), is another fine example, as is the famous "flushing" lavatory (a hole in the ground with drains to take the waste away – it was flushed by a bucket of water).

On the floor above the queen's domain, the Grand Staircase passes through a set of rooms which are generally described as the **King's Quarters**. These are chambers in a considerably sterner vein. The staircase opens into a grandiose reception area known as the **Hall of the Royal Guard**, its walls decorated in repeated shield motifs. Opening off it is the ruler's personal chamber, the **Hall of the Double Axes** – a room which could be divided to allow for privacy while audiences were held in the more public section, or the whole opened out for larger functions. Its name comes from the double-axe symbol, so common throughout Knossós, which here is carved into every block of masonry.

1

The drainage system

From the back of the queen's chambers, you can emerge into the fringes of the palace where it spreads down the lower slopes of the hill. This is a good point at which to consider the famous **drainage system** at Knossós, some of the most complete sections of which are visible under grilles. The snugly interconnecting terracotta pipes ran underneath most of the palace (here, they have come more or less direct from the Queen's Bathroom), and site guides never fail to point them out as evidence of the advanced state of Minoan civilization. Down by the external walls you get a clear view of the system of baffles and overflows designed to slow down the runoff and avoid flooding.

The Palace Workshops

From the bottom of the slope, you get a fine impression of the scale of the whole palace complex and can circle around towards the north, climbing back inside the palace limits to see the area known as the **Palace Workshops**. Here, potters, lapidaries and smiths appear to have plied their trades, and this area is also home to the spectacular **giant píthoi**; people queue to have their photograph taken with the jars towering over them. There's also a good view of the Bull Relief fresco set up by the north entrance.

Around the North Entrance

Circling around the palace, you can re-enter by the **North Entrance**. Beside the gateway is a well-preserved **lustral basin**, and beyond that, a guardroom. As you head up towards the central courtyard, a flight of stairs doubles back to allow you to examine the copy of the **Bull Relief** close up.

Just outside the North Entrance, the **Theatral Area** is one of the more important enigmas of this and other Minoan palaces. An open space resembling a stepped amphitheatre, it may have been used for ritual performances or dances, but there's no real evidence of this, and again there would have been very little room for an audience if that was its function.

Beyond it, the **Royal Road** sets out: originally this ran to the Little Palace (see p.68), and probably on across the island beyond that, but nowadays it ends after about 100m at a brick wall beneath the modern road. Alongside are assorted structures variously interpreted as stores, workshops or grandstands for viewing parades, all of them covered in undergrowth.

The south side

Of the lesser structures that crowd around the palace, a number of houses on the south side are particularly worth noting. The one known simply as the **South House**, reconstructed to its original three floors, seems amazingly modern, but actually dates from the late Minoan period (c.1550 BC). The dwelling is believed to have belonged to an important official or noble, since it encroaches on the palace domain. In the **Southeast House** of the same period, a cult room with a sacred pillar was discovered, as well as stands for double axes and a libation table.

Outlying remains

Numerous small sites dot the fields surrounding the palace, mostly of them barely visited, perhaps because unless you get lucky all you can do is stare in through their fences.

Caravanserai

Across a little valley from the south side of the palace, accessed from the road south

The **Caravanserai** was where travellers visiting Knossós would rest and water their animals. The restored building contains two elegant rooms, as well as a large stone footbath still with running water from an ancient spring. There's a good view of the palace from the surrounding fields.

1

Little Palace and Royal Villa

Off the road to Iráklio • Both occasionally open for special visits; details from ticket office

Among the most important of Knossós' outlying buildings are the **Little Palace**, on a site which also contains a mansion and many Roman remains, and the **Royal Villa**, facing the palace from the slope to the northeast.

Villa Dionysos

300m up the road to Iráklio from the site entrance

The first-century **Villa Dionysos** lay near the centre of the Roman city of Cnossus. The villa has extremely fine polychrome mosaics, and once restoration work is complete it is planned to open it up to the public. Details on the progress of this should be available from the Knossós ticket office or the Iráklio tourist office (see p.59).

Villa Ariadne

About 100m along the road to Iráklio from the site entrance • Not open to the public

The **Villa Ariadne** was built by Arthur Evans as his home-from-home during excavations. Later, the house served as a military hospital during the German siege of Iráklio and, following the city's fall, as the residence of the German commander of Crete. It was where General Kreipe was based when he was kidnapped (see p.340), and the villa's dining room was also where the German army signed the surrender on May 9, 1945. Although not open to the public, nobody seems to mind if you walk up the drive past the gatehouse to have a look at the house's exterior and lush gardens.

ARRIVAL AND INFORMATION   **KNOSSÓS**

By bus Local buses #2 and #4 set off (every 10min; €1.50 each way) from Iráklio's city bus stands (adjacent to Bus Station A), then proceed to Platía Eleftherías and out of town along Odhós-1821 and Evans.

By taxi A taxi from the centre of Iráklio will cost around €12.

By car From the centre of Iráklio head out through Evans gate; from anywhere else on the island turn directly off the bypass onto the badly signed Knossós road. There's a free car park immediately before the site entrance, which will enable you to avoid paying exorbitant rates for the private car parks dotting the road immediately before this (and whose touts will attempt to wave you in).

Opening hours July–Sept daily 8am–8pm; May, June & Oct Mon–Sat 8am–6pm, Sun 8am–3pm; Nov–April daily 8.30am–3pm.

Admission €6; €10 joint ticket with Iráklio Archeological Museum.

Contact ☎ 2810 231 940.

Guided tours Official guides can be hired at the site entrance; they are self-employed and expensive, but you can usually negotiate the price a little if you wish to use their services, and rope in other visitors to share the cost.

Websites The British School at Athens has a useful website dedicated to Knossós, with detail on its history and excavations in addition to a virtual tour; check out ⓦ bsa .ac.uk/knossos/vrtour/.

South of Iráklio: wine country

The countryside south of Knossós is dominated by the bulk of **Mount Yioúhtas** (811m), which rises alone from a landscape otherwise characterized by gently undulating agricultural country. Seen from the northwest, the mountain has an unmistakably human profile, and was traditionally identified with Zeus. The ancient Cretans claimed that Zeus lay buried underneath the mountain; given that the god is immortal, this furnished proof for other Greeks of the assertion that "All Cretans are liars" – it may even have been the original basis of this reputation.

As you leave Knossós behind, the nature of the journey south is transformed almost immediately: the road empties and the country becomes greener. Almost any of these roads makes a beautiful drive, past vineyards draped across low hills and through flourishing farming communities. Just a couple of kilometres from the archeological site, at the head of the valley, an extraordinary **aqueduct** arches beside the road. This looks medieval and was built on the line of an earlier Roman aqueduct, but is in fact less than two hundred years old, having been constructed during the brief period of Egyptian rule (1832–40) to provide Iráklio with water. A little further on, the junction where you turn right towards Arhánes seems a singularly unthreatening spot today, yet it was here, on April 26, 1944, that General Kreipe was kidnapped (see p.340). The site is now marked by a lofty modern monument.

Much of the interest in this region centres around Arhánes, where there's an **Archeological Museum** and easy access to three fascinating **Minoan sites** at Foúrni, Anemospília and on the summit of Mount Yioúhtas itself. Nearby at **Vathýpetro** the remarkable remains of a Minoan vineyard can be seen, at the heart of what remains one of the island's chief **wine-growing areas**: many a winemakers open their doors to the public, especially at **Pezá. Houdhétsi** has a music school and museum, while the village of **Myrtiá** boasts a museum devoted to Crete's most famous literary name, **Nikos Kazantzákis**.

East of Pezá, a road runs through hilly farm country well inland from the big resorts, a region known as the **Pedhiádha**. There's an important **pottery** centre at **Thrapsanó**, and other diversions include the ancient site of **Lýttos** and some notable **frescoed churches** around **Kastélli**.

Arhánes

ARHÁNES (Αρχάνες) is a large and prosperous agricultural centre, substantial enough to have a one-way traffic system and be served by hourly buses from Iráklio. The streets in the central area are narrow and confusing, and the best advice for drivers is to park up near the square and explore on foot. There are tavernas and cafés around the main square, as well as numerous flashy modern bars, reflecting the region's agricultural prosperity. In summer (mid-July to mid-August) a colourful daily **street market**, selling local crafts and delicacies, takes place in the old quarter.

WINE TASTING AROUND PEZÁ

Locals claim, with some justification, that **wine** has been being made in the area around Pezá for four thousand years (see p.73), probably using grape varieties not far removed from the Kotsifáli and Mandilariá (for red), Plytó and Vilána (white) that are extensively cultivated today. Cretan wines, traditionally very much *vin ordinaire*, are increasingly sophisticated, and a number of wineries open their doors to visitors, though most require appointments. The following are some of the largest, open to unplanned visits. For more information see Ⓦ winesofcrete.gr.

Boutari Skaláni, on the Myrtiá road some 4km beyond Knossós Ⓣ 2810 731 617, Ⓦ boutari.gr. Modern estate with state-of-the-art facilities and fancy multimedia show. Boutari is a big, national company with an excellent reputation, though this Cretan operation is still in its early stages. Tours €5. Mon–Fri 9am–5pm.

Miliarakis Vineyard House Sabás, about 10km east of Pezá on the Kastélli road Ⓣ 697 27 20 605, Ⓦ minoswines.gr. The fine wine label of Minos Wines (see below). Tasting takes place in a room furnished as a traditional *kafenío*, with expansive views over the surrounding countryside. You can also stroll, or take some more challenging hikes, through the local vineyards. Tasting €3, with cheese €5. April–Oct Mon–Sat 11am–6pm.

Minos Pezá Ⓣ 2810 741 213, Ⓦ minoswines.gr. On the main street in Pezá village, the epicentre of Cretan wine production, Minos is one of the island's biggest producers. There are tours of the winemaking plant approximately hourly (depending on the number of visitors), but at any time you can watch a video about the history of Cretan wine production, look at some traditional equipment, and taste and buy the house brands. €2. April–Oct Mon–Fri 9am–4pm, Sat 10.30am–3pm.

Peza Union Pezá, on the Kastélli road at the eastern edge of town Ⓣ 2810 741 945, Ⓦ pezaunion .gr. The union of agricultural cooperatives of Pezá produces olive oil as well as wine, from the vines and trees of many small producers. A tour of their exhibition centre is followed by wine tasting and a small meze. Free. May–Oct Mon–Sat 9am–5pm.

The richness of the land around Arhánes is nothing new: this area was a major centre of **Minoan civilization**, and there are a number of important sites in and around town, including a hypothesized fifth palace to rival those at Festós and Mália. Most are relatively recent discoveries, having been excavated over the last few decades, and not all of the excavations have been fully published. Consequently, these sites are neither particularly famous nor especially welcoming to visitors, but many of the finds are nonetheless important; indeed, some of the greatest treasures of the Iráklio archeological museum come from this region. A site described as the **Palace**, in reality more likely a large villa, lies right in the heart of modern Arhánes. Through the chain-link fence you can see evidence of a substantial walled mansion, representing only a small part of what once stood here. Piecemeal excavation is still going on at other sites in the centre too, but much is hidden beneath more modern buildings. If you make the Archeological Museum your first stop, you can find out more about the status of these sites, and pick up a leaflet on things to do in the area.

Arhánes Archeological Museum

Miháli Kalohristianáki, an alley between the two one-way streets, about 80m north of the main square • Wed–Mon 8.30am–2.30pm • Free

Imaginatively laid out in a single room, the **Arhánes Archeological Museum** displays some exceptional finds from the town and surrounding sites. Near the entrance are some well-preserved Minoan **larnakes** (clay coffins, complete with the bones found in them) from **Foúrni** (see below) dating from around 1800 BC. Displayed nearby is a replica of a **sistrum** (a simple, tambourine-like musical instrument; the original is in Iráklio) dating from around 2000 BC, also from the cemetery at Foúrni; it may well be the oldest surviving musical instrument in Europe. A photo shows a detail of the famous "Harvesters Vase" from the Iráklio museum, depicting a *sistrum* in use.

There are fascinating finds, too, from **Anemospília** (see p.72), where human sacrifices appear to have taken place in the temple. A copy of the **dagger** found lying on the sacrificial victim is displayed here, with a curious motif of a hybrid animal – resembling a deformed boar – carved on the blade. There's also a copy of the seal stone that the priest was wearing on his left wrist, and of the terracotta feet of a wooden statue that was destroyed in the fire that followed the destruction of the temple; again, the originals are in the Iráklio museum.

Other items to look out for include small terracotta cups that contained the ochres used to paint frescoes on the walls in the palaces and villas, and an imaginative display of **pottery shards** that evidences five thousand years of human occupation in this town: crude works of the third millennium BC are succeeded by the various Minoan periods, then Greek, Roman, Byzantine, Venetian and Turkish pieces, down to broken pots of the present day. There are also fragments of Minoan wall painting and many everyday domestic objects, ranging from a wine-press and giant *píthoi* to jewellery and jugs.

Arhánes churches

Numerous ancient churches are scattered through the town, though there's no guarantee that you'll find any open. Right on the main square an incongruous whitewashed clock tower marks out one, with a fine collection of icons; elsewhere, there are Byzantine frescoes in the church of **Ayía Triádha** on the fringes of town and at the church of **Asómatos** to the east, where the superb fourteenth-century works include a horrific *Crucifixion* and a depiction of the fall of Jericho with Joshua in full medieval armour.

Foúrni

Immediately west of Arhánes • July & Aug Tues–Sun 8.30am–2.30pm; at other times check with the Arhánes Archeological Museum (see above) • Free • Cross the bypass west of Arhánes and then walk for about 10min up a steep, very rocky trail

The size of the **burial ground at FOÚRNI (Φούρνι)** is evidence of the scale of the Minoan

ARCHEOLOGICAL MUSEUM, IRÁKLIO (P.54) >

1

HUMAN SACRIFICE IN ANCIENT CRETE?

The temple at Anemospília appears to have been destroyed in the midst of a ceremony involving **human sacrifice** – the only evidence of such a ritual found in Minoan Crete. This came as a severe shock to those who liked to portray the Minoans as the perfect peaceable society, but the evidence is hard to refute. Three skeletons were found in the western room: one had rich jewellery, indicative of a priest; another was a woman, presumably a priestess or assistant; the third was curled up on an altar-like structure, and, according to scientists, was already dead when the building collapsed and killed the others. A large bronze knife lay on top of this third skeleton. Outside the western room, another man was crushed in the corridor, apparently carrying some kind of ritual vase. These events have been dated to roughly the time of the earthquakes that destroyed the first palaces and, in the circumstances, it seems easy to believe that the priests might have resorted to desperate measures in a final attempt to appease the gods who were laying waste to their civilization.

community that once thrived around Arhánes; the site was used throughout the Minoan period, with its earliest tombs dating from around 2500 BC (before the construction of the great palaces), and the latest from the very end of the Minoan era. The structures include a number of early tholos tombs – round, stone buildings reminiscent of beehives – each of which contained multiple burials in sarcophagi and *píthoi*. Many simpler graves and a circle of seven Mycenaean-style shaft graves were also revealed at Foúrni, making it by far the most extensive Minoan cemetery known. In "Tholos A", a side-chamber was found that revealed the undisturbed tomb of a woman who, judging by the jewellery and other goods buried with her, was of royal descent and perhaps a priestess. Her jewellery is now on display at the Iráklio Archeological Museum, as is the skeleton of a horse apparently sacrificed in her honour.

Anemospília

2km northwest of Arhánes

ANEMOSPÍLIA (Ανεμοσπήλια) is enlivened by a spectacular setting and a controversial story, though the site itself can only be viewed through a fence. The approach road heads north from Arhánes: coming from Iráklio, you enter the one-way street and almost immediately turn sharp right, back on yourself, just past a small chapel. Following the road leading northwest out of the town, you begin to climb across the northern face of Mount Yioúhtas, winding around craggy rocks weirdly carved by the wind (Anemospília means "Caves of the Wind") until you reach the fenced site held in a steep curve of the road.

What stood here was a **temple**, and its interpretation has been the source of outraged controversy among Minoan scholars since its excavation at the beginning of the 1980s. The building, apparently destroyed by an earthquake around 1700 BC, is a simple one, consisting of three rooms connected by a north-facing portico, but its contents are not so easily described (see box above).

Mount Yioúhtas

A couple of kilometres south of Arhánes, a track leads towards the summit of **MOUNT YIOÚHTAS (Γιούχτας)**, a relatively easy drive. You can also climb the mountain in little over an hour from Arhánes, but it seems rather unsatisfying to do this only to discover other people rolling up on their motorbikes or in taxis (the summit is an optional diversion on the E4 European path as it crosses Crete: coming from the east it follows the track mentioned above, then winds steeply down to Arhánes, to rejoin the main route, via the footpath). At the summit, the **panoramic views** are the main lure, back across Iráklio especially, but also west to Psilorítis and east to Dhíkti. Up here, too, is a small chapel, and the trappings of the annual *paniyíri* (festival), which is celebrated on August 15 and attracts villagers from all around. The impressive remains of a **Minoan Peak sanctuary** dating from the early second millennium BC occupy the north side of the hill, partly built over by a telecommunications station. It very likely served as a cult centre, attracting pilgrims from Arhánes and Knossós, both of which can be seen from the summit. An enormous number of votive offerings, including jewellery, figurines and libation vessels, were unearthed in the excavations and are now on display in the museum at Iráklio. On the shoulders of the mountain, not easily accessible, are caves associated with the local Zeus cult.

Vathýpetro

Tues–Sun 8.30am–2.30pm • Free

The site of **VATHÝPETRO** (**Βαθύπετρο**) is well signposted off the road south of Arhánes, beneath Mount Yioúhtas. The remains of a large **Minoan villa**, which once controlled the rich farmland south of Arhánes, it was found when excavated to contain a remarkable collection of everyday items – equipment for making wine and oil, and other tools and simple requisites of rural life. Still surrounded by a vineyard with a valid claim to be the oldest in the world (winemaking has been carried on here since the second millennium BC), the house was originally a substantial building of several storeys, with a courtyard enclosing a shrine, and fine large rooms – especially on the east. The basement workrooms, however, were the scene of the most interesting discoveries, comprising agricultural equipment and a remarkably well-preserved **winepress**, which can still be seen *in situ*.

Houdhétsi

HOUDHÉTSI (**Χουδέτσι**) lies on a side road that links two major north–south thoroughfares, from Arhánes towards Pírgos and the road through Pezá and Arkalohóri towards Áno Viánnos. The village is distinguished from its agricultural neighbours by the presence of the museum/music workshop, **Labyrinth**.

Labyrinth

Just off the main square • April to mid-Oct daily 8am–4pm; mid-Oct to March Sun 10am–3pm • €3 • ☎ 2810 741 027, Ⓦ labyrinthmusic.gr

Labyrinth – partly a **museum of musical instruments** from all around the world and partly a music workshop with a programme of concerts and seminars throughout

---

THE IRISH *LYRA* PLAYER

One of the more remarkable stories of Cretan music is that an Irishman, **Ross Daly**, has become one of its most famous names. Born in England of Irish parents, he grew up in Asia and North America, the family settling wherever the work of his physicist father happened to take them. Daly first visited Crete in 1971 and was strongly attracted to its traditional music, studying in that same decade under master *lyra* player Kostas Mountakis, in Haniá. Part of his early career was spent in Anóyia teaching *lyra* to local children, but once he had become a *lyra* virtuoso he was not content to stay within the confines of Cretan music and began to synthesize what he had learned in Crete and Greece with music from other cultures such as Turkey, the Balkans, India and Afghanistan.

Daly now performs worldwide with his ensemble, Labyrinth, a unit comprising Russian, Greek and Cretan musicians, but always returns to his home in Crete. In addition to the *lyra*, he now plays a variety of instruments, including the *laoúto* (lute), *oud*, *rabab* (Afghan lute), *sarangi* (Turkish *bouzoúki*) and a special *lyra* with twenty-one strings instead of the usual three. More details, including a full discography, can be found on Ⓦ rossdaly.gr.

1

the summer – was founded by Irish *lyra* player Ross Daly (see box, p.73), who lives nearby, and is the focus for much of his musical energy. Housed in an elegant mansion, with a rare, emerald-green grass lawn, its museum consists of a collection of mainly string and percussion instruments (many very rare) from across the globe.

Myrtiá

The main reason to visit **MYRTIÁ** (Μυρτιά) is for the **Kazantzákis Museum**, dedicated to the writer and philosopher Nikos Kazantzákis (see p.52). Only the seriously committed will spend long here, but it's a lovely drive to the village on almost deserted roads. Myrtiá itself is larger than you'd expect – as are so many of these villages – and bright with flowers planted in old olive-oil cans.

Kazantzákis Museum

Village square • March–Oct daily 9am–5pm; Nov–Feb Sun 10am–3pm • €3

The **Kazantzákis Museum** occupies a cluster of buildings in the village square, where Nikos Kazantzákis's parents once lived. Its collection includes a vast quantity of ephemera relating to the great author and philosopher: diaries, photos, manuscripts, first editions, translations into every conceivable language, playbills, stills from films of his works, costumes and more. There's also a video documentary in Greek.

Thrapsanó

The large village of **THRAPSANÓ** (Θραψανό), 4km south of the Pezá–Kastélli road, has for centuries been an important **pottery-making** centre. Workshops still thrive in the village and along the roads out towards Vóni and Evangelismós, and many of them welcome visitors to admire the potters' skills, although there's not a great deal on offer to buy. There is, though, a good range of earthenware: *píthoi* are evident throughout Thrapsanó, not only in workshops but upturned in the main square and on the backs of parked pick-up trucks. Both Thrapsanó and Réthymno's pottery centre, Margarítes (see p.204), have found a new export market in recent years for these giant *píthoi*. In northern Europe, they have become popular decorative features for urban gardens, and both centres have been stretched to keep up with demand.

Kastélli and around

The chief village of the Pedhiádha, **KASTÉLLI** (Καστέλλι), or Kastélli Pedhiádhos, is a pleasant place to pause for a while. Chiefly an agricultural centre whose prosperity derives from the olive groves and vineyards spread across the surrounding hills, the town goes its own way, largely unaffected by the tourist zone on the coast below. But there's a good taverna and peaceful accommodation, far from the madding crowd. Otherwise the main attraction is the surrounding countryside, where winding lanes are traced by elderly oak and plane trees.

Áyios Pandeleímon

Less than 3km north of Kastélli, off the Hersónisos road, signed to "Paradise Tavern" • Daily 9am–3pm • Free

Should you decide to see only one of the many churches in this area, make it **Áyios Pandeleímon** (Άγιος Παντελεύμον), a large building set in a grove of oaks and planes around a spring which was very likely a sanctuary in ancient times. Inside the church are imposing though weathered frescoes of the soldier saints (on the north wall) and an unusual scene of Ayía Ánna nursing the infant Mary. The structure of the church, probably dating from the early thirteenth century, is interesting for the way it

FRESCOED CHURCHES AROUND KASTÉLLI

Many of the villages around Kastélli have frescoed medieval **churches**. Look out for signs as you drive around; they're usually worth seeking out simply for the journey off the main routes, even if you can't get in. In addition to the splendid **Áyios Pandeleímon** (see opposite), one of the more famous is the fifteenth-century **Isódhia Theótokon**, with fine Byzantine frescoes, near the village of **Sklaverohóri** just a couple of kilometres west of Kastélli. The key is available from the house with a vine trellis about 50m before the church, on the right. Some 6km further west, down a side road beyond Apostolí, **Moní Angaráthou** is in another pretty location. Although the monastery's church dates from the last century, the surrounding buildings date mainly from the sixteenth century and include a picturesque white-walled courtyard with palms, orange trees and cypresses. Another church is **Áyios Yeóryios** at **Ksidhás** (confusingly also known as Lýttos), about 3km east of Kastélli, which has frescoes dated by an inscription to 1321.

incorporates parts of the original tenth-century basilica and uses as columns some much older fragments, probably taken from Lýttos. The **aqueduct** that once transported water to the ancient city passes close by, and you may spot parts of it as you drive around. This idyllic spot also shelters the small *Paradise Taverna*, run by the eccentric Nikolaides family.

Ancient Lýttos

2km north of Ksidhás, east of Kastélli, between two small chapels that serve as useful landmarks as you approach

Ancient **LÝTTOS (Λύττος)**, occupying a magnificent position in the foothills of the Dhíkti range, was a prominent city of Dorian Crete, mentioned by Homer as leading the Cretan contingent in the Trojan War. Later it was one of the most powerful city-states of Classical Greece during the centuries prior to the Roman conquest, and was the bitter enemy of Górtys, Ierápytna (modern Ierápetra) and especially Knossós. When Lýttos engaged these three in a **war** for control of the island (221–219 BC), it overreached itself; while its army was launching an attack on Ierápetra, Knossós seized the opportunity to destroy the unguarded city, leaving it in ruins and taking its women and children into captivity. The historian Polybius vividly describes how, on their return to Lýttos, the troops broke down in tears at the sight, refused to enter their devastated homes and went for succour to Lappa (see p.198) near Réthymno, one of its few allies. The city was eventually rebuilt, however, and enjoyed a small-scale renaissance under the Romans through to Byzantine times.

The site

Sadly, what is visible above ground today in no way reflects Lýttos's ancient status, as no systematic archeological exploration has yet taken place. Nevertheless what you can see underlines the fact that when the riches of Lýttos are finally excavated – including what is said to be the island's largest theatre, now lost – it will be an important site. Below the church of Tímios Stavrós, built over a large fifth-century basilica with stones from the ancient city, are the bastions and curtain of an enormous **city wall**. The church is believed to mark the centre, or agora, of Lýttos. The church of **Áyios Yeóryios** (which has fragmentary frescoes) is also constructed from stones scavenged from Lýttos: incorporated into the outer wall is a fine fragment of carved acanthus foliage. Nearby, the ancient city's **bouleterion** or council chamber has been excavated, with visible platforms and benches. Spend half an hour roaming through the vines and olive groves on the surrounding slopes and you'll come across partially excavated dwellings, delicately carved tombstones, half-buried pillars and the enormous foundation stones of buildings waiting to be unearthed.

ARRIVAL AND DEPARTURE

By car The old road out via Knossós is much the most pleasant route, but directions can be confused by the presence of the new road, which cuts across the island via Pezá and Houdhétsi, often extremely close to the older road. The loop via Kastélli and the coast makes for a satisfying circuit.

By bus Buses from Iráklio (Bus Station A) can take you to Wine Country.

SOUTH OF IRÁKLIO: WINE COUNTRY

Destinations Arhánes (Mon–Fri 15 daily 6.30am–9pm, Sat 9 7am–7pm, Sun 8am, 1pm, 5pm); Kastélli (Mon–Fri 6 daily 6.45am–7pm, Sat 4 9am–7pm, Sun 2pm); Pezá & Houdhétsi (Mon–Thurs 6 daily 7am–3pm, Fri 7 daily 7am–8.15pm, Sat 4 9.30am–3pm, Sun 7.30am only).

ACCOMMODATION AND EATING

This is not remotely a touristy area, but you'll find somewhere to **eat** in most villages; if you **stay** you become very much part of the life of these thriving rural centres.

ARHÁNES

Arhontiko Villa Arhánes ☎2810 752 985, ⓦarhontikoarhanes.gr. A mansion on the edge of the village, converted to provide four beautiful duplex apartments for up to four guests, furnished with antiques and with dark wooden floors and ceilings, and plenty of exposed brickwork, as well as comforts including kitchenette, wi-fi, TV and a/c. **€90**

Kalimera Archanes Arhánes ☎2810 752 999, ⓦarchanes-village.com. Lovingly restored old house that now offers four villas and studios for two to five people around a tranquil, leafy courtyard. All have well-equipped kitchens and a/c; delicious breakfast included. **€150**

HOUDHÉTSI

Petronikoli Traditional House Houdhétsi ☎2810 743 203, ⓦpetronikolis.info. Traditional building in the heart of the village, whose bare stone walls have been scrubbed to within an inch of their lives. Comfy studios and apartments

are very well kitted out, with a/c, TV, wi-fi, CD players and more, and there's a café and good-sized pool. **€50**

KASTÉLLI

Taverna Irida West of the square on the inland road towards Iráklio. Authentic country taverna that serves up traditional dishes such as goat in tomato sauce, or rabbit in wine sauce, along with plenty of seafood. You can also simply stop in for coffee or a juice. Daily 11am–midnight.

Hotel Kalliopi Off the main road, close to the central crossroads ☎28910 32685. If you want to stay entirely away from tourist centres and get a taste of modern agricultural Crete, you'd be hard-pressed to do better. Despite initial appearances the rooms, and a couple of apartments, are as rural as they get, especially if you are in the annexe at the back, amid kitchen gardens and olive groves behind the small pool. Simple but comfortable tile-floored rooms with TV and a/c. **€35**

West of Iráklio

Heading west from Iráklio, the modern **E75 highway**, cut into the cliffs, is – in daytime at any rate – as fast and efficient a road as you could hope to find (see box opposite). In simple scenic terms it's a spectacular drive, but with very little in the way of habitation; there are only a couple of developed beach resorts and the "birthplace of El Greco" at **Fódhele** until the final, flat stretch before Réthymno. Once beyond the western city beaches, the highway starts to climb into the foothills of the Psilorítis range as they plunge straight to the sea. As you ascend, keep an eye out for the immaculately crafted medieval fortress of **Paleókastro**, built into the cliff right beside the road; it's easy to miss, so completely do the crumbling fortifications blend in against the rocks.

If you're in no hurry, try the **older roads west**, curling up amid stunning mountain scenery and archetypal rural Crete, with tracks tramped by herds of sheep and goats, isolated chapels or farmsteads beside the road, and occasionally a village. There's a choice of routes at Arolíthos (see p.79); the road that goes further inland, through the village of Týlissos and on via Anóyia (p.207), has more to see and passes through the **Malevísi**, a district of fertile valleys filled with olive groves and vineyards renowned from Venetian times for the strong, sweet Malmsey wine much favoured in western

1

THE E75 HIGHWAY

The **E75 highway**, which crosses the north of the island, linking Haniá in the west to Sitía in the east, is one of the most **dangerous** in Greece. The fact that it is a two-lane road with a hard shoulder has not prevented local drivers from turning it into an unofficial four-lane highway: slow-movers are expected to straddle the line demarcating the hard shoulder, thus allowing faster cars to overtake at will. A reluctance by some tourists to follow this unwritten rule often leads to dangerous tailgating until the way is cleared for the driver in a hurry. Other hazards on this road are posed by small or badly positioned **signs**, frequently posted far too late. Missing your exit can mean travelling a considerable distance to the next one, as they are not as frequent as you might expect. Further dangers can include unexpected traffic lights where the highway passes close to a town, and **left turns**, which can be particularly scary at night when you must deal with the dual hazards of crossing the opposite lane of traffic and the possibility of someone ploughing into your rear while you're waiting to do so.

Europe. England became a major market for the wine, and the growth of the shipping trade between Candia (Iráklio) and English ports caused Henry VIII to appoint the first ever British consul to the island in 1522.

Ayía Pelayía

AYÍA PELAYÍA (Αγία Πελαγία), some 15km from Iráklio, appears irresistibly inviting from the highway far above, a sprinkling of white cubes set around a deep blue bay. Closer up, the attraction is slightly diminished: development is rapidly outpacing the capacity of the narrow, taverna-lined beach, and is beginning to take its toll on the village. However, the water is clear and calm, the **swimming** excellent and there's a superb view, too, of all the ships that pass the end of the bay as they steam into Iráklio – spectacular at night, when the brightly lit ferries go by. Despite the development, and although the beach can get very crowded with day-trippers from Iráklio at weekends, Ayía Pelayía retains a slightly **exclusive** feel, partly thanks to a couple of upmarket hotels on the promontory immediately beyond the village.

Waterskiing, parasailing and motorboats are all available on the town beach; if you feel in need of a little more space, you can head to one of several other small beaches nearby, though none could be described as empty or unspoiled. As you continue out of the far end of Ayía Pelayía it is possible to walk to three small coves on the coast as it curls around to the north and west: **Kladhisós**, **Psaromoúra**, with just a summertime bar, and finally **Mononáftis**. In the other direction, **Ligariá**, to the east, has a little harbour and a number of tavernas – most of the time it's very quiet, but summer weekends can get busy. There's a turning off the E75 signed directly to Ligariá, or you can get there off the road down into Ayía Pelayía.

ARRIVAL AND DEPARTURE   AYÍA PELAYÍA

By car As it descends towards Ayía Pelayía, the road splits. The right-hand fork leads to a car park at the southern end of the beach; the other winds round to enter the town from the back, where there's an even larger car park (€2/day).

By bus There are just three direct buses a day from Iráklio, at 8.30am, 9.15am, 2.30pm, returning at 9.30am, 3pm and 6.15pm (30min; Bus Station A); if you take a long-distance bus bound for Réthymno or Haniá, you face a steep 3km walk down from the drop-off point on the highway.

INFORMATION AND ACTIVITIES

Travel agencies There's no tourist office here, but plenty of travel agencies who can help with rooms and general information as well as tours and car rental; JK Tours on Neofítou Pedhióti (the street between the northern corner

of the car park and the beach; ☏ 2810 811 400, ⓦ jk-tours .gr) is particularly helpful.
Website ⓦ agiapelagia-crete.com.
Scuba-diving There are two good diving centres: Divers

1

Club Crete (☎ 2810 811 755, ⓦ diversclub-crete.gr), in the middle of Ayía Pelayía's main beach, and the European Diving Institute (☎ 2810 811 252, ⓦ eurodiving.net) at Ligariá.

ACCOMMODATION

Almost every building in the centre of Ayía Pelayía seems to offer rooms, studios or apartments, but even so in peak season it can be hard to find anywhere. The greatest concentration of places is immediately **behind the beach**, especially on the road down from the car park by supermarket Vassilis ("Beach Road"); the more attractive hotels on the hill behind town tend to be block-booked through the summer. Out of season, prices can be low if you're prepared to bargain.

Creta Sun Hotel On the road behind the village ☎ 2810 811 626, ⓦ cretasunhotel.gr. Pleasant studio complex with a pool, and well-kept a/c rooms with fridge and balcony, most with fine views. Free wi-fi and friendly proprietors. **€41**

Irini Beach road ☎ 2810 811 455, ⓦ irini-hotel -apartments.gr. Cheery two-room apartments above *The Home*, a lurid pink ice-cream parlour/café, just a few metres from the beach. Apartments sleep 2–6, with a/c, balcony, TV and kitchen. **€45**

Out of the Blue ☎ 2810 811 112, ⓦ capsis.com. This five-star luxury resort complex sits on a private peninsula,

comprising five hotels, seven pools, luxury villas with private pools and three private beaches. It even has its own zoo. **€200**

Renia Beach road ☎ 2810 811 349, ⓦ renia.gr. Modern block comprising studios and apartments with a/c, TV and fridge overlooking a decent-sized pool. Decor is a little spartan, and wi-fi costs extra, but there's a tiny gym (and fish spa!) and breakfast is included. **€40**

Zorba's Beach road ☎ 2810 811 074, ⓦ zorbas.gr. Decent apartments and studios with balcony – many of which offer a sea view – above a shop just seconds from the beach. Facilities include a/c, kitchenette and fridge. Wi-fi available. **€53**

EATING, DRINKING AND NIGHTLIFE

For **food**, it's hard to look past the obvious attractions of Ayía Pelayía's seafront tavernas, which stretch in a solid row behind the beach, broken only by the odd bar. There are plenty of cheaper options in the village, including a number of takeaways and small supermarkets for the makings of a picnic on the beach. **Nightlife** is mostly based at the numerous waterfront bars.

Taverna Lygaria Ligaría Beach ☎ 2810 811 242. A good choice for plain, if rather touristy, dishes, in a great location right above the beach. They have loungers for customers' use and also some simple rooms. Daily 8am–10pm.

Mouragio Towards the southern end of the beach

☎ 2810 811 070. Also known as *Stella's* after its ebullient owner, this is among the better-value beachfront restaurants. It serves much the same Greek menu as all the others, with an emphasis on seafood, but is distinguished by the warmth of the welcome. Daily 11am–late.

Fódhele

FÓDHELE (Φόδελε) is firmly established on the tourist circuit as the birthplace of the painter **El Greco** (1541–1614), although there's virtually no hard evidence to substantiate the claim and most experts now believe that he was born in Iráklio. Nonetheless, it's an enjoyable place to visit: Fódhele is a lovely village in a richly fertile, peaceful valley, surrounded by orange and lime groves. On the far side of the river as you drive up are a couple of small Byzantine chapels, and there's an ancient church in the village, a number of craft shops and some tavernas with riverside terraces. While you're in the village, take a few minutes to study the plaque in the main square, made of stone from Toledo (where Domenico Theotokopoulos settled, produced the bulk of his most famous works and earned the name El Greco). The plaque was presented to Fódhele in 1934 by the University of Valladolid as an authentication of the locale's claim to fame, which must be responsible in some measure for its current prosperity, whatever the scholars may say now.

Museum of El Greco

Overlooking the valley, about 1km from Fódhele up a signed track • April–Oct daily 9am–7pm • €5 • ⓦ el-greco-museum-birthplace-fodele.gr

They used to claim that the ancient building housing the **Museum of El Greco** was the artist's birthplace: without that excuse the museum is, frankly, a shameless rip-off, with a few very poor reproductions of El Greco's work and almost nothing about his life and

1

times or how the works were created. It is a pleasant spot, though, and directly opposite is the charming church of the Panayía (see below).

Church of the Panayía
Directly opposite the Museum of El Greco • Usually locked

The mainly fourteenth-century **Church of the Panayía** is charming. This exquisite, drum-domed church was built over an eighth-century basilica and the baptismal font in the floor beside the church (deep enough for total immersion) dates from the earlier building. There are also restored thirteenth- and fourteenth-century frescoes. Beneath the orange groves surrounding the church are the remains of the medieval village it once served.

Rodhiá and around

RODHIÁ (Ροδιά) is a sizeable village looking back down over Iráklio; looking up from the city at night, you can see its twinkling lights on the hillside. Travelling on the old road west from Iráklio, you pass under the highway, and immediately start to climb south into the hills. Almost straight away, there's a right turn signed to Rodhiá, where a couple of *kafenía* allow you to rest up and enjoy the views.

Convent of Savathianá
5km northwest of Rodhiá • Daily 8am–1pm & 4–8pm • Free

The isolated **Convent of Savathianá (Σαββαθιανά)** is set amid barren mountaintops, reached only by narrow tracks. It's an extraordinary place, a lush oasis filled with flowers and birdsong, redolent of a more tranquil age. Founded in the Venetian period, the settlement is beautifully kept by its diligent nuns, who cultivate fruit trees and sell home-made jams to visitors. There are three small chapels within the complex, which gained further celebrity in 1991 when an eighteenth-century icon entitled *Lord Thou Art Great*, identical to the one at Tóplou (see p.156), was discovered; both were painted by Ioannis Kornaros.

Márathos and around

AROLÍTHOS (Αρολήθος) is a tacky and artificial "traditional village" aimed squarely at tourists. Just beyond it, the road forks; the route to the right seems far less used, though it used to be the main route from Iráklio to Réthymno. Some 9km northwest of Arolíthos the road passes through **MÁRATHOS (Μάραθος)**, famous for the honey that seems to be on sale at every house. Márathos is an attractive place with a couple of *kafenía* where you can break the journey (this road runs through very few other villages of any size); not far beyond the village, it's possible to cut down by an unpaved but reasonable track to Fódhele (see opposite).

Týlissos

15km southwest of Iráklio; the archeological site is signed to the left off the main street of the modern village of Týlissos • Daily 8.30am–3pm • €2 • Three daily buses to Týlissos village from Iráklio's Pórta Hanión (Bus Station B); they continue towards Anóyia

TÝLISSOS (Τύλισος) is a name famous in the annals of Minoan archeology as one of the first sites to be excavated, and the thriving modern village has a fair claim to four thousand years of continuous human occupation. Local archeologist Hatzidakis, working at the beginning of the twentieth century, revealed evidence of structures from the early pre-Palace period (c.2000 BC), but interest focuses primarily on three large villas (known as Houses A, B and C) from the **New Palace** era. They were probably not as isolated in the country-house sense as they seem today, but may well have been part of a thriving community, or even a staging post on the route west towards as yet

1

TÝLISSOS

undiscovered centres. The existence of a rather simpler villa at Sklavókambos, on the road halfway from here to Anóyia, may lend weight to this latter theory. Týlissos shared in the destruction of the palaces in about 1450 BC, but new buildings then arose, among which was the cistern in the northeast corner of the site. Following the arrival of the Dorians, Týlissos developed into a Greek city of the Classical period, issuing its own coinage. This later construction tends to make it a bit harder to get a clear picture of what's there today.

The site

While it's not always the easiest of sites to interpret, Týlissos is a lovely place to wander round, with few visitors, pine trees for shade, and some evocative remains, including staircases and walls still standing almost 2m tall. Immediately beyond the fence, vineyards and rich agricultural land suggest a seductive, but probably illusory, continuity of rural life. **Houses A and C** are of extremely fine construction and design (C is the more impressive), while little remains of **House B** apart from its ground plan, although it does contain some of the oldest relics here.

House A

A building of finely dressed ashlar stone, **House A** has a **colonnaded court** at its heart with a window lighting the staircase to the west side of this. In storerooms on the north side, some large reconstructed *píthoi* can be seen with holes near their bases for tapping the contents (probably oil). A number of Linear A tablets also came to light in this area. In the south wing, the main rooms open onto a light well, with the central room having a **lustral basin** – in this case more like a sunken bath – just off it. A stand for a double axe, similar to finds from Knossós, was found in the **pillar crypt**, along with the three enormous bronze cauldrons (now in the Iráklio Archeological Museum) that originally prompted the site's excavation. Throughout the house, fragments of painted stucco were found, leading archeologists to postulate the existence of a luxurious second storey to this dwelling, which had fallen in over time.

House C

House C, with a fair amount of concrete reconstruction, contains a **cult room** with a central pillar, storerooms and, at its northern end, the living area, where a paved main room would have been illuminated by a light well on its eastern side. At the end of one of many corridors (a Minoan speciality), a staircase would once have led to an upper floor. There is also evidence of a drainage system, while outside the house, beside the cistern, is a **stone altar** from the Classical period.

East of Iráklio

East of the airport and the city beach at Amnísos there's almost continuous development all the way to Mália, as what little remains of the coastal landscape is torn apart to build yet more hotels, apartments and beach complexes. You're in package-tour country here and the resorts of **Hersónisos** and **Mália**, above all, are big, brash and packed with visitors all summer long. There are one or two highlights and escapes along the way, though: the isolated **Skotinó cave** near Goúves, the impressive **Cretaquarium** at Goúrnes, the **old villages** in the hills behind Hersónissos, and, just beyond the clubs of Mália, a fine **Minoan palace** that will transport you back three and a half millennia. From Hersónisos or Mália, you can also head inland to climb towards the **Lasíthi plateau**.

GETTING AROUND
EAST OF IRÁKLIO

By bus Buses from Iráklio (Bus Station A) serve the coastal resorts, running at least every 30min through Háni Kokkíni and Goúves to Hersónissos and Mália (6.30am–9pm), with stops near all the major hotels. Major attractions like Cretaquarium and Water City also have tours from all the resorts.

By car The new E75 Highway runs a short way inland, bypassing all the major attractions and resorts; you'll need to turn off onto the old road to access any of them.

Háni Kokkíni

The first distinct centre east of Iráklio is **HÁNI KOKKÍNI** (Χάνι Κοκκίνι) a grubbily nondescript resort with a long but rather pebbly beach. There's a **Minoan villa** at the western end of town (Tues–Sun 8.30am–3pm; free) – known as Nírou Háni or simply Niros – which must have been beautifully sited above the water when it stood alone. With the road now cutting it off from the beach, it is harder to appreciate; what you see is a site the size of a large modern house, with walls standing to around waist height.

Goúrnes and around

At **GOÚRNES** (Γούρνες), 15km from Iráklio, there's a break in the overdeveloped coastal strip where, just west of the village, a mammoth former US air force base awaits redevelopment. The one thing that has been built here, and currently stands surrounded by broken fences and crumbling runways, is the **Cretaquarium**, a spectacular marine aquarium extensively signed from the highway.

Cretaquarium

Goúrnes • Daily: May–Sept 9.30am–9pm; Oct–April 9.30am–5pm • €9, children 5–17 €6; audio-guide €3, easily shared between two or three • ☎ 2810 337 788, ⓦ cretaquarium.gr

Boasting thirty tanks (some huge), the **Cretaquarium** houses everything from menacing sharks to dazzling jellyfish. Part of the Hellenic Centre for Marine Research, the venture is purely educational, scientific and non-profit making. Most of the island's fish and crustaceans are included among the 250 species and more than 2500 specimens on

1

display, and unless you're a marine biologist the audio-guide is pretty well indispensable, giving loads of fascinating background information on the creatures you're looking at.

Water City water park

Anópoli, 4km inland from Goúrnes and Háni Kokkíni, 15km from Iráklio • May–Oct daily 10am–6.30pm • €25, children 90–140cm €17 • ☎ 2810 781 317, ⓦ watercity.gr

The giant **Water City water park** is the largest and probably the most impressive on the island, with many of the rides taking advantage of the natural hillside over which the place is built. There's the usual array of slides, pools, snack bars and fast-food outlets, though they can struggle to cope with the crowds in high season.

The Skotinó cave

About 6km inland from Káto Goúves, 3km by road from the village of Skotinó • Open daylight hours • Free

The **Skotinó cave** is one of the largest and most spectacular on the island. It's an uphill hike from the coast (get detailed directions before you set out), or an easy drive, passing through **Goúves** village, which makes an encouragingly complete contrast to the coastal strip and is a good stop to pick up refreshments – there are a couple of decent tavernas. The cave itself is well signed from the village of **SKOTINÓ** (Σκοτεινό), which means "dark"), the last part on a rough track where the cave entrance is marked by a pair of chapels.

Some 160m deep, the cave is divided into four levels, with an awesomely huge main chamber; it's unattended and you can scramble down as far as you dare, with plenty of natural light at first, though you'd be brave to explore the further recesses alone. It was first investigated by Arthur Evans and more scientifically explored in the 1960s by French and Greek archeologists. A considerable number of bronze and ceramic **votive offerings** were found (the earliest dating back to early Minoan times), suggesting that this was an important shrine. The cave remained in use well into the Greek and Roman eras, when the fertility goddess Artemis was worshipped in what is thought to have been a substitution for an earlier Minoan female fertility deity, possibly Brytomartis. In the chapel of Ayía Paraskeví above, *taxímata* (ex-votos) left by pilgrims continue a tradition of supplication to the (now Christian) deity that has persisted on this same spot for well over four thousand years.

Hersónisos and around

HERSÓNISOS (Χερσόνησος) – more correctly **Límin Hersonísou**, the Port of Hersónisos; Hersónisos is one of the villages in the hills just behind – is the first of the big resorts east of Iráklio, a brash, sprawling and rather seedy place catering to mainly Dutch, Irish and Italian package tourists, replete with all the trappings of mass tourism. If you're looking for tranquillity and Cretan tradition, forget it; this is the world of concrete high-rise hotels, video bars, fast-food shops and eurodiscos. The town's main artery is a 2km-long street (Odhós Venizélou) parallel to the sea, a seemingly endless ribbon of bars, travel agents, amusement arcades, tacky shops, car and bike rental dealers and traffic jams. That said, the resort has plenty of life, lots of competition to keep food and drink prices down, and some really attractive rooms and restaurants in the hill villages behind; there are also decent sandy **beaches** both to the west and to the east. The one thing you may struggle to find in July or August is a room.

The esplanade

Along the modern seafront, a solid line of restaurants, bars, bars and more bars is broken only by the occasional souvenir shop or fish spa. In their midst you'll find a small **pyramidal fountain** with broken mosaics of fishing scenes. This dates from the Roman era and is the only real relic of the ancient town of **Chersonesos**, a thriving port from Classical Greek through to Byzantine times, handling trade from Lýttos (see p.75). The busy pleasure **harbour** to the west of the fountain is built over the ancient Roman one, and in odd places along the seafront you can see remains of Roman harbour installations, mostly submerged. The headland above the harbour is a popular spot to watch the sun set; you can explore the excavated remains of an impressively large, early Christian basilica here, complete with mosaic floors, while on the far side the remains of ancient Roman fish tanks can be seen cut into the rock. Other than these, most daytime interest is on the fringes of Hersónisos.

Star Beach Water Park

On the beach immediately east of the resort • Daily: April & May 10am–6pm; June–Sept 10am–7pm • Free entry, but charges for most activities • Ⓦ starbeach.gr

Star Beach Water Park hugs the coast immediately east of town, with some fine beach areas as well as pools, slides, bars and restaurants, and a wide range of watersports from bananas to kitesurfing. Activities for young children are generally free, as are the pools and wi-fi, but everything else has to be paid for, from loungers to bungee jumping.

Lychnostatis Open-Air Museum

On the eastern edge of town, beyond Star Beach • Mon–Fri & Sun 9am–2pm; guided tours every hour on the half-hour • €5; guided tours €1 • Ⓦ lychnostatis.gr

The entertaining **Lychnostatis Open-Air Museum** of folk culture is worth a visit, particularly if you haven't had a chance to see the "real thing" inland. A reasonably authentic-looking re-creation of a traditional Cretan village in a pleasant location next to the sea, the various exhibits relate to a way of life rapidly disappearing from the island. There are orchards and herb gardens, and live displays of local crafts, such as ceramics and weaving, as well as collections of lace, embroidery and traditional costumes within the main house. Concerts of traditional music and dance are frequent, and they occasionally stage more elaborate "dance spectaculars" in the evening, as well as seasonal special events like grape treading in the autumn.

Aqua World

Just off Venizélou, at the bottom of the road to Piskopianó • April–Oct daily 10am–6pm • €6, children €4 • Ⓦ aquaworld-crete.com

A small aquarium displaying many of the fish and sea creatures found off the island's coast, **Aqua World** also has a selection of snakes, lizards and tortoises outside in the reptile garden. Scots-run, Aqua World has an environmental message to deliver, and many of the creatures it houses have been rescued or were unwanted pets.

Acqua Plus

3km inland on the route to the Lasíthi plateau by the golf club • May–Oct daily 10am–7pm • €24, children 5–12 €16, cut-price late-entry deals • Ⓦ acquaplus.gr

Acqua Plus is a big water park that comes close to rivalling Water City (see opposite), but doesn't quite match up in terms of size or number of slides. It's good day out nonetheless, with an attractive setting in a natural bowl of hills and a fair amount of natural shade.

Piskopianó and around

In the hills immediately behind Hersónisos, the three pretty **hill villages** of **Koutoulafári**, **PISKOPIANÓ** (Πισκοπιανό) and **"old" Hersónisos** present a glimpse of a more traditional Crete. They're far from unspoiled – Piskopianó is directly above the harbour and an easy walk, with Koutoulafári a little further, so plenty of people come up here in the evenings to the pretty tavernas and to nights of Cretan dancing – but they're certainly more peaceful than the coast.

1

Museum of Rural Life

Piskopianó • Mon–Sat 11am–2pm & 4–8pm • €4 • ⓦ historical-museum.gr

The one real sight in the villages around Hersónisos, the impressive new **Museum of Rural Life** is one of the best of its kind. It's housed in a wealthy village mansion, modernized to form the bulk of the museum, and a more traditional workshop/barn; displays cover all aspects of rural life from carpentry to olive-oil and *raki* production, and above all there are some very fine examples of traditional weaving.

ARRIVAL AND DEPARTURE

By bus Buses run between Hersónisos and Iráklio (Bus Station A) virtually every 30min from 6.30am to 11pm, and to Áyios Nikoláos only marginally less frequently.

HERSÓNISOS AND AROUND

By taxi For short hops around town, or up to the hill villages, there's a taxi stand at the western end of Venizélou. You can also call on ☎ 28970 22098.

INFORMATION AND ACTIVITIES

Travel agencies In the absence of a tourist office, travel agencies are the best source of information; they're everywhere, offering a huge variety of local tours as well as horseriding, scuba, boat trips and car rental.

Boat trips A wide variety of boat trips to local beaches and islands are on offer from the harbour; it's around €20

for the popular day-trip to Sísi (see p.133).

Horseriding Finikia (☎ 28970 23555, ⓦ hersonissos -horse-riding.com) offer riding tours into the hills (around €60), riding on the beach and lessons from their base close to Star Beach.

ACCOMMODATION

Although you should have little problem finding somewhere to stay outside the peak season of July and August, much accommodation is allocated to package-tour operators and what remains is not cheap. Hotels in the centre are subject to a fair amount of **noise** both from traffic and – after dark – the vibrant nightlife. If you have a car or don't mind a short taxi ride or 20min walk, it's best to head inland to the hill villages for better quality and more peaceful surroundings.

Caravan Camping On the beach at the eastern end of Hersónisos, by Lychnostatis ☎ 28970 22025, ⓦ camping-caravan.doodlekit.com. Small campsite in a brilliant location right on the water. Not much room, so pitches for tents can be tight-packed; they also have hexagonal concrete "bungalows", with just enough space for a double bed, sink and fridge. Two people plus tent and vehicle **€21.50**, bungalow **€33**

Creta Maris ☎ 28970 22115, ⓦ maris.gr. The ritziest place in town, hogging the best part of the beach, with every facility you'd expect from a vast luxury all-inclusive resort, including bungalows designed to mimic a traditional village, seven pools and a wedding chapel. They're also proud of their green credentials. **€200**

Elgoni Apartments Piskopianó, right at the top of the hill above the museum ☎ 28970 21237, ⓔ elgoni _apartments@hotmail.com. Welcoming, good-value

family-run place offering well-equipped studios, apartments and maisonettes in a lovely setting with pool and bar, and great views. The downsides are that the decor is looking a bit tired, and despite the rural appearance there's some traffic noise from the new national road, which passes just above. **€30**

Galaxy Villas Koutouloufári, towards the eastern end of the village near the Sports Café ☎ 28970 22910, ⓦ galaxy-villas.com.gr. Comfortable, well-equipped modern a/c villa/apartments with kitchens, in a complex with pool and bar, and views down over the coast. **€80**

Ilios Omirou 2, on the western edge of town just back from the main road ☎ 28970 22500, ⓦ hotelilios.gr. Standard hotel in a relatively quiet area with a rooftop pool; there's an extra charge for a/c and wi-fi. As good as you'll find in this price range in Hersónisos itself. **€45**

EATING AND DRINKING

There's no shortage of places to eat and drink in the resort, although quality is not always a priority, especially among the **waterfront** places whose location is so irresistible that they don't need to try too hard. Better food and a more relaxed atmosphere is to be found out of town in the **hill villages**, where many tavernas have roof terraces with views towards the coast. The main square in old Hersónisos is closed off every evening and taken over by the tables of competing restaurants, with Cretan dancing most nights.

Argo Navárhou Neárhou 26, round the corner from the harbour ☎ 28970 22134. Much quieter and with a more

personal welcome and traditional Greek feel than anywhere on the main seafront. They offer home-made

1

Greek classics plus an international menu, and there's also a bar without loud music, popular with an older crowd. Daily 9am–midnight.

★ **Elliniko Estiatorio** Kaniadáki 4, off the south side of Venizélou slightly east of the church. The name means simply "Greek Restaurant", and that's exactly what it is – a place where locals come (many have takeaways) for a daily selection of freshly made *mayireftá* (trays baked in the oven, €6–7.50 for a main). There is a menu but no one uses it; simply look at the day's dishes displayed behind glass and choose from there; very little English is spoken. Come at lunchtime, because many dishes run out early. Mon–Sat noon–10pm.

Nikis 25 Mártiou 12, at the eastern end of the seafront ☎ 28970 22379. The international menu is not significantly better (or pricier) than elsewhere, but it's a little further from the centre so less manic than other places, with great views and a totally irresistible line in chat to draw in the punters. Daily 9am–1am.

Oniro Koutouloufári, on the lower street through the village ☎ 28970 23840. The terrace here has some of the best coastal views of all, which is reflected in the prices. Specials such as pork or lamb shanks (€12.80/€13.80) are slow-cooked in a wood oven; try also the aubergine stuffed with veal and cheese (€10.80) or *exohikó* (lamb in filo, €11.90). April–Oct daily 11am–midnight.

★ **Pithari** Koutouloufári, at the crossroads on the upper street through the village ☎ 28970 21449. Touristy, like everywhere up here, but with well-prepared authentic Cretan dishes and a large roof terrace. Try the likes of rabbit *stifádho* (€9.50) or lamb Pithari (baked in filo with potato and spinach; €13.50). April–Oct daily 11am–midnight.

La Scala Ayía Paraskeví 83, at the heart of the waterfront ☎ 28970 24777. The most glamorous of the central seafront restaurants, with candlelit tables right down on the sand as well as on a terrace above it, serving a huge menu of fresh fish, pizza (€6–11), pasta (from €10 to €25 for fettuccinie with crawfish, *féta* and honey) and Greek standards at much the same prices as its neighbours. Daily 10am–late.

NIGHTLIFE

Hersónisos is renowned for its **nightlife** and there's certainly no shortage of it. A night's partying kicks off around the many **bars** ringing the harbour; this is dancing on tables territory, so if you fancy a quiet drink, head for the fringes of town or to the hill villages. Later on, the larger **disco-pubs** and **clubs** in the streets leading up to and along Elefthériou Venizélou are the places to be seen. Many of these places change their name and decor annually, so those reviewed below are just a few of the longer-established options; you'll have no trouble finding others.

Matrix Towards the western end of Venizélou, ⓦ matrixclub.gr. The biggest club in town, attracting big-name international DJs. Every type of music from R & B to hip-hop to reggae depending on who's behind the decks. It's great when it's packed, but can be cavernously empty out of season.

New York Ayía Paraskeví 30, right on the water ☎ 28970 23415, ⓦ new-york.gr. Glamorous dance club that's also a café and beach club, with sunbeds, by day, and a sophisticated cocktail bar. DJ Yiannis plays funk, Greek pop and techno from around 11pm.

Star Water Park On the beach immediately east of the resort. The water park (see p.83) houses a megaclub, with wild foam parties on Sunday nights (free) and frequent appearances by international DJs.

Status Ayía Paraskeví 47 ⓦ statusclub.gr. Behind the street-facing bar (early-evening table-dancing activities) is a late-night dance club that sees occasional appearances by visiting DJs, playing predominantly house and club sounds. Right at the heart of the waterfront.

Mália

MÁLIA (Μάλια) is, perhaps, the most notorious resort in Crete: brash, commercial, with a reputation for wild nightlife. The **beach**, long and sandy as it is, becomes grotesquely crowded at times. Having said that, it can be a great place to stay if you're prepared to enter into the spirit of things – party all night and sleep all day – with the bonus of a genuine town that existed before the tourists came, and a fabulous **Minoan palace** just down the road.

The beaches

Beaches stretch either side of Mália. If you're prepared to walk a bit you'll be rewarded with better sands and fewer people; though solitude is a distant dream. The **central beach** stretches east from the bottom of Beach Road; in summer, you'll need to walk through the mass of bodies for about another fifteen minutes before you find

1

MÁLIA ORIENTATION

Mália consists of two distinct parts, lying on opposite sides of the old highway (Venizélou). The heart of tourist life lies to the north towards the **beach**, where two main streets snake for a good kilometre towards the sea: one, **Zahariádhi**, from the major junction near the western end of town; the other, **Dhimokratías**, a little further east. The streets merge into one after about 300m, and along them you'll find supermarkets, souvenir shops, travel agents, cafés, restaurants, video bars and nightclubs. To walk the length of this will take you about fifteen minutes – longer if you allow yourself to be enticed by the sales patter along the way, or after midnight, when it's at its busiest. At the end there's a car park, a small harbour and access to the beach.

South of the main road is the **old town**, with its narrow, twisting alleyways and whitewashed walls. Here you can still find traces of traditional life, as Mália determinedly clings to what remains of its self-respect.

somewhere to spread out. At this eastern end of the beach is a small **church** backed by dunes and patches of marshy ground alive with frogs. You can also swim out to a tiny **offshore islet**: the rocks here are sharp for barefoot exploring, but your efforts will be rewarded by a (perpetually locked) white chapel and rock pools alive with crabs, shellfish and sea urchins on the islet's seaward side.

There are beaches west of the resort centre, but the most tempting lie to the east: **Sun Beach**, about 2.5 km from the centre, where there are free trampolines and pools, plus plenty of loungers, drinks, amusements and watersports; **Tropical Beach**, with more loungers but fewer buzzing banana boats and parascenders; and finally **Potamos**, at the mouth of a small river very close to the palace, with loungers and a café.

The Palace of Mália

3km east of Mália, just off the old highway • Tues–Sun 8.30am–3pm • €4 • Any bus bound for Áyios Nikólaos will stop at the turn-off on the main road; moving on, buses pass on the main road at least hourly throughout the day – west towards Iráklio and east to Áyios Nikólaos

Though much less imposing than either Knossós or Festós, the **Palace of Mália** in some ways surpasses both. For a start, it's a great deal emptier, and you can wander among the remains in relative peace. And while no reconstruction has been attempted, the palace was never re-occupied after its second destruction, so the ground plan is virtually intact. The excavations are by no means complete; inside and beyond the fenced site to the north and west, digs are still going on, as an apparently sizeable town comes slowly to light.

Of the **ruins** you see today, virtually nothing stands much more than 1m above ground level apart from the giant *píthoi* that have been pieced together and left about the place like sentinels: the palace itself is worn and brown, blending almost imperceptibly into the landscape. With the mountains behind, it's a thoroughly atmospheric setting. It's also easier to comprehend than Knossós, and if you've already seen the reconstructions there, it's easy to envisage this seaside palace in its days of glory. Basking on the rich agricultural plain between the Lasíthi mountains and the sea, it retains a real flavour of an ancient civilization with a taste for the good life.

Though the palace is accessible by bus, it's also easily reached on foot – a 40min **walk** from Mália – or you could rent a **bike** for the easy, flat ride out to the site, and stop for a swim on the way back.

Brief history

First discovered by Joseph Hatzidhakis early in the twentieth century, the site's excavation was handed over to the French School at Athens in 1922. As at Knossós and Festós, there was an earlier palace dating from around 1900 BC, which was devastated by the earthquake of about 1700 BC. The remains you see today are those of the palace built to replace this, which functioned until about 1450 BC, when it was destroyed for the last time (see p.330). From this site came the famous **gold pendant** of two bees that can be seen in the Iráklio Archeological Museum and on any local postcard stand. It was allegedly part of a hoard that was plundered; the rest of the collection now resides (as the "Aegina Treasure") in London's British Museum. The beautiful **leopard's-head axe**, also in the museum at Iráklio, was another of the treasures found at Mália.

The West Court

The main palace is to the right of the site entrance, approached through the **West Court**. As at the other palaces, there are raised pathways leading across this, with the main one heading south towards the area of the eight circular **storage pits**. These probably held grain; the pillars in the middle of some would once have supported a protective roof. In the other direction, the raised walkway takes you to the building's north side, where you can pick up the more substantial paved road that apparently led to the sea.

Entering the palace itself through a "door" between two rocks and jinking right then left, you arrive in the **North Court**, by the storerooms and their elaborately decorated, much-photographed giant *píthoi*. Off to the right are the so-called Royal Apartments, on the far side of which is a well-preserved lustral basin or bath. Nearby lies the **Archive Room**, where a number of Linear A tablets were unearthed. Straight ahead is the

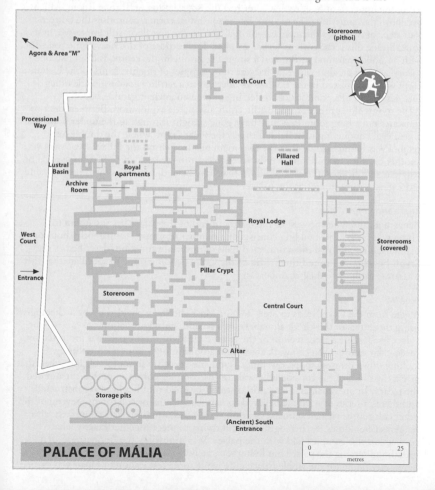

PALACE OF MÁLIA

1

Pillared Hall, which the excavators, encouraged by the discovery of some cooking pots, think may have been a kitchen (if correct, the relative location is almost exactly the same as that of the palace kitchen at Zákros). Above the hall, a grand dining room would have looked out over the courtyard.

The Central Court

Mália's **Central Court**, a long, narrow area, about 48m in length by 22m wide, is only slightly smaller than the main courtyards at Knossós and Festós. Look out for the remains of the columns that once supported a portico at the northern end, and for traces of a similar portico down the eastern side. Still-visible post-holes were discovered between these columns by the excavators, suggesting that the court could be fenced in – possibly to protect the spectators during the bull-jumping games that may have been held here. Behind the eastern portico are more storerooms, now under a canopy. In the centre of the court is a shallow pit that may have been used for sacrifices; if this was indeed its purpose then, along with Anemospília (see p.72), these are the only such Minoan sacrificial areas to have been discovered.

On the west side of the courtyard are the remains of two important stairways. The first led to the upper floor beside what is termed the **Royal Lodge** or Throne Room, which overlooks the courtyard. The second, in the southwest corner, comprises the bottom four steps of what was the main ceremonial stair to the first floor, still impressive in its scale. Beside this is the curious *kernos*, or **altar**. The purpose of this heavy limestone disc, with 34 hollows around its rim and a single bigger one in the centre, is disputed: one theory suggests an altar where, at harvest time, samples of the first fruits of the Cretan crops would be placed in the hollows as offerings to a fertility goddess, while other theories have it as a point for tax collecting or even an ancient gaming board.

The rooms along the west side of the court also merit exploration. Between the two staircases ran a long room that may have gone straight through to the upper floor, like a medieval banqueting hall. Behind this is the **Pillar Crypt**, where the double-axe symbol was found engraved on the two main pillars. Behind the Pillar Crypt runs yet another corridor of storerooms; only accessible through areas which had some royal or religious significance, these would doubtless have been depositories for things of value – the most secure storage at the palace.

Agora and Crypt

Beneath a canopy to the west of the northern end of the palace lies the **Agora** (or Hypostyle Hall). This building consists of a number of rooms – apparently shops or market stalls – and two interconnected halls of uncertain function, described as the **Crypt**. Benches run round three sides of the Crypt, leading some to speculate that this was some form of council chamber.

Area "M"

A gate from the Crypt leads to **area "M"** (or Mu – the site is divided up by archeologists using the letters of the Greek alphabet), in a second fenced area almost as large as the palace itself. Here a large section of the town dependent on the palace is protected by a spectacular canopy. You can walk above and around it on a suspended walkway, looking down on workshops, dwellings, some preserved up to roof level, and streets that give a clear idea of the considerable scale of the complex community that surrounded the palace. In one small area a section of wood-beamed roof has been reconstructed, and there's a series of what are believed to have been ritual or **cult rooms**. Several of the other cult rooms yielded statuary, libation vessels and other artefacts connected with religious ceremonies. Archeologists are still trying to piece together exactly what connection this complex had with the palace. Was it possibly the "monastery" of a priesthood serving the palace but living separately from it, or could it have served as a temporary home for the whole palace elite while some restoration or repair was carried out to the palace proper? Many of the most interesting finds from this area are displayed in the museum at Áyios Nikólaos, but at the site entrance there's a small **exhibition** on the excavations (especially the more recent ones) which is well worth a look, and includes a model of area "M" as it might have looked.

The Golden Pit

Turn right (west) on leaving the palace site, and then right again along a dirt track that heads northeast towards the sea; the fenced pit lies some 300m down the track, just before the islet of Ayía Varvára, visible offshore

Some 500m north of the palace, close to the sea and outside the main fenced area, is the *Chrysolakkos* or **Golden Pit**, apparently a large, multi-chambered mausoleum dating from the Old Palace period. Its elaborate construction suggests a royal burial-place, as does the wealth of grave goods discovered here, among them the gold honeybee pendant.

Area "E"

Between the palace and the main road, there are **new excavations** (fenced off) in **area "E"**, which further underline the scale of the urban area surrounding the palace. There are many substantial buildings here, including a large mansion where fragments of painted plaster were discovered, suggesting a sumptuously decorated interior.

ARRIVAL AND INFORMATION   MÁLIA

By bus Arriving by bus you'll be dropped at the central junction on the main road (Venizélou) heading through the town. There are services to and from Iráklio (Bus Station A) virtually every 30min from 6.30am to 11pm, and to Áyios Nikoláos at least hourly.

Travel agencies Artemis Travel, Venizélou 200 at the junction with 25 Martíou in the heart of town (☎ 28970 33767), can provide local information and help with rooms, as well as advice on local tours and car rental. Sunny Holidays, 25 Martíou 9 in the old town (☎ 28970 32120), are also helpful.

ACCOMMODATION

Many **rooms** are taken up by the package industry, and in peak season finding somewhere to stay may not be easy. Your best bet if you want any sleep is to avoid the Beach Road area: try one of the numerous rooms signed in the old town or on the fringes of the new. You'll save a lot of schlepping around by booking though a travel agent.

EATING AND DRINKING

Mália's **restaurant** owners jostle for your custom at every step, especially along the beach road; none particularly good, but they know their clientele – *moussaká*, pie and chips and all-you-can-eat Mexican, Indian or Chinese places abound. You're far better off in the **old town** where, around the Platía Ayíos Dhimítrios, you can choose from a variety of more elegant bars, tavernas and restaurants. If you're shopping for picnic food, look out for the tasty bananas sold at stalls throughout the centre: chances are they'll have been grown in the fields around the town.

Elizabeth and Stablos Platía Áyios Dhimítrios, old town ☎ 28970 31320. Elegant decor, decent *mezédhes* (mixed *meze* for 2 €25), good barrel wine and an attractive upstairs terrace opposite the little church make this a popular and appealing spot. Daily 5pm–midnight.

Kalesma Omiroú 8, off the top of 25 Martíou, old town ☎ 28970 33125. Located in a quiet backstreet with a classy terrace and blown-glass light fittings, this is Mália's most stylish restaurant. Famous for its *meze* (€3–7), it also offers well-prepared traditional dishes (*kleftikó* €11) and a good selection of Cretan wines. Daily 4pm–12.30am.

Pizza Zorbas 25 Martíou, near the Town Hall ☎ 28970 32433. Attractive, economical old-town pizzeria with a wood-fired oven and roof terrace; also simple grills, *yíros* and salads at this popular late-night spot. Daily 5pm–late.

NIGHTLIFE

Mália's beach road is transformed during the hours either side of midnight, when the profusion of **bars**, **discos** and **clubs** erupt into a pulsating cacophony. Most of them have touts outside trying to lure you in, and in most you can see through glass doors what you'll be letting yourself in for. The bigger, better clubs cluster around the point where the two beach roads meet. There are plenty of "English pubs", too. Vast crowds of 18–30s – many in organized groups – stagger between the bars and clubs, and while the worst excesses of past years have been left behind, you do still get the odd confrontation.

1

Camelot Castle Dhimokratías 82, at the junction on beach road ☎694 42 85 769. Right at the heart of the action, this is the daddy of the Mália clubs, with big-name DJs (Judge Jules and Westwood), foam parties and more. Daily 11pm–4am.

Candy Club Beach road ✆candyclubmalia.com. In the midst of the beach road madness, a huge venue with three bars, two dance stages, VIP area and more. House and electro, and performances featuring the likes of Ms Dynamite. Daily 11pm–4am.

Towards the Lasíthi plateau

The one inland route that visitors follow in any numbers is the drive up to the **Lasíthi plateau** (see p.135). The main route heads inland from Hersónisos, initially towards Kastélli (p.74), and then east through the Aposelémis valley to Potamiés and Goniés. The attractions are charmingly simple: scenery that becomes increasingly mountainous as you climb towards the plateau; old trees spreading beside the road, and still older churches in the villages. Alternative routes – dramatically wild and lonely, with spectacular views – wind up from Stalídha and Mália.

Panayía Gouverniótissa

The monastery of **Panayía Gouverniótissa** (Παναγία Γκουβερνιώτισσα; Assumption of the Virgin) is one of the oldest in Crete. The buildings are gradually being restored, and there's likely to be a workman or caretaker around to open any locked doors (if not, the key to the chapel is available from the *kafenío* at the edge of Potamiés). The tiny **chapel** stands close by in a peaceful garden with a lemon tree; inside are restored **frescoes** dating from the fourteenth century, with a fine *Pantokrátor* adorning the dome.

Avdhoú

In the village of **AVDHOÚ** (Αβδού) there are fine, very faded frescoes from the fourteenth and fifteenth centuries in three **churches**: Áyios Andónios, Áyios Konstantínos and Áyios Yeóryios. The churches should be open; if not, enquiries in the village cafés should produce the necessary keys.

Krási

The village of **KRÁSI** (Κράσι), just off the main road on the route to Mália, is curiously named – curious because Krási translates as "wine", but the village's fame is in fact based on water, in the form of a curative spring that is reputed to be especially good for stomach complaints. This is situated under stone arcading in the shade of an enormous **plane tree**, which is claimed to be two thousand years old and the largest in Europe, with a girth that cannot be encircled by twelve people. Flanking the tree are a couple of tavernas.

Panayía Kardhiótissa

Daily 8am–2pm & 4–8pm • €2

The convent of **Panayía Kardhiótissa** (Παναγία Καρδιώτισσα) – Our Lady of the Heart – is one of the most important places of worship on Crete, with an annual celebration on September 8. The buildings date from the twelfth century, and though the heavily refurbished exterior of the monastery looks like whitewashed concrete, the interior is undeniably spectacular, with restored **frescoes** throughout. These came to light only in the 1960s, when they were discovered beneath accumulated layers of paint. There is also a copy of a famous twelfth-century icon of the Virgin, the original of which was taken to Rome in 1498. According to legend, successive attempts by the Turks to steal this copy were thwarted when it found its way back to Kerá, despite being chained to a marble pillar; the pillar is now in the monastery yard, while the chain (kept inside the church) is believed to alleviate pain when wrapped around the bodies of the afflicted. There's an attractive little museum too.

The ascent to Séli Ambélou

Beyond the village of Kerá, the road winds on into the Dhiktean mountains, and the views become progressively more magnificent. To the left, **Mount Karfí** looms ominously, its summit more than 1100m above sea level. This spire-like peak (*karfí* means "nail" in Greek) was one of the sites where the Minoan civilization made its last stand, following the collapse of the great centres after the twelfth century BC. There's a scary-looking track to the site of **ancient Karfí** (see p.137), some 5km away, from the car park at the ludicrous **Homo Sapiens Village**.

The road continues to climb to the dramatic pass of **SÉLI AMBÉLOU** (Σέλι Αμπέλου), flanked by ruined stone windmills. Beyond, the Lasíthi plateau suddenly unfolds before you. Almost straight ahead, on the far side of the plateau, the highest peaks of the range dominate the landscape, with **Mount Dhíkti** – all 2148m of it – at their heart.

Southwest from Iráklio

Crossing the island on the southwest route is not, on the whole, the most exciting of drives: on the western outskirts of the city you turn south, under the highway, following the signs to Festós and Míres. From the beginning, the road climbs, heading up to the island's spine through agricultural country renowned for its vineyards. In the Middle Ages this was traditionally the **Malevísi**, or Malmsey, wine-producing region (see p.76): though some wine is still made, most of the grapes you'll see now are grown for eating rather than pressing or for turning into sultanas. Highlights along this route include an ancient site at **Rizinía**, as well as picturesque medieval **monasteries** at Veneráto and **Zarós**, the latter a particularly pleasant village with great accommodation choices, surrounded by fine **walking country** and with a small lake nearby.

GETTING AROUND
SOUTHWEST FROM IRÁKLIO

By car The main road is the fast route via Veneráto and Ayía Varvára, but you can also follow a scenic detour via Voutés, Áyios Míronas and Pírgou, a wonderful undulating ride through some lovely out-of-the-way villages.

By bus Buses from Iráklio's Bus Station B (Mon–Sat 11 daily 6.30am–8pm; fewer on Sun) follow the main road across the island, heading for Festós and Mátala or Ayía Galíni via Tymbáki. Míres, in the heart of the Messará plain, is the southern junction for switching between these various routes. Asites also has a bus service (Mon–Fri 6.45am, 1pm & 2.30pm, Sat 6am & 2.45pm).

Ancient Rizinía

To visit the site, continue beyond the hairpin bend to where a sign (to "Prinías archeological site") directs you up a short, just about driveable track, with the acropolis and chapel of Áyios Pandeleímon visible above

On a hairpin bend, 3km south of Ano Asítes and 2km north of Priniás, a pair of remarkable **rock-cut tombs** can be seen, part of the cemetery of **Ancient Rizinía** (Ριζινία), which occupied the flat-topped hill to the east. Founded at the end of the Bronze Age, possibly by Minoans fleeing the Dorian invasion of the north coast, Riziniá later flourished as a Greek city and the remains of two temples have been discovered on the acropolis. Although not a lot remains of the ancient town, the sheer quantity of broken shards littering the ground is evidence that this was once a substantial conurbation. Nosing around, you'll come across the footings of ancient dwellings, with steps and porches clearly identifiable. When you eventually reach the landmark whitewashed **chapel of Áyios Pandeleímon**, at the northern tip of the peak, you're greeted with astonishing **views** in all directions, especially north towards Iráklio, with the island of Dhía beyond.

Moní Paliani

MONÍ PALIANÍ (Παλιανή) is a well-signed 2km detour from the village of **Veneráto**. An ancient monastic foundation (dating perhaps from as early as the seventh century) and now a thriving convent, Paliani has at its heart a sacred ancient **myrtle tree** (said to be as much as 1000 years old), its every twig hung with *tamata* (ex-votos) and credited with healing powers. There's a powerful feeling that the rituals centred on the tree predate the monastery, and even Christianity itself, by some centuries. Around the tree is a tranquil, plant-filled courtyard with a thirteenth-century chapel to one side. You can also buy lace, embroidery and other items hand-crafted by the nuns in a small shop.

Ayía Varvára

AYÍA VARVÁRA (Αγία Βαρβάρα) is the chief village of this region, a place known as the **omphalos** (navel) **of Crete**. The great chapel-topped rock that you see as you arrive is held to be the very point around which the island balances, its centre of being. Not that this makes for any great tourist attraction. There are plenty of cafés and shops along the main street, but they cater mostly for local farmers in search of a bag of fertilizer or a tractor part.

Zarós and around

As a village, **ZARÓS (Ζαρός)**, 14km west of Ayía Varvára, is attractive enough, but at first sight little different from many others nearby. A number of things distinguish it, however. For locals, it is known above all for its **spring waters**, which are bottled and sold all over Crete (the bottling plant is at the far edge of the village); the spring waters also feed a small artificial lake. It's also an excellent **walking** centre, within easy reach of a couple of interesting **monasteries**, and has some excellent accommodation and food. To the west, a beautiful drive on relatively good, empty roads follows the flank of the Psilorítis range towards Kamáres (see p.212) and eventually on to Réthymno or down to Ayía Galíni.

Lake Vótomos

Just 1km or so out of Zarós, well signed for both walkers and drivers, deep-green **Lake Vótomos (Βότομος)** is overlooked by rocky heights. Tiny as it is, it's a lovely setting, and the lake, full of trout, is the starting point for numerous hikes. The lakeside bar and taverna *Limni* is run by the same family as the *Eleonas Resort* (see opposite), and they are also responsible for many of the excellent signs that help walkers find their way around.

Moní Áyios Nikólaos

The pick of the well-marked paths that start at Lake Vótomos is the climb past **MONÍ ÁYIOS NIKÓLAOS (Άγιος Νικόλαος**; 1km) and through the Roúvas Gorge (2.5km) to the chapel of Áyios Ioánnis (5.2km). You can also drive to the monastery by heading west on the main road out of Zarós, and then 2km up a signed road. The monastery itself is now dwarfed by a vast new concrete church, which seems totally out of place here. Nevertheless, the older institution behind remains very welcoming, and the elderly monks will usually offer some refreshment to passers-by as well as opening the chapel so you can view the fourteenth-century paintings within.

Roúvas Gorge

Above Moní Áyios Nikólaos, the track snakes back and forth across an increasingly steep mountainside before reaching the entrance to the **ROÚVAS GORGE (Ρούβας)**. The gorge is a spectacular walk on a good path, tough going at times despite the wooden walkways that help in the steeper sections. At the top lies the chapel of **Áyios Ioánnis**, on the main E4 trans-island walking route (the gorge walk itself is signed as the E4, but it's certainly not part of the main path). Here the easy option is to turn around and head down the way you came for a well-earned drink by the lake, a couple of hours away. With an early start and plenty of provisions you could take a more ambitious course and head east on the E4 to Áno Asítes, picking up a taxi back from there; but be warned that this is a good 20km of high-altitude mountain walking on rough paths – the rewards are spectacular views and plenty of bird and plant life.

Moní Vrondísi

3km west of Zarós; some signs read "Áyios Antónios" • Daily 8.30am–3pm

Fourteenth- to seventeenth-century **MONÍ VRONDÍSI** (Βροντύσι) is a gloriously peaceful foundation overlooking the Koútsoulidi valley with views towards Festós and the Gulf of Messará. A tranquil courtyard surrounded by monks' cells (mostly empty) and fronted by two fig trees, fronts the monastery's simple limestone **church**. Inside are some fine fourteenth-century **frescoes**, including a moving depiction of the Last Supper, and a collection of icons taken from the nearby church of Áyios Fanoúrios (see below). Vrondísi itself has given up the finest of its artworks, including the six great panels by Dhamaskinos, to the icon gallery of Ayía Ekateríni in Iráklio (see p.56). For most locals, however, the attraction of Vrondísi is not art, but the cool water gushing from a fifteenth-century Venetian fountain, with figures of Adam and Eve, near the entrance. Here you can fill up your empty bottles with fine mountain spring water (the same stuff that's bottled down the road) for free.

Moní Valsamónero

Signed from the village of Vorízia • Official opening hours Mon–Fri 8am–3pm; the guardian is on site most weekdays, but if not he can be found in the village

All that survives of **MONÍ VALSAMÓNERO** (Βαλσαμόνερο) is its church, Áyios Fanoúrios. It's some survival though; it houses some of the best **frescoes** in Crete, painted in the fifteenth century by Konstantinos Rikos and depicting scenes from the life of the *Panayía* (Virgin Mary), images of various saints and a fine *Pantokrátor*.

ACTIVITIES   ZARÓS AND AROUND

Cookery The *Vegera* restaurant (see p.94) in Zarós offers cookery lessons during which you prepare a five-course classic Cretan meal, then sit down and eat it (11am; approx. 4hr; €25 including food and drink).

ACCOMMODATION

★ **Eleonas Traditional Resort** In the hills behind Zarós – follow signs from the bottling plant or from the lake ☎28940 31238, ✆eleonas.gr. The traditionally built villas here are set in gardens where the native plants are labelled, at the base of the mountains. Built to resemble a village, they have every facility including kitchen, a/c, TV and a fireplace; the more attractive (and more expensive) original villas are slightly larger, with galleried bedrooms. There's also an excellent taverna using local produce (breakfast is included) and activities including a pool and five-a-side football pitch; guests are a curious mix of serious northern European hikers and elegant Irakliot weekenders. **€95**

Idi Hotel On the road to Lake Vótomos ☎28940 31301, ✆idi-hotel.gr. A comfortable place to get away from it all with a big garden pool (and indoor pool in winter) and tennis court. Pine-panelled rooms are a little old-fashioned. There's a roaring spring directly outside the hotel, and an abandoned watermill, while the hotel's taverna makes a speciality of the trout that splash around in the trout farm behind. Breakfast included. **€50**

★ **Rooms Keramos** Zarós village, signed off the main street ☎28940 31352, ✆studiokeramos-zaros.gr. A bourgeois house in the village has been converted into a warren of individually decorated rooms with fridge, a/c and heating. Most have balconies with village and mountain views, some have fine brass bedsteads. It's the exceptional warmth of the old-fashioned welcome that makes this place really special, though; that, and the amazing breakfasts with home-made pies and pastries. **€35**

EATING AND DRINKING

Limni Lake Vótomos ☎ 28940 31338. The only restaurant actually on the lakeside, *Limni* serves excellent food, beautifully presented; earthy bread comes with sage-flavoured olive oil, tzatziki, olives and tomato salsa, for example. The lake trout is the inevitable special, though it's a rather bland fish. Evenings here can be magical (providing you remember to bring your mosquito repellent) and it's perhaps the only place in Crete where you'll have geese begging for food alongside the usual cats. Daily noon–11pm.

Vegera Main street, Zarós village ☎ 28940 31730, ⓦ vegerazaros.gr. From the same hospitable family as *Keramos* (see p.93), and with an all-female kitchen, *Vegera* offers traditional, local food. There's no menu – instead, for €12, you get a selection of dishes to share, based on whatever is fresh and in season; usually excellent and including plenty of interesting veggie dishes but, despite the name, this is not a vegetarian restaurant. Daily 11am–5pm.

The Messará plain

South of Ayía Varvára the road becomes genuinely mountainous until, at the Vourvoulítis Pass (650m), you enter the watershed of the Messará. The **MESSARÁ PLAIN** (Μεσσαρά), a long strip running east from the Gulf of Messará, is the largest and most important of Crete's fertile flatlands. Bounded to the north by the Psilorítis range and the lower hills that run right across the centre of the island, to the east by the Dhiktean mountains, and to the south by the narrow strip of the Asteroússia and Kófinas hills, it is watered, somewhat erratically, by the Yeropótamos. Heavy with olives, and increasingly with the fruit and vegetable cash crops that dominate the modern agricultural economy, the plain has always been a major centre of population and a mainstay of the island's economy. There is much evidence of this, not only at the ancient sites of **Górtys**, **Festós** and **Ayía Triádha**, but at a wealth of lesser, barely explored sites; today's villages exude prosperity, too, surrounded by neat and intensive cultivation.

GETTING AROUND   THE MESSARÁ PLAIN

By car As you descend to the plain by a series of long, looping curves, the main road heads west through Áyii Dhéka towards Míres, Festós and Mátala. A left turn eastwards takes you across far less travelled country (see p.113) and all the way to Ierápetra.

By bus Buses from Iráklio's Bus Station B (Mon–Sat 11

daily 6.30am–8pm; fewer on Sun) head for Míres, the transport hub of the Messará plain. From here they continue variously to Mátala, Lendás or Ayía Galíni via Tymbáki; the majority of these buses call at Áyii Dhéka and Górtys, before Míres and many continue via Festós.

Áyii Dhéka

ÁYII DHÉKA (Άγιοι Δέκα) is the first village you reach on the Messará and the most interesting. The place takes its name from ten early Christians who were martyred here around 250 AD, at the behest of the Emperor Decius. The **Holy Ten** are still among the most revered of Cretan saints: regarded as martyrs for Crete as much as Christianity, they were the first in a heroic line of Cretans who laid down their lives to oppose tyrannical occupation.

On the west side of the village are two churches associated with the holy ten: the older, originally Byzantine **church** is signed to the south of the main road. Inside, there's an icon portraying the martyrdom of the saints and the marble block on which they are supposed to have been decapitated, complete with the imprints of their knees. Signed from here is a relatively modern **chapel** on the edge of the village beneath which, visible from the exterior, is a crypt where you can see six of their tombs. Both churches are gerally open in daylight hours; it's well worth taking the short walk between them to get a sense of how close to the busy main road rural Crete remains. You'll see reminders of the village's ancient past everywhere: Roman statues, pillars and odd blocks of masonry are reused in modern houses, propping up walls or simply lying about in yards.

1

Górtys

July & Aug daily 8am–8pm; April–June, Sept & Oct Mon–Sat 8am–6pm, Sun 8am–3pm; Nov–March daily 8am–3pm • €4

The remnants of the ancient city of **GÓRTYS** (Γόρτυς), known traditionally as Gortyn or Gortyna, are scattered across a large, fragmented area, covering a great deal more than the fenced site beside the road that most people see. The best way to get some idea of the ancient city's scale is to follow the path through the fields from the village. This heads out more or less parallel to the road, opposite the chapel of Áyii Dhéka, and is an easy walk of less than 1km to the main site; along the way you'll skirt most of the major remains.

Brief history

Settled from at least Minoan times, when it was a minor subject of Festós, Górtys began its rise to prominence under the **Dorians**. By the eighth century BC it had become a significant commercial power and in the third century BC it finally conquered its former rulers at Festós. The society was strictly regulated, with a citizen class (presumably Dorian) ruling over a population of serfs (presumably "Minoan" Cretans) and slaves. Even for the citizens, life was as hard and orderly as it was in Classical Sparta.

Evidence of early Górtys has survived thanks largely to the remarkable **law code** found here, and to a lesser extent through treaties known to have existed between the Górtys of this era and its rivals, notably Knossós. **Hannibal** fled to Górtys, where he stayed briefly after his defeat by Rome, and later the city helped the **Romans** to conquer Crete. It was during the Roman era that the city reached its apogee, from 67 BC onwards: as the seat of a Roman praetor, it was capital of the province of Crete and

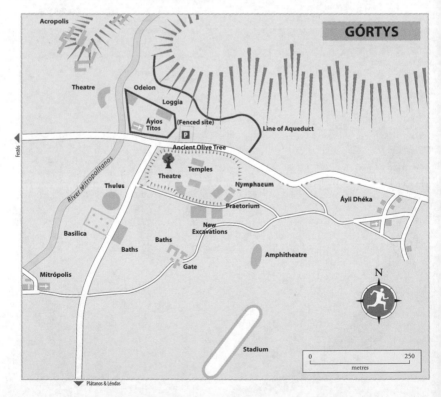

Cyrenaica, ruling not only the rest of the island but also much of Egypt and North Africa. It was here that **Christianity** first reached Crete, when St Titus was despatched by St Paul to convert the islanders, but after the **Saracen** invasion in the ninth century, when much of the city was razed, Górtys was abruptly abandoned.

South of the road: the Roman city

In the fields en route to the site, it is the **Roman city** that dominates: this once stretched from the edges of Áyii Dhéka to the far banks of the Mitropolitanos (then known as the Lethe) and from the hills in the north as far south as the modern hamlet of Mitrópolis, where a Roman basilica with good mosaics (now covered) has been excavated. For most people, though, the ruins along the main path, with others seen standing in the distance, and the tantalizing prospect of what lies unexcavated beneath hummocks along the way, are quite enough. Individually, or in another setting, these might seem unimpressive, but with so many of them, abandoned as they are and all but ignored, they are amazing – you almost feel as if you've discovered them for yourself. The sites that have been excavated here are mostly seen only through locked fences, but the ground everywhere is littered with pillars and broken masonry.

The **Praetorium** (the Roman governor's palace) has the most extensive remains, a vast pile built originally in the second century, rebuilt in the fourth, and occupied as a monastery right up to the time of the Venetian conquest. Excavations in this area have revealed impressive foundations, flights of steps, walls and marble columns once belonging to imposing buildings, all indicating how much more still lies beneath the olive groves waiting to be discovered. Within the same fenced area is a courtyard containing fountains and the **Nymphaeum**. Somewhere near here, too, was the terminus of the main aqueduct that brought water from the region of modern Zarós. About 100m to the west of the Praetorium area is the **Temple of Pythian Apollo**, the most important of the Roman city's temples, later converted to a church, while the nearby **theatre**, though small, is very well preserved. Some 50m north of here are the substantial remains of the **Temple of Isis and Serapis**.

The main site

Directly opposite the entrance to the main, fenced site, be sure not to miss the 1600-year-old **olive tree** that has grown around pillars from the ruins of the ancient site – a surreal attraction in its own right. Plenty of other trees that seem almost as venerable surround it; the bus stop sign is nailed to one. As you enter, there's an impressive collection of **statuary** in a small pavilion backing onto the site's **café**, demonstrating the high standard of work achieved here during the city's halcyon days.

Áyios Títos

The apse of the church of **Áyios Títos** is much the most famous image of Górtys, and the thing that immediately grabs the eye. This is the only part of the church that has survived intact, but the shape of the whole structure is easy enough to make out. When it was built (around the end of the sixth century), it would have been the island's chief church, and it is the best remaining example of an early Christian church in the Aegean: you can see the extent to which it is still revered from the little shrine at the end of one of the aisles. The church's capitals bear the monogram of the sixth-century Byzantine emperor Justinian.

The Odeion

Beyond the church lies an area that was probably the ancient forum, and beyond this the most important relic of ancient Górtys, the **Odeion** (or covered theatre) and its **law code**. The law code – a series of engraved stones some 9m long and 3m high – dates from around 500 BC, but it presumably codified laws that were long established by custom and practice. It provides a fascinating insight into a period of which relatively

1

little is otherwise known; the laws are written in a very rough Doric Cretan dialect and inscribed alternately left to right and right to left, so that the eyes can follow the writing continuously (a style known as *boustrophedon*, after the furrows of an ox plough). The code is not a complete system of law but rather a series of rulings on special cases, and reflects a strictly hierarchical society in which there were at least three distinct classes – citizens, serfs and slaves – each with quite separate rights and obligations. Five witnesses were needed to convict a free man of a crime, while one could convict a slave; the rape of a free man or woman carried a fine of a hundred *staters*, while the same offence committed against a serf was punishable by a mere five-*stater* fine. The laws also cover subjects such as property and inheritance rights, the status of children of mixed marriages (that is, between free people and serfs) and the control of trade.

The panels on which the law is inscribed are now incorporated into the round Odeion, which was erected under Trajan in around 100 AD and rebuilt in the third or fourth century (the brick terrace which protects the inscriptions from the elements is modern). The Odeion is just the latest incarnation of a series of buildings on this site in which the code has apparently always been preserved – obviously, this was a city which valued its own history.

The acropolis

With your own transport, you can reach the acropolis by following the road across the river towards Míres and Festós, taking a fork on the right signed "to the Acropolis of Górtys"; this road goes through the village of Ambeloúzos, where you should take a right turn immediately after the village sign; the route then climbs and you shortly need to make a right turn along a road signed to Apomarmá and Gérgeri; soon, a sign on the right will alert you to the acropolis, visible off to the right and a 5min walk away uphill

Beside the fenced site, the **river** runs by an abandoned medieval mill and on the far bank you can see a much larger **theatre**, in rather poor repair, set against the hillside. In Roman times, the river ran through a culvert here and you could have walked straight across; nowadays, you have to go back to the road-bridge to explore this area.

The guardians at the site will provide information on exploring the outlying areas, and will give directions to the easiest path up to the **acropolis** on the hilltop above the river. Hardly anyone makes the hike up there, shying away from such a stiff climb in the heat, but the ruins are surprisingly impressive, with Roman defensive **walls** and a building known as the *kástro* (though apparently not a castle) still standing to a height of 6m in places. The lesser remains are among the earliest on the site and include scant relics of a Greek **temple** that was later converted to a church. From this hilltop vantage point, you also get a fine overview of the layout of Górtys and the ongoing excavations, and it's possible to trace the line of the aqueducts coming in from the north.

Míres

The large market town of **MÍRES** (**Μοίρες**), 10km west of Áyii Dhéka, serves as a transport hub for buses further west and to the beaches of the south coast; if you're travelling to Mátala, or west beyond Phaistos, then you'll normally switch buses here. There are good facilities including a **bank**, a few **restaurants**, a couple of **rooms** places and a handy **internet** café right opposite the bus stop, though there's no particular reason to stay unless you are stranded while waiting for a bus.

ARRIVAL AND DEPARTURE	MÍRES
By bus The bus station is at the western end of town: actually a patch of ground behind a *períptero* (kiosk). You may need to change here for Léndas and Mátala on the coast, Zarós and Kamáres in the mountains, Tymbáki and Ayía Galíni, or Réthymno.	Destinations Ayía Galíni (4 daily 7.40am–3.10pm; 15min); Festós (8 daily 7.40am–4.40pm; 20min); Iráklio (11 daily 6.45am–7.30pm; Mátala (3/4 daily 10.10am–4.40pm; 45min)..

Festós

In a wonderfully scenic location on a ridge at the eastern end of the Messará plain, the **palace of FESTÓS** (Φαιστός) enjoys a stunning setting, overlooked by the snowcapped peaks of Psilorítis and with magnificent views east across the plain. While no traces of frescoes were found here, and few other artworks, this doesn't imply that the palace wasn't luxurious: the materials (marble, alabaster, gypsum) were of the highest quality, there were sophisticated drainage and bathing facilities, and remains suggest a large and airy dining hall on the upper floors overlooking the court. Bear in mind, as you explore, that part of the palace is missing: there must have been more outbuildings on the south side of the site, where erosion has worn away the edge of the ridge and a corner of the Central Court itself has collapsed.

The West Court

You enter the palace from above, approaching the northwest corner of the complex through the Upper Court, then into the **West Court** and integral **Theatral Area**. There are raised walkways leading across the courtyard, and one of them runs right up the steps that form the seats of the Theatral Area (accorded this title by archeologists who supposed it was used for viewing some kind of performance or spectacle). On the west side of the court are circular walled pits, probably for storing grain. The West Court itself is a rare survival from the original palace; the main walkway leads not up the stairs into the new palace but past them and into the entrance to the old palace. From there, much of the facade of the old palace can be seen as a low wall in front of the Grand Stairway which leads into the newer building. When the palace stood, of course, this would not have been apparent; then, the court was levelled at the height of the bottom step of the stairway.

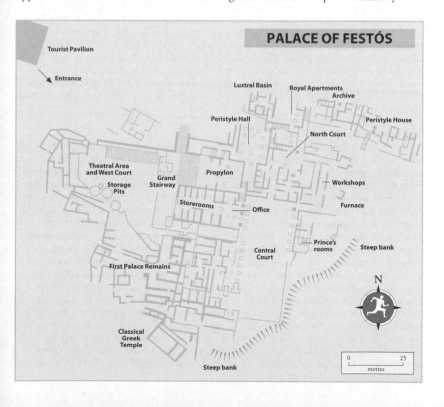

PALACE OF FESTÓS

1

EXCAVATING FESTÓS

In legend the home of Rhadamanthys, brother of King Minos, **Festós** was excavated by Federico Halbherr (also responsible for the early work on Górtys) at almost exactly the same time as Evans was working at Knossós. The style of the excavations, however, could hardly have been more different. Here, reconstruction has been kept to an absolute minimum, to the approval of most traditional archeologists: it's all bare foundations, and walls that scarcely rise above ground level.

As at Knossós (see p.63), most of what survives is what the excavators termed the **Second Palace**, rebuilt after its destruction around 1700 BC and occupied until c.1450 BC. But at Festós, the first palace was used as a foundation for the second, and much of its well-preserved floor plan has been uncovered by the excavations. Fascinating as these superimposed buildings are for the experts, they can make Festós confusing for casual visitors to interpret.

The Grand Stairway and storerooms

The **Grand Stairway** was a fitting approach to Festós, a superbly engineered flight of twelve shallow stone steps, 14m wide. Some of the steps are actually carved from the solid rock of the hill, and each is slightly convex in order to improve the visual impact. This remarkable architectural innovation anticipated similar subtleties of the Parthenon at Athens by twelve centuries. The entrance facade was no doubt equally impressive – you can still see the base of the pillar which supported the centre of the doorway – but it's hard to imagine from what actually survives. Once inside, the first few rooms seem somewhat cramped: this may have been deliberate, either for security purposes or as a ploy to enhance the larger, lighter spaces beyond. At the end would have been a blank wall, open to the sky, and a small door to the right which led onto stairs down towards the grand Central Court. Standing in the entrance area now, you can look down over the **storerooms**, and going down the stairs, you can get closer to them through a larger room that once served as an office. Exposed here is a storeroom from the old palace, with a giant jar still in place and another barred cellar to the right lined with more amphorae. At the far end, more *píthoi* stand in a room apparently used to store olive oil or other liquids; there's a stool to stand on while reaching in and a basin to catch spillage, while the whole floor slopes towards a hole in which slops would have collected.

The Central Court

From the stores "office", quite an elaborate room, you pass into the **Central Court**, which is by far the most atmospheric area of the palace. In this great paved court, with its scintillating **views**, there is a rare sense of Festós as it must have once been. Look north from here in the direction of the Psilorítis range and you can make out a black smudge to the right of a saddle between the two peaks. This marks the entrance to the Kamáres Cave (see p.211), a shrine sacred to the Minoans and the source of the famous hoard of elaborate Kamáres ware pottery. Even without the views – which would have been blocked by the two storeys to either side when the palace was standing – the courtyard remains impressive. Its north end, in particular, is positively and unusually grand: the doorway, flanked by half-columns and niches (possibly for sentries) covered in painted plaster, can be plainly made out. To the left as you face this are a couple of *píthoi* (left there by the excavators) and a stepped stone that some claim was an altar, or perhaps a block from which athletes would jump onto bulls, or maybe just a base for a flowerpot.

Along each of the lengthy sides of the courtyard ran a covered **portico** or veranda, the bases of whose supports are still visible. In the southwest corner are various rooms that probably had religious functions; beyond these are parts of the old palace that are mostly fenced off. Also here, right at the edge of the site, are the remains of a **Greek temple** of the Classical era, evidence that the site was occupied long after the Minoans and the destruction of the palace.

1

The Royal Apartments

Heading up through the grand north door – notice the holes for door pivots and the guardroom just inside – a corridor leads through the **North Court** toward the **Royal Apartments**. These have been covered and shut off to prevent damage from people walking through, and it's hard to see a great deal of the queen's rooms, or the king's rooms behind them. Above the king's quarters is a large **Peristyle Hall**, a colonnaded courtyard much like a cloister, open in the centre. On the north side, this courtyard was open to take in the view of Psilorítis: it must have been a beautiful place, and perhaps also one of some religious significance. Staircases linked the hall directly with the Royal Apartments (and the **lustral basin** on the north edge of the king's rooms); nowadays it's easier to approach from the palace entrance, turning left up the stairs from the Propylon.

Palace dependencies

Continuing past the royal quarters on the other side, you come to a series of buildings that almost certainly predate much of the palace. Among the first of these is the so-called **Archive**, where the famous **Festós Disc** (see p.55) was discovered in one of a row of mud-brick boxes. A little further on is the **Peristyle House**, probably a private home, with an enclosed yard similar in design to the Peristyle Hall. From here, stairs lead back down to the level of the Central Court, into the area of the palace **workshops**. In the centre of another large courtyard are the remains of a furnace, probably used for metalworking or as a kiln. The small rooms roundabout were the workshops, perhaps even the homes, of the craftsmen. As you walk back to the Central Court, another suite of rooms – usually described as the **Prince's Rooms** – lies on your left, boasting its own small peristyle hall.

ARRIVAL AND INFORMATION   **FESTÓS**

By bus Bus services to Festós are excellent, with 8 a day from Iráklio; there are also direct buses to and from Mátala and Ayía Galíni, or you can head back to Míres for more frequent connections.

Opening hours April–Oct Mon–Sat 8am–6pm, Sun 8am–3pm; Nov–March 8am–3pm.
Admission €4, joint ticket with Ayía Triádha €6.

ACCOMMODATION AND EATING

As you enter the site there's a **tourist pavilion** that serves drinks and food. **Rooms** can be found in villages such as Vóri (see p.103) and Kamilári (see p.108), as well as in Míres or Tymbáki. A major bonus of staying in the area is that if you get to the site early you may have a couple of hours of relative peace before the coaches start rolling in, some time after 10am. Áyios Ioánnis (see p.104), not far away on the Mátala road, makes a good **lunch stop** after or between sites.

Ayía Triádha

4km west of Festós on the far side of the hill • Daily: April–Oct 10am–5pm; Nov–March 8.30am–3pm • €3, joint ticket with Festós €6 • An easy drive or a walk of about 45min by a well-signed road around the south slope

In sharp contrast with unadorned Festós, **AYÍA TRIÁDHA (Αγία Τριάδα)** has provided some of the finest known Minoan **artworks**. These include frescoes, three famous vases of carved black steatite – the "Harvesters Vase", the "Boxer Vase" and the "Chieftain Cup" – and a unique painted sarcophagus, all of which are on display in the Iráklio Archeological Museum. Yet the site – discovered and excavated at the turn of the twentieth century by the Italian School under Federico Halbherr – remains something of an enigma. Nothing exists to compare it with, in what is known of Minoan Crete, nor does it appear in any records; even the name has had to be borrowed from a nearby chapel.

As ever, the ruins enjoy a magnificent **location**, looking out over the Gulf of Messará. The modern view takes in the coastal plain, with Tymbáki military airstrip in the foreground, but in Minoan times the sea would have come right up to the base of the hill, very close by. Despite this beauty and wealth, Ayía Triádha is clearly not a

1

construction on the same scale as the great palaces: the most commonly accepted explanation is that it was some kind of royal villa, but it may equally have been the home of an important prince or a wealthy ship-owing merchant, a building of special ceremonial significance, or even (as more recent theories have it, based on the quantity of records and storage found here) simply an administrative centre.

The remains, in which buildings of several eras are jumbled, are confused and confusing. This matters little, however, for it is the **atmosphere** of Ayía Triádha that really makes the place – the absence of crowds, the beauty of the surroundings and the human scale of the villa.

The site

To your left as you climb down to the site are the bare ruins of a **Minoan house** older than most of the other remains (the villa was broadly contemporary with the new palace at Festós), and beyond them a **shrine** that contained a frescoed floor and walls now on show in the Iráklio Archeological Museum. If you keep to the higher ground here, you come into the courtyard of the villa, perhaps the best place to get an impression of its overall layout. The L-shaped building enclosed the courtyard only on its north and west sides, and the north side is further muddled by a much later hall – apparently a Mycenaean megaron – built over it. To the south of the courtyard is the early fourteenth-century chapel of **Áyios Yeóryios**, in which there are fragments of some fine frescoes.

The Royal Villa

The **Royal Villa** now lies under covers below the level of the courtyard, but in Minoan times it would not have appeared this way: the builders made use of the natural slope to create a split-level construction, and entrances from the courtyard

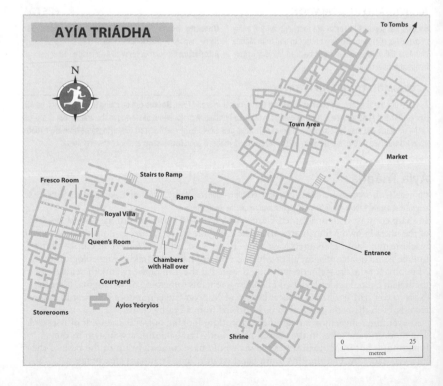

would have led directly into upper levels above those you see today. The finest of the rooms were those in the corner of the "L", looking out over the sea; here, the best of the frescoes were found, including the famous stalking cat. The quality of workmanship can still be appreciated in these chambers with their alabaster-lined walls and gypsum floors and benches. Beside them to the south is a small group of storerooms with a number of *píthoi* still in place; some bear scorch marks from the great fire that destroyed the palace about 1450 BC. From the hall and terrace out front, you can walk around the **ramp** that runs beneath the north side of the villa. The Italian excavators named this the *Rampa al Mare*, and it seems that it would have once run down to the sea.

The town area

By far the most striking aspect of the **town area**, which occupies the slope below the villa, is the **market**, a row of stores that are once again unique in Minoan architecture. The stores, identically sized and fronted by a covered portico, run in a line down the hill; in front of them is an open space and, across that, the houses of the town. There's only one problem with the easily conjured image of the Minoan populace milling around the market while their rulers looked benignly on from above: this area dates from the declining years of the Minoan culture and is contemporary not with the villa, but with the megaron erected over it. Beyond the stores (and outside the fence) lies the **Cemetery**, where remains of two tholos tombs and many other graves were found, including the one containing the Ayía Triádha sarcophagus.

Tymbáki

West of Festós the final stretch of the Messará plain, with its acres of polythene greenhouses and burgeoning concrete sprawl, must be among the ugliest places in Crete. **TYMBÁKI (Τυμβάκι)** may also be the island's drabbest town. It's a sizeable place, which means there are cafés and restaurants along the main street, stores and banks, and even a couple of hotels, but there's no reason to stay longer than you have to. Just beyond, a turning leads to **Kókkinos Pírgos** on the coast. Here, too, plastic and concrete are the overwhelming images, and the place is barely redeemed by a plentiful supply of cheap rooms and the lack of crowds on its none-too-beautiful beach. The more inviting **beaches** in this area are to the south around Kalamáki (p.109), Kommós (p.108) and the developed resort of Mátala (p.105).

Vóri

The road **north from Festós** confirms the rule that on Crete all you have to do is turn off the main road to escape into almost another world. **VÓRI (Βόροι)** is a sizeable place, very close to Festós and barely 1km off the main highway, yet it's almost entirely off the beaten track, a pleasant working village going about its daily routine. That some tourists do come here is largely due to its outstanding ethnology **museum**. If you're heading for the Amári valley and Réthymno from Vóri, you can spurn the main road and take a lovely, climbing drive via Kalohorafitís and Grigoría to **Kamáres** (see p.212); this also offers an alternate route back to Iráklio via Zarós (see p.92).

Museum of Cretan Ethnology

Hidden away in a pedestrian backstreet behind the church • April–Oct daily 11am–5pm • €3 • ⑩ cretanethnologymuseum.gr

Though much copied, Vóri's **Museum of Cretan Ethnology** is still probably the best example of its type on the island, worth seeking out for a comprehensive survey of traditional country life in Crete. The collection is a fascinating miscellany of agricultural implements, building tools and materials, domestic utensils, furniture, pottery, musical instruments, weaving and embroidery, all well labelled. There are sections on the production of olive oil, winemaking and the distillation of *raki*, as well as a display of the myriad herbs and medicinal plants used by Cretans since ancient times. A collection of baskets is especially interesting, the various designs including beehives, eel traps, cheese-drainers, animal muzzles and snail containers.

ACCOMMODATION AND EATING VÓRI

Taverna Alekos Well signed close to the centre of the village ☎ 28920 91094. Taverna with a pretty courtyard planted with pomegranate and olive trees, and serving straightforward Cretan village food, including grilled meats and snails, as well as schnitzels for the tourists. You can also stop in just for a drink, as an alternative to the *kafenía* in the village square. Daily 11am–11pm.

Pension Margit Towards the western edge of the village – look for the signs ☎ 28920 91129, ⓦ pension-margit.messara.de. Simple en-suite rooms in a modern house on a quiet street; very much away from it all. There's a communal kitchen, and breakfast available at extra cost; call ahead to ensure there's someone here to meet you. **€40**

Áyios Ioánnis

The road **south from Festós** passes the Ayía Triádha turn-off and soon approaches the village of **ÁYIOS IOÁNNIS** (Άγιος Ιωάννις) at the bottom of the hill. It's a handy stop for food or drinks, and it's worth taking the time to look at the venerable church of **Áyios Pávlos**. Right opposite the chapel a minor road heads west towards Kamilári (see p.108) and Kalamáki (see p.109), while the main route continues south towards Mátala.

Áyios Pávlos

500m beyond the Taverna Ayios Ioannis in a walled cemetery on the left side of the road • The church is normally open

Encircled by cypresses, the tiny, drum-domed church of **Áyios Pávlos** is one of the oldest on the island. Parts of it, in fact, date back to pre-Christian times, perhaps part of a Roman shrine to a water deity focused on the **well** at the back of the graveyard. The area to the rear of the church is the most ancient, with the dome probably added in the fourteenth century and the narthex, or porch – with its Venetian pointed arches – in the sixteenth. Inside some interesting **frescoes** are dated by a frieze to 1303 and have images of the Evangelists Matthew and Luke, as well as a lurid representation of the punishments of Hell with souls being molested by serpents. This is one of the very few churches on Crete dedicated to St Paul, who was none too taken with the islanders, describing them in one of his epistles as "liars, evil beasts and lazy gluttons". To the side of the church, a charnel house contains the (visible) bones of corpses removed from the nearby tombs after a period of time to "free up" space.

EATING ÁYIOS IOÁNNIS

Taverna Ayios Ioannis On the main road ☎ 28920 42006. Picturesque roadside taverna serving excellent food at tables set under a shady vine trellis; the house speciality of charcoal-grilled rabbit is recommended, and the lamb is tasty, too. Service tends to be slow at busy times. Daily noon–11pm.

The southwest coast

By far the best known of the beach resorts in the south of Iráklio province is **Mátala**, but this is far from the end of the story for this part of the coastline. There are much less crowded alternative sands at nearby **Kommós** with its fine Minoan site, and **Kalamáki**, and alternative bases just a short way inland at **Pitsídhia**, a well-established overflow for Mátala, and **Kamilári**, a charming hill village. Throughout this corner of Crete many properties have been bought by foreigners (Germans especially in this area), and many of the small villages have incongruously fancy villas in their midst.

1

Nonetheless head inland and you'll find lovely, quiet countryside, the villages surrounded by their crops of oranges, pomegranates or olives. One excursion well worth making is to the **Moní Odhiyítrias** and **Áyio Gorge**, where you can follow a verdant ravine down to the sea.

South of the Messará, two more beaches beckon – **Léndas** and **Kalí Liménes**. In an undeveloped way, Léndas is quite a busy place. Kalí Liménes, 20km south of Míres, is hardly visited at all, perhaps due to its role as a bunkering station for off-loading oil tankers. If you have your own transport, the roads around here are all passable but mostly very slow: the Asteroússia Hills, which divide the plain from the coast, are surprisingly precipitous. The only completely paved routes to this part of the coast are from Áyii Dhéka or Górtys to Léndas, and from Míres to Kalí Liménes via Pómbia. Both itineraries offer great views back over the Messará plain before toiling on through a quintessentially Cretan mountain landscape, where clumps of violet-flowering wild thyme cling to the verges in early summer, and shepherds slow your progress as they herd their flocks of goats along the road at dusk.

Mátala

You may still meet people who will assure you that **MÁTALA** (Μάταλα), with its cave-dwelling hippy community, is *the* travellers' beach on Crete. But that history bears about as much relation to modern reality as Mátala's role in legend as the place where Zeus swam ashore in the guise of a bull with Europa on his back, or its former glory as one of the chief ports of ancient Górtys. The entry to the village should prepare you for what to expect: a new road littered with very un-Cretan roundabouts, followed by a couple of kilometres of new hotels, "Welcome to Mátala" signs and extensive car and coach parking areas. In fairness it's far quieter at night, once the tour buses have paraded home, but the town never feels anything other than touristy. On the plus side, there's a spectacular **beach**, the atmosphere is boisterous and you'll never be short of somewhere to enjoy a cocktail at sunset; with the caves lit up at night, the beach is an impossibly romantic setting.

Red Beach

When the crowds on the town beach get too much, you can scramble over the hill for twenty or thirty minutes to **Red Beach**, which, with its reddish-gold sand, nudists and scruffy, seasonal *kantína*, does its best to uphold Mátala's traditions. To get there, simply follow "Hotel Street" away from town, where a track becomes obvious; it can be quite hard going in parts. There's a slightly longer, easier route from town – look for the white-painted arrows pointing up from the main street.

ARRIVAL AND DEPARTURE   MÁTALA

By car Coming in by car you'll need to use the car park by the beach (€2), signed on the right as you enter the resort; if this is full (as it often is in high season) there's limited paid parking in Hotel Street (€3), or you can retrace your route and seek a place on the entry road.

By bus Arriving by bus you'll be dropped right at the entrance to town.
Departures Míres and Iráklio (Mon–Sat 7am, 11.30am [9.30am on Sat], 3pm & 5.15pm; 5.15pm only on Sun).

MÁTALA ORIENTATION

For all its fame, Mátala is a very small place – you can walk through town and see all it has to offer in ten minutes. It consists basically of a single pedestrian street, running behind the **beach**: the **market** (where tourist tat has almost squeezed out the fruit and veg stalls) and many of the places to eat lie to the right, while the "**old town**", such as it is, is crammed against the rocks to the left. A widening of the main road close to the entrance to town we call the "first square"; the town's **main square** is immediately behind this.

1

THE MÁTALA CAVES

Nobody knows quite who originally built the **Mátala caves**, which are entirely artificial, but it seems likely that they were first hollowed out as Roman or early Christian **tombs**: they have since been so often reused and added to that it is virtually impossible to tell. The cliff in which they are carved is soft enough to allow surprisingly elaborate decor: some caves have windows and doorways as well as built-in benches or beds (which may originally have been grave slabs), while others are mere scooped-out hollows. Local people inhabited the caves, on and off, for centuries, and during the war they made a handy munitions dump, but it was in the 1960s that they really became famous, attracting a large and semi-permanent foreign community. Name a famous hippy, and there'll be someone who'll claim that they lived here – the most frequently mentioned are Cat Stevens, Bob Dylan and Joni Mitchell ("they're playin' that scratchy rock and roll beneath the Matala moon" crooned the latter on *Carey*, from her 1971 album, *Blue*).

It has, however, been a very long time since the caves were cleared, and nowadays they're a fenced-off **archeological site** (April–Sept daily 10am–7pm; €2), open by day to visitors but patrolled by the police – and floodlit – every night.

INFORMATION AND ACTIVITIES

Amenities Car and bike rental, ATM and currency exchange can all be found on the first part of the street as you enter town.

Travel agencies Cretan Travellers (☎ 28920 45732, ⊛ cretantravellers.gr) offers car and bike rental, ATM, currency exchange and information on rooms and excursions.

Boat trips There are daily boat trips from the tiny harbour in summer (weather permitting, ☎ 693 745 7439) to Red Beach and to Áyio (see p.110).

Horseriding Melanouri Stables (☎ 28920 45040, ⊛ melanouri.com), on the western edge of Pitsídhia (see opposite), offers a variety of rides, from a 1hr trip to the beach (€20) to an all-day tour to Áyio Gorge and beach (€170).

Shops Fanourios, on the main road close to the start of the market, sells English-language books as well as maps, guides and gifts; foreign newspapers, along with supermarket supplies and beach accoutrements, are available at Carrefour Express, which opens off the car park, below the *Hotel Zafiria*.

ACCOMMODATION

Finding a room should be no problem and, out of season, you may well be in a position to bargain. Most of the options below are on **"Hotel Street"**, left off the main road as you enter town, which is almost entirely lined with purpose-built places, all of them with parking, wi-fi and a/c.

Camping Kommos Off the seaward side of the road, roughly halfway between Pitsídhia and Mátala ☎ 28920 42596. If you don't mind being further from the action, this is a better site than *Matala Camping*, with a swimming pool and taverna. Two adults plus tent and vehicle €15

Fantastic Hotel St ☎ 28920 45362. Good value studios and rooms, some of which have been newly refurbished (and cost €5 extra). It's on the town side of the street, with a private entrance at the back almost directly on the town square. €40

Matala Bay Hotel On the entry road ☎ 28920 45300, ⊛ matalabay.gr. One of many bigger hotels that have sprung up along the road into town, this is close enough to be within easy walking distance of the beach, with a good-sized pool, pool bar, and comfortable a/c rooms and apartments. €52

Matala Camping Above the car park, close to the beach ☎ 28920 45720. Campsite with shady tamarisk trees. Fine if you don't mind camping on sand; there's a busy bar, and August can bring a rowdy party atmosphere. Two adults plus tent and vehicle €15

Matala View Hotel St ☎ 28920 45114, ⊛ matala -apartments.com. Simple rooms, mostly with small balconies, as well as some larger studios and apartments, on the quiet side of Hotel St. Breakfast available at extra cost. €35

Nikos Hotel St ☎ 28920 45375, ⊛ matala-nikos.com. The fanciest of the places on Hotel St, with very well kept rooms around a charming plant-filled courtyard and one "penthouse" with a sea view. Direct access to town from the back. €45

★ **Sunshine Matala** Hotel St ☎ 28920 45110, ⊛ matala-holidays.gr. Friendly, comfortable *pension* (formerly the *Iliaki*) with classily renovated rooms, with fridge, and one- and two-room apartments with kitchens, on the quieter side of the street. €40

Zafiria On the main street as you enter Mátala ☎ 28920 45366, ⊛ zafiria-matala.com. The largest hotel in town. The balcony rooms can be a little dark and old-fashioned, but they're comfortable and there's a good pool. Breakfast included. €45

EATING AND DRINKING

Anna & Alex First square ☎697 435 5609. A simpler place than its neighbour *Zwei Bruder*, with a short but good Greek menu and excellent daily specials, both fish and meat. Daily 11am–late.

Eleni Behind the central section of the beach. One of the smaller places with a terrace hanging over the beach, *Eleni* has, like all the others, a plastic menu with pictures of food that you can point at. However they also have a handwritten list of daily specials (fresh grilled sardines or traditional lamb casserole, for example, for around €8), often just scrawled on a notepad, and these are the ones to go for. Exceptionally welcoming too. Daily noon–midnight.

Giannis Main street beyond the market ☎698 361 9233. Usually the busiest place in town (partly because of a reputation for being inexpensive, which is no longer entirely justified), this is an earthy, family-run taverna specializing in grilled meats and fish (mixed fish plate €12). You may have to wait, though they can often find space to set up another table somewhere. Daily noon–late.

La Scala Far end of the beach above the harbour ☎28920 45489. Atmospheric little fish restaurant with a wonderful terrace overlooking the bay; more elegant than most and only marginally more expensive. Mixed fish for two €30, *kakaviá* (traditional fish soup) €8. Daily noon–midnight.

Zouridhakis Alley leading up to the main square ☎28920 45450. There appear to be two bakeries here but in fact it's just one big place, with bread, ice cream, cakes and fresh rice pudding. Good for breakfast of pastries, juice and coffee – they also serve eggs. Daily 8am–10.30pm.

Zwei Bruder First square ☎28920 45252. The swishest place in town, with bare-stone walls, candles, tablecloths and proper glassware. Lovely setting, even if, underneath it all, the food is standard Greek cooking at slightly higher prices than elsewhere. Daily 11am–late.

NIGHTLIFE

The chief entertainment in the early evening is watching the invariably spectacular crimson **sunset** from the beach or one of the beachfront cafés. Later on, the main square is ringed with quiet bars, while livelier places are crammed together at the far end of town, where on busy nights they merge into one big party.

Akuna Matata Main street at far end of town ☎694 73 43 688. A bar/café/taverna that's open all day, distinguished by the pirate ship's prow hanging out over the water, and the fact that you have to walk through to reach the far end of town. There's plenty of choice of food, but that's not really the point; the place really comes alive at night, serving cocktails (around €7) and with dancing and frequent live bands. Daily 11am–early hours.

Marinero Main street at far end of town. Next door to *Akuna Matata*, and also open all day, though with less emphasis on food; the music here tends to be more rock-oriented and they also have frequent live bands, often in competition. Daily 11am–sunrise.

Port Side Main street ☎694 59 83 886. A cocktail bar with an enviable location, its candlelit tables on a terrace hanging over the beach just at the start of the nightlife zone. Daily 5pm–late.

Pitsídhia

An alternative base to Mátala, marginally cheaper and certainly more peaceful, **PITSÍDHIA** (Πιτσίδια) sprawls around the main road about 5km inland. This is already a well-used option, and far from unspoilt, but it's a congenial Greek village with plenty of rooms, lively places to eat and an affable young international crowd. Head up the hill away from the main road for more peace and atmosphere – there are numerous rooms places and tavernas up here, and a **traditional Cretan night** in the square every Tuesday.

ACCOMMODATION   PITSÍDHIA

Pension Nikos Inland from the town square ☎28920 45130, ⍈pitsidia-nikos.gr. It's less fancy than it looks from outside, but this is a tranquil spot with comfy rooms and two-room apartments with balcony, fridge and a/c. There's a communal kitchen supplied with coffee and the basics, and a roof terrace with fabulous views. The same owners have a couple of villas in the countryside nearby. €35

Vrissi Studios Just off the main road, near the bakery ☎28920 45114, ⍈pitsidia-studios.com. Modern, a/c studios and one- and two-bedroom apartments accommodating up to five people, around a small pool; they also rent some nearby houses. €35

1

EATING AND DRINKING

Bodikos Pizzeria Main road through town ☎ 28920 45438, ⓦ bodikos.com. Something of a travellers' hangout, with good pizza from a wood-fired oven (€6–12), plus cheap pasta dishes and a full Greek menu. They also have rooms and apartments nearby. Daily 11am–11pm.

Mikes Taverna In an alley close to the town square ☎ 28920 45007. Probably the best food in town, freshly cooked from local ingredients. Check out the day's specials in the kitchen, rather than relying on the menu. Daily 6pm–1am.

Oneira Traumfabrik Signed, east of the town square ☎ 28920 45421. The "dream factory" is a café, bar and craft shop selling classy clothing and jewellery. There's a lovely terrace where they serve breakfast, omelettes and smoothies, and in the evening the cocktail bar is a favourite expat meeting place, with regular music and other events. Daily 9am–10pm.

Kommós

The archeological site of **KOMMÓS (Κομός)**, a Minoan harbour town that was probably the main port for Festós and Ayía Triádha, lies on the coast west of Pitsídhia, at the southern end of a sandy shore that extends all the way to Kalamáki (see opposite). The northwesterly winds that often lash the beach and fill the sea with whitecaps would suggest that this was not the best place for a harbour, but the sea level would have been a couple of metres lower in Minoan times, when a reef, still just about visible offshore, provided shelter. On calm days, the **beach** here is lovely, with great views, a taverna at one end, a few loungers, and plenty of room to escape the crowds.

Ancient Kommós

Though it's clear that this is a major site, and visitor facilities have been built, the excavations remain closed – though you can get a pretty good view through the fence. There are three main **excavation areas**, none of them more than a stone's throw behind the beach. The **northern area**, on a low hill close to the sea, contains domestic dwellings, among which is a large house with a paved court and a limestone winepress. The **central group** – behind a retaining wall to prevent subsidence – has houses from the New Palace era, with well-preserved walls and evidence, in the fallen limestone slabs, of the earthquake of around 1700 BC. A rich haul of intact pottery was found in this area, much of it in the brightly painted Kamáres style.

The most remarkable finds, however, came in the **southern sector**. Minoan remains here include a fine stretch of **limestone roadway**, 3m wide and more than 60m long, rutted from the passage of ox-drawn carts, heading away inland, no doubt towards Ayía Triádha and Festós. To the south of the road, one building contains the longest stretch of **Minoan wall** on the island: over 50m of dressed stone. The function of this enormous structure isn't known but it could conceivably have been a palace, or it may have had a storage purpose connected with the port. Some of the nearby dwellings to the north of the roadway were also of elaborate construction, and a substantial number of fresco fragments unearthed by the excavators hint at sumptuous interior decorations. Just south of here another large building was a ship shed or **dry dock**, 30m long and 35m wide, with its seaward end open to the sea; it's now partly overlaid by a later Greek structure – probably a warehouse.

Kamilári

The attractive hill village of **KAMILÁRI (Καμιλάρι)** has numerous attractive **accommodation** options, plus plenty of **bars and cafés**, some of which, thanks no doubt to the expat community, are surprisingly sophisticated. As you approach the village on the Festós road, you'll see signs (hard to follow; the final stretch is on foot, and the tomb at the top of a hill) to an early **Minoan tomb**, one of the oldest and best preserved in Crete. Dating from about 1900 BC, the tomb was a circular structure with a large dome, inside which communal burials took place, while cult rituals were

1

carried out in adjoining rooms. The stone walls still stand 2m high in parts; important clay models depicting worship at a shrine and a circular group of dancers unearthed here are now in the Iráklio Archeological Museum.

ACCOMMODATION KAMILÁRI

A large number of houses have been renovated by foreign owners – predominantly German – and there are plenty of tempting, inexpensive places to stay; just look out for the "Rooms" signs.

★ **Apartments Ambeliotissa** On the hill as you climb towards the village from the Festós road ☏ 28920 42690, ⊕ ambeliotissa.com. A very welcoming, child-friendly place with excellent a/c studios and apartments, some with mezzanine sleeping areas, in and around a house in its own grounds, with small pool and playground, café, communal barbecue and TV room. Studios €30, mezzanine apartments €55
Sifogiannis In the heart of the village ☏ 28920

42410, ⊕ sifogiannis.com. A flower-bedecked building where the simple rooms come with a/c, wi-fi, coffee-making facilities and fridge. There's also a roof terrace and communal kitchen. €30
Xenonas Apartments In the village ☏ 28920 42811, ⊕ xenonas.com. Four apartments sleeping two to four people, classily decorated in a traditional, blue-and-white Greek style. Potted plants and flowers abound in the outdoor areas. €50

Kalamáki

Some 3km from Kamilári, **KALAMÁKI** (Καλαμάκι) is a small beach resort, popular with locals, with a rather unfinished look. Though not particularly attractive, Kalamáki does have a large, uncrowded, windswept beach that stretches right down to Kommós, plenty of good-value **accommodation** and a pleasantly backwater atmosphere.

ACCOMMODATION KALAMÁKI

Along the **seafront** you'll find a fairly solid line of accommodation, almost all of it in four- or five-storey blocks of studios and rooms.

Alexander Beach At the southern end of the seafront ☏ 28920 45195, ⊕ alexandros-kalamaki.com. In a quiet spot on the edge of town, this beachfront hotel has a/c balcony rooms with fridge and wi-fi, plus its own restaurant. Breakfast included. €45
★ **Kiknos Studios** Beachfront in the centre of town ☏ 28920 45466, ⊕ kiknos.org. Exceptionally well-run place with classy touches, such as sheets and towels embroidered with the hotel name, that you'd expect in a far pricier establishment. Studios have kitchenette, fridge and

big balconies, most with sea view (the few that don't cost less); there's also a great rooftop room, with the entire roof and its fabulous views to yourself. Free loungers on the beach. €35, rooftop €45
Rooms Psiloritis Set back a little from the northern end of the main beach ☏ 28920 45693, ⊕ psiloritis -hotel.com. Great value – a rambling, slightly ramshackle hotel with numerous sea-view terraces and plain en-suite rooms with fridge. €35

EATING

For food, it's hard to look beyond the **seafront tavernas**, especially as eating there will allow you to use their loungers and umbrellas. All have standard Greek menus with an emphasis on fish.

Taverna Avra Northern end of the beach ☏ 28920 45052. A good choice if you want to use the sun-loungers, as it's in a quieter part of the beach away from the centre. Fresh fish and good Cretan standards are served on waterfront and roadside terraces. Daily 11am–11pm.

Taverna Delfinia Central beachfront ☏ 28920 45697. Small, popular fish taverna with a bright modern look – stripped pine tables, white chairs – serving excellent fresh fish and locally sourced meat and veg. Daily 11am–11pm.

Inland from Mátala

Though there's not a great deal to seek out, it's enjoyable simply to drive around the villages of the southern Messará. Just north of Pitsídhia you can turn off the main road

1

towards **SÍVAS**, a lovely village, but one of the most obviously affected by visitors, largely thanks to the rather bizarrely located *Shivas Village Resort*, a luxury resort on the edge of the village. Beyond Sívas you can continue to wander the back roads through villages like **Kousés**, where there are more rooms and places to eat, and on to the large agricultural centre of **Pómbia**, from where you can head south to the coast at Kalí Liménes (see below).

Moní Odhiyítrias

Just beyond Sívas, a paved road is signed south to Moní Odhiyítrias and Kalí Liménes – while the first half of this road, as far as the monastery, is excellent, the second half is a rough, mountainous dirt track • Daily during daylight hours • Free, though you're encouraged to buy their excellent oil, honey or *raki* (all €5)

Even with excellent road access, **MONÍ ODHIYÍTRIAS** (Οδηγύτριας) exudes a powerful sense of isolation, and except on summer weekends it sees few visitors. They make those visitors welcome, though, and there's usually someone to show you round this little walled oasis in the midst of the bare mountains: there's a flower-filled courtyard, fifteenth-century icons and frescoes in the church and a horse-powered olive-press, as well as a small collection of ancient agricultural implements and a crumbling tower to climb.

The Áyio Gorge

Opposite the Moní Odhiyítrias entrance you'll see signs for a track leading south to the Áyio Gorge • It's 1hr of relatively easy walking from Moní Odhiyítrias to the gorge entrance; you can also reach the gorge from a spot further down the (now unpaved) Kalí Liménes road, about 25min from the gorge entrance

ÁYIO GORGE (Άγιο) offers a lovely and relatively easy hike of about an hour (once you're in the gorge) down to a welcoming beach. The name ("Holy Gorge") refers to the fact that many of the caves that pockmark its sides are said to have been occupied by Christian hermits, especially during the period of the Turkish occupation. One of them, just 250m from the sea, was a site of early Christian worship, later enclosed in the fourteenth- to fifteenth-century church of Áyios Andónios. This is a beautiful building, with an ancient well outside (whose water, sadly, is not drinkable); the cave itself is not visible, locked within the inner sanctum of the church. Finally, the **beach** is ample reward for the walk, an expansive pebble cove with beautifully clear, calm water. Usually it's semi-deserted, though occasionally you may have the bad luck to coincide with a boat trip from Mátala.

ACCOMMODATION AND EATING   **INLAND FROM MÁTALA**

You'll find places to eat and tastefully restored houses, some of them for rent, in many of the villages you pass through. **Sívas** in particular has a couple of excellent tavernas and some good accommodation options.

Horiatiko Spiti (Village House) ✆ 28920 42004, ⊛ horiatiko-spiti.de. A converted old house with beautiful, fully equipped studios and a duplex apartment, all with full kitchen, a/c and wi-fi. In high season they may have a four-day minimum stay. **€43**

Kalí Liménes and around

KALÍ LIMÉNES (Καλοί Λιμένες) was an important port in Roman times, the main harbour of Górtys and the place where St Paul put in as a prisoner aboard a ship bound for Rome, an incident described in the Bible in Acts 27. Paul wanted to stay the winter here, but was overruled by the captain of the ship and the centurion acting as his guard; on setting sail, they were promptly overtaken by a storm, which drove them past Clauda (the island of Gávdhos) and on, eventually, to shipwreck on Malta. Today, Kalí Liménes is once again a port, for oil tankers this time, which has rather spoilt its chances of becoming a resort. It also has a real end-of-the-road feel, especially out of season, though summer weekends can see crowds of Irakliots descend.

This isolation and loneliness does have a certain appeal, and the procession of tankers gives you something to look at as they discharge their loads into tanks on an islet just offshore. There are a couple of somnolent **tavernas** behind the beach, but no rooms. Some small cove beaches are accessible beneath the cliffs to the west – on foot only – while to the east is a long, empty beach where people camp out around the *Taverna Gorgona*. With a full day you could also hike up to Moní Odhiyítrias and down through the gorge to Áyio beach (see opposite), having made arrangements at the harbour for a boat to pick you up at the end; you can also get a taxi-boat from Léndas (see below).

The coast road

Leaving Kalí Liménes to the east, a road follows the coast all the way to Léndas, smooth and temtping at first though later it becomes an extremely rough dirt track. In the first few kilometres, still on asphalt, you'll pass a few small tavernas, a couple of which have rooms, around the village of **Lassaia**, tumbling down a hill to a bay with a good sandy beach, and **Khrysóstomos**, the next bay. Beyond there are plenty more scruffy beaches, but the coast is blighted by plastic greenhouses and there's only one place with any sort of permanent habitation: **Platía Perámata**, a sandy little village with a couple of stores, a few basic rooms and usually the odd camper.

ACCOMMODATION	THE COAST ROAD
Villa Koutsakis Khrysóstomos ☎28920 97468, ⓦvillakoutsakis.com. Just twelve rooms in a modern building, with restaurant, immediately above the beach,	with balconies overlooking the sea, kitchenette, fridge and a/c (but no wi-fi). Very isolated, but very comfortable. **€40**

Léndas

The reputation of **LÉNDAS** (Λέντας) as a hippy resort, a fishing village where you can hang out by the beach and camp for free, is somewhat outdated: the hippies grew up and now they come back with their families to stay in comfortable rooms and eat at excellent restaurants. For a quiet break, you could hardly choose better: it's still small, low-key and a little alternative, but it's no longer especially cheap, nor the sort of place where campers are welcomed on the beach. Having said that, scores of people *do* camp on the sand at **Dytikós**, just over the headland to the west, a predominantly nudist beach where the old ethos is still very much alive and where there are some good taverna/bars with rooms: many of the visitors here are also second-generation hippies with their families, and a high proportion are German-speaking, as indeed they are in Léndas itself.

Léndas beaches

The **beach** in Léndas itself is narrow and grey: for better alternatives you can take the obvious path over the headland from the western end of the town beach to the 1km-long stretch of sand at **Dytikós** or head east, where a rough path or a dirt track (signed from the bend on the road) will take you towards **Petrákis Beach**, with rooms and taverna, and **Loutrá**, a bay 5km to the east with a decent beach, small fishing boat harbour and more places to stay and eat. From Loutrá you could take a more ambitious hike, 6km inland up the scenic **Trakhoúla gorge** to Krótos. From here you may find a bus (check the times in the village before leaving) or can take a taxi the 10km back to Léndas.

Ancient Levín

Just above the village, right on the main road • Tues–Sun 8.30am–3pm • Free

Ancient Levín (or Leben) was an important centre of healing, with an *Asklepion* sited by a spring of therapeutic waters – at its height, from the third century BC onward, the sanctuary maintained an enormous temple and was a major centre of pilgrimage. The

1

ruins spread over an extensive area (not confined to the fenced site – you'll see remains throughout the village) and include a temple and a bath complex with tunnels and arches through which the water once flowed. Above all, there's a lovely third-century BC Hellenistic black, red and white pebble mosaic (beneath a canopy) depicting a mythical creature: half horse, half sea-monster. Adjacent to the site are the more substantial remains of an early Christian basilica, with a much smaller eleventh-century chapel still standing in their midst.

ARRIVAL AND DEPARTURE
LÉNDAS

By bus Bus service to Léndas is uncertain, so you'll need to check; usually there is a weekday bus from Iráklio via Áyii Dhéka, leaving Iráklio around noon: the return, from Léndas to Míres, leaves around 6.15 am. The bus stop is a dusty square on the east side of the village – from here, a number of cobbled paths lead down towards the beach and the village's central platía.
By car The bus stop square also serves as a car park.
By taxi If there's no bus you'll have to take a taxi from Áyii Dhéka, for around €40.

INFORMATION AND ACTIVITIES

Amenities Most of the facilities you'll need, including a couple of supermarkets and internet cafés, are located on the square. There are few other facilities: no fuel or ATM, for instance.
Money and car rental To change money and for car rental, head for *Villa Tsapakis* at Dytikós (see below).

Boat trips Trips to local beaches can be arranged on the *Sandokan* (📞 28920 95345, 🌐 petrakisbeach.gr).
Cretan Outdoor Adventures Based at Dytikós, they organize adventure activities including trekking, canyoning, climbing and abseiling, from around €50 (📞 690 900 8502, 🌐 cretan-outdoor-adventures.com).

ACCOMMODATION

There's plenty of accommodation – most of it in good, modern studio-style **rooms** – though in peak season space can be at a premium. Unless stated, all of the following have a/c.

Casa Doria Loutrá beach 📞 28920 95376, 🌐 casadoria .net. Italian-run "slow life" hotel and restaurant right above the beach, with simple, brightly decorated rooms, a laidback atmosphere and Italian-influenced food. A fabulous place, but very isolated and relatively pricey for what you get. €60
New Levin Apartments Immediately to the east of the main part of the village 📞 28920 95237. Lovely modern studios and apartments, some with two bedrooms and big balconies overlooking the sea. €35
Nikis Rooms Centre of the village, behind Zorbas and El Greco 📞 28920 95246. Super-friendly place with inexpensive rooms equipped with kettle and fridge, around a lovely flower-filled courtyard; a couple of upper-floor ones have views (at extra cost), but there's a shared roof terrace for those who don't. €25
Studios Gaitani Western end of beach 📞 28920 95341, 🌐 studios-gaitani.gr. A/c studios and apartments

with kitchenette and satellite TV immediately above the beach, with huge, rickety-looking balconies hanging over it. Loungers for guests' use on the sand. The same owners have a more modern apartment complex in the hills immediately above town. €40
Villa Tsapakis Dytikós Beach 📞 28920 95378, 🌐 villa -tsapakis.gr. These bougainvillea-fronted rooms come with a sea view, fridge and TV, and reductions for longer stays. They also have studios and apartments, and their taverna, *Odysseas*, is the meeting point for everyone staying or camping at Dytikós. €35
Zorbas Towards the eastern end of the beach 📞 28920 95228, 🌐 zorbas-lentas.gr. Balcony rooms and studios directly above the beach, most with sea views, above a decent taverna, in conjunction with which they offer very good value half-board deals. €30

EATING

Tavernas in Léndas are generally very good, serving above-average Greek food with great **sea views**.

Akti Towards the western end of the beach 📞 28920 95206. Excellent, friendly taverna in a great location on the beach; check out the day's dishes in the kitchen, and the not-too-pricey fresh fish. Daily 8am–1am.
★**Taverna El Greco** 📞 28920 95322. A particularly good restaurant with a large leafy terrace above the beach.

The food is mostly traditional Greek – the day's baked dishes are on display in the kitchen – but cooked with exceptional care using the best local ingredients. There's an unusually good wine list, too, and they also have rooms. Daily 11am–midnight.

DRINKING AND NIGHTLIFE

Léndas **nightlife** is confined to a handful of bars, although in summer there are frequent beach events at Dytikós or Petrákis Beach (the latter often lays on minibus transfers from town) – look out for the posters.

Blue Café On the rocks past the western end of the beach ☎ 697 28 22 152. A romantic spot to lounge over evening drinks while watching the moon rise over the bay, as people have been doing here since the resort's earliest days. Daily noon–late.

Lions On the square. By day a quiet café with internet; at night the "dancing bar" behind opens its doors (from 9pm),

an incongruously modern place whose music, dancing and cocktails are about as wild as Léndas gets. Daily 9am–late.

Pink Panther On the square. A long-time Léndas favourite, *Pink Panther* has a sea-view roof terrace for breezy cocktails, and cranks up the music inside as the evening wears on. Daily 9pm–late.

The southeast coast

East of Léndas there's barely any access to the coast before the far east of the province, where there are low-key beach resorts at **Tsoútsouros** and **Keratókambos**, though for hardy walkers the secluded monastic community at **Moní Koudhoumá** is an escapist's dream. The road that gives access to these places, east across the Messará from Áyii Dhéka through Asími to Áno Viánnos, is an enjoyably solitary drive through fertile farming country in the shadow of the **Dhiktean mountains**. There's not a great deal to stop for along the way, but there are plenty of solid traditional villages with *kafenía* and places to eat. The more substantial village of **Áno Viánnos** has plenty of places for a lunch break and some ancient churches.

GETTING AROUND   THE SOUTHEAST COAST

By car The direct route from Iráklio to Áno Viánnos is via the featureless farming town of Arkalohóri, joining the west–east route at Mártha. Alternatively, you can head south from Houdhétsi (see p.73), joining the southern road near Pírgos.

By bus Buses run from Iráklio via Arkalohóri to Áno Viánnos (Bus Station A; Mon–Fri 9.30am, 1.15pm & 3pm, Sat 9.30am & 3pm, Sun 7.30am), but none follow the route across the Messará.

Moní Koudhoumá

The remote **MONÍ KOUDHOUMÁ (Κουδουμά)**, on the coast almost due south of Irákli, nestles in a seaside cove with an inviting pebble beach at the foot of a cliff, surrounded by pinewoods. Arriving here is a distinctly end-of-the world experience, and the handful of remaining monks spend most of the year alone. Donations by pilgrims and benefactors have financed a considerable rebuilding programme since the turn of the millennium and facilities for both monks and pilgrims have vastly improved. The monks see few visitors outside of the feast of the Panayía Koudhoumá in August (when up to 15,000 pilgrims descend on the monastery), but are extremely welcoming to those that do turn up, and will offer you food and a mattress in one of the dormitories set aside for "pilgrims". While the monks will not accept payment for their hospitality, a donation to monastery funds is unlikely to be refused. If you think the magic of the place may persuade you to prolong your stay, you should bring supplies with you. The nights here are exquisitely serene, broken only by the sound of the sea splashing against the rocks. While you're visiting the monastery, be sure to make the fifteen-minute walk west along the coast to the spectacular **cave** ("Avakospilios") where the founder monks lived during the building of the first monastery in the eighteenth century.

ARRIVAL AND DEPARTURE   MONÍ KOUDHOUMÁ

By car You can drive the 24km to the monastery on a reasonable unpaved road south from Stérnes, but the final

switchback cliff-face section is scary, with no barriers – allow at least 90min for the journey each way.

1

On foot It's possible to reach the monastery on foot, most easily by heading south from Hárakas on a paved road to the hamlet of Paranímfi, where you can get local directions onto the path that leads directly to the monastery, or continue on a reasonable dirt track to Trís Ekklisíes (tavernas and rooms), from where it's 7km or so along a coastal path. Alternatively, you can hike all the way from Pírgos via Priniás (20km; 4–5hr).

Pýrgos

PÝRGOS (Πύργος) is the biggest village in these parts, with plenty of facilities. Along the main street – which sees a lively **market** take place every Tuesday morning – you'll find a couple of decent **tavernas** and, at the eastern end of the thoroughfare, the fourteenth-century **church** of Áyios Yióryios and Áyios Konstantínos, with some interesting faded frescoes. The key is available from the house (no. 137) to the right of the church gate.

ACCOMMODATION

PÝRGOS

Hotel Arhontiko On the main road into town ☎ 28930 23118. Comfortable, modern hotel mostly used by local business travellers, hence plenty of parking and extras including a/c, TV and kitchenette. **€50**

Tsoútsouros

Some 11km of asphalt road winds alarmingly down from Káto Kastelianá, on the highway, to **TSOÚTSOUROS** (Τσούτσουρος). Despite the drama of the approach, Tsoútsouros itself is not immediately attractive; the central beach is narrow, rocky and grey, while the village straggles in an untidy line behind it, with an ugly concrete harbour/marina as a focus. Nonetheless the place is growing into a small resort, and the little bay does have its attractions – it's peaceful, with good stretches of beach backed by shady tamarisks in both directions. On summer weekends, and in the first two weeks of August, it can be very busy with local tourists; out of season, from October to April, most places close.

ACCOMMODATION AND EATING

TSOÚTSOUROS

For **accommodation**, the best places are generally at the eastern end of the village, where there's a better beach and it's generally more attractive despite the new development; prices tend to be dramatically lower out of season.

Mouratis Eastern end of seafront ☎ 28910 92244, ⓦ mouratis.gr. A large, modern place above a taverna with a/c studios and apartments with cooking facilities for up to six people, many with big seafront balconies. **€40**

Petra & Fos Western end of seafront near the harbour ☎ 28910 92345. Good pizzas from a wood-fired oven, plenty of well-prepared Greek dishes, and a comfortable café with breakfast, fresh juices and cocktails see this place lively throughout the day. Daily 9am–midnight.

Phaedra Apartments Far eastern end of seafront, beyond Zorba's ☎ 28910 92311. Simple two-room a/c balcony apartments with kitchenette, some with sea view. If there's no one around, ask at *Zorba's*. **€35**

San Georgio Central seafront, by the harbour ☎ 28910 92322, ⓦ sangeorgio.gr. Sizeable hotel (by Tsoútsouros standards) with simple, smallish a/c rooms with fridge; some have a balcony and sea view. There's a pleasant garden at the back. **€35**

★ **Zorba's** Eastern end of seafront ☎ 28910 92277, ⓦ zorbas-taverna.com. The best taverna and the best-value rooms in town, combined with an exceptionally warm welcome. Food and wine are home-produced or locally sourced; the rooms generously proportioned, with fridge and kettle and sea-view balconies. Open year-round, weekends only Nov–Feb. **€30**

Keratókambos

KERATÓKAMBOS (Κερατόκαμπος), 10km east of Tsoútsouros, is accessed by a spectacularly winding mountain road from Hóndhros, near Áno Viánnos, or on a good paved road along the coast from Tsoútsouros. Though you would not at first sight describe Keratókambos as a pretty place – a single street of mismatched houses interspersed with cafés and tavernas facing a narrow, grey, shingly beach – it grows on you if you stay long enough to get over first impressions; it's peaceful and friendly, with good food and rooms. The beach, too, is better than it appears, with sandy, shallow water for a long way offshore.

In theory Keratókambos is three separate villages, though in practice they run into one another. Keratókambos itself, with the best of the beach, is immediately east of the junction where the Hóndhros road meets the coast; **Kastrí**, immediately west, has most of the facilities, on the shore close to the junction; and **Pórto Kastrí**, where an ugly modern concrete harbour has been built, lies a couple of hundred metres west of here.

ACCOMMODATION

KERATÓKAMBOS

Filoxenia Kastrí ☎ 28950 51371. Clean, modern en-suite rooms for two to three people, right on the seafront behind a lovingly tended, flower-filled garden. Studio-style rooms come with a/c, TV and kitchenette. **€30**

Komis Studios In Keratókambos proper ☎ 28950 51390, ⓦ komisstudios.gr. Lovingly designed, multi-level

1

studio apartments with in a garden setting equipped with antique furnishings, minibar and TV. Beautiful, but starting to show their age slightly. €80

Pan Apartments Above the village around the road down from Hóndhros ☎ 28950 51220, ⓦ pan-appartments.de. There are numerous rooms places attractively sited above the village, with fine views out to the Libyan Sea. *Pan* is a good choice: modern studios and apartments come with kitchenette, spectacular sea view and a pretty garden. €35

EATING

Taverna Kriti Kastrí ☎ 28950 51231. One of the best local tavernas, serrving good, earthy, traditional Cretan food; try the special omelette, for example, with tomato, onion, potato and pepper. They also have simple rooms. Daily 9am–11pm.

Áno Viánnos

ÁNO VIÁNNOS (Άνω Βιάννος) clings to the southern slopes of the Dhíkti range, a large village where almost everyone seems to pull over to break their journey. Given the narrow streets and lack of parking this can be unfortunate, but the air of busy chaos seems appropriate, somehow, in what was traditionally the administrative and market centre of this part of southeastern Iráklio province. Its importance has waned as the coastal settlements have grown but it's still a busy place, and there are some interesting churches to see as well as plenty of places to eat or drink. The sharper, cooler air up here is refreshing too.

The **churches** are signed from the main street, up the narrow alleys in the upper part of the town. The most interesting is fourteenth-century Ayía Pelayía, with a magnificent, if damaged, fresco of the Crucifixion on the back wall.

ACCOMMODATION AND EATING   ÁNO VIÁNNOS

Kafenion O Platanos On the through road at the east end of the village. The most atmospheric of the local places to eat, serving *mezédhes* at tables under an ancient and gigantic plane tree. Daily 9am–6pm.

Káto Sými

East of Áno Viánnos the road to Árvi turns off at **Amirás**, alongside a giant memorial to the Cretans killed in World War II. A few kilometres further, 1km beyond Péfkos, you can turn left for a scenic detour to the village of **KÁTO SÝMI** (Κάτο Σύμη) and its atmospheric **ancient sanctuary of Hermes and Aphrodite**. The trip is worth it for the adventure as much as anything – an intimidating drive up into the mountains round first-gear hairpins, all on asphalt, with a rocky scramble around the site, surrounded by pine forest, to reward you at the end.

Káto Sými itself has another **war memorial**, commemorating five hundred people put to death in 1943 when it and six other settlements were destroyed in retaliation for an attack on a German patrol.

The Sanctuary of Hermes and Aphrodite

Known locally as **Kryá Vrísi** (cold spring), the **Sanctuary of Hermes and Aphrodite** is laid out on a series of broad ledges on the mountainside where a prodigious spring gushes clear, ice-cold water all year round. There is evidence of a **shrine** here dating back to prehistoric times. Adopted by the **Minoans**, it became a holy place of overwhelming importance, as evidenced by the thousands of votive clay and bronze figurines and vases brought here by pilgrims, many of which are now on display in the Iráklio Archeological Museum. In Greek and Roman times the shrine continued to be an important centre of pilgrimage, now to Hermes Dendrites and Aphrodite.

The spring still flows high up on the eastern side of the site, just outside the fence. Here too is an enormous hollow plane tree, which seems old enough to have witnessed many of the sacrifices and ceremonies that took place here in ancient times. The most obvious remains are in this corner of the site, including vestiges of temples, altars and cult rooms dating from all periods. Today most of the spring water disperses down the mountainside via plastic pipes to irrigate the olive groves below, but enough escapes to create several small waterfalls that you'll have passed on the way up.

ARRIVAL AND DEPARTURE

THE SANCTUARY OF HERMES AND APHRODITE

By car Start the ascent to the ancient site near the *Taverna Afrodite* in Káto Sými, with a fine terrace looking out over stands of plane trees, and where mountain honey is on sale; uphill beyond the taverna follow wooden signs to *Omalos Kristos*, a chapel much higher in the mountains. You may be confused by turnings and junctions as you climb higher, but remember to always stay on the asphalt. Eventually, some 3km above the village, a sign in Greek announces the site; the sturdy fence should be visible just above you, and although the site is almost always locked, the remains can easily be viewed by making a circuit of the exterior.

Lasíthi

VÁI

2

Lasíthi

Eastern Crete is dominated by the resort of Áyios Nikólaos and the upmarket tourism it attracts, but get beyond "Ag Nik" and its environs and you can experience some of the most striking highlands and wilderness coastlines on the island. Áyios Nikólaos itself, along with the pretty neighbouring resort of Eloúnda, offers some of Crete's best package holidays: lively and cosmopolitan, with the most luxurious hotels on the island as well as more ordinary rooms and apartments. It's easy to escape into the surrounding hills and mountains, too. North beyond Eloúnda and its beaches, you come to the brooding islet of Spinalónga, once a redoubtable Venetian and Turkish fortress, later a leper colony. The town of Kritsá, with its famous frescoed church and textile sellers, and the imposing ruins of ancient Lató , also make for an enjoyable short excursion, while slightly further afield the Lasíthi plateau – a high mountain plain with picturesque villages and abundant greenery – makes a great day-trip from the coast, even better if you stay overnight.

Towards the far east of the island the pace slackens as you enter an area which is under the sway not of Áyios Nikólaos but of **Sitía**, an attractive, traditional town where tourism has had little visible effect. The Minoan workers' village at **Gournía** is definitely worth a stop en route while, at the island's eastern tip, the famed palm-studded beach at **Vái** and the Minoan palace at **Káto Zákros** are the major tourist attractions. **Palékastro**, between the two, has plenty of accommodation within easy reach of isolated beaches while the island's southeast corner is about as escapist as you could wish.

Along the south coast, there is generally far less development. **Ierápetra** is the major town in these parts, with a scenic harbour from where boats sail to the offshore desert island of **Gaidhouronísi**. In both directions from here, towards **Mírtos** and **Makriyialós**, is a string of low-key resorts.

Áyios Nikólaos

The centre of Crete's most upmarket tourism, **ÁYIOS NIKÓLAOS** (Άγιος Νικόλαος) – "Ag Nik" as it's known to the majority of its English-speaking visitors – has obvious attractions. Set on a hilly peninsula around a supposedly bottomless **lake**, in a lovely setting overlooking the **Gulf of Mirabéllo** ("Beautiful View"), it is wonderfully picturesque, with dozens of excellent cafés, restaurants and bars around the lake, the

---

WINDMILLS ON THE LASÍTHI PLATEAU

Highlights

❶ Áyios Nikólaos A centre of upmarket tourism and one of the most attractive towns on the island, with good restaurants and buzzing nightlife. **See p.120**

❷ Spinalónga Fortified island whose impregnable isolation later made it an ideal location for a leper colony, chilling to visit even today. **See p.130**

❸ Lasíthi plateau This spectacular highland plateau is a verdant farming area, where cloth-sailed windmills, multicoloured wildflowers and soaring eagles compete for your attention. **See p.135**

❹ Kritsá Home to one of Crete's most famous frescoed Byzantine churches, this traditional village is also a centre of weaving and lacemaking. **See p.141**

❺ Sitía Set around a beautiful bay, this is an attractive and easy-going resort with a couple of interesting museums and plenty of after-dark diversions. **See p.150**

❻ Koureménos Beach Not far from the exotic palms and crowds of toursts at Vái, the island's best windsurfing spot offers simpler beach pleasures, with plenty of more sheltered sands nearby. **See p.159**

❼ Káto Zákros With a romantically sited Minoan palace flanked by a cluster of fish tavernas and simple places to stay, Káto Zákros is a delightful seaside hamlet. **See p.163**

HIGHLIGHTS ARE MARKED ON THE MAP ON P.122

LASÍTHI

HIGHLIGHTS
1 Áyios Nikólaos
2 Spinalónga
3 Lasíthi Plateau
4 Kritsá
5 Sitía
6 Koureménos Beach
7 Káto Zákros

N

0 — 10 kilometres

Kássos, Kárpathos & Rhodes

Iráklio

Áno Vianós

Gaidhouronísi

Naval Base

Cape Sídheros

Dionysádes Islands

Itanos
Vái
Maridháti
Hóni
Petsófas (215m)
Angathiá
Koureménos
Minoan Site
Palékastro
Hohlakiés
Modí (339m)
M. Tóplou
Ano Zákros
Voïgla Zákrou (714m)
Gorge of the Dead
Palace of Zákros
Káto Zákros
Lamnóni
Hametoúlo
Kerikámbos
Agriodomári
Ayiá Triní
Atherinólakos
Kaló Neró
Pilalímata
Goudhoúras
M. Kápsa
Pervólakia
Pervólakia Gorge
Lithínes
Etiá
Zíros
Handhrás
Voïla
Presós
Zóu
Sítanos
Karídhi
Ayía Fotiá
Petrás
Piskokéfalo
Sitía
M. Faneroméni
Áyios Pándes Gorge
Skopí
Épano Episkopí
Skordhílo
Hamézi
Mésa Moulianá
Mýrsini
Sfáka
Móhlos
Pláteau
Tholós
Kavoúsi
Thólos
Palía Ámmos
Gourniá
Vasilikí
M. Faneroméni
Ístro
Kaló Hório
Almirós
Amoudhára
Áyios Nikólaos
Eloúnda
Oloús
Pláka
Pínes
Vrouhás
Spinalónga Islet
Spinalónga Peninsula
Áyios Ioánnis Peninsula
Skiniás
Amigdáli
Sísi
Milátos
Cave
Selinári Gorge
Neápoli
Moni Aretíou
Dríros
Dóries
Kastéli
Foúrni
Lató
Panayía Kerá
Kritsá
Mílía
Mohós
Psyhró
Dhiktean Cave
LASÍTHI PLATEAU
Áyios Yeóryios
Tzermiádho
DHÍKTI
Mt. Díkta (2148m)
Katharó Tsivi (1564m)
Éxo Potámi
Mésa Potámi
Áyios Konstantínos
Tápes
Amigdáli
Plateó Koríú (1485m)
KATHARÓ PLAIN
Mális
Anatolí
Mýthi
Foúrnou Koryfí
Pýrgos
Mýrtos
Sarakinás Gorge
Káto Sými
Amirás
Áryi
Kalámi
Kserókambos
Tértsa
Gra Ligiá
Bramianá Reservoir
Kalamáfka
Ierápetra
Koutsonári
Férma
Ayía Fotiá
Ahliá
Áyios Ioánnis
Episkopí
Káto Hório
Koutsourás
Análipsi
Makrýyalos
Oríno
Peftí
Hrisopiyí
E4
THRÍPTIS
Aféndis Stavroménos (1476m)
Astoridiá (1237m)
ORNÓ
Psíra

Gulf of Mirabéllo

Gaidhouronísi

harbour and the nearby coast. Curiously, what the town doesn't have is a beach of any significance, so the five-star hotels are all some way out – mostly to the north, around Eloúnda – where they have private access to the coast.

By day, things to do in town are pretty limited –most people simply spend the day recovering from the night before. For the majority of visitors the days are taken up strolling the area around **Lake Voulisméni**, nosing around in the shops, or heading to one of the local **beaches**, all of which have Blue Flag status. There's also a wide choice of **boat trips** around the bay (see p.125).

Brief history

In antiquity, Áyios Nikólaos was the port for the city of **Lató** (see p.141), though this settlement faded in the Roman period and seems to have been abandoned in Byzantine times. The Venetians built a fortress – of which nothing remains – and gave the surrounding gulf its name, Mirabéllo. In succeeding years the town came slowly back to life, and by the nineteenth century the port was again busy; following union with Greece in 1913, Áyios Nikólaos was confirmed as the **capital** of Lasíthi province. A quiet harbour town for most of the last century, Áyios Nikólaos was discovered in the 1960s by international tourism, and has barely looked back since.

Áyios Nikólaos beaches

The beach closest to the heart of things is the shingly little cove of **Kitroplatía**, surprisingly pleasant despite being right in the heart of town, though invariably crowded. The main **municipal beach** (with entry fee), beyond the marina on the southwest side of town, is no less busy. Beyond here there's a constant stream of people walking to the excellent sandy beach at **Almirós**, 2km to the south, or using bus or bike to reach the good beaches at Kaló Hório and beyond (see p.143). In the other direction, heading north, many locals simply dive off the rocks along Aktí Koundoúrou, though the first real sand in this direction is at tree-shaded **Ammoúdi**, another municipally run beach about 1km out of town – again, usually packed. Beyond are more little beaches en route to Eloúnda.

Folk Museum

Paleológou 1, near the bridge • Mon–Sat 10am–2pm & 5–7pm • €3

The **Folk Museum** has a small but interesting display of handicrafts (especially embroidery), costumes, pottery, cooking utensils and old Cretan goat-leather bagpipes. The displays include a re-creation of a traditional Cretan bedroom, and a collection of weaponry with numerous revolution-era firearms.

The Archeological Museum

Paleológou 74, at the top of the hill north of the lake • Currently closed; contact the tourist office (☎ 28410 22357, ⓦ aghiosnikolaos.gr) for the latest

The town's **Archeological Museum** holds a great deal of interest, but is currently closed for renovation. Should it have reopened by the time you read this, highlights include the extraordinary **Goddess of Mírtos**, the museum's star exhibit, a goose-necked early Minoan clay jug (c.2500 BC). There's also gold jewellery from early Minoan tombs at Mohlós (2300–2000 BC) and some fine examples of Vasilikí ware, named after the early Bronze Age site on the isthmus of Ierápetra where it was first discovered. Recent finds from the palaces at Mália and Zákros are also displayed, though the major original discoveries are at Iráklio. These include a curious **model house** from Mália with a pitched roof and chimneys – both foreign concepts in Minoan architecture – and a beautiful **gold pin** (of unknown provenance) bearing an intricately crafted bramble motif and a tantalizingly long inscription in the undeciphered Linear A script on the reverse. There are fine late Minoan **clay sarcophagi**, or *lárnakes*, too, decorated with birds, fish and the long-tentacled octopus that seems to have so delighted Minoan artists. There's also a rare Minoan **infant burial** displayed exactly as found at its site at Kryá, near Sitía.

Áyios Nikólaos church

1km north of town in the grounds of the *Minos Palace Hotel* • Daily 4–8pm • Free • Ask for the key at the hotel's reception desk, leaving passport or other valuables as deposit

The Byzantine church of **Áyios Nikólaos**, from which the modern resort takes its name, is, perhaps appropriately, stranded in the grounds of a five-star hotel. It's worth the effort to get there, though, to see some of the earliest **fresco** fragments found in Greece,

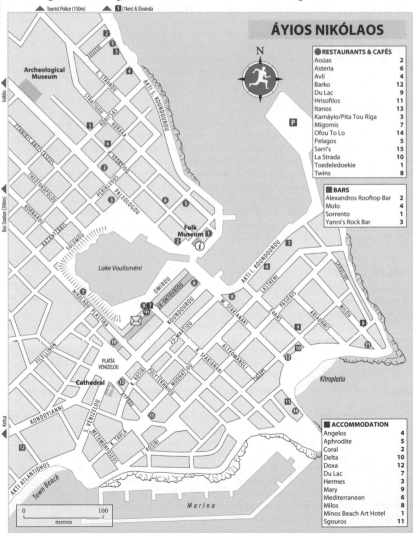

ÁYIOS NIKÓLAOS

Tourist Police (150m)   (1km) & Eloúnda

N

Archeological Museum

Iráklio

Bus Station (300m)

Khtsá

Folk Museum

Lake Voulisméni

PLATÍA VENIZELOU

Cathedral

Kitroplatía

Town Beach

Marina

0 — 100
metres

● **RESTAURANTS & CAFÉS**
Aoúas	2
Asteria	6
Avlí	4
Barko	12
Du Lac	9
Hrisofilos	11
Itanos	13
Karnáyio/Píta Tou Ríga	3
Migomis	7
Ofou To Lo	14
Pelagos	5
Sarri's	15
La Strada	10
Toedeledoekie	1
Twins	8

■ **BARS**
Alexandros Rooftop Bar	2
Molo	4
Sorrento	1
Yanni's Rock Bar	3

■ **ACCOMMODATION**
Angelos	4
Aphrodite	5
Coral	2
Delta	10
Doxa	12
Du Lac	7
Hermes	3
Mary	9
Mediterranean	6
Milos	8
Minos Beach Art Hotel	1
Sgouros	11

dating back to the eighth or ninth century. The geometric patterns and motifs that survive are the legacy of the Iconoclastic movement, which banned the representation of divine images in religious art.

ARRIVAL AND DEPARTURE

By bus The bus station is north of the centre in the new town. There are local buses to the centre roughly every 30min (7.15am–10pm), or it's a steep up-and-down walk; head uphill and turn right along Knossoú and its continuation Kornárou, which will bring you out high above the lake; taking a left here to join Paleológou will lead you back down to the harbour area. Check timetables on ⓦ bus-service-crete-ktel.com.
Destinations Eloúnda (hourly 7am–8pm; 20min); Ierápetra (7 daily; 6.30am–8.15pm; 1hr); Iráklio (18 daily; 6.15am–10.30pm; 1hr 30min); Kritsá (Mon–Fri 8, weekends 4; 7am–8pm; 15min); Pláka (6 daily; 9am–7pm; 30min); Sísi (Mon–Sat 3.30pm; 45min); Sitía

ÁYIOS NIKÓLAOS

(5 daily; 8.15am–7.30pm; 1hr 45min).
By car If you're driving in, follow the one-way system up the hill to Platía Venizélou, and then down into the picturesque areas past the souvenir stores that line Koundoúrou and parallel 28 Oktovríou. Parking in these central areas is a nightmare, however, especially in the evening, so you're better off leaving your vehicle in the car parks near the marina or at the harbour, or trying the marginally less busy streets to the east of Platía Venizélou. The lake marks the centre of town, in every way, and the narrow bridge over its channel is a notorious bottleneck for traffic and strolling visitors.

GETTING AROUND

Bike rental There are dozens of outlets, mainly in the harbour area. For scooters, small motorbikes and high-quality mountain bikes, try the friendly and reliable Mike Manolis, 25-Martíou 12, half a block from the harbour (☎ 28410 24940).

Car rental Clubcars, 28-Oktovríou 24 (☎ 28410 25868, ⓦ clubcars.net).
Taxis Ranks in Platía Venizélou and outside the Folk Museum; or call ☎ 28410 24000 or ☎ 28410 24100.

INFORMATION

Tourist information The tourist office (daily 8.30am–9.30pm; ☎ 28410 22357, ⓦ aghiosnikolaos.gr), by the bridge, is particularly helpful, if often busy. They have lots of maps and brochures, as well as currency

exchange at good rates and cheap internet access.
Tourist police The tourist police are at Eríthrou Stávrou 47 (☎ 28410 26900).

TOURS AND ACTIVITIES

Boat trips Trips to points around the Gulf leave from all around the harbour. There are daily trips to Spinalónga (€12–17), and various fishing, barbecue, beach and sunset tours, often with meals included. Longer trips to Mókhlos (see p.147) or even the island of Santoríni are also sometimes available. Cretan Sailing (☎ 28410 24376, ⓦ cretansailing.com) offer small-group trips to Spinalónga and Mókhlos as well as private charter of a small yacht.

Scuba diving Happy Divers (☎ 28410 82546, ⓦ happydivers.gr) are based on the beach in front of the *Hermes Hotel*; they can pick you up from your hotel. Pelagos Dive Centre is at the *Minos Beach Hotel* (☎ 28410 24376, ⓦ divecrete.com), while Underwater Crete is based in the *Hotel Mirabello* on the Eloúnda road (☎ 28410 22406, ⓦ creteunderwatercenter.com).

ACCOMMODATION

Except at the peak of the season you're unlikely to have a problem finding a **room** in Áyios Nikólaos; however, with accommodation scattered on hilly streets all over town you may get footsore. If you haven't booked, start at the tourist office, which has information on current availability.

★ **Angelos** Aktí S. Koundoúrou 16 ☎ 28410 23501. Welcoming small hotel on the seafront, offering excellent a/c balconied rooms with TV and fridge plus fine views over the Gulf. No breakfast, but there's a supermarket, owned by the same people, directly underneath; check in here for information if there's no one around. **€40**
Aphrodite P. Yeoryíou 34 ☎ 28410 28058. Cheap and

cheerful, old-school rooms place with shared bathrooms, lots of plants, a rooftop terrace and the use of a communal fridge. Little changed in twenty years. **€25**
Coral Aktí S. Koundoúrou 17 ☎ 28410 28363, ⓦ mhotels.gr. Comfortable three-star sister hotel of the nearby *Hermes*, with great sea views from rooms at the front (worth paying the extra); there's also a rooftop pool

2

and bar. Out of season, prices fall by up to 50 percent. Breakfast included. €95

Delta Tselépi 1 ☎ 28410 28893, ⊕ agiosnikolaos-hotels .gr. Modern, refurbished a/c studios and apartments overlooking Kitroplatía beach, a 5min walk from the centre of town. Rooms at the front have sea-view balconies. Facilities include full kitchen and TV. The same owners have good-value two-room family apartments at the nearby *Creta*. €60

Doxa Idomenéos 7, close to town beach ☎ 28410 24214, ⊕ doxahotel.gr. It's far from the best value in town, but this rather old-fashioned hotel, with a/c balcony rooms with satellite TV and fridge, often has rooms when others are full. Breakfast included. €75

★ **Du Lac** 28 Oktovríou 17 ☎ 28410 22711, ⊕ dulachotel.gr. Perhaps the most unexpected bargain in Áyios Nikólaos, with rooms and studios classily renovated in designer style with all facilities including a/c, TV and wi-fi (studios also have kitchenette) in a prime location overlooking the lake. Not all rooms have lake views, however, and night-time noise can be a problem, as you're right in the heart of things. €60

Hermes Aktí S. Koundoúrou 21 ☎ 28410 28253, ⊕ iberostar.com. Luxurious four-star seafront hotel with a large rooftop pool and every facility from minibar to satellite TV. Out of season, prices fall by up to 50 percent and there are often big online discounts. Breakfast included. €115

Mary Evans 13 ☎ 28410 23760. Very friendly place with basic, inexpensive en-suite rooms with fridge and use of communal kitchen, some with a sea view and balcony. Also some good-value apartments nearby sleeping up to four. €30

Mediterranean S. Dhávaki 27 ☎ 28410 23611, ✉ mannyspension@yahoo.com. On a hill between the lake and the seafront, these clean, economical rooms (most en suite, some with separate, private bath, some with balcony) are run by a welcoming Anglo-Greek couple. They come with fridges, a/c, TV and use of a communal kitchen. €30

★ **Milos** Sarolídi 24 ☎ 28410 23783. Sweet little *pension* east of Kitroplatía, with some of the best rooms in town for the price. Spotless, en-suite a/c balcony rooms (no. 2 is a dream) with TV, fridge and spectacular sea views over the Gulf. €35

Minos Beach Art Hotel On the promontory 1km north of town ☎ 28410 22345, ⊕ bluegr.com. One of the first of the luxury hotels to be built – in the 1960s – which means its rooms and bungalows enjoy a setting and spaciousness that younger rivals can only dream of, with almost 1km of private coastline just outside town. Original artworks sprinkle the grounds, and there's every facility you could hope for, including private pools in the fancier villas. Big online discounts on the quoted rates most of the year. €350

Sgouros Nikoláou Pagálou 3 ☎ 28410 28931, ⊕ sgourosgrouphotels.com. Modern hotel overlooking Kitroplatía beach, with a/c balcony rooms (sea view €10 extra) with fridge and TV, and plenty of tavernas nearby. €70

EATING

There are tourist-oriented **tavernas** (invariably employing overenthusiastic greeters) all round the lake, with little to choose between them apart from the different perspectives you get on the passing fashion show. Have a drink here, perhaps, or a mid-morning coffee – but choose somewhere else to eat. The places around Kitroplatía are generally fairer value, but again you pay for the location – the more authentic and better-value establishments tend to be less obvious, tucked away in the backstreets behind the tourist office or close to Platía Venizélou.

RESTAURANTS AND TAVERNAS

Aoúas Paleológou 44 ☎ 28410 23231. Very good, inexpensive traditional Cretan food (goat in red sauce for €7.50, for example), served in a plant-covered, trellissed courtyard. A bit out of the way, so can often be half-empty and lifeless. Daily 11am–midnight.

★ **Avlí** P. Yeoryíou 12 ☎ 28410 82479. Delightful garden ouzeri offering a wide *mezédhes* selection as well as more elaborate dishes such as *kounéli krasato* (rabbit in wine) or lamb slow-cooked in a traditional oven (both €9.80). Booking advisable. Daily 12.30–3pm & 7–11pm.

Barko Kitroplatía ☎ 28410 24610. This hip restaurant and bar, with a large terrace overlooking the beach, serves good-vale, modern Greek dishes with flair; share a mix of *mezédhes* such as stuffed courgette flowers, roast potatoes with leek, sausage and local cheese, and pork in wine. Daily noon–late.

Du Lac By the lake ☎ 28410 22414. Probably the best of the lakeside restaurants, with a local as well as tourist clientele

and good, fresh fish. It's expensive, though, and you may need to book in the evening. The café upstairs offers if anything better views, with music and drink. Daily 9am–1am.

Hrisofilos Aktí Pangálou ☎ 28410 22705. Attractive, stylish and creative *mezedhopolío* with reasonably priced fish, meat and veggie *mezédhes* served on a sea-facing terrace close to Kitroplatía beach. *Meze* from €4.50. Daily 3pm–2am.

Itanos Kýprou 1 ☎ 28410 25340. Popular with locals, this traditional taverna serves reasonably priced Cretan food such as *yemista* (rice-stuffed vegetables, €5) – check what's on offer from the trays in the kitchen – and barrel wine. The surroundings don't match up to the food, sadly, with a choice of tables on the street or in the cavernous, dark interior, decorated with huge barrels. Daily 11am–midnight.

★ **Karnáyio/Píta Tou Ríga** Paleológou 24 ☎ 28410 25968. What appear to be two separate establishments in fact share a colourful terrace above the lake, where you can order from either menu. *Karnáyio* is a modern incarnation of a traditional ouzerí serving tasty *mezédhes* (€4–5 each, or order the excellent value wine- or ouzo-*meze* combos), while *Píta tou Ríga* is an upmarket kebab joint – their speciality *píta tou ríga* (€3.80) comes with added bacon and cheese. The place attracts a young, local crowd and there's *lyra* and *laoúto* (lute) music most Fri and Sat evenings. Daily noon–2am.

Ofou To Lo Kitroplatía ☎ 28410 24819. Best of the moderately priced places on the seafront here, with consistently good food; it's usually crowded. Try their *loukánika me tirí* starter (spicy sausages with cheese; €5). Mains around €9.50. Daily 10am–late.

★ **Pelagos** Stratígou Kóraka and Kateháki 10 ☎ 28410 25737. Housed in an elegant mansion, this stylish fish taverna has an attractive leafy garden terrace that complements the excellent food. Pricey, but worth it; booking advisable. Daily noon–1am.

Sarri's Kýprou 15 ☎ 28410 28059. Great little economical neighbourhood café-taverna in a quiet corner, with a shady terrace across the road overlooking an ancient church. Good for breakfast, grills and *souvláki*, with good-value daily specials (*meze* and wine €8). Daily 9am–midnight.

La Strada N. Plastíra 5 ☎ 28410 25841. Decent pizza and pasta (€7–10) at this popular, Greek-Italian restaurant. Tables on the street are not in the prettiest setting, though, so you may want to eat inside. Daily 11am–midnight.

Twins Aktí I. Koundoúrou ☎ 28410 28201. Large and always buzzing pizzeria with tables right on the harbour and a busy takeaway business. The pizzas (€7–10) are good, and they also have sandwiches, salads, burgers and the like. Daily 9am–1am.

CAFÉS

Asteria Aktí I. Koundoúrou ☎ 28410 22452. Nicely old-fashioned café with a waterfront terrace fronting the harbour, and another on the second-floor balcony. One of the oldest in town and great for people watching. Daily 7.30am–late.

Migomis Nikoláou Plastíra 22 ☎ 28410 23904. High above the bottomless lake, *Migomis* has a matchless view, arguably the best in town, and prices not significantly higher than any other fancy café; a great place for afternoon or evening drinks. Their elegant piano restaurant next door is a little over-the-top in terms of both price and decor, but perhaps worth it if you've booked a terrace-edge table to feast on that view. Daily 8am–2am.

Toedeledoekie Aktí S. Koundoúrou 19 ☎ 28410 25537. Friendly, low-key café run by a Dutch-Greek couple. There are international papers to read, great sandwiches and milk shakes, and at night it morphs into a chilled bar. Daily 10.30am–2am.

DRINKING AND NIGHTLIFE

One thing that Áyios Nikólaos undeniably does well is **nightlife**. A string of bars along Aktí I Koundoúrou on the east side of the harbour play cool sounds to customers chatting on their waterside terraces, many with dancefloors inside that fill as the night wears on. There are bars on the opposite side of the harbour too, though fewer of them. More raucous music venues and clubs crowd the bottom of 25-Martíou (known as "Soho Street") as it heads up the hill – though few seem to survive in the same incarnation for long.

Alexandros Rooftop Bar Kondhiláki. The name says it all; a great eyrie for a relaxed drink overlooking the lake, becoming increasingly rowdy as the cocktails take effect and the music, dating from the 60s to present day but mostly oldies, gets louder. Happy hour till 10.30pm. Daily 8pm–early hours.

Molo Aktí I Koundoúrou 6 ☎ 28410 26250. One of a string of harbourside cafés with waterside terraces, *Molo* rarely closes; it's a café and local hangout by day and a cocktail bar in the evening; later on the action moves inside for dancing, club nights and occasional live music.

Daily 8am–early hours.

Sorrento Aktí S. Koundoúrou 23, on the west side of the harbour, near the tourist office ☎ 28410 24310. A long-established haunt of expats, loud and fun with plenty of happy-hour-style offers – it's fine, if that's what you're in the mood for. Daily noon–late.

Yanni's Rock Bar Aktí I Koundoúrou 1 ☎ 28410 23581. Long-running classic rock music bar, with a party atmosphere and a soundtrack of 70s and 80s music, blues, hard rock and heavy metal. Daily 10pm–4am.

DIRECTORY

Banks Banks and exchange places are mostly found along Koundoúrou and 28-Oktovríou, where there are several ATMs. The tourist office also changes money at reasonable rates.

THE LATO FESTIVAL

Each year, Áyios Nikólaos mounts a summer-long cultural festival, **"The Lato"**, which includes music, dance and theatre from Crete, Greece and other parts of Europe. Keep an eye out for posters advertising the various events, or ask at the tourist office.

Books and newspapers Anna Karteri, Koundoúrou 5 and 28-Oktovríou 4 near Platía Venizélou, has a good selection of books in English, and there are other bookshops nearby. Find foreign newspapers at World Press on the harbour next to *Twins* pizzeria.

Hospital The town hospital is at the northern end of Paleológou, one block beyond the Archeological Museum (☎ 28413 43000).

Internet There's wi-fi in virtually every hotel, café and restaurant; the best internet café is *Café du Lac* at 28-Oktovríou 17, a great place to hang out in its own right. There's cheap access at the tourist office, too.

Post office 28-Oktovríou, above the lake (Mon–Fri 7.30am–2pm).

Shopping The prime shopping street in town is Koundoúrou as it heads uphill from the harbour: head up to Platía Venizélou and then back down on 28-Oktovríou and you'll have seen most of what's on offer – from jewellery and fashion to souvenirs and sponges, photography to pharmacies and dive gear to delis.

The Gulf of Mirabéllo

North of Áyios Nikólaos, the swankier hotels are strung out along the **Gulf of Mirabéllo** coast road, above all as you approach the busy little resort of **Eloúnda**. The gulf's best-known attraction is the islet and former leper colony of **Spinalónga**, easily accessed from either Eloúnda or the hamlet of **Pláka**. Leaving Áyios Nikólaos, the road soon begins to climb; looking across the bay, you can make out the islands of Psíra and Mókhlos against the stark wall of the Sitía mountains, while nearer at hand mothballed supertankers are moored among the small islands sheltering in the lee of the peninsula. One of the largest of these islets, **Áyios Pándes**, is a refuge for the island's wild goat, the *kri-kri*. The animals have an elusive reputation and usually manage to avoid the cruise parties from Áyios Nikólaos that put in to see them.

Eloúnda

ELOÚNDA (Ελούντα) is distinctly schizophrenic: surrounded by the most expensive hotels in Crete, and by fancy apartment and villa developments, it has plenty of jewellery and fashion stores and some pricey seafront restaurants; on the other hand, on the fringes there's a much more earthy resort, with plenty of inexpensive rooms and cafés that compete to provide the biggest, cheapest English breakfast. There are small beaches all around, though many of the best are monopolized by the big hotels; a good, sandy **municipal beach** stretches out north from the centre, and there are numerous popular swimming spots further out in this direction, along the road to Pláka.

ARRIVAL AND DEPARTURE   ELOÚNDA

At the heart of town is an enormous seafront square ringed by cafés and restaurants, banks and post office, stores and hotels; virtually everything is here, or within a short walk.

By bus Buses stop on the main square, where tickets can be bought from the kiosk.
Destinations Áyios Nikólaos (15 daily; 7.20am–8.20pm; 20min); Pláka (6 daily; 9.20am –7.20pm; 10min).
By car The square is the best place to park.

INFORMATION AND ACTIVITIES

Boat trips Boats leave the harbour every 30min from 9am for the trip to Spinalónga (€10 return; ☎ 697 66 83 597, ⓦ eloundaboat.gr); longer day-trips taking in local beaches are also available.

Bookshop Eklektos, A. Papandréou 13 (Mon–Sat 9.30am–11pm, Sun 10.30am–11pm; ☎ 28410 42086), is a great little English bookshop 50m uphill from the square in the direction of Áyios Nikólaos, on the steps down to the water and *Poulis* restaurant; they sell new and secondhand books, offer credit for your old books, and stock guides, maps and gifts.

Internet There's internet access at *Babel* (see opposite).

Tourist information The municipal tourist booth may be open in the harbour square, though financial constraints had led to its closure at the time of writing. In its absence, travel agencies like Olous Travel (☎ 28410 41324, ⓦ olous -travel.gr), on the square next to the post office, can provide information and assist with finding accommodation, as well

as changing money and arranging tours and car rental.
Tours Rambles to discover the flora of Crete (from €45
including refreshments) are run by Julia Jones (☏ 28410

42177, ⓦ flowersofcrete.com). Two rival "happy trains"
offer local trips, starting from the harbour square, some of
which venture way up into the hills (from €10).

ACCOMMODATION

Many of the finest hotels in Crete are around Eloúnda, offering **spectacular villas** with private pools costing thousands
of euros a night, as well as more ordinary suites and rooms. These are almost always far less expensive booked as part of a
package. As for more ordinary accommodation, if you're having problems finding somewhere, try Olous Travel (see above)
or one of the other agencies in the centre of town.

Akti Olous On the road to the causeway ☏ 28410
41270, ⓦ eloundaaktiolous.com. An attractive seventy-
room seafront hotel where comfortable balcony rooms
come with a/c, TV and fridge. There's a bar and pool on the
roof, with great views, and a seashore terrace café flanked
by a small beach. Breakfast included. **€75**
Corali Studios Behind the far end of the town beach
☏ 28410 41712, ⓦ coralistudios.com. A sizeable
complex, *Corali* (together with neighbouring *Portobello
Apartments*, under the same management) has good
modern a/c studios and apartments with cooking
facilities, all with a sea view, and a pool and bar in the
garden area behind. **€65**
Delfinia Rooms On the waterfront just south of the
centre ☏ 28410 41641, ⓦ pediaditis.gr. A/c rooms,
studios and apartments in a great position right at the
heart of things and directly above the sea (most have
balconies with views). The decor is simple and perhaps in
need of a refurb, but it's reasonably priced. You can get info
at the Pediaditis Bookshop on the main square. Rooms
€40, apartments **€60**
Elounda Peninsula 2km south of Elounda ☏ 28410
68250, ⓦ eloundapeninsula.com. Spectacular all-suite
hotel draped across its own private peninsula.
Accommodation is in duplex suites or larger villas, all
with private pools, and there's virtually every facility you
could wish for, from an elegant spa to tennis courts,
9-hole golf course, sandy beach and kids' clubs and
activities. Part of a complex with the *Elounda Mare* and

Porto Elounda hotels, which share the same beaches and
facilities, but offer some more standard hotel rooms.
€520
Marin Studios Behind the town beach, close to town
☏ 697 23 14 067, ⓔ marinporoshotel@yahoo.gr. Bigger
and better than they appear from the front, these quiet
apartments and studios, set well back from the road, are
well equipped – with kitchens and a/c – and run by a
helpful family. **€45**
Milos Rooms In the upper part of town south of the
centre ☏ 28410 41641, ⓦ pediaditis.gr. Under the same
management as the *Delfinia*, this is a more modern
apartment complex with pool and bar. Rooms, studios and
apartments are all a/c, and larger units have kitchens. You
can get info at the Pediaditis Bookshop on the main square.
Rooms **€45**, apartments **€60**
Olive Grove Just off the square, on the road heading
inland ☏ 28410 41448, ⓦ olivegrove.com.gr. Big,
modern two-bedroom apartments with a/c, wi-fi and
full kitchen in a complex with pool and pool bar. The
latter is open to non-residents and hosts occasional
music nights. **€60**
Paradisos Taverna 2km out of town, poorly signed
down a dirt track off the Áyios Nikólaos road ☏ 28410
41631. Offering rural simplicity, this is an exceptionally
quiet spot with an idyllic setting on the landward side of
the Oloús lagoon. Simple rooms with fridge; a/c costs extra.
Also has an excellent garden taverna. **€40**

EATING AND DRINKING

Eloúnda has a good choice of **tavernas** and restaurants in all price categories, and just off the square you'll also find a
couple of excellent bakeries. **Nightlife** is quiet, centring on the cafés and bars around the main square; for anything
wilder, head to Áyios Nikólaos (see p.127).

Babel West side of the main square. A large and busy
bar/café/pub with big-screen sports, wi-fi and internet;
one of the liveliest spots in town, with music and dancing
as the night wears on. Daily 9am–late.
Dimitris On the square facing the church ☏ 28410
41822. It has all the atmosphere of a transport café, but
Dimitris' kitchen serves up good grilled meat and fish dishes,
as well as Greek standards, at economical prices; *moussaká*
€6.50, *kléftiko* €7.50. Daily noon–4pm & 6pm–midnight.

★ **Ferryman** Waterfront, south of the harbour
☏ 28410 41320. Glitzy place named for the 1970s BBC
TV series *Who Pays the Ferryman?* in which it featured.
Pricey, but worth it for the candlelit tables right above
the water and short menu of interesting variations on
traditional Greek recipes – lamb *stifádho* with rice
€12.80, *meze* for two €26.50. Daily 12.30–4pm &
7pm–midnight.
Kanali Far side of the Oloús causeway ☏ 28410 42075.

2

Lovely setting by the Oloús lagoon, for an ouzerí-style place serving *meze* (around €4), *staka*, a local smoked pork dish served with eggs or potatoes (€6), salads and fresh fish. It's also a great spot if you just want a drink. Daily 11am–late.

Megaro Waterfront, south of the harbour ☎ 28410 42220. Friendly place serving fresh, well-prepared fish, seafood (mussels €12) and steaks, inside or on a pontoon terrace on the water; notably cheaper than its fancier neighbours. Salads and starters are delicious too – try the halloumi and aubergine salad (€6). Daily 11am–late.

★ **Okeanis** Far end of the town beach ☎ 28410 42246. A very attractive terrace overlooking the town beach, with classy table settings, is matched by the quality of the cooking. Three-course menus for €9.90–16.90; *meze* for two €20. Daily 12.30–4pm & 6–11pm.

Old Mill In the Elounda Mare hotel, 2km south of town ☎ 28410 68200. If you want to push the boat out, this is the place to do it; one of the finest restaurants in Crete, dressy and relatively formal, though still in an outdoor garden setting with sea views. Superb modern Greek/Mediterranean cuisine, at a price – think starters like prawn "cappuccino" (around €20) or mains of rabbit in a honey and walnut sauce (around €40). There's an excellent local wine list too. Daily noon–4pm & 6pm–midnight.

Vritomartes Waterfront, main square ☎ 28410 41325. Occupying a plum spot on a floating pontoon in the centre of the harbour, this is one of the pricier places in town, with a heavily marked-up wine list. Fish is excellent, though, and there are some economical options such as the fish dish for two at €19.50. Daily 10am–midnight.

Peninsula of Spinalónga

The barren **PENINSULA OF SPINALÓNGA** (Σπιναλόγκα) – often known as "big Spinalónga" to distinguish it from the more famous island of the same name – lies directly offshore from Eloúnda, forming a huge sheltered bay in front of the resort. It is linked to the mainland only by a narrow causeway, all that remains of a once-substantial sunken isthmus less than 2km from the centre of Eloúnda; an easy walk along the coast or short drive (though the sharp turning off the main road can be hard to spot). Protected by the causeway are the remains of Venetian salt pans, now fallen into disrepair, which are worth checking for migrating birds in the spring. Also here are the remains of stone windmills and the "French" canal, while all around on both sides you'll find people swimming from small patches of **beach** or basking on flat rocks. On the far side of the peninsula there are more tiny patches of sand – you can walk across to the nearest in a further thirty minutes or so. These are lovely spots, and apparently isolated, but become horrendously overcrowded in the middle of the day when boat tours make their lunch stops here.

Oloús

The site of the ancient "sunken city" of **OLOÚS** (Ολούς) lay around the far end of the causeway to Spinalónga, mainly to the south and east, where a number of structures can be made out beneath the waves. Though it is known chiefly for having been the port of Dríros (see p.132), what little remains is **Roman**: there's a fenced enclosure behind the *Kanali* bar-restaurant (see p.129) in which you can see the floor of a fourth-century Roman **basilica** with an odd, almost patchwork-style black-and-white mosaic, and among the rocks a little further round (watch out for sea urchins) are traces of harbour installations, now submerged as a result of the rise in sea level over the past couple of millennia. The site has never been excavated, and this is about the extent of what is visible, but it's a worthwhile trip for the setting, especially if you combine it with a swim and a drink at the *Kanali*.

Spinalónga

Daily 9am–7pm • €2 • Boats run here every 30min in season from both Eloúnda (€10 return) and Pláka (€8); most give you 1hr on the island, though you can take a later boat if there's room; it's also on many day-trips from Áyios Nikólaos (€12–17)

The imposing fortress rock of **SPINALÓNGA** (Σπιναλόγκα) at the northern end of the bay protected by "big Spinalónga", is a prime target for boat trips from Áyios Nikólaos, Pláka and, above all, Eloúnda. The **fortress**, which entirely covers the island, was founded by the **Venetians** in 1579 to defend the approach to the gulf and the sheltered anchorages in the bay. With its battlements, guard towers and seemingly impregnable walls, it bears all the hallmarks of the Italian republic's brilliant military architecture. Like their other island fortresses, it proved impregnable and was only handed over to the Turks by treaty in 1715, some fifty years after the rest of Crete had surrendered.

The infamous part of the island's history is much more recent, however. For the first fifty years of the twentieth century, Spinalónga was a **leper colony**, the last in Europe. Lepers were sent as outcasts – long after drugs to control their condition had rendered such measures entirely unnecessary – to a colony that was primitive in the extreme and administered almost as if it were a detention camp (as described in *The Island*, a bestselling novel widely available in bookshops locally). Its jail was frequently used for lepers who dared complain about their living conditions.

Even today, if you can escape the visitors, there's an unnerving sense of isolation when the boat leaves you here, at a jetty from which a long tunnel leads up into the fortified centre. There are still just two easily sealed entrances: this tunnel, and a jetty on the seaward side (which you see if you approach from Áyios Nikólaos) leading up to the old **castle gate** with its lion of St Mark. Inside the castle a real town grew up – Turkish buildings mostly, adapted by the lepers using whatever materials they could find. Although everything is in decay, you can still pick out a row of stores and some houses that must once have been quite grand. A couple have been restored to make a small **museum**, with photos and artefacts outlining the island's history.

Pláka

PLÁKA (Πλάκα), about 5km north of Eloúnda, lies directly opposite Spinalónga and was once the mainland supply centre for the leper colony. Boats still make the short trip across, nowadays carrying tourists, and the formerly decaying hamlet has become quite chichi; overlooked by a vast luxury hotel and with many of its houses done up by foreign owners or villa companies. It's still an attractive, tranquil place, though, with a couple of excellent tavernas and crystal-clear water – though the beach is made up of large, uncomfortable pebbles.

ACTIVITIES AND TOURS   PLÁKA

Boat trips Boats cross to Spinalónga from the quaysides beside the *Gorgona* and *Spinalonga* tavernas (April–Oct every 30min 9am–6pm; €8 return); the *Spinalonga*'s boat also does a complete circuit of the island – allowing a fuller appreciation of the impregnable bastion – and offers fishing trips (€80/hr, up to four people) with the catch cooked up at the taverna on your return.

Watersports A cabin on the beach is the headquarters of a watersports centre (☎ 694 49 32 760, ⊛ spinalonga -windsurf.com), offering everything from windsurfing and ringos to kayaking and motorboat rental.

ACCOMMODATION AND EATING

Athina Villas ☎ 28410 41342, ⊛ spinalonga.eu. A modern complex of comfortable a/c studios and apartments with kitchens and balconies, with wi-fi and TV, many with sea views, right in the heart of the village. €50

Blue Palace Immediately south of the village ☎ 28410 65500, ⊛ bluepalace.gr. Spectacularly sited on a slope above the bay, the *Blue Palace* offers sybaritic luxury in its suites and villas, many with private pool. Watersports, spa, gym and tennis courts all on site. €320

Taverna Giorgos ☎ 28410 41353. The best setting in town, with a large terrace facing out to sea opposite Spinalónga island. You pay for it though, certainly if you go for fish (mixed fish plate €30 per person); meat and traditional Cretan dishes are less expensive. Daily lunch & dinner.

Taverna Spinalonga ☎ 28410 41804. With an outdoor terrace facing the sea and Spinalónga at the far end of the village, this taverna has perhaps the most economical fish meals, fresh from the day's catch, and very helpful owners. They can help with accommodation if you're stuck; their own rooms, though, are long overdue a makeover, and are not good value. Daily lunch & dinner.

The Áyios Ioánnis peninsula

The triangular **Áyios Ioánnis peninsula**, north of Áyios Nikólaos, inland from Eloúnda, is surprisingly wild and little travelled, with narrow roads running through remote farming hamlets with few facilities; the only sight of any significance is the remains of the ancient city of **Dríros**. The E75 north coast highway delineates the northern edge of the peninsula; coming from the west it leaves Mália behind and embarks almost immediately on a long climb inland – rising at first through the **Gorge of Selinári**, where travellers would traditionally stop at the chapel and pray to St George for safe passage. It's a tremendously engineered road, but bypasses the major town of **Néapoli** and anywhere else of note, and there's little to see until you emerge high above Áyios Nikólaos to spectacular views of the Gulf of Mirabéllo.

If you've time to dawdle, consider the minor roads across the peninsula: they make a great alternate route from Eloúnda to the west or to the Lasíthi Plateau. There's little specific to see, but there are wonderful views of the Gulf of Mirabéllo, while the larger villages offer plenty of places to eat and drink. A steep, narrow lane winds up from Eloúnda through **Páno Eloúnda** and **Pinés** towards **Fourní** and **Kastélli**, meeting up with the E75 highway outside Neápoli.

GETTING AROUND   THE ÁYIOS IOÁNNIS PENINSULA

By bus There's a steady stream of buses heading to and from Áyios Nikólaos along the E75 highway, most of which call at Neápoli (around 17 daily in each direction), but otherwise virtually no public transport on the peninsula; Sísi has just one bus a day in each direction, to Áyios Nikólaos and to Iráklio.

By car Road maps of Crete, unreliable at the best of times, seem particularly hopeless on the peninsula. Most significantly, there is no direct route around the coast, even on dirt roads, though some maps mark one. Follow the signposts and the asphalt, however, and you should eventually reach your destination.

Vrouhás and around

Beyond Pláka, the road leaves the coast and starts to climb towards **VROUHÁS** (**Βρουχάς**). Here, and in the surrounding country, you'll see many traditional stone windmills, mostly ruined: the winds that drove them are now being harnessed by a substantial **wind farm** (see p.168) on the ridges above. From Vrouhás and nearby **Skiniás**, rough tracks are signed to local **beaches**, plunging steeply down to isolated but unattractive pebble coves in a jagged, rocky coastline; there are small, seasonal tavernas at both.

Inland just beyond Skiniás, a signed, paved road climbs towards the lonely, fortress-like, sixteenth-century **Moní Aretíou**, surrounded by cypresses and cedars. Recently restored, it often appears deserted, though a couple of monks do remain and the gate and church of Ayía Triádha are usually open. Beyond, you can continue, on a paved road that initially winds through utterly barren mountain tops, to **Doriés**, where the church of Áyios Konstantínos holds an icon of the *Panayía* (Virgin), the oldest known on the island, dating from the fourteenth century. The church is sited near the heart of the village, and lies down a little path off the main road (marked by a small monument in the form of a church). The cream-and-brown-painted house next to it is that of the *papás*, who may be available to open the church for you.

Dríros

3km east of Neápoli • Open daylight hours • Free • On the northeastern edge of Neápoli, on the old road as it goes under the E75, is a road signed to Kouroúnes, Nofaliás and Skiniás; after 2km, a signed turn-off on the right leads a further 1km to a dead end beneath a rocky hillside – the stepped path up to the site can clearly be seen from the parking area inside the fence

The earliest remains found at ancient **DRÍROS** (**Δρήρος**) date back to the eighth century BC, and the city flourished for the next seven hundred years as an important ally of

Knossós, but a deadly enemy of Lýttos (see p.75). Dríros declined in importance prior to the end of the second century BC, when many of its citizens emigrated to Miletus in Asia Minor (see p.134).

The site
Scrambling over piles of collapsed stones – ruins of the ancient city – you come eventually to a stone building under a corrugated canopy: the eighth-century BC **Temple of Apollo Delphinios**, one of the earliest known temples in all of Greece, in the centre of which can be seen the remains of a sunken hearth. Among the discoveries here were three hammered bronze statuettes (some of the earliest known, now in the Iráklio Archeological Museum) and two Eteocretan inscriptions – Greek letters used to write a Cretan, possibly Minoan, tongue. The temple was dedicated to a cult that celebrated Apollo transformed into a dolphin, a guise the god used when guiding Greek sailors; that the chief sanctuary of Miletus in Asia Minor was devoted to the same cult is further evidence of a link between this area and the founding of the colony there. As you look around today, it's hard to believe that this temple once lay on the edge of the bustling **agora**, or market square. This was approached by a flight of steps – visible on the west side of the canopy, to the left of the doorway. Another flight of steps joined the temple on the east side, and to the south is a huge **cistern** constructed in the third century BC, now crammed with fig trees.

The path beyond the temple eventually guides you to a short scenic climb; vast cut stones on the hillsides all around show how extensive this city must have been. Hopefully one day the site will be properly excavated; until then, finding anything else of note among the thorny bushes and ruined dry-stone walls is very difficult, and deciphering it once you do virtually impossible. Nevertheless, if you make it to the top of the hill and the charming barrel-vaulted **chapel of Áyios Andónios**, the glorious views make the climb worthwhile, while the drab desolation of the surroundings is a startling contrast to the green country around Neápoli. The stunted oak tree standing before the chapel – which also serves as a belfry, with the bell attached to one of its branches – provides welcome shade for a picnic.

Neápoli

Despite its size, history – it was the birthplace of Pope Alexander V – and strategic location, **NEÁPOLI (Νεάπολη)** sees virtually no tourists other than those who stop for a coffee in the square between buses or as they drive through. A charming provincial town, it was formerly the capital of Lasíthi (a role now usurped by Áyios Nikólaos) and remains the seat of the local government and of the provincial courts; it's a peaceful place for a stopover, and it is from here that one of the roads up to the Lasíthi plateau sets out. Around the expansive, sleepy main square, where the buses stop, are a post office, banks, tavernas and *kafenía*. You'll also see signs to both a folklore and an archeological museum, but both have been closed for some time and show no signs of reopening.

Sísi

SÍSI (Σίσι), a fair-sized resort on the western edge of the Áyios Ioánnis peninsula, in many ways has more in common with the nearby holiday centres of Iráklio province than with the rest of Lasíthi. Certainly during the day it can be crowded with day-trippers from Hersónissos and Mália, whose tour boats moor up in the harbour. That gloriously picturesque **harbour**, overlooked by a string of cafés, bars and tavernas, is the chief attraction here, though there are also some attractive cove **beaches** to the east. The best of these has been taken over by the *Kalimera Kriti* resort, but you can still get there by going to Avláki beach (itself very pleasant), and following the path round the rocks from there.

ARRIVAL AND INFORMATION

By bus A single bus leaves Sísi daily at 9am, headed for Áyios Nikólaos and Irákio – passengers for the latter change buses at the highway; there are return journeys from each of those towns in the afternoon. If you walk or get a taxi the 2.5km to the highway junction, you can also pick up buses there; at least 17 daily in each direction.

Tourist information AIS Travel (☎ 28410 71712, ⓦ sisi-crete.com), 50m up the main street from the seafront, is a helpful travel agency that can sort everything from accommodation to tours. Nearby is everything else you're likely to need including ATMs, car and bike rental offices – and even a laundry.

ACCOMMODATION

Many of Sísi's visitors stay in modern **apartment complexes** scattered about the surrounding countryside. Because these are so widespread – and mostly pre-booked in high season – the best tactic is to ask around at the tavernas near the harbour or at AIS travel (see above). There are also plenty of "Rooms for Rent" signs along the roads as you approach the village.

Bella Vista Overlooking the sea from the hills just over 1km west of town ☎ 28410 71370, ⓦ bella vistasissi.com. Large, modern complex of a/c studios and apartments with a large pool and pool-bar. Wi-fi in communal areas. **€45**

Camping Sisi On the rocky shore just over 1km west of town ☎ 28410 71247, ⓦ sisicamping.gr. Campsite with a fabulous seafront location (though you can't actually swim from the shore here), shady pitches, and excellent

facilities including swimming pool, restaurant, kitchen, laundry and wi-fi. Two people plus tent and car **€22.50**

Porto Sisi Hotel Seafront east of the harbour ☎ 28410 71385, ⓦ portosisi.com. Luxurious hotel/apartment complex with the best location in town, right on the seafront. Comfortable, well-equipped and recently refurbished apartments come with kitchen and pool, though you pay for the privilege, especially if you want a sea view. **€78**

EATING AND DRINKING

Sísi's **harbour** is ringed by places to eat and drink, with more just round the corner facing out to sea; there are also plenty of bars and pubs on the inland streets. None really stand out as exceptional, though.

Angistri Facing out to sea, round the corner from the harbour ☎ 28410 71794. With the inevitable international menu featuring pizza and pictures of food to point at, *Angistri* also attracts locals for its competitively priced home-made food and fresh fish. Daily 10am–late.

Hemingway's Bar Harbour ☎ 28410 71068. With an immaculate setting hanging above the harbour, *Hemingway's* is a great place to admire the sunset over a cool drink, to a mostly oldies soundtrack (60s and 70s); it's also something of an expat hangout, with quizzes, live music and the like. Daily noon–late.

Mílatos

An unpretentious settlement with a line of tavernas fronting the sea, **MÍLATOS** (**Μίλατος**) is very little developed, possibly because of its uncomfortable pebble beach and its relative isolation – a good twenty-minute drive from the highway. Although you'd never guess from what remains today, the place has a distinguished past; **ancient Miletus** even earns a mention in Homer's *Iliad* as one of the seven Cretan cities that sent forces to fight at Troy. In mythology – backed up by recent archeological finds – it was from Mílatos that Sarpedon (King Minos's brother, whom the king had defeated to take the throne) sailed to found Miletus, which was destined to become one of the greatest of all cities in Asia Minor. The site of the ancient city lies to the east of the beach, but there's little to see there: the place faded into obscurity in antiquity and by Roman times no longer existed.

Mílatos Cave

3km east of Mílatos village • Open daylight hours • Free; bring a torch

More a series of caverns than a single cave, the **Mílatos Cave** is something of a place of pilgrimage for Cretans. It appears to go back indefinitely, and with adequate lighting you might be able to discover just how far. Less adventurously, there's a small chapel to explore right at the entrance, a memorial to the events that earned the cave its notoriety. In 1823, during one of the early rebellions against the Turks, some 2700 Cretans (that, at least, is the number claimed) took refuge in the cave, were discovered and besieged. Eventually, having failed to break their way out, they were offered safe conduct by the Turkish commander – only to be killed or taken away into slavery as soon as they surrendered.

ARRIVAL AND DEPARTURE   MÍLATOS

By car Mílatos is pretty much a dead end. Beyond the cave there are dirt roads that continue east, but there's no through route to the eastern half of the Áyios Ioánnis peninsula. What you can do, though, is zigzag directly up towards Neápoli, a beautiful drive on mostly good paved roads.

ACCOMMODATION AND EATING

Much of the accommodation is in **apartments** in the surrounding countryside, but there are also some excellent beachfront rooms. Almost everything clusters near the small church at the junction where the main road hits the waterfront: shops and car and bike rental places as well as tavernas, cafés and rooms.

Akrogiali Seafront, right by the junction ☎ 28410 81343. The tavernas lined along the seafront are almost all excellent; they're popular weekend outings for locals. *Akrogiali* is a particularly good spot, specializing in fish but with a broad menu for all tastes. Daily 10am–midnight.
Porto Bello Villas At the western end of the seafront ☎ 28410 81001, ⓦ portobello-villas.gr. Simple a/c apartments and studios in a lovely seaside setting close to the harbour with saltwater pool and satellite TV; exceptionally friendly welcome. **€45**
Rooms Taverna Sokrates East along the waterfront ☎ 28410 81375, ⓦ sokrati.de. Basic, sea-view a/c studios near the centre of things. The seafront taverna below serves good charcoal-grilled meat and fish dishes. **€35**

The Lasíthi plateau

Every day, scores of bus tours toil up to the **LASÍTHI PLATEAU** (Λασίθι) to view what is promoted as a sea of white-cloth-sailed windmills. In reality there are very few working mills left, and those that do operate do so only for limited periods; others are found as marketing features next to tavernas. Nevertheless, the trip is well worth making, even if you don't see a single unfurled sail.

If you **stay overnight** you'll see far more than on a day-trip, as the tour parties leave and a great peace settles over the plateau. The excesses of Mália or Hersónissos

THE LASÍTHI PLATEAU WINDMILLS

When you finally come upon the Lasíthi plateau laid out below you, it seems almost too perfect – a patchwork circle of tiny fields enclosed by the bare flanks of the mountains. Closer up, it's a fine example of rural Crete at work, with every centimetre given over to the cultivation of potatoes, apples, pears, cereals and almost anything else that could conceivably be grown in the cooler climate up here. The area has always been fertile, its rich alluvial soil washed down from the mountains and watered by the rains that collect in the natural bowl. In spring, there can be floods, which is why the villages all cluster on the higher ground around the edge of the plain, but in summer, the **windmills** traditionally come into use, pumping the water back up to the drying surface. Although the plateau was irrigated in Roman times – and inhabited long before that – this system was designed by the Venetians in the fifteenth century, bringing the plain back into use after nearly a century of enforced neglect (during which time cultivation and pasture had been banned after a local rebellion). Where they survive, the windmills have barely changed, and although many have been replaced by more dependable petrol-driven pumps, they have been making a comeback in recent years, thanks to EU funding and tourism. The 26 stone windmills standing guard on the ridges above the plain, also mostly ruined, were traditional grain mills.

2

seem a world away as you climb into your bed to the sound of braying donkeys and a tolling church bell, and wake to the cock's crow the next morning. Early in the day you'll often see a diaphanous white mist floating over the plain and its windmills sparkling in the sun. The winters are severe here – up to 50cm of snow is not unusual – so the **best time to visit** is at either end of the summer season. In late spring, the pastures and orchards are almost alpine in their covering of wildflowers, an impression reinforced by the snow lingering on the higher peaks, while in autumn, the fruit trees can barely support the weight of their crop. Whatever time of year you come, though, bring some warm clothing, as the nights can get extremely cold.

Tzermiádho

TZERMIÁDHO (Τζερμιάδο), on the plateau's northern edge, is the largest village and one of the least touristy; in the village centre old shops that seem virtually unchanged in fifty years are interspersed with embroidery and weaving sellers. There's also a post office and bank (with ATM) as well as an excellent old-fashioned bakery, several *kafenía* and good tavernas. In addition, Tzermiádho offers access to the Minoan site of Karfí and the Kronos Cave.

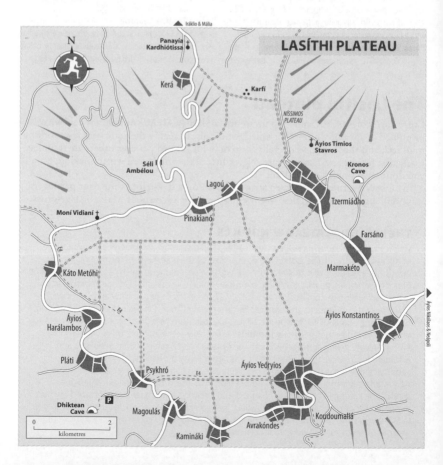

2

THE ASCENT TO KARFÍ

From Tzermiádho, there's an ascent to the ancient Minoan site of **Karfí (Καρφί)** one of the most dramatic places in Crete, perched on the southeast slope of Mount Karfí with an opportunity to see some of the area's spectacular birds of prey. The climb, some 6km, takes around 2hr on foot from Tzermiádho, less than half that if you drive as far as you can; you'll need sturdy footwear and, in summer, plenty of water. There are a number of shady places for a picnic on the way up, or even at the site itself.

The start of the route up is located on Tzermiádho's western edge at the side of the district health centre, opposite a blue sign marked, in English, "To the Timios Stavros church". Follow the road as it winds gently for the first couple of kilometres up to the Níssimos plateau. On this miniature plateau, turn left onto a dirt track and keep left, aiming for a small, whitewashed chapel. Leave any transport near the chapel, from just to the right of which the ascent begins, a final 30min through a rocky landscape patrolled by agile goats; there are no signs at the bottom, but the way is obvious and once climbing you'll come across numerous battered waymarkers.

THE SITE

At the end of the climb the archeological site, with magnificent views over the coast, spreads across the saddle between the summit of Mount Karfí (the location of an ancient peak sanctuary), to the west, and the pinnacle of Mikrí Kopróna (topped by a trig point), to the east. In this cluster of crude, stone-built, single-storey dwellings, founded in the twelfth century BC, Minoan refugees fleeing from the Dorian advance attempted to preserve vestiges of their ancestral culture. For the three thousand or so inhabitants who lived here prior to the site's peaceful evacuation around 1000 BC, life must have been a grim struggle, lashed by the winds and prey to the vicious winter elements. But this very inaccessibility was of great defensive value and preserved the settlement from attack, while the cultivation of the Níssimos plateau below provided food and pasture for livestock.

Among the ruins, excavated in the 1930s by John Pendlebury, it's hard to make out anything other than a mass of fallen stones intersected by paved alleyways. The most substantial structure is what the archeologist described as the Great House, an important building still retaining its walls and where a number of bronze artefacts were discovered. Behind this, just to the north, a shrine was located containing remarkable, metre-high terracotta goddesses with arms raised in blessing (now in the Iráklio Archeological Museum).

While you're up here there's a good chance you'll see the odd griffon vulture gliding majestically overhead, or maybe even the much rarer lammergeier, or bearded vulture, now down to a handful of isolated pairs.

Kronos Cave

Follow signs from the centre of Tzermiádho or from the edge of Marmakéto, on the main road southeast of Tzermiádho; a path and stone steps take you the final 500m to the narrow cave entrance • Open daylight hours • Free, though there's often a guide to show you around and lend out torches, who will expect a small payment

In the **Kronos Cave**, known to archeologists as Trápeza, Evans and Pendlebury discovered remains and tombs dating back to Neolithic times. Though the cave is small, footing is slippery and treacherous, so a guide (and torch) comes in handy: in any event it helps to have someone point out the ancient tombs (in Minoan times, communal burials took place here, and many funerary offerings were discovered).

Áyios Konstantínos

ÁYIOS KONSTANTÍNOS (Άγιος Κονσταντίνος) lies close to the point where the Neápoli road emerges onto the plain. As a result, it is the first (and last) village many people visit when doing a plateau circuit, and is therefore packed with souvenir stores. Some of the embroidery and weaving is very fine; in the best, natural dyes from onions, walnuts and other sources are still used. There's also an excellent taverna.

Áyios Yeóryios

ÁYIOS YEÓRYIOS (Άγιος Γεόργιος) is one of the largest and least touristy of the plateau villages, with a lovely, little-visited **Folk Museum** (April–Oct daily 10am–4pm; €3). Housed in a low-ceilinged, windowless farmhouse preserved much as it would have been in the early twentieth century, it's full of rural tools and artefacts including a great winepress, which doubled as the family bed. Below is a bourgeois house of the same period with displays of old pictures, including many photos of Cretan author Nikos Kazantzakis (see p.52), and between the two a section on shops and trade, including old barbers' and blacksmiths' equipment.

Psykhró

PSYKHRÓ (Ψυχρό), a simple community strung out along a tree-lined street, is the plateau's chief destination, the base for visiting the **Dhiktean Cave**, legendary birthplace of Zeus. There are tavernas along the main street, but in practice hardly anyone stops, preferring to continue straight to the cave itself.

The Dhiktean Cave

1km southwest of Psykhró • Daily: April–Oct 8am–7pm; Nov–March 8.30am–3pm • €4 • From Psykhró a signed side road takes you up to a car park (the €2 parking charges are strictly enforced) from where the cave is a 10m climb away on a steep, rocky path, or a longer but easier walk up a paved track; you can also go up by mule (€10 one way, €15 return)

According to legend, it was in the **Dhiktean Cave** that Zeus was born to Rhea. Zeus's father, Kronos, had been warned that he would be overthrown by a son, and accordingly ate all his offspring. On this occasion, however, Rhea gave Kronos a stone to eat instead and left the baby Zeus concealed within the cave, protected by the Kouretes (see p.344), who beat their shields outside to disguise his cries. From here, Zeus moved to the Idean Cave, on Psilorítis (see p.210), where he spent his youth. This, at least, is the version generally told here, and though there are scores of variations on the myth, it is undeniable that the cave was a cult centre from the Minoan period onwards, and that explorations around the turn of the twentieth century retrieved offerings to the Mother Goddess and to Zeus dating through to Classical Greek times.

Concrete steps and electric lighting have made the cave an easy place to visit, although some of the magic and mystery has inevitably been lost. The steps lead you on a circular tour, passing the bottom of the cave where you are confronted with an artificial lake. The one experience that has survived the alterations is the view back from the depths of the cave towards the peephole of light at the entrance, framed in a blue haze caused by the damp atmosphere. It's not hard to believe the tales that this was the infant Zeus's first sight of the world destined to become his kingdom.

To avoid the crowds and savour the cave's mystical qualities to the full, try to arrive early (coaches start to arrive around 11.30am) or after 5pm.

CLIMBING MOUNT DHÍKTI

A former guardian of the Dhiktean Cave, the genial Petros Zervakis leads regular ascents (May–Sept) of **Mount Dhíkti** (Δίκτι), which include an overnight stay at a refuge, supper under the stars and a 5am start for the summit. It's not a terribly difficult climb, but you'll need stout walking boots or shoes and a sleeping bag. The cost (around €50 per person) depends on the number of people in the group; he also organizes hikes to spot wildflowers (mid-April to mid-June) and birds (April–Sept). For details, ring or call in at his family's taverna *Petros*, facing the car park (☎ 694 70 22 216).

Moní Vidianí

Natural History Museum of Dhíkti Erratic hours, but usually open in summer • €1

Beyond Psykhró, you can complete a circuit of the plateau on a far less travelled road via the villages of Pláti, with its many tapestry sellers, Áyios Harálambos and Káto Metóhi, to meet with the direct route back to the coast at Pinakianó. Between Káto Metóhi and Pinakianó is the **Moní Vidianí**, one of whose restored buildings houses the tiny **Natural History Museum of Dhíkti** (aka Bearded Vulture Information Centre). Though not wildly inspiring, the informative display, well labelled in English, covers local fauna, concentrating especially on the lammergeier or bearded vulture and with many stuffed specimens.

ARRIVAL, DEPARTURE AND GETTING AROUND

THE LASÍTHI PLATEAU

By car The quickest and easiest routes up to the plateau are from the north and northwest, from Mália and Hersónissos (see p.90). The approach from Neápoli is far slower – a tortuous 30km climb, first south and then west into the mountains that ring the sunken plateau. Once you do finally make it, you'll find a circular road linking the villages on the plateau's edge.

By bus There are plenty of tours, but just two public buses a week between Iráklio and the plateau (where they circle the villages). These are designed to take villagers to town and back, rather than for tourists, so they leave the plateau at 5.45am on Mon & Fri, returning at 1.45pm.

On foot Once on the plateau, you can easily walk through the fields from one village to another – the paths between Áyios Yeóryios and Káto Metóhi via Psykhró even form part of the E4 Pan-European walking route. Whichever route you choose the path is rarely direct, but it's easy enough to pick your way by the trails: crossing the whole plain, from Psykhró to Tzermiádho, takes 90min or less. More ambitiously, you can also hike up to the plateau, most directly from Kritsá in the east, or on the E4 path from Kastélli in the west. A good time to take a walk here is the early evening, when you'll encounter the villagers on their carts, donkeys and pick-ups making their way back home.

ACCOMMODATION AND EATING

TZERMIÁDHO

Hotel Kourites On the eastern edge of the village ☎ 28440 22054, ⊛ kourites.net. One of the larger options on the plateau, with reasonably modern balcony rooms above a taverna, in a quiet setting on the edge of the village. They also rent pleasant, fully equipped apartments in the old village, sleeping up to four. Breakfast included. Room **€40**, apartment **€70**

★ **Kronio** Village centre ☎ 28440 22375. Traditional Cretan dishes with a French twist thanks to the proprietor's Gallic wife. It's excellent value – if you're hungry and in no hurry, try the *meze* selection, with 18 dishes, wine and dessert for around €15 – and excellent cooking. Watch out for the occasional coach party, though. Daily 11am–10pm.

ÁYIOS KONSTANTÍNOS

★ **Taverna Vilaeti** On the main street ☎ 28440 31983, ⊛ vilaeti.gr. A beautifully restored old stone building, much more elegant than you'd expect in this setting, serving exceptionally good traditional food (most of it local and organic) at standard prices (mains €10–14). Daily 9am–late.

Vilaeti Traditional Guesthouses Info at Taverna Vilaeti on the main street ☎ 28440 31983, ⊛ vilaeti.gr. Lovely, fully equipped restored village apartments and stone-built cottages, all with fireplaces for winter and full

kitchens with the basics supplied, sleeping up to seven. Two-night minimum. **€70**

ÁYIOS YEÓRYIOS

Hotel Maria Hidden away in the backstreets; information at Hotel Rea on the main street, run by the same family ☎ 28440 31774. Sweet, old-fashioned rooms place with framed embroidery on the walls and tiny bathrooms. Some of the double beds are exceptionally small too – they also have three- and four-bed rooms. **€35**

PSYKHRÓ

Taverna Halavro Above the Dhiktean Cave car park ☎ 28440 31402; hotel ☎ 697 29 81 782. Better than you'd expect, considering the captive audience; fresh juices and snacks for cave visitors as well as *meze* (€3–5), and lamb (€12) and pork (€10) roasted in a wood oven. Daily: April–Oct till 7.30pm; Nov–March till 3.30pm. **€30**

Taverna Dionysos Magoulás, around 1km east of Psykhró ☎ 28440 31672. Roadside taverna with quiet rooms with bath and balcony (a couple at the back have a great view over the plain), wi-fi and good food. **€30**

Zeus On the western edge of the village; enquire at Taverna Halavro (see above) ☎ 697 29 81 782. This small, seven-room hotel offers simple rooms, with views across the plateau. **€30**

Kritsá and around

The "traditional" village of **Kritsá**, 9km inland of Áyios Nikólaos, is a popular destination for tour buses and day-trippers. Despite some commercialization this is a trip well worth making, offering as it does a break from the frenetic pace of the coast; buses run frequently from the main station in Áyios Nikólaos. Along the way you'd do well to take a look at the remarkable church of **Panayía Kerá** and the ancient site of **Lató**, both of which are worthwhile sights in their own right.

2

Panayía Kerá

About 1km before Kritsá on the Áyios Nikólaos road • Tues–Sun 9am–4pm • €3

Inside the lovely Byzantine church of **PANAYÍA KERÁ (Παναγία Κερά)** is preserved perhaps the most complete and certainly the most famous set of **Byzantine frescoes** in Crete. They're originally from the fourteenth and early fifteenth centuries, though all have been retouched and restored to such an extent that they're impossible to date accurately. Those in the **south aisle**, through which you enter, depict the life of Anne, mother of Mary – her marriage to Joachim and the birth of Mary – and the early life of the Virgin herself up to the journey to Bethlehem. In the **centre** of the church, the oldest part, dating originally from the twelfth century, Mary's story is continued and there are scenes from the life of Christ, including the Nativity, Herod's banquet and a superb Last Supper. And in the **north aisle** there are vivid scenes of the Second Coming and Judgement, along with the delights of Paradise and assorted interludes from the lives of the saints (especially St Anthony). Throughout, the major scenes are interspersed with small portraits of saints and apostles.

Lató

4km north of Kritsá • Tues–Sun 8.30am–3pm • €2

Just outside Kritsá a surfaced road leads off for about 4km to the archeological site of **LATÓ (Λατώ)**. The city, originally Doric, flourished through to Classical times but its ruins are little visited, presumably because visitors and archeologists on Crete are more concerned with the Minoan era. That it was an important place is clear from the sheer extent of the ruins, which spread in every direction. It is also a magnificent setting, sprawled across the saddle between the twin peaks of a dauntingly craggy hill. Standing on the southernmost peak you get magnificent views down onto the white cluster of **Áyios Nikólaos** (Lató's ancient port), with the gulf and Oloús (a major rival of Lató in its heyday) beyond, as well as inland to the valleys and climbing peaks of the Dhiktean mountains.

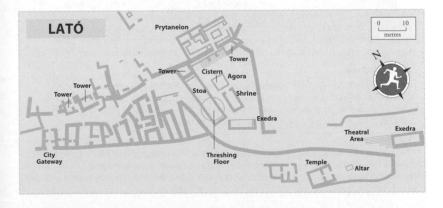

Lató's name derives from **Leto**, the mythical mother of Artemis and Apollo. Homer relates in the *Odyssey* how Eileithyia (the Minoan goddess of childbirth) attended Leto when she gave birth to the god Apollo on the island of Delos: it is thus fitting that Eileithyia became the patron goddess of Lató, as coins discovered here proved.

The site

You enter the site 200m or so below the ruins, following a rough path up to a rectangular area with a **gateway**, which would have been the city's original entrance. Continuing to climb up the street from here, you can see stores and workshops abutting the city wall on the right, with defensive towers and gateways into residential areas on the left. Higher up still, the pentagonal space of the **agora** was a meeting place for citizens that incorporates a tier of steps on its northern side, reminiscent of the theatral areas at Minoan sites such as Knossós and Festós. The steps ascend between the remains of two towers to the **prytaneion**, or town hall, with small rooms at the rear that held the city's archives. In the centre of the agora are a deep square cistern and a shrine, flanked on the western side by a colonnaded **stoa**, a shady place to shelter from the elements. The southern end of this has been cut through by a relatively modern circular threshing floor. The **exedra** nearby was a sort of public seating area, and in the southeast corner of the site is another exedra and a further broad flight of steps in the Minoan style, here officially dubbed the "Theatral Area". This leads to a raised terrace containing a well-preserved fourth-century BC temple.

Kritsá

KRITSÁ (Κριτσά), known as "the largest village in Crete", actually feels more like a small town, its main street lined with tourist stores selling local weaving, ceramics, carved olive wood, leather goods and embroidery. It enjoys a splendid **setting**, with views back over the green valley up which you arrived and the mountains rising steeply behind. You get little impression of this at street level, other than an awareness that you are climbing quite steeply, so try to get out onto one of the balconies or roof terraces of the *kafenía* and tavernas along the main street, from where you can look back over the town and towards Áyios Nikólaos. The more attractive part of the village is the upper half, beyond the square; this is also where you'll find the bulk of the better shops.

THE KATHARÓ PLAIN

If you have a couple of hours to spare, take the magnificent drive up to the **Katharó plain** (**Καθαρό**), 16km above Kritsá. From the top of the village, a winding asphalted road ascends steeply through woods of holm oaks where the air soon becomes sharper, even in summer. There are plenty of potential picnic spots, and roadside boards display maps of the various areas, some marking the routes of amazingly well-preserved Minoan trading paths, no doubt used to access the plateau in ancient times. When you finally reach the plain – a fertile upland similar to Lasíthi (see p.135), though far smaller, less intensely cultivated or visited and, at 1150m, some 300m higher – you will find a few scattered dwellings occupied in summer by farmers and shepherds.

INFORMATION

On the Katharó plain itself, the unexpected and welcome **Kafeníon Zervas**, run by the amiable Yiannis Zervas, an expert on all aspects of the plateau, displays photographs of the plateau's flora and fauna, as well as information about the fossils of large mammals found here: 500,000 years ago this was apparently the preserve of hippos and elephants.

TOURS

The plateau's **flowers**, including spectacular orchids, are exceptional; local expert Steve Lenton conducts guided walks to look at them, also taking in local wildlife, history, geology and paleontology (March–Nov pre-booked only; ☎ 28410 28263, ⊛ exploringkatharo.com).

ARRIVAL AND DEPARTURE

By bus Buses from Áyios Nikólaos to Kritsá (8 daily Mon–Fri, 4 Sat & Sun; 7am–8pm; 15min) terminate in the village square (they also drop off and pick up outside Panayía Kerá) and immediately turn round for the return journey.

KRITSÁ AND AROUND

By car If you arrive by car, use the signed car park on the way into the village, as there's no chance of finding a parking place in the narrow streets.

ACCOMMODATION

Argyro Main road as you enter Kritsá ☏ 28410 51174, ⓦ argyrorentrooms.gr. Clean, pleasant and economical en-suite rooms (plus a couple with shared bath), with wi-fi, some with TV, many with views across the olive-tree-lined valley. There's a small courtyard café. **€35**

East of Áyios Nikólaos: the isthmus

The main road south and then east from Áyios Nikólaos is not wildly exciting – a drive through barren hills dotted with new developments and villas above the occasional sandy cove – though in places the engineering of the new road (an ongoing process still years from completion) is breathtaking. Beyond the reed-fringed beaches at Almirós and Amoudhára (with watersports and giant inflatables) there's little temptation to stop until you reach the cluster of increasing development around **Kaló Hório**, 10km south of Áyios Nikólaos, which has tavernas and minimarkets, and paths winding steeply down to a couple of excellent small **beaches**. The next village is **Ístro**, soon followed by a turn-off to the isolated hilltop **monastery of Faneroméni**. The route then passes a remarkable Minoan site at **Gourniá**. Just beyond, the road south across the isthmus towards Ierápetra turns off, allowing detours to another important early Minoan site at **Vasilikí** and the ancient village of **Episkopí**, with its splendid Byzantine church.

Ístro and around

ÍSTRO (Ίστρο), a strip of development along the road, offers scattered accommodation and more superb **beaches**: follow the signs from town to Voúlisma or Áyios Pandelímon (or simply "to the beach"), down a variety of dusty tracks, for some lovely stretches of sand and crystalline water. There's a good beach café at Áyios Pandelímon.

Moní Faneroméni

5km east of Ístro, take the signed exit on the left; the route, asphalted in its early stages, later a track, climbs dizzily inland for 6km • Free

It's a bit of an effort to get to **MONÍ FANEROMÉNI** (Μονή Φανερωμένη), but the **view** when you finally arrive must be among the finest on Crete. To get into the rather bleak-looking monastery buildings, knock loudly. When you gain entry you will be shown (by one of the two monks currently in residence) up to the **chapel**, built into a cave sanctuary where a sacred icon of the Virgin was miraculously discovered, the reason for the foundation of the monastery in the fifteenth century. The **frescoes**, although seventeenth-century and quite late, are impressive – especially that of the *Panayía Theotókou*, the Mother of God.

Gourniá

Signed off the E75 • Tues–Sun 8.30am–3pm • €2

GOURNIÁ (Γουρνιά), slumped in the saddle between two low peaks on a dusty track by the highway, is the most completely preserved **Minoan town** in Crete, and in its small scale contains important clues about the lives of ordinary people and the nature of the communities from which the Minoan palaces evolved. A look at the map tells you much about ancient Gourniá's strategic importance, controlling the narrow isthmus and the relatively easy communication this gave with the southern seaboard at modern Ierápetra. The overland route avoided a hazardous sea voyage around the eastern cape

– a crucial factor in ancient times, especially in winter when sailing usually stopped because of rough seas.

As you leave Gourniá, it's tempting to cross the highway and take one of the paths north through the wild thyme to the sea for a swim. Don't bother – this seemingly innocent little bay acts as a magnet for every piece of floating detritus dumped off Crete's north coast. Do be sure to look back at the site, though; as the E75 climbs the hill opposite, its street plan is laid out like a map.

Brief history

There is evidence of occupation at Gourniá as early as the third millennium BC, but the remains you see today are those of a town of the **New Palace** period (c.1500 BC). Around 1450 BC, as happened elsewhere, the town was destroyed by fire. Limited rebuilding occurred during the era of **Mycenaean** rule at Knossós – and the shrine may date from this late period – but the site was soon abandoned again and disappeared beneath the soil where it lay unsuspected until the awakening of archeological interest in the nineteenth century. Arthur Evans, as usual, was the first to scent Minoan occupation of this area, and then a young American, Harriet Boyd-Hawes, started digging in 1901. The site, a budding archeologist's dream, made her reputation.

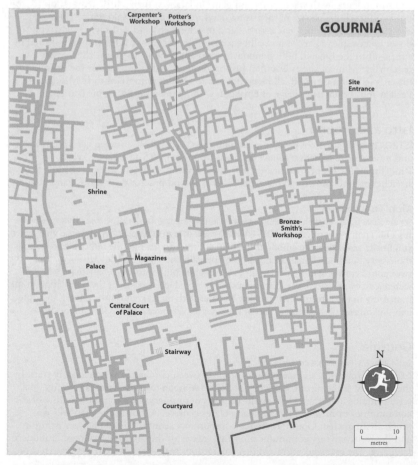

GOURNIÁ

Carpenter's Workshop
Potter's Workshop
Site Entrance
Shrine
Bronze-Smith's Workshop
Magazines
Palace
Central Court of Palace
Stairway
Courtyard

0 10
metres

N

The site

Gourniá's narrow, cobbled alleys and stairways – built for pack animals rather than carts – intersect a throng of one-roomed houses centred on a main square and the house of a local ruler or, more likely, governor. The settlement is not a large place, nor impressive by comparison with the palaces at Knossós and elsewhere, but it must have been at least as luxurious as the average Cretan mountain village of as little as fifty years ago. Among the dwellings to the north and east of the site are some which have been clearly identified, by tools or materials discovered, as the homes of **craftspeople**: a carpenter, a smith and a potter. It's easy to imagine a cramped and raucous community here three and a half thousand years ago, though worth remembering that the rooms may not have been as small as they appear – many of them are in fact basements or semi-basements reached by stairs from the main rooms above, and the floor plans of those that did not necessarily correspond with what you see today. The houses themselves were mainly built of stone on the lower courses and mud-brick above, with plaster-daubed reeds for roofing.

The Palace and shrine

The **palace** (or governor's quarters) occupied the highest ground, to the north of a courtyard containing a familiar L-shaped stairway. With a smaller court at its heart, the whole is a copy in miniature of the palaces at Knossós and Festós. About 20m to the north of the palace, a **shrine** was discovered. It is easily identified by the sloping approach path paved with an intricate pattern of evenly matched cobbles, and the shrine itself, up three steps, is a small room with a ledge for cult objects. Here, a number of terracotta goddesses with arms raised were unearthed, as well as snake totems and other cult objects, now on display in the Iráklio Archeological Museum.

Pahiá Ámmos and around

PAHIÁ ÁMMOS (Παχειά Άμμος), a rather windswept little place 2km east of Gourniá, makes for a good lunch or coffee stop, with a string of waterfront tavernas. There's a grey, pebbly beach, protected by a floating boom from the worst of the plastic rubbish that blights this stretch of coast. To the south, a fast road heads across the narrowest part of the island towards Ierápetra, with the awesome slopes of the Thriptí range bearing down from the east.

Vasilikí

3km south of Pahiá Ámmos • Daily 8.30am–3pm • Free

The Pre-Palatial settlement of **VASILIKÍ (Βασιλική)** dates from about 2650 to 2200 BC. The site may not be much to look at, but it's vitally important for the light that it throws upon the hazy millennium preceding the period of Minoan greatness. Remains from this period occur at Knossós and other palaces but cannot be properly excavated because of the important buildings constructed on top of them: Vasilikí was found in pristine condition, having being abandoned after a fire around 2200 BC. The **pottery** known as Vasilikí ware – ochre or red with dark, blotchy decoration – is named after this site, where the fine examples on display in the archeological museums at Iráklio and Áyios Nikólaos were discovered.

The site

The site contains two main buildings, originally surrounded by numerous smaller (and simpler) dwellings. The remains of the edifice nearest to the entrance, on the lower slope of the hill, are slightly earlier than those on the crown. The **Red House**, as the former is named, has a number of interesting features. It is oriented with its corners towards the cardinal points of the compass, a practice normal in Mesopotamia and the Near East but alien to Egypt and the Aegean (and thus possibly a clue to Minoan origins). In the southern corner, deep basement rooms allow you to gain an idea of early Minoan building techniques: holes to support the absent wooden beams are visible as well as large patches of hard, red lime plaster, the forerunner of what later artists were to use as the ideal background for the wonderful palace frescoes. On the southern flank of the Red House, excavations have revealed a bath, a stretch of roadway, more dwellings and quite a few hand-grindstones.

If you continue on up the lane into the **village** of Vasilikí, you'll find a friendly bar and a glimpse of traditional rural Crete well off the tourist trail.

Episkopí

Almost exactly halfway across the isthmus, **EPISKOPÍ (Επισκοπη)** makes a worthwhile diversion. Below the road, beside a raised platía where old men play *távli* in the shade of lofty eucalyptus trees, lies a charming **Byzantine church** dedicated to Áyios Yeóryios and Áyios Harálambos. The arched drum dome with elaborate blue-tile decoration, together with an unusual ground plan, make this church unique on the island. You may not be able to get in, but in any case it's the church's restored exterior which gives it its standing in Byzantine architecture.

ACCOMMODATION AND EATING	EAST OF ÁYIOS NIKÓLAOS: THE ISTHMUS
ÍSTRO	**PAHIÁ ÁMMOS**
Istron Bay Hotel 1.5km east of Ístro ☎28410 61303, ⓦistronbay.gr. Exclusive, long-established hotel hanging from the cliff above a spectacular cove with a fine sandy beach; extensive facilities include tennis courts, watersports and scuba. **€115**	**Zorba's Taverna** Pahiá Ámmos waterfront ☎28420 93455. Simple Cretan restaurant serving well-prepared local food at very reasonable prices. Also the usual array of coffees and juices, plus a warm welcome. Daily 10am–11pm.

The far east

The **far east** of Crete marks a dramatic change in scenery and tempo. Although much of it is rocky, barren and desolate, it is an area of great natural beauty, and on the whole the towns and villages are slower and quieter, with life conducted at an easier pace than in the rest of the province. **Sitía**, in particular, exudes a contented air, and is largely unperturbed by its visitors. The north coast has few beaches, and in the main the mountains drop straight to the sea; the drive towards Sitía is as dramatic as any in Crete. If you want a cooling dip, though, there are a couple of coves that are just about accessible, and a small resort at **Mókhlos**; there's more opportunity for swimming beyond Sitía, as the heights tail away.

This far eastern region is much visited only in two spots – the spectacular if rather too popular palm beach at **Vái** and the outstanding Minoan palace at **Zákros**; the small town of **Palékastro** makes an excellent base for both. Away from these, it's a great area for escapists, with some scenically rugged hill country around **Zíros**, the nearby Minoan site of **Presós** and Venetian remains at **Voilá** and **Etiá** to seek out, and the isolated coastal resort of **Xerókambos** and its surrounding coves.

The road to Sitía

The tawny bulk of the Ornó range of the Sitía mountains makes a formidable barrier to progress beyond the isthmus, and the road at first is carved into the cliff face, teetering perilously above the gulf. There's just one resort of any significance, at **Mókhlos**. Beyond here, lined in summer with a riot of pink and white oleander flowers, the road runs mostly a little further from the coast, toiling through villages clinging to the mountainside until the final approach to Sitía and a descent in great loops through softer hills. As you progress, the familiar olive groves are increasingly interspersed with **vineyards**, and there are some highly regarded local wines to be had in the village cafés, especially in **Mésa Mouliyaná** and its neighbour **Éxo Mouliyaná**. Most of the grapes, however, go to make sultanas; in late summer, when they are laid out to dry in the fields and on rooftops all around, the various stages of their slow change from green to gold to brown make a bizarre spectacle.

Kavoúsi

KAVOÚSI (Καβούσι), less than 6km from Pahiá Ámmos yet already high above the coast, is a pleasant village with Byzantine churches and a main street lined with oleanders and mulberry trees; at the far end of the village a map shows walks to various nearby places of interest, including a Minoan farmhouse and a vast, ancient olive tree. Many of the tempting **beaches** visible from on high are inaccessible, but **Thólos** – a quiet pebble-and-sand beach backed by tamarisk trees and a chapel, 3km below the village – can be reached by a good paved road.

Plátanos

As you travel east, the views back across the Gulf of Mirabéllo become more expansive all the time, until at **PLÁTANOS (Πλάτανος)** some 6km from Kavoúsi, you reach a famous viewpoint, with a couple of tavernas – *Panorama* and *Pixida* – where you can look down on the island of Psíra (see box below) and west across the gulf to Áyios Nikólaos to watch the sunset.

Mókhlos

MÓKHLOS (Μόχλος) lies way below the main road via 5km or more of dusty hairpin bends, but in a sleepy way it's a surprisingly developed spot. Small as it is, almost every house seems to advertise rooms for rent, and there are at least half a dozen good tavernas, and as many cafés. The whole place, in fact, is much fancier and more upmarket than you might expect, which is largely due to the presence of Minoan sites on two offshore **islets**. Not only do these attract tourists, but also American and Greek archeological teams, who often spend whole summers here.

There's not a great deal to do in Mókhlos – swim out to the islet from the rocky foreshore or hang out in the cafés – but it's a place where it's very easy not to do a great deal.

Mókhlos islet

Ⓦ uncg.edu/arc/Mochlos/first.html

When the weather is calm it's a reasonably easy swim across to the **islet of Mókhlos** – plenty of people do it – or you can arrange a ride across (see p.149). This barren rock,

---

PSÍRA

The island of **Psíra (Ψείρα)**, in the Gulf of Mirabello west of Mókhlos, is archeologically important, though these days it's almost impossible for tourists to visit. Like Mókhlos, Psíra was first excavated in 1907 by an American, Richard Seager, who revealed a Minoan port, occupied from the early Minoan era, with the remains of a town a little like Gourniá built amphitheatrically around a natural harbour. In one of a number of substantial dwellings – many containing hearths and with walls still standing up to 2m high in places – a fine relief **fresco** was found depicting female figures wearing richly embroidered dresses, the only known example outside Knossós.

No palaces or obvious public buildings were discovered, but the site did produce rich finds of **painted pottery**. One jar, now on display in the Iráklio Archeological Museum, is noted for its decoration of bulls' heads interspersed with the double-axe symbol. The remains of what is thought to be an ancient **well** have also been found, although the island is completely dry these days; even in ancient times, the islanders must have been heavily dependent on trade, with mainland Crete and further afield. The site was another of those destroyed about 1450 BC, though the **Romans** later used the island for strategic and navigational purposes, and the remains of their **lighthouse** and military settlement survive on the island's crown.

2

inhabited from the Pre-Palatial period, was in Minoan times almost certainly a much less barren peninsula, and the sandy spit linking it to the mainland would have been used as a harbour (anchorages which could be approached from either side were a great advantage for boats that could sail only before the wind). You can see remains of **late Minoan houses** on the south side of the island, and there are more below the current sea level where recent excavations have also identified remnants of the ancient harbour. But the important discoveries at Mókhlos were in the much more ancient **tombs** built up against the cliff. Here, very early seal stones were found (including one from Mesopotamia), as well as some spectacular gold jewellery now in the Iráklio Archeological Museum and a fine collection of marble, steatite and rock-crystal vases on display in the Áyios Nikólaos and Sitía archeological museums.

Myrsíni

MYRSÍNI (Μυρσίνι) is a resolutely traditional village whose attractive church is built around, and entirely encloses, a frescoed fourteenth-century chapel – fascinating, but you'll need to find the priest if you want to look inside; ask at the *Taverna Kathodon* (see p.150).

Hamézi and around

The sleepy village of **HAMÉZI (Χαμέζι)** spreads uphill to the north of the road some 10km west of Sitía. In the narrow streets (don't try to bring a car up here) plants are festooned over buildings and down whitewashed steps. The local **folk museum** (daily 9am–1pm & 5–8pm; €1) is worth a visit for its collection of ancient farm implements and rooms filled with furniture and utensils from the nineteenth century. To get there, walk up the main street, passing the brilliant-white **church**, and turn left up a charming stepped street. For the path through the Áyios Pándes gorge (see below), ask for directions locally.

Hamézi Minoan House

1.5km west of Hamézi village, near the ruined stone windmills on the final crest before the Bay of Sitía, a track on the right is signed "Middle Minoan House"; follow this winding track (driveable, or about a 15min walk), keeping right at a restored windmill, to the site • Unfenced • Free

The grey-stone **Minoan house** at Hamézi, dating from the Pre-Palatial period (c.2000 BC), is the only known Minoan structure to have had an oval ground plan, possibly dictated by the conical shape of the hill. It was thought at first to be a peak sanctuary, but the discovery of a **cistern** made a dwelling, or even a fortress, seem more likely. The ground plan sketched out by the walls – more than 1m high in places – consists of a number of rooms grouped around a central courtyard, where the cistern is located. A paved entrance is visible on the south side. Whatever the building's function, it certainly had a commanding view over the surrounding terrain from its spectacular hilltop setting. While you're taking this in, keep an eye out for the rare **Eleanora's falcon** that breeds on the offshore island of Paximádha – the valley to the east is one of its favourite hunting grounds.

Moní Faneroméni

About 6km west of Sitía, immediately east of the village of Skopí, a track heads north towards the **MONÍ FANEROMÉNI (Μονή Φανερωμένη)**. This partly asphalted 5km road leads, via some alarming hairpin bends, to a picturesque rocky cove lapped by a

---

HIKES AROUND HAMÉZI AND MONÍ FANEROMÉNI

There are a number of attractive **hiking** possibilities in the area around Moní Faneroméni. A well-marked path leads from the coast (there's a parking area by the road), up the Áyios Pándes gorge beneath the monastery, and eventually to Hamézi, from where you should be able to get a bus back to Sitía. You can also walk to Sitía in 2–3hr, or walk the whole way from Hamézi, via the gorge, to Sitía.

turquoise sea. From the cove, the track climbs inland to the monastery. If you're coming from Sitía, you can join this route by following the signs down a narrow lane shortly after you leave the town.

The charming **monastic church** stands at the heart of a tiny, isolated community, built into the rock on the very lip of a gorge. Standing as a metaphor for recent Cretan history, the church has been battered but still stands unbowed. In 1829, monastery and church were looted and burned by the Turks, and most of the frescoes destroyed. They're now blackened and graffitied, but the beauty of what was lost can be glimpsed in one remaining fragment, depicting a saint reading. Behind the church, shoals of silver *taxímata* (ex-votos), hung on the icon of the Virgin in a small cave, attest to the continuing importance of the shrine.

ARRIVAL AND INFORMATION   THE ROAD TO SITÍA

MÓKHLOS

By bus If you're hoping to get to Mókhlos by bus, be warned that you'll be dropped on the main road, a full hour's walk above the village (and a sweaty slog back up);

there's a good chance of getting a lift, however.

Tourist information ⓦ mochlos.eu is an informative local website.

ACTIVITIES

MÓKHLOS

Boat trips Mochlos Boat Tours (ⓣ 697 78 37 803) – a rather grand name for one tiny fishing boat – takes people to and from the islet for €5 per person. The boat and captain are usually in the harbour; if not ask at one of the nearby tavernas.

Walks and tours Anne le Brun and Yannis Petrakis (ⓣ 28430 94725, ⓦ kastelas.com), run primarily Francophone botanical guided walks in the vicinity (from €15/half day), as well as mountain bike, trail bike and 4WD tours (from €75/day). There are also guided walks with donkeys (ⓣ 699 83 00 784, ⓦ mochlos-donkeys.net).

ACCOMMODATION

KAVOÚSI

Tholos Beach Taverna Halfway down the Thólos road, 1.5km from Kavoúsi ⓣ 28420 94785, ⓕ 28420 94810. There are several rooms places on the main road in Kavoúsi, but this modern block with simple, good-value a/c rooms (and wi-fi) offers peaceful nights, isolated in the middle of nowhere. Decent taverna food too. **€35**

MÓKHLOS

Though it's far busier than its isolated location would lead you to expect, you'll almost always be able to find a room in Mókhlos. The best approach if you arrive without a booking is to head for the harbour – the tavernas there act as agents for most of the cheaper rooms scattered around the back-streets.

Blue Sea Coast road, less than 1km east of the village ⓣ 28430 94237, ⓦ blueseamochlos.com. Sparkling a/c rooms and apartments with fridge, satellite TV and balcony overlooking the sea and small pool. The only problem is that the pool bar is a popular meeting place for locals, and music often goes on to the early hours (daily late July to mid-Aug, weekends rest of year). **€45**

To Kyma Beyond the harbour ⓣ 28430 94177, ⓔ soik @in.gr. New block of modern, good-value a/c studio rooms with kitchen, TV and balcony, just round the corner from the harbour. Ask at supermarket Anna, next door. **€35**

★ **Limenaria** On a rise overlooking the new harbour,

600m west of town ⓣ 28420 27837, ⓦ mochlos-crete .gr. A tranquil hideaway with attractive, fully equipped sea-view terrace apartments sleeping up to four; big balconies front and back allow you to appreciate the view. **€55**

Meltemi By the road as you enter the village ⓣ 28430 94200. Attractive studios with kitchenette and sea view from just above the village. The same owner has a couple of wonderful new apartments – built in 2011 – right on the harbour, with full, modern kitchens (including washing machine) and big balconies looking over the action. Information at *Taverna Bogazi*. Studio **€40**, apartment **€70**

Mochlos Set back from the waterfront in the heart of the village ⓣ 28430 94240, ⓔ hotel.mochlos@gmail .com. Exceptionally welcoming hotel with simple a/c rooms and studios with fridge and kitchenette. Some have sea views from the balcony, at extra cost. **€35**

Mochlos Mare Coast road 500m east of the village ⓣ 28430 94005, ⓦ mochlos-mare.com. Peaceful, well-equipped one- and two-bedroom apartments with kitchen for up to six people, set back from the road in the midst of the owner's lovingly tended kitchen garden. There's a separate lounging area above the sea. **€50**

Sofia On the harbour ⓣ 28430 94554, ⓔ sofia -mochlos@hotmail.com. This friendly hotel with simple balcony rooms with sea views, a/c, fridge and TV, is situated above a harbourfont taverna; they also rent studios and apartments nearby. Room **€40**, apartment **€55**

EATING AND DRINKING

MÓKHLOS

Food is excellent at almost all of Mókhlos' tavernas. Many places feature *achinosalata*, something of an acquired taste, made from the roe of the sea urchins that flourish in the clear, unpolluted water here (most people wear plastic shoes or flippers, sold at the local minimarkets, when they swim).

To Bogazi On the harbour ☎ 28430 94200. With an unbeatable seafront position, *To Bogazi* is run by a Greek-Swiss couple; the shortish menu, heavy on fish, includes interesting "specials" and some good vegetarian dishes. Live music Thurs & Sun evenings in summer. Daily 9am–late.

Le Grand Bleu Waterfront, on the west side of the village. There's little in the way of nightlife in Mókhlos, but

this quiet bar-café is a prime spot for a sundowner. Daily 5pm–late.

Mesostrati On the harbour ☎ 28430 94170. Traditional Cretan cuisine from family recipes, as well as fresh fish, served on a pretty seaside terrace; also good breakfasts. *Meze* €3–5, mixed *meze* €13. Daily 9am–late.

MYRSÍNI

Taverna Kathodon Immediately above the road in Myrsíni ☎ 28430 94766. A classic Cretan menu with everything from snails (€5) and octopus to *souvláki*, burgers and lamb chops, served on a terrace with stunning views across the coast – down to Mókhlos and out across the Gulf – and tremendous sunsets. Daily 10am–10pm.

Sitía and around

After the excesses of Mália or Áyios Nikólaos, arriving in SITÍA (Σητεία) can seem something of an anticlimax. But allow yourself to adjust to the more leisurely pace of life here and you may, like many other visitors before you, end up staying much longer than intended. An ideal base from which to visit the local attractions, Sitía hasn't entirely escaped the tourist boom; many of the visitors are French or Italian (as they are, in fact, throughout the far east of Crete), a legacy perhaps of the French troops who garrisoned the place under the Great Power protection at the end of the nineteenth century, and the Italians who occupied it during World War II.

The town is set on a hill tumbling down towards the western end of the picturesque **Bay of Sitía**. Its oldest sections, hanging steeply above the harbour, look east over the bay and the ribbon of new development along the coast. For visitors, life concentrates on the **waterfront**. A seafront promenade crowded with the outdoor tables of rival tavernas and cafés spreads in either direction from Platía Iróon Polytehníou, in the corner of the bay; northeast towards the port and ferry dock, south towards the town beach. The narrow streets behind the seafront feature the everyday scenes of a Cretan provincial town: villagers stocking up on news and necessities, and stores catering to their every conceivable need, from steel drums to wooden saddles, seed to pick-up trucks.

Brief history

This area was settled, as Éteia, in Classical times, but may be identified with the **Minoan** *se-to-i-ja* inscribed on clay tablets found locally. That there was a substantial Minoan presence hereabouts is borne out by the excavations at **Petrás**, the town's southern suburb, where a settlement dating to the early second millennium BC has been unearthed and where, in the later Neo-Palatial period, there was a fine town with sophisticated buildings and roads (for full details see ⓦ petras-excavations.gr). A couple of **Minoan villas** have also been excavated immediately south of the city (see p.153). Knowledge of the subsequent Greek and Roman settlements is sketchy, although a substantial chunk of **Hellenistic Sitía** has recently been discovered on the outskirts (see p.153). Apart from some tombs and fish tanks (now incorporated into an artificial pond on the harbour promenade), little tangible survives from the **Roman** town.

It was under the **Venetians** that the port really took off (they called it *La Sitia* – hence Lasíthi), as part of a conscious attempt to exploit the east of the island. For all their efforts, the area remained cut off by land from the rest of Crete and, although what was in effect a separate fiefdom developed here, it never amounted to a great deal. Perhaps the most significant event of this era was the birth of Vitzentzos Kornaros, author of the epic Cretan poem, the *Erotókritos*. More physical remains are few, due to earthquakes and the raids of **Barbarossa**. Where once there was a walled city, now you'll find only the barest remains of a fortress.

The beach

Sitía's **town beach** is surprisingly excellent; sandy, with beautifully clear water, and stretching far into the distance south of town. In summer the heat eventually seems to

2

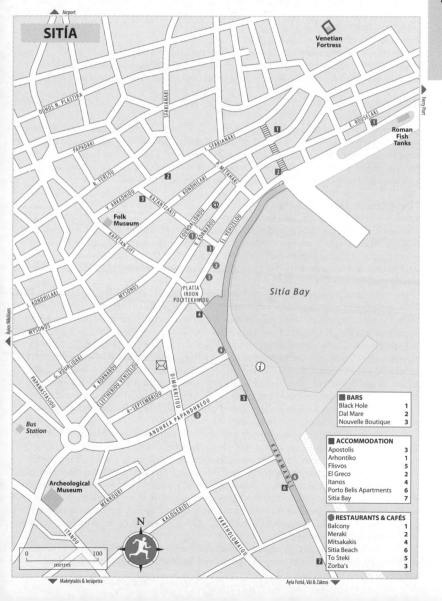

SITÍA

Airport

Venetian Fortress

Ferry Port

Roman Fish Tanks

Sitía Bay

ODHOS N. PLASTIRA

SFAKIANAKI

E. ROUSELAKI

I. SFAKIANAKI

PAPADAKI

R. FEGLOU

METAXAKI

V. ARKADHIOU

I. KONDHILAKI

KAZANTZAKIS

Folk Museum

FOUNDALIDHOU

V. KORNAROU

EL. VENIZELOU

KAPETAN SIFI

PLATÍA IROON POLYTEKHNÍOU

I. KONDHILAKI

MYSONOS

MYSONOS

G. VOURLIAKI

V. KORNAROU

ELEFTHERIOU VENIZELOU

PAPANASTASIOU

DIMOKRITOU

4-SEPTEMBRIOU

ANDRHREA PAPANDHREOU

KARAMANLI

Bus Station

Archeological Museum

MERKOURI

ITANOU

KALOGERIDI

VARTHOLOMAIOU

N

0   100
metres

Makriyialós & Ierápetra

Ayía Fotiá, Váï & Zákros

■ BARS	
Black Hole	1
Dal Mare	2
Nouvelle Boutique	3

■ ACCOMMODATION	
Apostolis	3
Arhontiko	1
Flisvos	5
El Greco	2
Itanos	4
Porto Belis Apartments	6
Sitia Bay	7

● RESTAURANTS & CAFÉS	
Balcony	1
Meraki	2
Mitsakakis	4
Sitia Beach	6
To Steki	5
Zorba's	3

draw half the town's population down here by late afternoon, but it's never unbearably crowded, and there's room to escape if you walk far enough along.

The Folk Museum
Kápetan Sífi 28 • Mon–Sat 10am–2pm • €2

The **Folk Museum** offers an entertaining look at traditional life, with displays of antique furniture, costumes, kitchenware and ceramics from the region, and above all textiles and embroidery. There's a working loom on which museum staff demonstrate; the finished items are on sale in the little shop.

Venetian fortress
On the hill above the harbour • Tues–Sun 9am–4pm • Free

The restored **Venetian fortress**, known as Kazarma (from Casa di Arma) dominates the town from its hilltop setting. Now used as an open-air venue for concerts, theatre, lectures and exhibitions, it doesn't offer a great deal to see, though the views are superb.

Roman fish tanks
Seafront, north of the centre

The seafront promenade north of the centre – heading towards the vast concrete ferry jetty – leads past the ruined remains of some **Roman fish tanks**: freshly caught fish were kept in these semicircular constructions until they were needed. The tanks have been incorporated into an artificial **pond** along the concrete promenade, and are used as a preening perch by the resident colony of swans, ducks and geese.

The Archeological Museum
400m south of the centre on the Ierápetra road • Tues–Sun 9.30am–4pm • €3

Eastern Crete is rich in ancient peak sanctuaries and Minoan villas or country houses. Many finds from these, as well as from the palace at Zákros and from excavations in and around Sitía itself, are gathered in Sitía's little-visited **Archeological Museum**, a modern building surrounded by construction and new development.

The museum's greatest treasure, the **Palékastro koúros**, is on display as you enter. This little male figure is an exquisitely delicate work dating from c.1500 BC, made from eight interlocking pieces of hippopotamus ivory; when complete it would have been decorated with a gold Minoan belt, bracelets and shoes. Note that the left leg is placed slightly forward, following the Egyptian convention for the portrayal of this form of statue. Left from here is the **main room**, where finds from the early Minoan cemetery at nearby Ayía Fotiá are displayed, as well as some fine stone vases from Mókhlos and its island neighbour, Psíra. There are also recent discoveries from Petrás, Sitía's southern suburb, where important buildings from the Minoan Neo-Palatial period have been unearthed. One large building there stored giant *píthoi* (earthenware jars), many of which are stationed around the museum.

The **Zákros** section includes a bronze saw and a winepress from a Minoan villa near the palace. Here too is a case full of rare **Linear A tablets**, discovered in the archives room at the palace, on which Minoan characters were delicately scratched into soft clay. Some show evidence of being burned by the fire that destroyed the palace; in fact, it was the fire that preserved them – as unbaked clay tablets they would have crumbled to dust. A nearby case illustrates the **kitchen**, the only one so far positively identified at any palace, featuring a superbly preserved terracotta grill, probably used for cooking some form of *souvláki* – a method used in the Greek world since pre-Mycenaean times and mentioned by Homer.

After the Hellenistic and Roman sections, don't miss the barnacle-encrusted tangle of **Roman pots** (probably from a wreck), preserved by placing it inside a fish tank of salinated water.

Hellenistic Sitía

2km east of town off the main coast road; a signed track (marked "Archeological Site") leads 100m to a farm building where you can park
• Open daylight hours • Free

The recently discovered remains of **Hellenistic Sitía**, dating from the third century BC and later, are substantial. Remains so far unearthed include easily identifiable ruins of dwellings, rooms and streets, and continuing excavations will no doubt add to these in the years ahead.

Minoan graveyard

Ayía Fotiá, about 4km east of town: follow signs at the eastern edge of the village • Open daylight hours • Free

In 1971, the largest **Minoan graveyard** yet found in Crete was excavated, close to the sea on the edge of the village of Ayía Fotiá. More than 250 chamber tombs from the early Pre-Palatial period were revealed; among the outstanding finds of vases, fish hooks, daggers and stone axes (now in the Sitía and Áyios Nikólaos archeological museums) were a number of lead amulets, which suggests that these early Minoans regarded lead as a precious metal, as well as silver.

Piskokéfalo Minoan villa

Well signed 2km south of town on the Ierápetra road • Open daylight hours • Free

Near the village of **Piskokéfalo**, the main road cuts straight through a **Minoan villa**. Dating from the late Neo-Palatial period (1550–1450 BC), it had two floors and is terraced into the hillside, with a well-preserved staircase giving access to an upper floor. The villa's view would have encompassed the river valley below the road, where its farmlands were probably located.

Zoú Minoan villa

6km south of Sitía • Unfenced • Free • From Piskokéfalo a dirt road is signed to the village of Zoú: it crosses a dry riverbed and then turns right (signed), eventually becoming asphalt as it winds up into the hills; the villa – not easily spotted and with no sign – lies on a high bank to the right of the road just before the village.

The **Minoan villa** at Zoú, dating from the late Neo-Palatial period (1550–1450 BC), was excavated by Nikolaos Platon, the archeologist who unearthed the palace at Zákros. This one is more a farmhouse – cultivating the land in the valley to the east – than simply a country dwelling, with rooms that appear to have been divided between those for domestic life and others for work and storage of farm equipment. A pottery kiln (perhaps used for making olive-oil containers) was discovered in one room, while two deep pits near the entrance probably stored grain.

ARRIVAL AND DEPARTURE
SITÍA AND AROUND

By plane Sitía Airport (☎ 28430 24424) lies immediately north of town. There's no public transport, but it's a taxi ride of just 5min (less than €10). Although it can cater for international flights, so far there's only a very occasional charter.

By bus The bus station (☎ 28430 22272; timetables on ⓦ bus -service-crete-ktel.com) is on the southwest fringe of the centre; head north along Odhós Venizélou to get into town.

Destinations Ay. Nikólaos (5 daily; 5.30am–5.30pm; 1hr 45min); Ierápetra (4 daily; 6.15am–7.15pm; 1hr 30min); Iráklio (5 daily; 5.30am–5.30pm; 3hr 15min); Káto Zákros (Mon, Tues & Fri 6am & 2.15pm; 1hr); Makriyialós (4 daily; 6.15am–7.15pm; 1hr); Palékastro (3 daily; 6am–2.15pm; 30min); Vái (2 daily; 11am & 2.15pm [4pm weekends]; 30min).

By ferry The ferry dock is 500m northeast of the centre. Just one ferry currently calls at Sitía, the *Prevelis* (☎ 28430

28555, ⓦ anek.gr). Check timetables on ⓦ openseas.gr or ⓦ ferries.gr.

Destinations The *Prevelis* departs Wed & Sat to Kássos (3hr), Kárpathos (5hr), Hálki (8hr) and Rhodes (10hr); Sun to Iráklio (3hr), Anáfi (7hr), Santoríni (9hr), Mílos (13hr) and Pireás (19hr).

Destinations Astra Airlines (☎ 2310 489392, ⓦ astra -airlines.gr) fly daily (except Wed) to Athens and 4 times weekly to Thessaloníki. Olympic (☎ 801 801 0101, ⓦ olympic air.com) fly daily in summer to Kássos, Kárpathos and Rhodes. Sky Express (☎ 2810 223 800, ⓦ skyexpress.gr) have flights Mon, Wed & Fri to Iráklio, Alexandhroúpoli and Préveza.

By car You're required to display a card to park anywhere in the centre on weekdays; cards can be purchased from kiosks and some shops. Most of the hotels on the beach road have off-street parking.

2

GETTING AROUND

Bike rental Scoot Bydoo, Karamánli 26 (☎ 698 100 2224, ⓦ scootbydoo.com) has excellent modern scooters (€25/day) and mountain bikes (€10/day).
Car rental Club Cars, Papandréou 3 (☎ 28430 25104; ⓦ clubcars.net); Petras, Papandréou 8 (☎ 28430 24849; ⓦ petras-rentals.gr).
Taxis There's a rank at the corner of the harbour by the *Hotel Itanos*, or call ☎ 28430 22700.

INFORMATION

Tourist office The municipal tourist office, on the seafront along the Beach Road (Mon–Fri 9.30am–2.30pm & 5–9pm, Sat 9.30am–2.30pm; ☎ 28430 28300, ⓦ sitia.gr) can supply accommodation lists, town maps and a free guide to the region that also describes some walking routes.
Tourist police Therisou 31 (summer daily 7.30am–2.30pm; ☎ 28430 24200).

Travel agents Agents for ferry and airline tickets are mostly on Kornárou, one street inland from the harbour. Try Dikta Travel, Kornárou 150, corner of Filellínon (☎ 28430 25080), or Sitian Holidays, Kornárou 83 (☎ 28430 28555, ⓦ sitianholidays.gr). They can also help with accommodation, but the seafront Porto Belis, Karamánli 34 (☎ 28430 22370, ⓦ portobelis-crete.gr) is better for that.

ACCOMMODATION

Except at the busiest times (principally the first two weeks of Aug), you should have no trouble in finding a **room**. Several old-fashioned places, generally quiet and good value, can be found in the older streets leading northwest up the hill from the waterfront; more modern hotels are on waterfront Karamánli.

Apostolis Kazantzákis 27 ☎ 28430 22993. Friendly rooms place that feels like a hangover from an older Crete; scrupulously clean a/c, en-suite rooms in an apartment block – effectively in the owners' apartment – sharing a huge balcony and a fridge and kitchen where coffee and basics are supplied. **€35**
★ **Arhontiko** Kondhiláki 16 ☎ 28430 28172. The pick of the budget places, in a lovely, little-modernized traditional house with a shady garden. Only one of the rooms is en suite, but they're spotless and attractive. **€30**
Flisvos Karamánli 4 ☎ 28430 27135, ⓦ flisvos-sitia .com. Small hotel fronting the sea at the start of the Beach Road. A/c rooms with TV, wi-fi and fridge face either the sea or a patio garden behind; those at the back are larger and more modern, and cost the same as a sea-view option. Breakfast included. **€60**
El Greco G. Arkadhíou 13 ☎ 28430 23133, ⓦ elgreco -sitia.gr. Small hotel in the upper town with an old-fashioned feel; en-suite, a/c balcony rooms have fridge,

wi-fi and TV, and a couple have sea views. They also offer studios and apartments sleeping up to five. **€45**
Itanos Platía Iróon Polytehníou ☎ 28430 22900, ⓦ itanoshotel.com. Smart hotel just off the town's main square. A/c balcony rooms mostly have good views, but be sure to check out a few as not all have been refurbished. Free wi-fi in reception area. Breakfast included. **€60**
Porto Belis Apartments Karamánli 34 ☎ 28430 22370, ⓦ portobelis-crete.gr. Studios and two-room apartments with kitchens for up to four people, plus some rooms. All are modern and well equipped, and some have sea-view balconies, though most overlook a small garden. Room **€42**, studio **€48**, apartment **€68**
★ **Sitia Bay** Trítis Septemvríou 8 ☎ 28430 24800, ⓦ sitiabay.com. Purpose-built apartment complex overlooking the town beach, with a large pool. Lovely modern studios and two-room apartments, all with sea-view balconies and fully equipped kitchens, plus a very warm welcome. Substantial discounts out of season. **€100**

EATING AND DRINKING

SITÍA

Balcony Foundalídhou 19, corner of Kazantzákis ☎ 28430 25084, ⓦ balcony-restaurant.com. Stylish restaurant on the upper floor of an elegant townhouse, with a menu that combines traditional Cretan dishes with Mexican- and Asian-influenced cuisine, usually to great effect; pricey, but worth it. Expect the likes of grilled goat's cheese with a sesame crust and fresh basil as a starter, with prawns and mushrooms with lemon-garlic saffron rice to follow; also home-made pasta and veggie dishes. Four-course menu for two, €32. Mon–Sat noon–3pm & 7–11pm.
★ **Meraki** Venizélou 151 ☎ 28430 23640. The first of a

group of fashionable *rakádhika* (like an ouzerí, but serving *raki*) to open on the seafront, and the best. You can order (by ticking items off on a sheet) from a substantial menu combining modern and traditional, but the best deal is go for a drink with *meze* (around €7), which will come with about five small dishes of whatever is fresh that day; not quite a meal, but you'll probably want another drink anyway, or you can order a few extras. The bulk wine from Toploú monastery is also excellent. Daily 9am–late.
Mitsakakis Karamánli 6, at 4-Septemvríou ☎ 28430 22377. Wonderful traditional *zaharoplastío* with a terrace facing the harbour, always busy with locals. Try their

2

KORNARIA FESTIVAL

Sitía's **Kornaria cultural festival**, from the beginning of July to mid-August, features concerts, dance and theatre by Greek and international performers. Many are held in the castle, and there are also "traditional feasts" staged in nearby villages; ask at the tourist office (see opposite) for details.

delicious *loukoumádhes* (dough fritters) with vanilla ice cream; they also have sandwiches and crêpes. Daily 8am–midnight.

Sitia Beach Karamánli 28 ☎28430 22104. Touristy-looking place that promotes itself as a pizzeria (pizzas €7–13) but also has pasta and good Greek dishes, served on a terrace overlooking the town beach. Decent barrel wine, and reasonably priced bottles. Daily 11am–midnight.

To Steki Papandréou 10 ☎28430 223857. Traditional place popular with locals for its good-value *souvláki*, grills and *mezédhes*; not the prettiest setting, though, with tables on the grassy centre-strip of the road. Daily noon–11pm.

Zorba's Venizélou 56 ☎28430 22689. Occupying the prime position in the corner of the harbour, this is the biggest and busiest place on the seafront, with far more authentic food than you might expect from the touristy appearance. Daily 11am–late.

PISKOKÉFALO

I Plateia Main square, Piskokéfalo ☎28430 22644. An excellent taverna whose specialities include *kolokithóanthi* (stuffed courgette flowers), along with a good variety of *meze* and traditional baked dishes. Sit on the terrace and watch village life go by. Daily noon–11pm.

NIGHTLIFE

Sitía's nightlife, mostly conducted at an easy pace, centres around **café-bars** concentrated at the north end of Venizélou, towards the Roman fish tanks.

Black Hole Karaveláki 7, on the continuation of Venizélou ☎28430 20422. A meeting place for Sitía's alternative crowd, this is a rock music bar in an old harbour building with exposed stone walls. Loud rock and occasional live performances as the action moves inside from around 10.30pm. Daily 6pm–early hours.

Dal Mare Venizélou 193 ☎28430 23640. Big café-bar with three separate seaside terraces, open most of the day

and night. By day there's coffee, snacks – burgers, club sandwiches – and sofas for lounging, and at night there's cocktails and music. Daily 9am–early hours.

Nouvelle Boutique Venizélou 161 ☎28430 28758. One of the liveliest bars in town, with a big dancefloor and a terrace. Mainstream music, lurid pink decor and a young crowd. Daily 9am–early hours.

DIRECTORY

Banks and exchange There's a bank with ATM at the bottom of Kápetan Sífi, facing Platía Iróon Polytechníou, and others inland along Venizélou.

Books and newspapers The minimarket at Karamánli 22, corner Kaloyerídhi, stocks foreign newspapers and paperbacks.

Hospital Off the Áyios Nikólaos road on the town's western edge (☎28433 40100).

Internet Java, Kornárou 113.

Market A colourful weekly market (Tues 7am–2pm) takes place along Odhós Itanou near the archeological museum.

Post office Dhimókritou 8 (Mon–Fri 7.30am–2pm).

The northeast

Crete's northeast corner is among its most tempting destinations, at least if it's beaches and isolation you're after. You won't find much solitude at **Vái beach** which, with its famous grove of palm trees and silvery sands, features alongside Knossós, the Lasíthi plateau and the Samariá Gorge on almost every Cretan travel agent's list of excursions. But it remains a beautiful spot, and there are plenty of escapes nearby. If you're planning to stay at this end of the island, **Palékastro** is a lovely small town within easy reach of many less-known beaches, as well as some of Crete's best windsurfing. There are also small **archeological sites** at Ítanos and Palékastro, as well as the ancient monastery of **Touploú**, one of the most revered on the island.

Leaving Sitía, the road runs along the coast for about 10km, turning inland by the extraordinarily ugly *Dionysos Village* holiday complex. Here you start to climb into deserted, gently hilly country, the slopes covered in thyme, heather and sage with the occasional cluster of strategically sited beehives. In summer, the sweet-scented, deep-violet thyme flowers prove an irresistible attraction for the bees that feed on them almost exclusively, thus creating the much-sought-after **thimarísio** (thyme honey).

The Monastery of Toploú

Not long after the main road leaves the coast a side road switchbacks steeply up to the left, signed to Vái and the Monastery of Toploú • Daily: April–Sept 9am–1pm & 2–6pm; Oct–March closes 4pm • €3

Standing defiant in a landscape that is empty, save for a line of wind turbines along the ridge behind, the **Monastery of Toploú** (Τοπλού) looks more like a fortress than a religious institution. Which is appropriate: the name Toploú is Turkish for "with a cannon", a reference to a giant device with which the monks used to defend themselves and uphold the Cretan monastic traditions of resistance to invaders. Highlights of the monastery's adventures include being sacked by pirates and destroyed in 1498; captured by the Turks in the 1821 rebellion, when twelve monks were hanged from the gate as an example; and serving as a place of shelter for the resistance in World War II. The monastery is also reputed to be incredibly wealthy – it owns most of the northeastern corner of the island – which is no doubt how they can afford the extensive restorations that render the place so spotless.Forbidding exterior and grim history notwithstanding, Toploú is startlingly beautiful within. Stairways lead up from the flower-decked, cloister-like **courtyard** to arcaded walkways, off which lie the cells. The blue-robed monks stay out of the way of visitors as far as possible, and in quieter periods their cells and refectory (with spectacular modern frescoes) are left discreetly on view. In the **church** is one of the masterpieces of Cretan art, the eighteenth-century **icon** *Lord Thou Art Great* by Ioannis Kornaros. This marvellously intricate work incorporates 61 small scenes full of detail, each illustrating, and labelled with, a phrase from the Orthodox prayer that begins with this phrase. There's a small **museum**, too, and a shop where you can buy expensive reproductions of the famous icon, as well as postcards, books and the monastery's own wine and olive oil.

As you leave the church, take a look at the **inscription** set into the exterior wall. It records an arbitration by Magnesia, a city in Asia Minor, dating from the second century BC, concerning a territorial dispute between nearby Ítanos and Ierápytna (modern Ierápetra). At this time, when the Romans held sway over Crete, these deadly rivals clashed constantly, and finally Rome, unable to placate the two, called in the Magnesians to act as honest brokers. The inscription records part of their judgement (in favour of Ítanos) and was placed in the monastery wall at the suggestion of the English traveller and antiquarian Robert Pashley, who found it being used as a gravestone in 1834.

Beyond Toploú, the road descends towards Vái through the same arid, rock-strewn landscape as before. There's a chance here that you could spot the rare **Eleonora's falcon**, which breeds on the Dionysádes islands to the north – Toploú and Cape Sídheros (a closed military zone) are its regular hunting grounds.

Vái

The beach at **VÁI** (Βάι), famous above all for its **palm trees**, makes for a thoroughly secular contrast to the spiritual tranquillity of Toploú – and the sudden appearance of what is claimed to be Europe's only indigenous wild date-palm grove (the palms here are a local species, present on the island for millennia) is indeed an exotic surprise. As you lie on the fine sand in the early morning, especially in early spring or late autumn, you could almost imagine yourself to be on a Caribbean island.

In summer, however, the beach fills to overflowing as **buses** – public ones from Sitía and tours from all over the island – pour into the **car park** (€2.50), and cars unable to squeeze in line the access road for hundreds of metres. On the beach itself, only the boardwalks guarantee a route through the mass of baking bodies. Pricey sun-loungers are available and a watersports centre offers waterskiing, ringos and other high-speed rides. There's a café and expensive taverna, and you'll pay again to have a shower or use the toilet. That said, for a couple of hours at each end of the day, you should be able to enjoy Vái the way it ought to be. Alternatively, avoid the high season if you can. For a bit more peace you can climb the steps cut into the rock behind the taverna to the less shaded cove to the south or, with rather more difficulty, clamber over the rocks to the north.

Ítanos

The sand may not be as good as at Vái, but the relative emptiness of the three small beaches at **ÍTANOS** ('Ítανος), 1.5km north of the turning to Vái, makes them far more enjoyable. There's still the odd palm tree scattered around here, and you can explore the remains of the **ancient city** too; there are no facilities of any sort, though.

Ancient Ítanos

Scattered over the hill above the beach • Free

Inhabited from Minoan times, **ancient Ítanos** became important later, flourishing through the Classical Greek and Roman eras, when it vied with Ierápytna (modern Ierápetra) for control of eastern Crete. One twenty-year squabble between these two led to the arbitration of Magnesia in 132 BC, part of the stone record of which is preserved at Toploú Monastery (see opposite). The settlement then remained prosperous until the medieval Byzantine era, when it was destroyed, most likely by Saracen pirates. All sorts of messy ruins strewn with potsherds survive beneath the twin acropoli, but little which retains any shape. You might be able to make out two early **basilicas**, as well as the beautifully cut lower courses of a **Hellenistic wall** on the western hill.

Cape Sídheros

The wilderness of **CAPE SÍDHEROS** (Σίδερος), Crete's northeastern tip, lies to the north of Ítanos. At the end there's a naval base, strictly off-limits and no photography permitted, but you can drive quite a way up the excellent asphalted road towards it, across a wild and craggy peninsula where there are coves with tempting beaches and some likely places to snorkel. This area, owned by the Toploú monastery, is under threat from international developers who – with the consent of the monks and the Greek government – drew up plans for a mammoth 7000-bed tourist "village" with casinos, yacht harbour, golf courses and luxury hotels. Despite a chorus of protest from environmental and political groups, construction work was supposed to start in 2009. This was finally stalled when the Greek Supreme Court intervened at the eleventh hour, putting a stop to the project. In September 2012, however, the government used emergency powers introduced as a result of the financial crisis to give fast-track approval to a slightly reduced development plan, and at the time of writing the project appeared set to go ahead, despite fierce local opposition.

Palékastro and around

A substantial village with easy access to numerous excellent beaches, and with plenty of accommodation both in town and in the surrounding area, **PALÉKASTRO** (Παλαίκαστρο) makes an excellent, quiet base. There are several good tavernas and just about every other facility you might need, but just one real sight, an interesting little **folk museum** (Tues & Thurs–Sun 9am–5pm; €2), housed in a restored traditional cottage. Inside, rooms are decorated with period furnishings, and there are the usual displays of tools and agricultural equipment.

Angathiá

The hamlet of **ANGATHIÁ** (Ανκαθιά), barely ten minutes' walk east of Palékastro, is smaller and even quieter than its neighbour. There are good rooms and tavernas here, but little else – though it is convenient for Hióna Beach, the Palékastro archeological site and the Petsofás peak sanctuary.

Ancient Palékastro

Close to Hióna Beach, about 20min walk from Palékastro village • Usually unlocked in daylight hours • Free

For archeologists the Minoan site of **Palékastro** (aka Roussólakkos) is a very significant excavation, the largest Minoan town yet discovered and a rich source of information about everyday Minoan life. It may seem disappointing for the casual visitor when compared with the spectacular palace sites elsewhere on the island, but there's still plenty to see (though signage could be improved), and continuing excavation means that new finds are still coming to light. Recent explorations on the site's northern side, for example, have revealed a road leading from the town to the nearby harbour (no trace of which has yet been found), while beneath the olive groves to the south and west more of the Minoan town lies waiting to be revealed – geophysical surveys have indicated the existence of a very large building, maybe a palace.

Set on a fertile agricultural plain on a bay offering harbourage beneath the protection of the high, flat-topped bluff of Kastrí, this is an obvious place to settle – and indeed the area was extensively inhabited both before and after the Minoan era. Water was available too; the site is dotted with deep wells, so superbly constructed that they still contain water today. **Building 5**, now under cover to protect its plaster walls, lies at the heart of a complex of streets, dwellings and small squares around the harbour road. Here archeologists discovered the **Palékastro koúros** (see p.152), a stunning ivory statuette now in the Sitía museum. To the south, the limestone-paved "main street" was the town's principal artery; around it a number of impressive dwellings with stone walls and column bases have been revealed, and the fine, Marine-style vases found in the

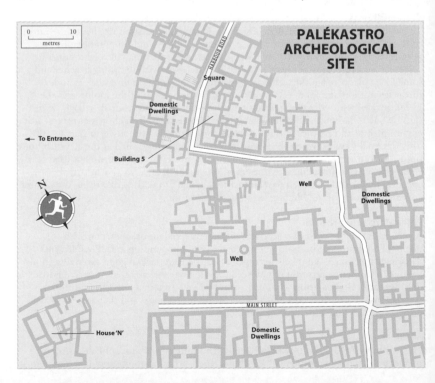

ruins of some of them are evidence of the status and wealth of the owners. House N, at the site's western end, is dated to the late Neo-Palatial period, and excavations revealed horns of consecration and double-axe stands that had fallen from a shrine room on an upper floor. The room at the rear produced hundreds of cups as well as jars and cooking pots, suggesting that it may have been some form of communal eating club, or perhaps an early taverna.

Hióna Beach

A good stretch of EU blue-flagged pebble and sand, **HIÓNA (Χιώνα)** is the closest beach to Palékastro, less than 2km east, or fifteen minutes' walk beyond Angathiá. Consequently it's often relatively busy, though still far from crowded. A couple of the region's finest tavernas overlook the beach (see p.162), and to the south a rough track follows the coast past more lovely little beaches, where for most of the year you can easily claim a cove to yourself.

Petsofás peak sanctuary

The summit of **PETSOFÁS (Πετσοφάς)** gives you a great overview of the ancient Minoan town of Palékastro, and was itself the site of a Minoan **peak sanctuary**. Many small clay figurines were found here, representing the people who made offerings at the sanctuary, and these have provided a great deal of information about the dress and hairstyles of the period. Today there's not a great deal to see, but it's an enjoyable hike of some 3km on a path signed either off the road south of Angathiá or from the coastal path south of Hióna.

Koureménos Beach

KOUREMÉNOS BEACH (Κουρεμένος), north of Hióna beyond the flat-topped hill of Kastrí, is one of Crete's top **windsurfing** spots. Not surprisingly, it can be windy (a funnel effect creates ideal windsurfing conditions; Hióna is far more sheltered), but it's a fine, long sand-and-pebble beach, with several tavernas and rooms places – even a bar – directly behind. There's also quite a community of camper vans in summer, and an excellent windsurf centre, too. You can get to Koureménos on a sandy track from Hióna, but if you're starting from Palékastro head out on the Vái road and follow the signs; it's barely a thirty-minute walk.

Maridháti Beach

The most easily accessible of the beaches north of Koureménos, off the Vái road, is **MARIDHÁTI (Μαριδάτη)**, about 1km down a signed track. Mostly pebbly, with a few trees for shade, it's a tranquil spot, very sheltered, and little enough visited that at least part of the beach is usually nudist. There's a taverna halfway down the access track.

ARRIVAL AND DEPARTURE   THE NORTHEAST

By bus There are buses from Sitía to Vái via Toploú (2 daily; 11am & 2.15pm [4pm weekends]; return at 11.30am & 4.15pm [4.30pm weekends]) and to Palékastro (3 daily; 6am–2.15pm; 45min; on Mon, Tues & Fri the first and last of these continue to Zákros).

By car Watch where you park in Palékastro – they give tickets for parking around the main square.

INFORMATION AND ACTIVITIES

PALÉKASTRO

Facilities Almost everything you might need in Palékastro is gathered around or close to the main square; an ATM, several minimarkets, two bakeries (just off the square on the Vái road) and a laundry.

Bike and scooter rental Moto Kastri (☎ 28430 61477), on the eastern edge of Palékastro along the Vái road.

Internet Many places have wi-fi; there's internet access at the *Hotel Hellas*.

Newspapers and souvenirs Art et Lumiere (daily 9am–10.30pm), not far from the square on the road signed to Zákros and Hióna, sells high-class souvenirs, the arty photos of co-owner Manolis Tsantakis, books and foreign papers.

2

Tourist information Palékastro's tourist office had closed at the time of writing, but a number of locally run websites have details of attractions and accommodation: check out wpalaikastro.com, weastcrete-holidays.gr and wwww.eastern.cretefamilyhotels.com.

KOUREMÉNOS

Windsurfing Freak (t697 92 53 861, wfreak-surf.com), an excellent if pricey windsurf centre at Koureménos Beach, rents high-quality equipment for all levels by the hour (€40), day (€100) or week (€250) and offers lessons (from €60) and other activities.

ACCOMMODATION

As well as plenty of **rooms** in Palékastro itself (you'll see signs throughout the village), there are many apartment complexes in the surrounding countryside and at the nearby beaches. July and August get very busy here, so advance booking is advisable. See also wpalaikastro.com, weastcrete-holidays.gr and wwww.eastern.cretefamilyhotels.com.

VÁI

Metohi Vai Village On the Palékastro road about 15min walk from the beach t28430 61071, wmetohi -vai.gr. Former shepherds' shelters, owned by the Monastery of Toploú, have been converted into well-furnished, traditional-style apartments, which retain many original features including fireplaces and wooden beams. Rooms come with a/c, fridge, cooker and TV; there's an excellent garden taverna attached. €55

PALÉKASTRO

Hellas On the main square t28430 61240, wpalaikastro.com/hotelhellas. Simple a/c rooms come with balcony, TV, wi-fi and fridge; a little impersonal, but could hardly be closer to the action and there's a good taverna downstairs. €40

House Margot Set back from the Sitía road on the edge of the village t28430 61277, wpalekastro.gr. Family-run accommodation in a garden setting, with en-suite, a/c balcony rooms with fridges and wi-fi. Clean, friendly and good value. €35

Ostria Outskirts of the village on the Vái road t28430 61022, wostria-itanos.gr. An incongruously modern, brightly furnished hotel in a garden setting. The tile-floored rooms have a/c, wi-fi, fridge and balcony. €45

HIÓNA

Marina Village Off the Hióna Beach road, about 600m from Hióna, 800m from Koureménos t28430 61284, wmarinavillage.gr. A peaceful haven with well-furnished,

a/c balcony rooms, surrounded by olive groves and a garden of bougainvillea and banana plants, plus pool and tennis court. They also have a tiny house (for up to four people) right by Hióna Beach. Buffet breakfast included. €64

KOUREMÉNOS

Grandes Apartments Koureménos Beach t28430 61496, wgrandes.gr. Small group of simple a/c apartments with attractive terraces, right behind the beach. Each can sleep up to four, with bedroom, sitting area with sofabeds, and kitchen. There's a taverna out front. €45

Kouremenos Beach Apartments Koureménos Beach t28430 56825, wkouremenosbeach.gr. A couple of small studios for two in the olive groves immediately behind the beach, as well as some larger apartments for up to six people, all with a/c, TV and fridge, the larger ones with separate kitchen. Studio €40, apartment €45

★ **Kouremenos Villas/Panorama Apartments** On the hillside beyond Koureménos Beach t28430 61370, wpalaikastro.com/kouremenos_apts. A glorious setting with great views over beach and countryside, and an exceptionally friendly welcome, make this place special; very comfortable apartments with modern kitchen, a/c, satellite TV, and a pool. €61

Porto Heli apartments Inland from the Vái road, 1km from Palékastro, 450m from Koureménos t28430 61275, wporto-heli.eu. Two-room apartments in a tranquil garden setting (no. 5, with sea view, is a peach) with a/c, TV and well-equipped kitchens, sleeping up to five. €50

EATING AND DRINKING

PALÉKASTRO

Hellas On the main square t28430 61455. A traditional taverna on the terrace beneath the hotel, in the heart of the village, serving Greek and Cretan dishes made from locally sourced ingredients; rabbit with garlic €8.50. Daily 10am–late.

Mythos On the main square t28430 61243. This friendly, family-run taverna serves good traditional food on a streetside terrace, with meat, fish and plenty of

vegetarian options. Friendly service and economical prices. Daily 10am–midnight.

Sticky Minds On the Zákros road, 50m from the square t28430 61528. As wild as Palékastro's nightlife gets – a café-bar with a classic 60s and 70s rock soundtrack and a courtyard shaded by mulberry trees. Daily 4pm–early hours.

ANGATHIÁ

Taverna Vaios Up the hill from the bridge leading into

the village, on the right ☎ 28430 61043. A very popular place (you may need to book in high season), with home-cooked traditional food and charcoal-grilled meats (from €5.50) served on a large roadside terrace. Daily 6pm–midnight.

HIÓNA

Hiona Hióna Beach ☎ 28430 61228. Stunningly beautiful spot on a promontory at the northern end of the beach, a touch more formal than anywhere else in the area and a little pricier, but worth it. Fresh fish and seafood are the specialities; try the *kakaviá* traditional fish stew (€25 for

two). Often booked up in season. Daily noon–midnight. **Kakavia** Hióna Beach ☎ 28430 61227. A less glamorous setting than nearby *Hiona*, but locals reckon that the fish here is more expertly cooked. It's also marginally less expensive, and more likely to have a table. Daily noon–midnight.

KOUREMÉNOS

To Votsalo Koureménos Beach ☎ 28430 61282. The pick of several tavernas behind the beach, *Votsalo* serves good Cretan dishes, fish and grills on a large terrace facing the sea, shaded by tamarisk trees. Daily 9am–late.

Zákros and around

South of Palékastro, a winding road offers a beautiful drive through countryside where the soil is a strange pinkish-purple colour, as if indelibly stained with grape juice (although actually it's olives which grow around here). The few hamlets you pass along the way are so tiny that they make **Áno Zákros** seem positively urban when finally you get there. This is the point where you turn off for **Káto Zákros**, the tiny seaside village that's home to the magnificent **Minoan palace of Zákros**, either walking down the gorge or by a spectacular cliff road.

Hokhlakiés gorge

For a fine **gorge walk**, make a stop at tiny **HOKHLAKIÉS (Χοχλακιές)**, halfway between Palékastro and Áno Zákros, from where you can follow a well-signed route through the gorge to Karoúbes Bay and beach, 3km below. From the bottom you can either return up the gorge or strike out along the coast in either direction; north to Palékastro, south to Káto Zákros, each about 6km further. For the one-way walk, you could get dropped at Hokhlakiés by the early morning Zákros bus (Mon, Tues and Fri only); drivers in small cars (only a small car will squeeze through the village streets) can follow a track 200m from the main road to a parking place at the start of the trail.

Áno Zákros

A slow-moving little country town, **ÁNO ZÁKROS (Άνω Ζάκρος)** – "Upper" Zákros – boasts three or four tavernas around its central square which, throughout the summer at weekends, host numerous wedding feasts accompanied by dancing to *bouzoúki* and *lyra*; should you arrive then, you'll most likely have a glass of wine thrust into your hand by one of the multitude of smartly dressed revellers filling the square. The little trade these establishments see the rest of the time, however, is almost exclusively passing through, since the far more obvious attractions of Káto ("Lower") Zákros and the celebrated palace are on the coast 8km further southeast.

Locally, Áno Zákros enjoys a certain fame for the numerous **springs** that feed the lush vegetation hereabouts and which were also an attraction for the Minoans. If you follow the sign up to the right as you come into the town, or simply climb the hill from the centre, you'll reach a little **chapel** from where, in five minutes' walk, a path leads beside the stream to its source and some shady picnic spots. Information on how to get to it or to reach the start of the "Gorge of the Dead" walk (see below) is available from the town's small central hotel, the *Zakros*.

The Gorge of the Dead

There are plenty of ways to get to Káto Zákros, but perhaps the most satisfying is to walk, in about two hours altogether, via a beautiful ravine known as the **Gorge of the Dead** (but just as likely to be signed "Zákros Gorge"). This path is also the final stage of the E4 trans-European footpath, so it's pretty well marked, at least once you get out of Áno Zákros. The easiest way to get on to it is to follow the signs from the south end of the village, opposite the *Napoleon* taverna. Alternatively there's a parking place beside the road about halfway to Káto Zákros, from where a steep path plunges down into the gorge, cutting off half the distance but still giving you the most spectacular portion of the hike.

Leaving from Áno Zákros, the first half-hour or so is through olive groves and lovingly tended smallholdings, gradually becoming lonelier and wilder as the valley closes in. The trail for the most part is easy to follow beside the stream bed, marked by the usual red waymarks and the occasional signpost in case of confusion. It's a solitary but magnificent walk, brightened especially in spring by plenty of plant life. High in the cliff walls you'll see the mouths of **caves**: it is these, used as tombs in Minoan times and earlier, which give the ravine its name. At the bottom you join a dirt road, which runs through groves of bananas and olives past the palace and into Káto Zákros.

Káto Zákros

From the first spectacular view as you approach along the cliff-top road, **KÁTO ZÁKROS** (Κάτω Ζάκρος) – "Lower" Zákros – is a delight. There's a pebbly sand beach, half a dozen waterfront tavernas and café-bars, and a few places offering rooms and apartments; along with a tiny harbour with a few fishing boats, this is about all the place amounts to. It's best to bring cash and anything else you might need: there's a cardphone kiosk on the seafront and they'll change money and offer local information in the tavernas, but there's no shop, or anything else much. If it's laidback tranquillity you're after, you've come to the right place.

The Palace of Zákros

Daily: April–Oct 8am–5pm; Nov–March 8.30am–3pm • €3

Though the **Palace of Zákros** is small, it is full of interest, and can match any of the more important Minoan centres for quality of construction and materials. It's also much easier to understand than many of the other Minoan sites: here, the remains are of one palace only, dating from between 1600 and 1450 BC. Although there is an earlier settlement at a lower level, it is unlikely ever to be excavated – mainly because this end of the island is gradually sinking. The water table is already almost at the palace level, and anything deeper would be thoroughly submerged. Even the exposed parts of the palace are marshy and often waterlogged: there are terrapins living in the green water in the cistern. When it's really wet, you can keep your feet dry and get an excellent view of the overall plan of the palace by climbing the streets of one of Zákros's unique features; the **town** – a place very like Gourniá (see p.143) – that occupied the hill above it.

The destruction of the palace appears to have been very violent, with only enough time for the inhabitants to abandon it, taking almost nothing with them. This contributed to the enormous number of artefacts found here, but more importantly the nature of the destruction, in which the palace was flattened and burned, is an

EXCAVATING ZÁKROS

The valley behind Káto Zákros was explored by a British archeologist, **David Hogarth**, at much the same time as the other great Cretan palaces were being discovered, around the turn of the century. But Hogarth gave up the search, having unearthed only a couple of Minoan houses, and it was not until the 1960s that new explorations were begun by a Cretan archeologist, **Nikolaos Platon**. Platon found the palace almost immediately, just metres from where Hogarth's trenches ended. The Palace of Zákros thus benefited from modern techniques in its excavation and, having been forgotten even locally, it was never looted. As a result, the site yielded an enormous quantity of treasures and everyday items, including a religious treasury full of stone vases and ritual vessels, and storerooms with their giant *píthoi* still in place.

important prop in the theory that it was the explosion of Thíra (see p.330) that ended the Minoan civilization. Large lumps of **pumice** found among the ruins are supposed to have been swept there by the tidal wave that followed the eruption. However, many archeologists take issue with this hypothesis and question both its chronological accuracy and the type of destruction, seeing the palace's demise as more consistent with human than natural causes.

The harbour road

The **site entrance** is on the south side, but the following description starts on the east, where a paved road came into the palace, leading directly towards the main gateway. The **harbour**, now lost beneath the sea, was the chief reason why a palace existed here at all; this must have been a significant port, the first landfall on Crete for trade from Egypt, the Nile Delta and the Middle East. Among the ruins were found ingots of copper imported from Cyprus, elephant tusks from Syria, and gold and precious materials from Egypt.

Before entering the palace, the harbour road passed various dwellings on each side as well as a **foundry** dating from the Old Palace period; the remains stand beneath a

PALACE OF ZÁKROS

N

Upper Town

Magazines

Portico

Central Shrine

Light Well

Archives Room

Latrine

Dye House

Kitchen

Storerooms

HARBOUR ROAD

Bathroom

Altar Base

Courtyard

Main Gate

Foundry

Entry to West Wing

Queen's Megaron

Treasury

Lustral Basin

Banquet Hall

Central Court

Ceremonial Hall

Light Well

Workshop

Cistern

Well

Workshops

Well

Portico

King's Megaron

Royal Apartments

To Entrance

0   25
metres

protective canopy on the left. The road (part of which has been reconstructed) then curves round into the town, passing the palace entrance on the left.

The Central Court

As you enter the **palace**, the **main gate** leads to a stepped ramp, followed by a **courtyard** that may have served as a meeting place between the palace hierarchy and the townspeople. Here, in the northeast corner beneath another canopy, is a **bathroom** where visitors to the palace may have been required to wash or purify themselves before proceeding. To the west of the courtyard lies the main or **Central Court**, a little over 30m by 12m, or about a third the size of that at Knossós. Crossing the north edge of the court, you come to an **altar base**, with the lower courses of the west-wing wall in grey ashlar stone beyond.

The west wing

The **west wing** (actually the northwest, as Zákros is not truly aligned north–south), entered between two pillars, is where, as usual, the chief ceremonial and ritual rooms were located. A **reception room** leads into a colonnaded **light well**, the hallmark of Minoan architecture. The light well's black stone crazy paving survives, as do the pillar bases and a drain in the northwest corner. It was here that the excavators unearthed what was arguably Zákros's single most important find: the **Peak Sanctuary Rhyton**, a carved stone vase depicting a peak sanctuary with wild goats, from which valuable information about Minoan religion was gleaned. The light well illuminated the **Ceremonial Hall**, beyond which lay the **Banqueting Hall**, originally a lavish room with frescoed walls and an elaborate floor. Platon gave the room this name because of the large number of cups and drinking vessels discovered scattered about the floor.

At the heart of a complex of rooms behind the Banqueting Hall is the **Central Shrine** (with a canopy), which contains a ledge and niche, similar to the shrine at Gourniá, where idols would have been placed. Nearby is the **lustral basin**, necessary for purification before entering the shrine. Here, too, was the **Treasury** – probably the most important discovery from the excavators' viewpoint as it is the only one so far positively identified. In a number of box-like compartments (which have been partially restored), almost a hundred fine stone jars and libation vessels were discovered, including the exquisite rock-crystal rhyton with its delicate crystal bead handle and collar – found crushed into more than three hundred fragments – that the Iráklio Archeological Museum is so proud of.

Next to the Treasury, in the **Palace Archive**, hundreds of Linear A record tablets had been stored in wooden chests. Sadly, only a handful of the top layers survived the centuries of rain and flooding; the rest had solidified into a mass of clay, depriving the archeologists of potentially priceless clues in their attempts at deciphering the script. On the opposite side of the treasury is a **workshop** where pieces of raw marble and steatite were found. The remaining stone slabs most likely supported a craftsman's workbench. More workshops and storerooms lay to the west of the shrine – one of these has been identified as a **dye-house** – and a **lavatory** with a cesspit outside the wall was found nearby. Further west, beyond the palace confines, new excavations are still going on.

The kitchen and south wing workshops

On the north side of the Central Court was the palace **kitchen**, the first to be positively identified at any of the palaces. Bones, cooking pots and utensils were found strewn around the floor both here and in the storeroom or pantry next door. The south wing was devoted to **workshops**: for smiths, lapidaries, potters and even, according to Platon, perfume-makers – possibly a borrowing from Egypt. The **well** that serviced this area still flows with drinkable water, and an offering cup was found close by, containing olives preserved by the waters. Platon and his team devoured the 3500-year-old olives, which shrivelled upon contact with the air, and said that they tasted as fresh as those in the nearby tavernas.

2

Royal apartments

Two large rooms regarded as **royal apartments** flank the east side of the Central Court behind a portico. The larger of the two, to the south, is called the King's Room and the smaller is described as that of the queen. However, one of these may have been the throne room, and there would have been elaborate rooms on the upper floor, possibly with verandas overlooking the courtyard below where the rulers may have lived. Next to a light well in the eastern wall of the King's Room lay the colonnaded **Cistern Hall**, with eight steps leading down to water contained in a plaster-lined basin, which may have served as a royal aquarium or even a swimming pool (if so, the only one known). It is ingeniously designed to maintain the water at a constant level, with the excess draining into the well to the south, which, being outside the palace wall, was probably used by the townsfolk. The water from the spring was, as at Knossós, piped throughout the palace, and traces of the pipework can still be seen.

Residential areas

Beyond the royal apartments lay other **residential areas**, though much has been destroyed by centuries of ploughing combined with frequent waterlogging of the land here. In the steep **upper town** more survives and, close to the perimeter fence, a **narrow street** running east to west passes an impressive doorway and gives you some idea of how the town may have looked when twin-storey buildings overlooked these narrow thoroughfares. Quite a few grindstones found in the excavations are to be seen here, and nearby there's also a charming **stone bench**, now exposed, which would have looked into a light well. It's not hard to imagine someone sitting here, enjoying the cool shade of a summer evening. Near to the bench, there's a well-preserved stairway climbing tantalizingly a couple of metres towards the now disappeared second storey. Both the stairway and the bench are close to the perimeter fence on the eastern (or seaward) side of the upper town.

ARRIVAL AND INFORMATION

ZÁKROS AND AROUND

By bus Buses run from Sitía to Káto Zákros via Palékastro and Áno Zákros (Mon, Tues & Fri 6am & 2.15pm; return journeys at 7am & 3.30pm).

On foot The gorge walk between Áno and Káto Zákros (see p.162), about 2hr each way, is just the start of the local hiking possibilities: the owners of *Stella's* (see below) have waymarked several other 3–4hr walks in the surrounding

hills; there's a map at the entrance to the apartments. A good map to bring if you're thinking of doing a lot of walking is the *Anavasi* 1:25,000 Zákros–Vái map, widely available from bookshops on Crete.

Tourist information *Taverna Akrogiali* (see below) is a handy source of local information, and acts as agent for a number of rooms places nearby.

ACCOMMODATION AND EATING

Although there are several places to eat in **Áno Zákros** – handy if you're just passing through on the road – and some cheap, basic rooms, the quality of accommodation and the setting of the tavernas is infinitely better down on the coast at **Káto Zákros**. You'll pass a number of accommodation options on the way down, some perched high above the coast with spectacular views; in the village there are older rooms places right by the water and more modern apartments scattered inland on the track that heads past the palace. If you have trouble finding somewhere – August can be very busy – try at the various waterfront tavernas, especially *Akrogiali*, which act as agents for many of the local places, or check out ⓦ eastcrete-holidays.gr.

★ **Akrogiali** End of the beach road ☎ 28430 26893, ⓦ kato-zakros.gr. The last of the places on the waterfront, with a particularly attractive waterfront terrace away from the road. Excellent food and helpful management. Daily 9am–late.

Coral & Athina On the rise immediately beyond Taverna Akrogiali ☎ 28430 26893, ⓦ kato-zakros.gr. Rooms right above the beach, with great sea views from

large communal terraces; clean and simply furnished, with a/c, fridge and TV. Ask at the taverna. **€45**

★ **Stella's Traditional Apartments** About 500m inland, beyond the palace ☎ 28430 23739, ⓦ stelapts .com. Large, elegantly decorated, stone-built a/c apartments, with hammocks and lovely views in the verdant gardens, and some slightly simpler studios. Exceptionally well equipped, well run and friendly. Studio **€70**, apartment **€80**

Yianni's Retreat About 500m inland, beyond the palace ☎28430 25726, ⓦkatozakros-rooms.com. Sharing a site with sister *Stella's* (see above), *Yianni's* offers simpler, smaller a/c studios, with slightly less magical views, though they're still classily constructed and fitted out. **€60**

Zakros Palace Apartments On the entry road above the village ☎28430 29550, ⓦkatozakros-apts.gr. Perched high above the coast with spectacular views; a/c rooms have balconies overlooking both the bay and the gorge, TV, fridge (kitchenette in studios) and wi-fi. **€50**

The southeast

Few tourists venture south of Zákros, and indeed there's little in the way of habitation in the whole of the southeastern corner of the island, and barely any public transport. The effort of getting to these remote parts is rewarded with a barren, empty landscape and numerous excellent **beaches** – mostly deserted. Along the road from Áno Zákros to **Xerókambos**, agricultural country of olive groves and plastic greenhouses gradually gives way to a harsher mountain environment until finally you emerge high above the coast, and a brilliant turquoise sea and white sandy beaches divided by rocky outcrops appear below. Beyond Xerókambos you can circle back round to Sitía, taking in an archeological site at **Presós** along the way, or on towards the south coast.

Xerókambos

Straggling across a little coastal plain in the lee of the Sitían mountains, the tiny hamlet of **XERÓKAMBOS** (Ξερόκαμπος) is not especially attractive, but it's as isolated and peaceful as you could wish for. There's no real centre, just a street along which, between fields of olive groves, are spaced some houses, a few tavernas and a couple of basic minimarkets, with rooms and apartment places scattered along the road and down by the beach. Despite the stirrings of development, this **main beach** is more than long enough to find seclusion if you want it, and there are isolated coves either side where you might never see another soul. The crystal-clear waters here are great for **snorkelling** too – the minimarkets sell the basic equipment.

Away from the sea, you could stretch your legs with a walk to the tiny chapel on a low hill to the south of the beach. Surrounding this are the ruins of an extensive **Minoan settlement** not yet fully explored or documented. Archeologists argue as to whether Xerókambos is the site of ancient Ambelos (in spite of a location of this name nearby), but artefacts discovered both here and at a looted peak sanctuary in the hills certainly suggest this was a settlement of some significance in ancient times, possibly connected with Zákros palace to the north.

Hamétoulo

A good paved road – populated by herds of goats who, despite the arrival of the asphalt, still regard it as their domain – switchbacks up into the barren, desolate mountains behind Xerókambos, offering dramatic views before heading down towards Zíros. Almost at the highest point lies the primitive hamlet of **HAMÉTOULO** (Χαμαίτουλο), a piece of living Cretan folklore with twenty dwellings, a cobbled street and a church. Beyond here all views are dominated by a giant radar dome on the mountaintop, and the road itself is dotted with "No Photography" signs – this is a military zone and the site of NATO's main intelligence gathering post for the eastern Mediterranean.

Zíros

The farming village of **ZÍROS** (Ζίρος), in the midst of a high inland plain, is the administrative centre of this region. That doesn't amount to a great deal, but it's a fair-sized place, tumbling down a hillside towards a neat platía circled by willow and acacia trees with whitewashed trunks. Facilities here include banks and fuel, and should you come in late July you might be lucky enough to catch the annual **festival**, when the women of the village produce huge trays of delicacies that are laid out on tables in the square and washed down with gallons of *raki* to the accompaniment of *bouzoúki* and

2

THE WIND TURBINES OF EASTERN CRETE

The **wind turbines** that stretch across the hills and ridges of many areas of eastern Crete – visible here above Handhrás – have helped turn the island into a world leader in renewable energy. A response to the acute electricity shortages the island experiences in high summer when its population doubles – and power demand increases more than twofold – the turbines can now supply a good proportion of the island's electricity. Ironically, however, the very success of the programme may be damaging it. There is now overcapacity for most of the year, meaning that a significant proportion of the power generated is not used, which has a financial impact on the (mostly private) windfarm operators. The concentration of wind power in the east also means that generation is very dependent on local wind conditions. With the upgrading of the conventional power stations at Iráklio and Haniá, plus a new one at Atherinolakós, a remote site in the far southeast, power shortages are not expected in the foreseeable future.

---

lyra. For quieter times, there are sixteenth-century frescoes to be seen in the church of **Ayía Paraskeví**, or you may prefer simply to soak up the atmosphere with a drink at a table in the square. In the early evening, when the rocky heights seem to crowd in on all sides, places like Zíros feel like the real heart of Crete.

Handhrás

The olive groves and vineyards around Zíros are said to be among the best on the island; the villages are still prosperous, though you feel that their best days are several hundred years behind them. **HANDHRÁS (Χανδράς)**, another tidy farming village, is entered past its sail-less and derelict irrigation windmills whose modern counterparts – a phalanx of mammoth wind turbines spaced out along the ridge above the village – make a surreal addition to the landscape.

Etiá

At **ETIÁ (Ετιά)**, a **Venetian mansion** stands in memorial to the glory days of the Italian city's power in Crete. Built by the Di Mezzo family (whose arms decorate the doorway) in the late fifteenth century, this once elegant edifice was badly damaged in 1828 when the local populace vented their rage on the Turks who had been using it as an administrative base, and later fell into almost complete ruin, along with the rest of the village. The mansion has been completely refurbished – or at least its exterior has, as you can rarely get in – and is one of the very few Venetian buildings to survive outside the cities. Around it is effectively a ghost town of one-room stone shacks; the last of what were once over five hundred permanent residents left in the 1970s. Only a seasonal roadside taverna, a Byzantine chapel and the church of **Ayía Katerína**, with an elegant carved stone tower, show any signs of life.

Voilá

The ruined medieval village of **VOILÁ (Βοιλά)** is signed up a lane just outside Handhrás. With its Gothic arches and silent paved streets, this is a distinctly eerie place to wander round; two ornamental drinking **fountains** with beautiful brass taps still function, one at each end of the village, a Turkish contribution to this Venetian stronghold. The only building still standing with a functional roof is the twin-naved **Áyios Yeóryios** church, inside which (if you can get in) you can see an interesting sixteenth-century gravestone fresco. The church and a tower of the Turkish period dominate the site; you can also climb to a ruined Venetian fort above the village.

Ancient Presós

From the centre of the village of Néa Presós, opposite a *kafenío* with a raised terrace, a dirt road is clearly signposted downhill; after about 2km you'll come to a signed gate for the "First Acropolis", where you can park • Open daylight hours • Free

The archeological site of **PRESÓS (Πραισός)** is another of those sites where what you see

– in this case very little – cannot begin to match the interest and importance of the history. But even without ruins, it would be worth taking the walk around the site for the **scenery** alone.

Brief history

Presós first came to light in 1884, when the Italian archeologist Federico Halbherr turned up a large number of clay idols and some unusual inscriptions written in an unknown tongue – very likely the same as that of the Linear A tablets – using Greek characters. Set out with lines reading alternately right to left and left to right, these **Eteocretan** (true Cretan) inscriptions are now believed to be evidence of the post-Bronze Age Minoans who fled from the Dorian invasions to remote locations in the east of the island in an attempt to preserve their civilization. Presós seems to have been one of their principal towns, controlling the sanctuary of Dhiktean Zeus at Palékastro, probably an earlier Minoan shrine. With harbours on the north and south coasts of the island, its power eventually led to conflict with the leading Dorian city of the region, Ierápytna (modern Ierápetra). Following final victory about 155 BC, Ierápytna razed Presós to the ground and the city was never rebuilt. With this defeat, the long twilight of Minoan civilization, lasting more than a thousand years after the palaces had fallen, came to an end.

The site

From the entrance, follow the signed path west to a saddle between the two hills where the ancient city lay; the defensive wall that encircled these two hills can still be made out in places. On the summit of the **First Acropolis** are the foundations of a temple. Further on, the path forks and to the right – on the western slope of the same hill – are the remains of a substantial **Hellenistic house**. Dating from the third century BC, the outer walls of superbly cut stone define the main living rooms at the front of the house, with workrooms at the rear. In the largest workroom, an olive press was found together with a stone tank for storing the oil. A stairway to the left of the main door led down to a cellar. Turning left at the fork brings you – after a hundred-metre walk across the saddle – to the **Second Acropolis** where cuttings in the rock on the south side formed the foundations of dwellings.

ARRIVAL, DEPARTURE AND GETTING AROUND   THE SOUTHEAST

By bus The only buses in this region, apart from those that run along the main road from Sitía to the south coast, are two weekday services from Sitía to Zíros (6am & 1.15pm), returning 1hr later).

By car Approaching the region directly from Sitía, the main road across the island to the south coast cuts high between the east and west ranges of the Sitía mountains. Along the way are a number of sturdy agricultural hamlets where you can stop for a snack and a drink, and short detours will take you to Presós or Etiá, and to Zíros beyond. From Xerókambos there are three potential routes. On the

outskirts of Zíros, a newly paved road heads directly for the south coast at Goúdhouras (see p.171), through very lonely country. Continue through Zíros and the older road divides at Handhrás, both picturesque branches continuing to meet the main Sitía–Ierápetra road; the southerly route, the logical direction if you're heading for Makríyialos, Ierápetra and the south coast, goes via Etiá; the northerly, back toward Sitía, passes Voilá and ancient Presós.

On foot The E4 path passes through Handhrás and Zíros, before turning northeast to end at the Gorge of the Dead and Zákros.

ACCOMMODATION

Apart from one highly seasonal place at **Handhrás**, the only good accommodation in the region is at **Xerókambos**, where it's scattered across the countryside behind the beach; many local options are listed at ⓦ xerocamboscreta.com and ⓦ eastcrete-holidays.gr. None stay open over winter.

XERÓKAMBOS

Asteras In the hills above the main road ☏ 28430 26787, ⓦ asterasapartments.gr. Set in their own garden, above the olive groves, these modern a/c studio rooms and

two-room apartments all come with kitchenette, fridge and good sea views. €40

Faros On the main road ☏ 28430 25612. Pleasant a/c rooms, studios and apartments with TV and wi-fi, some

with sea view. There's also a bar, and a garden with children's play area. **€35**
Lithos Main road towards the south end of Xerókambos ☎ 28430 26729, ⊛ lithoshouses.gr. The village's most luxurious option, whose elegantly furnished stone-built sea-view duplex apartments (bedroom upstairs, living quarters below) come with kitchen, satellite TV, sound system and wi-fi; free olive oil, wine and *raki* are provided. **€60**
Liviko View Off the main street ☎ 28430 27000, ⊛ livikoview.gr. These excellent rooms (and taverna) are run by a couple of Greek-Australians. Rooms come with

a/c and balcony sea view, and there are some more expensive apartments sleeping up to four. Internet access available. **€35**

HANDHRÁS
Lemon Tree By the roundabout on the edge of the village ☎ 28430 31066, ⊛ lemontree.crete.com. The taverna (see below) has a couple of excellent, stone-walled, a/c rooms with fridge, a handy stop for anyone walking the E4. However, you'll need to check in advance if it's open. **€30**

EATING

XERÓKAMBOS
Akrogiali On the beachfront, at the south end. This taverna serves up fresh fish, seafood, salads and Cretan dishes on a large terrace set back from the beach with good sea views. Daily 11am–10pm.
Liviko View Off the main street ☎ 28430 27000, ⊛ livikoview.gr. Below the apartments of the same name (see above), offering great food, made from organic ingredients grown on the family farm, and a wonderful terrace. Vegetarian dishes from €4. Daily 10am–late.

HANDHRÁS
Lemon Tree By the roundabout on the edge of the

village ☎ 28430 31066, ⊛ lemontree.crete.com. English-run taverna with professional chef Mark Cardnell manning the stoves, and turning out food infinitely better than you'd expect in these surroundings. Expect the likes of confit chicken with noodles or home-made garlic spaghetti with walnut pesto, as well as comfort food for British visitors – fish and chips or curry and rice. Also excellent home-made desserts (plum pie, chocolate bread-and-butter pudding), all using local seasonal ingredients (mains around €15, puddings €7). However, it will only open during occasional English school holidays in future, so check the website or call ahead. Lunch & dinner.

The south coast

There are three main approaches to Lasíthi's south coast: the long haul across the centre of the island from Iráklio via Áno Viánnos to approach from the west; the short cut across the isthmus from Pahiá Ámmos to **Ierápetra**; or the road south from Sitía that emerges on the coast at **Pilalímata**, close to **Makríyialos**.

Makríyialos and around

At first sight, **MAKRÍYIALOS (Μακρύγιαλος)** seems just another example of ruinous strip development, and even on better acquaintance it's never wildly attractive. However, it does have its compensations: the development is almost exclusively along the road, so get away from that and there are some quiet corners and congenial places to stay; there's an attractive little harbour, and right in town is one of the best **beaches** at this end of Crete, with sand that shelves so gently you might imagine you could walk the 320km to Africa. There are plenty of other beaches nearby, too, and attractive walks into the hills behind.

Much the most appealing part of town is in the west, where the **harbour** shelters under a little bluff, just off the main road. Nearby are the Roman and Minoan **villas**. There's a patch of beach right by the harbour, and another around the corner of the bluff, to the west, but the main sands stretch out eastwards, where Makríyialos merges almost imperceptibly into **Análipsi**.

Beaches around Makríyialos
Should the town beaches get too crowded, there are plenty of alternatives nearby. To the west, the village of **Koutsourás** is effectively part of the same resort (albeit the poor relation), and though its beach may not be the most attractive, it does offer some

excellent places to eat right by the water. Better places to swim and to escape the crowds lie to the east. The first of them, **Dhiaskári**, is at the eastern edge of town just beyond the *Sunwing Hotel*, an easy walk. The taverna here rents out little shelters with hammocks for a truly sybaritic experience, or walk further along the sand to get away from people altogether. Further east, there are numerous attractive little coves along the road to Moní Kápsa; to find them, simply look out for where the locals have parked alongside the road. A couple of the better ones are at **Kaló Neró**, where there are two small cafés, not far beyond the large *Dragon's Cave Taverna*, whose signs you can't miss.

Makríyialos Minoan villa
Signed at the western end of the village, inland from the main road

The **Minoan villa** in Makríyialos – sadly, you can usually only see it through the fence – was discovered in 1971 by Costis Davaras. An important house of the late Neo-Palatial period (1550–1450 BC), it had strong outer walls and some fine stone-flagged floors. The ground plan is not unlike that of the palaces, with rooms situated around a **central court**, where an **altar** was also identified. The excavation also revealed that the house was destroyed by fire – yet more evidence for the endless debate over what caused the downfall of the Minoans.

Makríyialos Roman villa
On the bluff above the harbour, at the western end of the village

The extensive and impressive remains of Makríyialos's **Roman villa** are a reminder that this was an important trading port in Roman and Byzantine times. The trade was based on **Koufonísi**, an island to the southeast that's currently off-limits, and on the murex, a type of sea-snail found there from which valuable purple dye was extracted. As you stroll around the neglected site enjoying the sea views you can make out the remains of mosaic floors and – at the southern end – an elaborate suite of bathing rooms complete with hypocaust and furnace to provide underfloor heating. In other rooms, traces of plasterwork are visible on the walls along with fragments of the original marble that would have covered them. On the villa's west side, an atrium or ornamental garden underlines the fact that the owner was a person of elevated status.

Moní Kápsa
8km east of Makríyialos • Daily 6.30am–12.30pm & 3.30–7pm • Free; modest dress required

MONÍ KÁPSA (Μονή Κάψα) enjoys an abiding reputation for miracles as well as a spectacular setting on a ledge in the cliffs where a gorge emerges into the sea (see p.172). You can easily imagine the isolation of this place when no real coast road existed, and even the paved road and extensive restoration can't entirely destroy the romance. The original monastery, probably founded in the early Venetian period, was destroyed by **Turkish pirates** in 1471. It was rebuilt, but most of the present buildings were constructed in the nineteenth century, thanks to the energies of **Yerontoyiannis**, a monk who earned himself a name as a Robin Hood-style hero as well as a healer. Locally he is revered as a saint, and although he never conducted a single service due to his illiteracy and is denied canonization by the Church, Cretans flock to leave offerings beside his silver-encased cadaver and skull in the monastery chapel. You can also visit a **cave** behind the church to which he often retreated and from where there's a fine view towards the island of Koufonísi.

Goúdhouras
The village of **GOÚDHOURAS (Γούδουρας)** marks the end of the coast road, though you can continue inland to Zíros (see p.167). Numerous grandiose modern villas in finest mock-Classical style attest to a recent local economic boom, thanks in part to the dusty plastic greenhouses scattered along the coast, and in part to the small fishing fleet, but above all to the new oil- and gas-fired power station in an isolated spot 5km

further round the coast, at Atherinolakós. There's a long stretch of pebbly, rather windswept beach.

Péfki gorge

The hike up the **Péfki gorge** to the village of Péfki is the most straightforward of several gorge walks you can make from Makríyialos, and the easiest. It starts up the valley of the Áspro Potámos (White River), on the track past *White River Cottages* (see opposite) towards the eastern edge of town; the gorge starts where the track ends, and though rocky in places a relatively straightforward hike will see you at the top in around two hours. **PÉFKI** itself (**Πεύκοι**) is a lovely village, where a number of houses have been bought and done up by foreigners. There are relaxing places to sit and eat or drink to take in the views and, right at the top of the village, a little **folklore museum** is housed in the old schoolhouse, full of traditional artefacts including a working loom.

Pervolákia gorge

The **Pervolákia gorge** emerges at the sea by Moní Kápsa (see p.171) where there's a tiny pebble beach offering a chance to cool off. This is the deepest and most spectacular of the gorges around Makríyialos, and a slightly more challenging hike; two hours for the 3.5km up to the village of **KÁTO PERVOLÁKIA** (**Κάτο Περβολάκια**) a little less back down. Since there's no transport at either end, you'll need to walk both ways or arrange a pick-up time with a taxi.

Butterfly Gorge

West of Koutsourás, keep an eye out on the right for the poorly signed **Koutsourás Communal Park**. This is at the bottom of **Butterfly Gorge**, and the start of a three- to four-hour walk up to the village of Orinó. Despite the name, butterflies have not been much in evidence in recent years, perhaps because the slopes higher up were devastated by a massive fire in 1993, from which they have still not recovered. Some believe that the fire was not the accident it appeared (see box below); many of the nearby villagers would prefer to see olives planted here or some other "sensible" use of the land.

It's easy enough to stroll a short way into the park (which, since it's on the main Ierápetra road, can be reached by bus) but the finest scenery, flora and fauna are to be found further up. In effect there are two gorges here: set out from the park through the first one, then across flatter, cultivated land to a final steep climb. In this final section

---

THE FIRES OF CRETE

Forest fires are an all-too-common occurrence in Crete. Understandable, perhaps, given the summer heat and tinderbox conditions but, depressingly, not all are the accidents they seem to be. Figures from the Greek Agricultural Ministry attribute no less than 57 percent of all fires to unknown causes or arson; the number also increases prior to general elections. This, of course, is when the politicians – in a desperate scramble for votes – are willing to recognize the claims to land of those who may have started the fires in the first place. Under Greek law, there is no organized system of land registry for publicly owned land, which means that if an area of woodland is burned down, the barren territory left behind becomes a no-man's-land that can be claimed under squatters' rights. Once olives or other crops have been planted, a foothold towards possession has been attained, with local politicians often smoothing over the obstacles to the land transfer. This callous attitude to the environment, where trees are little regarded for their beauty and their environmental benefits ignored or not understood, has a long history. In his book *Wild Flowers of Crete*, biologist George Sfikas writes of the Greek view that "a green wood is useless because the trees drink valuable water and don't produce anything". Attitudes are slowly changing as environmental awareness grows, especially among the young, but for now fires continue to plague the island.

there are waterfalls (in spring these can become torrents that make the way impassable, so check before setting out) and spectacular mountain scenery.

Orinó

The village of **ORINÓ** (Ορεινό) lies 2km further up the road from the top of Butterfly Gorge – you can also drive up there, on a road west of the park. Surrounded by lush greenery and wildflowers and at a height of nearly 1000m, the village is noticeably cooler than the coast; there's an excellent *kafenío* as well as a couple of rustic bars where you can slake your thirst after the climb.

Ayía Fotiá

AYÍA FOTIÁ (Αγία Φωτιά) is almost exactly halfway between Makríyialos and Ierápetra, where a poorly signed turning (hazardously situated halfway round a bend) leads down to an excellent small, sandy **beach** hidden from the road in a wooded valley. The tiny resort here is quiet at night, but the beach can get very crowded on summer weekends, when parking is also a nightmare. Nearby **Ahliá**, with a taverna and other facilities, is another lovely cove beach.

ARRIVAL AND DEPARTURE   MAKRÍYIALOS AND AROUND

By bus Six buses a day run between Makríyialos and Ierápetra; 4 to Sitía. They stop at various points on the main road behind the beach; get off at the harbour for the western end of town, or near the *Villea Village Hotel* for Áspros Pótamos and places at the eastern end of town.

By boat In summer, there are daily trips from Makríyialos to Gaidhouronísi – Chrissi Island (see p.177) – with the *Sofia* (☎ 697 44 09 511).

ACCOMMODATION

Thanks to its popularity with the **package holiday** market (generally the more exclusive end of it), Makríyialos is not overflowing with accommodation for anyone on a modest budget. There are some very good midmarket choices, though; many more can be found on ⓦ makrysgialos.com.

MAKRÍYIALOS

⭐ **Aspros Potamos Traditional Houses** 600m up a signed track at the eastern end of town ☎ 28430 51694, ⓦ asprospotamos.com. This back-to-nature version of *White River Cottages* (see below) is slightly further up the valley. Here another group of tiny stone houses cut from the rock has been delightfully converted into studios and apartments, but in this case there's only solar power; rooms have a fridge, single bathroom light and LED reading lamp (plus solar hot water), and in reception there's wi-fi and power for rechargers, otherwise you are reliant on oil lamps and candles for lighting, and a fireplace to warm you in winter (extra charge for firewood). **€50**

Asteria Studios Beachfront west of the harbour, close to the Roman villa ☎ 28430 51926, ⓦ relaxincrete .com. English-run a/c studios right by the beach: bright, airy and exceptionally well kitted out, with wi-fi and everything from toasters to hairdryers. **€50**

Maria Tsankalioti Apartments Seaward side of the main road, halfway through town ☎ 28430 51557, ⓦ makrigialos-crete.com. The friendly proprietor offers bright beachfront studio rooms and apartments – some with sea view and terrace – with kitchenette, a/c, TV and wi-fi. **€40**

Miramare Studios Eastern end of the town beach, down a track opposite the turning to Áspros Pótamos ☎ 28430 51049, ⓦ miramare-studios.gr. Bright, white-and-blue a/c studios with kitchenette, TV, wi-fi and large balconies directly above the beach, where they have free sunbeds. **€55**

Oasis Rooms Beachfront west of the harbour, close to the Roman villa ☎ 28430 51918. Spacious sea-view a/c rooms with wi-fi, kitchenette, fridge, terrace and balcony, right on the beach. **€40**

⭐ **White House** On the harbour ☎ 28430 29183, ⓦ makrigialos.com. Three houses and two apartments in beautifully restored harbour buildings, each one architect-designed and unique. Equipment includes everything from wi-fi and washing machine to champagne glasses. **€120**

White River Cottages 500m up a signed track at the eastern end of town ☎ 28430 51120, ⓔ wriver@otenet .gr. An abandoned hamlet of traditional stone dwellings has been restored as a warren of studios and apartments (for up to four people) around a small pool. Built partly into the rocks, with the original stone floors and whitewashed walls, they come with kitchens, a/c, wi-fi and private terraces. Minimum three-day stay. **€78**

AYÍA FOTIÁ

Markos Studios Built into the cliff on the east side of the bay, overlooking the beach ☎ 28420 61906, ⓦ markos-studios.com. Modern a/c studios and

2

apartments for up to four people, with kitchenettes and balconies with awesome views. €44

Taverna Agia Fotia Right by the beach ☎ 28420 61288, ⓦ agiafotia.gr. These simple a/c studios are set back a little from the beach, behind the taverna, which is probably the best of the places to eat here. €40

EATING AND DRINKING

The majority of tavernas in **Makríyialos** itself offer fairly standard, touristy food; options improve if you're prepared to travel a bit further. There's not much happening in the way of nightlife, but a number of **bars** on the harbour play soft music and serve cocktails.

MAKRÍYIALOS

Faros Overlooking the beach beside the harbour ☎ 28430 52456. Big taverna in a great position, with everything from pizza and pasta to octopus and kalamari; good fish from their own boat too (fish dishes €10–12). Daily noon–late.

Ilios Overlooking the beach beside the harbour ☎ 28430 51280. Housed in a refurbished carob warehouse, this bar-café serves breakfast but is better later on, when it's the perfect place for a sundowner. Daily 9am–1am.

Cafe Olympio Overlooking the beach beside the harbour ☎ 28430 52135. Friendly bar-café that's a good source of information on the local area, and has sunbeds on a sandy strip of beach. Breakfasts, light lunches, cocktails and draft beer. Daily 8am–late.

KOUTSOURÁS

★ **Kalliotzina** Towards the western end of the village ☎ 28430 51207. An absolutely classic old-fashioned taverna, serving home-cooked food and excellent fish on a tree-shaded terrace right by the sea. There's no written menu, so check out what's on offer in the kitchen or listen carefully as the day's dishes are reeled off at speed; mains are around €7, or less for the veggie options. There's often musical accompaniment at weekends in summer. Daily 11am–late.

Votsalakia In the middle of the beach by the mouth of

the stream ☎ 28430 51247. Old-fashioned food and barrel wine, but smarter than average decor, with cream-coloured awnings and dark-blue check tablecloths. Daily noon–11pm.

DHIASKÁRI

Diaskari Western end of the beach ☎ 694 43 18 803. Worth visiting for the magnificent setting, right above the beach, rather than because there's anything particularly special about the food, which is good, standard Greek cooking. Daily 10am–10pm.

PERVOLÁKIA

Aposperida Káto Pervolákia ☎ 28430 31010. Arriving at this *kafenío* is a worthwhile reward for climbing the Pervolákia gorge – a simple place for a drink or home-cooked food. Daily, but ring ahead to check they're open if you want to go in the evening, or out of season.

PEFKÍ

★ **Piperia** Upper part of the village ☎ 28430 52471. A lovely spot under a spreading pepper tree, with authentic, traditional food and great views over the coast. Mains like okra with lamb or rabbit in wine sauce go for around €8; they have live Greek music some summer evenings (with a set menu); and they sell their own jams, olives and liqueurs. Daily noon–midnight.

Ierápetra and around

IERÁPETRA (Ιεράπετρα) has various claims to fame – the southernmost town in Europe, the most hours of sunshine, the largest town on the south coast of Crete – but until recently, charm was not one of them. Though there's an excellent Blue Flag **beach**, it's a big, sprawling place and a major supply centre for the region's numerous farmers who have grown rich on the year-round cultivation of cucumbers, tomatoes and peppers in the plastic greenhouses that scar the landscape along this coast (see box, p.178). In recent years some resources have been devoted to smartening the town up, and, on the **seafront**, where a string of restaurants and bars stretches out in either direction, Ierápetra can be genuinely picturesque. However, tourism seems very much an afterthought, and things to do by day – apart from lie on the beach – are limited.

Brief history

Although you'd hardly know it to look at the town today, Ierápetra has quite a history. Early knowledge is sketchy, but it's almost certain that there was a settlement here, or at least a port, in **Minoan** times. A look at the map suggests a link across the isthmus with Gourniá, and it was probably from Ierápetra and other south-coast harbours that the Keftiu, as the Egyptians called the Cretans, sailed for the coast of Africa.

However, it was as a **Doric** settlement that **Ierápytna**, as the place was then known, grew to real prominence. By the second century BC it occupied more territory than any other Cretan city and had become a bastion of the Greek Dorians against their bitter enemies the Eteocretans: the final victory over Eteocretan Presós in 155 BC ended the last Minoan presence in eastern Crete. Only Ítanos, near Vái, now stood between Ierápytna and the complete domination of the eastern end of the island. Prolonged wars and disputes rumbled on for almost a century, and were finally brought to an end only by Rome's ruthless conquest of the entire island. Even then, Ierápytna stubbornly resisted to the last, becoming the final city to fall to the invading legions.

When **Rome** then joined Crete to Cyrene in northern Libya, forming the province of Cyrenaica, Ierápytna embarked on a new career as an important **commercial centre**, trading with Greece and Italy as well as Africa and the Near East. During this period,

IERÁPETRA

ACCOMMODATION	
ByCaptain's	7
Camping Koutsounari	2
Cretan Villa	1
Erotokritos	6
Ersi	5
El Greco	4
Katerina	3

RESTAURANTS & CAFÉS	
Gorgona	4
Levante	6
Napoleon	5
Oxo	3
Parados	2
Veterano	1

2

much impressive building took place – theatres, amphitheatres, temples – of which virtually nothing survives today, save for piles of fractured pillars and column capitals scattered in odd corners around the town.

From the Romans to the tourists is a chronicle of steady decline. The Venetians (who favoured Sitía as their administrative centre in the east) left behind a small **fortress**, now restored, defending the harbour entrance. The Turks, under whom Ierápetra languished as a backwater, are represented by a nineteenth-century **mosque** and nearby Ottoman fountain.

The Archeological Museum
Just off Platía Kanoupáki • Tues–Sun 8.30am–3pm • €2

Ierapetra's **Archeological Museum**, housed in the former Turkish school, is poorly labelled and doesn't take long to see, but does boast some high-quality exhibits. Among the highlights are numerous Minoan **lárnakes**, or clay coffins, the finest example of which was excavated at nearby Episkopí. Dating from the very end of the Neo-Palatial period (c.1300 BC), it has fascinating painted panels, one of which depicts a mare suckling her foal; other scenes revel in the stalking of the *kri-kri*, or wild goat, by hunting dogs. Look out too for some interesting **Vasilikí ware** (see p.145), including typical jugs and vases, as well as some potters' turntables from the early Minoan settlement at Fournoú Korýfi (p.179). The Greek and Roman section contains a selection of statuary, mostly headless because iconoclastic Christians tended to regard the stone craniums as places where the spirit of the devil was lurking. One more recent discovery, a wonderful second-century statue of **Persephone**, holding an ear of corn in her left hand, managed to hang on to her head, which is crowned by a small altar encoiled by two serpents, symbols of her divinity.

The Kalés
Tues–Sun 8.30am–3pm • Free

A restored fortress known as the **Kalés** guards the harbour. Reputedly built by the Genoese pirate Pescatore in 1212, the present structure is basically a seventeenth-century Venetian defence, later used and modified by the Turks. Atmospheric as it is, it's simply an empty shell, with no signage or anything else apart from some public toilets.

The old quarter

A labyrinth of narrow streets inland from the harbour constitutes the **old quarter**. You'll almost certainly get lost here, but it's so tiny that a couple of minutes later you'll emerge at some recognizable landmark. Places to look out for include **Napoleon's House**, where Napoleon Bonaparte allegedly spent a night in 1798, and the twin-domed church of **Aféndis Christós**, a fourteenth-century building with a fine carved and painted wooden iconostasis. In a small square opposite a Turkish fountain, the **Tzami**, or mosque, has been painstakingly restored (it had been converted to a church). It retains a substantial chunk of its minaret and – inside – the original mihrab.

Beaches around Ierápetra

Much the best beaches accessible from Ierápetra are on Gaidhouronísi (see opposite), but there's a small **town beach** right in the centre in front of the old quarter, and more along the coast in either direction, with good bus services along the main road behind them. Most of the tourist development lies to the east, where aptly named **Long Beach**, a windswept line of sand (and the wind can really blow here) stretches virtually unbroken for 5km from the edge of town. There's more sand at **Koutsonári**, just beyond.

Roman fish tanks
Between Koutsonári and Férma, about 9km east of Ierápetra • Look for a sign for "Roman Fish Tanks" in front of the *Kakkos Bay Hotel*

The remarkable **Roman fish tank** carved out of the rock near the village of Férma is some 4m square, with the sea still sloshing through an ancient sluicegate in the bottom.

The carved steps leading down into the tank would have been used by the fish sellers to net the fish demanded by their customers; the pools in the surrounding rocks were no doubt used for the fish to be sold that day, while the smaller ones could be fattened up in the larger tank below.

Gaidhouronísi

The most popular way to escape Ierápetra's often stifling summer temperatures is to take a boat trip (see below) to **GAIDHOURONÍSI** (Γαιδουρονήσι) – Donkey Island, more often known locally as **Chrissi** – some 10km offshore. A real desert island a little over 4km in length, with a fine cedar forest and a couple of tavernas, Gaidhouronísi has some excellent sandy **beaches** and plenty of room to escape – although you wouldn't want to miss the boat back. There's a waymarked **walking route** around the island on which you should spot quite a few examples of the varied flora and fauna, as well as fossils and the fabulous "**Shell Beach**" covered with discarded shells from countless generations of molluscs (no souvenir-taking allowed).

2

ARRIVAL AND DEPARTURE

IERÁPETRA AND AROUND

By car Ierápetra has a complex one-way system and the usual shortage of parking. The easiest plan is to follow the signs to the "Archeological Collection" and from there to the seafront, where there's a large car park.

By bus The bus station (☎ 28420 28237) is on Lasthénous – the Áyios Nikólaos road. The centre is to the northeast, a 5min walk away, reached by heading down towards the water, past the souvenir stores and stalls selling foreign newspapers, to the seafront and promenade.

Destinations Ay. Nikólaos (7 daily; 6.30am–8pm; 1hr); Iráklio (7 daily; 6.30am–8pm; 2hr 30min); Makríyialos (Mon–Fri 6, 6.15am–8.30pm; Sat 5, 6.15am–6pm; Sun 9.30am, 2.30pm & 6pm; 30min); Mýrtos (Mon–Fri 5, 5.45am–5pm; Sat 8am & 12.30pm; 30min); Sitía (Mon–Sat 4, 6.15am–6.15pm; Sun 9.30am & 2.30pm; 1hr 30min).

GETTING AROUND

Boat trips Two competing companies, Chrysi Cruises (☎ 28420 20008, ⓦ chrysicruises.com) and Zanadu (☎ 28420 26649), run daily trips to Gaidhouronísi, on large boats with on-board bars, from the jetty on the seafront (May–Oct; peak-season departures 10.30am, 11am & 12.30pm, returning 4pm, 5pm & 6pm; 55min). Tickets are sold by agents throughout town, or at the boat; officially they cost €24 but off-season, or if you bargain with the agents, you may get them for as little as €15. From the harbour, small boats offer more personalized trips and private charters; they include a traditional fishing *kaïki* (the *Nefeli*; ☎ 694 27 91 474, ⓦ bateaucrete.canalblog.com) and a fast modern motor-yacht (the *Nautilos*; ☎ 697 28 94 279, ⓦ nautiloscruises.com), both of which charge €45 a head for the day-trip to the island.

Taxis There's a taxi rank on Platía Kanoupáki, or call ☎ 28420 26600.

INFORMATION

Tourist information The municipal tourist information booth in the seafront car park (ⓦ ierapetra .gr) may be open in summer, financial crisis permitting. In its absence, the Ierapetra Express travel agency (Mon–Fri 8am–2pm & 5–9pm, Sat 9am–2pm & 5–7pm; ☎ 28420 28673), on Platía Eleftherías, is another useful source for general information, as well as local accommodation and car rental.

ACCOMMODATION

ByCaptain's Stratígou Samouíl 54 ☎ 697 90 80 154, ⓦ bycaptains-studios.gr. Newly converted a/c studios above a seafront souvenir shop, close to the town beach, with TV, modern kitchenette, and big seafront balconies. **€45**

Camping Koutsounari Koutsounári, off the coast road 7km east ☎ 28420 61213, ⓦ camping-koutsounari .epimlas.gr. The only campsite on this stretch of the south coast, with a taverna, store and pool, and although the ground is a bit gritty there's a good beach and plenty of shade. Two people plus tent and car **€21**

★ **Cretan Villa** Lakérda 16 ☎ 28420 28522, ⓦ cretan -villa.com. Close to the bus station; sparkling a/c rooms with TV and fridge overlook the flower-bedecked patio of a beautiful 180-year-old stone house. **€45**

Erotokritos Parodós Stratígou Samouíl, signed off the seafront beyond Taverna Napoleon ☎ 28420 28151. Decent, old-fashioned en-suite rooms and apartments with kitchenette, fridges and fans (some with a/c), tucked away in the old quarter. **€35**

Ersi Platía Eleftherías 19 ☎ 28420 23208. The good-value rooms at this refurbished hotel come with fridge, a/c

2

(€5 extra), TV and balcony – the higher the better for peace and sea views. The owner also has some apartments nearby, which come with kitchen and lounge, for the same price. **€35**

El Greco Kothrí 42 ☏28420 28471, ⌨elgreco-ierapetra.gr. Beachfront hotel that's been done up, designer-style, with harmoniously toned rooms and snazzy bathrooms; balconies at the front have great sea views,

although rooms facing inland are substantially cheaper. It also has its own café and restaurant (discounts for guests) and wi-fi in public areas. Breakfast included. **€65**

Katerina Markópoulo 95, on the seafront ☏28420 28345, ⌨katerina-rooms.gr. Recently refurbished inside (but in need of a lick of paint outside), offering smart rooms and studios with a/c, TV, wi-fi, fridge and balcony with sea view. **€50**

EATING AND DRINKING

Along Markópoulou, the seafront promenade stretching behind the beach northeast of the town hall, there's a string of **café-bars** with outdoor seating, many of which serve breakfast. Samouíl, the promenade south of the ferry terminal, has a number of more traditional **tavernas** facing the sea. In town itself there are plenty of more basic café and fast-food options between Platía Kanoupáki and Platía Eleftherías. Nightlife is pretty quiet, though there are plenty of late-opening **bars** in the centre, especially around Platía Kanoupáki, by the Archeological Museum and south along Kírva.

Gorgona Stratígou Samouíl 12 ☏28420 26619. Near the harbour and fort, directly on the beach, this reliable, well-known and locally popular taverna serves good fish, seafood (try the octopus, €8) and Cretan dishes at reasonable prices. Daily 11am–late.

Levante Stratígou Samouíl 38 ☏28420 80585. Fish taverna that also serves plenty of classic Greek dishes using locally sourced ingredients. Slightly more elegant than the neighbouring places with terraces on this seafront. Daily 11am–late.

★ **Napoleon** Stratígou Samouil 26 ☏28420 22410. One of Ierápetra's oldest tavernas, usually busy with locals at lunchtime. Freshly cooked dishes, a good choice of appetizers – try a mixed plate of their cheese and vegetable pies – and reasonable prices. Daily 11am–late.

Oxo Kírva 15 ☏28420 80089. Colourful *rakádhiko* (like an ouzerí, but with *raki*) packed late at night with young locals; one of a number of fashionable restaurants here, with tables looking out towards the jetty for the island boats. Good, inexpensive *meze*, plus kebabs, *pansetta* (pork ribs) or meat or mushroom pies. Daily 7pm–early hours.

Parados Off Platía Kanoupáki, by the Archeological Museum. A lovely bar-café with an ambience as laidback as the jazz that is played there; also sells arty books. Daily 10am–3pm & 6pm–late.

★ **Veterano** Northern end of Platía Eleftherías. An elegant and excellent bakery/*zaharoplastío* with an outdoor terrace where you can sit and watch the world go by. Great cakes, plus ice cream, coffee and sandwiches. Daily 9am–11pm.

Mýrtos and around

The coastline west of Ierápetra is, even more than usual, swathed in plastic (see box below), and holds plentiful signs of the wealth this form of agriculture has brought to the region: gleaming car and kitchen showrooms line the road. At the end of this stretch **MÝRTOS** (Μύρτος) lies just off the main road, which here turns inland, heading up towards Áno Viánnos. Razed to the ground by the German army in 1944 as a punishment for resistance activities, Mýrtos today is an unexpected pleasure after the drabness of what has gone before; a charming, white-walled village with a long shingle

---

THE PLASTIC REVOLUTION

The **plastic greenhouses** that disfigure much of the coastline around Ierápetra are a great source of wealth for local farmers. The system was introduced in the 1960s by a Dutch farmer named Paul Kuypers, who correctly surmised that the mild climate and fertile soil along this coast would perfectly suit greenhouse crops, which could be produced all year and sold to supermarkets in northern Europe in the depths of winter. The plastic tents were initially ridiculed, but once the canny Cretan farmers saw the size and quality of the tomatoes that emerged from them in the middle of January, the revolution began. The new system had hardly got going when Kuypers died in a road accident in 1971. However, in typically Cretan fashion, the farmers did not forget who had brought them this horn of plenty – they erected a statue to Kuypers on the site of his first greenhouse.

beach. Even in August, when the place can get pretty full, the pace of life remains slow, the atmosphere pleasantly laidback.

Apart from topping up your tan, swimming, renting a boat or lingering over a drink, there's not a great deal to do in Mýrtos, but the surrounding countryside offers a couple of important **Minoan sites**, as well as the opportunity for mountain **hikes**. Above the beach at the western edge of the village there's evidence of a **Roman-era settlement**: a brick-built circular tank construction that may be part of a Roman baths complex, walls and, closer to the water, harbour installations – all awaiting archeological investigation.

2

Mýrtos Museum
Western side of the village, beside the church • Mon & Fri 10am–2pm, Wed 5–8pm • Free

Mýrtos Museum was put together by a much-loved and respected local schoolmaster, Yiorgos Dimitrianakis, who taught most of the older folk in the village prior to his death in 1994. Throughout his life, he spent much of his free time wandering the fields and hills around Mýrtos collecting a wealth of finds, including ancient statuettes and vase fragments, and it was he who brought the Fournoú Korýfi and Pýrgos sites (see below) to the attention of archeologists. Inside are minor finds from those sites, as well as a folklore section with tools, kitchen and farming implements once used by the villagers. There's also a superb clay model of the site at Fournoú Korýfi created by John Atkinson, a British potter who now looks after the museum.

Pýrgos
Immediately west of Mýrtos, just beyond the bridge over the Mýrtos Rriver; take the signed track and follow a waymarked footpath to the right, which climbs to the site, atop a low hill

The Minoan villa at **PÝRGOS** (Πύργος) was inhabited, like nearby Fournoú Korýfi (see below), in the early Pre-Palatial period (c.2500 BC), and destroyed by fire around 2200 BC. Unlike Fournoú Korýfi, however, Pýrgos was reoccupied and rebuilt following its destruction, when it appears to have incorporated the former's lands. By the time of the Neo-Palatial period (c.1600 BC), the community occupying the lower slopes was dominated by a two- or three-storey country villa spread over the crown of the hill.

The path up circles around the back of the hill and past the remains of an enormous plastered **cistern**, the largest found in Minoan Crete, dating from the Pre-Palatial era (c.1900–1700 BC). When it burst over the northern side of the hill in ancient times, it was not repaired. Beyond this, a fine stretch of **paved road** survives from the early period: this led to a burial pit, now excavated. Continuing up, a **stepped street** flanked by some well-cut lower courses of the villa's outer wall leads into a **courtyard**, partly paved in the purple limestone of the region. At the rear of the villa (furthest away from the sea) on the west side, it's possible to make out a **light well** floored with the same purple limestone. Many of the walls carry marks of the ferocious blaze which destroyed the villa around 1450 BC, lending credibility to the Thíra explosion theory, (see p.330) especially since volcanic material was discovered amid the rubble. But it now seems that while the villa was burned, the surrounding settlement was untouched – another puzzle to contemplate as you savour the magnificent sea view from the courtyard.

Fournoú Korýfi
Signed inland a couple of kilometres west of Mýrtos, near the village of Néa Mýrtos • The gate is generally left open • The site is on the peak, reached by scrambling up a gully (signed), then heading towards a stand of pine trees just before which a path heads to the right across a flat expanse of brush towards a hill where the fenced site is clearly visible

At **FOURNOÚ KORÝFI** (Φουρνού Κορύφι) – Kiln Hill, also known as **Néa Mýrtos** – a Minoan site excavated in the 1960s by a British team yielded important evidence concerning early Minoan settlements. The excavations – which are not always easy to make sense of – revealed a **stone-built village** of nearly one hundred rooms, spread over

2

the hilltop. Probably typical of numerous other settlements sited on the coast of eastern Crete during the early Pre-Palatial period (c.2500 BC), these rooms contained stone and copper tools, carved seals and over seven hundred **pottery vessels**. Some of these were Vasilikí-type jugs (see p.145), and many were no doubt used to store the produce of the surrounding lands, then less arid than today.

In a room in the southwest corner of the site was located the oldest known Minoan domestic shrine, which produced the most important of the finds here: the **goddess of Mýrtos**, a clay idol with a stalked neck carrying a ewer. (It's now in the Áyios Nikólaos museum, along with most of the other finds from this site and Pýrgos.) Around the goddess, broken offering vessels were strewn about the floor, many of them charred by the fire that destroyed the site in about 2200 BC. The riddle of the fire, which seems to have left no casualties and provoked no rebuilding, is yet another of the unresolved Minoan questions.

ARRIVAL AND INFORMATION

By bus There are 5 buses to and from Ierápetra on weekdays, just two on Sat (8.20am & 12.50pm) and none on Sun.

Travel agencies Several travel agencies in Mýrtos offer local information and help with rooms, villas for rent, money exchange, car rental and the like. Perhaps the most

MÝRTOS AND AROUND

helpful is the friendly Prima Tours (☎ 28420 51530, ⓦ sunbudget.net), on a side street near the beach towards the eastern end of the village, where the bus timetable and lots of other information is posted; they also run a used book exchange, lead guided walks, rent out mountain bikes and provide internet access.

ACCOMMODATION

Most of the time there are plenty of **rooms** advertised throughout Mýrtos – on every street, it seems. Many of the places we review here, and more, are listed on the Prima Tours website (see above).

Big Blue Apartments West side of village ☎ 28420 51094, ⓦ big-blue.gr. Lovely rooms with fridge, studios with kitchenette, and larger two-bedroom apartments, all with a/c and sea-view balconies in a stunning position high above the beach. Room **€45**, apartment **€80**

Mirtopolis On the hill above the village ☎ 28420 51183, ⓦ mirtopolis.com. New group of studios and apartments of varying sizes, some with raised sleeping galleries, all with outdoor terraces, in an airy rural spot just behind the village, with tremendous views. A/c costs extra. **€56**

Nikos House At the heart of the village near Hotel Mirtos ☎ 28420 51116. Very simple studios or two-room apartments with fans, both and kitchenette; the upstairs studio, especially, is lovely, and you feel very much part of village life here. **€40**

Panorama At almost the highest point at the west end of the village, above Big Blue ☎ 28420 51362. Studios with kitchenette, TV, a/c (€3 extra) and balconies; exceptional sea views from those at the front. **€35**

Villa Elena High at the west end of the village, next to Panorama ☎ 28420 51396. A welcoming place offering well-equipped a/c studios and one-bedroom apartments with large balconies, many with good sea views. **€45**

Villa Nostos Eastern edge of the village, signed as you enter from the main road ☎ 28420 51569, ⓦ villanostos.nl. Garden complex with plain but very good-value a/c balcony studios and apartments with TV and wi-fi right behind the beach, some with sea view. **€35**

EATING AND DRINKING

Along the main street several **minimarkets** and bakeries provide all the essentials, while **cafés**, **bars** and **restaurants** line the seafront promenade behind the beach. Once the sun goes down, there's little to do but prolong your eating and drinking into the night, although the odd bar sometimes risks breaking the late-night curfew with a blast of soft rock, and in summer there's the occasional *lyra* and *bouzoúki* concert on the beach.

Beach Café Western end of the promenade ☎ 699 54 34 848. The last spot at the western end of the village, right above the beach. It's all too tempting to linger here for hours over a drink; they also serve breakfast and full meals. Daily 9am–late.

Katerina's On a pedestrian alley in the heart of the

village ☎ 28420 51451. Self-described as "the only gourmet restaurant in the region", colourful *Katerina's* attempts to be a cut above the rest and mostly succeeds, with dishes like Martini-marinated pork filet mignon as well as old favourites such as *kléftiko*, and plenty of veggie choices. Only slightly more expensive than elsewhere. Chef

INLAND ESCAPES FROM MÝRTOS

The **mountainous terrain** behind Mýrtos offers plenty of opportunity to escape the crowds and heat of the coast, or to stretch your legs, as well as some spectacular scenery. If you're driving to or from Ierápetra, the route through **Mýthi** and **Máles** to Gra Ligiá offers a beautiful, if extremely slow, alternative to the plastic-strewn coast road.

SARAKINÁS GORGE

The scenic, 150m-deep **Sarakinás gorge** starts close to the village of **Mýthi**, some 5km north of Mýrtos. To reach the start of the walk, drive or take a taxi to the village and then follow the signs to the gorge; there's a small parking place five minutes downhill, just before the bridge, where the walk begins. Depending on the rains, the water level in the gorge may mean you'll have to do some wading in parts, so waterproof footwear, sandals or rubber shoes would be useful. It's about 2km or one hour's climb to the top of the gorge and a little less coming back down, by which time the *kafenío* in Mýthi will be an irresistible stop. Should you not wish to repeat the scramble back down, it's possible to pick up an asphalt road back to Mýthi by following the river a further 300m upstream from the top of the gorge to where it's feasible to wade across. A path heads off from the opposite bank to meet the road.

MÁLES

Above Mýthi, with transport, you can continue to climb to **Máles**, a village clinging to the lower slopes of the Dhíkti range. The climb takes in some stunning rock formations and – as you get higher – there are views of Chrissi Island (see p.177) far out to sea, as well as the expanse of plastic greenhouses along the coastal strip. Máles would be a good starting point if you wanted to take a **walk** through some stunning mountain terrain (the E4 Pan-European footpath passes just 3km north of here).

BRAMIANÁ

The reservoir of **Bramianá**, 3km inland from Gra Ligiá, has become a major stopover for migratory birds. Large numbers of waterfowl and birds of prey can be seen here, especially in spring when there's also plenty of vivid plant life. Facilities for birdwatchers include a car park that gives access to various hides and pathways around the lake.

Yiannis Zervakis also runs half-day cooking workshops and excursions into the mountains to forage for herbs and wild greens. Daily 6–11pm.

Myrtos Taverna Main thoroughfare, below Hotel Myrtos ☎ 28420 51227. An excellent, family-run taverna offering a range of home-cooked dishes and tasty *mezédhes*, with some outdoor tables along the pavement. Daily 9am–11pm.

Votsalo Seafront in the middle of the beach ☎ 28420 51457. A likeable place with a great position at the centre of the beachfront promenade; hand-painted menus detail a good traditional set of choices, washed down with home-produced wine (starters €3–4, mains €7–10). Also breakfast, and coffee and drinks throughout the day. Daily 9am–late.

Tértsa

The narrow coast road west from Mýrtos runs for some 6km, past some tempting cove beaches, to the tiny resort of **TÉRTSA (Τέρτσα)**. Technically, this is in Iráklio province, and there is a paved road that winds inland to meet the main Áno Viánnos road, but practically everyone who gets here has come from Mýrtos. There's an excellent long beach, partly nudist, a couple of fine tavernas, and some get away from it all apartments.

ACCOMMODATION AND EATING   TÉRTSA

Lambros Apartments Set back down a side road from the centre of the village ☎ 28950 61437, ⊛ tertsa.gr. Modern a/c studios and apartments with cooking facilities, in a rural setting at the back of the village. Get info from *Lambros Taverna*. €35

Lambros Taverna In the centre of the village ☎ 28950 61437, ⊛ tertsa.gr. Family-run taverna with a beachside terrace serving home-made traditional food till late. Also acts an unofficial information centre, and as agent for many of the local rooms; free sunbeds on the beach for customers. Daily 9am–late.

2

Réthymno

RÉTHYMNO HARBOUR

Réthymno

The province of Réthymno has something for everyone. The island's intellectual and cultural capital, Réthymno itself is a relaxed university town dominated by one of the most imposing Venetian fortresses on the island. It also retains a picturesque old quarter, redolent of traditional urban life, as well as an excellent folklore museum and a fine beach. However, probably the greatest attraction of this province is its interior, dominated by mountains that provide stunning vistas at almost every turn. The provincial borders are defined by the island's highest peaks in the west by the far reaches of the Lefká Óri, the White Mountains, and to the east by the looming mass of Psilorítis, Crete's highest mountain. The villages ranged around the Psilorítis massif provide ideal bases for spectacular wilderness hikes, and are highly recommended for casual ramblers and committed hikers alike.

The peaks themselves are approached most easily from **Anóyia**, a high mountain town known for its sheep-breeding, weaving and embroidery. From here, you can hike across to the south side of the mountains or down, via the summit of Psilorítis, to the pretty villages of the lushly fertile **Amári valley** – some of the least visited and most traditional places in Crete. Southwest of Réthymno town you're on the fringes of the Lefká Óri, studded with traditional hill villages such as **Argiroúpolis** and **Asigonía**, surrounded by more magnificent **hiking** country.

By road, the Amári valley also offers access to the south coast. Not far out of Réthymno in this direction is the revered **Moní Arkádhi**, a beautiful, ancient monastery whose history makes it the emblem of Crete's nineteenth-century struggle for independence against the Turks. The main road south, though, goes via the Minoan cemetery at Arméni to the attractive hill town of **Spíli**, another centre for walkers with many fine hikes in the surrounding hills.

The **south coast** has no fancy hotels, but if all you want is sea and sand it's a far more attractive prospect than the north. There are two sizeable resorts, crowded **Ayía Galíni** and its more easy-going rival, **Plakiás**. Along the coast between them is a string of secluded pockets of sand – sometimes with a village attached – often hard to access but well worth it for a few lazy days. One of them, **Palm Beach**, is among the most picturesque on Crete, though far from undiscovered. Above it is **Moní Préveli**, an illustrious seaside monastery that played a pivotal role during the Battle of Crete.

AMÁRI VALLEY

Highlights

❶ Fortezza, Réthymno The provincial capital has fine Venetian and Turkish monuments and is dominated by a magnificent fortress, the largest Venetian castle ever built. **See p.188**

❷ Moní Arkádhi & Moní Préveli Two of Crete's most important monasteries, the imposing Moní Arkádhi and the seaside Moní Préveli are inextricably bound up with the island's history. **See p.191 & p.228**

❸ Margarítes A major centre of ceramics production, this is the place to buy anything from an egg cup to a massive Minoan-style *píthos*. **See p.204**

❹ Anóyia The gateway to Mount Psilorítis, this charming village is famous for its woven rugs and tapestries. **See p.207**

❺ Mount Psilorítis Dominating the province, Crete's highest peak provides some spectacular hikes. **See p.210**

❻ Amári valley A delightfully scenic stretch of country, where white-walled villages with frescoed Byzantine chapels are surrounded by orchards, vineyards and olive groves. **See p.214**

❼ Plakiás & Ayía Galíni The province's twin but contrasting south-coast resorts are ideal seaside getaways. **See p.224 & p.219**

HIGHLIGHTS ARE MARKED ON THE MAP ON P.186

N

MEDITERRANEAN SEA

Iráklio
Iráklio
Ayía Varvára
Pýrgos
Górtys

Týlissos
Márathos
Dhamásta
Fódhele
Goniés
Zarós
Síses
Anóyia
Vorízia
Kamáres
Vóri
Axós
Sendóni Cave
Zoniná
Idean Cave
Timbáki
Garazó
Livádhia
Kamáres Cave
M. Dhiskoúri
Nídha Plateau
Melidhóni
Ayios Ioánnis
Koúsana (1850m)
Cave
Krasoúnas
Bali
Pánormos
Pérama
Psilorítis (2456m)
Fourfourás
Ayía Galíni
PSILORITIS
Margarítes
Eléfthenó
Arhéa Eléftherna
Kouroútes
Vathiakó
Kouroútes
Nithavris
Apodhoúlou
Pidzános
Roúpes
M. Arkádhi
Thrónos
M. Asomáton
Monastiráki
Ayios Ioánnis
Ayia Paraskevi
Melambés
Loutrá
Koúles (1091m)
Amári
Kardháki
Vrisses
Ayios Yeóryios
Piyí
Maroulás
Ayía Fotíni
Mévonas
Yerakári
Ano Méros
Akoúmia
Stavroménos
Patsós
Soros (1186m)
Kédros (1777m)
Saktoúria
Cave
Kalínes
Spíli
Asidérato (1162m)
Triópetra
Perivólia
Mili Gorge
Ayía Pelayía
Mourtzé
Ayios Pávlos
Mili
Homonastíri
Lampíni
Frati
Ayia Fotini
Ligres
Arméni
Mixorroúma
Drimískos
Palm Beach
Réthymno
Minoan Cemetery
Megalopótamos
M. Préveli
Ayios Konstantíne
Ano Vasamónero
Kánevos
Lefkóyia
Sóchinaria Beach
Yeráni
Asómatos
Myrthios
Dhamnóni
Vlandhrédho
Sellía
Plakiás
Soudha Beach
Epískopi
Kótsifoú Gorge
Arhontikí
Kóto Póros
Ayios
Mourtzé
Kourtaliótiko Gorge
Argoúpolis
Pátima
Rodhákino
Minokéfala
Kroneritis (1312m)
Kefalás
Kournás
Asigoná
Almirídha
Patsós
Kallikrátis
Yamás
Yeoryioúpolis
Pátima
Argoúlés
Frangokástello
Haniá
Vríses
Haniá
Dhriú
Imbros
Soústos
Hóra Stakíon
E75
E4

0   10

Réthymno town and around

Although it's the third largest town in Crete, **RÉTHYMNO** (Ρέθυομνο) never feels like a city, as Haniá and Iráklio do. Instead, it has an easy-going provincial air; it's a place that moves slowly and, for all the myriad bars springing up along the seafront, the **old town** still preserves much of its Venetian and Turkish appearance. Here the streets are a fascinating mix of generations of **architecture**, the Venetian buildings largely indistinguishable from the Turkish and all of them adapted by later generations. Ornate wooden doors and balconies and ancient stonework crop up everywhere, and there are a number of elaborate **Turkish fountains** hidden in obscure corners. You'll also stumble across curious old stores, and craftsmen – often manufacturing *lyras*, the Cretan "violin" – working away in their traditional get-up of high boots, baggy trousers (*vrákes*) and black headscarves (*tsalvária*). Arriving, especially if you approach from the east in the evening, the town looks exactly as it does in old engravings or in Edward Lear's watercolours – dominated by the bulk of a colossal **Venetian fortress**, the skyline picked out with delicate minarets.

All of this is increasingly under commercial threat, but for the time being it's an enjoyable place to spend some time, with a wide, sandy **beach** and palm-fringed promenade in front of the tangled streets of the old town. There are hundreds of tavernas, bars, cafés and clubs, but the big hotels are all out of town, stretching away along the shore to the east.

Numerous attractions lie within easy striking distance of Réthymno town. In the hills to the southeast, the **Monastery of Arkádhi** is a potent symbol of the Cretan struggle for independence and an atmospheric detour on a journey into the mountainous hinterland of the province. A short way south of town, there is a fascinating Minoan cemetery at **Arméni**, and in the hills immediately above the developed coastline are old villages with tremendous views. The gorge at **Míli**, meanwhile, gives at least a hint of what awaits on the south coast.

The harbour

The Venetian or inner **harbour** is the most attractive part of Réthymno's waterfront, although these days its elegant sixteenth-century lighthouse looks down on a line of fish tavernas that have taken over the former quayside, rather than the sailing ships and barges of bygone eras. The nearby and impressive breakwaters, which are constantly being extended, reveal some of the problems with the harbour. Soon after its completion the Venetians discovered the dock's tendency to silt up, and this has been a constant hindrance ever since: until relatively recently it was unable to handle really big

---

RÉTHYMNO CITY CENTRE ORIENTATION

Réthymno **city centre**, at least as far as tourists are concerned, is the area around the seventeenth-century Venetian **Loggia**, a shop selling high-quality (and pricey) reproductions of classical art; more shops, restaurants and bars radiate in every direction. The **Rimóndi Fountain**, nearby at the western end of Paleológou, is also seventeenth-century Venetian. Half-hidden under a blocked-off arcade, the fountain's lion-head spouts still splash water down to a marble bowl, and nowadays they look out over **Platía Petiháki**, one of the liveliest areas in town. South from the fountain, a line of cafés and tavernas leads into Ethníkis Andistásis, the **market** street. Turn right just before this and the backstreets lead to the fine **Nerandzés Mosque** (used for concerts but not open to the public) with its iconic minaret dominating the skyline. Up through the market area, the old city ends at the only surviving remnant of the city walls, the **Porta Guora**. Through the gate you emerge into the busy **Platía Tessáron Martíron** with its unprepossessing modern church. Almost directly opposite are the quiet and shady **Public Gardens**, a former Turkish cemetery now laid out with a fine variety of palms and other trees.

ships or ferries. When the locals decided to set up their own ferry service to Pireás (the first vessel, *Arkadhi*, was bought by public subscription) the whole harbour had to be completely cleared out, and only a constant dredging operation keeps it open. Even now, big ships must dock in a specially constructed outer harbour; the inner harbour is today given over to small fishing *kaïkia*, pleasure craft and tourist cruise boats.

The Fortezza

Odhós Katehaki (entrance) • Daily: April–Sept 8am–7.30pm; Oct–March 8am–6pm • €4

Looking down on the old town from behind its walls on a lofty hill at the western end

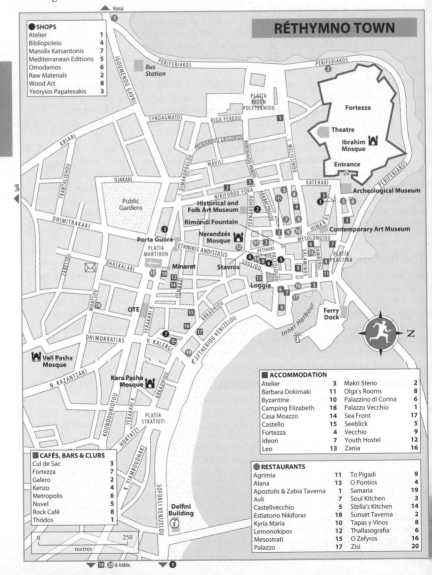

RÉTHYMNO TOWN

● SHOPS

Atelier	1
Bibliopoleio	4
Manolis Katsantonis	7
Mediterranean Editions	5
Omodamos	6
Raw Materials	2
Wood Art	8
Yeóryios Papalexakis	3

■ ACCOMMODATION

Atelier	3	Makri Steno	2
Barbara Dokimaki	11	Olga's Rooms	8
Byzantine	10	Palazzino di Corina	6
Camping Elizabeth	18	Palazzo Vecchio	1
Casa Moazzo	14	Sea Front	17
Castello	15	Seeblick	5
Fortezza	4	Vecchio	9
Ideon	7	Youth Hostel	12
Leo	13	Zania	16

● RESTAURANTS

Agrimia	11	To Pigadi	9
Alana	13	O Pontios	4
Apostolis & Zabia Taverna	1	Samaria	19
Avli	7	Soul Kitchen	3
Castellvecchio	5	Stella's Kitchen	14
Estiatorio Nikiforas	18	Sunset Taverna	2
Kyria Maria	10	Tapas y Vinos	8
Lemonokipos	12	Thallasografia	6
Mesostrati	15	O Zefyros	16
Palazzo	17	Zisi	20

■ CAFÉS, BARS & CLUBS

Cul de Sac	3
Fortezza	7
Galero	2
Kenzo	4
Metropolis	6
Nuvel	5
Rock Café	8
Thódos	1

0   250
metres

18, 20 & Iráklio   8

of the seafront stands the massive **Fortezza** or **Venetian Fortress**. Although much is ruined now, the fort remains thoroughly atmospheric, with **views** from the walls over the town and harbour, or in the other direction along the coast to the west. Walk around the outside, preferably at sunset, to get an impression of its vast bulk; there are more great views along the coast, and a pleasant resting point around the far side at the *Sunset Taverna* (see p.195).

Brief history

Said to be the largest Venetian castle ever built, the Fortezza was a response, in the last quarter of the sixteenth century, to a series of **pirate raids** (by Barbarossa in 1538 and Uluch Ali in 1562 and 1571) that had devastated the town. Designed by the Italian engineer Sforza Pallavicini, the mammoth edifice took a full ten years to build at a crippling cost and was large enough for the entire population to take shelter within its walls. Whether it was effective is another matter; in 1645 the Venetian city fell to the Turks in less than 24 hours (they simply bypassed the fort), and when the English writer Robert Pashley visited in 1834 he found the guns, some of them still the Venetian originals, to be entirely useless.

Visiting the Fortezza

As you walk through the impressive gateway in the walls you pass what must have been some sort of **guardhouse** within the bastion, and then you emerge into the vast open interior space, dotted with the remains of barracks, arsenals, officers' houses, earthworks and deep shafts. At the centre is a large domed building which was once a **church** and later – following the fall of the town to the Turks – converted into a **mosque** dedicated to the then ruling sultan, Ibrahim. Recently renovated, it has a truly fabulous **dome** and a pretty carved mihrab (a niche indicating the direction of Mecca), both of which are Turkish additions. Just north of the church/mosque are some fine arched foundations and a **stairway** leading down to a gate in the seaward defences. Among the most impressive remains are the **cisterns** where rainwater would have been collected: they are deep and cool, and dimly lit by slits through which shafts of sunlight penetrate.

The Archeological Museum

Odhós Katehaki • Tues–Sun 9am–4pm • €3

Réthymno's **Archeological Museum** lies almost directly opposite the entrance to the Fortezza, in a building built by the Turks as an extra defence, and which later served as a prison. It's now entirely modern inside – cool, spacious and airy – and well worth a visit. There's an interesting collection of Minoan pottery and sarcophagi, as well as Roman coins, jewellery, pots and statues, all of them from Réthymno province. Take a look beneath the central atrium at an unusual unfinished Roman **statue of Aphrodite**, with the sculptor's chisel marks still plain to see, allowing you to glimpse the goddess's features – never completed – emerging from the stone.

The Historical and Folk Art Museum

M. Vernárdhou 28 • Mon–Sat 9.30am–2.30pm & 6–9.30pm • €3

The enjoyable **Historical and Folk Art Museum**, in a beautifully restored seventeenth-century Venetian mansion near the Nerandzés Mosque, has two rooms filled with musical instruments (including the *lyra* of Nikos Piskopakis, one of its greatest-ever exponents), old photos, basketry, farm tools, traditional costumes and jewellery, lace, weaving and embroidery, knives and old wooden chests and pottery (with early examples from Margarítes, still one of Réthymno's most important pottery centres today). A newer section includes entertaining reconstructions of a traditional *kafenío*, plus recreated barbers' and blacksmiths' shops. It's a fascinating insight into the island's fast-disappearing lifestyles, many of which had survived virtually unchanged from Venetian times to the 1960s.

The Contemporary Art Museum

Himáras 5 • Tues–Fri 9am–2pm & 7–9pm, Sat & Sun 11am–3pm • €3 • ⓦ rca.gr

The interesting **Contemporary Art Museum** features works by Greek and Cretan sculptors and painters, with oils and watercolours by Réthymno-born artist Lefteris Kanakakis (1934–85) forming the core of the collection. They also stage frequent special exhibitions.

The beach

Flanking the north side of the old town, you can't miss **Réthymno beach**, an invitingly broad swathe of tawny sand stretching away to the east. There are showers and cafés, and the waters protected by the breakwaters are dead calm (and ideal for kids). Sadly, they're also crowded and often none too clean. Outside the harbour, less sheltered sands stretch for kilometres, only marginally less crowded but with much cleaner water. Interspersed among the hotels along here is every facility you could need – travel agents, bike rental, bars and restaurants.

Hromonastíri and around

One of the most attractive drives you could take out of Réthymno is to Míli and **HROMONASTÍRI (Χρομοναστήρι)**, hill villages to the southeast of town, with the chance to walk down the Míli Gorge on the way back. The road up to Hromonastíri (a couple of buses run from town on weekdays) winds attractively up the side of the gorge to arrive at the ancient and beautiful village. Its numerous, well-signposted sights include an ancient olive mill, two Byzantine churches and the Villa Clodio, a striking Venetian mansion that has been restored as a local history museum.

The Míli Gorge

The entry to the **Míli Gorge (Μύλοι Φαράγγι)** is signed off the road below Hromonastíri, just beneath the village of **Míli**. Considering that you're barely 5km from the centre of Réthymno here, the gorge is pretty impressive, though obviously it can't compare with the great south-coast ravines. Starting the descent to the bottom of the gorge, you'll find a friendly café-snack bar from where the path down is well signed. In the early sections you'll see the abandoned buildings of an old hamlet, including the mill from which the gorge takes its name; there's plenty of water in the stream, so this is a lush and shady walk. After about an hour, you arrive at the bottom. Here you can either walk back up, or if you walk about twenty minutes more, taking minor roads along the bottom of the gorge, you will come to the main road outside Perivólia, where you can pick up a bus or taxi.

Arméni Minoan cemetery

Arméni, 10km south of Réthymno • Tues–Sun 8.30am–3pm • Free

The little-visited but fascinating **Minoan cemetery** at **ARMÉNI (Αρμένοι)** features more than two hundred rock-cut tombs dating from the Late Minoan period, after the fall of the great palaces. Most of the tombs, pleasantly sited today in a shady oak wood, are of the *drómos* (passage) and chamber type. One large tomb under a cover on the

GERMAN BEER COMES TO CRETE

When German Bernd Brink decided to build a **brewery** in Arméni after marrying a local girl, many thought he had bitten off more than he could chew. But using tact, diplomacy, and not a little tenacity, he started work on what is now **Brink's Brewery** (☎ 28310 41243, ⓦ brinks-beer.gr) in 2001. Today this glittering stainless steel model of Teutonic efficiency receives orders from as far away as Cyprus and Denmark. He produces two very tasty brews, a blonde and a dark – both organic and made in accordance with sixteenth-century German beer purity laws. Unfiltered and unpasteurized, they are made only with water, hops, yeast and malt. The brewery is 3km south of the village of Arméni and is open for visits (and tastings) on the first Sat of the month (10am–1pm). If you call by at other times and the proprietor isn't too busy he will still give you a tour (and most likely a tasting). The beer is widely available in bars and tavernas throughout Réthymno and Haniá provinces. For a bite to eat after you've visited the brewery, head to the excellent **taverna** in the nearby village of Goulediana (see p.195).

3

south side of the site has a particularly spectacular *drómos* and finely cut chamber, and may well have belonged to a royal personage. Many others are almost as impressive, although at some only the *drómos* has been cut, and work seems for some reason to have been abandoned. A number of important discoveries have been made here, including many *lárnakes* (clay coffins) and rich grave goods – weapons, jewellery, vases and a rare helmet made from boar's tusks – now on display in the archeological museums at Réthymno and Iráklio. One mystery is still to be solved: the location of the sizeable settlement that provided this necropolis with its customers.

The Monastery of Arkádhi

25km southeast of the city in the foothills of the Psilorítis range • Daily 8am–8pm • €2.50 • There are tours from Réthymno, plus 3 daily buses (2 at weekends); if driving, watch out for the road layout at the approach to the monastery, the road from Réthymno passes the monastery on one side, and the Amári/Eléftherna road on the other, and they're connected by the unpaved track through the monastery's car park

The **Monastery of Arkádhi** (**Μονή Αρκαδίο**) is effectively a national Cretan shrine to the nineteenth-century struggle for independence. Historical resonance apart, the monastery's striking architecture and highly scenic location are reason enough to visit. It won't take you long to see the place: you can peer into the roofless **vault** beside the cloister where the 1866 explosion (see p.192) took place, and wander about the rest of the well-restored grounds in less than half an hour. The bulk of the buildings were relatively unscathed by the explosion and Arkádhi is still a working monastery. Of the surviving buildings the **church** is the most impressive, its rich mix of styles placing it among the finest Venetian structures left in Crete. The rest of the monastery is mainly seventeenth-century (though it was originally founded as early as the eleventh) and more familiar in layout and style. Across the courtyard from the scene of the explosion a small **museum**, devoted to the exploits of the defenders of the faith, contains a variety of mementoes and tributes, blood-stained clothing and commemorative medals. Opposite the monastery (next to its cafeteria-taverna) is a monumental **ossuary** where skulls and bones of many of the explosion's victims are displayed behind glass.

Food is available from the monastery's rather unappealing **cafeteria-taverna**, and there are plenty of picnic spots nearby. More attractive places to eat can be found in almost any direction, with onward routes south to the Amári valley (see p.214) or northeast to Eléftherna (see p.205), just 5km away, and the potters' village of Margarítes (see p.204).

3

A SHRINE TO CRETAN INDEPENDENCE

Historically, Arkádhi was one of the richest monasteries in Crete and a well-known stopover for travellers, as well as a centre of resistance. In the 1820s eighty Muslims, who had occupied the monastery to pacify local rebels, were captured and put to death; in retaliation, many of the buildings were burned.

It is the events of **1866**, however, which guarantee Arkádhi a place in history. In the rebellion of that year the monastery served as a Cretan stronghold in which, as the Turks took the upper hand, hundreds of Cretan guerrillas and their families took refuge. Here they were surrounded by a Turkish army until, after a siege of two days, the defences were finally breached on November 9, 1866. As the attackers poured in, the ammunition stored in the monastery exploded – deliberately fired, according to the accepted version of events, on the orders of the abbot. Hundreds were killed in the initial blast, Cretans and Turks alike, and most of the surviving defenders were put to death by the enraged assailants. This incited a wave of international sympathy for the cause of **Cretan independence**. Figures as disparate as Victor Hugo, Garibaldi and the poet Swinburne were moved to public declarations of support, and in Britain money was raised for a ship (the *Arkádhi*) to run the Turkish blockade. Though Crete's liberty was still some way off at that stage, the monastery remains the most potent symbol of the struggle (and the anniversary of the blast is commemorated on November 7–9 each year). More recently the monastery lent assistance to guerrilla fighters during **World War II**: George Psychoundakis, for example, describes handing over supplies from a parachute drop to the monks.

ARRIVAL AND DEPARTURE

RÉTHYMNO TOWN AND AROUND

BY CAR

Most people arrive in Réthymno by road, turning off the main E75 highway and descending the 1km into the town. You can often find a parking place near Platía Plastíra near the ferry dock (where there is also a pay car park with plenty of space), around the public garden (with another pay car park) or in the streets surrounding Platía Stratioti at the east end of the seafront.

Car rental Ellotia Tours, Arkadhíou 155 (☎ 28310 51981, ✆ rethymnoatcrete.com), are very reliable, with a ten percent discount for *Rough Guide* readers with this Guide. They also do collection and drop-off at Iráklio or Haniá airports.

BY BUS

Coming in by bus it's easy to get your bearings: walk north along the seafront towards the fortress, then right onto Vlastou, left along Riga Ferou and right again along Melissinou, or one of the narrower alleys of the old town. There's left luggage available (Mon–Fri 9am–11pm, Sat & Sun 9am–5pm; ☎ 28310 57766; €1/item/24hr).

Destinations Amári (Mon, Wed & Fri; 5.30am & 2.15pm; 1hr); Anóyia (Mon–Fri; 5.30am & 2pm; 1hr 30min); Arkádhi (3 daily; 6am, 10.30am & 2.30pm; 50min); Ay. Galíni (5 daily; 5.30am–5.30pm; 1hr 30min); Haniá

(17 daily; 6am–10.30pm; 1hr 30min–3hr); Hóra Sfakíon (change at Vrísses; 3 daily; 8am, 10am & 1pm; 1hr 45min); Iráklio (17 daily; 6.30am–10.15pm; 1hr 30min–2hr); Moní Préveli (2 daily; 11.30am & 6pm; 45min); Omalós (daily at 7am; 2hr 30min); Pánormos & hotels en route (34 daily; 1hr 15min); Plakiás (5 daily; 6.15am–6pm; 45min).

BY FERRY

If you arrive by ferry you'll come in at the western edge of the harbour, with the old town directly ahead of you. For information and tickets, visit the very helpful Ellotia Tours, Arkadhíou 155 (☎ 28310 51981, ✆ rethymnoatcrete.com). The ANEK Lines office is at Arkadhíou 250 (☎ 28310 29221, ✆ anek.gr).

Destinations There are direct sailings to Piraeus on the Elli-T (Tues, Thurs, Sat & Sun, 9pm). In summer there are two fast catamarans a week to Thíra (Santoríni; Tues & Sat; 2hr 30min; around €140); cost includes a meal and island bus tour.

BY PLANE

The nearest airports to Réthymno are at Haniá (60km) and Iráklio (78km). Airline information and tickets can be obtained from local travel agents (see p.197).

INFORMATION AND ACTIVITIES

Tourist office In the Delfini Building, a 5min walk east from the harbour along the seafront (Mon–Fri 8.30am–2.30pm; ☎ 28310 29148).

Boat trips The Dolphin company runs 4 daily trips on the

Dolphin Express to Pánormos, Balí and the Skaléta "pirate" caves (adults €25, under-12s €10), along with trips to Yeoryioúpolis, evening cruises and fishing expeditions. The *Barbarossa* makes similar trips on a more touristy "Jolly

Roger" vessel, complete with sails, which is great fun for kids (adults €22, kids €17). Both boats are on the inner harbour.

Diving Paradise Dive Center (☎ 28310 26317, ⓦ diving -center.gr), 10km west of town off the E75 highway, offers PADI-certificated scuba courses for beginners and facilities for certified divers. They will collect you and return you to your hotel. Kalypso Diving Centre, Sofoklés Venizélou 4, near Platía Stratioti (☎ 28310 20990, ⓦ kalypsodivingcenter.com), also offers PADI beginners and advanced courses. Fees include transfers to and from their dive centre near Plakiás on the south coast.

Fishing trips The Dolphin company (see above) runs 4hr fishing trips (€25), which includes a meal cooked from the catch, eaten on board with wine and salad.

Mountain climbing The local EOS mountain climbing club is at Dhimokratias 12 (☎ 28310 23666); besides advice on climbing, it also organizes walking tours and easy climbs that anyone can join.

Walking tours The Happy Walker, Tombázi 56 (☎ 28310 52920, ⓦ happywalker.com), a long-standing Dutch operation near the youth hostel, offers walking tours from one day to two weeks. Single-day guided walks cost €30 (lunch €10 extra), including transport to and from your hotel to the start point.

ACCOMMODATION

There are many places to stay in Réthymno, with the greatest concentration of **rooms** in the tangled streets west of the inner harbour, between the Rimóndi Fountain and the museums. There are also quite a few places on and around Arkadhíou. The higher-category **hotels** are all modern and businesslike and some boutique places are very attractive indeed; the downmarket hotels are, on the whole, less good value than the rooms places, though more likely to have space – there are several along or just off Arkadhíou. For central, rock-bottom budget accommodation, the only option is the **youth hostel** (see p.194).

AROUND THE HARBOUR AND THE FORTRESS

★ **Atelier** Himáras 25 ☎ 28310 24440, ⓦ frosso -bora.com. This small place near the fortress is run by a talented potter with a studio in the basement and a store on the other side of the building (see p.196). The attractive en-suite a/c rooms come with kitchenette and satellite TV. Free wi-fi. **€45**

Barbara Dokimaki Platía Plastíra 7 ☎ 28310 22607, ⓦ barbarastudios.gr. Strange warren of a place, with one entrance on Platía Plastíra, just off the harbourfront behind the *Ideon*, and another on Dambergi. Offers a/c studios with kitchenette and TV; the more attractive options are on the top floor. Free wi-fi. **€55**

★ **Fortezza** I. Melissínou 16 ☎ 28310 55551, ⓦ fortezza.gr. Stylish, top-of-the-range but good-value hotel in a central location with everything you'd expect for the price, including a/c rooms (most with balcony, some with terrace), bar, pool and restaurant. Breakfast included. Free wi-fi. **€88**

Ideon Platía Plastíra 10 ☎ 28310 28667, ⓦ hotelideon .gr. Upmarket hotel in an excellent location just north of the ferry dock – try to get a balcony room with a sea view. Rooms come with a/c, TV and internet and there's a pool. Advance booking essential in high season. Breakfast included. Free wi-fi. **€90**

Makri Steno Nikiforou Foka 54 ☎ 28310 55465, ⓦ www.makristeno.gr. A rambling but welcoming and nicely renovated mansion, with light, fresh a/c en-suite rooms and studios with fridge and TV and a huge roof terrace. Also some slightly more expensive apartments. Free wi-fi. **€45**

Palazzino di Corina Dambergi 7–9 ☎ 28310 21205, ⓦ corina.gr. Sumptuous luxury suites with a/c, minibar and satellite TV in a stunningly restored Venetian palace; the charming patio squeezes in a small pool. Breakfast included. Free wi-fi. **€114**

Palazzo Vecchio Junction of Iróon Politehniou and I. Melissínou ☎ 28310 35351, ⓦ palazzovecchio.gr. A delightful small apartment/studio boutique hotel in a restored Venetian mansion, where elegantly furnished rooms come with full bathroom, a/c and TV; there's also a small pool. Breakfast included. Internet bookings get a discount. Free wi-fi. **€110**

Seeblick Platía Plastíra 17 ☎ 28310 22478, ⓦ seeblick .rethymnon.com. On the seafront as you walk round from the inner harbour towards the outer wall of the fortress. En-suite a/c studio rooms come with kitchenette and, if you're lucky, a balcony sea view – there are cheaper rooms without views. Good value for the location, although the owners prefer to rent by the week, and won't even consider a single-night stay in Aug. Free wi-fi in reception. **€40**

Vecchio Daliani 4, near the Rimóndi Fountain ☎ 28310 54985, ⓦ vecchio.gr. Elegant Venetian mansion tastefully transformed into an enchanting small hotel. Rooms come with a/c, balcony and fridge, and are set around a pool. Free wi-fi. **€60**

ALONG AND BEHIND THE BEACH

Castello Karaoli 10 ☎ 28310 23570, ⓦ castello -rethymno.gr. A very pleasant small *pension* in a 300-year-old Turkish mansion; a/c en-suite rooms come with fridge and TV and there's a delightful patio garden for taking breakfast (extra). **€50**

3

Leo Vafe 2 ☎ 28310 26197, ⓦ leohotel.gr. Charming boutique hotel in yet another restored Venetian mansion with eight luxurious and individually styled rooms featuring lots of exposed stonework. All are equipped with fridge and satellite TV and some come with jacuzzi. Breakfast included. Free wi-fi. €107

Olga's Rooms Souliou 57 ☎ 28310 54896, ⓦ rethymnoguide.com/olgas. Set in a nice old building with roof garden on this touristy street, the en-suite studios overlooking the sea are very good, with a/c, kitchenette and TV. There are also a/c en-suite rooms and cheaper rooms without bath, plus a great breakfast bar/ diner, *Stella's Kitchen* (see below). €35

Sea Front Arkadhíou 159 ☎ 28310 51981, ⓦ rethymnoatcrete.com. Good a/c en-suite rooms in a restored old house, some with sea-view balconies (others overlook Arkadhíou), and all with fridge and TV. The welcoming owners also have a number of excellent sea-view apartments nearby. *Rough Guide* readers can claim a ten percent discount. Free wi-fi. Rooms €45, apartments €50

Zania Pavlou Vlastou 3 ☎ 28310 28169. A refurbished old Venetian mansion, on the corner of Arkadhíou, run by courteous, French-speaking proprietors. The elegant high-ceilinged rooms come with a/c and their own fridge, but bathrooms are shared. €35

NEAR THE PUBLIC GARDENS

Byzantine Vosporou 26 ☎ 28310 55609, ⓦ byzantine hotel.gr. Light and airy a/c en-suite rooms in a renovated old Byzantine palace, which also has a tranquil patio bar. Free wi-fi. €60

Casa Moazzo Tombázi 57 ☎ 28310 36235, ⓦ casamoazzo.gr. Delightful boutique hotel with a friendly female proprietor, offering six luxurious and stylish suites with king-size beds, sitting area and jacuzzi plus coffee- and tea-making facilities. Breakfast included. Free wi-fi. €100

Youth Hostel Tombázi 41 ☎ 28310 22848, ⓦ yhrethymno.com. The cheapest beds in town, in dorm rooms, in this large, clean, friendly and popular hostel. There's a café for food, free hot showers, internet access, and even a library. Free wi-fi. €11

CAMPSITE

Camping Elizabeth About 4km east of town ☎ 28310 28694, ⓦ camping-elizabeth.net. A large, appealing beach site with all facilities, and regular connections to the city using the hotel bus (marked "Scaleta/El Greco") which runs between here and the town bus station. Two people plus tent and car €24.40

EATING

Immediately **behind the town beach** are arrayed the most obvious of Réthymno's restaurants, all with illustrated menus out front and most with waiters who will run off their patter in a variety of languags. These places are sometimes reasonable value – especially if you hanker after an "English breakfast" – but they are all thoroughly touristy. Around the inner harbour there's a cluster of rather more expensive and intimate fish tavernas with annoyingly persistent greeters. The more authentic places are found away from the waterfront in and around the **old town**. With your own transport, should you fancy a bite to eat before or after visiting the Minoan site or brewery (see p.191) you can try the excellent taverna in the village of **Goulediana**.

AROUND THE RIMÓNDI FOUNTAIN

Agrimia Platía Petiháki, ☎ 28310 24735. Studio-workshop selling creative modern ceramics from local potter Frosso Bora. Daily 10am–midnight.

★ **Avli** Xanthoudidou 22 ☎ 28310 26213. Réthymno's top restaurant is an upmarket place in a Venetian mansion with an exquisite garden patio. The food – prepared under head chef Aristea Dafnomili – is top-notch, offering carefully prepared traditional dishes from Crete as well as creative dishes from Greece and further afield. Try the *Avli* salad or their own version of *moussaká*. Prices are on the high side (mains €13–29), but the food is outstanding. There's also an extensive wine list. Daily 11am–1am.

Kyria Maria Moshovitou 20 ☎ 28130 25681. Pleasant, unassuming small taverna tucked down an alley behind the Rimóndi Fountain serving wholesome Cretan food. After the meal everyone gets a couple of María's delicious

tiropitákia topped with honey, on the house. Daily 8am–midnight.

Lemonokipos Andistásis 100 ☎ 28310 57087. A charming garden restaurant serving a variety of tasty meat and fish dishes at tables under the lemon trees, with a decent selection of (slightly pricey) wines. April–Oct daily 10.30am–midnight.

★ **To Pigadi** Xanthoudidou 31 ☎ 28310 27522. Excellent taverna in the old town, with an attractive garden terrace containing an ancient well (*pigadi*). Reasonably priced traditional dishes are cooked with flair, plus there's very good house wine (€8/litre) and a decent wine list. April–Nov daily noon–1am.

★ **Stella's Kitchen** Souliou 55 ☎ 28310 54896. A great-value and welcoming little diner run by the eponymous and ebullient proprietor. Stella serves up six daily specials (at least two of which are vegetarian) each day; it's also good for breakfast. Daily 8am–8pm.

Tapas y Vinos Melissinou 14 ☎28130 58554. An expatriate *malagueña* (from Málaga) has given Réthymno its first genuine Spanish tapas bar, complete with varied tapas, excellent *jamón serrano* and superb Spanish wines. March–Sept daily 6pm–1am.

INNER HARBOUR AND FORTRESS

Alana Salaminas 11. An attractive, tree-filled courtyard provides the setting for very good Cretan and Greek cuisine served at competitive prices. Try the *arnaki aginarato* (lamb with artichokes in an egg-lemon sauce). Also very good house wine and a range of bottled vintages. May–Oct daily noon–2am.

Castellvecchio Himáras 29 ☎28310 55163. Inviting small family taverna next to the Fortezza, offering carefully prepared dishes (any with lamb are recommended) and quite a few vegetarian choices. There's also a pleasant terrace with a view over the city. March–Oct daily 6–11pm.

Palazzo At the inner harbour. One of the nicest settings on the harbour, with tables on a rooftop terrace, but rather overpriced for what you get – simple fish and Cretan standards. April–Oct daily 11am–midnight.

O Pontios I. Melissinou 34. A tiny, economical and unassuming place near the Archeological Museum and the fortress, serving surprisingly good food – a worthwhile lunchtime stop. Daily 10am–midnight.

Soul Kitchen Junction of Katehaki and Himáras near the fortress ☎28310 30533. Réthymno's newest restaurant, a café-diner, is dedicated to organic vegetarian cuisine. The menu lists salads, veggie burgers, omelettes and local cheeses as well as grilled vegetables and daily specials and there's a daily all-you-can-eat buffet for €15. Frequent live music at weekends, and they also offer yoga classes in an annexe. April–Oct daily 9am–10pm.

Sunset Taverna Periforiakos ☎28310 23943. Frequented more for its spectacular sunset views than its food, but the meals aren't bad value and there's usually a decent selection of fish. The terrace tables are right by the shore – the waiters have to cross the road from the kitchen. It's an ideal place for an ouzo and *mezédhes* at sunset with the breakers splashing over the rocks below. April–Oct daily 9am–11pm.

★**Thallasografia** Kefalogianidon 33 ☎28310 52569. Best approached from the car park fronting the fort entrance (although there are steps from the road below), this is a superb new-style taverna perched on a cliff overlooking the sea. The views are sensational and service is slick – recommended dishes include grilled sardines, *arní sti stamna* (jugged lamb) and *rizóto me múdia* (mussel risotto). There's also a cocktail bar (evenings only) above the dining area. Daily 10am–midnight.

O Zefyros At the inner harbour ☎28310 28206. If you're determined to eat by the water, you could do worse than this, one of the more reliable of the harbourside fish tavernas, offering reasonably priced (for this location) fish and seafood. March–Oct daily 10am–midnight.

SEAFRONT AND NEW TOWN

Apostolis & Zabía Taverna Junction of Periferiakos and Igoum Gavril ☎28310 24561. Highly popular – and good-value – local taverna specializing in lunchtime *mayireftá* (pre-cooked dishes), served until they run out. Evenings tend to be more subdued with standard meat and fish dishes served on a seafront terrace. Daily 11am–midnight.

Estiatorio Nikiforas Moatsou 40 ☎28310 55403. Typical town *estiatório*, off the tourist trail and with a nice shaded terrace, where the hearty (low-priced) food is made daily and you choose from the heated trays behind a glass display. Daily 9am–6pm.

★**Mesostrati** Yerakári 1 ☎28310 29375. An excellent and economical little neighbourhood taverna-ouzerí serving well-prepared country dishes on a shady small terrace. Try their tasty *apákia* (smoked pork) or *loukánika* (sausage). Live Cretan *lyra* and *laoúto* (lute) performances most Fri and Sat eves, with big-name performers known to drop in for impromptu jam sessions. Daily 10am–3pm & 6pm–2am; closed Sun eve.

Samaria Venizélou, almost opposite the tourist office. One of the few seafront places patronized by locals (and tellingly the only one that stays open all year), serving well-prepared taverna standards at reasonable prices. Daily 24hr.

★**Zisi** Missíria village, 2km east of town along the coast road ☎28310 28814. *Zisi* is one of the great Réthymno institutions, where local families get together for celebrations and feasting, especially on Sunday lunchtimes, when booking is advised. The place is large and elegant with real table linen, *mayireftá* laid out in heated display cabinets and a menu filled with other tempting fish and meat dishes; both food and wine are economically priced. It's accessible by taxi from the centre. Daily 11am–midnight.

GOULEDIANÁ

Goules Taverna Main square, Gouledianá ☎28310 41001. An outstanding country taverna that uses local ingredients to create traditional Cretan cuisine often with a creative twist, with good meat, fish and vegetarian options. It also serves Brinks beers (see p.191). The taverna lies down a turn-off heading east 2km south of Arméni. June–Oct Tues–Fri 5–10.30pm, Sat 2–10.30pm, Sun noon–10.30pm; Nov–May Tues–Sat 2–10.30pm, Sun noon–10.30pm.

3

RÉTHYMNO'S SUMMER FESTIVALS

The nominal entrance fee for the annual **Réthymno Wine Festival**, held in the Public Gardens in the second half of July – and which celebrates Cretan wine, foods and olive oil – includes all the wine you can drink from barrels set up around the gardens, with food stalls and entertainment laid on. Meanwhile, every August Réthymno puts on its **Renaissance Festival** (Anagennisiakó). The fortress and venues around the old town host folk and classical music concerts and theatrical events, as well as performances of Classical tragedies and comedies; a full programme is available from the tourist office.

DRINKING, NIGHTLIFE AND ENTERTAINMENT

Réthymno's bars and nightlife are concentrated in the same general areas as the restaurants. At the western end of Venizélou, in the streets behind the inner harbour, pavements soon fill with the overflow from a cluster of noisy **music bars** where partygoers gather before the clubs open. The café-cum-cocktail places around the Rimóndi Fountain are great for people-watching, but the cacophony of late-evening noise from competing bars is less than relaxing. A few less raucous **cocktail bars** can be found up Salaminos towards the fortress and below the *Ideon* hotel on Platía Plastíra, although students tend to colonize this latter area during term time. Larger **clubs** are mostly out to the east, among the big hotels, but there are one or two in town as well.

CAFÉS, BARS AND CLUBS

Cul de Sac Platía Petiháki. Stylish *kafenío* overlooking the Rimóndi Fountain. The prices are higher than average, but it's a great place to people-watch over a coffee or a sundowner. Daily 8am–3am.

Fortezza Inner harbour. A big, glitzy disco-bar, where the action kicks off after midnight. Daily 9pm–late.

Galero Platía Petiháki. Large beers, toasted sandwiches and snacks served on one of the town's most popular terraces for seeing and being seen. Daily 8am–2am.

Kenzo Platía Plastíra 4. Music café with lively terrace favoured by the town's students. Similar stylish bars fill the rest of this square. Daily 9am–2am.

Metropolis Nearchou 24. A loud rock-music bar just round the corner from the *Fortezza* disco-bar, on an alley which connects with Arkadhíou. Daily 10pm–late.

Nuvel Near the old harbour pier at the western side of the inner harbour. Chic, all-day drinks and music bar playing Greek and international sounds. They turn up the volume around 10pm. Daily 9am–2am.

Rock Café Petiháki 8, near the inner harbour. Big, brash dance club attracting large crowds in high summer for R&B, house and hip-hop. Daily 11pm–5am.

Thódos Nikiforou Foka 86. A great new music bar inside a cavernous Venetian-Turkish building with many original features including an eighteenth-century Turkish bathhouse. The playlist ranges from blues and jazz to rock and reggae, and there's usually live music at weekends. Daily 9pm–3am.

SHOPPING

Atelier Atelier pension, Himáras 25 ☎ 28310 24440, ⓦ frosso-bora.com. Studio-workshop selling creative modern ceramics from local potter Frosso Bora. Mon–Sat 10am–2pm & 5–9pm.

Bibliopoleío Souliou 43. A handy place for secondhand English-language books in the old town. Mon–Fri 9am–2pm & 6–9pm, Sat 9am–2pm.

Manolis Katsantonis V. Kalergi 38, near the junction with Arkadhíou. Réthymno is a centre of *lyra* and *laoúto* (lute) production. This is one of the dozen or so workshops in town where you can see Crete's beautiful "national" instruments being made by a master craftsman. Mon–Sat 9am–2pm & 5.30–9pm.

Mediterranean Editions Paleológou, near the Rimóndi Fountain. A good selection of books in English, as well as many foreign newspapers. Mon–Sat 8am–9pm.

Omodamos Souliou 3. Innovative handmade ceramics produced in Crete and elswhere. Mon–Sat 8.30am–2pm & 5.30–9pm.

Raw Materials Arabatsoglou 38 ⓦ www.avli rawmaterials.gr. The speciality Cretan and Greek food shop of the *Avli* restaurant (see p.194), just a stone's throw away from the restaurant, it stocks many of the island's best wines and olive oils in addition to herbs, cheeses and lots more. Mon–Sat 10am–2pm & 5.30–9.30pm.

Wood Art Petalioti 2 ⓦ siragas.gr. Internationally recognized woodturner Nikos Siragas produces wonderful creative sculptures in olive, eucalyptus, walnut and carob woods. His creations are on show at his gallery-workshop and most are for sale. April–Oct Mon–Sat 10.30am–2.30pm & 6–10.30pm.

Yeóryios Papalexakis Dimakopolou 6, near the Porta Guora. One of Réthymno's *lyra*-makers whom you can watch while he works. Prices for these stunningly crafted instruments range from €150 to more than €1000. Mon–Sat 9am–2pm & 5.30–9pm.

DIRECTORY

Banks ATMs are to be found throughout the centre; the National Bank, at the foot of Dhimokratias west of the Public Gardens, has a 24hr ATM which takes MasterCard and Eurocard. Over the road, the Interamerican Bank has another ATM, with more along nearby Koundouriótou.

Bike rental Stavros Paleológou 14 (☎ 28310 22858). Mountain bike rental for €7/day.

Internet Galero on Platía Petiháki by the Rimóndi Fountain (daily 9am–midnight), or Cybernet, Kalergi 44 (daily 10am–midnight).

Pharmacies Plenty on the main shopping streets, especially Koundouriótou and Arkadhíou. Check the rota on the door for late/weekend opening. The tourist office has a list of English-speaking doctors.

Post office The main post office (Mon–Fri 7.30am–8pm) is on Moátsou, opposite the *Brascos* hotel.

Taxis There are ranks in Platía Tessáron Martíron and Platía Stratioti, or call ☎ 28310 25000.

Travel agents There are several travel agents along Paleológou, Arkhadhíou and Koundouriótou, and also around Platía Stratioti and along Venizélou. The following can all arrange excursions and domestic flight and ferry tickets: Ellotia Tours (☎ 28310 51981); Creta Connection, Kallergi 15 (☎ 28310 24977); Apoplous Travel, Giampoudaki 11 (☎ 28310 20476).

West of Réthymno

Heading **west from Réthymno** the roads are easy and efficient, but offer little in the way of diversion. The main E75 **highway** initially climbs above the coast before dropping back to sea level at **Yeráni**, 6km from Réthymno, with a rocky cove good for swimming. Beyond, after another brief flirtation with the hills, the road finally levels out beside the **Gulf of Almirós**, from where it traces the shore, flat and straight, the rest of the way to Yeoryioúpolis (see p.260). A long and windswept **sandy beach** follows it all the way, separated from the road by straggling bushes of oleander. The beach is virtually deserted much of the way, but there can be dangerous currents so don't venture too far out; it gets further from the road and considerably more sheltered as you approach the development at Yeoryioúpolis.

The scenic **old road**, which peels off to head inland soon after you leave the city, is by comparison quite populous. You'll pass through five or six prosperous little villages before arriving, after 23km, at **Episkopí**, a local market centre with narrow, twisting hilly streets at its heart. Here you're approaching the foothills of the White Mountains, which rise with increasing majesty ahead. Beyond Episkopí the road soon divides, the main way descending steadily towards Yeoryioúpolis, a secondary route climbing through the village of Kournás (see p.261) and then dropping steeply to the lake. Alternatively you can head **south** towards **Argiroúpolis**, **Asigonía** and a series of small mountain villages, a rarely travelled route where the old life continues, and where there are good opportunities for **hiking** in the surrounding hills. This road, which in the other direction is a short cut to the coastal highway, turns off just before Episkopí, bypassing the narrowest streets.

Argiroúpolis

ARGIROÚPOLIS (Αργυρούπολη), 6km south of Episkopí and 22km southwest of Réthymno, is a strikingly scenic village with a split personality: the lower village congregates around its famous **springs**, while the upper village is founded on the ruins of the prestigious ancient Greco-Roman city of **Lappa**. With lovely views over the Mouséllas river valley and surrounded by some fine **walking** country in the foothills of the White Mountains, it is one of the most attractive villages in this part of Crete.

The lower village

The **lower village**, reached by taking a right downhill when you come to a fork (the Asigonía road), is effectively comprised of five **tavernas** in a spectacular wooded setting where gushing spring water cascades in every direction from the hill above. Vegetation is abundant in this fertile environment and, as well as great numbers of chestnut and plane trees, there are even banana plants. The roar of water is impressive; there's so much of it here that it supplies the whole of Réthymno town.

The Venetian Fulling Mill

Go through the grounds of the *Vieux Moulin* taverna and pass through a barred wooden gate; at the chapel in the field opposite, fronted by a Roman pillar, turn left downhill to find the mill on the right facing a great plane tree

The remarkable seventeenth-century **Venetian fulling mill**, complete with a rare wooden fulling machine, was accidentally discovered in 1994 by a British team. Once driven by water from the spring, it was used for shrinking, beating and preparing cloth. Plans to save and restore this unique piece of Crete's industrial history have so far come to nothing and the mill and its wooden machinery are further damaged each passing winter by the elements. Between the mill and the springs are the scanty remains of the **Roman baths** of ancient Lappa – ask at the *Vieux Moulin* taverna if you have problems finding these.

The upper village

Argiroúpolis's **upper village**, reached by taking the left fork uphill (or by climbing a path which ascends steps from the springs), lies around a tranquil square overlooked by the elegant seventeenth-century Venetian church of **Áyios Ioánnis**. This segment of the village is built over the celebrated ancient city of **Lappa** (see below), parts of which can be seen near the church; archeologists have been busy over recent years excavating and documenting the city's ancient necropolis in the valley to the north, where they have unearthed a wealth of grave goods. Beyond the church, the village's **folk museum** is also worth a look (daily 10am–7pm; free).

Heading downhill from the west side of the square along narrow, stepped streets, you come to a smaller square (the old **marketplace**), with a couple of tiny churches en route. At the northern end of the village beyond the *Morfeas* guesthouse, a pleasant walk will bring you to the delightful chapel of **Áyios Nikólaos**, dating from the eleventh century, with fourteenth-century frescoes by Ioannis Pagomenos (John the Frozen). To get there, take the first track on the right off the road beyond the pension which heads down into the valley; then take the first track on the left and descend to the church (which is unlocked), some 300m further.

Ancient Lappa

Originally a Dorian settlement, **Lappa** was an ally of Lyttos (see p.75) in the latter's wars against Knossós. When it fiercely opposed the Roman invasion in 67 BC, the city was destroyed by the conquering legions. Later, when Lappa aided Octavian-Augustus in his struggle against Antony for the control of the Roman world, the victorious

---

ARGIROÚPOLIS'S UPPER VILLAGE: A CIRCULAR TOUR

You can begin a **tour** of the upper village in the main square, opposite the church. Pass beneath a stone arch where there is a store, Lappa Avocado, who offer an excellent free **map** (see opposite). Beyond the arch, keep ahead to pass an elegant Venetian dwelling (perhaps part of the once extensive villa of the Clodio family) on the left with a fine **portal** bearing the legend *Omnia Mundi Fumus et Umbra* (All Things in This World are Smoke and Shadow). The street eventually climbs and the houses become brilliant white. This is not a tourist village, however, and discreet glances inside open doorways will reveal the everyday work of the village women – rolling *bourekákia* pastries for the evening meal, peeling corncobs, or embroidering and repairing family clothing. The route will lead you past more crumbling Venetian houses, some being refurbished, to a superb **Roman mosaic floor** beneath a canopy on a street corner. Part of a third-century bathhouse, its quality is not only an indication of the wealth of the ancient town, but also of how much still lies buried beneath the modern village. Following the same street around the hill leads back to the arch and the main square.

emperor permitted the Lappans to rebuild their town and gifted them a **water reservoir** in 27 BC which, incredibly, still supplies the village today. The city flourished for many centuries, even outlasting Roman rule, but was razed again by the Saracens in the ninth century. It recovered during the Venetian occupation and was an important centre, as is evident from the numerous villas left behind by Venetian landlords. Remnants of buildings from all periods of the village's history have been incorporated into most of the houses: you'll spot classical inscriptions, ancient columns and bits of Venetian stone carving in the most unlikely places.

The necropolis

Just over 1km north of Argiroúpolis • Access is by a signed footpath from the upper village and is detailed on the free map from Lappa Avocado (see below)

Ancient Lappa's **necropolis** is located at a site known as the Five Virgins, after a nearby chapel. Hundreds of **tombs** – currently being investigated by archeologists – have been cut into the rock cliffs here, many of them with elaborate interior and exterior decoration. One, opened only recently after its discovery by a goatherd, was found to contain a stunning gold diadem. The chapel takes its name from five young women put to death by the Romans in the third century for secretly practising Christianity in the tombs. Nearby, alongside yet another spring, stands a gigantic 2000-year-old **plane tree** (claimed by locals to be the oldest in Crete), with a path cut through it.

ARRIVAL AND INFORMATION ARGIROÚPOLIS

By bus Buses to Argiroúpolis (Mon–Fri only) leave Réthymno at 11.30am and 2.30pm, and return (from the upper village) at 12.30pm and 3.30pm.

Tourist information Beneath a stone arch in the main square, Lappa Avocado (☎28310 81070), a shop selling local wine, herbs and olive oil as well as various avocado products, can provide you with an excellent free map and information on accommodation.

ACCOMMODATION

Despite being in the midst of such spectacular walking terrain, there's usually no problem finding a **room** in Argiroúpolis – in fact you're spoilt for choice. A couple of good tavernas overlooking the Moussélas river valley to the south offer rooms, and for longer stays there are a number of attractive **apartments** and houses in the village; Lappa Avocado (see above) has information.

Argiroupolis Rooms Near the springs ☎28310 81148, ✉argiroupolis@yahoo.gr. Pleasant option offering en-suite studios with balcony, a/c, TV and kitchenette overlooking a large garden. Also apartments sleeping up to four. Free wi-fi. Breakfast included. Studios €40, apartments €50

Maria's Villas 2km south of the village ☎28310 81070, ✉jmsmanou@otenet.gr. New, fully equipped three-room apartments in stone-built houses in a magnificent setting. The views are stunning and facilities include veranda or terrace balcony, a/c, heating, satellite TV and internet access. €75

Morfeas Upper village, 1km along the Miriakéfala road off the main square ☎28310 81172, ⍟morfeas-rooms.gr. Good-value, a/c en-suite balcony rooms with fridge and TV – rooms 1 and 2 are the ones to go for – with a fantastic view down the valley from its taverna terrace. Closed Nov–April. €25

Taverna-Rooms Zografakis Upper village, 50m along the Miriakéfala road just off the main square ☎28310 81269, ⍟ezografakis.gr. Very nice en-suite balcony rooms with fridge and TV above a decent taverna. Breakfast (extra) available. €25

EATING AND DRINKING

The village's main cluster of restaurants is at the **springs**, where tavernas have all incorporated water features into their terraces – walls of tumbling water, oriental wooden water bells, water wheels and the like. The whole scene is especially magical at night. The **upper village** can't really compete for ambience but there are a couple of places well worth a try.

Bar Maria Main square, upper village. The village's main bar, which serves breakfast and snacks. A speciality is their avocado and tuna salad prepared with organic village-grown avocados. Daily 9am–10pm.

Taverna Arhéa Lappa Upper village, 200m along the Episkopi road below the main square ☎28310 81004. Good local taverna with an outdoor terrace serving Cretan and Greek cuisine including *moussaká*, *loukánika* sausages and various lamb-based dishes. April–Oct daily noon–midnight.

Taverna Zografakis Upper village, 50m along the Miriakéfala road just off the main square ☎ 28310 81269. Attached to the *pension* of the same name, this is a good choice for solid Cretan cooking prepared daily by Kiría Zografakis. Daily 11am–11pm.

Vieux Moulin At the springs in the lower village ☎ 28310 81209. Perhaps the most atmospheric of the many good tavernas at the springs, with its tables arranged around a gushing spring. Specialities include *tsigariasto* (Sfakian braised mountain goat) and fresh trout, and there are plenty of vegetarian options. July & Aug daily 11am–11pm; April–June & Sept 11am–8pm; Oct–March Sat & Sun 11am–8pm.

Miriokéfala

The road leading out of Argiroúpolis's upper village beyond the church allows visits to more villages and interesting churches. After 7km – with possible stops en route to explore the hamlets of Maroulού and Arolíthi, just off the road to left and right – the road passes through **MIRIOKÉFALA (Μυριοκέφαλα)**, whose former monastery church of the **Panayía Antifonitria** has ancient **Byzantine frescoes** depicting the Passion which are among the earliest examples on the island, dating from the eleventh and twelfth centuries. The tiny drum-domed edifice – in a courtyard at the bottom of the village – also has an icon of the Virgin which is highly venerated locally. The church should be open, but the bar a little further along will be able to advise if not. With your own transport (or on foot) you can take a stunningly **scenic route** west from here to **Kallikrátis** – now asphalted – and from there head to the south coast or to **Asigonía**.

Asigonía and around

Beyond the lower village of Argiroúpolis, the road continues southwest for 6km to **ASIGONÍA (Ασηγωνιά)**, an isolated and perpetually cloudy rustic settlement. The lovely road winds through the verdant cleft of the Gipari gorge where trees thrust skywards from a riverbed flowing with water all winter, but which lies arid in the summer drought. This habitat breeds a profusion of **birdlife**: as well as blue rock thrushes, pipits and the ubiquitous tits, you may also spot griffon vultures and hawks hovering around the crags.

The road finally arrives in Asigonía's broad platía – ringed by **busts** portraying Venizélou and associated village heroes, but curiously not its most celebrated recent son, **George Psychoundakis** (see p.353) who died in 2006 aged 85. From the square, the **main street** climbs uphill between simple stone dwellings, their yards piled with the firewood needed to stave off the bitterly cold winters here. Many of the men still wear the traditional *saríki* black headdress, baggy *vraka* trousers and high boots, and almost all still dress in black.

ACCOMMODATION AND EATING   ASIGONÍA AND AROUND

The **bars** overlooking the square and along the main street – usually the haunt of taciturn card-playing farmers and shepherds at the end of the working day – are welcoming. However, there is no **accommodation**.

Taverna Asitiko Main square ☎ 28310 82217. Good local taverna where any of the *arni* (lamb) dishes such as *païdhákia* (chops) are delicious. Daily 9am–midnight.

Kallikrátis and around

Beyond Asigonía, the road via the hamlet of **KALLIKRÁTIS (Καλλικράτης)**, 10 km away, to Ímbros, a further 17km, is a magnificent, lonely mountain drive. It also forms a branch of the E4 Pan-European walking route, though less attractive to walkers now that it is completely asphalted; in the other direction the E4 continues through Argiroúpolis before striking east, across country. You can also drive due south from Kallikrátis to emerge at Patsianós, just above the coast at Frangokástello (see p.291). Again, this is a spectacular journey, closely tracing the Kallikráti gorge, and yet another branch of the E4 goes this way, following the road at first, but then dropping to the bottom of the gorge while the tarmac loops around the slopes above. An alternative, circular **hike** (not following the E4) heads along the track that turns off just north of Kallikrátis to Miriokéfala (see opposite), 8km away. From here it's possible to return to Asigonía by way of Maroulóu (5km), or continue 7km north to Argiroúpolis along the road.

East of Réthymno: the coast road

Leaving Réthymno to the east, you can strike almost immediately onto the **coast road**, which runs fast, flat and dull along the coastal plain, or follow the old road, squeezed into the narrow gap between this and the sea. On the latter route you'll pass through a string of village suburbs, connected now by an almost continuous string of hotel development for some 10km. At **Stavroménos** the old road cuts under the highway and heads inland; the new road continues to hug a featureless coastline dotted with rocky beaches, stands of reeds and piecemeal development, plus the odd luxury hotel. **Pánormos** and **Balí** are both welcoming places to rest up for a while, though with very different characters. Behind Pánormos, and from the highway between Pánormos and Balí, roads head up to Pérama (p.204) and the nearby mountain villages. **East of Balí**, the next access to the coast is at Ayía Pelayía (see p.77), 25km further on. Nor is there much else to stop for: **Síses**, 12km east of Balí, has wonderful views from its perch beside the highway and a few rooms, but little else.

Pánormos

PÁNORMOS (Πάνορμος), 22km east of Réthymno, marks a distinct break in topography: to the west is a long stretch of level coastline, to the east a spectacular, swooping mountain drive on the E75 highway which continues virtually all the way to Iráklio. The village is just a short (poorly signed) detour off the road, a pretty little place with pedestrianized streets and a tiny harbour, with a couple of small beaches either side. Perhaps because the beaches don't amount to much, Pánormos does not attract big crowds even in high season and as a result holds on to its appealing tranquillity; many visitors rent apartments and stay for weeks or months. The better of the beaches is to the west of the harbour, with a bar-café and sunbeds. Surprisingly, this

---

SAVE THE TURTLE

The beaches east of Réthymno make up the second largest nesting area in the Mediterranean for the endangered **loggerhead sea turtle**. Loggerheads, once common throughout the Mediterranean, are today under serious threat from the damage wrought by tourism and industry on their breeding habitats.

A seagoing creature for most of its life, the turtle must return to a beach – always the same one – in order to lay its eggs. Unfortunately, nesting occurs from early June to the end of August, coinciding with the high tourist season. Once the female has buried her eighty to a hundred eggs on a nocturnal visit to the beach, the eggs must then remain undisturbed for a period of two months before the hatchlings emerge to head for the sea. But even should they avoid being skewered by a beach umbrella or crushed by the feet of bathers – both common hazards – further dangers lie ahead for the newborn turtles. When they emerge, many of them, instead of heading for the sea, are lured inland by artificial lights from hotel and tourist developments. Emblematic of Crete's and Greece's problem of balancing tourist development and the needs of the environment, it remains to be seen whether the loggerhead turtle will avoid the fate of the dodo.

For **information** on programmes to protect the turtle, making donations or becoming a volunteer, contact the Sea Turtle Protection Society of Greece (☎28310 72288, ⊚archelon.gr).

is also an ancient settlement (a minuscule river runs through to the sea) with the ruins of what was once a large sixth-century **basilica**, probably destroyed in the ninth-century Saracen invasion, and of a later **Genoese castle**.

ARRIVAL AND DEPARTURE
PÁNORMOS

By bus The Réthymno hotel zone bus runs as far as Pánormos (16 daily); there are also highway buses.
Boat trips Departing from the harbour with Captain

Lefteris (see p.203), boats explore the coast en route to Réthymno (Mon, Thurs & Sat 10am; €26).

ACCOMMODATION

Captain's House Right on the harbour ☎ 28340 51352, ⊛ captainshouse.gr. Comfortable seafront studios and apartments with the best location in town, directly above the water, though those on the harbourside can be noisy; there's also a beautiful three-bedroom suite. Free wi-fi. Studios **€50**, apartments **€60**, suite **€150**
Grecotel Club Marine Palace On the western edge of Pánormos ☎ 28340 51610, ⊛ grecotel.gr. The last of the large hotels that dot the coastline all the way from Réthymno; an excellent, if pricey, all-inclusive resort above a small bay and beach. It tends to be block-booked by upmarket tour

operators during high season. Free wi-fi. **€350**
Lucy's Pension In the village proper ☎ 28340 51212, ⊛ lucy.gr. Excellent and good-value a/c studio rooms with kitchenette and balcony (one with a sea view) near the centre of the village. The very friendly eponymous proprietor lives in an apartment below. Free wi-fi. **€45**
Villa Andreas West end of the seafront ☎ 28340 51212, ⊛ lucy.gr. Modern five-bedroom luxury villa sleeping up to ten with sumptuously furnished rooms (including four bathrooms) plus sea views, a pool and fully equipped kitchen. **€300**

EATING AND DRINKING

There are some rather touristy traditional **tavernas** on the harbour and a clutch of more interesting places in and around the pedestrianized main street, **Dhrómos Agorás**.

Angyra East side of the harbour ☎ 28340 51022. Taking its name from the huge *angyra* (anchor) parked outside, this is a reliable waterfront option for fresh fish as well as more mainstream dishes such as *moussaká* and stuffed tomatoes. Daily 11am–11pm.
Captain's House West side of the harbour ☎ 28340 51352. The best of the more touristy places around this side of the harbour, all with international menus. Daily noon–11pm.
Oasis Dhrómos Agorás ☎ 28340 51390. This very pleasant garden café makes an ideal place for breakfast or a nightcap. They show occasional original-version films on a garden screen and host frequent live guitar music. Daily 9am–1am.

Stavroula Just off Dhrómos Agorás ☎ 28340 51565. The best place for *souvláki* and grills served on a bougainvillea-draped street terrace, plus salads to accompany them. Daily 6pm–midnight.
★ **To Steki tou Sifaki** Dhrómos Agorás ☎ 28340 51230. Good taverna with an attractive garden terrace serving well-priced lamb dishes (try the succulent *kléftiko*, baked lamb) as well as fresh fish and a good selection of *orektiká* (appetizers). Daily noon–11pm.
★ **Taverna Geronymos** Dhrómos Agorás ☎ 28340 51338. Popular taverna serving quality Cretan food on an atmospheric street terrace beneath a spreading vine. Try the *pastítsio*, *stifádho* or chicken in white wine sauce. Daily 1.30–11pm.

Balí

BALÍ (Μπαλί) is a resort set around a series of little coves, 9km east of Pánormos. The place is much bigger than it first appears, especially as the streets are winding and hilly – it's a couple of kilometres from the main road to the village, more to the best beach. Sadly, although the beaches are spectacular, they're very much overrun, and Balí has become a package resort too popular for its own good. It's lively and friendly, but only really tempting well out of season, when there are bound to be bargains given the number of rooms.

Balí's beaches

The first beach, immediately below the road, is **Livádhi** (aka Paradise Beach). An extensive stretch of gritty sand, with a row of bars and tavernas behind, it's the most recently developed and the least attractive part of town, though lively at night. Balí proper is centred around three west-facing **coves** with pebbly beaches on the promontory beyond. The first is known as **Varkotopos**; the second, at the centre of the old village, is itself divided in two by a rocky outcrop into **Limáni**, where the harbour is, and Limanákia beaches; a long loop of road then winds round to the final cove (there are short cuts if you walk), which is nameless. This is barely developed and much the most pleasant place to swim – with a patch of sand and, on either side, crags of rock with level places to sunbathe – but still very crowded and overlooked. Two shady **tavernas** just above the beach make reasonable lunch stops.

Moní Áyios Ioánnis

Sat–Thurs 9am–noon & 4–7pm • Reached by turning inland on a good road (though a dangerous exit from the E75) that turns off the highway a short distance west of the resort

A good viewpoint to appreciate Balí's setting is the tiny part-ruined, part-restored seventeenth-century **Monastery of Áyios Ioánnis (Μονη Αγιος Ιωάννης)**. The monastery church has some fragmentary seventeenth-century frescoes and there's a serene garden fronting the monks' cells (only one monk now remains), but its reputation among Cretans today is for its energetic role in the struggle against Turkish rule, for which it was bombarded in 1866 by the Turkish navy.

ARRIVAL AND DEPARTURE   BALÍ

By bus Buses will drop you by a large service station at the junction with the road into town. It's quite a walk to the centre, so it may be worth considering a taxi.

INFORMATION AND ACTIVITIES

Internet There are internet connections (screens and wi-fi) at Bali Netcafe (daily 8.30am–3am), in the old village, and free wi-fi at several of the bars at Livádhi and at *Mambo* in Varkotopos (see p.204).
Boat trips and watersports Captain Lefteris (☎ 28340 94102; all trips half-price for kids) offers a daily sail (€59 including lunch and drinks) or sunset cruise (€30 including drinks) in a catamaran; day-trips to Réthymno via

Pánormos (Mon, Thurs and Sat; €26); and motorboat, kayak, pedalo and jet-ski rental.
Diving Just behind the harbour, Hippocampos (☎ 28340 94193, ⓦ hippocampos.com) is a PADI dive centre offering courses, trial dives and more.
Car rental Car rental outlets and travel agencies are liberally scattered throughout the resort.

ACCOMMODATION

Bali Beach Hotel Behind Limanákia ☎ 28340 94210, ⓦ balibeach.gr. Taking over much of Limanákia beach, with rooms tumbling down the slope behind it, this is by far the fanciest hotel in town. With two pools and balcony rooms with sea view, a/c, TV and fridge it's quite a bargain, especially out of season. Buffet breakfast included. Free wi-fi in lobby only. **€103**
Bali Blue Bay Hotel On the ridge between Varkotopos cove and Limáni ☎ 28340 20111, ⓦ balibluebay.gr. Comfortable, modern hotel with great views from most rooms and even better ones from the rooftop pool. Buffet breakfast included. Free wi-fi in lobby. **€55**
Dimitris Apartments High above the north side of the harbour ☎ 694 78 65 459, ⓦ apts-dimitris.gr. Well-equipped studios and two-room apartments, with good views from their balconies. Studios **€40**, apartments **€48**
Mira Mare Above Varkotopos cove ☎ 28340 94256. Handily located above a supermarket, these a/c, en-suite balcony rooms with fridge and sea views are excellent value. **€35**

EATING, DRINKING AND NIGHTLIFE

There are supermarkets, cafés and tavernas throughout the resort. A couple of the best **tavernas** are in the old village by the harbour. **Nightlife** tends to consist of late-night drinks at a number of music bars behind the beaches.

TAVERNAS

Panorama In the old village by the harbour ☎ 28340 94217. Occupying a renovated old warehouse, with a superb view from its terrace overlooking the water, *Panorama* offers well-prepared fish and meat dishes. Specialities include a good-value assorted *mezédhes*

plate (€8) and baked aubergine with *féta*. April–Oct daily 9am–11pm.

Valentino In the old village by the harbour ☎ 28340 94501. Pleasantly situated harbourfront taverna with a lively terrace serving up the usual standards as well as fresh fish. April–Oct daily 8am–11pm.

BARS

Mambo Varkotopos cove. All day (and most of the night) beachfront music bar serving cocktails, drinks and juices into the small hours. Daily 9am–4am.

Porto Paradiso Varkotopos cove. A good spot for an early or late-evening cocktail, with the waves lapping the shore a mere 20m from the terrace tables. Daily 9am–4am.

The foothills of the Psilorítis

Taking the old roads east from Réthymno, through the **foothills of the Psilorítis** range, there are a variety of routes to choose from or combine. The former main road, heading towards Dhamásta, has least to offer, though it's a pretty enough drive. Striking higher into the mountains is more rewarding. For a combination of interest and relatively easy driving, the best option is the road up through Garázo and Axós to Anóyia, though you can also reach Anóyia on the even higher, stunningly scenic road from **Pérama**. Possible detours along the way include the potters' village of **Margarítes** and scenic archeological site of **Arhéa Eléftherna**, and the remarkable caves of **Melidhóni** and **Sendóni**. Anóyia, famed for its textiles, is the gateway to the summit of Psilorítis. The northern branch of the E4 footpath winds through this area, offering numerous attractive short walks: from the monastery at Arkádhi it heads through Eléftherna to Margarítes, and from there via Houméri to Garázo, and onwards past the Moní Dhiskoúri and Sendóni Cave to Anóyia.

Margarítes

A very pretty place on the edge of a ravine, with views back towards the coast, **MARGARÍTES** (Μαργαρίτεζ) has a long tradition of making pottery. Workshops are scattered throughout the village, and you can buy the results in a dozen or more outlets along the steep main street. One of the best is the workshop of **Nikos Kavgalakis**, just beyond the far (southern) edge of the village. Jovial Nikos not only turns out a variety of pots, but also the enormous Ali Baba jars, or *píthoi*, similar to those found in the Minoan palaces and still used throughout agricultural Crete today. Another creative potter, **Yiorgos Dalamvelas**, has his studio and shop on the main street and derives inspiration for his traditionally made ceramics from Minoan and Byzantine originals.

Monastery of Sotíros Chrístos

Lower village • Daily 9am–dusk • Free • Reached from the lower square (with huge central eucalyptus) by following a signed lane uphill for 70m

Off the village's lower square, a steep path leads to the **Monastery of Sotíros Chrístos** (Μονή Σοτήριος Χριστός), or Áyios Gedeón, a ruined monastery that has been partly restored by its last remaining monk. The ancient church is usually open; take a wander through the delightful surrounding gardens, filled with a cornucopia of flowers and plants – complete with peacocks – which are all the work of the same monk.

ACCOMMODATION | **MARGARÍTES**

Irini Rooms ☎ 28340 92494, ⊛ irini-apartments.com. Welcoming proprietors offer good-value en-suite studio rooms with kitchenette, a/c and TV plus a fully equipped apartment (for the same price) in the lower village. Breakfast included. **€30**

Kapsilania Village Hotel On the Pérama road on the northern edge of the village ☎ 28310 83400, ⊛ kapsalianavillage.gr. The olive oil factory of a former

monastery has been transformed into a chic boutique hotel where luxurious individually styled rooms and suites – with a/c, satellite TV and plenty of exposed stonework – are surrounded by gardens with a pool. There's a cafeteria, bar and restaurant. **€175**

Kouriton House In the hamlet of Tzanakianá, immediately north of Margarítes ☎ 694 57 22 052, ⊛ kouritonhouse.gr. A beautifully restored eighteenth-century stone-built house where each room is unique and furnished in traditional style. €60

Taverna I Velanidia Just out of the southern edge of the village, almost opposite the workshop of Nikos

Kavgalikis ☎ 28340 92520, ⓦ belanidiahotel.gr. Good-value, a/c, en-suite balcony rooms with fridge and TV above a decent taverna in a leafy setting. €30

EATING AND DRINKING

Cafe Mella 50m downhill from the main square. Small German-run diner offering Mitteleuropean coffee, cake and snacks. Wed–Sun 10.30am–6pm.

Taverna Mantalos Main square ☎ 28340 92294. On the village's attractive upper platía, this great little taverna

has a shady terrace offering fine views over the valley. Friendly proprietors cook up tasty traditional Cretan food including delicious *kolokithoánthi yemistá* (stuffed courgette flowers). Daily 9am–10.30pm.

Arhéa Eléftherna and around

Beyond Margarítes, the road climbs for 4km to the village of **ARHÉA ELÉFTHERNA** (Αρχαία Ελεύθερνα). Just a couple of hundred metres from the centre of the village is the spectacular acropolis of ancient **Eléftherna**. The ancient city that stood here was one of the most important in eighth- and seventh-century BC Dorian Crete; when the Romans came in search of conquest in 67 BC it put up a stiff resistance, and later flourished as the seat of a Christian bishop. The Saracen invasions finished it off, however.

Acropolis of Eléftherna

A couple of hundred metres from the centre of the village down a signed road

At the entry to the acropolis, a path leads across a stretch of level rock, carved in ancient times to resemble paving stones, to a hefty *pírgos* or **tower** (which in large part still stands) protecting the narrow entrance to the **acropolis of Eléftherna** itself. This enjoys a magnificent defensive position, on a long, steep-sided promontory surrounded by narrow ravines. The E4 path climbs out of the valley onto the acropolis – very close to where it meets the path from the entry, remarkable **Roman cisterns** are carved into the hill's west side, with enormous pillars of solid rock supporting a cavernous interior. Further out along the promontory (it's a good fifteen-minute walk to the end) are numerous scattered fragments of massive walls and ancient buildings, not always easy to make sense of, as well as the roofless ruined ancient church of **Ayía Ánna**, still revered as a shrine by locals.

In the valley below you can see both the **main site of ancient Eléftherna**, to the east, and, to the northwest, its **necropolis**. Both have impressive-looking visitor facilities but most of the excavated remains are fenced off, although you can get a reasonable view through the fences. At the necropolis, archeologists made a potentially very significant discovery: traces of a **human sacrifice** made in front of the funeral pyre of some local magnate. It apparently dates from the late eighth century BC, about the same time that Homer was describing very similar sacrifices of Trojan prisoners in front of the funeral pyre of Achilles. The victim, who was bound hand and foot before ritually having his throat cut, may well have been expected to serve the dead man in the next world: also found in front of the pyre were sacrificed animals and offerings of perfume and food. Other cremations on the site (some twenty have been found, though only one human sacrifice) had offerings including gold, jewellery and fine pottery, as well as four tiny, superbly crafted **ivory heads** which are among the best work of their time (c.600 BC) yet discovered anywhere. These and other finds are displayed in the archeological museum at Réthymno.

Sotíros Chrístos

Signed where the road from Margarítes comes into Arhéa Eléftherna, a turning on the left is signed to the chapel of Sotíris Christos

Sotíros Christos (Σωτήρος Χριστός) is a beautiful tenth-century Byzantine chapel in a picturesque setting beside a spring-fed pool. Inside there's a fine twelfth-century

Pantokrátor in the dome, the only surviving **fresco** of what must once have been a glorious painted interior.

The Hellenistic bridge

North of Sotíros Chrístos • The bridge is more easily reached from Arhéa Eléftherna's twin village, Eléftherna, where a track (initially the E4 path, signed "Ancient Eléftherna") heads steeply downhill; as you descend, the E4 continues down and across towards the acropolis, while the (driveable) track heads north following the valley; keep left on a couple of occasions where the track forks, and after a couple of kilometres you'll reach the bridge

The valley below the acropolis of Eléftherna has a track leading to a remarkable stone-built **Hellenistic bridge**. Standing 5m high and 3m deep, its vaulted arch is almost perfectly intact, still capable of carrying traffic across the river. Beneath the arch is a washing and bathing place cut into the rock, probably dating from the same era.

ACCOMMODATION AND EATING	ARHÉA ELÉFTHERNA AND AROUND
Acropolis Taverna At the entry to the acropolis. Good taverna with attractive terrace serving Greek and Cretan standards; just the place for a meal or a cool beer after a look around Eléftherna acropolis. Daily noon–10pm.	**Villa Katerina** At the northern end of the village ☎ 28310 27216. A lovely renovated, two-bedroom stone house with fully equipped kitchen and garden pool. A week: approx **€1000**
Villa Antigoni At the northern end of the village ☎ 28340 23517, ⊛ antigonivillas.com. Excellent-value, roomy studios and apartments with kitchen and balcony set around a pool with great views. If there's no one around, check at the *Bar Apollion* in the village square. **€35**	**Villas Magda** By the entrance to the acropolis ☎ 28340 22877, ⊛ villamagda.gr. Two well-equipped and furnished new stone villas, one two- and one three-bedroom, with pools. **€110**

The Melidhóni Cave

Daily: June–Aug 9am–8pm; April, May, Sept & Oct 9am–7pm • €3 including map

The village of **MELIDHÓNI** – 5km northeast of Pérama on a road which continues to the main highway near Balí – is unremarkable, but from here a thirty-minute walk (or a drive, signed from the village) climbs to the **Melidhóni Cave** (Μελιδόνι Αντρο), one of the most impressive on the island. In mythology this was the legendary home of **Talos**, a bronze giant who protected the coasts of Crete by striding around the island hurling rocks at unfriendly ships; the Argonauts were greeted thus when they approached. Excavations in the cave have shown that it was inhabited during the Neolithic period and later was an important shrine for the **Minoans**, who may have worshipped their fertility goddess Eileithyia here. The Greeks and Romans

THE MELIDHÓNI MASSACRE

The **Melidhóni Cave** was the setting for one of the most horrific **atrocities** in the struggle for Cretan independence. Here, in 1824, around three hundred villagers took refuge, as they had often done before at time of war, in the face of an advancing army. This time, however, the Muslim commander demanded that they come out. When the Cretans refused, and shot two messengers sent to offer safe conduct, he tried to force them out by blocking the mouth of the cave with stones and cutting off the air supply. After several days of this, with the defenders opening new air passages every night, the troops changed their tactics, piling combustible materials in front of the cave and setting light to them; everyone inside was asphyxiated. The bodies were left where they lay for the cave to become their tomb; ten years later traveller and historian Robert Pashley, one of the first to enter after the tragedy, found "the bones and skulls of the poor Christians so thickly scattered, that it is almost impossible to avoid crushing them as we pick our steps along". This grisly event was far from unique: numerous other caves around the island have similar histories, although none claimed so many victims.

transformed it into a shrine to the god **Hermes Tallaios**, evidenced by thousands of inscriptions etched into the walls of one of the cave's inner chambers.

Today, the awesome central chamber is a geological cathedral thick with gigantic stalactites, stalagmites and bunches of mighty "organ pipes" soaring between petrified "draperies", spectacular curtain-like folds formed by the calcium deposits. A **shrine** near the entrance commemorates the martyrs of 1824 (see box opposite).

EATING   THE MELIDHÓNI CAVE

Melidhóni Cave Café Next to the ticket office. A small café, run with diner-style efficiency and banter by a friendly Greek family who used to live in the United States. Daily: June–Aug 9am–8pm; April, May, Sept & Oct 9am–7pm.

Axós

AXÓS (Αξός) is an attractive village, occasionally swamped by lunching tour bus passengers, and it has an ancient history: a significant Dorian city stood here from around the seventh century BC, and thrived through to the Byzantine era, hence the many early churches. Beside one of them, **Ayía Iríni**, a signed path leads up to the "Akropolis", where there's not a great deal to see. The fourteenth-century church is more interesting, with significant, if damaged, frescoes.

Sendóni Cave

April–Oct daily 10.30am–5pm; Nov–March Sat & Sun 10am–2pm; guided tours every 40–50min • €4 • ⓦ zoniana.gr

Beyond Axós a road heads south to **Zonianá**, where you'll find the **Sendóni Cave** (**Σεντόνη**). The cave interior is spectacular with a magnificent display of stalactites, stalagmites and petrified waves, many more than five million years old. Enthusiastic and knowledgeable guides conduct you through a vast tunnel-like cavern, fitted with a series of walkways extending some 500m or so into a spur of Mount Psilorítis. Local legend has it that the cave was discovered by an eight-year-old girl who, lured away by fairies, was later found dead in its darkest recesses. At the entrance there's a giant visitor centre with a café and shop.

Anóyia

ANÓYIA (Ανώγεια), a small town perched beneath the highest peaks of the Psilorítis range, is the obvious place from which to approach the **Idean Cave** (see p.210) and, for the committed, the **summit of Psilorítis** itself (see p.211). The weather, refreshingly cool when the summer heat lower down is becoming oppressive, is one good reason to come, but most people are drawn by the proximity of the mountains or by a reputation for some of the best woven and embroidered **handicrafts** in Crete. The last is greatly exaggerated but this exceptionally friendly town still makes a pleasant break from the coast. It's also a noticeably prosperous place, thanks to stockbreeding; the sheep farmers here are some of the richest in Greece, as evidenced by the giant cheese factory on the eastern edge of town.

On first impression it seems that Anóyia has two quite distinct halves: coming from the west you enter what appears to be the older, lower town, before the road takes a broad loop around to re-emerge near the upper town's large, modern-looking **Platía Meídani**, lined with youthful bars. The upper town has almost all the accommodation as well as the bank (with ATM) and post office, police and most of the non-tourist stores. In many ways this appearance is deceptive. A series of steep alleys connect the two directly, and however traditional the buildings may look, closer inspection shows that most are actually concrete. This reflects a tragic history – the village was one of those destroyed in 1944 as a reprisal for the abduction of **General Kreipe** (see p.340), when all the men who could be rounded up here were executed.

THE *LYRA* IN ANÓYIA

Anóyia is a noted centre of *lyra* **music** – many of the greatest performers on the instrument have come from here. Among them, the late, self-taught Nikos Xylouris was a shepherd who made his own *lyra*, and whose performances and compositions made him a Cretan legend in the 1960s and 1970s. The house where he was born, on Platía Livádhi, is now the *Kafenion Xylouris*, where you can get a glass of *raki* or house wine.

Platía Livádhi

The local handicrafts tradition – shops and stalls line a street leading off **Platía Livádhi** – partly arose from bitter necessity, with so large a proportion of the local men killed in 1944. As a way of surviving it seems to have worked, and a few elderly widows (accompanied now by their daughters) remain anxious to subject any passing visitor to their aggressive sales techniques. The traditional feel of the lower town is reinforced by the elderly men, baggy trousers tucked into their black boots, moustaches bristling, who sit at the *kafenía* tables around the square.

Anóyia Museum

Just behind Platía Livádhi • Mon–Sat 9am–7pm • Free

The **Anóyia Museum** is dedicated to local sculptor Algiliadi Skoulas, who died in 1996. As well as guiding visitors around his father's sculptures and paintings which display a striking and naive simplicity, museum curator Yéorgos Skoulas frequently treats visitors to a deft performance on the *lyra*.

ACCOMMODATION   ANÓYIA

Anóyia sees a lot of day-trippers, but most stay only an hour or so. Linger a while, or stay overnight, and it's surprisingly uncommercial. It shouldn't be hard to find a **room** in the upper town, where the best places line the road (Periferiakos) that climbs parallel to the main road on the east side of the village.

Rooms Aris Periferiakos ☎ 28340 31817, ⓦ aris.anogia .info. A pleasant flower-bedecked place with cosy, en-suite, a/c rooms with balcony views and fridge. Free wi-fi. €40

★ **Hotel Aristea** Upper town ☎ 28340 31584, ⓦ aristea -studios.gr. Friendly, modernized hotel offering smart a/c en-suite rooms with TV and sensational balcony views, as well

as studios and apartments for up to six people. Free wi-fi. €35
Hotel Marina At the top of the hill ☎ 28340 31817, ⓦ marinahotelanogia.gr. Three-star modern hotel with studio rooms with kitchenette and fabulous views from the terrace balconies. Free wi-fi. Enquire at *Rooms Aris* if no one's around. €40

EATING AND DRINKING

Wherever you eat, ask to sample the delicious local *anthogalo* **cheese**. In the lower village, head for the grill places on the Platía Livádhi, where the choice will usually be limited to whatever's on the spit (usually succulent lamb).

★ **Aetos** Upper village, just beyond Platía Meídani ☎ 28340 31262. Excellent local taverna with a wood-fired grill and spacious terrace. Specialities include *souvláki* and goat dishes as well as a mouthwatering *ofto* (wood-fire-roasted lamb). Daily 11am–11pm.
Gagaris Upper village, at start of the Psilorítis road ☎ 28340 31280. Good taverna specializing in *ofto* (the

glass-sided wood oven is a feature out front) along with other traditional dishes. Daily 10am–midnight.
Taverna Skalomata By the road junction leading to Mt Psilorítis ☎ 28340 31316. It's worth the climb to the eastern end of the main street to this large taverna, which has a fantastic view from its terrace and serves excellent barbecued lamb. Daily 9am–11pm.

SHOPPING

Tarrah Glass Upper village ☎ 28340 31357, ⓦ www .tarrahglass.com. The studio-shop of creative glass designers Marios Chalkiadakis and Natasha Papadogamvraki, who, besides glasses, vases and the like, also produce larger exotic

glass sculptures. An immaculate 1968 sky-blue Triumph Herald usually stands outside. Mon–Fri 9am–2pm & 5.30–9pm, Sat 9am–2pm.

Mount Psilorítis

It's 21km from Anóyia to the **Nídha plateau** (1400m), at the base of **Mount Psilorítis** (Ορος Ψηλορείτης), also known as Mount Ida – which, at 2456m, is the highest mountain in Crete. It's a steady climb most of the way, along a road travelled little except by the shepherds who pasture their sheep up here. In late spring, as the snow recedes, you'll see myriad wildflowers and, at all times, quite a few birds, including vultures and magnificent golden eagles. The *mitáta* or stone huts near the roadside – many of them ruined – are former shepherds' dwellings; many are now used as dog kennels and chicken coops.

Somewhere near the highest point a signed road leads off left for 3km to the **Skinakas Observatory**, sitting atop the peak of the same name (open on occasional Sundays in summer – dates should be posted on a board at the start of the road; ⓦwww.skinakas .org.gr). A little further along, a track to the right goes to the **ski area**, which sees plenty of snow in season. Soon after, the small plateau and its bare summer pastures fan out below you, and the road drops to skirt around its western edge.

At what is effectively the end of the road (shortly beyond, it peters out in a network of trails across the plateau), overlooking the plain, stands a neglected **visitor centre** and the *Taverna Nida* (see p.212).

The Idean Cave

A 15min walk along a path opposite the *Taverna Nida*

The celebrated **Idean Cave** (Ιδεον Ανδρον) rivals that on Mount Dhíkti (see p.138) for the title of **Zeus's birthplace**. Although scholarly arguments rage over the exact identity of the caves in the legends of Zeus, and over interpretation of versions of the legend, locals are in no doubt that the Idean Cave is the place where the god was brought up, suckled by wild animals. Certainly this hole in the mountainside, which as Cretan caves go is not especially large or impressive, was associated from the earliest times with the cult of Zeus, and at times ranked among the most important centres of pilgrimage in the Greek world. Pythagoras visited the cave, Plato set *The Laws* as a dialogue along the pilgrimage route here, and the finds within indicate offerings brought from all over the eastern Mediterranean. First signs of occupation go back as far as 3000 BC, and though it may then have been a mere place of shelter, by the Minoan era it was already established as a shrine, maintaining this role until about 500 AD.

Sadly the cave and its surroundings are disappointing. Remains of earlier archeological digs have left miniature railway tracks leading into the cave, while attempts to create a taverna and parking area lie abandoned. Even the cave itself turns out to be fairly uninspiring, and certainly not a patch on the dramatic Dhiktean Cave (see p.138).

THE MEMORIAL TO PEACE

At the northern end of the Nídha plateau, German artist Karen Raeck has constructed a **rock sculpture** entitled *Immortal Freedom Fighter of Peace*, commemorating the suffering of the town of Anóyia at the hands of the German army in 1944 (see p.207). A one-woman reconciliation mission between her homeland and Anóyia, Raeck has spent most of the last thirty years living in the town and has gained the respect and trust of its inhabitants. The monument, measuring 30m by 9m, consists of a large number of huge boulders in an impressionistic image which, when viewed from the air, create a winged figure. The shepherds of the plateau assisted Raeck in carrying and positioning the stones, and during the work's assembly she lived in one of their stone huts. The sculpture is visible from the terrace of the *Taverna Nida*, where staff can tell you about it; an excursion to see it at close quarters makes for a very pleasant stroll across the plateau.

THE DESCENT FROM NÍDHA TO KAMÁRES

While most people are here to climb **Psilorítis**, there is also a good 5hr hike down from Nídha to Kamáres, via the huge **Kamáres Cave**, where the first great cache of the elaborate pottery known as Kamáres ware was found – it's now in the Irákjo Archeological Museum. You can either follow the E4 towards the summit for around an hour and a half, until you reach a basin (Kollita) where the trails meet, and descend south from there, or you can take the track which heads south from the *Taverna Nida* (see p.212). This is a much flatter route, but also significantly harder to follow in the later stages, so you're advised to check directions first; get it right and you will eventually approach the cave (a short detour off the E4) from the east. The track initially leads to a gully, which shortly after becomes a considerable ravine. Here, large red arrows direct you towards Kamáres and the cave. For **Vorízia**, follow the ravine for about an hour until a faint trail climbs out on the left (soon after this, the stream bed becomes impassable). Above the ravine there are fine views and a heady drop for another hour, when you must turn left (east) again. This is not obvious, but you should begin to see signs of life – goat trails and shepherds' huts. You cut past the top of a second, smaller ravine to a stone hut and then descend, zigzagging steeply, to a dirt road and Vorízia village.

Neither Kamáres nor Vorízia has a lot to offer when you arrive. In Kamáres the trail emerges at the eastern end of the village, opposite a very basic taverna. Ask here and you may be able to find a room; the only other facilities are a couple of old-fashioned *kafenía*. Vorízia has neither food nor accommodation.

3

Climbing Psilorítis

The *Taverna Nida* (see p.212) and visitor centre mark the start of the way (now forming a stretch of the E4 path) to the **summit of Psilorítis**. Though it's not for the unwary or unfit, the climb should present few problems to experienced, properly equipped hikers, and there are also **guided ascents** (including by moonlight) from Thrónos (see p.215). The route, which diverts from the path to the Idean Cave just beyond the small spring and chapel, is marked with red arrows in addition to the E4 waymarkers – a guide who knows the mountain would be useful, since it's not always obvious which is the main trail, but is by no means essential. The *Anavasi Psilorítis* map (see p.40) is the best available for this area and clearly marks the routes described here. Don't attempt the ascent alone, however, as you could face a very long wait for help if you were to run into trouble. If you do make the climb, allow for a six- to eight-hour return trip to the chapel at the summit, and be prepared in spring for thick snow to slow you down. Carry enough food, water and warm gear to be able to overnight in one of the shelters should the weather turn; a night at the top, with the whole island laid out in the sunset and sunrise, is a wonderful experience.

Only in the last twenty minutes or so of the climb does the peak of Psilorítis itself become visible and the ground start to fall away to reveal just how high you are. The **summit** is marked by a shelter and the chapel of **Tímios Stavrós** ("Holy Cross" – a name by which the peak is sometimes known locally), inside which Nikos Kazantzákis famously claimed to have lost his virginity. Nearby there's water in a cistern, which you should boil or purify before drinking. On a (rare) clear day the spectacular **panoramas** from the summit – including the Lefká Óri (White Mountains) rising in the west and the Dhíkti massif to the east – make the climb well worthwhile.

Alternate routes

There are any number of **alternate routes** up and down the mountain. From the west the obvious departure point is Fourfourás in the Amári valley, along the route of the E4. This is relatively straightforward in the sense that you can see the peak almost all the way, though it can be hard to find the start of the path, or to work out which is the main trail at times, despite the waymarking: it's also much further, a 2000m ascent and at least five or six hours climbing. There's a mountain hut about halfway up, run by the EOS in Réthymno (see p.193). The proprietors of the *Windy Place* taverna-rooms in

3

THE WILDEST CAT IN CRETE

In Cretan myth and legend there have long been told tales of the **fourokattos** ("furious cat"), a mountain wildcat. Although in 1905 two skins from such a beast were bought at the market in Haniá by a British woman attached to a scientific mission, for most of the last century scientists regarded the existence of such a creature as unlikely. They also dismissed the stories of shepherds and goatherds who claimed to have seen this wild cat.

Then, in 1996, an Italian university team studying the carnivores of the Cretan mountains were astonished when they returned to their traps one morning to find they had snared a 5.5-kilo wildcat. The news created a sensation as the beast was taken to the University of Crete for study before being released back into the wild equipped with a radio tracking device. Tawny and with small lynx-like tufts, the cat does not belong to the subspecies of cats on the mainland of Greece and the rest of Europe; its nearest relative is a species inhabiting North Africa and Sardinia. Scientists believe that it is an extremely reclusive and nocturnal animal, which explains why it is so rarely seen.

The cat's discovery has not only proven generations of Cretans right, but has turned the zoological history of the island upside down. Recent research has produced evidence of more wildcats, but there are serious concerns for the future as its natural environment is encroached upon by development. Scientists are now puzzling over how the animal got to Crete in the first place – was the cat perhaps brought over as a domesticated beast by the ancestors of the Minoans, or has it been on Crete since the island became separated from the mainland?

Fourfourás (p.216) can provide details of a short cut, which involves taking your car a good way up the mountain along a track that ascends from a turn-off on the right, 5km north of Fourfourás and 2km beyond the village of Platánia. With care you can take a vehicle to the tree line (about 1hr), from where it's about a three-hour trek to the summit, two hours back down. They can also advise on a 15km gorge walk along the Plátis river valley to Ayía Galíni and will collect you (if you are a guest) from there to return you to Fourfourás. South of the mountain, **Kamáres** is another possible trailhead, on yet another branch of the E4. Again, this is a much more substantial ascent than from the plateau, starting from around 900m, and with some stiff climbing in the early stages.

ARRIVAL AND DEPARTURE   MOUNT PSILORÍTIS

By bus One or two buses a day run between Kamáres and Iráklio, passing through Vorízia.

ACCOMMODATION AND EATING

Taverna Nida In the visitor centre, Nídha plateau ☎ 28340 31141. Serves hearty taverna standards and has a couple of rooms sharing a bathroom. Stelios Slavrakakis, the proprietor, is a fount of information on the plateau and can advise (in Greek) on the viability of walking routes in the mountains, as well as likely weather conditions. If you stay here or camp on the plateau (there's plenty of water but it can be very cold), you could tackle the peak up and down in one day, and continue south next day to Kamáres or Vorízia. April–Sept daily; Oct–March Sat & Sun. **€25**

Spíli and around

The main road south from Réthymno heads through Arméni (see p.190) towards Plakiás (p.224), Spíli and Ayía Galíni (p.219). If you take this main road, the pleasant country town of **SPÍLI (Σπίλι)**, tucked into the folds of the Mount Kédhros foothills 30km south of Réthymno, is the obvious point to break a journey.

The trailhead for plenty of wild country **hikes**, and a popular overnight stop for groups of ramblers, the town doesn't look much as you drive through, though the mountainside which towers over the houses is impressive. If you get off the main road, however, into the white-walled alleys that wind upwards towards the cliff, it can be very attractive. A sharp curve in the road marks the centre of town, by a small platía overlooked by lofty plane trees. Just above this there's a prodigious 25-spouted **fountain**, a replacement for the elegant Venetian original, which has been removed to a less exalted position beside the health centre (see box below). Beyond the fountain begins a steep mosaic of flowered balconies, cobbled lanes, shady archways, giant urns and whitewashed chimneypots. Spíli can become quite crowded – many of the bus tours passing along the road make a brief stop here, usually for lunch – but between times and in the evenings it is quiet and rural.

ARRIVAL AND INFORMATION   SPÍLI AND AROUND

By bus The main road passes right through the centre of Spíli, and the Ayía Galíni bus will drop you in the heart of town.
Amenities Every facility you're likely to need is clustered around the fountain square, and if not at some point along the main road: post office, banks (with ATM) and a souvenir/newspaper store that sells foreign press are all on the main street close to the fountain. There's internet at several of the bars overlooking the fountain (see p.214).

WALKS AROUND SPÍLI

Plenty of challenging **hikes** start in Spíli. Heracles at **Heracles Rooms** (see p.214) can advise on many of the local walking possibilities, has maps of some, and can help with route information. Both here and the nearby *Green Hotel* can book taxis back to Spíli (around €25 from either Yerakári or Moní Prevéli, for example). None of the available **maps** have enough detail to be really useful: best are the *Petrakis* or *Anavasi* 1:100,000 versions.

TO THE AMÁRI VALLEY VIA MOUNT KÉDHROS

The direct route to **Yerakári** in the Amári valley is on the paved road, but there's also a spectacular walk there on the E4 (which passes through Spíli). This heads south, initially along the road, to the village of Kissós and then up via the summit of Kédhros (1777m). A slightly easier route bypasses the summit, but this is still a tough, all-day, 19km trek with plenty of climbing.

SPÍLI CIRCULAR LOOP

Other attractive options include an easy 2hr **loop walk** via the ancient chapel of Áyios Pnefma. This sets out from Spíli's health centre, up a side road on the left, 200m south of the centre (a road to the right just before the health centre leads 75m to the site of the Venetian fountain that once stood in Spíli's central platía), and meanders into the hills to meet the Spíli–Yerakári road, from where you can descend along narrow lanes to the central square; Heracles has details and a map.

NORTH FROM MIXÓRROUMA

West of Spíli, the E4 follows the road for 4km to the village of **Mixórrouma**, where you can loop back either north or south of the main road. The northern route is all on roads, initially signed for Karínes. This brings you to the pretty village of **Lampiní** and its domed Byzantine **church of the Panayía**, the scene of a terrible massacre in 1827 (marked by a plaque) when the Turks locked the congregation inside the church before setting fire to it. You can head back to Spíli from here or continue for 5km to **Karínes**, another attractive village with a friendly *kafenío*, and **Patsós**, 7km beyond. A turn on the left 1km before Patsós leads for ten minutes to the **Áyios Andónios cave**, which was a Minoan and later Dorian and Roman sanctuary, close to a beautiful gorge. From Patsós it's less than 10km to Thrónos in the Amári valley (see p.215), or about 7km back to Spíli.

SOUTH FROM MIXÓRROUMA

The southern route from Mixórrouma, via **Fratí** and **Mourné**, takes in some superb scenery and four ancient churches. It's probably easier tackled in the other direction – by road from Spíli to Mourné (4km), cross-country from there to Fratí (8km; you'll need directions), then an easy route above the Kissanos river valley to Ayía Pelayía and Mixórrouma (4km).

TO MONÍ PRÉVELI

You can also walk the 15km southwest from Spíli to **Moní Préveli** and **Palm Beach** (see p.229). Head to Mourné, from where a track leads south towards **Drímiskos**; just before the village a cross-track heads west to the Megapótamos River. Follow the River to reach the beach.

3

ACCOMMODATION

Costas Main street, 70m north of the square ☎28320 22040. Simple rooms with TV and fans above a taverna, where breakfast (extra) is served. Free wi-fi. **€35**

Green Hotel Main street, 100m north of the square ☎28320 22225, ⓦmaravelspili.gr. Comfortable place with decent rooms, although lacking a/c and TV; those at the back have fine views across the valley. **€30**

★ **Heracles** Just off the main street, below the Green Hotel ☎28320 22111, ⓔheracles papadakis @hotmail.com. Friendly *pension* with spotless a/c balcony rooms with TV and fridge; excellent breakfast (extra), and internet; they also rent mountain bikes.

Heracles himself is an authority on walking in the area; he can usually be found in his small shop on the main street nearby, where he sells quality souvenirs and local food products. Ten percent reduction for *Rough Guide* readers. **€40**

Rastoni At the bottom of the Yerakári road, north end of the village ☎28320 22744, ⓦrastoni-hotel.gr. New, comfortable a/c rooms around a superb pool; wonderful views from the poolside and many of the rooms. Even if you're not staying, you can have a swim (day and night) for the price of a drink. Occasionally, this can mean it gets noisy. Breakfast (extra) available. **€30**

EATING AND DRINKING

Numerous **tavernas** are spread out along the main road, hoping to tempt drivers; there are a couple of good places among them. **Cafés** cluster around the central platía, and by the fountain.

Babis At the bend in the main road south of the fountain. Lively bar-café with a street terrace ideal for watching the village's coming and goings. Daily 9am–1am.

Fabrica Opposite the fountain ☎28320 22766. One of several places around the fountain, this modern bar-café is slightly livelier at night, and has internet access and free wi-fi. You can also try a Brinks beer here (p.191). Daily 8am–1am.

Giannis Main road, 50m south of the fountain. Close to the heart of things, this is a decent, straightforward taverna for solid Cretan cooking served on a streetside terrace. Daily 11am–11pm.

Mylos Opposite the fountain ☎28320 22481. A lovely place to sit and watch the world go by, serving snacks,

juices, coffee, light meals and beers all day and into the night. Plus internet and free wi-fi. Daily 8.30am–1am.

★ **Panorama** To the right of the main road, about 500m out of Spíli to the south ☎28320 22555. Family-run taverna with great views and an excellent kitchen serving up traditional dishes such as *katsikaki krasatos* (kid in wine) and *hortopitakia* (vegetable pies). Often stages big-name Cretan traditional music events. June–Sept Mon–Fri 6–11pm, Sat & Sun noon–11pm; Oct–May Sat & Sun noon–11pm.

Café Plateia Above the fountain ☎697 92 26 668. Pleasant, relaxing bar-café with an elevated "crow's nest" terrace owned by the proprietors of the *Panorama* (see above) and serving lots of the same menu items. Daily 9am–1am.

The Amári valley

Far less travelled than the route from Réthymno to Spíli is the route through the **Amári valley**, which turns off south at Perívolia on the eastern fringe of Réthymno. Amári is one of those areas, like Sfakiá, which features prominently in almost everything written about Crete – especially in tales of **wartime resistance** – yet which is hardly explored at all by modern visitors. Shadowed by the vast profile of Psilorítis, its way of life survives barely altered by the changes of the last twenty or even fifty years. Throughout the valley, isolated hamlets subsist on the ubiquitous olive, with the occasional luxury of an orchard of cherries (especially around Yerakári), pears or figs, and throughout there are a startling number of richly frescoed **churches**. It's an environment conducive to slow exploration, with a climate noticeably cooler than the coast, and in midsummer the trees, flowers and general greenery make a stunning contrast to the rest of the island.

There are two **roads** through the valley, one following the **eastern** side from the village of **Thrónos** and clinging to the flanks of the Psilorítis range, the other tracing the edge of the lesser Kédhros range on the **western** side. Both are scenically spectacular, but the eastern route probably has the edge in terms of beauty and places of interest.

FESTIVITIES AND DANCE IN THE AMÁRI VALLEY

Whenever you come to the Amári valley, but in July or August especially, you may be lucky enough to stumble on a village wedding (something not to be missed) or a **festival** in honour of the local saint, the harvest or some obscure historical event; the latter are worth going out of your way for, so keep an eye out for notices pasted in *kafenío* windows. Beginning with a distorted cacophony of overamplified Cretan music, *lyra* and *laoúto* to the fore, the celebrations continue until the participants are sufficiently gorged on roast lamb and enlivened by wine to get down to the real business of **dancing**. Cretan dancing at an event such as this is an extraordinary display of athleticism and, as often as not, endurance – and if the party really takes off, locals will dig out their old guns and rattle off a few rounds into the sky to celebrate.

Thrónos and around

The first of the real Amári villages on the **eastern side** of the valley is **THRÓNOS** (Θρόνος), just off the main road at the head of the valley. It's here that you'll emerge if you've come south from Moní Arkádhi (see p.191). Thrónos stands on the site of ancient Sybritos, and like so many of these villages seems lost in the past, with its beautifully frescoed **church of the Panayía** and majestic views. In the Byzantine era this was the seat of a bishop (hence *thrónos*, throne) and these early Christian days are recalled by the remains of a mosaic which is partly under the village church and spreads beyond its walls, with traces both inside and out. The later building, in fact, is only about a quarter of the size of the original church, whose floor plan, guarded by a low rail, can be clearly seen. The keeper will usually appear with the key as soon as you start to take an interest in the church; if not enquire at the shop next door or *Rooms Aravanes*.

The acropolis of Sybritos

On the hill above the village are the remains of the **acropolis of ancient Sybritos** (Συβριτος), easily reached by following a path signed on the left beyond the church. Founded in the twelfth century BC in the troubled Late Minoan period, the original settlement seems to have been more a refuge from mainland invaders (similar to those at Karfí and Présos in eastern Crete) than a real town. Most of the remains visible today, however, date from the substantial Greco-Roman town that flourished from the fifth century BC into the early Byzantine period, when the modern resort of Ayía Galíni served as its port. The town was destroyed by the Saracens in the ninth century. At the top of the hill is a radio mast and plenty of ancient ruins, but above all there are spectacular views in all directions.

Moní Asomáton

Daily 10am–6pm • Free

Outside Thrónos, a confusing slew of roads converge at a junction by the **Moní Asomáton** (Μονή Ασωμάτων), just a couple of kilometres away. The *Kafenio Klados* here is a wonderfully old-fashioned place, full of local farmers. A palm-lined drive leads into an agricultural school (which occupies the monastery's lands) and the abandoned monastery, an ancient foundation whose ruinous Venetian buildings are gradually being restored. The church has a beautiful carved and painted iconostasis (altarpiece). Close to the junction is an attractive new place to stay (see p.218).

Monastiráki archeological site and around

Tues–Sun 9am–3pm • Free

There are numerous fine, big trees around the **Moní Asomáton** junction, and a line of fir and eucalyptus marks the beginning of the 3km road to Amári. This is a beautiful drive or manageable walk, although the second half climbs quite steeply up the hill of

3

HIKES FROM THRÓNOS

The proprietor of *Rooms Aravanes* (see p.218) conducts **guided treks** to the peak of **Mount Psilorítis** (see p.211). Although he does take groups up in the daytime, his preferred approach is during the full moons of June, July and August, which avoids the extreme summer temperatures. Phone in advance for details; it's not a difficult climb, but you'll need sturdy footwear and a sleeping bag. On the **night walks**, the summit is reached at around dawn, and the sunrise is always spectacular. On the route down, you'll visit a goatherd's *mitáto* (stone mountain hut) where you see and sample delicious cheese made on the spot.

You can also get details at *Aravanes* of other **hikes** from Thrónos. These include a relatively easy route north through the foothills in a couple of hours to the monastery of **Arkádhi** (see p.191). The first half of this follows the road, before you head off cross-country to the east. South from Thrónos an extremely easy stroll on a paved road runs into the main valley via **Kalóyeros**. Fifteen minutes' walk beyond Kalóyeros, a narrow path on the left leads uphill to the small stone church of **Áyios Ioánnis Theológos**, whose fine but decayed frescoes date from 1347 – the church should be open. This walk can be extended into a two-hour trek back to Thrónos.

Samítos, which rises right in the middle of the valley. On the way you pass through the picturesque villages of **Monastiráki** and **Opsigiás**. In **MONASTIRÁKI (Μοναστηράκι)** the antiquity of the region is proved by a poorly signed **archeological site**, below the village on a narrow track. The site is usually locked, but when you arrive the caretaker will emerge from the last house on the track: what you see, under covers, is a substantial Middle Minoan settlement that apparently was a centre of wine and cloth production.

Amári

The village of **AMÁRI (Αμάρι)** has fair claim to be the prettiest in the valley: it looks like nothing so much as a perfect Tuscan hill village – note the steeply sloping roofs to cope with the winter snows and the chimneys for wood fires. There's very little to do here – though the *Cafe Petrakeion*, on the central platía, serves good simple food – but there are scintillating views across to Psilorítis and west towards Méronas. For a bird's-eye view, climb the **Venetian clock tower** that dominates the narrow alleyways (the door is always open). Just outside the village, the church of **Ayía Ánna**, reached down a lane on the western edge opposite the police station, has some extremely faded **frescoes** – dating from 1225, they are among the oldest on Crete.

South of Amári

South of Amári, there are more lovely villages on the eastern side of the valley, with the peak of Psilorítis almost directly above and the softer lines of Mount Kédhros on the other side. After 9km the road arrives at **Fourfourás**, a substantial village with facilities including an ATM and a friendly, excellent-value **taverna** and **rooms** place. From here the E4 heads up to the summit of Psilorítis (see p.211) and is also the trailhead of some arduous hikes to the lesser peaks.

Kouroútes, 15km southeast of Amári, is a tiny place with two things going for it: hereabouts you get your first views of the south coast, and there's an excellent **place to stay** (see p.219). From here another just about driveable track heads up towards the peaks – this one going to the mountain hut at Prínos, the halfway point of the E4.

At the small village of **Níthavris**, 4km south of Kouroútes, the road divides. It's worth taking the road south to the village of **Apodhoúlou**, 3km further. Head west at Níthavris and you can again choose to head to Ayía Galíni, or curve round to complete a circuit of the Amári valley through the villages on the lower slopes of **Mount Kédhros**. The roads divide at the hamlet of **Áyios Ioánnis**: on the route south, **Ayía Paraskeví** has fine sixteenth-century **frescoes** in the small **church of the Panayía**. The road to Hordháki, on the western side of the valley, is narrow, winding and neglected.

Apodhoúlou and around
On the way into the village of **APODHOÚLOU** (**Αποδούλου**) there's a Late Minoan **passage tomb**, signed on the left, with its lintel still intact. Beyond here – opposite a fountain – lies an interesting, partly ruined mansion known as the **House of Kalítsa Psaráki** (see box below).

The church of **Áyios Yeóryios**, signed from the village centre and currently undergoing restoration, lies around 1.5km from the village along a lane and dirt track. Inside are some damaged but wonderful **frescoes** from the fourteenth century by Iereas Anastasios, one vigorously portraying its eponymous saint slaying the dragon. Around 1km beyond the turn-off for the church you can see an **ancient Minoan site** beneath a number of metal canopies; unfortunately it is currently fenced off and closed. Excavations have revealed the impressive remains of a Minoan settlement dating from the early second millennium BC, with many substantial dwellings and all the familiar features of Minoan architecture including light wells, benches and narrow corridors. Back on the main road just south of Apodhoúlou you can head down to Ayía Galíni (see p.219) or follow the flank of the mountains east around through Kamáres (see p.212).

The western Amári valley
The villages on the **western** side of the Amári valley look little different from those on the eastern side, but they are in fact almost entirely **modern** – rebuilt after their deliberate destruction during World War II (see box, p.218).

Méronas
As you come through the western Amári valley from the north, **Méronas** (**Μέρωνας**) is the first substantial village, sited where a road cuts across the valley through Amári. Here, the soft-pink Venetian-style **church of the Panayía** (daily except Thurs 10am–2pm) shelters frescoes from the fourteenth century. It takes time for your eyes to adjust to the dim interior and take in the painstaking detail of the artwork, darkened with age: a torch would allow you to see a great deal more than the candles or nightlights which usually provide illumination. There's an excellent **taverna** here, too (see p.219).

Yerakári and around
Yerakári (**Γερακάρι**) is a bigger, more modern and prosperous-looking village than most, with several places to stop for a drink, food and accommodation. The village's **cheeses**, *thimárísio* (thyme honey) and pickled cherries are all for sale on the main square and recommended, although their cherry brandy is probably an acquired taste.

THE HOUSE OF KALÍTSA PSARÁKI
Apodhoúlou's once substantial **House of Kalítsa Psaráki** gets its name from the daughter of a local official who, in the 1821 rising against Turkish rule, was abducted by Muslims and sent to the slave market at Alexandria. By chance she was seen there by Robert Hay, a wealthy Scottish gentleman traveller and Egyptologist, who secured her freedom and – after he had paid for her to be educated in Britain – proposed. They married in Malta, after which Kalítsa accompanied him on his archeological trips to Egypt. Later, when they returned to Crete, an overjoyed family built this house for them to live in. Now a crumbling pile, it's nevertheless possible to see evidence of former grandeur. The stone lintel of a window facing the road bears both Hay's and Psaráki's initials and the date of 1846, when the house was completed.

3

WAR IN THE AMÁRI

The Amári villages suffered gravely during **World War II**, particularly towards the end of the German occupation in the latter part of 1944 when – with an Allied victory assured – the occupiers carried out many wanton atrocities. George Psychoundakis (see p.353) watched the outrage from a cave on the slopes of:

I stayed there two or three days before leaving, watching the Kedros villages burning ceaselessly on the other side of the deep valley. Every now and then we heard the sound of explosions. The Germans went there in the small hours of the twenty-second of August and the burning went on for an entire week. The villages we could see from there and which were given over to the flames were: Yerakari, Kardaki, Gourgouthoi, Vrysses, Smiles, Dryes and Ano-Meros. First they emptied every single house, transporting all the loot to Retimo, then they set fire to them, and finally, to complete the ruin, they piled dynamite into every remaining corner, and blew them sky high. The village schools met the same fate, also the churches and the wells, and at Ano-Meros they even blew up the cemetery. They shot all the men they could find.

Other villages around Psilorítis, from Anóyia to Kamáres, were also burned and destroyed. Officially these atrocities were in reprisal for the kidnap of General Kreipe, four months earlier. But Psychoundakis, for one, believed that it was a more general revenge, intended to destroy any effective resistance in the closing months of the German occupation. Today the villages of Méronas, Elénes, Yerakári, Kardháki and Vrísses mark the southward progress of the German troops with etched stone **memorials** dated one day apart. Áno Méros has a striking war memorial of a woman wielding a hammer and chisel as she carves the names of the dead into the monument.

A spectacular road heads west from here to Spíli (see p.212), offering tremendous views along a valley between the heights of Kédhros and Sorós towards the distant and magnificent Lefká Óri. Continuing south, though, the road beyond Yerakári narrows and is increasingly neglected. Just 1km before **Kardháki**, you'll come to the unusual **Monastery of Áyios Ioánnis Theológos**, with a spreading oak tree providing shade for a tapped spring – a beautiful spot to stop for a breather, or a picnic. Its church has been painstakingly repaired and restored and its remaining thirteenth-century **frescoes** preserved for posterity. Traces of the medieval stone road on which the church was originally aligned can still be made out behind it. Some 6km south of Kardháki the larger village of **ANO MÉROS** makes a pleasant place for a pause and has a place to eat, and 3km south from here lies **Hordháki**.

ARRIVAL AND DEPARTURE   THE AMÁRI VALLEY

By bus Two buses a day on Mon, Wed & Fri (plus one per day at weekends) run from Réthymno to Thrónos and along the eastern edge of the valley past the main villages.
By car Driving is a pleasure; main roads are fine and well

maintained, and the views are magnificent.
Walking The Amári is ideal for exploring on foot. A water bottle, and the best map you can find (see p.40) are essential.

ACCOMMODATION, EATING AND DRINKING

Officially, there are **rooms** only in Amári-Asomáton, Thrónos, Fourfourás, Méronas, Yerakári and Kouroútes, but don't let this deter you from asking in other villages: locals are often only too happy to have a paying guest for a night or two, and traditional hospitality is rife.

AMÁRI-ASOMÁTON
Cottages Panakron 100m from Moní Asomáton (p.215), along the Thrónos road, 3km fron Amári ☎ 28330 22120, ⓦ agrotourismos-kriti.com. A wonderful new cottage complex with five modern a/c cottages (sleeping up to 5) with TV, CD player, kitchen and minibar), in a leafy rural setting. There's also a pool and free wi-fi. **€70**

THRÓNOS
★ **Rooms Aravanes** ☎ 28330 22760, ⓔ aravanes2thronos@yahoo.gr. Signs in Thrónos will guide you to this welcoming bar-taverna whose terrace and en-suite balcony rooms have the best view in the village; they have more rooms (same price) in an attractive stone-built house nearby. Books on the local area are available for

perusal, while the owner, Lambros Papoutsakis, who builds and plays *lyras*, also organizes herb-collecting rambles in the mountains and distils his own *raki*. The distilling season begins in October; you can visit his and other local stills to see the process, with a few samples thrown in. **€40**

Aravanes Shop Attached to Rooms Aravanes ☎ 28330 22760, ✉ arvavanes2thronos@yahoo.gr. The hotel shop sells mountain herbs collected by proprietor Lambros as well as home-made honey, *raki*, olive oil and lots more. Daily 9am–9pm.

Aravanes Taverna Attached to Rooms Aravanes ☎ 28330 22760, ✉ arvavanes2thronos@yahoo.gr. Very good taverna with a nice terrace offering traditional Cretan cuisine. They periodically host big *bouzoúki* get-togethers, with dozens of tables put out and fires lit for barbecuing. Daily 9am–11pm.

Kafepantopolíon Near the church. Basic, friendly village store for food and vegetables, drinks and picnic items. They also have a couple of tables and serve coffee and stronger beverages. Daily 9am–2pm & 5.30–9pm.

FOURFOURÁS

Windy Place Taverna and Rooms At the northern edge of the village ☎ 28330 41366. The taverna serves up hearty meals on an attractive terrace, while the en-suite rooms – in another building in the village proper – come with a/c and heating. The proprietors can describe a short cut (with your own vehicle) to the Psilorítis peak (see p.211) and advise on a 15km gorge walk along the Plátis river valley to Ayía Galíni; they can even collect you from there to return you to Fourfourás. Taverna daily 8am–11pm **€30**

KOUROÚTES

Studios Kourites At the northern edge of the village ☎ 28330 41305. Modern balcony rooms with kitchenette, TV and fans in a detached house surrounded by a garden. Some larger apartments are also available, sleeping up to four. **€35**

MÉRONAS

Elia Hotel Above the main street ☎ 28330 22229, ✉ eliameronas.gr. New, swish apart-hotel offering six twin-roomed balcony apartments, with fully equipped kitchens and fine views, ranged around a large pool. The complex also has its own bar and taverna. Breakfast included. **€50**

Moskovolies Main street, close to the church of the Panayía ☎ 28330 22526. Excellent taverna offering meat (delicious *païdhákia*) and fish dishes served with organic veg from their own smallholding. Daily 8am–midnight.

YERAKÁRI

Alexander Hotel The main street ☎ 28330 51160, ✉ alexanderhotelgerakari.gr. Indubitably the poshest place in town, even if slightly over the top for a Cretan mountain village. If the staidly furnished public areas are a bit off-putting, the balcony rooms are a tad more user friendly with a/c, fridge and coffee-making facilities. The hotel hopes to become an outdoor activity (including hiking) centre and there's a large pool (open to all for the price of a drink) and tennis court in its ample grounds. It also has its own bar and taverna. Free wi-fi. Breakfast included. **€50**

Taverna Rooms Gerakari The main street ☎ 28330 51013. Simple rooms sharing bath above a bar-taverna. The female proprietor's taverna kitchen is a veritable pickling and bottling factory for the fruits of the region – especially cherries, for which the village is famous – that are spread out to dry on every available rooftop during the picking season. **€25**

ANO MÉROS

Bar o Stinos Southern end of the main street ☎ 28330 51063. Friendly family bar-taverna serving solid traditional food – anything from the grill should be good – on a pleasant terrace with a fine view across the valley. Daily 9am–11pm.

Ayía Galíni

Forty years ago, **AYÍA GALÍNI** (Αγια Γαλήνη) must have been an idyllic spot: an isolated fishing community of some five hundred souls nestling in a convenient fold of the mountains which dominate this part of the **south coast**. Although this was the port of ancient **Sybritos** (see p.215), the modern village is barely a hundred years old, its inhabitants having moved down from the mountain villages of Mélambes and Saktoúria as the traditional threat of piracy along the coast receded.

Catch it out of season and the streets of white houses, crowded in on three sides by mountains and opening below to a small, busy **harbour**, can still appeal. But this is a face which is increasingly hard to find. Swarming with package tourists throughout the season, and confined by the limits of its narrow situation, the village has seen many of its older houses squeezed out by apartment buildings and uninspiring hotels. And for a place that bills itself as the province's major resort, the **beach** here is surprisingly small, and was

3

AYÍA GALÍNI ORIENTATION

Few of the streets in Ayía Galíni village are named and such names as there are seem rarely used. Three streets which run down to the harbour form the heart of the place: the first of these (Venizélou) is a continuation of the main road into town; the narrow street parallel to this to the east (we'll call it "Shopping Street") is lined with stores, jewellery shops, bars and travel agencies; while the next street along, for obvious reasons, is known locally as "Taverna Street" although the economic crisis of recent years has drastically reduced the number of eating places. All of this falls within a very small area where nothing is more than a couple of minutes' walk away.

never a major asset anyway. If you're looking for strands with space to breathe you'll need to use the resort as a base for trips to nearby beaches or opt for a shorter stay. The lack of a decent beach is a shame, as is the use of the potentially picturesque harbour area as a car park, for otherwise there's something engaging about Ayía Galíni's relatively staid and respectable brand of tourism. With a **vibrant nightlife** plus plenty of bars and tavernas, the resort is a more inviting place than you'd expect from first impressions, largely because the people have stayed friendly and the atmosphere, despite the development, Cretan. All this attracts a surprising number of long-term expat residents.

The beach

The **beach** at Ayía Galíni lies to the east of the village, ten minutes' walk on a narrow path that tracks around the cliff from the harbour, or by a path that descends from the top of the town. You can also drive round and park by *Camping Agia Galini*. Walking round by the cliffs, you'll pass **caves** that in World War II served as gun emplacements. Although less than 1km long and bisected by the River Platís (spanned by a footbridge), outside August there's usually no problem with finding a patch of soft sand. However, in busier times once these have been claimed you'll have to rent a sunbed if you hope to lounge in any comfort. Various **watersports**, from waterskiing to jet skis and pedaloes, are available from the *Café Acrogiali*, close to where the paths arrive on the strand.

ARRIVAL AND DEPARTURE   AYÍA GALÍNI

By bus Frequent daily buses to and from Réthymno, Iráklio and Spíli terminate at the platía on Venizélou, about 250m above the harbour.

Destinations Festós and Mátala (4 daily; 30/45min); Iráklio (4 daily; 2hr).

By car Coming in by car, head for the large car park on the harbour. Close to the bus halt on Venizélou are several travel agencies and car rental places; Alianthos (☎ 28320 32033, ⊛ alianthos-group.com) is reliable and good value, as is Ostria Rent a Car (☎ 28320 91555, ⊛ ostria-agiagalini .com), higher up the street.

ACTIVITIES

Boat trips Most people who stay here end up making regular excursions elsewhere. In season, boats from the harbour (tickets on board) run to the beaches of Áyios Yeóryios (€5) to the west, and for around €30, east to Palm Beach at Préveli (see p.229), with occasional tours to the Paximádhia islands (around €52 including on-board meal), 12km offshore, which have wonderful fine-sand beaches but little shade (take a parasol).

Fishing and dolphin-spotting There are regular fishing and dolphin-spotting trips (around €30 including meal) with the *Elizabeth* boat. For these contact Captain Vasilis via the *Aerostato* bar on the harbour. Outside peak times, only the occasional boat runs.

ACCOMMODATION

There are so many **rooms** in Ayía Galíni that you'll find exceptional bargains for much of the year – though perhaps not in August when many are pre-booked by tour operators. Probably the best place to start is at the top of the town where the road from Réthymno enters from the east. Other possibilities line the road descending to the harbour, although there aren't many places close to the waterfront. Dozens of places, including almost all of those that we review here, are represented on the excellent ⊛ agia-galini.com.

Camping No Problem Behind the beach ☎ 28320 91386. Big campsite with a pool, shop and restaurant, with sandy, tree-shaded pitches. Two people plus tent plus car €19

Glaros Main road just beyond Agapitos ☎ 28320 91151, ⓦ glaros-agiagalini.com. One of the fanciest places in town, this hotel offers designer communal areas and a/c balcony rooms complete with fridge, some with views. Also squeezes in a small pool. Free wi-fi. Breakfast included. €70

Hariklia On entry road from Réthymno just before the descent ☎ 28320 91257, ⓦ hotelhariklia.gr. Delightful, spotless *pension* with good harbour views and refurbished en-suite a/c rooms with fridge. Guests also have use of kitchen to prepare breakfasts and snacks. Free wi-fi. €35

Irini Mare 100m behind the beach ☎ 28320 91488, ⓦ irinimare.com. All rooms at this upmarket, resort-style hotel are a/c, most have balconies with sea view, and there's a big pool and kids' playground. Free wi-fi in lobby and around pool. Buffet breakfast included. €100

★ **Minos** Entry road from Réthymno on left ☎ 28320 91292, ⓦ agiagalini.com. Welcoming hotel with excellent,

newly refurbished a/c rooms with fridge, TV and room safe. Many enjoy the best sea views in town (cheaper rooms have partial views). Breakfast available. Free wi-fi. €30

Palazzo Greco Entry road from Réthymno on left ☎ 28320 91187, ⓦ palazzogreco.com. Boutique hotel done up in bright colours with marble floors, designer bathrooms and gorgeous sea views from many rooms. Also squeezes in a small pool; the suites are fabulous, the standard rooms a little cramped for the price. Free wi-fi. Rooms €80, suites €110

Romantika Across the bridge and behind the beach ☎ 28320 91388, ⓦ romantika-creta.com. Attractive modern rooms and apartments just 30m from the beach. Rooms come with a/c, fridge, satellite TV and balcony views; the apartments add an extra room and fully equipped kitchen. Free wi-fi. Rooms €50, apartments €65

Tropika Across the bridge and behind the beach ☎ 28320 91351, ✉ tropika@otenet.gr. Good-value studios and apartments behind the beach with the added attraction of a big pool. Studios have a/c, TV and kitchenette while the more spacious apartments also have a kitchen. Rooms €40, apartments €50

EATING AND DRINKING

Ayía Galíni's vast range of **food** and **drink** – one major and undeniable benefit of the resort's popularity – is often excellent and, thanks to the competition, not overpriced. There are plenty of options on **Taverna Street**, but these are not generally the best. There's a good bakery opposite the post office.

O Faros Shopping St ☎ 28930 91346. The resort's best and most unpretentious fish restaurant, with a small street terrace, where the friendly family who run it serve up what they catch themselves. House speciality is *astakomakaronada* (lobster with spaghetti). Daily 6pm–midnight.

Madame Hortense Overlooking the harbour, bottom of Taverna St, above Zorba's bar ☎ 28320 91215. Slightly pricier and more stylish than the competition and named after Zorba the Greek's floozy in the classic novel. An upstairs timber-floored dining room offers great views over the harbour, while the bar downstairs is good for a pre-meal drink. The menu is sprinkled with Greek, Mediterranean and Cretan specialities (try the house *kléftiko* and chicken with olives) and includes a few more exotic, mildly curried dishes from Asia. Daily 11am–midnight.

Mezetzidiko On the harbour ☎ 694 42 85 836. One of the best of the harbourfront places for fish and meat *mezédhes*. Daily 8am–midnight.

Onar Bottom of Taverna St ☎ 28320 91288. Perhaps the best place on Taverna St for wholesome, traditional food – charcoal-grilled fish and meat is a speciality. The bonus is a

great setting, overlooking the harbour from a rooftop terrace. Daily noon–1am.

★ **To Petrino** Just off the platía. Friendly little gem of an ouzerí whose proprietor is an ex-sea captain. Serves breakfast and coffee plus excellent *mezédhes* later in the day, and retains some of the flavour of the pre-tourist days. Daily 8am–1pm & 4.30pm–midnight.

Platía On a small square slightly south of the bus stop ☎ 28320 91185. This café is famed for its breakfasts (omelettes, fruit salads and muesli all feature), and later in the day also does snack meals and *mezédhes* (which it calls tapas). Daily 8.30am–2pm & 6pm–1am.

Romantika Romantika Hotel, across the bridge and behind the beach ☎ 28320 91388, ⓦ romantika-creta .com. One of several enjoyable bar/tavernas behind the beach, attached to a hotel; the nearby *Tropika* is also good. April–Sept daily noon–midnight.

La Strada Shopping St. Good pizza and decent pasta and risotto served on a street terrace; the brothers who run it are accomplished performers on the *lyra* and *laoúto* and often treat their customers to an impromptu concert. Daily 6pm–midnight.

NIGHTLIFE

Aerostato Harbourfront. New-style bar serving breakfasts, snacks and salads by day and cocktails and

juices by night. Pleasant seafront terrace with easy-on-the-ear rock and jazz music. Daily 8.30am–3am.

Blue Bar Shopping St. This enjoyable bar attracts a slightly more mature crowd, getting down to jazz and pre-1980s classics. Daily 6pm–2am.

C'est la Vie Harbourfront. Laidback harbourfront bar serving breakfasts, drinks and snacks, and stronger stuff as the day progresses. Daily 8am–2am.

Juke Box Bottom of Taverna St. Late-night clubbing venue with a mainstream, crowd-pleasing playlist. Daily 6pm–2am.

Kafenío Elpida Shopping St. Almost the last traditional *kafenío* in the village, stubbornly clinging to its identity in the face of the surrounding tumult; a good place for *mezédhes* and people-watching. Daily 9am–11pm.

Zanzibar Platía, by the bus stop. As well as an internet café (with free wi-fi), this bar is a home from home to many English-speaking expats, with a real pub atmosphere. Daily 11am–1am.

Zorba's Overlooking the harbour, bottom of Taverna St. A pleasant place for an early-evening drink, or an ouzo before your meal in the restaurant above, with a veranda overlooking the harbour, dartboard, piano and shrine to the Beatles. It changes character later, when dancing starts around midnight. Daily noon–2am.

DIRECTORY

Banks and money You'll find banks with ATMs near the platía, on Venizélou.

Books and newspapers Le Shop Kalliopi, close to the north end of Shopping St, is a bookshop with English fiction, books about the island and foreign newspapers.

Doctor Near the platía.

Internet Numerous bars offer internet access. Try *Alexander* (10am–1am) on the east side of the harbourfront. Both also offer free wi-fi, as do most of the bars and tavernas around the harbour.

Post office Near the platía bus halt (Mon–Sat 8am–7pm).

West of Ayía Galíni

In high summer visitors seeking space to breathe tend to head west to the beaches of **Áyios Yeóryios**, **Áyios Pávlos** and beyond. Áyios Yeóryios can be reached on foot and is currently the only western beach accessible by boat from Ayía Galini. If you're aiming for Áyios Pávlos, or the even more isolated beach settlements further west still, at **Triópetra**, **Lígres** and **Ayía Fotiní**, you'll need your own transport.

Áyios Yeóryios

About 8km west of Ayía Galíni, the seaside hamlet of **Áyios Yeóryios** (Άγιος Γεώργιος) is fairly easily reached on foot, by a marked and well-trodden path that leaves town from the top of the main street, near the *Hotel Ostria*. The beach is almost two hours away, a shingle cove with a taverna (see opposite). Daily boat trips from Ayía Galíni also visit, and you can drive here, on a paved road that turns off the Ayía Galíni–Mélambes road (accessed from the highway north of Ayía Galíni). When you get here, though the water is startlingly clear, the beach is not especially attractive, and has little shade (although parasols can be rented). If you have a vehicle you're better off heading further west.

Áyios Pávlos

Áyios Pávlos (Άγιος Πάυλος), 8km from Áyios Yeóryios as the crow flies, but quite a few more along the meandering back roads via Mélambes and Saktoúria, is an attractive proposition, with some striking rock formations around a sheltered bay, and excellent snorkelling. The lovely **beach** can be subject to strong winds, which you can escape by climbing over the headland to the west, where you can scramble down a sandy slope to two fine-sand beaches, one very sheltered, one nudist. In addition to the visitors arriving by car from the surrounding hinterland, Áyios Pávlos is home to a colony of New Age practitioners who run **yoga** and related courses at their centre, Yoga Plus (bookable in advance only; ⊛yogaplus.co.uk).

West of Áyios Pávlos

West of Áyios Pávlos it's possible to drive all the way to Palm Beach (see p.229). Most of this is on paved roads, and though they can be steep, winding and narrow in places (and the route not always obvious), it's not an especially hard drive – by far the toughest section comes after you reach Palm Beach, where the road around the back of the beach is very rough, though this is also much the busiest part of the route. Along the way are a series of long beaches, with only the first stirrings of development.

Triópetra

As far as the coastal hamlet of Triópetra the road west from Áyios Pávlos is mostly inland; once here you simply turn right along the beach, following signs to Lígres. As for **TRIÓPETRA (Τριόπετρα)** itself, if you wanted to hole up for a couple of days in a tranquil haven, with a lovely small cove and a huge but exposed beach, this would be as good a choice as any. There's quite fancy yoga retreat here (Wastanga.gr), and tavernas with **rooms** (see below). You can also reach Triópetra (and Áyios Pávlos) directly from the main road south of Spíli, via the village of Akoúmia.

Lígres and around

Lígres (Λίγρες), 4km west of Triópetra, is another isolated strand with two taverna-rooms places behind a grey-sand beach that seems to stretch for miles to the west. Considering the isolation here, the tavernas are remarkably busy and comfortable. Finally, a couple of kilometres beyond Lígres lies the even simpler **Ayía Fotiní,** the last stop before the celebrated Palm Beach. Beyond here, the final section of coast road is unpaved.

ACCOMMODATION AND EATING   **WEST OF AYÍA GALÍNI**

ÁYIOS YEÓRYIOS

Nikos ☎28320 91001 or ☎694 45 04 852, Waggeorgios.gr. En-suite a/c rooms with fridge. The eponymous proprietor serves his daily seafood catch, including langoustine and lobster, on the attractive terrace above the sea. Free wi-fi. Daily 9am–11pm. **€45**

ÁYIOS PÁVLOS

★ **Ayios Pavlos Hotel** ☎28320 71104, Wagios pavloshotel.gr. A great place to stay with lovely a/c sea-view rooms and some cheaper, more basic options; another complex in a slightly less perfect setting has modern, well-equipped apartments for up to four people. The café-restaurant boasts a terrace on the rocks directly above the sea. Basic rooms **€28**, superior rooms **€40**

Mama Eva Immediately above the beach. Simple a/c rooms without views and a good taverna with a shady terrace looking out to sea. **€30**

TRIÓPETRA

Apanemia Around the cove ☎697 21 22 186. One of the most attractive tavernas, with attractive, a/c rooms with fridge and balcony. Daily 9am–11pm. **€30**

Pavlos Around the cove ☎28310 25189, Wtriopetra .com.gr. A friendly seafront taverna-rooms place that offers appealing a/c rooms with fridge and balcony. The taverna specializes in fresh fish caught with their own boat. Daily 9am–11am, noon–4pm & 6.30–11.30pm. **€40**

To Yiroyiali Behind the main beach ☎697 64 30 145. This place has an attractive dining terrace and some quite fancy a/c rooms with fridge and TV in a separate two-storey block overlooking a garden. Daily 9am–11pm. **€35**

LÍGRES

Ligres Beach ☎697 42 34 509, Wligres.gr. Modern, a/c rooms with fridge and sea-view balconies, and a reliable taverna serving fresh fish. Daily 9am–11pm. **€35**

Villa Maria ☎28320 22675, Wligres.eu. Perhaps the best of the places here, a stone-built affair with welcoming rooms and studios with a/c, TV and fridge – and, unexpectedly, a rushing stream running beside them – as well as some great two-room apartments. The taverna offers good food (they catch their own fish) and icy spring water from the waterfall outside. Daily 7.30am–11pm. **€35**

AYÍA FOTINÍ

★ **Taverna Agia Fotini** ☎28320 22675, Wagiafotini.net. A lovely, isolated and tranquil option that's a throwback to the Crete of thirty years ago; the excellent taverna, with a terrace out front, offers a range of traditional Cretan dishes as well as fresh fish. Upstairs are four simple but spotless rooms overlooking the sea that come with a/c and a fridge. Free wi-fi. Breakfast included. **€40**

Plakiás and around

Around 35km south of Réthymno, and 30km from Ayía Galíni as the crow flies (although longer by a road that diverts inland via Spíli) the major resort of **PLAKIÁS** (Πλακιάς) is the biggest attraction on Réthymno's south coast. A well-established resort, it's still a long way from the big league, and commercialized as it is, has a very different feel to anywhere on the north coast, or even Ayía Galíni – the accommodation is simpler, less of it is booked up in advance, the beaches are infinitely better and it attracts a younger crowd. Don't come for sophisticated nightlife or for a picturesque white Greek island village: what you'll find is a lively, friendly place that makes a good base for **walks** in the beautiful countryside – especially around the gorges – and trips to some great **beaches**.

Virtually everything in Plakiás lies along or just off the **main road** that enters from the east, running beside the sea, or on one of the lanes connecting it to the single street that runs inland, rapidly deteriorating into paths which wind up towards Selliá and Mírthios.

Plakiás beaches

Getting to the **beach** involves no more than a two-minute walk. The town is set at the western end of the bay, and east of the paved harbour grey sand curves around in an unbroken line to the headland 1km or more away, with an increasing amount of development behind it. Unfortunately, this beach looks better from a distance than from close up – the long open sweep of the bay means it can be exposed and gusty, and the strong summer **winds** seem to affect Plakiás more than other places along this coast. There's plenty of space – especially towards the far end – but you'll find much better sands beyond the headland at Dhamnóni (see p.228), or to the west at Soúdha Beach.

Soúdha Beach

Soúdha Beach (Παραλία Σούδα) is just over half an hour's walk west of Plakiás, past signs of encroaching development, with places to stop for a swim along the way. The sand is mostly grey and coarse, but there's plenty of room and the water at the far end is sheltered by rocks; closer to town, where there are fewer people and less development, it's largely nudist.

Mírthios

The village of **MÍRTHIOS** (Μύρθιος) hangs high above Plakiás, with wonderful views over the bay. There are few facilities beyond a couple of small shops and a post office, so you really need transport. You can, however, walk down to Plakiás, about twenty minutes heading steeply downhill, or to several of the nearby beaches – the walk back up is considerably tougher, though.

ARRIVAL AND DEPARTURE   PLAKIÁS AND AROUND

PLAKIÁS

By car Three routes towards Plakiás branch off from the main Réthymno–Ayía Galíni road. The main one, signed to Plakiás, heads down towards the coast via the spectacular Kourtaliótiko Gorge; an alternative route, signed to Selliá, comes through the only slightly less impressive Kotsifóu Gorge, where there is an excellent taverna in the village of Kánevos (see p.226). This route eventually opens out to leave you on the main coast road west of Plakiás; turn right for Selliá (p.230), left for

Mírthios and Plakiás. The road enters Plakiás from the east, behind the beach, and heads straight into the heart of things along the seafront. Continuing through town, the coast road westwards ends after 3km or so at Soúdha, though you can turn off to head up to Selliá and the main road west via a vertiginous series of narrow hairpin bends.

By bus Buses arrive and depart from a stop just east of the little bridge, roughly halfway along the seafront opposite the big Forum supermarket: the timetable is usually pinned up and is also displayed at nearby travel agencies. There are currently four buses daily between here and Réthymno.

By taxi There's a taxi office at the bottom of the street to the post office, or try Taxi4you, on the main street inland from the harbour (☎ 28320 31777, ⓦ taxi4you.gr).

Car and mountain bike rental There are many car rental outlets, including several on the seafront; Alianthos, at the *Alianthos Beach Hotel* (☎ 28320 318510, is excellent,

or try Anso Travel (☎ 28320 31712), who also have mountain bikes.

MÍRTHIOS

Ideally you need your own transport to get to Mírthios. However, the Plakiás bus usually comes up here after it has dropped most of the passengers (or it may drop you at the junction below, about 10min walk away).

INFORMATION AND ACTIVITIES

Travel agencies Alianthos Travel (☎ 28320 31851, ⓦ alianthos-group.com), on the seafront, and the nearby Anso Travel (☎ 28320 31712, ⓦ ansotravel.com).

Boat trips and fishing Several boats a day (except Wed) head to Préveli and Áyios Pávlos; you can buy tickets in advance at local travel agencies, or simply turn up at the harbour. The *Finikas*, leaves daily at 10.20am and 12.30pm, returning at 3pm and 5pm; get details from *Smerna* bar at the western end of the seafront. *Tassos* – information at *Tassomanolis* taverna (see p.227) – also goes daily to Préveli Palm Beach in season (€15 return) and once a week to Frangokástello and Rodhákino; fishing trips are also on offer when demand is sufficient.

Diving Some of Crete's best diving is near Plakiás, and there are also easy beaches for learners. Dive2gether is a

Dutch company with an office on the front, east of the bridge (☎ 28320 32313, ⓦ dive2gether.com); Kalypso Rocks Dive Centre (☎ 28310 54135, ⓦ kalypsodivingcenter .com) organizes dives at the nearby *Kalypso Cretan Village* resort (see below).

Horseriding The country around Plakiás is great to explore on horseback; arrange pony trekking and lessons through the *Alianthos Beach Hotel* (☎ 28320 31196).

Walking Organized walks are available through many local travel agencies (see above), and there's an excellent walking guide of the local area by Lance Chilton (see p.355). This is not currently available locally; buy it at ⓦ marengowalks.com. Several local walks are also described in detail at ⓦ peter-thomson.co.uk/crete /contents.html.

ACCOMMODATION

While there are scores of **hotels** and **rooms** in Plakiás – indeed at times it seems there's little else – you may have difficulty finding a vacancy in high season. The places on the backstreets lack sea views but are quieter and usually the last to fill; many of these are on the street parallel to the coast, heading towards the youth hostel – get there from behind the *Alianthos Garden Hotel*, or by following the street past the post office. There are also lots of new studio-apartment complexes on the road as you approach town and along the coast towards Soúdha Beach to the west and, slightly further afield, options at the beaches to the east such as Dhamnóni or Amoúdhi. You can find an excellent **list** of local accommodation at ⓦ plakias-filoxenia.gr.

PLAKIÁS

Alianthos Beach At the start of the seafront road ☎ 28320 31196, ⓦ alianthosbeach.com. Friendly hotel above a good taverna. The comfortable rooms have a/c; those at the front have balconies overlooking the beach. Breakfast included. €55

Anthos Apartments East of town, above the beach ☎ 28320 32018, ⓦ anthos.kreta-sun.com. Comfortable a/c apartments with kitchen, balcony and satellite TV sharing a small pool. €60

Aphrodite Pension Two blocks in from the beach next to the Porto Plakias hotel ☎ 28320 31266, ⓦ plakiasrooms.4ty.gr. Charming, gleaming white *pension* with spotless en-suite rooms and apartments in a tranquil garden location with cascading bougainvillea. Good-value rooms come with a/c, fridge, strongbox and coffee-making facilities. Free wi-fi in lobby. €34

Camping Apollonia On the right as you approach town ☎ 28320 31318, ⓦ apollonia-camping.gr. Small,

rather cramped site, but the location is excellent, and facilities include a minimarket and pool. Tents and caravans available to rent. Two people plus tent plus car €23

Gio-ma At the western end of the seafront ☎ 28320 32003, ⓦ gioma.gr. In a prime position overlooking the harbour, these fabulously sited, if small and simple, rooms (with bath, fridge and a/c) sit above the taverna of the same name, right on the water. Over the road are comfortable modern studios (with kitchenette) and two-room apartments with sea views – more expensive, but still good value. Rooms €25, studios €35, apartments €45

Ippokambos On the inland street parallel to the sea ☎ 28320 31525, ⓔ amoutsos@otenet.gr. Modern, friendly place with simple, but spacious and well-presented rooms, all with bath, balcony and fridge. Parking on site. €40

Kalypso Cretan Village On the promontory south of town, 4km or so by road ☎ 28320 31296, ⓦ kalypso hotels.com. All-inclusive hotel in a stunning, rocky,

3

seaside setting with its own tiny secret cove. It's good value considering the facilities – though rooms vary in quality. Breakfast included. Free wi-fi in public areas (but €3/hr in room). There's also a good dive centre here, and other activities including mountain biking. **€104**

★ **Morpheas Apartments** On the seafront, above Plakiás Market ☎ 28320 31583, 🌐 morpheas -apartments-plakias-crete-greece.com. Fine modern rooms, studios and duplex apartments with balconies overlooking the beach (although not all have sea view). Double-glazed against the potentially noisy location, with a/c, TV, fridge and, in the larger apartments, even a washing machine. Rooms **€45**, studios **€50**, large apartments **€72**

Paligremnos Beach At the eastern end of the town beach, about 500m from town ☎ 28320 31835, 🌐 paligremnos.com. Small studio complex with its own taverna and garden with kids' play area in a quiet location right by the beach. Good-value a/c studios and apartments have kitchenette and balcony overlooking the sea. **€45**

Phoenix Apartments 1.5km west, near Soúdha Beach ☎ 28320 32108, 🌐 phoenix-plakias.com. Tranquil complex with a good-sized pool in a great spot above the sea. Studios and three-room apartments are all a/c and well equipped. Studios **€42**, apartments **€63**

Skinos Apartments Two locations on the road to Soúdha Beach, about 300m and 500m from town ☎ 28320 31737, 🌐 skinos -plakias.com. *Skinos I* is a simple rooms place, *Skinos II* has slightly more modern apartments with kitchen; all are very quiet, with shower,

a/c, fridge and large balconies looking out to sea. Free wi-fi. Rooms **€40**, apartments **€45**

Souda Mare Just before Soúdha Beach ☎ 28320 31931, 🌐 souda-mare.blogspot.com. Friendly hotel in a beautiful spot above the water, with a/c rooms with balconies and sea views. Free wi-fi in the bar. **€55**

★ **Youth Hostel** Inland a little way behind town ☎ 28320 32118, 🌐 yhplakias.com. By far the best hostel on Crete – friendly, relaxed and well run, in an attractively rural setting, with a terrace for breakfast and evening drinks and a busy social scene. Hot showers included; wi-fi and internet. Dorms **€10**

KÁNEVOS

Iliomanolis Kánevos, right at the head of the Kotsifóu Gorge, 7km north of Plakiás ☎ 28320 51053. An excellent and inexpensive taverna with simple but clean rooms in a tiny settlement near the Kotsifóu Gorge. **€30**

MÍRTHIOS

★ **Apartments Anna** ☎ 6973 324775, 🌐 annaview .com. A variety of different-sized, attractive and well-equipped a/c studios and apartments, many with spectacular balcony views. All are equipped with satellite TV and there's a pleasant garden to lounge in. Free wi-fi. **€48**

Village Apartments ☎ 28320 31835, 🌐 village.kreta -sun.com. Pleasant place with well-appointed studios and apartments, all with kitchenette or separate kitchen. Free wi-fi. **€35**

EATING

Plakiás's seafront street is lined with **tavernas**, cafés and bars, but the prime spot is towards the harbour right at the centre of town, where a strip of places have tables next to the water. You'll pay a bit more here than at other places in the resort – but the setting is worth it. For breakfast, there are a number of **bakeries** along the seafront too, and many of the **cafés** open early. The biggest **supermarkets** are Forum, immediately east of the bridge, Plakiás Market, between the *Livikon* and *Lamon* hotels, and one on the edge of town by the *Alianthos Beach* hotel, which has an excellent bakery and a wonderful fruit shop.

PLAKIÁS

Candia Bakery Between the hotels Livikon and Lamon on the seafront. A good place for breakfast, and throughout the day for coffee, juices and takeaway snacks and pies. Daily 8am–1am.

Gio-Ma Overlooking the harbour at west end of the seafront ☎ 28320 31261. Along with neighbouring *Christos*, *Gio-Ma* has probably the best location of the seafront places, sharing a pleasant tamarisk-shaded terrace; it's noted for its seafood. Daily 9am–11pm.

Kastro High on the hill behind the town ☎ 28320 32246. This taverna's fine terrace with great views complements friendly service and some original and tasty dishes such as *kounéli lemonato* (rabbit with a lemon and garlic sauce). It's signed by road, or on foot you can follow

the path through the olive groves beside the *Alianthos Garden Hotel*, looking out for the taverna's crenellated roofline above you. Daily 11am–midnight.

Kri Kri Near the bridge on the seafront ☎ 28320 32223. Good pizza from a wood-fired oven as well as all the taverna standards such as *stifádho* and *kléftiko*. Daily noon–1am.

★ **Medousa** At the eastern end of the inland street, near the back of the Alianthos Garden hotel ☎ 28320 31521. A welcoming and traditional taverna with an excellent kitchen (try the delicious *moussaká* or any of the lamb dishes) and prices noticeably lower than those on the seafront. Also decent bottled wine in addition to the usual barrelled house wine. Daily noon–3pm & 6.30–10.30pm.

Nikos Souvlaki By the post office on the street running inland from the front. Probably the cheapest place in town, serving up excellent *souvláki* or fish and chips to take away, or eat in at one of the few small tables. Daily 6pm–midnight.

On the Rocks Overlooking the beach at the western end of town ☎ 28320 31023. Café-bar serving good breakfasts, and later in the day day, ice cream and cocktails. Free wi-fi. Daily 8.30am–1am.

Plateia Main road just east of Forum supermarket ☎ 979277229. Café by day, with good breakfasts, and a popular late-night drinking spot. Daily 8am–1am.

Sofia On the seafront near the bus stop ☎ 28320 31226. The best of the tavernas right by the sea, with a slightly less touristy menu than some of its neighbours. House specials include Cretan *saganáki*, *kotópoulo Sofia* (pot stewed chicken) and *piri-piri* (spicy oven-baked beef). Daily noon–midnight.

★ **Tassomanolis** Facing west along the shore beyond the harbour ☎ 28320 31229. One of three or four good places around this end of the beach. Seafood is king here, most of it caught by the proprietor from his own boat. Try the oven-baked *dorada* (bream) or their three-fish *souvláki*. Daily noon–midnight.

MIRTHIOS

Panorama Slightly uphill from Taverna Plateia. A straightforward taverna offering well-cooked standards. A decent substitute when the *Plateia* is full, with equally fine vistas from its terrace. Daily noon–10.30pm.

★ **Taverna Plateia** Village square ☎ 28320 31560. The village's oldest restaurant, recently refurbished and taken distinctly upmarket, although prices remain very reasonable and the view from its inviting terrace has to be a candidate for the best in Crete. An outstanding kitchen produces tasty traditional Cretan cuisine with the odd creative twist. Their mixed *mezédhes* starter makes an excellent (and economical) light lunch for two, and there are more elaborate dishes such as *kokinistós arni* (lamb cooked with tomato and wine). It can get busy, especially at Sunday lunchtimes, so turn up early if you don't want to wait (they don't accept bookings). Daily noon–11pm.

DRINKING AND NIGHTLIFE

Frame Up steps next door to the Forum supermarket. Stylish and relaxed new bar with easy listening and a great sea view through panoramic windows. Also billiard tables, internet and free wi-fi. Daily 10am–3am.

Notus Café On the waterfront, near the harbour. A chilled place, with free wi-fi and occasional live music. Daily 6pm–6am.

Ostraco On the waterfront, close to the harbour.

Ostraco has been here for ever, it seems, with a rock-based playlist and fun atmosphere. It's one of the best places in town, with two floors of bars and a balcony. Daily 9am–3am.

Paralia On the waterfront, close to the harbour. A rather cooler version of its neighbour *Ostraco*, with an upstairs balcony and more club-oriented music. Daily 7pm–3am.

DIRECTORY

Books and newspapers International press and books in English are widely available; the best selection is at the Forum supermarket, east of the bridge.

Doctor A private doctor's surgery (9am–1pm & 5–9.30pm; ☎ 28320 31770) and a pharmacy are in the street by the post office.

Internet Several of the bars around the harbour have internet, and the *Notus* café here has free wi-fi. Frame, above the Forum supermarket, has the fastest connection.

Money There's no bank in Plakiás, but there are four ATMs along the seafront street and you can change money at most travel agents and some supermarkets.

Post office On the street running inland near *Hotel Livikon* (Mon–Fri 7.30am–2pm).

Travel agents Anso, with offices in the two main streets running inland, from the harbour and by the post office (☎ 28320 31712, ⊛ ansotravel.com); Alianthos Travel, next to the Forum supermarket (☎ 28320 31851).

East of Plakiás

Just east of Plakiás Bay, beyond a headland riddled with caves and wartime bunkers and gun emplacements, lie some of the most tempting **beaches** in central Crete, albeit a very poorly kept secret. Three splashes of yellow sand, divided by rocky promontories, go by the general name of **Dhamnóni**. Five kilometres east from here (although it's a good 8km along the inland road you're forced to follow) lies the **Moní Préveli** and, 1km further, **Palm Beach**, one of Crete's most celebrated strands.

Dhamnóni beach and around

Dhamnóni beach (Δαμνόνι) is the first beach east of Plakiás, and the only one that has so far really seen much development: the western half has been colonized by an ugly Swiss-owned holiday village, *Hapimag*, while the road down to the sand has an increasing number of new **rooms** places.

The **beach** is a wonderfully long strip of yellow sand and super-clear water with a couple of **tavernas**. At the far eastern end you're likely to find a few people who've dispensed with their clothes, at least out of season, and the little cove that shelters the middle of the three beaches (a scramble over the rocks, or a very rough track) is almost entirely **nudist**. This enclave can get very crowded, but they're a good-humoured bunch and, unusually, often include quite a few Greek naturists too. The water is beautiful and there are caves at the back of the beach and rocks to dive from, with some great snorkelling to be had.

Skhínaria beach and around

If you continue over the rocks beyond Dhamnóni you will pass another tiny pocket of sand (also nudist) before **Amoúdhi beach**, where there's a rather more sedate atmosphere and another **taverna** attached to the *Ammoudi Hotel*. **Skhínaria beach** (Σχοίναρια) is almost adjacent, but to get there you have to drive several kilometres round, via Lefkóyia. Another fine, sandy cove, it's popular with Greek families at holiday times and weekends, and occasionally hosts groups learning to scuba dive, but is otherwise delightfully quiet. There's a taverna open during the day.

Monastery of Áyios Ioánnis

Ten kilometres east of Plakiás a paved road descends into the fertile valley of the Megalopótamos River, which, unusually for Crete, flows throughout the year. Where it meets the river, the road turns south to climb past the fenced-off ruins of the **Monastery of Áyios Ioánnis** (Μονή Άγιος Ιωάννης), also called Κáto, or Lower, Préveli. This is the site of the original sixteenth-century monastery of Préveli, until it was left behind in the following century when the monks decided to move to the greater safety of the present site further uphill. Torched by the Turks in the nineteenth century and long abandoned, only the church now stands complete amid the broken walls, cattle mangers and derelict dwellings of the former monastic community. A project has been mooted to restore the ancient buildings; Moní Préveli (see below) will have information on this.

Moní Préveli

April & May daily 9am–6pm; June–Oct Mon–Sat 9am–1.30pm & 3.30–9pm, Sun 8am–7pm; in winter, knock for admission • €2.50 • In summer two daily buses run from Réthymno to Préveli (11.30am & 6pm); you can also get here by taking a boat to Palm Beach from Plakiás and Ayía Galíni and climbing up steps in the cliff – a strenuous 30min or so to the monastery, reached via the car park

The celebrated **Moní Préveli** (Μονί Πρέβελη), perched high above the sea, lies 16km by road from Plakiás. Justifiably proud of its role in centuries of Cretan resistance, it is famed above all for the shelter provided to Allied troops, many of them Australian, stranded on the island after the Battle of Crete in World War II. The monks supported and fed many soldiers and helped organize them into groups to be taken off nearby beaches by submarine. There's a startling **monument** to these events, overlooking the sea just before the monastery, depicting a life-sized rifle-toting abbot and an Allied soldier cast in bronze. More commemorative plaques decorate the monastery interior and alongside the icons in the church are a number of offerings from grateful individuals and governments. The church also houses a cross said to contain a fragment of the True Cross; there's a small **museum** with other relics and religious vestments; and a fountain in the courtyard with the palindromic Greek inscription "Wash your sins, not only your face". There are also fine views out to sea towards the distant and chunky-looking Paximádhia islands, which take their name from the tooth-cracking lumps of twice-baked bread served up with *mezédhes* in the *kafenía*.

Palm Beach

A sand-filled cove right at the end of the Kourtaliótiko gorge, where a freshwater estuary feeds a little oasis complete with palm grove and cluster of oleanders, **Palm Beach** certainly looks beautiful – but for much of the year there are far too many visitors, with loungers, sun umbrellas and pedaloes diminishing the natural charm of the place. Behind the beach, you can escape up the palm-lined riverbanks on foot or take a pedalo through the icy water. Further upstream, before the gorge becomes too steep to follow, are a couple of deep pools nice to swim in. On the beach, a small **bar-taverna** provides basic food and sells drinks, snacks and a few basic provisions. It's strange to think, as you bask on the crowded sands, that from here, in 1941, many of the Allied soldiers who sought refuge at Moní Préveli (see opposite) were evacuated by submarine.

ARRIVAL AND DEPARTURE   EAST OF PLAKIÁS

THE DHAMNÓNI BEACHES

By car Driving to the Dhamnóni beaches from Plakiás you have to go much further round than if you were to walk: follow the road towards Lefkóyia and turn down at the sign for Dhamnóni or, further on, for Amoúdhi.

On foot From Plakiás follow the main road east and turn right along a track which leads through the olive groves. After a while you'll see the beach below you and a path which runs down to it – about 40min in all.

PALM BEACH

By car Driving from Plakiás, after 9km the road bends right into the Megalopótamos river valley and shortly beyond this you'll pass an ancient-looking bridge across the river (actually a nineteenth-century copy of a Venetian original), where a sign indicates a left turn to Palm Beach. Immediately (across the river) you turn right, soon crossing another cobbled Venetian bridge, beyond which the track leads – after perhaps 15min tortuous, rough driving – to the *Amoudi Taverna*. From here, Palm Beach is a 5min climb around the cliff via a stairway carved into the rock – and your first view of it as you reach the crest is quite stunning. An alternative, easier, route is to continue past the turn off by the bridge towards Préveli Monastery and follow signs on the left to a car park (€2). From here a well-marked, stepped path with dramatic views clambers steeply down over the rocks – a 10min descent to Palm Beach, a sweaty, muscle-taxing 15 or 20min getting back up.

By boat Boats from Plakiás and Ayía Galíni can take you to Palm Beach.

ACCOMMODATION AND EATING

Ammoudi Hotel Amoúdhi beach ☎28320 31355, ⓦammoudi.gr. A fabulous place to get away from it all, with a/c balcony rooms with fridge and TV plus apartments 100m from the shore. Breakfast is available in their taverna. It also has a dive centre, and this is an ideal spot to learn. Taverna daily 8am–10pm. **€45**

Amoudi Taverna Palm Beach ☎6945 704654. One of two places that offer basic rooms with and without private bath, some with a great view, on a not terribly attractive beach alongside Palm Beach. **€20**

Damnoni Paradise Dhamnóni Beach ☎28320 31480, ⓦdamnoni-paradise.kreta-sun.com. One of the oldest places to stay is this charming, family-oriented place surrounded by a dense garden whose palms, jasmine and bougainvillea offer welcome shade; a variety of en-suite rooms are available, as well as a couple of larger apartments. Free wi-fi in lobby. **€40**

Lybian Star Skhínaria, behind the beach. Friendly, family-run beach taverna specializing in fresh local fish and dishes made with olive oil and vegetables from their own *kípos*. Daily 11am–7pm.

Taverna Gefyra By the "Venetian" bridge on the Préveli–Palm Beach road ☎693 72 32 189. A pleasant taverna on the way to Palm Beach serving *mezédhes*, snacks and drinks on a shady terrace. Daily 9am–10pm.

West of Plakiás

West of Plakiás the terrain becomes more mountainous as you near the district of Sfakiá and the foothills of the Lefká Óri or White Mountains. Historically this area always had an unhealthy reputation for lawlessness, and its fighting men were feared both by other Cretans and successive invading powers. Heading west from Plakiás towards Frangokástello (see p.291), it's a stiff climb up towards Mírthios and then round, hugging the mountainside, to **Selliá**. You can also approach Selliá direct by an alarmingly steep, winding road climbing from the coast west of Plakiás.

Selliá

Looking up from Plakiás or across from Mírthios you would imagine that **SELLIÁ** (Σελλιά) had the best views of all across this area, but if you drive through you see nothing: these are exclusively enjoyed by the backs of the houses which face out across the sea towards Africa. If you want to stop and take a look it's easy enough to find a path through; better still, pause for a drink or a bite to eat at the tiny and excellent taverna on the main street (see below). Nearby, the "folk art museum" is actually a private **gallery** and studio belonging to resident painter Marianne Morris; her canvases and hand-painted postcards are for sale. You can walk from the centre of the village down to Plakiás, a steep thirty minutes below, or you could include Selliá in a long circular hike from Plakiás via Mírthios.

Rodhákino and around

Beyond Selliá the country changes and there's a real feeling of the approach of western Crete. The road runs high above a series of capes and small coves, where the only village of any size is **RODHÁKINO** (Ροδάκινο), whose two halves are set on steep streets divided by a dramatic ravine. Below is the sand-and-shingle beach of **Koráka**, where General Kreipe was finally taken off the island after his kidnap in 1944 (see p.340). Some development has started on the coast around here, and if you want to get away from it all there are a few good **rooms** places.

Polirízos and around

The beach road west of Koráka continues as far as **POLIRÍZOS** (Πολυρίζος) in the next bay along, where there are more rooms places and villas above a small sandy beach. Continuing west from Polirízos, the main road winds high above the coast, from where a number of beaches look tempting, though hardly any are accessible. Signs of development increase as you cross the provincial border into Haniá and approach Frangokástello, with villas, a few isolated rooms places and even the odd taverna. New tracks connecting these places pop up all the time, which makes things confusing: however, if you drive towards the coast you can often find a way through, though the last bit may be on foot. Some of the best are found by following the sign from the main road to **Lákki beach** – follow the dirt road straight on (avoid being seduced by new bits of tarmac or signs to tavernas) and you'll reach a headland from which you can easily walk down to a couple of beautiful patches of sand.

ACCOMMODATION AND EATING   WEST OF PLAKIÁS

SELLIÁ

★ **Elia** Main street by the "folk art museum" ☎ 697 42 95 193. Excellent little ouzerí-taverna where the home-cooked food (try the *mezédhes* or *loukánika* sausage) is every bit as good as the stunning terrace view. Daily 10.30am–10pm.

RODHÁKINO

Arokaria Behind the beach ☎ 28320 32161, ⊛ arokaria-rodakino.gr. A very good and friendly taverna whose pleasant en-suite a/c rooms have views as well as TV and kitchenette. The taverna serves fresh fish and some Sfakián specialities such as *katsikapsito* (mountain goat stewed in wine). Don't miss their home-made orange liqueur. Daily 8am–11pm. €30

Sunrise A short way up the hill above the beach ☎28320 31787, ⓦsunrise-hotel-crete.gr. Attractive rooms, studios and apartments with sea views, as well as a pool and a taverna (daily 8.30am–midnight) with a rooftop terrace. Rates include breakfast. Rooms €40, studios €45, apartments €60

POLIRÍZOS

Panorama Above the small sandy beach ☎28320 31788. A decent taverna offering clean and simple rooms without a/c. Daily 7am–11pm. €30

Polyrizos ☎28320 31334, ⓔpolyrizo@otenet.gr. Relatively fancy hotel complex, with a pool and good restaurant where any of the lamb dishes are worth a try. Free wi-fi. €40

3

Haniá

BALOS BAY, GRAMVOÚSA

Haniá

Haniá, Crete's westernmost province, is still its least visited, which is a significant part of its attraction. Although tourist development is spreading fast, and has already covered much of the coast around the city of Haniá, the west is likely to remain one of the emptier parts of the island, partly because there are few beaches suited to large resort hotels, and partly because the great archeological sites are a long way from here. In their place are some of the most classic elements of the island: scattered coves, unexploited rural villages, and a spectacular vista of mountains.

The city of **Haniá**, island capital until 1971, is unequivocally the most enjoyable of Crete's larger towns, littered with oddments from its Venetian and Turkish past, and bustling with harbourside life. To either side, along virtually the whole **north coast** of the province, spreads a line of sandy beach – at times exposed, and increasingly developed, but still with numerous stretches where you can escape the crowds. Three peninsulas punctuate this northern coastline: **Akrotíri**, enclosing the magnificent natural harbour of **Soúdha Bay**; **Rodhopoú**, a bare and roadless tract of mountain; and, at the western tip of the island, **Gramvoúsa**, uninhabited and entirely barren. Akrotíri is overshadowed by NATO air bases and naval installations, but it's still worth a day-trip, with a couple of excellent beaches and two beautiful monasteries. Most tourists stay to the west, on the coast between Haniá and Rodhopoú, in one of a number of former villages now linked by an ever-expanding strip of low-rise development centred on **Ayía Marína** and **Plataniás**, with the villas and apartments thinning out as you head further from the city.

The south is overshadowed by the peaks of the **Lefká Óri** – the White Mountains – whose grey bulk, snowcapped from January through to June, dominates every view in western Crete. Although marginally less high than the Psilorítis range, they're far more rewarding for walking or climbing. Along the south coast the mountains drop straight to the Libyan Sea and the few towns here lie in their shadow, clinging to what flat land can be found around the bays. Through the heart of the massif there's no road at all, nor is there any driveable route along the south coast: unless you want to travel back and forth across the island you'll have to rely on boats, or on walking. The hike through the National Park in the **Samariá Gorge**, Europe's longest, is stunning, despite the summer hordes. With a little spirit of adventure and preparation you can take scores of other, deserted **hiking** routes.

The south-coast communities beneath the mountains see plenty of visitors, mostly gorge-trippers passing through, but none could really be described as a resort. **Ayía**

VIEW OF THE LEFKÁ ÓRI

Highlights

❶ Haniá Old Town The island's second-largest city has a delightful Old Town filled with Venetian and Turkish buildings lining narrow alleys and stepped streets leading down to a scenic harbour. **See p.239**

❷ Lefká Óri Crete's most impressive mountains offer a huge range of hiking opportunities – the famous Samariá Gorge is just one option. See p.273

❸ Loutró Accessible only on foot or by boat, the tiny village of Loutró epitomizes the isolated appeal of the southwest coast. See p.279

❹ Frangokástello A stunning seaside castle with a backdrop of stark mountains. **See p.291**

❺ Falásarna and Elafonísi The remote west coast boasts two of the island's finest beaches. **See p.298 & p.305**

❻ The Enneachora Touring the "Nine Villages" offers a spectacular drive through green, wooded countryside, circling back via a spectacular cliff-top corniche. **See p.302**

❼ Byzantine churches Ancient churches, many of them with remains of original frescoes, are found throughout the region, particularly in Sélinos. **See p.306**

❽ Paleohóra The only real resort in the southwest, with a great beach, lively atmosphere and an enjoyable end-of-the-road feel. **See p.307**

HIGHLIGHTS ARE MARKED ON THE MAP ON P.236

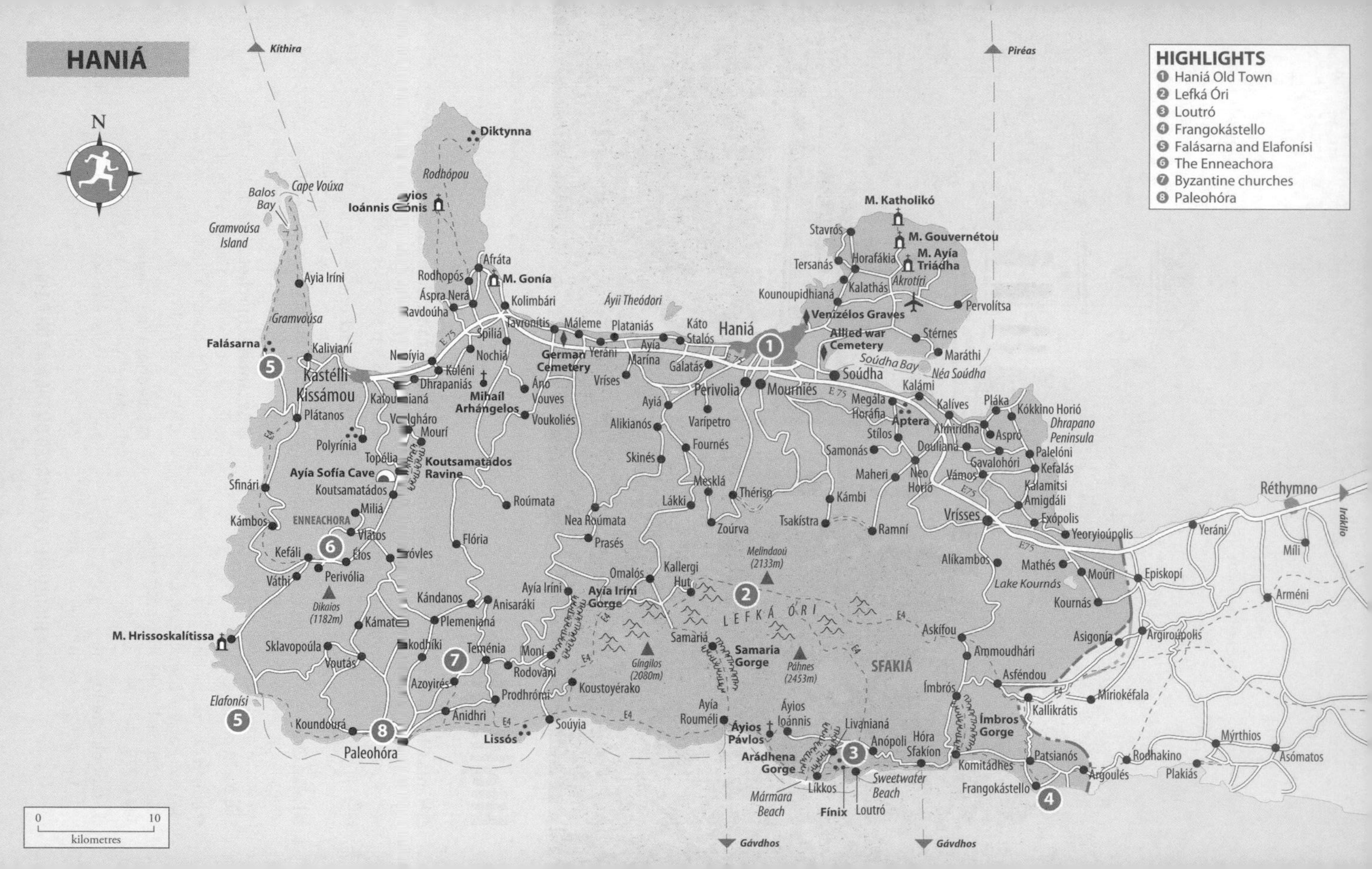

HANIÁ
HIGHLIGHTS
1 Haniá Old Town
2 Lefká Óri
3 Loutró
4 Frangokástello
5 Falásarna and Elafonísi
6 The Enneachora
7 Byzantine churches
8 Paleohóra
N
Kíthira
Piréas
Gávdhos
Gávdhos
Iráklio
Diktynna
Rodhópou
Cape Voúxa
Balos Bay
Gramvoúsa Island
Gramvoúsa
Ayia Iríni
Falásarna
Kaliviani
Kastélli Kissámou
Plátanos
Polyrínia
Sfinári
Kámbos
ENNEACHORA
Kefáli
Váthi
Perivólia
Élos
Vlátos
Miliá
Koutsamatádos
Ayía Sofía Cave
Topólia
Koutsamatados Ravine
Mourí
Dhrapaniás
Koléni
Kaloudianá
Afráta
M. Gonía
Rodhopós
Áspra Nerá
Kolimbári
Tavronítis
Spiliá
Nochiá
Mihaíl Arhángelos
Áno Vouves
Voukoliés
Máleme
German Cemetery
Yeráni
Platanias
Áyii Theódori
Ayía Marína
Vríses
Káto Stalós
Galatás
Haniá
Perivolia
Mourniés
Soúdha
Allied war Cemetery
Venizélos Graves
Kounoupidhianá
Kalathás
Tersanás
Stavrós
Horafákia
Akrotíri
M. Katholikó
M. Gouvernétou
M. Ayía Triádha
Pervolítsa
Stérnes
Maráthi
Soúdha Bay
Néa Soúdha
Kalámi
Megála Horáfia
Aptera
Kalíves
Almirídha
Pláka
Aspró
Kókkino Horió
Dhrapano Peninsula
Stílos
Samonás
Douliana
Palelóni
Gavalohóri
Kefalás
Vámos
Kalamitsi
Amigdáli
Maheri
Neo Horió
Vrísses
Exópolis
Yeoryioúpolis
Réthymno
Yeráni
Míli
Arméni
Episkopí
Mathés
Mourí
Lake Kournás
Kournás
Alíkambos
Asigonía
Argiroúpolis
Askífou
Ammoudhári
Asféndou
Ímbrós
Ímbros Gorge
Kallikrátis
Miriokéfala
Patsianós
Argoulés
Rodhakino
Mýrthios
Asómatos
Plakiás
Frangokástello
Komitádhes
Hóra Sfakíon
Anópoli
Livanianá
Sweetwater Beach
Loutró
Fínix
Líkkos
Árádhena Gorge
Mármara Beach
Áyios Pávlos
Áyios Ioánnis
Ayía Rouméli
Páhnes (2453m)
SFAKIÁ
Samaria Gorge
Samariá
LEFKÁ ÓRI
Melindaoú (2133m)
Kallergi Hut
Omalós
Gíngilos (2080m)
Koustoyérako
Soúyia
E4
E75
Lissós
Ayía Iríni
Ayía Iríni Gorge
Prasés
Nea Roúmata
Roúmata
Flória
Kándanos
Anisaráki
Plemenianá
Teménia
Moní
Rodováni
Prodhrómi
Anídhri
Azoyirés
Paleohóra
Koundourá
Elafonísi
Sklavopoúla
Voutás
Dikaios (1182m)
M. Hrissoskalítissa
Alikianós
Skinés
Ayiá
Varípetro
Fournés
Mesklá
Thériso
Lákki
Zoúrva
Tsakístra
Kámbi
Ramní
0
10
kilometres

Rouméli, the sometimes frenetic end-point of the Samariá Gorge walk, and serene **Loutró** can be reached only on foot or by boat. **Hóra Sfakíon**, the capital of the wild region known as Sfakiá, is a pleasant place to stay if you can handle the influx of day-trippers; more peace is to be found down the coast a little, at the superb beaches by the Venetian castle of **Frangokástello**.

The west end of the island, beyond Rodhopoú, is very sparsely populated. The port of **Kastélli** is the only town of any size, and there's a growing resort at **Paleohóra** in the south. **Soúyia** may be the next in line, but for the moment it seems in a rather charming state of limbo. The whole of the mountainous southwestern corner, an area known as **Sélinos**, is worth exploring, with rough roads leading to untouched mountain villages and little-known ruins and churches. On the west-facing coast – hard to get to but well worth the effort – are two of Crete's finest beaches, **Falásarna** and **Elafonísi**. Finally there's **Gávdhos**, an island some 30km off the south coast that is Europe's southernmost point, caught somewhere between the eighteenth and the twenty-first centuries.

Haniá town

HANIÁ (Χανιά), as any of its residents will tell you, is the spiritual capital of Crete, even if the political title is now officially bestowed on Iráklio's urban sprawl. With its shimmering waterfront, crumbling masonry and web of alleys, it is an extraordinarily attractive city, especially if you can catch it in spring when the Lefká Óri's snowcapped peaks seem to hover above the roofs. The permanent population – fast expanding into hill and coastal suburbs – always outnumbers the tourists, although in August visitors seem to run them pretty close. Haniá has plenty to fill a good day or two's sightseeing; highlights include the **Venetian harbour** and a quartet of **museums**, as well as plenty of Minoan ruins. But the greatest pleasure of all, perhaps, is to be had wandering the narrow streets and stepped alleyways of the **old quarters**, filled with Venetian and Turkish architectural gems. Add plentiful accommodation and tavernas, excellent **markets**, shopping and nightlife, and you'll almost certainly want to stay longer than you intended.

Haniá's **old city** clusters around the harbour, and most tourists confine themselves to this area or the fringes of the **new town** up towards the bus station. You may get lost wandering among the alleys, but it's never far to the sea, one of the main thoroughfares or some other landmark. The closest **beaches** lie in a string to the west of the city.

The main annual **festival** is the commemoration of the Battle of Crete around May 20 (when accommodation is at a premium), with folklore and other events mostly in the Public Gardens.

Brief history

Haniá is one of the longest continuously inhabited city sites in the world, though its convoluted and often violent history has left it with little to show for it. Only recently has the arrival of **tourism**, amid a rare period of peace and prosperity, inspired the will – if not the resources – to save the city's crumbling architectural heritage.

Ancient Kydonia and La Canea

Ancient **Kydonia** was an apparently substantial **Minoan** community about which little is known: only scattered remnants have so far been brought to light, but many believe that there was a major palace here, probably beneath the modern buildings in Kastélli, overlooking the harbour. After the collapse of the Minoan palace culture, Kydonia grew into one of the island's most important cities – well enough known for its citizens to warrant a mention in Homer's *Odyssey* – and remained so through the Classical Greek era. When **Rome** came in search of conquest, the city mounted a stiff resistance prior to its eventual capitulation in 69 BC, after which it flourished once more. The Kastélli hill served as the Roman city's acropolis, but dwellings spread at least as far as the extent of

HANIÁ TOWN

● **SHOPS**
Daily Market	3
Mediterranean Editions	1/4
Street Market	2

■ **ACCOMMODATION**
Alcanea	2
Amphora	10
Anastasia	8
Anemi Suites	18
Artemis	22
Camping Hania	13
Casa Delfino	16
Casa Veneta	9
To Dhiporto	25
Doma	26
El Greco	15
Helena	7
Ifigenia	6
Ionas	19
Kasteli	12
Lucia	17
Maro	21
Nefeli	27
Neli	23
Nora	3
Palazzo	14
Porto Veneziano	1
Rooms 47	11
Splanzia	20
Stella	5
Thereza	4
Vilelmine	24

● **RESTAURANTS**
Akrogiali	10
Amphora	9
Anna's	21
Doloma	8
Enetikon	15
Faka	6
Karnayio	7
Khrisostomos	1
Mathios	3
Ta Merakliklia tou Boureki	28
Mihalis	2
Nikteridha	24
To Pigadi Tou Tourkou	18
Portes	22
To Staki	4
Tamam	17
Tholos	20

● **CAFÉS & CAFÉ-BARS**
Alcanea	5
Dekatria	25
Iordanis Bougatsa	26
To Kafenio	16
Kentrikon	23
Kormoranos	11
Muses	12
O Platanos tis Splantzias	13
Spirit Lounge	19
Thea	14
Time Out	27

■ **BARS & NIGHTLIFE**
Fagotto	2
Ippopotamos	1
To Monastiri tou Karolos	10
El Mondo	8
Notos	4
Rudi's Bierhaus	3
Synagogi	7
Tesseres Epoches	5
Thelma	6

Map labels

Outer Harbour
Inner Harbour

Firkas
Byzantine Museum
Naval Museum
Mosque of the Janissaries
Renier Gate
Center of Traditional Folk Art
Cretan House Folklore Museum
Archeological Museum
Cathedral
Minoan Excavation
KASTÉLI
Arsenali
Minoan Ship
CMA
San Rocco
Ayios Nikolaos
Ayii Anaryiri
SPLANTZIA
Minaret
Market
Schiavo Bastion
Supermarket
Open-air Theatre
Stadium
KOUM KAPI
Bus Station
Dhimarhio
Bus Stop for Soudha
Bus Stop for City Beaches

Platía Katehaki
Platía Sindriváni
Platía 1821
Platía Ay. Venizélou

4

N

0   200
metres

26 (300m), 24 (5km), Airport & Akrotiri
Platía Eleftherías
New Road, Soudha, Réthymno & Iráklio
27 (20m)
Beaches, Plataniás & Kastélli
30 (500m), 13 (5km) & City Beach

the walled city that can be seen today: Roman mosaics have been discovered beneath Cathedral Square and up near the present market.

In early **Christian** times Kydonia was the seat of a bishop, and under the protection of Byzantium the city flourished along with the island. As the Byzantine Empire became increasingly embattled however, so its further outposts, Kydonia included, suffered neglect. Not much is heard of the place again until the thirteenth century, when the **Genoese** seized the city from the Venetians and held it from 1263 to 1285.

When the **Venetians** finally won the city back they turned **La Canea** (as it was now known) into a formidable bulwark, as well as probably the island's most beautiful city. The city walls were built in two stages: in the fourteenth century Kastélli alone was fortified; in the sixteenth century, new walls were constructed as a defence against constant raids by pirate corsairs – in particular against the systematic ravages of Barbarossa. It is these defences, along with the Venetian harbour installations, that define the shape of Haniá's old town today.

Occupation and resistance

In 1645, after a two-month siege with terrible losses (the Turkish commander was executed on his return home for losing as many as forty thousand men), Haniá fell to the **Turks**. It was the first major Cretan stronghold to succumb, becoming the Turkish island capital. Churches were converted to mosques, the defences more or less maintained, and there must have been at least some new building, though today it is barely possible to distinguish Venetian from Turkish workmanship.

For the rest, it is a history of struggle. In the **independence** campaign, the city's most dramatic moment came in 1897, following the outbreak of war between Greece and the Ottoman Empire, when the Great Powers (Britain, France, Russia and Italy) imposed peace and stationed a joint force in the waters off Haniá. From here, they bombarded Cretan insurgents attempting prematurely to raise the flag of Greece on the hill of Profítis Elías (see p.250). When the Turks were finally forced to leave, Prince George, the high commissioner chosen by the powers, established his capital here for the brief period of his regency.

During **World War II**, with most of the German landings and the bulk of the fighting on the coast immediately west of the city, Haniá suffered severe bombardment, the destruction eventually compounded by a fire, which wiped out almost everything apart from the area around the harbour.

Around Odhós Hálidhon

Odhós Hálidhon is perhaps the most touristy street in Haniá, and the major junction at the inland end (Platía 1866) marks the centre of town as well as anywhere. If you stand facing north at this junction, everything in front of and below you is basically the old, walled city; behind and to either side lie the newer parts. To the east, **Odhós Yiánnari** leads past the market and eventually out to the main road or onto the Akrotíri peninsula, while to the west, **Skalídhi** leads out of town towards Kastélli Kissámou. Ahead of you, Hálidhon descends to the **harbour** and into the heart of the old town; some 70m from the junction is the animated **Odhós Skridhlóf** ("Leather Street"), where, traditionally, leather-makers plied their trade. While many shops are now geared to tourists, prices for leather sandals, bags and the like remain the best in Crete.

Cathedral

Set back from the road, the **cathedral**, a modest 1860s building with little architectural merit, presides over **Platía Mitropóleos**. This attractive square, surrounded by outdoor cafés – more peaceful if you head round to the back of the cathedral – was where, around 1770, the rebel Dhaskaloyiannis (see p.284) was tortured to death.

Archeological Museum

Hálidhon 21 • Tues–Sun 9am–6pm • €2, combined ticket with Byzantine Museum €3

Haniá's **Archeological Museum** is housed in the Venetian-built church of San Francesco. Though it doesn't look like much now, with its campanile gone and a crumbling facade, this building was once one of the island's grandest. Inside, you get a better sense of its former importance. The Turks converted the church into a mosque, from which a beautiful fountain and the base of a minaret have survived in the flowery garden.

The museum boasts a large collection of **Minoan metalwork and pottery**, including a few huge storage jars or *píthoi* and a collection of Minoan clay coffins (*lárnakes*), some wonderfully decorated, and one containing two small skeletons. For archeologists, the most significant items are the **inscribed tablets** excavated in Kastélli: this is the only place other than Knossós where examples of Linear A and Linear B script (see p.329), have been found together and is regarded as evidence supporting the existence of a palace here. Another important recent find in the Kastélli excavations is the **"Master Impression" seal**. Dating from the Late Minoan period (1500–1450 BC), it is almost unique in depicting a townscape – a long-haired male figure in Minoan loincloth, holding a sceptre, is shown standing over a great complex of multi-storey buildings (the Kastélli hill?) with a rocky seaside landscape below.

Towards the back of the church, the collection is arranged chronologically, progressing through a large group of Classical **sculptures**, a case full of Greco-Roman **glassware** and some third-century Roman **mosaics**. The latter are truly lovely, particularly those of Dionysos and Ariadne, and of Poseidon and Anemone.

The museum is scheduled to move to a spectacular **new building** in the eastern suburb of Halepa in 2013 or 2014. Designed by renowned Greek architect Theofanis Bobotis, the new edifice will add exhibition space and provide library and laboratory facilities for researchers. Check with the tourist office (see p.245) for the latest.

Cretan House Folklore Museum

Hálidhon 46 • Mon–Fri 9am–3pm & 6–9pm, Sat & Sun 9am–3pm • €2

The **Cretan House Folklore Museum** is a cluttered collection of artefacts, tapestries and traditional crafts equipment set out in a replica of a "traditional" house (though few can have been quite so packed). Embroidered cloths and tapestries made on site are on sale. On your way out, take a look at Haniá's elegant **Roman Catholic church** in the same courtyard, an interesting contrast to the city's Orthodox churches.

The outer harbour

Hálidhon ends at a square by the harbour – officially called Platía Sindriváni, but known simply as **Harbour Square**. To the left, Aktí Koundouriótou circles around the outer harbour, crowded with outdoor cafés and tavernas. The **harbour** comes into its own at night, when the lights from bars and restaurants reflect in the water and the animated crowds – locals as much as tourists – parade in a ritualistic volta of apparently perpetual motion. Stalls sell everything from seashells to henna tattoos, and buskers serenade the passers-by. By day, especially in the hot, dozy mid-afternoon, it can be less appealing – often deserted and with the occasional whiff of decay from the rubbish washing up against the quayside.

Mosque of the Janissaries

Aktí Tombázi • Usually daily • Free

The curious, domed profile of the **Mosque of the Janissaries** (aka Hassan Pasha mosque) dominates the Harbour Square view. Built in 1645, the year Haniá fell to the Turks, it is the oldest Ottoman building on the island, and has been well restored – apart from the jarring concrete dome. It is usually open as a gallery, housing temporary exhibitions, while a more long-term plan is considered. Inside, the main feature is the **mihrab** (a niche indicating the direction of Mecca) complete with Koranic inscription.

Naval Museum

Aktí Koundouriótou • Mon–Sat 9am–7pm, Sun 10am–6pm • €3

The hefty bastion at the western end of the outer harbour houses Crete's **Naval Museum**. Although largely of specialist interest, the enthusiasm here is infectious, and the model ships, maquettes of the town in Venetian times, old maps and working exhibits like the old harbour light are hard to resist.

Whether visiting the museum or not, it's worth going through the main gate (usually open in daylight hours) to see the compound of the small naval garrison. Here you can climb onto the renovated seaward fortifications of the **Fírkas**, as this part of the city defences is known. It was on this spot that the modern Greek flag was first raised on Crete – in 1913 – and there are fine sea views.

Byzantine Museum

Theotokopólou 78 • Tues–Sun 9am–4pm • €2, combined ticket with Archeological Museum €3

The **Byzantine Museum**, in the Venetian chapel of San Salvatore, has a tiny but beautifully displayed collection of mosaics, icons, jewellery, coins, sculpture and everyday objects, giving a fascinating insight into an era that's largely overlooked – the entire period from early Christian to the end of the Venetian occupation in the seventeenth century.

City walls

West of the Byzantine Museum, Odhós Pireós cuts inland outside the best-preserved stretch of the **city walls**, impressive, weighty and threatening. Following them on the inside is rather trickier, but far more enjoyable. This is where you'll stumble on some of the most picturesque little alleyways and finest Venetian houses in Haniá, and also where the pace of renovation and gentrification is most rapid. The arch of the **Renieri Gate** is particularly elegant. There are also interesting art and craft stores around here, along Theotokopóulou and the many alleys that run off it down towards the harbour.

Evraiki

Between the Renieri Gate and Hálidhon the emphasis is on tavernas, bars and cafés: **Kóndhilaki** is one of the busiest streets. This area was the medieval Jewish ghetto (the quarter is still officially known as **Evraiki**).

Synagogue

Párados Kóndhilaki • Mon–Fri 10am–6pm • Suggested donation €2 • ⓦ etz-hayyim-hania.org

Signed at the end of a small alley off the west side of Kóndhilaki is Haniá's fifteenth-century Etz Hayyim **synagogue**, renovated by a fraternity of local Christians, Muslims and Jews after falling into ruin. All but one of the city's Jews were rounded up by the Nazi occupation forces in 1944; they met their end (along with around five hundred members of the captured Cretan resistance) when the transport ship taking them to Auschwitz was torpedoed by a British submarine off the island of Mílos. The synagogue is entered through the original Venetian doorway, and its garden, *mikveh* (purification fountain), reconstructed interior and *bimah* (speakers' platform) have been sensitively restored. The names of the 276 Jews who perished in the ship are remembered on a plaque in a garden cemetery at the rear.

The inner harbour

Beyond the mosque, harbourfront Aktí Tombázi curves round to the right to the **inner harbour**, where pleasure boats, private yachts and small fishing vessels are moored, and where sixteenth-century Venetian arsenals look out towards the breakwater alongside a cluster of restaurants and bars. Many of the arched **Arsenali** are still in a ruinous state, but others have been sensitively restored: one, the sixteenth-century Great Arsenal, is occupied by the **Center for Mediterranean Architecture** (CMA), with offices, a café and a glitzy space for temporary exhibitions (times and prices vary).

For a nice stroll you can follow the sea wall for almost 1km as far as the minaret-style **lighthouse**, en route to which there are excellent **views** back over the city. At the eastern end of the inner harbour there are more signs of regeneration and refurbishment; this is now a fashionable part of town. Aktí Miaoúli, following the shore eastwards beyond the city walls (an area known as **Koum Kápi**), is packed at night with bars and cafés, mostly frequented by young locals. Behind the harbour, though, the streets are still pretty run-down, and in some ways the most atmospheric in the old town.

Exhibition of Traditional Naval Architecture

Inner harbour • Mon–Sat 10am–3pm & 6–9pm, Sun 10am–6pm • €2

One Arsenali, at the extreme eastern end of the harbour, houses the Naval Museum's **Exhibition of Traditional Naval Architecture**, the highlight of which is a reconstruction of a fifteenth-century BC **Minoan ship**; the *Minoa* was rowed to Athens for the start of the 2004 Olympics and it, together with the vast boat shed itself, easily outshines the rest of the exhibits.

Kastélli

The bluff that rises behind the mosque and the inner harbour, known as **Kastélli**, was the site of the earliest habitation in Haniá. Favoured from earliest times for its defensive qualities, this little hill takes its name from a fortress that originally dated from the Byzantine era. Later it was the centre of the Venetian and of the Turkish towns, but very little survived a heavy bombardment during World War II.

HANIÁ'S BEACHES

Haniá's beaches lie west of town. The town beach can be reached by foot, while the others are accessible by bus #21 from Platía 1866.

Néa Hóra The city beach is about a 10min walk from the harbour, round past the Naval Museum and on by the city's open-air swimming pool and a small fishing-boat harbour. The beach has clean sand and sheltered water, showers, and usually crowds of people. Cafés and restaurants line the seafront, while offshore (a longer swim than it looks) is a tiny islet with a sandy beach large enough for about five people at a time.

Áyii Apóstoli Around 3km west of Néa Hora – about 20min on foot. En route you'll pass plenty of new development but it's not got out of hand. There's a good long stretch of yellow sand, the city's campsite and a much more established, if low-key, cluster of development; the only drawback (as at most of these beaches) is the crashing breakers, which can become vicious.

Hrissí Aktí Some 2km beyond Áyii Apóstoli you'll reach the next section of beach, known as Hrissí Aktí (Golden Beach). Here there's more good sand, which has attracted the apartment-builders. But it's not yet overcrowded, has some good tavernas and is popular with locals.

Oasis Beach and Kalamáki Beyond the Hrissí Aktí headland lies a tiny sand cove, another small promontory, and then the long curve of Oasis Beach running on round to Kalamáki. This is justly crowded – the swimming is probably the best in the area, with a gently shelving sandy bottom and a fossil-covered (and very sharp) rocky islet/reef that fends off the bigger waves. There's a string of cafés and tavernas, and other facilities including windsurf rental and lessons. Kalamáki is the furthest beach accessible by city bus, and it's right by the main road.

Beyond Kalamáki There are even finer beaches at Ayía Marína (see p.264) to the west, or Kalathás and Stavrós (p.250) out on the Akrotíri peninsula, all of which can be reached by KTEL buses from the main station.

Walking up Kaneváro from Platía Sindriváni you'll pass various remains, including a couple of fenced-off sites where **Minoan Kydonia** is being excavated. The Swedish-Greek archeological team have traced the outline of substantial buildings engulfed by a violent fire about 1450 BC, similar to that which destroyed Knossós. Many believe that this could be the site of the **palace** long thought to have existed here – if so, it would complete a pattern across the island – but as yet no trace of a "Central Court", the defining feature of Minoan palaces in Crete, has come to light. However, recent trial excavations in the nearby Odhós Dhaskaloyiánni at the end of Kanevaró revealed the whole area to be covered with Minoan remains, so there is a possibility that a Minoan palace could lie somewhere here. In the period following the Minoan demise it is also likely, given its proximity to the mainland, that this may well have been the focus of Mycenaean power on Crete.

Among pottery finds were some dating back to the Neolithic era, but the greatest prize uncovered was an archive of clay tablets bearing Minoan Linear A script (see p.329), the first to be found so far west in Crete. All around the Kastélli hill various other **trial excavations**, usually on vacant lots between existing houses, reveal further tantalizing glimpses of the substantial Minoan conurbation that lies beneath the modern town, and there are plans for much more extensive excavations once all the relevant property has been acquired. The alleys up to the left, onto the rise, end up going nowhere, but it's worth looking up here for the traces of the old city that survive, and tantalizing glimpses of the views that the old buildings afford. Lithinón, for example, has various Venetian doorways and inscriptions and, at the top, a fine old archway beyond which the rather derelict hilltop area allows fine **views** over the harbour and out to sea.

Splántzia

Inland from Kastélli, you can head through the backstreets towards the **market**. This area, still known by its Turkish name **Splántzia**, is full of unexpected architectural delights, with carved wooden balconies and houses arching across the street at first-floor level. Many of the streets between here and the inner harbour have recently been recobbled and refurbished, and they're among the most atmospheric and tranquil in the old town.

Platía 1821 and around

The tranquil **Platía 1821** features the refurbished church of Áyios Nikólaos whose **minaret** is missing its top. Built by the Venetians, the church was converted to a mosque under Sultan Ibrahim and reconverted after Crete's reversion to Greek authority. The square itself – whose name recalls the date of one of the larger rebellions against Turkish authority, following which an Orthodox bishop was hanged here – is a shady space set with café chairs. Nearby are two more old churches: San Rocco, at the square's northeast corner, is small and old-fashioned, while **Áyii Anáryiri**, which retained its Orthodox status throughout the Turkish occupation, has some very ancient icons.

The modern town

Modern Haniá sprawls in every direction, encircling the old town. The areas southwest of the **market**, on the way to **Platía 1866** and the bus station, have an attractively old-fashioned commercialism about them, full of stores stocking life's essentials.

Public Gardens

Between Odhós Tzanakáki and Odhós Papandreou, southeast of the market

Laid out by a Turkish pasha in the nineteenth century, the **Public Gardens** include a few caged animals – Cretan wild goats, or *kri-kri*, ponies, loud monkeys and birds – a café where you can sit under the trees and a children's play area. The open-air auditorium is often used as a cinema, and also hosts local ceremonies and folklore displays.

Platía Eleftherías and around

At the end of Sfakianáki, about 500m southeast of the Public Gardens, **Platía Eleftherías** has a statue of Venizélos in the centre and an imposing court building along the south side, which was originally the government building of Prince George's short-lived administration (see p.337). **Iróon Politehníou** runs due north from Platía Eleftherías down to the sea. A broad avenue divided by trees and lined with large houses, interspersed with several expensive garden restaurants and a number of fashionable café-bars, it makes for an interesting walk in a part of the city very different from that dominated by the tourist crowds of Hálidhon.

ARRIVAL AND DEPARTURE   HANIÁ TOWN

BY BUS

Bus station South of the walls on Odhós Kydhonías, within easy walking distance of the centre; there's a left-luggage office.

Destinations Almirídha (4 daily; 8.45am–5pm; 30min); Ayía Marína (every 15min; 6.30am–11.40pm; 20min); Elafonísi (1 daily; 9am; 3hr); Falásarna (7 daily; 8.30am–6.30pm; 2hr); Frangokástello (1 daily; 2pm; 2hr 30min); Haniá airport (17 daily 5.45am–9pm; 30min); Hóra Sfakíon (2 daily; 8.30am & 2pm; 2hr); Iráklio (16 daily; 5.30am–9pm; 2hr 30min); Kalíves (8 daily; 6.45am–8pm; 45min); Kastélli (15 daily; 6.30am–10pm; 1hr); Kolimbári (every 30min; 6.30am–11.30pm; 1hr); Limnoupolis water park (7 daily; 9.45am–5.45pm; 30min); Máleme (every 30min; 6.30am–11.30pm; 45min); Mesklá (2 daily Mon–Fri; 6.45am & 2pm; 30min); Omalós, for the Samariá Gorge (3 daily; 6.15am, 7.45am, & 8.45am; 1hr 30min); Paleohóra (4 daily; 5am–4pm; 2hr); Plataniás (every 15min; 6.30am–11.40pm; 30min); Réthymno (16 daily; 5.30am–9pm; 1hr); Soúyia (2 daily; 5am & 2pm; 2hr); Stavrós (via Horafákia; 4 daily; 6.50am–8.15pm; 30min); Thériso (Mon, Wed & Fri 2 daily; 6.45am & 2.15pm; 30min); Vámos (6 daily; 6.45am–8pm; 30min); Yeoryioúpolis (16 daily; 5.30am–9pm; 40min); Yerani (every 15min; 6.30am–11.40pm; 40min).

BY FERRY

Ferry dock You'll dock at the port and naval base of Soúdha, 10km east of Haniá. Frequent buses will drop you by the market on the fringes of the old town, or you can take a taxi (around €11); KTEL buses to Réthymno and Kastélli also meet most ferries. If you are stuck in Soúdha you can find just about everything you need on the square right by the ferries, but it's not an attractive place.

Ferry tickets From most Travel agencies, or the ANEK line office (on Venizélou, opposite the market; ☎ 28210 27500); Hellenic Seaways are represented by STC at Platía 1866 14 (☎ 28210 75444).

BY PLANE

Haniá airport About 15km northeast of the city, in the middle of the Akrotíri peninsula, the airport is served by frequent local buses (roughly hourly 6.15am–10.40pm; €2.30), and taxis (about €20 to Haniá). The driving route into Haniá is pretty clear: for all destinations other than the city, it's quicker and easier to take the left turn signed to Soúdha at the roundabout some 7km from the airport; this will take you down past the head of Soúdha Bay and out onto the main E75 highway, bypassing Haniá's congestion.

Airlines Olympic (Mon–Fri 9am–4pm; ☎ 28210 63818, ⓦ olympicair.com); Aegean (☎ 28210 63366, ⓦ aegeanair .com).

Destinations Athens (3–4 daily on Olympic; 3 daily on Aegean); Thessaloníki (1 daily on Aegean).

DRIVING

Parking Arriving by car can be a nightmare once you hit the harbour area and get tangled up in the one-way system and no-parking zones. As a car is near-useless inside the old walled city and distances are easily walkable anyway, the least stressful solution is to park outside the old town and walk in. Longer-term parking places can usually be found along Aktí Kanári to the west of the Naval Museum near the seafront, or on the side streets off Pireós leading down there, and to the north of the open-air theatre on the east side of the old town; there are also signposted pay car parks in the new town. Much of the old town is off-limits to vehicles, and parking within the walls is almost impossible in high season – get advice from your hotel if you are driving, as they may help you with your luggage, or have a temporary space where you can unload.

Car rental For cars try around the top of Hálidhon, where Tellus Rent a Car, Hálidhon 108 (☎ 28210 91500, ⓦ tellustravel.gr) is one of many. Alianthos is another reliable outlet (☎ 28320 32033, ⓦ alianthos-group.com) with offices at the airport and in Ayía Marína.

GETTING AROUND

Walking The best way to get around the old town and the city centre just outside the walls is to walk.

Buses For excursions further afield the terminus for most city buses, especially those heading west (including the beaches; bus #21), is at Platía 1866 just south of the walls; for Soúdha and the eastern side of town you may find it easier to get on at one of the stops by the market.

Longer-distance buses, to the coastal resorts around Plataniás (see p.264), run from the bus station.

Taxis The main taxi ranks are in Platía 1866 and at the bottom of Karaiskáki, just off Yiánnari. For radio taxis call ☎ 18300, 28210 94300 or ☎ 28210 98700.

Cycling Summertime, Dhaskaloyiánni 7 (☎ 28210 45797, ⓦ strentals.gr), has a huge range, including mountain bikes.

INFORMATION AND ACTIVITIES

Tourist offices The very helpful Municipal Tourist Office (Mon–Fri 8.30am–2.30pm; ☎ 28213 41666, ⓦ chania.gr) is in the *dhimarhío* (town hall), four blocks east of the bus station – the entrance is at 53 Odhós Milonoyiánni at the side of the building. They have timetables for buses, sites and museums, as well as details on excursions. In summer they run two booths – one on the Platía Mitropóleos near the cathedral harbour (June–Sept daily 10am–2pm), the other in front of the market (July–Sept daily 10am–1.30pm).

EOT The Greek National Tourist Office has an office close to the municipal one at Kriári 40, just off Platía 1866 (Mon–Fri 8am–2pm; ☎ 28210 92943), along with an office at the airport in summer (July–Sept Mon–Sat 9am–9pm).

Travel agencies Concentrated around the top of Hálidhon and on Platía 1866, as well as around the bus station. Try Tellus Travel, Hálidhon 108 (☎ 28210 91500, ⓦ www .tellustravel.gr), or in the old town El Greco Travel, Theotokopóulou 50 (☎ 28210 86015, ⓦ elgreco.gr).

Boat trips A number of boats run trips from the harbour

(around €15 for 2hr), mainly to the nearby islands of Áyii Theódori and Lazarétta, for swimming and *kri-kri* (ibex) spotting: you're unlikely to escape the attentions of their stalls around the harbour. Alternatives include sunset cruises and all-day trips to the Rodhopoú peninsula.

Climbing and walking The local EOS mountaineering club, Tzanakáki 90 (☎ 28210 44647, ⓦ eoshanion.gr), provides information about climbing in the Lefká Óri and takes reservations for the mountain refuge at Kallergi, near the Samariá Gorge (see p.275). They also try to maintain and mark a number of easier trails.

Diving Blue Adventures Diving, Dhaskaloyiánni 69 (☎ 28210 40403, ⓦ blueadventuresdiving.gr), is a PADI centre with a modern, purpose-built dive boat. They run daily diving and snorkelling trips.

Water park The expansive Limnoupolis (adults €23/€16 after 3pm, kids €17/€13; ⓦ limnoupolis.gr) is near to the village of Varipetro, 8km southwest of the city. There are regular buses from the station.

ACCOMMODATION

There are thousands of **rooms to rent** in Haniá and, unusually, quite a few comfortable, elegant **boutique hotels**. Even so you may face a long search for a bed at the height of the season (especially in the first half of August). Perhaps the most desirable rooms are those overlooking the **harbour**, which are sometimes available at reasonable rates: this is often because they're noisy at night. Most are approached from the streets behind; those further back are likely to be more peaceful. **Theotokopóulou** and the alleys off it make a good starting point. The best of the more expensive places are here, too, equally set back but often with views from the upper storeys. In recent years the popularity of this area has led to anyone with a room near the harbour tarting it up and attempting to rent it out at a ridiculously inflated price. You'll often be touted in the street for these; don't commit yourself until you've made some comparisons. In the **addresses** below, Párodhos means side street, so 2 Párodhos Theotokopóulou, for example, is the second alley off Theotokopóulou. If you're having trouble finding somewhere, ask at the tourist office. Many places drop their **prices** outside August, some quite dramatically; it's always worth enquiring.

HARBOUR AREA: WEST OF HÁLIDHON

★ **Alcanea** Angélou 2 (☎ 28210 75370, ⓦ alcanea .com. Charming eight-room boutique hotel, which once served as the office of Cretan statesman Venizélos, in a great situation on the far side of the harbour near the Naval Museum. Refurbished, pastel rooms come with a/c, minibar, satellite TV and galleried beds and almost all have stunning views. Prices depend on size, from small rooms to a family suite with private terrace, but all are excellent value. Popular café-wine bar below. Free wi-fi. Breakfast included. **€85**

★ **Amphora** 2 Párodhos Theotokopóulou 20 (☎ 28210 93224, ⓦ amphora.gr. Hotel in a beautifully renovated fourteenth-century Venetian building, with spiral staircases and four-poster beds. Balcony rooms (such as Room 20) with harbour view are the best value; those without a view are cheaper. Free wi-fi. **€100**

Anastasia Theotokopóulou 57 (☎ 28210 79530, ⓦ anastasia-apartments.com. Attractive a/c en-suite rooms and fully equipped apartments in buildings on each side of this atmospheric street. Free wi-fi. Rooms **€45**, apartments **€55**

Artemis Kondhiláki 13 ☎28210 91196, ⓦartemisrooms.gr. A/c rooms with bath, fridge and TV plus use of kitchen in this touristy street running inland from Zambelíu. Free wi-fi. **€55**

Casa Delfino Theofánous 9 ☎28210 87400, ⓦcasadelfino.com. Over-the-top hotel offering big, deluxe suites with elegant decor, marble or polished-wood floors, satellite TV, wi-fi and jacuzzis. **€196**

Casa Veneta Theotokopóulou 57 ☎28210 90007, ⓦcasa-veneta.gr. Very well-equipped, comfortable studios and apartments with kitchenette, TV and (some) balcony sea views behind a Venetian facade; the large duplex apartment is particularly attractive. Helpful, friendly proprietor. Free wi-fi in reception area. Studios **€50**, apartments **€60**

El Greco Theotokopóulou 49 ☎28210 90432, ⓦelgrecohotel.eu. Comfortable hotel with nicely furnished, compact rooms with fridge, a/c and TV. Some have balconies. There's a roof terrace. **€65**

Helena 1A A Párodhos Theotokopóulou 14 ☎28210 95516 or ☎697 33 21 762, ⓦhelena-hotel.gr. Charming hotel in a quiet street with a/c balcony rooms with TV; some with views. Free wi-fi. **€50**

Ifigenia A. Gamba 21 ☎28210 94357, ⓦifigeniastudios.gr. A small empire of rooms, studios and apartments at various prices, in old Venetian buildings scattered across the old town. Most have elegant, quirky decor and come well equipped (some with jacuzzi). Free wi-fi in room or reception. Rooms **€40**, studios **€70**, apartments **€120**

Lucia Aktí Koundouriótou ☎28210 90302, ⓦloukiahotel.gr. Harbourfront hotel with a/c balcony rooms with fridge; the furnishing is basic at best, hence much less expensive than you might expect for one of the best views in town, and – thanks to double-glazing – reasonably soundproof. Free wi-fi. With harbour view **€62**, without harbour view **€50**

Maro Párodhos Pórtou 5 ☎28210 54981 or ☎693 62 30 053. Probably the cheapest rooms in the old town, hidden away in a quiet, unmarked alley off Pórtou not far from the Schiavo Bastion. En-suite rooms come with a/c and fridge. Friendly and clean. **€30**

Nora Theotokopóulou 60 ☎28210 72265, ⓦpension-nora.com. Charming a/c en-suite rooms in a refurbished wooden Turkish house. Also appealing studios (same price) in a building nearby. Nice café below. **€40**

Palazzo Theotokopóulou 54 ☎28210 93227, ⓦpalazzohotel.gr. An old mansion conversion, with wood-beamed ceilings and dark wood floors. Good-sized, simple rooms, most with balconies, plus a roof terrace with harbour views and tasty breakfasts. Free wi-fi in reception. Breakfast included. **€80**

Stella Angélou 10 ☎28210 73756 ⓔchania256 @yahoo.gr. Creaky, eccentric old house above an eclectic

gift shop, with en-suite rooms equipped with a/c and fridge. **€45**

Thereza Angélou 8 ☎28210 92798, ⓦpensiontheresa .gr. Beautiful old *pension* in a great position with stunning views from its roof terrace and some rooms; classy decor too, and a kitchen for guests' use. Very popular, so book ahead in high season. Free wi-fi. Buffet breakfast included. **€45**

EAST OF HÁLIDHON

Anemi Suites Sarpáki 41 ☎28210 53001, ⓦanemisuites.gr. Inviting one- and two-room apartments inside a restored Turkish wooden house; all are a/c with kitchen. Prices vary, but the cheapest (No. 4) with a superb terrace is the one to go for. **€81**

To Dhiporto Betólo 41 ☎28210 40570, ⓦtodiporto.gr. The "Two Doors" runs between Betólo and pedestrian Skridhlóf: the balcony rooms over the latter, especially, are quiet. Friendly and good value, with a/c, TV, fridge and coffee machine in the rooms, which include singles and triples. Free wi-fi. **€45**

Ionas Sarpáki, corner of Sórvolou `☎28210 55090, ⓦionashotel.com. Small boutique hotel in a lovingly restored Venetian mansion. Very comfortable rooms and beautiful architectural detail, though service is occasionally lacking. **€85**

★ **Kasteli** Kaneváro 39 ☎28210 57057, ⓦkastelistudios.gr. Comfortable, modern, reasonably priced *pension*, very quiet at the back. All en-suite rooms come with a/c and fridge. The proprietor is very helpful and also has a few studios, apartments and a couple of beautiful houses to rent nearby. Discount for *Rough Guide* readers. Private free parking. Free wi-fi. Rooms **€50**, studios **€75**, apartments **€90**

Neli Isódhion 21–23 ☎28210 55533, ⓦnelistudios .com. Larger and fancier than it appears, this hotel rambles through three lovingly restored old buildings, with stylishly decorated studio rooms with balconies, a/c and kitchenette. Free wi-fi. **€50**

Porto Veneziano Overlooking the inner harbour ☎28210 27100, ⓦportoveneziano.gr. The plushest hotel on the east side of the old town, part of the *Best Western* chain. Very comfortable, if bland, rooms, many with balcony views (extra) over the harbour. Breakfast included. **€100**

Rooms 47 Kandanoléon 47 ☎28210 53243. Quiet, traditional and simple rooms place on a street leading up from Kaneváro into Kastélli. All rooms have a/c and some have balconies with fantastic sea views. **€40**

★ **Splanzia** Dhaskaloyiánni 20 ☎28210 45313, ⓦsplanzia.com. Attractive and friendly boutique hotel (taking its name from the old Turkish quarter) in an elegantly refurbished Venetian mansion, with stylish rooms (some with four-poster beds draped with mosquito nets). Free wi-fi. Breakfast, included, is served in a pretty courtyard. **€115**

★ **Vilelmine** Betólo 32 ☎ 28210 46048, ⓦ vilelmine .gr. New hotel in a *fin-de-siècle* building linking Betólo St with the Cathedral Square. Lovingly furnished and reasonably soundproofed rooms and suites; great service. Free wi-fi. **€90**

THE MODERN TOWN

★ **Doma** Venizélou 124 ☎ 28210 51772, ⓦ hotel-doma.gr. Elegant seafront hotel inside a late nineteenth-century building that served as the Austrian Embassy and later the British consulate until it was taken over by the Germans during World War II. There are fine sea views from some rooms and a serene patio garden. Comfortable rooms (and more expensive suites) are tastefully furnished and the hotel is filled with fascinating photos of old Haniá. Breakfast included. Parking nearby. **€130**

Nefeli Zimvrakákidhon 47 ☎ 28210 70007, ⓦ nefelihotel.com. Decent-value, if rather bland, three-star business hotel with functional a/c balcony rooms with TV and minibar; several similar places all around. Street parking nearby; handy for the bus station. Free wi-fi. Breakfast included. **€60**

CAMPSITE

Camping Hania Behind the beach in Áyii Apóstoli, 5km west of the city ☎ 28210 31138, ⓦ camping-chania.gr. A rather small site, hemmed in by new development, but with a pool and all the usual facilities, just a short walk from some of the better beaches. Also rents tents (€10). Two people plus tent & car **€22**

EATING AND DRINKING

Evenings in Haniá for most visitors centre around the harbour, and you need not stray far from the waterfront to find a cocktail before **dinner**, a meal, a late-night **bar** and a **club**. These places tend to be pricey, however, and the quality at many leaves a lot to be desired. The most fashionable waterfront area these days, particularly with locals, is towards the far end of the inner harbour, around **Sarpidhónos** spreading east into the Koum Kápi quarter. Away from the water, there are plenty of attractive, slightly cheaper restaurants and tavernas on (among others) Kondiláki, Kaneváro and most of the streets off Hálidhon, some of them restored or partially restored ancient buildings. The abundant **cafés** round the harbour tend to serve cocktails and fresh juices at exorbitant prices, though breakfast can be good value. There are more traditional cafés by the cathedral, at the market – where you also find a couple of good *zaharoplastía* (one on Tsoudherón, the other, *Kronos*, on Mousoúron, down the steps from the side entrance of the market) – and along Dhaskaloyiánni, where Platía 1821 is a delightfully tranquil oasis.

TAVERNAS AND RESTAURANTS

Akrogiali Aktí Papanikoli 19, behind the city beach ☎ 28210 73110. Excellent, reasonably priced seafront fish taverna, with a summer terrace, that's well worth the 15min walk or short taxi ride. Often packed with locals, so it may be worth booking – though there are plenty of alternatives along the same stretch including the equally good *Achilleas* (slightly west at the corner of Moní Goniás). Free wi-fi. Daily noon–midnight.

Amphora Aktí Koundouriótou 49, under the Hotel Amphora ☎ 28210 71976. One of the most reliable places on the outer harbour, with good, simple Greek food and no hard sell. April–Oct daily 10am–midnight.

Anna's Daliáni 21 ☎ 28210 50844. New, retro-style *mezedhopolío* serving traditional *meze* in a fast-gentrifying part of town. Daily 7pm–midnight.

Doloma Kapsokályvon 5 ☎ 28210 51196. Excellent, friendly little taverna with a nice terrace serving well-prepared, economical Cretan dishes. April–Oct noon–11pm.

Enetikon Zambelíu 57 ☎ 28210 88270. A very good taverna whose proprietor is a wine buff and where the house wine comes from the excellent Lyrarakis vineyard in Pezá. The food is also top-notch and anything with lamb is recommended: try a *árni me stamnágathi* (lamb with chicory). April–Oct daily noon–midnight.

Faka Arholéon 15 ☎ 28210 42341. Set back from the harbour, so significantly less touristy than many near neighbours, *Faka* serves good traditional local food, often with live Greek music. Check out the daily specials, made using seasonal ingredients. April–Oct daily 11.30am–12.30am.

Karnayio Platía Kateháki 8 ☎ 28210 53366. Not right on the water, but one of the best harbour restaurants nonetheless, with an inviting terrace. Its touristy looks belie very good food, a friendly atmosphere and reasonable prices. House specials include *dákos*, *loukánika* (country sausage) and *kalamaría* (grilled squid) and there's an extensive wine list. April–Oct daily noon–midnight.

Khrisostomos Dheukalíona and Ikárou ☎ 28210 57035. Not a very attractive setting, but interesting traditional recipes (using Sfakian meat) served in a thoroughly untouristy environment. In summer, the proprietor can be found running the isolated taverna at Mármara Beach (see p.283). Oct–April daily noon–11pm.

4

Mathios Aktí Enóseos 3 ☎28210 54291. The fish tavernas at the inner end of the harbour are rated much more highly by locals than those further round – this is Haniá's oldest.

Ta Meraklíkia tou Boureki Ipsiladhon 3 ☎28210 73814. Great little eatery run by a friendly Sfakian family and away from the tourist beehive, hence very reasonable prices. The lamb dishes are excellent as are other specialities such as *pastítsio* and *stifádho*. Mon–Sat 10am–11pm.

★ **Mihalis** Aktí Tombázi ☎ 28210 58330. Arguably the best waterfront place on the outer harbour, with a varied menu and a good selection of Cretan specialities and *mezédhes*, the latter available as mixed platters. Also a good wine selection at reasonable prices. *Monastiri*, next door and open all year, is another excellent place highly rated by locals. April–Oct daily 9am–1am.

★ **Nikteridha** 5km east of town in the village of Korakiés ☎28210 64215, ⚲nykterida.gr. Head for Akrotíri and, at the top of the hill after the Venizélos tombs, follow the signs to the village, off the airport road. Founded in 1933, this upmarket and stylish taverna is a Haniá institution, serving traditional Cretan standards (try the *kalitsoúnia* or any of the lamb dishes). It also has a wonderful setting with stunning views over Soúdha Bay. April–Sept daily 7pm–1am; Oct–March Tues–Sat 7pm–midnight.

To Pigadi Tou Tourkou Sarpáki 1 ☎28210 54547. Greco-Moroccan fusion restaurant with an interesting menu combining the two cuisines as well as adding a few dishes – such as Tunisian, Egyptian and Lebanese *mezédhes* – from the wider Middle East. Somewhat pricey, but with an attractive small terrace. April–Oct Wed–Mon 7pm–12.30am.

★ **Portes** Portoú 48 ☎28210 76261. A small group of restaurants nestles under the walls along Portoú. *Portes* is smarter than most, with an adventurous menu putting a modern twist on age-old dishes: rabbit with prunes, cuttlefish with fennel, and traditional pies with unusual fillings. See their blackboard for daily specials. Excellent house wine. April–Oct Mon–Sat 12.30pm–1am, Sun 5pm–1am.

To Staki Defkaliona 5 ☎28210 42589. Atmospheric new organic vegetarian diner where welcoming proprietor-chef Stelios Michelakis prepares tasty dishes including vegetarian *moussaká*, *dolmadakia* (stuffed vine leaves), *bouréki* (Cretan veggie and cheese bake), pizzas and lots more. Also herbal teas, and organic beer and wine. Daily 1pm–11pm.

Tamam Zambelíu 49 ☎28210 96080. Excellent food from an adventurous Cretan kitchen, with plenty of vegetarian options and reasonably priced specials. Unfortunately there are only a few cramped tables outside where you often get jostled by the passing multitude, and

it can get hot inside (although a/c has been installed), so at its best in cooler months. Decent wine list. Daily 12.30pm–1am.

Tholos Ay. Dhéka 36 ☎28210 46725. A stone's throw north of the cathedral, this is yet another recycled Venetian ruin with tables outside in a courtyard. The food is good, too: *moskhári tis yiayiás* ("grandma's veal") is a house speciality, and there are lots of seafood options. Daily 4pm–midnight.

CAFÉS, CAFÉ-BARS AND SNACKS

Alcanea Angélou 2. Appealing terrace bar with great harbour view beneath the hotel of the same name; it's good for breakfast, and locals (especially expats) while the day away here playing *távli*. Serves *mezédhes* and, after sunset, cocktails and Cretan wines. Occasional live acoustic music at night. March–Sept daily 8am–2am.

Dekatría Platía 1866 on the corner with Yiánnari. Excellent, stylish *zaharoplastío* with a small street terrace on this key square, serving delicious cakes, pastries, ices and traditional Cretan confectionery. Daily 7.30am–midnight.

To Kafenío Platía 1821. Perhaps the best of the relaxing cafés on this great old square. It certainly has the lowest drink prices, which is why its terrace tables tend to fill up first. Daily 7.30am–3am.

Kentrikon Betólo 6. Relaxed café with tables outside on the pedestrianized street, also serving salads, pizzas, gyros and full meals. Daily 8am–1am.

Kormoranos Theotokopóulou 31 & 46. A bakery/café/ouzerí occupying two small sites on opposite sides of the street. Breakfast, sandwiches and pastries washed down by juices, herb teas and coffee during the day, and delicious *meze* to go with your drinks at night. Daily 8am–1am.

Muses Platía Sindriváni. Long-established favourite café-ouzerí in a prime people-watching position, serving drinks, breakfast and light meals. April–Oct daily 6am–3am.

O Plátanos tis Splantzias Platía 1821. Retro bar-ouzéri on this quiet square serving interesting Thai food and snacks alongside more traditional *mezédhes*. April–Oct daily 8am–2am.

Spirit Lounge Isodhíon 14. One of several chilled bars at the bottom of this narrow old town street – this one serves baguettes, burgers, Magners and Guinness, with a happy hour till 10pm; despite all that, a laidback atmosphere prevails. Daily noon–2am.

Thea Platía Sindriváni. Café-bar overlooking the harbourside crowds from a first-floor terrace, for peaceful people-watching. Daily 9am–3am.

Time Out Platía 1866. Fast food Cretan style, serving everything from *yíros píta* to lamb stews, sandwiches and spaghetti, day and night. Daily 24hr.

NIGHTLIFE AND ENTERTAINMENT

As you might expect, the harbour area contains plenty of beautifully set but touristy **bars**. Locals head east, to Koum Kápi and the scores of bars and cafés lining Aktí Miaoúli, the seafront outside the walls – these are heaving by 11pm. Sometime after midnight, action will move on to the **clubs**, and where these are depends on the time of year. In summer, many of the downtown venues close and the action moves to the vibrant scene at **Plataniás** and **Ayía Marína** on the coast west of town (see p.266).

Fagotto Angélou 16. Very pleasant, laidback jazz bar, often with live performers in high season. Daily 9pm–late.

Ippopotamos Sarpidhónos 6. Comfy, popular bar-café in a street full of similar places that attract a slightly older crowd than nearby Aktí Miaoúli. Outdoor terrace and Mexican food, too. The neighbouring *Duo Lux* is also good. Daily 9am–3am.

★ **To Monastíri tou Karolos** Daliáni 22 ⓦ karolos.gr. The art and performance centre of internationally acclaimed artist/hairdresser Karolos Cambelopoulos whose works – including bronzes of Maria Callas and Kazantzákis – decorate the building. In a restored sixteenth-century monastery, the centre's theatre (with bar) showcases music groups from Crete, Greece and the Balkans, as well as mounting art shows. The café-bar is open from noon onwards. Mon–Sat 1pm–2am (or later), Sun 8pm–2am; closed Nov.

El Mondo Kondiláki. A survivor from the days when this street was very rowdy, and still popular with military types in from the bases; lively till late. Daily 8pm–3am.

Notos Aktí Koundouriótou 31. Harbourside music bar with terrace, serving up snacks and soft drinks along with even softer music. Daily 9am–2am.

★ **Rudi's Bierhaus** Kalergón 16. Haniá's beer shrine: Austrian – and longtime Haniá resident – Rudi Riegler's bar stocks more than a hundred of Europe's finest brews, plus excellent *mezédhes* to accompany them. The next-door *Bar Raki* is also good for a change of scene. July & Aug daily 8.30am–3am; Sept–June Tues–Sat.

Synagogi Between Kondiláki and Skúfon. Taking its name from the restored Jewish synagogue next door, this is an appealing bar in a beautiful setting in a Venetian mansion bombed in World War II. Good music, too. May–Sept daily 9pm–4am.

Tesseres Epoches Aktí Koundouriótou 52. The "Four Seasons" is a relatively quiet café and bar by day, with outdoor seating on the outer harbour, but hosts club and rock nights later on, in a soundproofed room behind. Daily 8am–3am.

Thelma Ipeírou 31–35 at Aktí Míaouli. There are dozens of cafés, bars and *mezedhopolía* in Koum Kápi: this sizeable café-bar is perhaps the archetype, with coffee and frappé at outdoor tables by day and early evening, and the volume, crowds and alcohol intake increasing as the night goes on. Daily 8am–1am.

SHOPPING

Stores aimed at tourists are mainly found in the old town, especially **jewellery** and **souvenirs** on Hálidhon and all around the harbour. The **leather** goods on Skridhlóf are excellent value, while along Sífaka just to the north the traditional shops of Haniá's cutlers will sell you fearsome **Cretan knives** with goat-horn handles or even something less vicious for the kitchen. The various arty-crafty stores around the harbour on Kaneváro, Zambelíou, Kondiláki and Theotokópoulou are also worth a browse. Around the junction of Hálidhon and Yiánnari and down towards the market you'll find pharmacies, newspaper stores, photographic shops and banks, and there's a sizeable **supermarket** at the top of Pireós, close to the Schiavo Bastion. The major thoroughfares heading south off Yiánnari – Apokorónou, Tzanakáki and Papandreou – are full of clothes and furniture stores, car rental places and more banks, while the streets around Platía 1866, especially towards the Town Hall and market, have more interesting local shops, from food and fashion to pet shops and printers. English and other foreign-language **newspapers** are sold at a number of places, including a couple around the junction of Hálidhon and Yiánnari.

Haniá market Odhós Yiánnari, with another entrance on Tsoudherón. Haniá's market, an imposing and rather beautiful cross-shaped structure, dating from around 1900, is in full swing on weekday mornings, when it's a wonderful kaleidoscope of bustle and colour, and there are some good souvenirs to be had among the stalls of meat, fish and veg. At the back is a small shaded square where locals sit outside a couple of *kafenía*. Mon–Sat 8am–2pm.

Mediterranean Editions Bookshop Aktí Koundouriótou 57, near the Naval Museum; also at the top of Hálidhon at the junction with Yiánnari. Lots of English-language titles; their Hálidhon branch also sells international press. Daily 8am–11pm.

Street market Minöos. There's a fabulous weekly street market inside the eastern city wall, where local farmers sell their produce. Sat mornings.

DIRECTORY

Banks The main branch of the National Bank of Greece, with two ATMs, is opposite the market. There's a cluster of banks with more ATMs around the top of Hálidhon, and lots of out-of-hours exchange places on Hálidhon, in the travel agencies.

Hospital For an ambulance, dial ☎ 166. The main hospital is in the village of Mourniés, 1.5km south of the centre (☎ 28210 22000).

Internet Good internet cafés include: Triple W, Odhós I Baladhinou just off Hálidhon; Café Notos, Aktí Koundouriótou 31 under the *Hotel Lucia*; and Cosmos, on Koronéou near the bus station. Most bars and many restaurants have free wi-fi.

Pharmacies Several on Yiánnari between the market and Platía 1866; others up Tzanakáki.

Post office The main post office is on Odhós Péridhou just off Kydhonías (Mon–Fri 7.30am–8pm, Sat 9am–1pm).

Tourist police Iraklíou 23 (emergency ☎ 100, ☎ 28210 25803 or ☎ 28210 25700), some way south of the centre in the new town.

Akrotíri peninsula

The hilly, undulating **Akrotíri peninsula** (Ακρωτήρι Χερσονήσος) loops round to the east of Haniá, protecting the magnificent anchorages of the **Bay of Soúdha**. It's a somewhat strange amalgam, with a couple of developing **resorts** along with burgeoning suburbs and a new university on the north coast, several ancient **monasteries** in the northeast, and military installations and the airport dominating the centre and south. This is very much apartment and villa country, geared to families staying at least a week at a time; outside August you should be able to find something on spec, but you'd be well advised to try phoning ahead, as few of the places have regular reception hours.

The Venizélos Graves

City bus #11 from Haniá market (about 20min)

The **Venizélos Graves** are the simple stone-slab tombs of Eleftherios Venizélos, Crete's most famous statesman, and his son Sophocles. The immaculately tended garden setting, looking back over Haniá and the coast for miles beyond, is magnificent and also historic – the scene in 1897 of an illegal raising of the Greek flag in defiance of the Turks and the European powers. The flagpole was smashed by a salvo from the European fleet, but the Cretans raised their standard by hand, keeping it flying even under fire. Two stories attach to this: one that the sailors were so impressed that they all stopped firing to applaud; the second that a shell fired from a Russian ship hit the little church of Profítis Elías, which still stands, and that divine revenge caused the offending ship itself to explode the next day.

EATING AND DRINKING	THE VENIZÉLOS GRAVES
KouKou Vayia ☎ 28210 27449. Excellent café with a fabulous view from its terrace over Haniá. They specialize in	cakes and tarts (try the walnut cake) as well as various teas and coffees. Daily 10am–2am.

The Akrotíri beaches

The road by the **Venizélos Graves** divides: straight ahead takes you east across the peninsula towards the **airport**, while the left fork heads north to Horafákia and the beaches, culminating at **Stavrós**, Akrotíri's most popular resort. This is lovely country to drive around, gently rolling and dotted with villages that are clearly quite wealthy – many city workers live out here or build themselves country villas.

Kalathás

Just beyond the village of **Kounoupidhianá**, the road suddenly plunges down and emerges by the **beach** at **KALATHÁS** (Καλαθάς), two little patches of sand divided by a rocky promontory, with a bar and taverna right on the sand. This makes a fine place to spend a lazy day, marred only slightly by the proximity of the road: there's an offshore island to which you can swim, and good snorkelling.

Horafákia and around

HORAFÁKIA (Χωραφάκια), inland, a little over 1km beyond Kalathás, has the bulk of the local facilities including shops and a travel agent/car rental place. From here a road leads down to the coast at **Tersanás** where there's a tiny cove beach, shallow and safe for small children, as well as a couple of tavernas.

Stavrós

Some 3km beyond Horafákia, you finally reach **STAVRÓS (Σταυρός)** and its near-perfect beach, an almost completely enclosed circular bay. The sea is dead calm with gently shelving sand underfoot, making it ideal for kids. It's an extraordinary-looking place, too, with a sheer, bare mountainside rising just 100m away from you on the far side of the bay. This is where the cataclysmic climax of *Zorba the Greek* was shot (the hill is known locally as Zorba's Mountain) and is also the site of a **cave**, whose entrance can just about be seen from the beach, in which there was an ancient sanctuary.

Stavrós beach is often crowded – sometimes unpleasantly so as it doesn't take many people to fill it up – but even so it's a great place to bask for a few hours, and is the one place on the peninsula that's easily accessible by bus. There's a far less visited patch of sand facing directly out to sea if you do find it oppressive. Stavrós has relatively few facilities beyond a couple of minimarkets and snack bars, while the apartments and rooms places are mostly pre-booked.

ARRIVAL AND DEPARTURE

By car You'll need your own transport; there are buses along the coast to Stavrós, and occasional tours to the monasteries, but little else.

THE AKROTÍRI BEACHES

By bus There are services to Stavrós (Mon–Sat 5 daily) from Haniá's bus station.

ACCOMMODATION

Accommodation is widely scattered in the flat plain lining the coast between Stavrós and Tersanás. If you have your own transport you can drive around, checking out the numerous **apartment complexes**; without it, you'll find it much harder, though a few of the options below are within walking distance of Stavrós. If you're coming from Haniá, it's worth checking at travel agencies there (see p.245).

STAVRÓS AND TERSANÁS

Blue Beach Apartments On the edge of Stavrós, on the seafront at the western end of the sea beach ☎ 28210 39404, ⊛ bluebeach.eu. Two-person studios up to three-room apartments with a tiny sand beach, small pool and a seaside terrace where meals are served. To get here by road, you have to drive some way round inland. Free wi-fi in public areas, a/c €8/day. Studios **€75**, apartments **€120**

★ **Georgia-Vicky Apartments** Stavrós near Blue Beach Apartments ☎ 28210 39006 or ☎ 697 85 16 341, ⊛ georgia-vicky.com. Excellent-value, mid-sized and welcoming apartments and bungalows (sleeping five), all with stunning views over a rocky shore from terraces and balconies. There's also a large seawater pool. Free wi-fi. Apartments **€65**, bungalows **€95**

Kavos Hotel ☎ 28210 39255, ⊛ kavos-hotel.com. On a rocky cape not far from Stavrós main beach, this is a very attractive, recently refurbished apartment complex with saltwater pool, café and well-equipped apartments and

studios. Scuba diving and other activities on offer. Free wi-fi. Breakfast included. Studios **€84**, apartments **€128**

Perle Roi Spa Hotel Seafront, 1km west of Stavrós ☎ 28210 39400, ⊛ perle-spa.com. Large, luxury hotel and thalassotherapy centre with five indoor and outdoor pools, plus gym, bars and restaurants, a kids' club, and almost every other facility you could think of. It seems very out of place here but represents excellent value for what you get. **€100**

Villa Eleana 1km west of Stavrós ☎ 28210 39480, ⊛ eleana-villas.gr. Friendly apartment/studio hotel with two wheelchair-accessible studios as well as larger apartments and a good-sized pool and bar surrounded by well-tended gardens. Free wi-fi. Studios **€45**, apartments **€60**

Zorba's Apartments On the edge of Stavrós, on the seafront at the western end of the sea beach ☎ 28210 39010, ⊛ hotel-zorbas.gr. Less attractive than the neighbouring *Blue Beach* apartments but also less expensive, with pool and tennis court. **€45**

KALATHÁS

Giorgi's Blue Apartments Signed from the road ☎28210 64080, ⊚blueapts.gr. Very comfortable apartments, and a pool and bar beautifully situated above

a rocky coastline. Free wi-fi. Breakfast included. **€85**

Lena Beach ☎28210 64750, ⊚lenabeach.com. The big hotel immediately above the beach, with pool and attractive a/c rooms with fridge, balcony with sea views. Free wi-fi. **€70**

EATING AND DRINKING

Almyriki Stavrós, behind the beach ☎28210 29489. Attractive new taverna with tables spread beneath the shady tamarisk tree that gives it its name. Specialities include a range of *mezédhes* as well as Cretan dishes such as *bouréki* (veggie and cheese bake) and stuffed tomatoes. May–Oct daily noon–11.30pm.

Bahar Horafákia, on the road out towards Stavrós ☎28210 39410. One of the few restaurants on the peninsula with any pretensions, this stylish new place turns out a variety of exotic salads, heading a varied Cretan and international menu. Their "Aphrodisiac" plate – mussels, prawns and lobster bisque with pasta – is a bargain at €16.50 for two. There's also an excellent wine selection, and a house wine from noted Pezá grower

Lyrarakis. The attached bar hosts live music (jazz, soul, Greek) on summer weekends. April–Sept daily noon–midnight; bar stays open later.

Thanassis Taverna Stavrós, on the seafront ☎28210 39110. Good taverna for Cretan classics and fresh fish, with a decent wine selection. There's a lovely terrace above the water, and a tiny strip of sand with free loungers for clients. April–Oct daily noon–midnight.

Zorba's Stavrós, behind the beach ☎28210 39402. Wonderful place that's been here since the film was made from which it takes its name. Run by an enthusiastic and friendly family, the purely Cretan kitchen turns out tasty treats including *katsikaki* (kid) stew and good fresh fish. May–Nov daily 9am–midnight.

Monastery of Ayía Triádha

5km east of Horafákia • Daily 7am–7pm • €2

Ayía Triádha (Μονή Αγίας Τριάδας), sometimes known as Moní Zangarólo after its founder, was established in the seventeenth century and built in Venetian style. Today, while not exactly thriving (it has only five monks), it is one of the few Cretan monasteries to preserve real monastic life to any degree. Its imposing ochre frontage is approached through carefully tended fields of vines and olive groves – all the property of the monastery, which now bottles and markets its own wine and organic olive oil.

You can walk right through the complex and sit on benches shaded by orange trees in the patio. The **church**, which appears strangely foreshortened, contains a beautiful old gilded altarpiece and, around the walls, ancient wooden stalls; like most of the monastery it is built from stone that glows orange in the afternoon sun. By the entrance a small **museum** exhibits silver chalices, vestments, relics and manuscripts, mostly dating from the eighteenth or nineteenth centuries, and a few icons that are considerably older. In the courtyard there's a water cooler; in quieter times, if you're lucky, the traditional hospitality might extend to a glass of *raki* and a piece of *loukoúm* (Turkish delight) in the hall where you sign the visitors' book. A small shop sells postcards along with the monks' olive oil and wine.

Monastery of Gouvernétou

Some 4km north of Ayía Triádha • Easter–Oct Mon, Tues & Thurs 9am–noon & 5–7pm, Sat & Sun 9am–noon & 5–8pm; Oct–Easter afternoon hours are 4–7pm • Free • The monastery is enclosed within a compound; leave any transport at the gate and approach via a path through a garden (around 100m)

The lonely road to the **Monastery of Gouvernétou (Μονή Γουβερνέτου)** ascends through a biblical landscape of rocks and wild olives; the final section is paved but horribly rutted as it twists through a steep rocky gully. The monastery itself, a simple square block of a building, is older than Ayía Triádha (a Greek inscription above the entrance is dated 1573), with the usual refreshingly shaded patio and ancient frescoes in the church; there's a tiny museum, too. Despite its more remote location, Gouvernétou feels like a thriving community: beautifully renovated and with carefully tended flowerbeds and chapel. Nevertheless, the stark surroundings help to give a real sense of the isolation that the remaining monks must face for most of the year, and their life is contemplative and strict; visitors are expected to respect this.

St John the Hermit's cave

500m beyond the Gouvernétou monastery heading towards the sea

Immediately above Gouvernétou is a simple marble war memorial. Beyond this, you can follow (on foot) a paved path that leads down towards the sea; after about ten minutes you reach the cave in which **St John the Hermit** is said to have lived and died. This large, low cavern, stark, dank and dripping, features hefty stalactites and stalagmites and a substantial bathing tank, probably for baptisms. Excavations revealed that this had been an important Minoan shrine too, and in the Greek period it became a sanctuary dedicated to the goddess Artemis.

Monastery of Katholikó

About 1km north of Gouvernétou monastery

From St John the Hermit's cave a path continues for a further 0.5km to the amazing **ruins** of the **Monastery of Katholikó (Μονή Καθολικού)** founded in the eleventh century and one of the oldest – if not the oldest – monasteries on the island. Descending beyond the cave the path deteriorates as the going gets steeper, rockier and sharper. After some fifteen minutes you reach the ruins of the monastery, built into the side of, and partly carved from, a craggy ravine of spectacular desolation. This older monastery was abandoned more than three hundred years ago when the monks, driven by repeated pirate raids, moved up to the comparative safety of Gouvernétou. The valley sides are dotted with caves, which formed a centre of still-earlier Christian worship, at least one of which (just before the buildings) you can explore if you have a torch.

Spanning the ravine by the ruins is a vast **bridge** leading nowhere, evocatively captured by Edward Lear in one of his Cretan watercolours (see p.353). Cross it and you can scramble down to the bottom of the ravine and follow the stream bed for about another fifteen minutes to the sea. There's a tiny natural **harbour**, a fjord-like finger of water pushing up between the rocks, where remains of a port can still be made out. Hewn from the rock, and with part of its roof intact, is what appears to be an ancient boathouse or slipway. There's no beach, but it's easy enough to lower yourself from the rocks straight into the astonishingly clear green water. The walk back up takes perhaps an hour in all – and is much more strenuous than it might have seemed on the way down.

Soúdha Bay

On the **south side** of the Akrotíri peninsula there are beaches near Stérnes, pretty isolated, but not as deserted as you might hope. Almost all of this region is a **military zone**, and the beaches are popular with the NATO personnel based here. There's an R&R base and officers' club at **Maráthi**, for example, which has sheltered, if not particularly attractive sandy beaches with views across the mouth of the bay. This has grown into a resort of sorts, with rooms places and tavernas, the latter often overloaded in high summer, but has few charms. Boat trips from Haniá or the resorts across the bay occasionally run to the little harbour here, only adding to the crush for space on the beach. The views of **Soúdha Bay (Όρμος Σούδας)** are best on the descent towards Maráthi – above all, of a little **island** (Néa Soúdha), bristling with Venetian and Turkish fortifications which, from a distance at least, appear miraculously well preserved.

The Allied war cemetery

1km northwest of Soúdha, down a short lane signed "Soúdha Cemetery"

Surrounded by eucalyptus trees and beautifully sited at the water's edge with Soúdha Bay stretching away beyond, **the Allied war cemetery** is a melancholy and moving spot. With its row upon row of immaculately tended headstones, many of them to unknown soldiers and very young men, the serene and dignified cemetery brings home with some force the scale of the calamity of the Battle of Crete in which most of them perished. A grave in row 10E on the cemetery's northern side is that of the distinguished archeologist John Pendlebury, who took over at Knossós after Arthur Evans retired; he died fighting alongside Cretans during the German assault on Iráklion in 1941.

ARRIVAL AND DEPARTURE   SOÚDHA BAY

By bus The ferry port is served by frequent daily buses to and from Haniá and extra buses meet incoming boats.

By ferry ANEK Line runs to Pireás (daily 9pm; peak summer also daytime sailing; 9hr).

EATING

Don Rosario Just east of Soúdha on the National Road ☎ 28210 23663. Soúdha has the usual array of run-of-the-mill tavernas, but this is not one of them. An upscale Italian restaurant run by a Sicilian family, the kitchen serves a range of well-prepared pasta dishes in addition to meat and fish (try the beef marsala or fish baked in a salt crust). Also has a good selection of Italian wines plus a pleasant leafy terrace. Pricey, but worth it; main dishes €10–20. Mon–Fri 4.30–11.30pm, Sat & Sun 1–11.30pm.

East from Haniá to Yeoryioúpolis

Heading east out of Haniá you can either make your way through the new town to pick up the main E75 road on the south side of town, or follow the buses and most of the other traffic along the old road to **Soúdha**, beyond which the routes merge. The new road is fast, but you'll see little through the screen of trees and flowering shrubs until you emerge on the coast at **Yeoryioúpolis**. If you're in no hurry, or you simply want an attractive circular drive, then the minor roads that head inland or out onto the **Dhrápano peninsula** have much more to offer.

Megála Horáfia and around

Some 6km east of Soúdha, and 1km (and a steep climb) inland, the village of **MEGÁLA HORÁFIA (Μεγάλα Χωράφια)**– which has officially changed its name to Áptera, though no one seems to pay this much attention – is a popular spot for villa holidays, with numerous houses and apartments (many with pool) offering spectacular hilltop views. Just 2km away, signed from the main square, is the archeological site of **Áptera**.

Áptera

Signed off the E75 highway, the site is 2km above Megála Horáfia • Tues–Sun 8am–3pm • Free

The archeological site of **Áptera** (Άπτερα), occupying the table top of a mesa-like hilltop, has little shade and can be very hot in high summer – visit in the early morning if you can. This location appears in Linear B inscriptions, and therefore seems to have been **continuously occupied** from as early as the fourteenth century BC right up to 1964, when the monastery here was finally abandoned. Áptera from the fifth century BC into early Christian times was one of the island's most important cities. Work on the extensive remains is continuing, so new areas may be opened up, or others fenced off for excavation. The main entrance is by the **Monastery of Áyios Ioánnis Theólogos** – the most obvious building at the site. Here the biggest of the fenced areas includes the monastery, the cisterns, a bath complex and, right by the entrance, a fifth-century BC Classical Greek **temple** marked by huge stone slabs. The Roman **cisterns**, brick-lined and mainly underground, must be among the largest surviving – an awesome, cavernous testament to Roman engineering genius. Below spreads an extensive **Roman bath** complex, all of which raises the question of just how enough water to fill the vast cisterns and feed the baths was collected on what is now a barren hilltop, although it could be that long-gone aqueducts were the source.

Numerous other remains are scattered around the immediate area, mostly signed but not all accessible. Check the map at the site entrance (or there may be a leaflet). Many are reached by a well-signed path on the opposite side of the car park from the monastery (and outside the fenced site). There are remains of a small **theatre** here, and of a **Roman villa** full of collapsed pillars. To reach the latter head along a path through the olives for 150m in a roughly southwest direction. When you reach them, the remains of the first- or second-century peristyle villa are impressive and the size of the collapsed stone columns show how grand it must once have been. You also pass a World War II machine-gun post, which, if it weren't signed, could easily be mistaken for another restored Roman ruin. The path continues down towards Megála Horáfia and ends, right on the edge of the village, by a substantial section of the ancient city **wall**, complete with defensive tower and gate.

ACCOMMODATION AND EATING   MEGÁLA HORÁFIA AND AROUND

There are a number of tavernas in the village; they may be able to steer you towards local accommodation (though much is pre-booked in high season).

Aptera Apartments 1km up the road leading to the Áptera site ☎ 28210 90237 or ☎ 697 74 23 350, ⓦ aptera-apartments.com. Attractive, fully equipped rooms and apartments in a garden setting, with spectacular veranda views over the bay. Often pre-booked in July & Aug. You can take a swim and enjoy the view at their pool bar for the price of a drink. Studios €55, large apartment €90

Taverna Aptera Centre of the village, where the road turns up to the site ☎ 28250 31313. Very good taverna, with a shaded terrace, serving the usual Cretan and Greek staples. Daily: April–Oct 10am–midnight; Nov–March 5–11pm.

Stílos and around

South from Áptera you can follow minor roads inland to circle round via the Dhrápano peninsula, a very attractive drive. The first place of any size is **STÍLOS (Στύλος)**, which is where the Australian and New Zealand rearguard made their final stand during the Battle of Crete (this was then the main road south), enabling the majority of Allied troops to be evacuated while they themselves were mostly stranded on the island. Many found refuge in the villages in the foothills around here and were later smuggled off the island – some of these villages were destroyed in retribution. Today Stílos is an unremarkable agricultural centre, but there are a couple of *kafenía* with shady tables beside the road, and some excellent tavernas. The local spring water is bottled under the Samariá brand (it comes in jugs in the restaurants here), and there's a very ancient church – usually locked – with a still more ancient Minoan or Mycenaean tholos tomb signed nearby.

Áyios Nikólaos

Kiriakosélia • To fix a visit head for the *kafenío* in Samonás – preferably in late afternoon after the *ipnákos* (siesta) – and they'll phone for a keyholder (Kostas or Roussa), who'll accompany you to the church; neither accept money for their time, but a contribution towards the upkeep of the church is unlikely to be refused

At a right fork on the edge of Stílos, a twisting and turning ride of 4km – with 180-degree hairpins – climbs dizzily, offering better views at every turn, to **SAMONÁS (Σαμωνάς)**, from where you can visit the isolated Byzantine church of **Áyios Nikólaos** at Kiriakosélia. For location and artworks, this is one of the most beautiful churches on the island. The restored church, nestling in a valley, contains fantastic **medieval frescoes**, as good as any on Crete. Painted in the thirteenth century, these have not been touched by the restorers – at least not recently – and are patchy and faded against their deep-blue background, but parts still seem as vivid as the day they were created. A *Madonna and Child*, at eye level on the left-hand side, and a dramatic *Christ Pantokrátor* in the drum dome stand out.

4

Faragi On Stílos' main square ☎ 28250 41462. Excellent, welcoming little taverna offering delicious, traditional Cretan cooking. Any of the lamb dishes are recommended and you'll usually get a dessert (often fresh fruit) on the house. Daily 9am–11pm.

★ **Moustakia** On Stílos' main square ☎ 28250 41190. An unpretentious, outstanding taverna with terrace tables

beneath giant plane trees. Everything is as fresh as it can be; among mouthwatering dishes try the Greek salad topped with *mizíthra* sheep's cheese (a meal in itself) or the *bekrí meze* (slow stewed pork in wine). The spit-roasted lamb is finger-licking good and the chips are gourmet standard. Daily 9am–11pm.

The Dhrápano peninsula

A multitude of roads crisscrosses the **Dhrápano peninsula (Χερσόνησος Δράπανο)** east of Haniá, almost all of them scenic and well surfaced. Also known as the **Apókoronas** region (its provincial name), this is rich agricultural land, a countryside of rolling green, wooded hills interrupted by immaculately whitewashed, and obviously wealthy, villages. Part of this wealth was fuelled – prior to the post-2010 slump – by a real estate boom and a huge amount of new villa construction; today many of these projects lie derelict and unfinished. There are few attractions to detain you long, but all these settlements have *kafenía* where you can sit and wonder at the rural tranquillity away from the main-road traffic.

Kalíves

KALÍVES (Καλύβες) is both a resort and an agricultural market centre of some size. As you approach, you pass a long sandy beach in the lee of Áptera's castle-topped bluff, which looks attractive but is hard to reach. The main **beach** stretches in both directions from the centre of the village, best at the eastern end where it curves round to a small harbour in the shelter of a headland. The village itself is not particularly attractive at first sight, a rather straggly development lining the main road for over 2km. It's very much a package resort, although the mainly low-rise apartments and studios keep it low-key; along with Almirídha (see below), Kalíves has become a focus for the mainly British villa-owning community in the surrounding hills and there are a number of businesses and bars with English names.

The centre of town is marked by a small square with a church, just to the east of which a river runs through to the sea. The most attractive parts are round here, especially if you cut down to the seafront just one block away.

Almirídha

ALMIRÍDHA (Αλμυρίδα), the next village along the coast from Kalíves, is smaller, marginally more of a resort, and considerably more attractive. The beach, lined with tavernas and cafés, is a popular spot for **windsurfing**, with a fairly reliable breeze once you're slightly offshore. It's worth looking at the remains of an **early Christian basilica** dating from the fifth century, with a wonderful mosaic floor. It lies beside the road as it enters the western end of the village close to the *Lagos* taverna (see p.259).

Pláka and around

Beyond Almirídha the coast becomes increasingly rocky, with cliffs almost all the way round to Yeoryioúpolis denying access to the sea. The roads and the signage also deteriorate if you go this way, but as you climb the views become increasingly worthwhile. The first place you reach is **PLÁKA (Πλάκα)**, a beautiful hamlet a little over 1km east of Almirídha, with a couple of tavernas and a tempting cake shop on a sleepy central platía; nearby *Sunset Taverna* has fabulous views back over Almirídha and the coast. There are also a couple of particularly good places to **stay** (see p.258).

Further around the coast, **KÓKKINO HORIÓ**, on the steep height above Pláka, is if anything even more picturesque – both villages were used as backdrops for the film *Zorba* *the Greek.* Passing through Palelóni you reach, after 6km, **KEFALÁS**, another absurdly pretty place perched along a road above the sea with spectacular views towards Réthymno.

Aspró

Good roads head inland from both Kalíves and Almirídha towards Vámos. It's interesting driving, with numerous villages worth a brief stop on the way. Immediately inland from Almirídha you pass below **ASPRÓ (Ασπρó)**, a tiny, ancient hamlet looking down over the coast. This is the old Greek village as you've always imagined it, with lots of bougainvillea-draped backstreets and dozing dogs stretched out in the road. A handful of foreigners have snapped up the only empty houses but it seems only a matter of time before the remaining local residents decide to cash in, too.

Doulianá

DOULIANÁ (Δουλιανά), a couple of kilometres southwest of Aspró as the crow flies but a few more along the back roads you're forced to take to reach it, is a delightful hamlet. Overflowing with plants and flowers and crisscrossed by winding lanes lined with fine old houses, it's yet another place where time seems to stand still.

Gavalohóri

The evidence that **GAVALOHÓRI (Γαβαλοχώρι)**, 2km south of Aspró, is an ancient settlement is scattered throughout the village's narrow, winding streets: there are Byzantine wells and Roman tombs on the outskirts, and on the corner by the museum you can see the cleverly preserved remains of a Turkish coffee shop. In the central square look out for the store run by the **Women's Agrotourism Co-operative**, an organization dedicated to reviving many of the region's disappearing arts and crafts; the results of their work – glass, ceramics and *kopanéli* (silk lace made by bobbin-weaving) – are on sale.

Folklore museum

Mon–Sat 9am–7pm, Sun 11am–6pm • €2

Housed in a beautifully restored Venetian building with Turkish additions, Gavalohóri's small but excellent **folklore museum** clearly documents the history and culture of the village, with items labelled in English and Greek. Of special interest are the examples of stone-cutting, woodcarving and **kopanéli**, which is being revived in the village. The mulberry trees planted around here by the Turks still produce silk from the silkworms that feed on their leaves – although the worms themselves are now imported from Japan and China.

Vámos

The main agricultural centre of the peninsula, and the capital of the Apokóronas district, **VÁMOS (Βάμος)** is hard to miss – the roads converge here, and from all over the region signs direct you to the local health centre. Only size really distinguishes it from all the other villages, however, and the *kafenía* round the crossroads are as peaceful as any you'll find.

An interesting and laudable venture here is **Vámos S.A.**, a co-operative founded to promote eco-tourism and rebuild and restore houses in the village. While you're here, make sure to see the upper part of the village which is where most of the population lives, as it is easy to get the idea that the co-operative's half is all there is. The upper village's main square has a number of lively *kafenía* with street terraces.

INFORMATION	THE DHRÁPANO PENINSULA

KALÍVES

Banks Banks with ATMs can be found along the main street.

Internet Many central bars and cafés offer free wi-fi to customers. Floppy Internet Cafe, by the junction on the

main road just east of the square also has screens (daily 9am–midnight).

Travel agencies Flisvos Travel (☎ 28250 31337, ⊕ flisvos .com) and Valeria Travel (☎ 28250 32392) both close to the main square. They can arrange car rental, money exchange and excursions, and are good options if you want to stay, representing apartments slightly further out which can be very good value.

ALMIRÍDHA

Car and bike rental Flisvos, at the bottom of the inland road (daily 8.30am–8.30pm; ☎ 28250 31100).

Watersports UCPA (☎ 28250 31443, ⓦ www.ucpa .com), on the seafront, rents out boards (€8/hr) and kayaks (€8–12/hr). Dream Adventures, with a desk under the tamarisks at the eastern end of the seafront (☎ 694 43 57 383) run speedboat and snorkelling (both

€22) trips to inaccessible parts of the nearby coast.

VÁMOS

Vamos S.A. tourist office 75m from the *Tou Bloumosifi* taverna up a road alongside it (☎ 28250 22190, ⓦ vamosvillage.gr). Helpful tourist information, walking tours, cookery courses and mountain bike rentals; they also sell an excellent local walking guide, *Discover Vamos On Foot*, detailing seven walks between 7–10km.

Internet Boulis, on the left at the top of the steep main street, beyond the upper square (daily 11am–2pm & 6pm–1am).

ACCOMMODATION

KALÍVES

Akti Galini On the seafront next door to the Kalives Beach Hotel ☎ 28250 32066, ⓦ aktigalinis.gr. Well-equipped studios and apartments with balcony sea view. Studios €45, apartments €50

Kalives Beach Hotel On the seafront in the centre of town, beside the river ☎ 28250 31285, ⓦ kalyvesbeach .com. There's a fair amount of choice in town, but this rather out-of-place hotel, whose facilities include indoor and outdoor pools plus a tiny gym and beach bar, has by far the highest profile. Free wi-fi. Breakfast included. €95

Mana On the seafront at the western end of the village ☎ 28250 31519, ✉ mana_rooms@hotmail.com. Old-fashioned place with marble-floored a/c sea-view studios with kitchenette in someone's house. €35

Zourpos Apartments 200m inland ☎ 6978 764353, ⓦ zourpos.gr. Simple but fully equipped studios with balcony and kitchenette plus a larger apartment in a garden setting in a quiet spot. Studio €35

ALMIRÍDHA

Almyrida In the centre ☎ 28250 32284, ⓦ almyrida beach.com. The centre of town is marked by two incongruous modern hotels, the four-star *Almyrida Residence* and slightly more downmarket *Almyrida Beach* which, together with the beachfront *Almyrida Studios*, are all under the same management and extremely comfortable. Free wi-fi. All rates include breakfast. *Studios* €90, *Beach* €105, *Residence* €118

Marianna On the street that runs inland beside the Almyrida Residence, about 100m from the junction ☎ 28210 92509, ⓦ almyrida-apartments.gr. One of a number of apartment complexes set back from the beach; a friendly option, where apartments come with kitchenette, fridge and TV. Plus a small pool. Free wi-fi. €80

Rooms Pothoulakis Between Marianna and Dimitra

☎ 28250 32132 ⓦ ypothoulakis.gr. Simple a/c studios and apartments (with TV and kitchen) in a peaceful spot. Studios €30, apartments €50

PLÁKA

★ **Bicorna Family Hotel** Pláka ☎ 28250 32073, ⓦ bicorna.gr. Wonderfully friendly hotel with a lush garden, small pool and recently refurbished light and airy balcony rooms with fridge. Free wi-fi. €50

Studios Koukouros Pláka ☎ 28250 31145, ⓦ studios koukouros.gr. Pleasant a/c rooms with balcony and fridge, and a stunning garden filled with palms, cacti and bougainvillea. €35

DOULIANÁ

Natalia's Houses On the edge of the village ☎ 28250 23356, ⓦ nataliashouses.gr. Lovely, traditional-style villas and apartments (sleeping two to six people) in a beautifully restored house surrounded by a lush garden. Both options come with a/c, TV and fully equipped kitchen. €120

GAVALOHÓRI

Agrotourism Apartments ☎ 28250 22038. The Women's Agrotourism Co-operative rent out fully equipped apartments, sleeping four, for stays of two days or more, and can provide information on good-value country villas in and around the village. €50

VÁMOS

★ **Vamos S.A.** 75m from the Tou Bloumosifi taverna ☎ 28250 22190, ⓦ vamosvillage.gr. The co-operative's tourist office has rooms, apartments and guesthouses to rent, all in carefully restored traditional houses and all very comfortably equipped with bath, TV and cooking facilities plus, in some, jacuzzis, steam bath or a pool. €75

EATING AND DRINKING

KALÍVES

Cafe Arena y Mar Eastern end of the beach. Café-bar

with TV sport, free wi-fi and free sunbeds on the beach for customers. April–Oct daily 9am–1am.

Elena Eastern end of the beach ☎ 28250 32544. The best of a bunch of traditional tavernas here, with free sunbeds for customers. April–Oct daily 11am–midnight.

Il Fourno Eastern end of the beach ☎ 28250 32520. Excellent pizza from a wood-fired oven, plus free sunbeds for customers. Daily 10am–midnight.

Kritiko In the centre of town, on the main road between the square and the river ☎ 28250 31096. Very good taverna offering well-prepared dishes and packed with locals at weekends; a lovely terrace overlooks the beach at the back. Daily 10am–midnight.

Potamos Overlooking the river close to the square. *Kafenío* serving snacks and drinks in an attractive waterside setting. Daily 8.30am–10pm.

Provlita 500m west of the centre on the rocky seafront ☎ 28250 31835. Excellent taverna with an attractive seafront terrace. The speciality is perfectly cooked fish but meat dishes are also served – try the *bekrí meze* (slow stewed pork). Good wine list. April–Oct daily noon–midnight; Nov–March Sat & Sun noon–midnight.

Zorba's At the back of the main square, opposite the church. No great shakes to look at, but the kitchen is wholeheartedly Cretan and the terrace fronting the church is often lively. Generous helpings of taverna staples and a great chicken pie make this a popular hangout for expats. Daily 9am–11pm.

ALMIRÍDHA

Café Françoise Towards the eastern end of the seafront close to the UCPA diving centre ☎ 28250 32591. Vibrant little café-patisserie serving a wide range of tasty snacks including salads, omelettes and pizzas. They also do a mammoth "English breakfast", as well as pastries and ice cream. April–Oct daily 8am–11pm.

★ **Dimitri's** In the centre of the seafront ☎ 28250 31303. Long-established, traditional taverna, specializing in fish and highly popular with locals. Service is efficient and there's a choice of white or wholemeal bread. Non-fish dishes include a tasty tuna salad, as well as very good *païdhákia* (lamb chops) and *kolokithakeftedhes* (fried zucchini balls). March–Oct daily 11am–midnight.

Lagos On the main road at the western edge of the village ☎ 6977 391778. "The Hare" taverna has an attractive garden setting and a meaty, traditional menu, plus excellent kalitsoúnia cheese pies and green peppers with six different fillings. May–Oct daily noon–midnight.

Psaros Central seafront ☎ 28250 32430. Excellent fish restaurant that also does a fair line in *mezédhes* – try their tasty *dákos* with soft goat cheese. The good selection of fresh fish and seafood specials includes *astakomakoronáda* (lobster with pasta). Daily 11.30am–midnight.

Thalami Central waterfront ☎ 28250 31287. Along with *Dimitri's*, this is the best of the waterfront tavernas, offering a wide range of fish, meat and vegetable dishes as well as a decent selection of *mezédhes*. April–Oct daily noon–midnight.

Tsunami On the waterfront at the western end of the seafront. All-day beach bar with music and cocktails at night – about as wild as the local nightlife ever gets. April–Oct daily 9am–1am.

PLÁKA

Sunset Taverna At the entrance to the village coming from Almirídha ☎ 28250 32047. Very good taverna serving a variety of fish and meat dishes on a terrace with fabulous panoramic views and – of course – sunsets. Daily 8am–midnight.

DOULIANÁ

★ **Ta Douliana** Down a narrow track close to Natalia's Houses on the edge of the village. A friendly taverna with tables on a leafy terrace. Great local dishes include *arní krasáto* (lamb stewed in wine) and don't forget to try their *to mandí* (meat pie with a garlic sauce). Daily 11am–midnight.

GAVALOHÓRI

Aposperitis At the edge of the village on the Vámos road ☎ 28250 23095. The village's best taverna has a shady garden terrace and a good Cretan kitchen. House specials include *kókoras to krasáto* (rooster in red wine sauce) and *kounéli stifádho* (spiced rabbit stew) plus excellent lamb dishes. May–Sept daily 6.30–11.30pm.

VÁMOS

To Liakoto Around the corner from the taverna near the tourist office. The Vámos S.A. co-operative's café-bar, with regular exhibitions, live music and spectacular terrace views; next door is a grocery store selling beautifully packaged cheeses, herbs, honey, oil and wine from the region. Daily 9am–11pm.

Marouvas On the main street ☎ 697 22 00 246. Good taverna with an attractive terrace serving well-prepared Cretan standards. Pork baked in a wood-fired oven and *moussaká* are popular specials. Daily noon–midnight.

★ **Sterna Tou Bloumosifi** Main road, near the centre of the lower village. This outstanding taverna with a superb tree-shaded terrace is run by the Vámos S.A. co-operative and dedicated to Cretan cuisine. A varied menu offers salads, *mezédhes* (try the *fáva* – pureed split peas) and plenty of vegetarian options. Standouts among the mains include oven-baked or pan-fried lamb, pork and chicken and delicious stuffed mushrooms. They have a decent wine list, and the *hyma* (barrelled) house wine (red or white) is pretty good, too. Daily noon–midnight.

4

SHOPPING

GAVALOHÓRI
Women's Agrotourism Co-operative Shop Main Square ☎ 28250 22038. The co-operative's handmade products for sale, including *kopanéli*, embroidery, lace and lots more. April–Oct daily 10.30am–10pm.

Vrísses and around

VRÍSSES (Βρύσες), on the south side of the E75 highway, was a major junction on the old road and is still at the crossroads for the route south to Hóra Sfakíon (if you're coming from Réthymno or anywhere else to the east, you usually have to **change buses** here), though nowadays bypassed by much of the traffic. Set on the banks of the Almirós River, Vrísses is a wonderfully shady little town, its streets lined with huge old plane trees and busy with the life of a local agricultural centre. On the riverside are a number of inviting cafés and **tavernas**.

Alíkambos

About 4km south of Vrísses, along the road to Hóra Sfakíon, is the turn-off to the traditional village of **ALÍKAMBOS (Αλίκαμπος)**, which has a couple of *kafenía*. Just before the village, the **church of the Panayía** (signed "Kimisis tis Theotokou") is beautifully set in a steep valley. In its nave are outstanding, remarkably well-preserved **frescoes** by the fourteenth-century master, Ioannis Pagomenos; they depict the Virgin and Child, Áyios Yeóryios and Áyios Dimítrios. The paintings around the altar are by a later artist. You can see the frescoes reasonably well even if the church is locked; if it is, the key should be available in the village.

EATING   VRÍSSES AND AROUND

O Progoulis Next to the Almirós River, Vrísses ☎ 28250 51806. With a terrace overlooking the river and its pools filled with entertaining ducks and geese, this is a very good taverna for Cretan standards, as well as the house speciality, rotisserie chicken, and other grills. Daily 9am–1am.

Yeoryioúpolis and around

YEORYIOÚPOLIS (Γεωργιούπολη) – or Georgioupolis – lies at the base of Cape Dhrápano where the Almirós flows into the sea. It's named after the ill-starred Prince George, a son of the Greek king who was appointed High Commissioner to Crete in 1898 (see p.337). These days, the place has a distinctly split personality: on the one hand is a pretty **old town** by the river, with a tree-lined approach and ancient eucalyptus trees shading the huge square in the centre; on the other is a lively **package resort**, with development spreading further every year along the beach to the east of town. For the moment the two sides maintain a comfortable balance and Yeoryioúpolis remains an extremely pleasant place to spend a few days: small-scale, yet with plenty of action, and with the freshwater **Lake Kournás** an easy trip away.

HIKING AROUND YEORYIOÚPOLIS

If you want to do some walking in the area around Yeoryioúpolis, *Walks in Rethymnon and Georgioupolis, Crete* by Lance Chilton (see p.355) is recommended. As a taster, you could try hiking up the Almirós valley towards Vrísses or tackling the steep climb to Exópolis on the road to Vámos, where there are some wonderfully sited tavernas with magnificent views. Hikes to and around Lake Kournás (see opposite) are another possibility. An excellent local walking guide *Discover Kavros and Georgioupolis On Foot* details ten walks of between 3–10km in the hills around the town. It should be on sale at local shops and supermarkets and is available from the Vamos Co-operative tourist office (p.258).

Yeoryioúpolis beaches

The main course of the river runs into the sea on the northern edge of Yeoryioúpolis, by a small harbour protected by a long rocky breakwater, and there are numerous smaller streams crossing the **beach** all around, some of which have wooden bridges to let you cross without getting your feet wet. These can make swimming cold in places, and they also create little quicksands, mostly only ankle-deep. This area is also a favoured nesting ground of the loggerhead **sea turtle** (see p.201). Close to town it can be hard to find space between the sunloungers, but several **beach bars** offer these for free as long as you pay for the odd drink; the best of these are probably *Corissia Park*, right in town, which also has a pool, and the *Tropicana Beach Club*, at the start of the long eastern stretch. Beyond *Tropicana* a large stream crosses the beach, and more beach bars and hotels stretch into the distance; you may find more space here, but you should swim close to a lifeguard as there are **dangerous currents** in places: don't venture too far out, and take heed of any warning notices.

A second, much more sheltered, **beach** lies to the north of the river in a small bay. Swimming here is safer and there are generally fewer people, but the water can be extremely cold.

Lake Kournás and around

Crete's only freshwater lake, **Lake Kournás (Λίμνη Κουρνά)**, shelters in a bowl of hills 4km inland from Yeoryioúpolis. As lakes go, it's small and shallow, but it nevertheless makes for an interesting excursion. Its appearance varies greatly according to when you visit: during the day its colours change remarkably as the sun shifts around the rim of the bowl, and its size alters over the course of a year. In late summer the level drops to reveal sand (or dried mud) beaches all around, and a number of popular camping spots. Earlier in the year, the water comes right up to the tidal ring of scrubby growth and it's much harder to find anywhere to camp or to swim from. The lake and the surrounding hills are also a good place to seek out some of the more unusual island wildlife. In summer it's possible to make a circuit of the lake using a path and the dried mud beaches where this runs out – about an hour's walk.

On the lakeshore where you arrive there are a few simple **tavernas** on the shore – popular with the locals for outings, with lamb barbecued on spits – and a few pedaloes and canoes for rent.

Kournás

The village of **KOURNÁS (Κουρνάς)**, a charming hill settlement fanning out around its inclined main street, is a stiff 4km climb beyond Lake Kournás. After you've eaten at the *Kali Kardia* taverna (see p.264) you could take a look at the church of **Áyios Yeóryios**. A fine old Byzantine structure with Venetian additions, it has some impressive fresco fragments. If it's locked, ask around and someone should produce a key.

ARRIVAL AND INFORMATION

YEORYIOÚPOLIS AND AROUND

YEORYIOÚPOLIS

By bus Buses drop you on the main road, just a couple of minutes' walk from the square and crossroads at the centre of town – a booth here sells tickets for onward buses.

Banks As you head up towards the square from the highway, you'll find a couple of banks with ATMs.

Internet Planet Internet Café on the edge of the square towards the river or (coin-operated) *Tito's* on the square. Both are open daily 11am–2am.

Shops There are minimarkets liberally scattered around and a couple of slightly larger supermarkets, including

handy Kafkalas right on the square; several of them sell English books and newspapers.

Travel agencies Ethon Tours on the square (☎ 28250 61269, ⊛ ethon.gr) offers everything from car, mountain and motorbike rental to its own ATM.

LAKE KOURNÁS

To get to the lake from Yeoryioúpolis you could take the tourist train or rent a bike, or it's an easy walk, nice enough once you've crossed the E75 highway. The best route is via the hamlet of Mathés. From here there's a waymarked rambling route to the lake's northern edge, linking in with the route around it – ask the villagers at Mathés to direct you to the path, should you have difficulty.

TOURS AND ACTIVITIES

YEORYIOÚPOLIS

Boat trips Sofía Cruises (☎ 28250 61100) runs boat trips from the river just below the bridge: in particular "turtle trips" up the river (they're actually terrapins), or a day's outing to the beach at Maráthi (10am; €39, €49 with lunch), at the mouth of Soúdha Bay (see p.253).

Cycling Adventure Bikes (daily 9.30am–1pm & 6–10pm; ☎ 28250 61830, ⓦ adventurebikes.org) organizes easy bike tours all around the western end of the island with transport to get you up the steep bits.

Horseriding Horserides along the beach or up to Lake

Kournás, for example, can be arranged through local Travel agencies or direct with Zoraïda's (☎ 28250 61745, ⓦ zoraidas-horseriding.com).

Train tours Two small trains transport visitors along the seafront and to various places of interest inland, including the lake, and even as far as Argiroúpolis (p.197).

Watersports You can rent jet skis on the beach just beyond the *Tropicana*, by the mouth of the stream; *La Palma* beach bar, a little further, has a kids' playground and mini-soccer, and many of the other beach bars offer similar enticements.

ACCOMMODATION

There are rooms to rent everywhere in **Yeoryioúpolis**, it seems, and only at the height of season are you likely to have any trouble finding a vacancy. The competition generally keeps prices low. **Mosquitoes** can be a problem if you're staying near the river, but the wildlife on the banks is some compensation and kingfishers are regular visitors. With your own transport, the hill village of nearby **Exópolis** becomes a viable alternative to staying in town. The big hotels are mostly out to the east, espcially in and around the village of **Kavrós**. The best thing you can say about Kavrós, which is almost entirely purpose-built, is that it has plenty of nightlife, and there's a frequent road-train into Yeoryioúpolis.

YEORYIOÚPOLIS

Andy's Rooms Near the church, on the road towards the beach from the south end of the square by the supermarket ☎ 28250 61394, ⓔ andymaliarakis @gmail.com. Friendly place shaded by trees with good-value a/c balcony rooms with fridge and balcony, plus a couple of well-equipped apartments with kitchenette. Rooms **€35**, apartments **€65**

Anna Just across the river from town, on the main road; information at Anna Market, between the square and the bridge ☎ 28250 61556, ⓦ annashouse.gr. Excellent-value and well-presented, if basic, balcony en-suite a/c rooms in a garden setting, with kitchenette and fridge. A new complex 200m further along the same road offers modern, fully equipped apartments sleeping six around a full-size pool, with free wi-fi. Rooms **€30**, apartments **€80**

Eligas On the first cross street below the square, heading towards the beach ☎ 28250 61541, ⓦ eligas .gr. Simply furnished but well-maintained studios and apartments in a bougainvillea-draped building; upper floors have good views from the back. Free wi-fi. **€40**

Georgioupolis Beach Hotel On the seafront at the bottom of the road from the north corner of the square ☎ 28250 61056, ⓦ gbhotel.gr. Good value considering the location and facilities – a/c rooms with beach views and satellite TV, plus a pool. **€70**

Marika Studio Apartments In the hill village of Exópolis, just above the main road, 3km northwest of town ☎ 28210 61500, ⓦ georgioupoli-apartments.gr.

With your own transport, this attractive option with a/c studio rooms around a pool and a truly spectacular view becomes a possibility. They operate a pool bar during the day, so you can swim and enjoy the view for the price of a drink. Ten percent discount for *Rough Guide* readers. **€40**

Porto Kalivaki Behind the beach on the far side of the river ☎ 28250 61316, ⓦ kalivaki.com. Great-value a/c studios in a tranquil spot right behind a sandy beach, with pool and lovingly tended gardens with scale models of the Acropolis and Arkádhi monastery, among others. **€40**

Sofia Seafront by the mouth of the river ☎ 28250 61325, ⓦ river-side.gr. Peach-coloured apartment complex with modern two-room a/c apartments with kitchen and TV, most with sea views. The same owners run the adjacent *Riverside Villa*, with similar facilities but inland views, and have other places nearby and in the hills. Free wi-fi. **€70**

Sunlight Seafront, just east of the centre ☎ 28250 61396, ⓦ sunlight-geo.gr. Modern apartment complex that's ugly from the outside, but friendly and comfortable within, with good sea-view balconies and rooms for 2 to 6 people. Free wi-fi. **€45**

Zorba's Taverna Close to the square on the road towards the church ☎ 28250 61381, ⓦ zorbashotel.gr. Larger than average a/c rooms and apartments above a taverna. The rooms come with kitchenette, the family apartments with a complete kitchen, and there's a tiny courtyard swimming pool. Breakfast included at both. Rooms **€65**, apartments **€75**

MATHÉS

★ **Taverna Villa Kapasa** ☎ 28250 61050, ⓦ villa
-kapasas.com. Delightful place with a/c, en-suite rooms
overlooking the leafy garden of an ancient restored house;
they also do meals. **€40**

LAKE KOURNÁS

Most of the tavernas have en-suite rooms
upstairs overlooking the water. If these are full, you
could try for rooms at the village of Mourí, which is
straight up from the junction with the path that leads
down to the lake.

Korissia North end of the lake ☎ 28250 61653,
ⓦ kournas-lake-apartments.gr. Superbly sited taverna-
rooms place with a/c lake-view balcony rooms above a
taverna; very comfortable if you have insect-repellent. Free
wi-fi. **€35**

KOURNÁS

Villa Stella On the right coming in from the lake ☎ 6947
407181, ⓦ villas-kournas.com/en/location.html. Luxury
studios (sleeping two) and apartments (sleeping six). As the
proprietor lives off site you'll need to make contact in
advance. Tends to be pre-booked in high summer. **€80**

EATING, DRINKING AND NIGHTLIFE

There are plenty of restaurants and tavernas in Yeoryioúpolis, mainly between the square and the river or along the
waterfront; the square itself is ringed by cafés. There are a number of tavernas up in the hill village of **Exópolis** too, with
stunning views over the coast. In terms of **nightlife**, Yeoryioúpolis itself is pretty quiet, though there are plenty of **bars**
open late. There are regular Greek dance nights and other events at the *Tropicana Beach Club*, while the *Hawaii Beach Bar*
sometimes has all-night weekend beach parties. There's much more of a late-night scene in nearby Kavrós, where there are
numerous **clubs**, some of which lay on transport to and from Yeoryioúpolis: the *Maeva Coffee Club*, for example, has regular
themed club nights; otherwise, look out for posters around town.

YEORYIOÚPOLIS

Babis First left off the road leading down towards the
beach from the square's southwest corner; it's then on
the first corner on the right ☎ 28250 61760. Traditional
taverna with good-value, simple Cretan food. The same
family have another branch further along the same street
on the left opposite *Stelios Rooms*. Daily 9am–11pm.

Blue Moon By the river, just upstream from the bridge
☎ 697 27 05 310. Café-bar with a riverside terrace for
breakfast (made with produce from their own farm) or a
sundowner. May–Oct daily 7.30am–1pm & 6–10pm.

Corissia Park On the seafront in the centre of town
☎ 28250 83010. A somewhat bland international menu is
made up for by one of the best locations in town and a free
pool for customers; there's a breakfast buffet for €7 or a
daily all-you-can-eat dinner buffet (6–9pm; €15).
Frequent live music. Daily 8am–midnight.

Efthimis On the road heading east out of town,
parallel to the highway ☎ 28250 61886. Friendly little
diner serving good wood-fired pizza and decent Greek
dishes. Daily 5.30pm–midnight.

O Fanis Near the bridge ☎ 699 87 95 979. Very good fish
restaurant offering the freshest catch from the quayside,
30m away. Also good meat dishes – excellent roast lamb.
April–Sept Daily 11am–midnight.

Oasis Café Bar East of the centre behind the beach –
follow the signs. A pool, good snacks and light meals, plus
night-time entertainment including live music and
karaoke. Daily 10am–2am.

Paradise Down by the river west of the square
☎ 28250 61313. Reliable taverna with an attractive
garden setting. The Cretan kitchen turns out a range of

popular standards from *dákos* to *païdhákia*. May–Oct daily
7am–11pm.

Perastikos Behind the beach, beyond Tropicana Beach
Club. Tranquil café-restaurant with a terrace over a
tributary of the river, where terrapins come to be fed in the
evening. Daily 9am–midnight.

To Pikantiko On the road from the square (by Mythos
Taverna) down to the beach. An excellent bakery, selling
the usual *tyrópita* and *spanakópita* as well as filled
croissants and other temptations. Mon–Sat 9am–2pm &
6–10pm.

Poseidon Taverna 70m down an alley on the right
from the road south of the square ☎ 28250 61026. In a
lovely riverside setting and serving "every day fish from our
own boat" at reasonable prices, this is definitely worth a
try. There's no menu; enter the kitchen and choose your fish
carefully (sold by weight) to avoid a nasty surprise when
the bill arrives. April–Oct daily 6–11pm.

Sirtaki Near the bridge ☎ 28250 61382. Excellent
taverna-ouzerí with a raised terrace serving well-prepared
mezédhes and taverna standards. April–Oct daily
noon–midnight.

Sunlight Taverna Overlooking the beach, east of the
centre ☎ 28250 83075. Fantastic seafront setting for
decent, plain Cretan food (including fresh fish) with great-
value daily specials. In the evening, tables are set up across
the road by the water. April–Oct daily 8am–11pm.

EXÓPOLIS

Thymari Exópolis ☎ 28250 61777. New, stylish taverna
with a creative slant offering breakfasts and snacks
throughout the day and more elaborate food in the

evenings. Try their *manites* (grilled mushrooms with sweet-sour sauce) or *márathopita* (fennel-stuffed pastries) or their house special, Haniá meat pie. Daily 8.30am–midnight.

MATHÉS

Taverna Mathes Centre of the village ☎ 28250 61514. A fine terrace with a stunning panoramic view and daily specials such as braised lamb in wine. Also does

charcoal-grilled meat and fish. April–Oct daily 10am–11pm.

KOURNÁS

★ **Kali Kardia** At the top of the main street ☎ 28250 96278. Some of the best lamb and sausages in the province, together with tasty *souvláki* and super salads – and don't forget to try their noted *galaktoboúreko* dessert, a lemony egg-custard pudding. Daily 9am–11pm.

West of Haniá

West of Haniá, the E75 speeds you towards Kastélli with little to see along the way. The **old road**, meanwhile, also served by **buses**, follows the coastline more or less consistently, through a string of small towns and growing resorts, all the way to the base of the Rodhopoú peninsula. Occasionally it runs right above the water, more often 100m or so inland, but never more than easy walking distance from the sea. There are hotels and apartments the whole way, but the first real resort area starts at **Káto Stalós**, which runs into **Ayía Marína** and then into **Plataniás** without a break, creating the most built-up, touristy strip in the west of the island. This is better than it sounds: it's all fairly low-rise, there's a decent beach almost all the way along (with facilities including jet skis, windsurfers and parascending) and, by resort standards, it's pretty quiet. The end of the Haniá coastal strip is marked by the **Rodhopoú peninsula**, which is best explored on foot.

Ayía Marína and Plataniás

The coastal half of **AYÍA MARÍNA (Αγία Μαρίνα)** – the older village lies a little inland – is distinguished by a beautiful beach, curving round a little promontory with a fine view of the sunset and of **Áyii Theódori**, a little offshore island that's a sanctuary for *kri-kri* or wild goats (you're not allowed to come ashore). From the west of the islet a great cave gapes like the jaws of a beast; legend has Áyii Theódori as a sea-monster which, emerging from the depths to swallow Crete, was petrified by the gods. Remains found in the cave suggest that it was a place of Minoan worship in antiquity, while in more recent times the Venetians turned the island into a fortress. As for Ayía Marína itself, there's every facility and tour you could want on offer.

Seamlessly following to the west, **PLATANIÁS (Πλατανιάς)** is an even busier place boasting a delightful old quarter perched high on an almost sheer bluff above the road.

TOURS   **AYÍA MARÍNA AND PLATANIÁS**

Bike tours Hellas Bike, in Ayía Marína (☎ 28210 60858, ⓦ hellasbike.net) offer bike rental and easy bike tours

(€38/half day; €58/day) around this area and into the mountains.

ACCOMMODATION

The best accommodation deals in **Ayía Marina** are on packages; there are a few old-fashioned rooms places but, out of season at least, you'll be better off at one of the many modern, well-appointed apartment complexes (most have pools). Outside July or August there may well be bargains available in **Plataniás**. Any of the travel agencies along the main street should be able to arrange a deal.

AYÍA MARÍNA

Minerva Beach Eastern end of the beachfront ☎ 28210 68813, ⓦ minerva-dore.gr. Good-value hotel fronting the beach offering well-presented rooms with a/c,

TV and kitchenette-fridge. **€45**

Villa Life Upper village inland, near Villa Life apartments ☎ 28210 95986, ⓦ villa-life.gr. Welcoming, modern, a/c balcony apartments around a nice pool. The

largest have two rooms and all come with a kitchenette. Free wi-fi. €60

PLATANIÁS
Ermis Suites On the beach ☎28210 60101, ⓦermishotel.com. Fairly simple studios and apartments, many with sea view and all with balcony or veranda. Larger apartments have two rooms and fully equipped kitchen; studios come with a kitchenette. Free wi-fi. Studios €75, apartments €110

Pelagos Holiday Apartments Halfway up the hill above the main square ☎28210 60075, ⓦpelagosholidays.gr. Modern, exceptionally well-fitted-out duplex apartments – designed by the Finnish architect-husband of the owner – these are a step up in price and quality from most of the accommodation here. Designer furnishings (including Scandinavian beds) complete the picture and all apartments come with balcony sea views, kitchenette and satellite TV. Free wi-fi. €105

EATING, DRINKING AND NIGHTLIFE

A number of tavernas in **Plataniás** attract evening and weekend visitors from Haniá. The best views, if not cuisine, are from the eagles' eyries right at the top of the village, including the terraces of *Vigli* and *Astrea*. The best food, however, is down below. For most young people in Haniá, Plataniás means **clubs**, and a great exodus from the city takes place in summer at around midnight. The top places here include *Mylos* (ⓦmylos-chania.com) and *Splendid* (ⓦwww.splendid-hania.gr), while in in Ayía Marína *Villa Mercedes* is a popular option. There are also dozens of beach bars open much of the day and most of the night.

Manolis Taverna Ayía Marina, upper village inland, near Villa Life apartments ☎28210 68311. Excellent little family taverna away from the seafront maelstrom, with a nice outdoor terrace. Solid Cretan cooking includes dishes like *bouréki* and *kounéli stifádho* (stewed rabbit) and there's a decent selection of reasonably priced bottled wines, too. April–Oct daily 6–11.30pm.

★ **0 Milos tou Kerata** Main road, just west of the centre ☎28210 68578. A restaurant of repute that opened its doors in 1960, *Milos* is dedicated to quality and expensive by Cretan standards – but worth it. Specialities here, and elsewhere in the village, are *yíros* and *kokorétsi* – Cretan-style doner kebab cooked on huge spits over charcoal – plus *haniótiki kreatópita* (Haniá meat pie) and a

variety of salads. You eat in a delightful walled garden with an old millstream running through it. Their bar next door, *Café Nero*, is an ideal place for an aperitif or a nightcap. April–Oct daily 6pm–1pm.

★ **Taverna Drakiana** 3km along the road heading inland from beside Milos, near the tiny church of Áyios Yioryíos ☎28210 61677. The food – organic and based on traditional recipes – may not be quite up to the same standard as *Milos*, but the prices are more palatable and the riverside setting, in wooded surroundings couldn't be more romantic – especially at night. It's an easy walk inland, but they also offer a free minibus from Plataniás or Ayía Marína that will also bring you home after you've eaten; simply call ahead. April–Oct daily 10am–midnight.

Máleme and around

Beyond Plataniás the development thins out, though there are still regular clusters of apartments, along with isolated hotels and villas and one or two slightly more concentrated developments in places such as **Yeráni**. These on the whole are pleasantly low-key, but the beach is rarely that great, being very open to wind and waves and with rather gravelly, grey sand. **MÁLEME (Μάλεμε)** is perhaps the place you're most likely to stop.

German war cemetery

Just beyond Máleme a narrow lane leads up to a **German war cemetery**, set on a hillside below the ridge known as Hill 107. This ridge played a pivotal role in the defence of, and the battle for, the nearby **airfield**, which saw much of the early fighting in the Battle of Crete and where the German invasion began on May 20, 1941 – the loss of the airfield in controversial circumstances was crucial to the German success.

Overlooking the battleground where so many of the four and a half thousand buried here lost their lives, the lines of flat headstones, each marking a double grave, lend a sombre aspect to an otherwise peaceful scene. In a piece of almost grotesque irony, the cemetery's keepers were for many years George Psychoundakis, author of *The Cretan Runner*, and Manoli Pateraki, who played a leading role in the capture of General Kreipe (see p.340).

Late Minoan tomb

Follow the lane down from the cemetery to the first left bend, where a track (signed) on the right leads 100m along a terraced hillside to the tomb on the right

The discovery in 1966 of a splendid **Late Minoan tomb** near Máleme demonstrated that this area had already been a graveyard for more than three thousand years. The *dhrómos* or entrance passage of the stone-built tomb and its enormous heavy lintel are well preserved.

The Rodhopoú peninsula

Half a dozen villages cluster near the base of the **Rodhopoú peninsula (Χερσόνησος Ροδωπού)**, and are beginning to be discovered by tourists. But for the most part it's a barren, harsh landscape, with no roads penetrating northwards; if you want to explore here, you'll have to do so on foot.

Kolimbári and around

KOLIMBÁRI (Κολυμπάρι), just off the main road, is much the most developed village on Rodhopoú, but still has far more appeal than anything that has preceded it along the north coast. If there were a sandy beach, it would be a perfect resort: as it is, there's a long strip of pebbles and clear water looking back along the coast towards Haniá in the distance. It's little spoiled, and from the narrow main street, where there are a couple of good tavernas, you can walk through to a concrete seafront promenade lined with more restaurants and cafés. Nearby, the vast new concrete harbour is entirely deserted most of the time.

Inland, a road south from Kolimbári towards Episkopí tracks the valley of the Spiliakos River and offers an opportunity to see an impressive **cave** and a trio of superb **churches**.

Moní Goniá

June–Sept Sun–Fri 8am–12.30pm & 4–8pm, Sat 4–8pm; Oct–May Sun–Fri 8am–12.30pm & 3.30–5.30pm • Free; museum €2; respectable dress required (no shorts)

A short walk from Kolimbári on the main road out onto the peninsula, the seventeenth-century **Moní Goniá (Μονή Γωνιάς)** occupies a prime site, with stupendous views and a scramble down to a sandy cove – rumoured to be the monks' private beach. Every monk in Crete can tell tales of a valiant heritage of resistance to invaders, but here the Turkish cannonballs are still lodged in the walls to prove it, a relic of which the good fathers seem far more proud than any of the icons. That said, the church has a splendid series of seventeenth- and eighteenth-century icons (plus a few modern examples); Áyios Nikólaos, in a side chapel, is particularly fine. More are kept in the small **museum**, along with assorted vestments and relics.

From Afráta to Ravdoúha

AFRÁTA (Άφράτα) is a tiny place with a couple of tavernas, and the first stirrings of development. Keep right down an increasingly steep, narrow road, and after little more than 1km you'll reach a rocky cove at the far end of the gorge you can see from the village. There's a *kantína* here and the exceptionally clear water offers great swimming, although it's a tiny space and can get crowded.

From Afráta you can head across the penisula on good roads to **Astrátigos** and **Áspra Nerá**, with a turn-off to the village of **RODHOPÓS**, all pleasant if unremarkable settlements with places to eat and drink. From here **RAVDOÚHA (Ραβδούχα)** and the peninsula's west coast is accessible (though you can also get here directly from the main road). En route you'll pass the ancient church of **Ayía Marína** with some fine fresco fragments and, next to it, an old communal washing place, evoking a Crete long gone. **Ravdoúha Beach**, a dizzying drop below the village proper, is something of a misnomer, but there are patches of rocky foreshore to swim from, and a couple of places to eat.

4

The tip of the peninsula

Towards the tip of the peninsula you'll find no easily driveable roads, although a rough track (for which you'll need a 4WD) heads north out of Rodhopós up the spine of the peninsula to Diktynna (see below) 20km distant. There are, however, a couple of sites you might consider taking a major hike or a **boat trip** to reach. The latter is certainly the easier option – in summer the terrain is frighteningly hot, barren and shadeless – and there are regular trips to **Diktynna**, almost at the top of the peninsula above a little bay on the east side. An important Roman sanctuary to the goddess of the same name, this was probably built over more ancient centres of worship, and though it has never been properly excavated there's a surprising amount to be seen. The boats come here mainly because it's a sheltered spot to swim (when the sea is rough, fishing boats often shelter here too), but they allow plenty of time to explore.

Church of Áyios Ioánnis Giónis

If you've come to Diktynna by boat, there's a challenging 14km hike over to the isolated **Church of Áyios Ioánnis Giónis (Άγιος Ιωάννης Γχιώνας)** on the western side of the peninsula from where you could then continue back to Rodhopós (7km) or Kolimbári (a further 7km) but let the boatmen know your plans to save them sending out a search party. On August 29, the church plays host to a major pilgrimage and a mass baptism of boys called Yiannis (John), marking one of the most important festivals of the Cretan religious calendar. At this time the two- to three-hour walk (each way) from Rodhopós among crowds of people is definitely worth it. Although you can approach from Afráta, the main track up the spine of the peninsula starts in Rodhopós.

Spiliá and around

A little over 3km south of Kolimbári lies the rural village of **SPILIÁ (Σπηλιά)**. High above the village, close to the hamlet of Marathókefala, the **Cave of Áyios Ioánnis Ermítis** (St John the Hermit), is a sizeable grotto with a church, dedicated to the eleventh-century evangelist, built inside it. There's a terrace with fine coastal views and, on weekends and holidays, when this is a popular outing, a café and museum. On Spiliá's southern edge signs lead to the charming fourteenth-century church of the **Panayía**, raised on the lower slope of a hill and ringed by junipers. Inside the dark interior is decorated with fine fourteenth-century **frescoes**. Just over 2km south of Spiliá and beyond the village of **Drakoná**, a signed path ("To Holy Stephen") leads to the delightful **chapel of Áyios Stéfanos**, a tiny tenth-century white-walled chapel squatting beneath overhanging oak trees. Inside you'll find the heavy stone walls decorated with exquisite **frescoes** dating from the period following the Arab conquest, when the Christian faith was being triumphantly restored

Mihaíl Arhángelos Episkopí

4km southwest of Spiliá on the outskirts of Episkopí • Free

The most impressive church in the area around Spiliá, and one of the oldest in Greece, is the remarkable church of **Mihaíl Arhángelos Episkopí (Μιχαιλ Αρχάγγελος Επισκοπή)** whose concentric stepped **dome**, unique in Crete, gives the structure its local name, "The Rotunda". The church was, as its official name suggests, a bishop's seat during the Venetian period, but the edifice is much older than this. The core rotunda section dates to the first Byzantine period, completed perhaps as early as the sixth century, and originally stood alone; the rest of the building was added after the end of the Arab occupation in the tenth century. Recent excavations in the adjoining graveyard yielded evidence that the present church was built over the remains of a still earlier Christian basilica, with various layers of burials from all periods of the church's history. Inside, fragmentary **frescoes** dating back to the tenth century include a poignant head and partial wing of Áyios Mihaíl, the church's patron. Take a look also at mosaic floor fragments (thought to date to the earliest period), and an impressive double-seated marble **font**.

THE WORLD'S OLDEST OLIVE TREE

Áno Voúves, 4km east of Episkopí and reached via back roads, has become famous throughout Greece as the location of one of the oldest olive trees in existence. Having seen the zenith of Minoan Crete and being seriously venerable at the time of Christ, the gnarled and contorted tree looks every one of the 4000-plus years attributed to it by experts from the University of Crete (the 3000 years quoted on information boards at the site is thought to be a conservative estimate). Still vigorously producing foliage and fruit, the ancient tree has become a source of huge pride for Áno Voúves, and there's a café-information centre for visitors. In 2004 a branch from the tree was carried to Athens on a reconstructed Minoan boat (see p.242) and two victory wreaths fashioned from its leaves were used to honour the first and last winners of events in that year's Olympic Games.

ACCOMMODATION

THE RODHOPOÚ PENINSULA

KOLIMBÁRI

Aphea Village On the road to the upper village ☎ 28240 23344, ⓦ aphea-village.gr. A sizeable complex, where two- or three-room a/c apartments come with TV and there's a pool. Free wi-fi. **€50**

Grand Bay Beach Resort At the eastern end of the beach ☎ 28240 83380, ⓦ grandbay.gr. Rather characterless four-star hotel – albeit in an attractive location – with mundanely furnished balcony rooms around a pool. Sea-view rooms cost extra. **€110**

Lefka On the road junction at the entrance to the village ☎ 28240 22211, ⓦ lefka-kolimbari.gr. A friendly taverna with balcony rooms that are clean if uninspiring and come with fridge and a/c. Taverna daily 8am–11pm. **€40**

Villa Polichna Upper village ☎ 28210 74191, ⓦ villa-polichna.gr. Small but serviceable modern a/c

apartments done out in traditional style with TV, kitchenette and a communal Lilliputian pool; the same proprietor rents villas nearby. **€50**

RAVDOÚHA

★ **Brakhos Sto Kyma** "Waves on the Rock", signed off the left fork at the foot of the hill ☎ 28240 23133, ⓦ wavesontherock.eu. A delightful and excellent taverna (daily 9am–midnight) fronting a pebble beach shaded by tamarisks, serving up tasty Cretan dishes and fresh fish. Also lets five simple, a/c studio rooms. Staying here affords you utter tranquillity; it's worth reserving, as they have many repeat guests. Breakfast (€4) is available and a daily three-course menu for €10. Taverna daily April–Oct; Nov–March Fri–Sun only. **€38**

EATING AND DRINKING

KOLIMBÁRI

★ **Argentina** Main street, behind the harbour ☎ 28240 22243. One of the best tavernas in the village, with a raised street terrace in the main building or a sea-view terrace at their extension across the road. Excellent fish and meat dishes and salads plus very good house wine. April–Oct daily noon–11pm.

Diktina Main street, behind the harbour ☎ 28240 22611. With a terrace at the rear overlooking the old harbour, this good taverna serves fresh fish and *mezédhes* along with the usual standards. April–Oct daily noon–11.30pm.

Mylos On the promenade overlooking the beach ☎ 28240 22210. Converted from an old olive-oil mill, and with a seafront terrace, this is an appealing, stylish café-bar

bar for a sundowner or late night drinks and *mezédhes*. Daily 9.30am–1am.

Palio Arkhontiko Overlooking the beach ☎ 28240 22124. Decent taverna with a seafront terrace for the usual food and fresh fish, and a good (if slightly pricey) wine list. Daily noon–11pm.

RAVDOÚHA

Neratzia Taverna On the road leading to the northern beach, reached by turning right at the bottom of the hill ☎ 28240 23988. This simple family-run taverna is a good alternative to the excellent "Waves on the Rock" (see above), offering a range of hearty Cretan dishes plus fresh local fish. April–Oct daily 10am–midnight.

South of Haniá

The obvious route inland from Haniá is on the road that heads south towards Omalós, the Samariá Gorge and the heart of the White Mountains. This is agricultural country, growing oranges above all, and paying little heed to tourism, though there's a wealth of history here. Coastal villages like **Dharátsos** and **Galatás** may seem unattractive as you drive along the main road, but in most cases there is a real village up in the hills behind, where traditional life survives to a remarkable degree. This whole area was the scene of the fiercest fighting in the **Battle of Crete**, and the bridgehead from which the Germans established their domination, while the inland villages also have a much longer history of resistance. In particular, many are associated with **Eleftherios Venizélos**, the revered Cretan statesman who, as prime minister of Greece for most of the period from 1910 to 1932, finally brought Crete into the modern Greek nation. You'll need your own transport to explore the remoter areas inland.

Galatás

Following the Alikianós road southwest out of Haniá, after 5km a turn-off on the right is signed to the hilltop village of **GALATÁS** (Γαλατάς) one of the major battlegrounds in the Battle of Crete when poorly armed villagers and a contingent of New Zealander soldiers stood between Haniá and the might of the German army. Heroically, and against all odds they held back the German army for almost a week with huge loss of life. The village today is a pleasant and fair-sized place, with a tiny, one-room **Battle of Crete museum** (usually daily 9am–2pm; free), sited on the main square dedicated to the events of 1941. It's basically a collection of rusty guns, helmets, photos and newspaper cuttings, fascinating nevetheless. Outside is a memorial to those who died here, including 145 New Zealand soldiers. If the museum is closed, enquiries at any of the nearby *kafenía* should soon produce the key (and possibly a guided tour).

The Ayiá Reservoir

On the edge of the village of Ayiá

The **Ayiá Reservoir** (Λίμνη Αγιά) is arguably the best **birdwatching** spot on Crete. This watery marshland is home to a rich variety of species, including crakes, avocet, marsh harrier, spotted flycatcher and squacco heron in season. The kingfishers are a particular delight and not at all put off their diving tricks by human visitors. Terrapins too, are residents here and when not squelching around in the marshy pools they can often be spotted sunning themselves on a raised mud bank. The best sightings should be in the early morning or a couple of hours before dusk, though there's plenty of birdlife year-round, at almost any time of day; binoculars are helpful. There are number of walkways around the lake, and a couple of upmarket and rather incongruous cafés on the banks. The *Limni* café is signed off the main road, but you are better off continuing into the village, where a swan-shaped sign to the lake and *Erasma* café will take you to the best viewing areas.

Alikianós

Shortly beyond Ayía there's a junction for Alikianós and, ultimately, Soúyia. Beside this turning there's a large **war memorial**, commemorating local members of the irregular forces that defended this area, known as "Prison Valley", in the Battle of Crete (you can't miss the prison; it's the big white building bristling with aerials). Cut off from any other Allied units – who believed that resistance here collapsed on the first day of the battle – the Greeks fought on even as everyone else was in full retreat. By doing so they prevented the Germans getting around the mountains to cut the road and guaranteed that the evacuation from Hóra Sfakíon could go ahead. In much earlier history, Alikianós was also the site of the wedding massacre that ended the Kandanoleon revolt (see box opposite).

ALIKIANÓS (Αλικιανός) itself has a couple of churches worth a look. Once in the village, follow the Koufós road (signed) for a short distance to reach the small

THE KANDANOLEON REVOLT

The village of Mesklá (see p.272) was the centre of one of the great legends of Cretan resistance, the **Kandanoleon revolt**. According to the story (which is certainly not historically accurate, though probably has some basis in fact), much of western Crete rose against the Venetians early in the sixteenth century. They elected as their leader one George Kandanoleon, who established a base in Mesklá and from here ran a rebel administration, controlling much of the west. In order to legitimize his authority, Kandanoleon arranged for his son to marry the daughter of a Venetian aristocrat, Francesco Molini. During the wedding celebrations Kandanoleon and several hundred of his supporters ate and drank themselves into a stupor – at which point, by pre-arranged signal, a Venetian army arrived and captured the Cretans as they slept. Their leaders were hanged at villages around the countryside, and the revolt was over.

You can visit the alleged scene of the massacre in Alikianós. Ask directions to the ruins of the **Da Molini castle**, in an orange grove over the road from the church of Áyios Yeóryios. To reach the castle, with your back to the church gate turn right to a new porticoed building on the left. Follow a narrow alley to the left of this for 50m: the castle ruins lie in an orange grove off to the right. Impressive walls still stand, festooned with weeds, and the overgrown entrance lintel carries the inscription *Omnia Mundi Fumus et Umbra* ("All in the World is Smoke and Shadow"), a sentiment to which the Venetians were particularly attached, and which ultimately turned out to be grimly accurate regarding their Cretan possessions.

fourteenth-century church of **Áyios Yeóryios**, close to the road on the right, whose frescoes were destroyed during World War II. Continue along the same road for 1km to **Áyios Ioánnis**, 50m down a signed track into orange groves on the right. A beautiful fourteenth-century building (recently restored) on the site of at least two previous churches dating back to the sixth century, the church employs parts of the previous basilica in the construction of its apse. Inside, surviving **frescoes** depict the Ascension as well as a number of saints.

Thériso and around

One of the the most attractive trips you can make around Haniá is the 14km drive up to the traditional country village of **THÉRISO** (Θέρισο), one of the cradles of Cretan independence and hometown of Eleftherios Venizélos's mother. Here in 1905 the Revolutionary Assembly was held (all baggy black shirts and drooping moustaches, as depicted in so many Cretan museums) that ousted Prince George and did much to precipitate union with Greece. The trip out to Venizélos's little house (signed off the main street; daily noon–1.30pm & 7–8.30pm; €1), with its plaque commemorating the famous son, is all but obligatory for Cretans, and the village is frequently crowded with busloads of schoolkids. There's also a one-room **resistance museum** (signed off the main street; irregular hours; €1) and numerous **tavernas**, some of them huge, mostly empty except at weekends and holidays.

Thériso Gorge

Once in Thériso, it's worth heading out to **Thériso Gorge**. In terms of spectacle this can't, of course, compare with Samariá and, in any case, the bed of the ravine is given over to the road. But it is exceedingly pretty in the lower reaches, gentle and winding with the stream crossed and recrossed on concrete bridges, and surprisingly craggy towards the top where the walls are cracked and pocked with caves.

Zoúrva

The drive south of Thériso is a spectacularly heady climb along a newly asphalted road into the foothills of the mountains and over what feels like an impressively lofty ridge. Alternatively, the route makes a wonderful long **hike**, occasionally traversed by rambling groups but quite possible on your own. Right at the top lies **ZOÚRVA** (Ζούρβα), a cluster of whitewashed houses with stupendous views over the surrounding valleys and a lovely taverna.

ARRIVAL AND DEPARTURE

By bus or on foot There are buses to Thériso from Haniá, and the walk between here and Mesklá via Zoúrva, where there's accommodation, takes less than 3hr. Given

THÉRISO AND AROUND

the vagaries of the timetable, though, the trip is liable to take all day if you do it by bus.

ACCOMMODATION AND EATING

THÉRISO

Andartis Main street, near the village centre ☎ 28210 78833. Good taverna with Cretan dishes including spit-roasted lamb, *singlino* (cured pork), *stifádho* and *sfakiano* (lamb casserole). Daily: July & Aug 11am–10.30pm; Sept–June 11am–6pm.

Madares Taverna-Rooms Main street, near the village centre ☎ 28210 89207. En-suite a/c rooms with fireplace (this is also a winter destination, when rooms cost more) and kitchenette. The speciality in the decent taverna below is tasty charcoal-grilled *arní* or lamb. Taverna and rooms daily April–Sept 11.30am–10pm; Oct–March Fri–Sun only. **€40**

ZOÚRVA

Amilia Entrance to village ☎ 28210 67470. Very appealing taverna with a terrace. Cretan specials include *katsíka yuvétsi* (goat in tomato) and charcoal-grilled lamb. April–Oct daily 9am–midnight.

Zourvas Traditional Hostel Centre of village ☎ 694 44 14 710. Spanking new place offering well-equipped studio apartments and twin-room maisonettes (sleeping four). Phone the proprietor (who lives in Haniá) to book accommodation at least a day before you arrive. Studios **€80**, maisonettes **€180**

Mesklá and around

From Zoúrva the way spirals slowly down to **MESKLÁ** (Μεσκλά), another beautiful village, set on a swift-flowing brook and surrounded by lush agricultural land and orange groves. There are several café-tavernas here.

Under the Venetians, Mesklá was a place of considerably more importance than it is now, as indicated by the tiny chapel of **Metamórphosis Sotírou** (Transfiguration of the Saviour), which lies at the bottom of the village. The chapel itself is unprepossessing, but inside are preserved the remains of fourteenth-century **frescoes**: many have been severely damaged by damp and mould, but parts remain clearly visible and are all the more remarkable for their ordinary surroundings. At the top of the village there's another chapel dedicated to the **Panayía** (next to a large modern church of the same name), which was constructed in the fourteenth century over a fifth-century basilica which had, in its turn, been raised over a Roman temple to Aphrodite.

Fournés

Beyond Mesklá, if on foot, you could tackle the steep climb to Lákki (see p.274). The road, however, heads back towards the coast, rejoining the Haniá–Omalós road at the substantial and prosperous village of **FOURNÉS** (Φουρνές), home to Crete's first botanical garden.

Fournés Botanical Park

4km south of Fournés on the Omalós road • May–Oct daily 8.30am–8.30pm; Nov–April Sat & Sun 9am–6pm; last admission 1hr before closing • €5 • ☎ 697 68 60 573, ⊕ botanical-park.com

After the four Marinakis brothers lost their olive groves in a disastrous fire in 2003, instead of replanting the olives they decided to create a botanical park on the land to enable Cretans to understand and learn to care for the natural environment. Making use of the valley's unique microclimate they imported plants and trees from all over the world, the fruit from which is used in the lovely **taverna-café**, along with ingredients grown on the park's organic farm. A complete route around the park takes about four hours, depending on how many information boards you choose to read. A shop sells honey and other farm produce.

ARRIVAL AND DEPARTURE

By bus or on foot There are buses to Mesklá from Haniá. Walking here from Thériso takes less than 3hr,

MESKLÁ AND AROUND

with glorious mountain views along the way. If you do it by bus it will take all day.

EATING

Taverna Halari At the top end of Mesklá beyond the modern church ☎ 28210 67480. A fine little taverna in a woodland setting with tables spread under the trees. The traditional cooking uses many home-grown ingredients, with specialities including *bouréki*, *stifádho* and – according to proprietor Manolis – the best *païdhákia* in the province. Daily 9am–midnight.

The Lefká Óri

The **Lefká Óri** (Λευκά Ορι), or White Mountains – make a formidable barrier to reaching the south of the province. Just a couple of metres short of the highest point of the Psilorítis range, these are in every other way more impressive mountains: barer, craggier and far less tamed. There is just one road into the heart of the area, climbing up to the cold, enclosed plateau of **Omalós** in the heart of the mountains. From here any further progress south must be done on foot – and the most spectacular, and spectacularly popular, is the descent through the great cleft of the **Samariá Gorge**. Famous as it is, this is just the largest of a series of ravines by which streams make their escape to the coast. Far less beaten tracks lead, for example, down the **Ímbros ravine** towards Hóra Sfakíon, or from **Ayía Iríni** to Soúyia. With more preparation you could also go climbing among the peaks or undertake an expedition right across the range. Bear in mind that this is a genuinely wild mountain zone – venture nowhere alone or without adequate equipment. The 1:25,000 *Anavasi* **maps** are highly recommended for anything other than the most obvious routes.

4

The Omalós plateau

From Haniá the road up to Omalós forks at Alikianós, passing Fournés and its botanical garden (see p.272) and then begins to climb in earnest to the Lefká Óri through a series of sweeping great loops with increasingly alarming drops. **LÁKKI**, the only village of any size you pass, has stupendous views from its leafy churchyard, to the rear of a small platía. A bracingly exposed place, it makes an ideal base for walking in the surrounding hills, especially in spring when wildflowers abound. Eighteen steeply ascending kilometres beyond here you eventually reach the the **Omalós plateau,** at more than 1000m high – a cold, flat expanse dotted with stunted vegetation, and with the enclosing ring of stone peaks clearly visible all around.

Omalós

OMALÓS (Ομαλός), at the heart of the Omalós plateau, is largely unaffected by the daily dawn procession in summer when up to fifty buses pass through, transporting walkers from all over the island to the Samariá Gorge entrance. Once the hordes have gone it settles back into the tranquil rustic settlement it remains for most of the year. Walk out into the plain in almost any direction and within five minutes you'll have left all traces of modern life behind, with only the jingling of the occasional goat's bell or the deliberate piling of stones to remind you of human presence. Few people live here year-round: in winter everything is deep in snow and deserted. In spring the land is marshy and waterlogged – almost becoming a lake if there's a sudden melt. Only in summer do most residents move here full-time, coming up from Lákki and other villages on the lower slopes to pasture sheep and goats or to cultivate, on a small scale, cereals and potatoes.

HIKING AROUND OMALÓS

The area around Omalós is excellent for **walking**. The paths into the hills surrounding the plateau (a branch of the E4 Pan-European footpath crosses the southern edge of the village) are strewn with wildflowers in season, birdlife is profuse year-round and temperatures even in high summer are refreshingly cool. Despite this, as so often in places like this in Crete, you'll usually find that most of the excellent, good-value accommodation is empty throughout the season.

If you are not planning to walk from Omalós to the Samariá Gorge (see opposite), you can take a spectacular surfaced road that cuts west through the mountains to link up with the Soúyia–Haniá road just north of Dimitrianá and Ayía Iríni. You can also walk **to Soúyia**, starting either from the top of the gorge or from Omalós and descending via the Ayía Iríni gorge (see p.316) or on a slightly tougher, higher route through Koustoyérako (p.316). These are alternate branches of the E4, so reasonably well signed – though take care not to miss the point where you turn off the road. Either route is a full day's walk and both are detailed on the excellent Anavasi 1:25,000 Lefká Óri (White Mountains) map (see p.40).

SCALING THE PEAKS

The **Kallergi Refuge** (see box opposite) acts as the base for climbing into the highest peaks, and the staff here are the best source of information on doing so. As well as the high-mountain treks from the hut, there are also walks to the west of the Samariá Gorge. Most impressively, you can tackle the climb to the peak of **Mount Gíngilos** (2080m), beginning from the top of the gorge. Its north face, the one everyone sees, is a near-vertical slope of solid rock; round the back though, you can reach the summit with only a little scrambling. It's hard work and you need confidence with heights, especially if it's windy, but no special mountaineering skills are necessary. A large yellow sign points the way from the back of the *Tourist Lodge* and the path should be easy enough to follow for the two and a half hours to the top. The final ascent is signalled with red paint – stick to the path as there are hidden hazards and even the official route needs hands as well as feet. The rewards are an all-round panorama from the summit and, with luck, the chance to spot some of the rarer animal life that the crowds have driven from the gorge itself.

THE KALLERGI REFUGE

If you are staying on the Omalós plateau for a couple of days a hike to the wonderful **Kallergi Refuge** (April–Oct daily; Nov–March Sat & Sun; ☎ 28210 33199 or ☎ 693 66 57 954, winter ☎ 28210 44647, ⓦ eoshanion.gr; €12) is a bracing introduction to the high mountains. Perched high over the eastern edge of the Samariá Gorge at 1680m, it's a fairly easy (if unrelenting) ascent for 5km from the Omalós plain and once you're there makes an excellent base for many other mountain treks.

To get to the hut from Omalós, follow the road towards the gorge entrance for 3km (about 20–30min), then turn left onto the dirt track signed to the hut, a further hour's climb (with a 4WD vehicle you can also drive this, along – in the early stages – a badly rutted dirt road); alternatively, from the top of the Samariá Gorge a signed path leads up in about 90min along the same route. From Kallergi you can peer down into the gorge, looking exceptionally impressive from the isolation of the bare stone peaks up here, a slash of rich green in an otherwise remorseless landscape of grey and brown. On clearer days both the Libyan and Aegean seas can also be seen from the hut, while the nights are spectacular, with the whole dome of the starry heavens arranged above you.

There's usually no problem finding a bed at the refuge (although it's best to ring ahead) and the hut is comfortably equipped with wood-burning stoves and space for fifty in cosy two- and four-bed dorms. There's also an excellent **taverna**. The refuge is supervised by the helpful Austrian guardian and mountaineer, Josef Schemberger, who can advise on **hikes** from Kallergi including the 5hr circular waymarked route to **Melindaoú** (2133m) via Mount Psarí (1817m), or the 12hr hike to Anópoli via **Mount Páhnes** (at 2453m, just 3m short of Psilorítis for the title of loftiest in Crete: Haniot mountaineers regularly add stones to the cairn on the peak in an attempt to catch up) with an overnight stop at a refuge en route. Both follow the E4 much of the way.

4

The Samariá Gorge

The one trip that every visitor to Crete – even those eminently unsuited to it – feels compelled to make is the hike down the **Samariá Gorge** (Φαράγγι Σαμαριάς) which, at 16km, is claimed to be the **longest in Europe**. Protected as a National Park since 1962, this natural wonder was formed by a river flowing between Mount Volakiás to the west and the towering bulk of the heart of the Lefká Óri to the east. In summer the violent winter torrent reduces to a meek trickle and this is when the multitudes descend. If you're expecting a wilderness experience, think again; Friday and Saturday are the days attracting fewest visitors. Bear in mind that this is not a gentle stroll to be lightly undertaken; especially in spring when the river is roaring, or on a hot midsummer day, it can be a thoroughly gruelling test of fitness and stamina. The mules and helicopter standing by to rescue the injured are not mere show: anyone who regularly leads tours through the gorge has a stack of horror stories to regale you with – broken legs and heart attacks feature most frequently. To undertake the walk you need to be reasonably fit and/or used to lengthy walks, and you should have comfortable, sturdy shoes that will stand up to hot, sharp rocks.

The gorge hike itself is some **18km long** (the final 2km to reach the sea from the mouth of the gorge) and the **walk** down takes between four and seven hours, depending on your level of fitness, and how often you stop to admire the scenery, bathe your feet and take refreshment. Be wary of the kilometre markers – these mark only distances within the park, not the full extent of the walk.

The Samariá Gorge hike

The gorge begins, with startling suddenness, on the far side of the plateau. After the dull tranquillity of the plain you are faced with this great cleft opening beneath your feet and, across it – close enough to bounce stones off, it seems – the gaunt limestone face of Mount Gíngilos. The descent starts on the **Xilóskalon** ("wooden stairway"), a stepped path cut from the rock and augmented by log stairs and wooden handrails, which zigzags rapidly down to the base of the gorge, plunging 350m in the first 2km or

FLORA AND FAUNA IN THE SAMARIÁ GORGE

Gorge **wildlife** means most famously the *kri-kri* (variously the *agrimi*, *Capra aegagrus*, the Cretan wild goat or ibex), for whose protection the park was primarily created. You are unlikely to see one of these large, nimble animals with their long backswept horns, though you may well see ordinary mountain goats defying death on the cliff faces. In addition, almost four hundred varieties of **birds** are claimed to have been seen here, including owls, eagles, falcons and vultures; birdwatchers after a coup should look out for the endangered lammergeier (or bearded vulture). On the ground lizards abound, there's also the odd snake and you may just spot a beech marten, spiny mouse or weasel.

The multifarious **trees** – Cretan maple, pine and cypress – provide the backdrop to an often dazzling array of **wildflowers**; the purple *Tulipa saxatilis* and rock plants such as aubretias, saxifrages and anemones stand out, and there are wild irises and orchids too. **Herbs** are also in abundance; besides the aromatic thyme and rosemary, common sage and oregano, there are half a dozen species that exist exclusively here. Also to be found – and usually growing in the most inaccessible places – is **Cretan dittany**, a celebrated medicinal herb referred to by Aristotle and Hippocrates and taken by women in ancient times as a method of abortion.

Two **books** on the gorge can prove useful and are portable enough to take along. *The Samariá Gorge Yesterday and Today* (Toubis, Athens) documents the history of the gorge and includes an illustrated guide to its flora and fauna, while *The Gorge of Samariá and its Plants* by Albertis Atonis (Albertis, Iráklio) provides a step-by-step description of the flora. Both are widely available from bookshops on the island.

so of the walk. Near the bottom the chapel of Áyios Nikólaos stands on a little terrace of coniferous trees where there are benches from which to enjoy the view, and fresh water. Beyond, the path begins gradually to level out, following the stream bed amid softer vegetation which reflects the milder climate down here. In late spring it's magnificent, but at any time of year there should be wildflowers and rare plants (no picking allowed), including the endangered large white peony, *Paeonia clusii*. The stream itself is less reliable: there are places where you can be sure of icy fresh water and pools to bathe sore feet all year round (particularly in the middle sections), but what starts in spring as a fierce, even dangerous torrent has dwindled by autumn to a trickle between hot, dry boulders, disappearing beneath the surface for long stretches.

The abandoned village of **Samariá** lies a little under midway through the walk, shortly before the 7km marker. One of the buildings here has been converted to house the wardens' office, another has been pressed into (inadequate) service as a public toilet, but for the most part the remains of the village are quietly crumbling away. Its inhabitants, until they were relocated to make way for the park in 1962, were predominantly members of the Viglis family, who claimed direct descent from one of the twelve aristocratic clans implanted from Byzantium. Certainly this settlement, as isolated as any in Crete and cut off by floodwater for much of the year, is a very ancient one – the church of **Óssia María**, from which both gorge and village take their name, was founded in the early fourteenth century.

After Samariá the path is more level, the walls of the gorge begin to close in and the path is often forced to cross from one side of the stream to the other, on **stepping stones** which at times may be submerged and slippery. Beside you, the contorted striations of the cliffs are increasingly spectacular, but the highlight comes shortly after the Christós resting point with the **Sidherespórtes** (Iron Gates) where two rock walls rise sheer to within a whisker of a thousand feet: standing at the bottom, one can almost touch both at once. For this short stretch, there's a wooden walkway raised above the stream, whose swirling waters fill the whole of the narrow passage. Almost as suddenly as you entered this mighty crack in the mountain you leave it again, the valley broadens, its sides fall away, and you're in a parched wilderness of rubble deposited here by the spring thaw.

Before long – 8km beyond Samariá – you reach the fringes of **Ayía Rouméli,** where there's a gate by which you leave the park and a couple of stalls selling cool drinks at crippling prices. Frustratingly, however, this is not the end of the walk: old Ayía Rouméli has been all but deserted in favour of the new beachside community, a further excruciatingly hot, dull twenty minutes away. The arrival of a **shuttle bus service** (€1.50) means that you can now avoid this final rather tedious stretch; the bus drops you in the coastal settlement.

Ayía Rouméli

Arriving finally by shuttle bus or on foot in **AYÍA ROUMÉLI (Αγία Ρουμέλη)** proper, you face the choice between plunging into the sea or diving into a taverna for an iced drink. Once your senses adjust, you'll find that the village isn't all that appealing – but that drink, and the first plunge in the sea, are likely to live in the memory as the most refreshing ever. Once you've drunk and eaten your fill (a couple of the tavernas have showers which they'll let you use if you eat there), lain on the beach for a while and rested, Ayía Rouméli's attractions soon begin to pall. It's a pretty unattractive example of over-rapid development, with a rash of concrete tavernas and rooms spreading over a large shingly beach, though at night it's very peaceful. The village is attempting to be environmentally conscious: the pile of huge concrete tank traps behind the beach shields a solar energy plant; at night, or other times when this system can't cope, a diesel generator cuts in.

Although there was an ancient settlement here – **Tarra**, inhabited probably from the fifth century BC through to the fifth AD – and more or less constant later habitation, very little remains to be seen. Tarra straddled the stream where it ran into the sea, just to the east of the present village – the only obvious remains are the foundations of an early Christian basilica by the present **church of Panayía**, around which you may also spot a few tiny fragments of mosaic. This, supposedly, was the site of a much earlier temple of Apollo.

Ascending the gorge

Starting from the bottom, the hike **up the gorge** to **Omalós** is not as hard as some imagine, though it will take rather longer – six to seven hours at a reasonable, steady pace. Few people do it all the way, which means that at the top you may well find the gorge almost empty; on the way up, however, you'll have had to pass the hordes charging down. You could also walk a short way up and come back – an outing offered as a day-trip known as "Samariá the Lazy Way". This will show you the Iron Gates, the most spectacular individual section, but it means a lot of walking in the dullest parts down by the coast (unless you make use of the shuttle bus) and none of the almost alpine scenes nearer the top.

ARRIVAL AND DEPARTURE

THE LEFKÁ ÓRI

THE SAMARIÁ GORGE

Trips and tours The vast majority of people who walk through the gorge do so as part of a day-trip: a very early bus to the top, walk down by early afternoon, boat from Ayía Rouméli to Hóra Sfakíon and bus from there back home. Most go with one of the guided tours offered by every travel agent on the island – certainly if you're staying in a hotel anywhere in the east of Crete this is much the simplest method, and probably the only way of doing it in a single day. Most tours will include all bus and ferry connections, but not food or the park entrance fee. They can be very good value adding only €5–10 to the cost of doing it yourself (from Haniá, the cost of bus, ferry and entry tickets adds up to about €30). If you're planning to stay on the south coast, the tour bus can save you the effort of carrying your bags; simply stow them underneath and retrieve them in Hóra Sfakíon. Do let them know your plan, though, both to guard against an unexpected switch of bus and to prevent search parties being sent out.

By bus From Haniá, or marginally less straightforwardly from Iráklio, Réthymno, Soúyia or Paleohóra, it's also easy to take the public bus, which runs a daily service during the periods when the gorge is open and avoids the need to walk in a large group.

From Haniá There are three departures a day (6.15am, 7.45am & 8.45am), arriving at the top about 75min later. You'll normally be sold a return ticket, including the return leg from Hóra Sfakíon (which needn't necessarily be used the same day), so if you don't want this you'll have to make your intentions very clear; the bus station is very busy when the first buses leave. There's a lot to be said for taking the earliest bus: more of the walk can be completed while it's still relatively cool, there's no need to force your pace, and if you're planning to stop over anywhere at the bottom you've more chance of being among the first to arrive. On the other hand, everyone does this – there's often a procession of as many as four full buses leaving Haniá before dawn, there are queues and confusion when you arrive, and you're unlikely to escape from crowds the whole way down. It may be hotter, but it's also quieter if you set out later.

From other destinations The first buses of the day from Iráklio (5.30am) and Réthymno (7am) travel to Haniá bus station where you will board another bus for the journey to Omalós. There are also services from Paleohóra (6.15am) and Soúyia (7am) and these meet in Ayía Iríni from where one continues to the gorge and the other direct to Haniá, so you may have to change.

By ferry Having reached the south coast you can continue to walk in either direction, but it's a great deal easier to get around by boat. From the bottom of the gorge, boats run from Ayía Rouméli to Hóra Sfakíon, calling at Loutró, and also head west to Soúyia and Paleohóra (see p.307). Buses from Hóra Sfakíon back to Haniá currently leave at 7am, 11am and 6.30pm. It's also possible to get back to Haniá via Soúyia, with a bus currently running at 6pm. There should always be enough capacity on the boats, and the buses wait for the boats to arrive. The kiosk selling boat tickets is marked down by the beach. If you're catching the bus back to Haniá or elsewhere from Hóra Sfakíon, you could get a ticket for the last connecting boat when you emerge from the gorge, and spend the afternoon on the beach. If you plan to stay elsewhere on this coast, in July & Aug take the first boat available for the best chance of finding a room at your destination.

Destinations Loutró/Hóra Sfakíon (April–June, Sept & Oct daily 5.30pm; July & Aug daily 9am, 3.45pm & 6pm; Nov–March 3 weekly; 40min/1hr); Soúyia/Paleohóra (April–Oct daily 5.30pm; 45min/1hr 20min).

Independent travel If you want to see the gorge using your own transport, or while staying in Omalós, it's possible to walk down (most of the hotels will take you to the gorge entrance for free if you're a guest), take the boat to Soúyia, and then get a taxi back up to Omalós or the gorge parking area from there – Soúyia taxis generally charge about €60 for this.

INFORMATION

THE SAMARIÁ GORGE

Opening months Conditions permitting, the gorge is open from May to October between 7am and sunset. In the first few weeks after opening and the last couple before closure, entry will depend on weather conditions, and the gorge is also closed in extremely hot weather, for safety reasons. You should ring ahead to save a wasted journey. Outside the official season, and at the discretion of the wardens, you may be allowed through if the weather is good, but there will be very little transport. At any time, if you enter after 3pm you're only allowed into the first couple of kilometres from each end and wardens patrol to enforce this.

Admission €5 (under-15s free).

Gorge office Check conditions by calling ☎ 28210 67179 or ☎ 28210 92287.

Rules and regulations There are a whole series of National Park rules (posted at the entrance), of which the most important are: no camping, no fires (or smoking outside the designated areas), no alcohol, no hunting and no interfering with the wildlife or collecting plants. Wardens patrol to ensure these rules are obeyed, that no one wanders too far from the main path (only allowed with a permit obtained in advance from the Haniá Forest Service), and that no stragglers are overtaken by nightfall. At the entrance, you'll be given a date-stamped ticket in return for your entrance fee, which you should hand in at the gate when you leave; this, too, is partly to check that nobody is lost inside, and partly to make sure no one tries camping.

Supplies Carry the minimum possible. A water bottle is essential (there are springs at regular intervals and ice-cold water in the stream, but for long periods you'll find neither – especially over the last, hottest hour) and something to munch on the way definitely worthwhile, as is some means of carrying clothes you discard en route (7am at the top feels close to freezing; 1pm at the bottom may hover around 38°C/100°F). If you plan to stay a day or two at the bottom you should leave your luggage elsewhere, taking only what's essential.

Facilities There's a café near the gorge entrance and an official tourist lodge (with substantial meals and a fine terrace view) on the heights above this, plus stalls for hot drinks, bottled water and snacks, while Ayía Rouméli is more than equipped to feed everyone arriving at the bottom; there are toilets at regular intervals along the walk.

ACCOMMODATION AND EATING

LÁKKI

★ **Taverna-Rooms Nikolas** Main square ☎ 28210 67232. The village taverna serves magnificent food, including great breakfasts, catering for hearty appetites generated by mountain air and whetted with the prospect of strenuous activity. The en-suite a/c rooms are less impressive than the food, but they are clean, and come with wonderful views. Taverna daily 7am–11pm. **€30**

OMALÓS

A couple of newish hotels look very out of place alongside the chapel and few crude stone houses of the original settlement. All three hotels listed below will usually drive you the 5km to the top of the gorge the following morning if you're staying with them, but make sure to confirm this on arrival. Each has its own bar and taverna serving up hearty mountain food, though not all may be open at quiet times. They also have heating, which is more often in demand at this altitude than a/c.

Hotel Exari Omalós village ☎ 28210 67180, ⓦ exari.gr. The biggest and most obvious of the new hotels – with comfortable, modern en-suite balcony rooms with TV. Free wi-fi in bar. Taverna daily 6am–midnight. €30

Hotel Gigilos Omalós village ☎ 28210 67181. Modern en-suite a/c rooms, some with balcony view, above a taverna. Taverna daily 6am–11.30pm. €30

Hotel Neos Omalos Omalós village ☎ 28210 67269, ⓦ neos-omalos.gr. Perhaps the best of the bunch, with the busiest taverna, this has nice en-suite balcony rooms with bath, central heating and satellite TV. Free wi-fi. The taverna does tasty *souvláki*. Closed Nov–March. Taverna daily 7am–10pm. €35

Taverna Xyloskalo Gorge entrance ☎ 28210 52122, ⓦ omalos.com. Perched above the gorge entrance, with magnificent mountain views from its terrace, this is a good place to take breakfast or lunch before heading down the gorge. They also have comfortable rooms with kitchenette in a modern stone building nearby. Free wi-fi. Closed Nov–April. Taverna daily 9.30am–8pm. €50

THE SAMARIÁ GORGE

The nearest bed you can get to the entrance is in Omalós (see above) or in the excellent *Kallergi Refuge* (see p.275). Alternatively you could simply sleep out: there are usually quite a few people trying to find a flat space for their sleeping bags around the entrance. This has few real advantages however; you'd have to be up very early to steal a march on the first arrivals from Haniá (for much of the year this would mean setting off before daylight) and from Omalós you face an extra 5km walk to reach the top of the trail (or the early buses will stop and pick you up on their way through). Nonetheless, it does make quite a change to stay up here and freeze for a night, and of course it gives you the opportunity to explore more than just the gorge. Staying on the south coast for a night or more after your exertions makes more sense: in addition to Ayía Rouméli (see below), there are rooms at Loutró (p.283) and Hóra Sfakíon (p.290) or westwards in Soúyia (p.317) and Paleohóra (p.310).

AYÍA ROUMÉLI

Just east of the village (near the solar plant) is a clump of trees where a few people are usually camped; you will also find people sleeping out in the caves on the beach nearby. The three options below, all under the same management, are among the more comfortable places.

Hotel Agia Roumeli West end of seafront ☎ 28250 91432, ⓦ agiaroumelihotel.com. Slightly more upmarket than other places in town, but offering very similar facilities. Free wi-fi. €50

Hotel Kalypso West end of seafront ☎ 28250 91231, ⓦ agiaroumeli.gr. Clean and tidy a/c balcony rooms with fridge and sea view, above a taverna with a nice terrace. Free wi-fi. Taverna daily 8am–11pm. €35

Taverna Tarra West end of seafront ☎ 28250 91231, ⓦ agiaroumeli.gr. Functional and clean a/c en-suite rooms with fridge above a taverna. Free wi-fi. Taverna daily 8am–11pm. €30

The Sfakiá coast

A series of paths thread their way along the **Sfakiá coast**, linking Ayía Rouméli in the west with Hóra Sfakíon in the east. **Loutró**, accessible only on foot or by boat, lies close to the heart of this network. Anyone who spends any time at all here is eventually taken with the urge to explore – even if it's just climbing up to the ruins on the headland. With not much more effort you can walk or get a boat to a nearby beach, but there are also plenty of long, tough treks available. Most real traffic nowadays goes by boat, of course, and, with the exception of Loutró itself, virtually every local hamlet can be reached on some kind of driveable track. But the old paths and trails remain, to give a variety of marvellous **hikes**, even the easiest of which can be demanding in the heat of high summer. You'll need, at the very least, decent boots or shoes to cope with rough, rocky terrain and a water bottle, which you should fill at every opportunity. You should also have a companion, since some of these paths are pretty isolated, and outside help cannot be relied upon.

Loutró and around

Of all the south coast villages, **LOUTRÓ** (Λουτρό) perhaps best sums up what this coast ought to be all about. It's a soporific place, where there's nothing to do but eat, drink and laze – and where you fast lose any desire to do anything else. The big

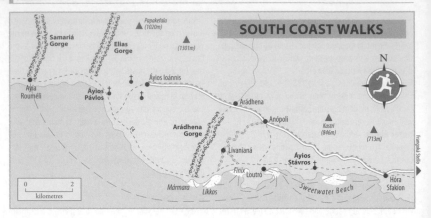

excitements of the day are the occasional arrivals and departures of the ferries. Little happens all summer long to interrupt this easy-going idyll, but if you're here for the great **feast of the Panayía** on August 15 the small church is the place to head for. From early dawn, the formidable local priest conducts the service which lasts until after midday. The small churchyard then fills up with all those who had intended to come earlier – and each of whom receives a disapproving glare from the *papás* – as biblical quantities of *arní* (roast lamb), *psomí* and *krasí* are doled out and everyone enjoys a great feast.

The waterfront

The short **waterfront** arching around a beautiful little bay consists of a row of perhaps a dozen tavernas and cafés and a similar number of rooms places and small hotels; the mountains rise immediately behind the waterfront. There's no road in – everyone here has either come on the boat or walked, which helps to keep things very low-key, prices reasonable, big groups rare and the people genuinely friendly. Although the transparent blue water is always inviting, perhaps Loutró's main drawback is its lack of a real **beach**. There's a stretch of pebbles in front of the tavernas and a much smaller, more private beach immediately beyond the last of the buildings. But the sheltered bay is otherwise ideal for **swimming**, clear and warm, and people bask nude on the rocks around the point, far enough out to avoid offence. Other excellent beaches are within walking distance, with small boats or rented canoes ferrying visitors to the best, at **Sweetwater** to the east (see below), and **Mármara** to the west (see p.282).

Sweetwater Beach

East of Loutró, **Sweetwater Beach (Γλυκά Νερά)** lies in the middle of a barren coastline, approximately halfway to Hóra Sfakíon. From the sea, as you pass on one of the coastal boats, it appears as a long, extremely narrow slice of grey between sheer ochre cliffs and a dark, deep sea. Closer up, the beach seems much larger, but there's still a frightening sense of being isolated between unscaleable mountains and an endless stretch of water.

The beach takes its name from the small springs that bubble up beneath the pebbles to provide fresh, cool drinking water. You can dig a hole almost anywhere to find water, but take care not to pollute the groundwater with soap. Daily boat services bring in quite a few people, but so far these have not spoilt the place – the beach is easily big enough to absorb everyone – and the nudist campers who once had Sweetwater practically to themselves remain, for once doing a good job of keeping

WALKING THE COASTAL PATH FROM LOUTRÓ

The **coastal path** – now part of the E4 Pan-European Footpath – is the most obvious hike from Loutró, the most frequently used by tourists and, in terms of not getting lost, the simplest to follow. There's not a great deal to see en route, however, nor is it an easy walk – the path is often frighteningly narrow and uneven as it clings to the cliff face, and in summer it is very, very hot, offering no shelter at all from the sun. In Loutró the path runs inland, behind most of the houses; to find it, climb up until you see the signs.

LOUTRÓ TO HÓRA SFAKÍON

Heading east from **Loutró to Hóra Sfakíon** is barely a problem: it's the most heavily travelled part, the whole walk takes less than two hours (8km), and there's a rest stop at Sweetwater Beach (see opposite) halfway. Loutró to Sweetwater is straightforward and fairly well beaten: beyond here the path clambers over a massive rockfall and then follows the cliffs until it eventually emerges on the Hóra Sfakíon–Anópoli road about thirty minutes' walk above Hóra. This is easy to find from the other direction too, the path (to the left) leaving the road at the first hairpin bend.

LOUTRÓ TO AYÍA ROUMÉLI

Heading west, **Loutró to Ayía Rouméli** is an altogether tougher proposition. You can expect to be walking for at least four hours solid, a real sweat in high summer, and after the tavernas at Líkkos the only chance of refreshment is at Áyios Pávlos (see below). After Mármara (see p.282) you climb again to track along the exposed cliff face for around an hour before reaching the first sign of civilization, a solitary cottage and a few trees. In about another hour, you'll arrive at the eleventh-century cruciform chapel of **Áyios Pávlos**, yet another site where St Paul is supposed to have landed. Here he allegedly christened locals in a spring close to the church (now only a trickle). The chapel itself is ancient and rather beautiful, set on a ledge above the water, and surrounded by dunes; inside are fresco fragments dated to the thirteenth century. You could cool off in the sea here before setting out on the final hour to Ayía Rouméli, and there is a simple **taverna**, *Saint Paul* (June–Sept only), which also rents out tents for nearby camping.

Returning from Ayía Rouméli this path is well marked, heading east out of the village. Ten to fifteen minutes after Áyios Pávlos it splits, heading left to climb inland to Áyios Ioánnis and Anópoli, right or to continue along the coast back to Mármara.

4

things pristine: signs warn against leaving rubbish, and people make an effort to pick up any junk that is left behind.

The long-term residents (including local goats) tend to monopolize the only shade, in the **caves** at the back of the beach, but you can always escape the sun at the small **bar-taverna**, which also rents out sun umbrellas.

Fínix

Immediately west of Loutró, in the beautiful little bay on the other side of the promontory, stood **ancient Fínikas (Φοίνικας)**, now known as **Fínix** or Phoenix. This was a major town during the Roman and Byzantine periods, and a significant port long after that: it was the harbour at Fínix, a more comfortable place to wait out the winter storms than Kalí Liménes, which St Paul's ship was hoping to reach when it was swept away. A local story has the saint actually landing here and being beaten up by the locals he tried to convert. There is very little to be seen and it's hard to believe there could ever have been a population of any size here. Up on the headland, though, there's certainly evidence of later occupation, principally in the form of the **Venetian fortification** on the point. Nearby are traces of a Byzantine basilica and other scattered remains.

Fínix manages to remain exceptionally languid, a tranquil hideaway with its own frescoed chapel, while the bay itself, with its rocky beach, has a fashionable **taverna** and **rooms** place (see p.283).

Líkkos

West of Fínix, the path continues over cliffs for about half an hour to another, much longer bay, **LÍKKOS** (Λύκος), with a couple of ultra-cheap **taverna-rooms** places – there's plenty of fresh water too, which there may not be in Loutró.

Unfortunately Líkkos is not a very attractive **beach**, with rocks and pebbles, and is awkward to swim from unless you wear shoes. Behind, you can look up and see the village of Livaniáná, perched on the eastern flank of the Arádhena Gorge (see p.286); there's a rough new dirt road down from there.

Mármara Beach

The Arádhena Gorge emerges at the sea in the next bay west of Líkkos, **MÁRMARA BEACH** (Μάρμαρα), which takes its name from marble deposits visible near the jetty where you land. Just fifteen minutes' walk or so beyond Líkkos, this is a fairly small cove, with a sandy beach surrounded by interesting rock formations full of caves and slabs to dive from or sunbathe on. What with boats from Loutró and people walking down the Arádhena Gorge which hits the coast here, some days in summer can bring more people than can comfortably be accommodated. Even when busy it's charming, though, with a simple **taverna-rooms place** to give the place focus, as well as providing sun umbrellas, loungers and tempting cool drinks. The owner is a good source of information on the many **walking** possibilities in this area: from Mármara you could walk up the Arádhena Gorge to Livaniáná (see p.286), about a three-hour hike, or you could take the coastal route to Áyios Pávlos (see p.281) – about 2hr 30min – and Ayía Rouméli (1hr further).

ARRIVAL AND DEPARTURE

LOUTRÓ

LOUTRÓ

By ferry and taxiboat The ferry (€7 return) doesn't stay long in Loutró, so be ready to disembark as it arrives: tickets are sold from a kiosk behind the dock at the extreme western end of the seafront, which opens only for a few minutes before each departure. A taxi-boat service from Hóra Sfakíon costs around €35 and can be arranged by any of the seafront tavernas in either village.

SWEETWATER BEACH

By boat Boats from Loutró and Hóra Sfakíon arrive once in the morning and again at 5pm. A taxi-boat (one way) from Loutró costs around €15. Kayaking to the beach is also possible but you'll need sun protection and a hat in summer.
On foot It's a very hot and shadeless 45min walk from Loutró, an hour from Hóra Sfakíon (p.288) – boats back to each leave at 5pm in summer (see above). In Loutró the path runs behind the houses – climb the hill to find it.

FÍNIX

On foot To walk to Fínix by the most direct route, join the path – now part of the E4 – that runs behind Loutró, up behind the beachside kiosk and the church. This will lead you straight up, past the castle and directly over the headland, in around fifteen minutes; if you're continuing beyond Fínix, you don't have to go down to the water as a path continues straight past the back of the bay, but it's only marginally shorter. It's also possible to get there by walking out past the last house in Loutró and simply following the rocky coast around. This is a much longer and tougher walk, but it does pass plenty of good rocks to swim from, and extensive remains of old buildings which you can imagine are, and may indeed be, ancient Fínikas.

By boat Boats to Mármara occasionally call in at Fínix, bringing supplies, and the *Old Phoenix* (see opposite) will pick you up from Loutró, if you're staying there. A taxi-boat (one way) will cost about €10 (ask at tavernas in Loutró).
By car It's possible to drive here, on a hair-raising barrierless dirt road that descends from Livaniáná, though this is only advisable in a 4WD.

MÁRMARA BEACH

By boat A boat back to Loutró leaves at 5pm in summer. The proprietor of *Chrisostomos* rooms will collect guests from Loutró. A taxi-boat (one way) to or from Loutró costs around €15.

INFORMATION AND ACTIVITIES

LOUTRÓ
Boat trips Small boats depart from the jetty daily at 11am (after the arrival of the ferry) to Sweetwater and Mármara beaches, returning at 5pm.

Canoes You can rent canoes for expeditions to the nearby coves and beaches, or arrange a taxi-boat to any nearby beach or to Hóra Sfakíon (about €35); ask at *Ilios* or *Blue House* tavernas.

LOUTRÓ AND AROUND

4

Internet Free wi-fi is available along the whole seafront, and expensive internet access is available at the *Daskalogiannis Hotel*.

Money There's no ATM, so you should bring sufficient cash to see you through your stay. At a pinch your hotel or rooms place may give you cash on a credit card or change money.

ACCOMMODATION

Rooms in Loutró seem uniformly basic and comfortable, though you should book ahead or arrive early – an increasing number are **pre-booked**. Try for one with a balcony (the *Porto Loutro* and *Blue House* offer top-floor rooms with huge roof terraces); the quietest places are generally the furthest round to the east, but nowhere is exactly loud or stays open late. You'll find links to much of the local accommodation at ⓦ loutro.net/accommodation.

LOUTRÓ

★ **Blue House** ⓣ 28250 91127, ⓔ bluehouseloutro @gmail.com. One of the original places here, and still one of the friendliest and best. Good-value, a/c, en-suite sea-view rooms with fridge, plus superior rooms in a wonderful (more expensive) top-floor extension. Free wi-fi and a good restaurant. **€30**

★ **Nikolas** Eastern end of the seafront ⓣ 28250 91352. Virtually the last building in Loutró and probably the quietest you'll find; friendly proprietors rent simple but comfortable a/c rooms at the back and some lovely top-floor a/c balcony rooms with fridge above the water. Free wi-fi. **€38**

Notos In the middle of the village above the beach ⓣ 28250 91501. Very simple sea-view en-suite rooms with fridges and fans. Free wi-fi. **€35**

Hotel Porto Loutro In the middle of the village above the beach ⓣ 28250 91433, ⓦ hotelportoloutro.com. Run by Anglo-Greek proprietors, this hotel – one of the few with any pretensions at all – is a lovely place whose white cubes fit in surprisingly well with the surroundings; as the a/c rooms are pretty accurate reproductions of a simple Greek room you may question whether it's worth paying the extra. Includes breakfast. Free wi-fi in bar. They have more rooms higher up, above the ferry dock. **€65**

Protopapas Inland above the eastern end of the seafront ⓣ 28250 91400 ⓔ protopapas-loutro @hotmail.com. Simple, good-sized rooms with a/c and fridge, some triples and quads; it's not right on the water, which keeps the prices down, and often has vacancies when others are full. Partial sea views from some rooms. Free wi-fi. **€40**

Villa Niki Inland from the centre of the seafront ⓣ 28250 91529, ⓦ loutro-accommodation.com.

En-suite a/c studios and fully equipped apartments with an attractive patio garden; the pricier upper floors have great views. Also an attractive villa sleeping six. Studios and apartments **€45**, large apartment **€70**, villa **€125**

FÍNIX

★ **Old Phoenix** ⓣ 28250 91257, ⓦ old-phoenix.com. This charming hotel is the epitome of a peaceful haven. En-suite rooms come with a/c and fridge; the very good taverna below is open for breakfast. They also rent sun umbrellas and loungers as well as canoes. Free wi-fi. Taverna daily 9am–10.30pm. **€45**

Rooms Manousoudakis ⓣ 28250 91482. A basic place to stay with simple but clean en-suite rooms with fans and fridge. Free wi-fi. **€30**

LÍKKOS

Akrogiali ⓣ 28250 91446. Refurbished a/c balcony rooms with fridge, above a decent taverna. They can pick you up from Loutró by boat. Closed Nov–March. **€35**

★ **Small Paradise** ⓣ 28250 91125. The first place you see, run by a friendly Irish-Cretan couple, this offers simple en-suite balcony rooms above a taverna. They can pick you up from Loutró by boat. Closed Nov–March. **€25**

MÁRMARA BEACH

Chrisostomos ⓣ 28250 91387 or ⓣ 694 22 01 456. Simple en-suite cabins lit with oil lamps and candles (there's no electricity here). You'll probably need insect repellent. Call ahead (on the mobile) and the owner will collect you in his boat from Loutró if you intend to stay. The owner also operates a taverna. Closed Nov–March. Taverna Oct–April daily 9am–10pm. **€25**

EATING AND DRINKING

Because most of its visitors come from northern Europe, Loutró's tavernas tend to be busy earlier on and start to close by 9.30pm. Many places have a better than usual **vegetarian** selection.

LOUTRÓ

Café Bistro Almost the westernmost building in Loutró, beneath Sifis hotel ⓣ 28250 91501. There are several cafés at the west end of Loutró, serving breakfast, juices and coffee, and beers and cocktails in the evening.

This, although not the cheapest, is probably the pick of them. April–Oct daily 7am–midnight.

★ **Blue House** Central seafront. Probably the best restaurant in Loutró, serving an array of Cretan specialities plus fresh fish and plenty of vegetarian options; owner brothers Vangelis and Yiorgos are among the village's friendliest characters. April–Oct daily 8am–10.30pm.

Ilios Eastern end of the seafront. Good fresh fish caught from their own boat as well as a range of taverna standards served on a waterfront terrace. It's also a good breakfast stop with overhead fans keeping temperatures down. Daily 7.30am–11.30pm.

★ **Notos** Central seafront. Excellent *mezédhes* including plenty of vegetarian possibilities (try their tasty *fáva* or *saganáki*) served on an attractive small terrace. April–Oct daily 7am–11pm.

Stratis Inland from the centre of the seafront ☎ 28250 91348. Superb charcoal-grilled meats and traditional specialities including snails and good *kalitsoúnia* (pies) served on a terrace. April–Oct daily 7am–10pm.

LÍKKOS

★ **Small Paradise** ☎ 28250 91125. Good traditional Cretan food (Cretan *mizíthra* sheep's cheese is a speciality) as well as breakfast, in this taverna with rooms. April–Oct daily 9am–10.30pm.

Anópoli and around

ANÓPOLI (**Ανώπολη**), high above Loutró, is a quiet country village, not much used to visitors, dominating a small upland plain with a few rare vestiges of forest. If you're hiking for its own sake, or for that matter if you want to take the easiest route from Ayía Rouméli to Hóra Sfakíon without necessarily calling at Loutró, then the inland trails centring on Anópoli have a great deal to be said for them: it also makes a good base for an exploration of the **Arádhena Gorge** and for walks into the heart of the White Mountains. The village itself is a wonderful location to sample the simple delights of rural Crete, and except at the busiest local holiday periods you should have no problem finding somewhere to stay, away from the hustle of the coast.

Arádhena

West of Anópoli, a paved road continues northwest to the virtually abandoned hamlet of **ARÁDHENA** (**Αράδαινα**), some 3km away. This is also a pleasant forty-minute walk, with plenty of obvious short cuts close to the little-travelled road. With the coming of the paved road, one or two people have moved back and started to restore some of the setttlement's crumbling buildings.

The bridge

Bungee jumping: June–Aug Sat & Sun noon–dusk • €100, including video • ⓦ bungy.gr

The first thing to grab your attention in Arádhena is a steel **bridge** across a dramatic gorge – a remarkable construction, all the more so when you discover that it's a bridge to nowhere, as the road on the far side soon peters out at nearby Áyios Ioánnis (see p.286). Built in 1986 by the local wealthy Vardinoyiannis family, controllers of an international business empire, the bridge was a gift to provide a lifeline to the outside world without which their home village, Áyios Ioánnis, would probably have died. Rumble across it in a car and the terrifying crack of the wooden boards against metal

---

DHASKALOYIANNIS

Anópoli was the home of the first of the great Cretan rebels against the Turks, **Dhaskaloyiannis** – the subject of a celebrated epic ballad. To cut a very long story extremely short, Dhaskaloyiannis, a wealthy ship-owner, was promised support by Russian agents if he raised a rebellion in Sfakiá, support which in the event never materialized. (The Russians hoped only to divert attention from their campaigns against the Ottoman Empire elsewhere.) The revolt, in 1770, was short-lived and disastrous for Sfakiá, which for the first time was brought well and truly under the Turkish heel: Dhaskaloyiannis went to the Turks in an attempt to negotiate acceptable surrender terms. Instead the Turkish authorities seized and then tortured him in the Cathedral square at Haniá, following which he was skinned alive and executed. There's a statue honouring him in the square at Anópoli.

thunders around the gorge below. The **views** from the bridge down into the gorge – one of Crete's most precipitous – are vertiginously spectacular, and you can even take a **bungee jump**, plunging 138m into the ravine.

Miḥaíl Arḥángelos

Right on the rim of the Arádhena Gorge • The church is locked following a number of thefts; to ask about access consult Andonis, who runs the *kantína* at the bridge's northern end

The romantically picturesque Byzantine church of **Miḥaíl Arḥángelos (Μιχαήλ Αρχάγγελος)**, with its curious "pepper-pot" dome, stands proud above the gorge with against the Lefká Óri's heights as a backdrop. The white-walled church dates from the fourteenth or fifteenth century and was constructed on the ruins of a much earlier basilica. Inside, outstanding **frescoes** depict the life and crucifixion of Christ as well as the church's patron saint. Scattered round about, beyond the nearly deserted village, are a few traces of ancient Araden, a still unexcavated Greco-Roman town from whose stones the church is said to have been built.

The Arádhena Gorge

Standing on the Arádhena bridge you can see the old path, negotiable only on foot or by pack animals, zigzagging down to the bottom of the **Arádhena Gorge** and back up the other side. For well over two millennia this was the only way across the gorge, and it's still the path you take to follow the gorge down to the sea, a walk of around two and three-quarter hours. This is a superb hike, and though it has been tamed in recent years and is fairly well trodden, it's still reasonably tough, with steep staircases and scrambles over rocks in places. Parts can be scary too, not helped by the ominous presence of picked-clean skeletons of goats, which presumably have either fallen from the top or been washed away in spring floods. The sense of achievement, however, is immense, and the gorge, though far smaller than that of Samariá, is in physical terms almost as impressive. There isn't much in the way of wildlife, but the rocky riverbed is forced into an extremely narrow gap between sheer walls almost all the way down – and there'll be hardly anyone else around.

4

LOUTRÓ TO THE ARÁDHENA GORGE: THE CIRCUIT

The **circuit from Loutró**, up to Anópoli, through the gorge and down to Mármara Beach (see p.282), from where you can get a boat back to Loutró, is about 11km in total and will realistically take at least 6hr; significantly more if you make many stops along the way. Add an extra 3km (or 90min) if you walk back to Loutró from Mármara. You can cut out the hardest part (the initial climb), by taking a boat to Hóra Sfakíon and a taxi from there to Anópoli or Arádhena. A shorter but less spectacular route from Loutró would be to head out past Fínix and from there follow the road to Livianá (see p.286), clearly visible above you; from there a path descends into the lower reaches of the gorge.

The start of the **descent** into the gorge at Arádhena is not obvious: you need to turn right off the road before the bridge comes in to view, following a narrow trail above a pine coppice and heading straight towards the pepperpot church. This will lead you to the stepped stone path down to the bottom (this side should be used rather than the track on the other side, which is deteriorating fast). The impressive stone path and the relatively flat section as you head under the bridge through a very deep ravine, conspire to lull you into a false sense of security: as it gets steeper further down, you find yourself jumping from rock to rock or taking narrow steps around dry cascades. Look out as you go for the paint marks indicating the route – these often seem to take you over unnecessarily tricky terrain, but you usually discover the reason further on when you reach an impassable portion. Fill up with water at every opportunity, as there's none towards the end of the gorge.

Livanianá

Just before the bridge in Arádhena, a signed mostly asphalted road on the left heads for **LIVANIANÁ (Λιβανιανά)**, a hamlet perched above the lower reaches of the Arádhena Gorge, some 4km away. There are a few potholed patches, but the road is easily driveable as far as Livanianá. Beyond, rough dirt roads continue to Fínix (see p.281) and Líkkos (see p.282). In the village there's a path (signed "Mármara") down into the gorge. It starts beyond a gate just above the church and emerges fairly near the bottom of the gorge, having bypassed all the hardest bits. The red markings show you the best path down and you'll reach the beach after about 45 minutes.

Áyios Ioánnis

Beyond Arádhena, the paved road from the bridge climbs westward for about an hour on foot (5km) to **ÁYIOS IOÁNNIS (Άγιος Ιωάννης)**, beneath the massed peaks of Páhnes, Troharís and Zaranokefála. The village has a good rooms place, the *Alonia* hostel, and a couple of **Byzantine churches** with fourteenth-century frescoes; enquire at the hostel (see opposite) for information on getting in. There are also several impressively large **caves** nearby: a signed track leads up to the Kormokopos cave, some two hours climb above the village.

The onward path to Ayía Rouméli (see p.277) is also signed, at least initially, though it becomes hard to follow for a while until it emerges on top of the cliffs. From here it loops down as a rough but obvious path to join the coastal trail before the chapel of **Áyios Pávlos**. You should be able to complete the approximately 17km walk from Anópoli to Ayía Rouméli in about four hours, though with rest stops and wrong turnings it could well take much longer; leave plenty of leeway if you need to catch a boat back. If you are undertaking this walk in reverse, start early so as to complete the climb of the cliffs before it gets too hot.

ARRIVAL AND DEPARTURE

ANÓPOLI AND AROUND

ANÓPOLI

By car Getting to Anópoli is not easy unless you have a car.

On foot from Hóra Sfakíon There's a good new road from Hóra Sfakíon, 12km away, but it's still a very steep climb; having to follow the road means it's not a very attractive walk, but you may have little choice.

On foot from Loutró The climb up from Loutró looks terrifying – you can see the path tracking back and forth across an almost vertical cliff – but is not as bad as it appears though it will take about 2hr, climbing steeply most of the way. This is best done very early,

before the sun gets too hot. The path diverges from the coastal route immediately outside Loutró, by the gate at the edge of the village; near the top the old path has been disrupted by fencing and a new farmers' track – the easiest course is to follow this to the paved road (the Hóra Sfakíon–Anópoli road), and turn left on that into the village. If you continue to climb you'll go right over the top of the ridge and into Anópoli from above.

By bus The lone daily bus from Hóra Sfakíon drives up around 4pm and down again at 6.45am.

By taxi A taxi from Hóra Sfakíon will cost around €25.

ACCOMMODATION AND EATING

ANÓPOLI

There are several rooms places along the road as you approach from Hóra Sfakíon. Both places listed below can advise on excursions and walking routes in the area and have good tavernas. Any of the goat, lamb or sausage dishes are mouthwatering. Around the square you'll also find a couple of traditional *kafenía* and a small general store.

Panorama On the road entering the village from Hóra Sfakíon ☎ 28250 91100. Functional rooms place with clean rooms lacking a/c or fridge. **€25**

Taverna Plátanos By the statue of Dhaskaloyiannis

on the main square ☎ 28250 91169, ⓦ anopoli-sfakia.com. You'll get a warm Sfakiá welcome here, along with comfortable a/c rooms with fridge. The taverna below is excellent. Taverna daily 8am–11pm. **€30**

Xenonas Bakery On the left of the road as it enters the village proper ☎ 28250 91189. Excellent bakery for good bread and a range of other tasty treats – try the delicious almond cookies. Mon–Sat 8am–8pm.

ARÁDHENA

Kantína On the far side of the bridge. Nice little meeting place with a cosy terrace serving drinks and snacks with a view. April–Oct daily 8am–9pm.

LIVANIANÁ

Taverna Livanianá Centre of village ☎ 6974 286 641. Very good village bar-taverna offering well-prepared Sfakian cooking including a traditional meat stew and Sfakía meat pie. Veggie options include salads and a range of *mezédhes*. Daily 9am–10pm.

ÁYIOS IOÁNNIS

★ **Alonia Mountain Hostel** Take a left fork on the way through the village; ☎ 6938 792695 ✆ www .alonia.gr. Appealing hostel with an "end of the world" feel, offering stone-built en-suite doubles with terrace – it's tricky to find, so you may need to ask. The welcoming owner is a great source of information on local walking, and meals (including the occasional barbie) are available. **€30**, including evening meal **€50**

From Vrísses to the Sfakiá coast

The easy way **into Sfakiá** from the north coast is by a good road that cuts south from Vrísses, almost immediately beginning to spiral up into the mountains, passing first Alíkambos and the **Dourakis Winery** before climbing again towards the **plateau of Askífou**. The climb seems straightforward from a vehicle, but the country has a history as bloody as any in Crete: you pass first through a little ravine where two Turkish armies were massacred, the first during the 1821 uprising, the second in 1866 after the heroic events at Arkádhi (see p.192); the road itself is the one along which the Allied troops retreated at such cost in the final stages of the Battle of Crete. This chaotic flight has been described in detail in just about all the books covering the battle (and also in Evelyn Waugh's *Officers and Gentlemen*).

The final descent to the coast is stunning, running high above the **Ímbros Gorge** until the road breaks out of its confinement, way above the sea, and plunges down through a series of hairpin bends. Frangokástello can be made out on the broad plain to the east and ahead are immense vistas out towards Africa, with Gávdhos hazy on the horizon.

Dourákis Winery

2km from the village of Alíkambos • Daily 10am–2pm & 4–6.30pm; visits with tasting Thurs & Fri 10am–noon • Free • ☎ 28250 51761, ✆ dourakiswinery.gr

Part of the Cretan wine "revolution" which has seen the emergence of many prize-winning vineyards on the island over the past fifteen years, the **Dourakis Winery (Ντουράκη Οινοποιείο)** was founded in the 1990s and produces red, white and organic wines. The visit (often guided by amiable owner Andreas Dourákis) includes the cellars and production processes and on Thursdays & Fridays a visit to the tasting room.

Askífou plateau

The **Askífou plateau (Οροπέδιο Ασκύφου)** is dominated by a ruined Turkish castle on a hill – a hill so small and perfectly conical it almost looks fake, put there expressly to raise the castle above its surroundings. Chief among the several small villages up here, all bypassed by the main road, is **AMMOUDHÁRI**, with a couple of small tavernas. There are more tavernas in nearby **ASKÍFOU**, along with home-made signs to an equally home-made Battle of Crete **museum**. Gathered in the home of the late Yiorgos Hatzidakis, who witnessed the German invasion as a child, this is a fascinating jumble of weapons, helmets, badges and photos, much of it picked up in the immediate area. Don't miss the *Norton* motorbike captured by the Germans from the Allies and then put to work for the invading forces. Yiorgos' children seem a lot less keen on his collection than he was, however, and their tours can be perfunctory at best.

Ímbros Gorge

April–Oct 8am–sunset; Nov–March unmanned • April–Oct €2; Nov–March free • The official entrance to the ravine is some 500m south of Ímbros, by the *Taverna Porofarago* (see p.288), where you can park your vehicle while you do the walk – from here a well-trodden trail soon passes a booth where you will be charged the entry fee

On the far side of the Askífou plateau lies **ÍMBROS ('Ίμπρος)**, the entry point for the

---

HIKING ON THE ASKÍFOU PLATEAU

For keen **walkers**, the most obvious hike is the Ímbros gorge (see p.287), but there are also a couple of more serious treks into the Lefká Óri. A branch of the E4 Pan-European footpath passes through Ammoudhári: to the west it climbs into the foothills – initially easy walking with good opportunities for bird-spotting and then climbing seriously into the heart of the mountains to eventually reach the Kallergi Hut (p.275), a two-day trek with a possible overnight stop at the Katsiveli or Svourihti refuge (if open). In the other direction the E4 heads south across the plain to Ímbros, where one branch follows the gorge down to meet the coastal path while another heads east to Asféndou and from there to Asigonía (p.200). A shorter route leads east from Ammoudhári to the nearby village of **Goní**, from where a track leads to Asigonía, some 10km away. From **Petrés**, immediately south of Ammoudhári, you could alternatively take a long day's hike (18km) to Anópoli, through the mountains via the hamlet of **Kalí Láki**. Though detailed on the *Anavasi* Léfka Óri map (see p.40), it's not a terribly easy route to follow and you should attempt to get thorough directions locally before setting off.

Ímbros gorge. Not even a village as such, it consists of a clutch of tavernas and rooms places strung out along the road.

The **gorge walk** is clearly signed from here, and there are several ways down into it. Once in the gorge, you are following a **track** that was once the district's main thoroughfare. The hike to the end – emerging at the village of Komitádhes – is easily enough done in less than three hours. Provided you don't coincide with a tour bus (set out early), it can still be a wonderfully quiet walk, certainly in contrast to the crowds at Samariá. In its own way the gorge is as interesting as its better-known rival, albeit on a smaller scale: narrow and stiflingly confined in places, speckled with caves in others and at one point passing under a monumental, natural stone archway. Through the ravine you simply follow the stream until, emerging at the lower end, an obvious track leads away again towards Komitádhes.

KOMITÁDHES itself is full of huge, usually empty, tavernas waiting for the occasional tour party to arrive. They'll order you a taxi if you want to be taken back up to Ímbros (about €20) or on to Hóra Sfakíon (about €10). You can also walk to Hóra Sfakíon easily enough, though this final 5km makes a hot, boring anticlimax to what has gone before.

Note that it's possible to walk the gorge as a half-day trip from Hóra Sfakíon (or Loutró, by getting the first boat from there): simply take the early bus to Haniá, and get off at Ímbros.

ACCOMMODATION AND EATING

ASKÍFOU PLATEAU
Lefkoritis Resort ☎ 28250 95455, ✆ lefkoritis.com. Incongruously luxurious modern resort offering a restaurant, bar and all kinds of activities from horse- and mountain bike-riding to organized hikes. The twin room "apartments" are comfortable if bland, with minibar and TV but no cooking facilities. Larger three-room apartments (no kitchen) sleeping 5 cost more. **€60**

ÍMBROS
A couple of excellent rooms places allow a quiet night's stay before attempting the gorge. If you're walking the gorge

FROM VRÍSSES TO THE SFAKIÁ COAST

and want to leave your car here, the proprietor of the *Kalinorisima* should be able to help you organize a taxi to bring you back to the hotel from Komitádhes (around €20).
Hotel Kalinorisima ☎ 694 47 99 859. This impressive new hotel has comfortable rooms with TV and fridge; the taverna does good food and has an appealing terrace. Taverna April–Oct daily 9am–10pam. **€40**
Taverna Porofarago ☎ 28250 95450. A very good, friendly taverna with an attractive shady terrace overlooking the gorge. Sfakian specialities include goat *stifádho* and meat pie, and they're also open for breakfast. April–Oct daily 7am–11pm.

Hóra Sfakíon

Squeezed between the sea and the mountains, **HÓRA SFAKÍON (Χώρα Σφακίων)** – often known simply as Hóra, meaning "chief town" – couldn't grow even if it wanted to.

CLOCKWISE FROM TOP FALASÁRNA BEACH (P.298); WILD KRI-KRI; HIKING IN SAMARÍA GORGE (P.275)

Nevertheless it's a surprise to find the capital of Sfakiá quite so small. It is, though, a thoroughly commercial place: restaurants cram the seafront promenade between the square where the **buses** stop and the pier where the **boats** dock, and half the houses in town seem to display a large "Rooms" sign. That said, it's inexpensive and pleasant, and relatively quiet by the end of the day, though the beaches are small and pebbly and there is little else to distract you.

There are just two pedestrian streets leading off the square into town, one along the waterfront with an unbroken row of tavernas leading round to the harbour, the other just inland, lined with shops and rooms places. You can visit the **Cave of Dhaskaloyiánnis**, one of several large caves in the cliffs west of Hóra. Always a hideout in times of trouble, this was where the rebel leader (see p.284) set up a mint to produce revolutionary coinage.

ARRIVAL AND DEPARTURE HÓRA SFAKÍON

The road into Hóra Sfakíon ends at a small square just above the water. This is where the **bus** will drop you, and there's expensive paid **parking** (you can park for free around the bay to the east).

By ferry Ferries leave from the concrete jetty beyond the town square to the east; always confirm schedules. The ticket booth at the top of the jetty opens about 1hr before departure. Destinations Gávdhos (11.30am: May Wed & Thurs; June Tues & Fri; July–Sept Tues, Fri & Sun; Oct Wed & Thurs; for rest of year and to confirm schedules visit ⓦ anendyk.gr); Loutró/Ayía Rouméli (April daily 10.30am & 1pm; May, June, Sept & Oct daily 10.30am & 1pm; July & Aug daily 10.30am, 1pm & 6.30pm; for rest of year and to confirm schedules visit ⓦ www.sfakia-crete.com/sfakia-crete/ferries).

By boat A boat runs from the old harbour to Sweetwater Beach and Loutró (summer daily 10.15am, after the bus arrives; return 5.30pm; tickets on the boat, €4/€6); you'll see taxi-boats advertised here too, or ask at the information kiosk on the square.

By bus Tickets are sold on the bus. Anyone who has walked the gorge and already has a ticket should get on the bus and secure a seat.

Destinations Haniá (3 daily; 7am, 11am & 6.30pm; 2hr).

INFORMATION AND ACTIVITIES

Information A tourist information kiosk (April–Sept daily 9.30am–1.30pm & 3.30–6.30pm) on the main square can provide information on ferries (but not tickets) and taxi-boats along with general information about the town and the surroundings.

Amenities Directly ahead of the small square the *Delfini* café-restaurant is an obvious landmark; also on the square are the post office (Mon–Fri 7.30am–2pm) and (in the southeast corner) a small supermarket (one of several in town) which sells foreign newspapers, and which has an ATM outside; there's another nearby at the top of the seafront street.

Diving Notos Mare is a good dive place at the new concrete harbour beyond the ferry dock (☏ 28250 91333, ⓦ notosmare.com). They also run a 24hr taxi-boat service.

Internet *Damoulis* café-bar (also the nightlife hotspot), on the west side of the main square, and *Tria Adelfia* (see opposite).

Travel agencies Sfakiá Tours (April–Sept daily 9am–10pm; ☏ 28250 91272), next to the *Delfini*, is a useful source of local information, offering car rental and help with finding accommodation.

ACCOMMODATION

Hotel Stavris Follow the inland street around, or climb the steps behind the waterfront tavernas ☏ 28250 91220, ⓦ stavris.com. A variety of en-suite rooms and studios, all with balconies, increasing in price as you add a/c, kitchenette, or sea views; plus smarter apartments on the edge of town. Free wi-fi in bar. €35

Tria Adelfia On the inland street ☏ 28250 91450, ⓦ three-brothers-sfakia-crete.com. Overlooking the cove on the edge of town, offering a similar range of comfortable, a/c en-suite rooms and apartments to *Stavris*. €25

★ **Hotel Xenia** At the far end of the seafront promenade, just above the harbour ☏ 28250 91490, ⓦ xenia-crete.com. A refurbished former state-owned hotel with the best location in town, offering modern, a/c sea-view rooms with balcony, fridge and TV; also apartments nearby. Steps at the rear let you swim off the rocks, and the bar-taverna terrace is a great place to watch the harbour activity. Breakfast included. Free wi-fi. €48

EATING AND DRINKING

Finding food is never a problem, and all the tavernas have a good array of **vegetarian** options. There's little to choose between them: a couple, the *Samariá* and *Livikon*, are in fact run by the same people and served from the same kitchen. You'll find cheaper cafés and **takeaway** places on the east side of the bay, towards the ferry jetty.

Lefka Ori Corner of the harbour ☎28250 91209. Probably the best seafood, with a decent terrace by the water. April–Oct daily 9am–11pm.

Niki's Bakery On the inland street ☎28250 91268. A Hóra institution, offering a superb range of breads, cookies and other sweet temptations. There's a supermarket almost next door, with better prices than those on the front. Daily 3am–midnight.

Samariá On the harbour ☎28250 91261. The oldest taverna in town; a reliable place for Cretan standards. March–Oct daily 8.30am–11.30pm.

Tria Adelfia On the inland street ☎28250 91450, ⓦthree-brothers-sfakia-crete.com. In a quiet spot, with a great terrace above the sea, this taverna serves good food with a wide range of salads, pasta and vegetarian dishes. *Mezédhes* include a tasty *melitzánes tiganites* (fried aubergine), while *kounéli stifádho* (rabbit stew) is just one of many Cretan specials. Outside eating times the terrace is a nice place to get away from the crowds for a sundowner. Free wi-fi. Daily 9am–11pm.

Xenia At the far end of the seafront promenade, just above the harbour ☎28250 91490, ⓦxenia-crete .com. The taverna of the hotel (see opposite) has a limited but well-prepared menu supervised by owner-chef and all-round good guy Yiorgos Lykogiannakis. House specials include charcoal-grilled lamb, goat and pork, and the grilled fresh fish is excellent. Daily 8.30am–11.30pm.

Frangokástello

FRANGOKÁSTELLO (Φραγκοκάστελλο) lies 14km east of Hóra Sfakíon, about 3km south of the road heading east towards Plakiás (see p.224). A series of isolated dwellings dotted across a plain between the mountains and the Libyan Sea, it's a curious place, with a fabulous **beach** but no real centre, leaving you with little option but to head for the **castle** – the imposing silhouette of which comes into view long before anything else.

The beach

For peaceful lassitude the **beach** at Frangokástello is among the best spots in Crete, with fine sand, crystal-clear water (with good snorkelling opportunities), and very little effort required either to get here or to find food and drink once you've arrived. Once here, if you want company you'll find it around the castle, where the best part of the sand is sheltered and slowly shelving. For solitude, head west along the shoreline, where there's less soft sand and more wind, but it's still very pleasant. There are beaches to the east too: follow the coastal path for ten to fifteen minutes and you'll arrive at the top of a low cliff overlooking perhaps 1km of beautiful, deserted sand and rocks.

The castle

Centre of the village fronting the sea • May–Oct daily 10am–8.30pm • €1.50

The **castle**, so impressively four-square from a distance, turns out close up to be a mere shell. Nothing but the bare walls survive, with a tower in each corner and, over the seaward entrance, an escutcheon which can just be made out as the Venetian lion of St Mark. Still, it's some shell. The fortress was originally built in 1371 to deter pirates and in an attempt to impose some order on Sfakiá: a garrison was maintained here throughout the Venetian and Turkish occupations, controlling the plain as surely as it failed to tame the mountains – even today, the orange-pink walls look puny when you see them with the grey bulk of the mountains towering behind. In 1828, Frangokástello was occupied by **Hadzimihali Daliani**, a Greek adventurer attempting to spread the War of Independence from the mainland to Crete. Instead of taking to the hills as all sensible rebels before and since have done, he and his tiny force attempted to make a stand in the castle. Predictably, they were massacred and their martyrdom became fuel for yet more heroic legends of the *pallikári*. Locals claim that to this day, around May 17, the ghosts of Daliani and his army march from the castle: they are known as *dhrossoulítes*, or dewy ones, because they appear in the mists around dawn.

ARRIVAL AND GETTING AROUND — FRANGOKÁSTELLO

By bus A bus runs from Haniá to Frangokástello on weekdays at 2pm, returning at 4.30pm.

Vehicle rental You can rent cars, scooters and mountain bikes at *Blue Sky* (see below), an apartment complex signed inland off the main road.

ACCOMMODATION

Many of the **places to stay** and other facilities lie along the road that heads in from Hóra Sfakíon: a turn-off immediately before the castle leads to another little group of seaside rooms places and tavernas. If you're approaching from the east, the monstrous two-storey modern eyesore *Taverna Kriti* ruins most views of the castle: you'll see signs to a number of newer rooms places along the way. Wherever you stay, come prepared for **mosquitoes**.

Babis & Popi Main road west of the castle ☎ 28250 92092, ⓦ babis-popi.com. Sited right above a rocky shoreline, this friendly taverna/minimarket offers simple en-suite rooms, studios (with TV and kitchenette) and attractive apartments (sleeping 6) all with a/c, a short walk from the beach. Free wi-fi. Rooms €28, studios €45, apartments €70

Blue Sky Apartments Signed inland off the main road, west of the castle ☎ 28250 92095 ⓦ blue-sky-kreta.de. Very attractive modern two-room apartments (sleeping five) with a/c, kitchen and TV in a tranquil location. Free wi-fi. Ten percent discount for *Rough Guide* readers. €70

Kali Kardia Main road almost next to the castle ☎ 28250 92311. Popular taverna with simple a/c rooms (with fridge) at the back – there's direct access from these to the beach. €35

Maria's Studios Side road by the castle ☎ 28250 92159, ⓦ marias-studios.net. Prime beachfront position and friendly management at this somewhat characterless but well-presented and -equipped modern block. En-suite a/c rooms have kitchenettes, and many have balcony sea views; there are also some larger apartments. €45

Milos Side road by the castle ☎ 28250 92162, ⓦ milos-sfakia.com. A variety of a/c rooms (with fridge), studios and apartments (sleeping 4) – some of them right on the beach. Popular, and often booked up. Rooms €40, studios €40, apartments €60

Oasis Main road west of the castle ☎ 28250 92136, ⓦ oasisrooms.com. A good taverna with very pleasant a/c studios and apartments facing the sea, with a path to the beach; the two-room apartments with full kitchen are particularly good value. Taverna April–Oct daily 8am–11pm Studios €35, apartments €50

Paradisos Signed off the road east of the castle ☎ 28250 92078, ⓦ paradisos-kreta.com. Tranquil modern studio and apartment complex in an olive grove very near the sandy eastern beach; well-equipped accommodation with kitchen, a/c and TV, plus a tennis court and free bikes for guests. Larger three-room apartments can sleep six. Studios €50, apartments €65

EATING, DRINKING AND NIGHTLIFE

For eating and drinking, most of your options lie within a few minutes' walk of the castle; places further out tend to be less expensive. There are also a number of **minimarkets** dotted along the main road. There's little in the way of **nightlife**.

Babis & Popi Main road west of the castle ☎ 28250 92092, ⓦ babis-popi.com. Very good, very friendly taverna for traditional Cretan cuisine and fresh fish. *Astakomakoronáda* (lobster with spaghetti) is a house special, while Saturday, barbecue night, offers charcoal grilled fish, meat and sausage. Free internet. April–Oct daily 7am–11pm.

Blue Sky Café-Taverna Signed inland off the main road, west of the castle ☎ 28250 92095, ⓦ blue-sky-kreta.de. One of the better tavernas in the village, with a good terrace, serving creative Cretan cooking with some more internationally slanted dishes. Try their *kotópoulo me síka* (chicken in wine with figs) or *arní melitzána* (lamb with aubergines); they also cater for vegetarians. The adjoining café serves tasty ice cream and pastries and

has a nice pool that customers can use. April–Oct daily 9am–10pm.

Kali Kardia Main road almost next to the castle ☎ 28250 92311. The "Good Heart" started life as the village's *kafenío*, and is still the place you're most likely to see locals, enjoying the usual standards as well as fresh fish and a tasty tomato soup (Cretan tomatoes taste like no others). This is also a good stop for breakfast, drinks and snacks, including takeaway pizza. March–Nov daily 8am–midnight.

Milos Side road by the castle ☎ 28250 92162, ⓦ milos-sfakia.com. Enjoying probably the best position near the beach, this is a reliable place for fresh fish and the usual staples. Good selection of bottled wines. April–Oct daily 8am–11pm.

Sunrise Taverna On the clifftop east of the castle ☎ 28250 92041. Great views from its position hanging above the shore, and good food; all the meat (goat and lamb) comes from its own herds (try the tasty Sfakian lamb casserole). The *mezédhes* are recommended, too, and there are many vegetarian possibilities. April–Oct daily 8.30am–11pm.

Western Haniá

Crete's **far west** has, to date, attracted surprisingly little attention from tourists or developers, and though that is beginning to change, such development as there is consists of mostly low-key apartments and rooms rather than big hotels. The one town of any size west of Haniá is **Kastélli Kissámou**, a port with a ferry service to the Peloponnese, very regular buses to Haniá and a fine new museum. To the northwest of Kastélli the long, slender finger of the **Gramvoúsa peninsula** reaches out into the Aegean with, on its western flank, the fabulous white-sand beach of **Balos Bay**. Extending to the south of this peninsula, Crete's west-facing coast remains remote: there's little public transport and virtually nothing in the way of luxurious facilities. However, here you'll find two of the finest **beaches** on the island – **Falásarna** and Elafonísi – both of them, sadly, beginning to suffer from over-exploitation.

The Gulf of Kissámou

Kastélli lies some 20km beyond the crossroads at Kolimbári (see p.267) on the coast of the **Gulf of Kissámou** (Κόλπος Κισσάμου). If you're in a hurry to head west, the new highway is fast and efficient, taking you right to the edge of Kastélli, where it finally ends. It has also left the **old road** – always a beautiful drive – as a delightful backwater. Going this way you wind steeply up a rocky spur thrown back by the peninsula and emerge through a cleft in the hills to a magnificent view of the Gulf of Kissámou, with Kastélli in the middle distance. Caught with the sun setting behind the craggy heights of **Cape Voúxa** at the far west of Crete, this is a memorable panorama. There's a roadside restaurant from which you can contemplate the view, and further along a number of quite large, entirely unvisited villages, such as Nochiá, Koléni or Kaloudhianá, where you could also stop for a drink or a bite to eat at a number of inviting tavernas.

As it leaves the height, the road loops back out of the hills onto the fertile **plain of Kastélli**. Almost as soon as you hit level ground you'll see turnings to the beach, a long stretch of grey sand which, while not the best in Crete, is at least clean and uncrowded. The village of **Kaloudhianá**, 4km further along, marks the turn-off for the inland route to Topólia and Elafonísi.

ACCOMMODATION   GULF OF KISSÁMOU

There are scattered rooms places on the plain of Kastélli, and two attractive, well-equipped **campsites** on the coast about 1km from the road. There's a regular bus service to and from Kastélli, and though the sites are popular with people arriving in Kastélli on the ferry, there should always be space.

Camping Mithimna Between Nopíyia and Dhrapaniás ☎ 28220 31444, ⊕ campingmithimna .com. *Mithimna* takes its name from the ancient Minoan town of Mithymna, thought to have been approximately where Nopíyia now stands; excavations near the junction have revealed a Minoan building. A largish site, with studios and apartments (sleeping 4) to rent nearby. Two adults plus tent and vehicle €21.50, studios €45, apartments €60
Camping Nopigia Near Nopíyia village ☎ 28220 31111, ⊕ campingnopigia.gr. A newish campsite with a pool and taverna. Two adults plus tent and vehicle €21.50

Kastélli Kissámou and around

KASTÉLLI – also known as Kíssamos after its region, and officially Kastélli Kissámou (Καστέλλι Κισσάμου) seems at first sight to offer little to get excited about. It's a busy

4

KASTÉLLI KISSÁMOU

RESTAURANTS, CAFÉS & BARS	
Aéras	10
To Akrogiali	7
Aqua	4
Aretousa	6
Babel Café	5
Captain	2
Kastello	8
Papadakis	1
Petra	9
Pixida	3

ACCOMMODATION	
To Akrogiali	5
Argo	2
Bikakis	7
Galini Beach Hotel	4
Maria Beach	1
Mirtilos	6
Revekka	3

little town and port with a long seafront, a rather rocky strand to the east and a small sandy beach to the west. This very ordinariness, however, has real charm: it's a working town full of stores used by locals and cafés not entirely geared to outsiders. **Kisámos** was the Greco-Roman city-state that stood here in ancient times – the name Kíssamou ("of Kísamos") was appended to plain Kastélli to avoid confusion with towns of the same name in both Crete and Greece. Ongoing excavations in the town centre – whose finds are displayed in an outstanding **museum** – are revealing just how important the ancient city was.

The Archeological Museum

Platía Tzanakáki • Tues–Sun 8.30am–3pm • €3

Housed in the former Venetian governor's palace on the main square, the fine **Archeological Museum** is Kastélli's major attraction. The lower floor exhibits finds from the pre-historic and Minoan periods as well as items from **Polyrínia** (see opposite) through to the destruction of the town by a gigantic earthquake in 365 AD, but the second floor – devoted to the Roman town – holds the highlights of the collection.

KASTÉLLI ORIENTATION

On the eastern outskirts the old and new roads merge to head straight through town as Iróon Politehníou, south of the centre. This is lined with stores and supermarkets, and there are cafés and banks on **Platía Venizélou**, where it passes through the centre of town. The heart of Kastélli's life, however, lies a couple of blocks towards the sea from here, around **Platía Tzanakáki** and the main street that runs through it, **Odhós Skálidi**. This is also where the **buses** pull in. There's a further cluster of development along the **waterfront**, directly down from the main squares, with an attractive promenade separating the town's **beaches** to the east and west.

Here, in Room 4 are two spectacular **Roman mosaics** from the period when Kísamos thrived as an important municipality in the Roman Empire. During the first and second centuries many wealthy aristocrats embellished their luxurious villas here with sculptures, frescoes, inlaid marble floors (*opus sectilis*) and fine mosaics. Many of these arts and crafts are exhibited in the museum, but it is the mosaics that steal the show. The huge polychromatic, so-called **Dyonysiac mosaic** covers most of Room 4 and depicts various scenes in a Dyonysiac ritual. Interestingly, the mosaic had been restored many times by the various owners of the villa that housed it.

Horae and the Seasons
The museum's star exhibit is **Horae and the Seasons**, one of the finest mosaics on Crete. A brilliant work, its colours still remarkably vivid, the almost perfectly complete mosaic depicts a trio of dancing *horae* (goddesses of the seasons). There were only three seasons (spring, summer and winter) in the old Hellenic calendar but at the four corners the mosaicist has added depictions of the four seasons of later antiquity.

At least a dozen other, equally splendid, mosaics have been discovered in recent excavations throughout Kastélli, but the museum has no space to exhibit them. There are, however, plans to open an extension on the **Villa of Phidias** excavation site nearby (see below). Kísamos was a key centre of mosaic production, and once all the floors are on display this will undoubtedly become one of Greece's most important museums of Greco-Roman mosaics.

Archeological excavations
Originally the port of nearby Polyrínia, Kísamos grew to become the more powerful city; various **archeological excavations** have revealed substantial remains of the ancient town (and more mosaics). However, as the mosaics have been covered in sand and gravel to protect them until they are removed for display in the museum, all you can do is stare at the dirt, a few foundation walls and the odd stretch of ancient roadway, through a chain-link fence. One villa that will be opened to the public is the **Villa of Phidias**, so named from the owner whose name has been found on a mosaic. An enormous place, now partly covered by the town's health centre, it has six fine mosaics that will be viewed from a walkway. Check with the museum regarding the opening date.

The Venetian and Ottoman town
Immediately north of Platía Tzanakáki, where the ground falls sharply away towards the coast, are substantial **defensive bastions** connected with a Venetian castle here (which gave the town its name) and which was largely destroyed by Turkish pirates in the early sixteenth century. In the streets surrounding the square, particularly to the west, surviving sections of city wall from the same period can still be seen. There's also a beautiful old **Venetian fountain,** inscribed with the date 1520, about 100m east of the main square in a small courtyard to the left off Kampouri.

Polyrínia
7km south of Kastélli above Polyrínia village • No bus; without transport your best bet is to take a taxi up (around €8) and walk back down
You can still see substantial vestiges of the ancient city of **POLYRÍNIA (Πολυρρήνια)** of which Kástelli was the port, around 7km inland. In spring, especially, the hike down from the site back to town is lovely, with alpine flowers and abundant water from springs: it's part of the E4 path, which continues west until it hits the coast road, which it follows all the way down the coast to Elafonísi (see p.305).

The site
It's something of a climb from the village to the **hilltop site**, where ruins are scattered across two horns of high ground that seem to reach out to enclose the Gulf of Kissámou. Originally an eighth-century BC Dorian colony occupied by settlers from

the Peloponnese, Polyrínia – a name meaning "rich in lambs" – remained a prosperous city down to Roman times and beyond. One of its main claims to fame, however, would not endear it to most Cretans: an inscription found here and dated to 69 BC tells of how the Polyrinians created a statue in honour of the Roman conqueror of Crete, Quintus Metellus, referring to him as the "saviour and benefactor of the city". It seems that Polyrínia did not join in the resistance put up by Haniá and other cities to the Roman invasion, and as a result was spared destruction.

The most obvious feature, right at the summit, is the **Acropolis**, reached via a circuitous track starting east of the church. There are stunning **views** of the coast from here, and though much of what you see is in fact a Venetian defensive structure, the site is dotted with ancient remains including Roman **cisterns** and the vestiges of an **aqueduct**. Miscellaneous Roman and Greek masonry is incorporated into the **church** that now stands below the Acropolis. The church is itself constructed on the base of what must have been an enormously impressive Hellenistic building, possibly a fourth-century BC temple. The sheer amount of work involved in cutting and dressing these stone blocks and transporting them to places as inaccessible as this makes you wonder at the phenomenal scale of manpower at the service of these towns in antiquity. The unsightly breezeblocks used for the cemetery wall of the modern church make a starkly ironic contrast. Just below the church are the remains of Hellenistic **dwellings** with cisterns and cave-like storage cellars.

ARRIVAL AND DEPARTURE

By bus Buses drop and collect passengers in Platía Tzanakáki. Destinations Elafonísi (1 daily; 9.30am; 1hr 30min); Élos (2 daily; 10.30am & 2pm; 1hr 30min); Falásarna (4 daily; 9.45am, 12.15pm, 2pm & 4.30pm; 30min); Haniá (14 daily; 6am–8.30pm; 1hr); Omalós (Mon–Sat 1 daily; 6am; 3hr); Soúdha (daily to meet the ferries; 1hr 15min).

By ferry The ferry harbour, for ferries to the Peloponnese, is 3km west of town –a cheap taxi ride. Day-trips to the island of Gramvoúsa and Balos Bay (see p.298) also depart from here (May, June, Sept & Oct 10.20am & 10.40am; July & Aug 10.20am, 10.40am & 12.30pm; €23; ☎ 28220 24344, ⓦ gramvousa.com). Thursday and Friday seem to

KASTÉLLI KISSÁMOU AND AROUND

be especially popular with coach trips; tickets are available from travel agencies in town, on the quayside or online. Destinations Kíthira (4 weekly; 4–5hr); Pireás (2 weekly; 11–12hr); Yíthio (1 weekly; 7hr).

Bike and car rental For cars, motorbikes, scooters and mountain bikes try the longstanding and helpful Motofun/Autofun (☎ 28220 23440, ⓦ auto-motofun.info) on Platía Tzanakáki; they offer remarkably cheap deals for a week's rental with special offers undercutting most Haniá dealers' prices by over fifty percent. They will also deliver to Haniá airport. Horeftakis Tours (see below) and others on Skálidi also rent cars.

INFORMATION AND TOURS

Taxis The main rank is on Platía Venizélou, or try ☎ 28220 22324 or ☎ 28220 22069.

Tours In spring and autumn Strata Tours (☎ 28220 23700, ⓦ stratatours.com) offer walking and wildlife tours of the beautiful country around Kastélli; contact To Kelari taverna on the waterfront. Balos Travel, Papayiannakis 54 (behind

the Aéras kafenío on Platía Tzanakáki; ☎ 28220 22655) runs cycling tours to Falásarna, Polyrínia and other areas, with plulk lunch and guide included.

Travel agencies Several along Skálidi: Horeftakis Tours at no. 33 (☎ 28220 23250, ⓦ horeftakistours.com) sells ferry tickets and offers car rental.

ACCOMMODATION

Kastélli has an abundance of **accommodation** and is rarely filled to capacity, even in high season. The beachside places tend to fill before those in town. The nearest **campsites** are near Nopíyia, 7km east (see p.293).

To Akrogiali On the coast east, about 2km beyond the Galini Beach hotel ☎ 28220 31410. Attractive sea-view a/c rooms with fridge and TV above an excellent restaurant (see opposite). Really only worth considering if you have your own transport. €40

Argo Central seafront ☎ 28220 23563, ⓦ papadaki.biz. Great location for sea-view a/c en-suite balcony rooms

with fridge and TV. Free wi-fi. €40

Bikakis Kampouri, east of the centre ☎ 28220 24257, ⓦ familybikakis.gr. Ignore the unattractive streetside frontage – the quiet rooms at the back have uninterrupted sea views. Family-run, with well-equipped, a/c rooms and studios along with cheaper rooms sharing bath; the owner often meets the ferry, and will collect you on request. €35

★ **Galini Beach Hotel** On the eastern beach, just past the football pitch ☎ 28220 23288, ⓦ galinibeach.com. Friendly, good-value hotel with easy parking, sparkling light and airy en-suite, a/c rooms with TV, balcony and sea views. It also offers an excellent breakfast (extra) served on its seafront terrace. The friendly proprietor has lots of information on hiking in the area. Free wi-fi. **€50**

★ **Maria Beach** On the western beach ☎ 28220 22610, ⓦ mariabeach.gr. The best location in town, right on the sandy beach. A couple of separate buildings include some fairly plain rooms (some with fridge) as well as new,

fully equipped sea-view studios (with kitchenette and TV) and apartments (sleeping 5) with kitchen and a/c. Free wi-fi. Rooms **€40**, studios **€50**, apartments **€75**

Mirtilos Platía Tzanakáki ☎ 28220 023079, ⓦ mirtilos .com. Appealing new apartment complex round a large pool, right off the main square. Often block-booked in high season, but worth trying at other times – all apartments with a/c, TV and kitchenette. Free wi-fi. **€70**

Revekka A block back from the seafront ☎ 28220 24213. These a/c en-suite balcony rooms with kitchenette and fridge are much nicer than the view from outside suggests. Free wi-fi in reception. **€44**

EATING AND DRINKING

There are many **places to eat** in Kastélli, the best of which tend to be away from the centre; many of the seafront places are disappointing. For light meals and breakfasts, though, the area around Platía Tzanakáki offers plenty of choice. There's a good **bakery**, *Hairetis*, on the square's south side next to the *Aéras kafenío*. Wherever you eat, you'll probably be offered the local **red wine**. Made from the *roméïko* grape, believed to have been brought to the island by the Venetians, it is as good as any produced on Crete. Although the central seafront area often has a listless, end-of-season air by day, it comes to life at night when the locals pile in to drink at the **cafés and bars** along the central promenade; *Babel Café* and *Aqua* (both with free wi-fi) are among the best.

KASTÉLLI

★ **Aéras** Platía Tzanakáki ☎ 28220 22913. "Winds" is the town's oldest *kafenío* and meeting place, serving customers for over a century. Remarkably, it's still in the hands of the same family and remains a great place for a breakfast coffee in the atmospheric bar (with photos of old Kastélli) or a sundowner on its terrace on the square, beneath the spreading rubber tree. Daily 6.30am–1am.

★ **To Akrogiali** On the coast east, about 2km beyond the Galini Beach hotel ☎ 28220 31410. Excellent fresh seafood (caught by the friendly proprietor with his own boat), served on a terrace with the waves almost lapping the table legs. It's immediately east of a seafront soap factory whose chimney stacks are visible from some distance. They also have rooms (see opposite). April–Oct daily 11am–midnight.

Aretousa Eastern end of the seafront promenade ☎ 28220 23569. Serving fish (try the grilled sardines) and meat dishes, including a tasty *kounéli stifádho* (rabbit stew), with a flourish, this is one of the best of the in-town tavernas. Also good *mezédhes*, a decent wine list and a nice terrace. Daily 9am–midnight.

Captain At the small-boat and fishing harbour, about halfway to the main port ☎ 28220 22857. Along with *To Akrogiali* (see above) this place, a short drive or taxi ride west of town, probably has the freshest (if not the cheapest) fish in town – the catch is landed on the quayside, 10m from the taverna's terrace tables. They also

have rooms. Free wi-fi. Daily 9am–11pm.

Kastello Skálldi 96, immediately west of Platía Tzanakáki (behind the museum) ☎ 28220 24083. Highly popular place with cost-conscious locals who queue for tasty takeaway *souvláki* and *yíros*; there are also tables in a small garden for sit-down meals. Daily 10am–1am.

Papadakis Western end of the seafront promenade ☎ 28220 22340. The best choice at this end of the seafront, with decent, reasonably priced seafood and courteous service. You can also bring your own wine. April–Nov daily noon–midnight.

Petra Platía Tzanakáki ☎ 28220 24387. Simple, inexpensive taverna next to the bus station, serving hearty meals and grills at tables out on the square. Daily 8.30am–midnight.

Pixida Central seafront promenade ☎ 28220 22850. Traditional Cretan dishes and seafood, and decent house wines from the barrel. April–Nov daily 11am–midnight.

POLYRÍNIA

Acropolis Taverna At the foot of the hill close to the site ☎ 6949 476237. A good lunch stop, serving a range of *mezédhes* and the usual Greek standards on a shady terrace. They can also arrange a taxi back to Kastélli. May–Sept daily noon–10pm.

Old Kafeníon On the way up to the site from Polyrínia village. This small café serves snacks and drinks and has site information. April–Oct daily 9am–6pm.

DIRECTORY

Banks There are several with ATMs on Platía Venizélou, and a couple more along Skálidi.

Internet Bit Planet (daily 10am–midnight) upstairs on the south side of Platía Venizélou; Gamers, next to the

4

museum (daily 9.30am–2pm). Some of the waterfront cafés also offer free wi-fi.
Laundry Papayiannakis, between the two squares (Mon–Sat 8am–2.30pm & 5–9.30pm).

Newspapers Fountoukakis on Skálidi, east of Platía Tzanakáki sells foreign newspapers and some English books (Mon–Sat 9am–2pm & 6–9pm).
Post office Iróon Politehníou (Mon–Fri 7.30am–2pm).

The Gramvoúsa peninsula

Leaving Kastélli Kissámou for the west, the Plátanos road climbs back into the hills again, cutting southwest across the base of the **Gramvoúsa peninsula (Γραμβούσα)**. Along this first stretch there are plenty of signs of development, with new apartment blocks and small hotels. After 7km a turn-off for Kalivianí marks the start of a 9km track up the Gramvoúsa peninsula towards **Cape Voúxa** and the **island of Gramvoúsa**, on which the Venetians built an important fort, and which is only accessible by boat. The track is just about driveable in a standard vehicle – and no problem at all for a 4WD. You can also walk it in around three hours. The track ends at a car park on the east coast (with a seasonal drinks stall), from where a well-marked path leads across to west-facing **Balos Bay** (around ten minutes' walk), where there's a really spectacular white-sand **beach** (sadly with a recurring tar problem) more or less opposite Gramvoúsa island. If you're on an organized **boat trip** from Kastélli, you will arrive at Balos Bay after calling in at the island.

Walking on the extraordinarily barren and quite unpopulated peninsula is great – but lonely, so take plenty of water and all the other provisions you're going to need. Apart from the car park stall and a spring near the chapel of Ayía Iríni, about 6km out (neither of which it's safe to rely on), there's nothing to be had beyond Kalivianí. Note that you can also walk along the western side of the Gramvoúsa Peninsula from Falásarna but this is a much tougher route and you'll need a head for heights (see opposite).

Gramvoúsa Island

Along with the fortified islands of Néa Sóudha and Spinalónga, the formidable **castle** on **Gramvoúsa Island** was one of the points that held out against the Turks long after the Cretan mainland had fallen. When the Venetians left, the fort was allowed to fall into disrepair until it was taken over by Greek refugees from other Turkish-occupied islands (notably Kásos) who used it as a base for piracy. It took a major Turkish campaign to wrest the fortress back, and thereafter they maintained a garrison here. In the War of Independence it became a base for the Turkish ships attempting to maintain a blockade of the coastline. Today you can climb up to the fort (a gruelling fifteen- to twenty-minute ascent in high summer), walk around its well-preserved ramparts with stunning **views**, and examine the huge water cisterns and chapel. There are lovely wildflowers in season.

In summer, many visitors arriving by boat, upon seeing the climb to the fort high above, opt instead to spread out on the island's small beach. Another slightly larger and wilder island, **Agría Gramvoúsa**, lies to the north just off the cape; boat trips currently don't call there.

Falásarna and around

The descent from Plátanos, 10km southwest of Kastélli, to the the beautiful beach at **FALÁSARNA (Φαλάσαρνα)** is via a spectacular series of hairpin bends above a narrow coastal plain where farmers grow tomatoes, melons and the like in plastic greenhouses. Below, you can see two main **beaches**, with several smaller patches of sand between – the southern one (enterprisingly named "Big Beach") is much bigger, but the best and most sheltered sand is reached by continuing to the end of the asphalt, where there's a car park, the bus stop and a couple of taverna-rooms places above a broad crescent of yellow sand lapped by turquoise waters. You can either head straight down to the sand here, or walk a bit further north, past the *Orange & Blue* bar. Although the beach can occasionally be afflicted by washed-up oil, tar and discarded rubbish, this doesn't detract from the overall beauty of the place. When it gets too crowded (and on Sundays in summer it will, as half of Haniá seems to head here) you can find other patches of sand within easy walking distance in either direction.

Following the (driveable) main dirt track for 1km beyond the car park, and through olive groves, at the edge of the archeological site you will pass a large stone "**throne**" that has puzzled experts for a century – there is still no satisfactory explanation for its function.

Ancient Falásarna
1km north of the car park by the *Falassarna Beach* hotel

The westernmost of the cities of ancient Crete, **Falásarna** was founded prior to the sixth century BC and remained the sworn enemy of nearby Polyrínia (see p.295). What you see today are the scattered remains of a city built around a large depression – its inner **harbour** – and the bed of a canal that once joined this to the sea. The entire site is now high and dry, offering conclusive proof that Crete's western extremities have risen at least 8m over the last 24 centuries or so. Excavators discovered large stone blocks thrown across the entrance to the old harbour; current thinking suggests that this was carried out in the first century BC by the Romans to prevent pirates using the port as a base.

The harbour was defended by part of the city wall linked by a number of towers to a harbour mole, with the **South Tower**, the nearest to the sea, a formidable bastion built of huge sandstone blocks. More ruined structures can be seen ascending the acropolis hill behind, and near the chapel of Áyios Yeóryios a recently excavated building (beneath a canopy) revealed a number of well-preserved **terracotta baths**. On the southwest side of the site (after scrambling over rocks) you can see the impressive remains of the Roman quarries where the stone was hewn to build the harbour and surrounding town. Nearer the sea here you can also view huge fish tanks carved in the rock where captive fish were maintained alive until they were required. Near the guardian's hut (always closed) by the entrance a couple of trial trenches have been dug revealing footings of buildings from the ancient town, which is still to be exacavated.

Walks around the peninsula
If you continue on the best of the tracks past the Falásarna archeological site, you pass under Cyclopean walls to emerge above a small bay. Tempting as it is, this is too sharp and rocky to be able to get to the sea, but it does give you views to the north, over Cape Voúxa, which are shielded from Falásarna itself. Towards the top you can see the island of Gramvoúsa (not to be confused with the uninhabitable rock of Pontikonísi, a more distant islet which can sometimes be seen from the beach at Falásarna). It's possible to hike on from here up the **western side of the Gramvoúsa peninsula** (see opposite) on an occasionally scary path above the coast, marked by blue paint and cairns. After about four and a half hours you reach a crest, the highest point on the walk, with breathtaking views over the islands. If you do try this, don't do it alone, and take plenty of water.

ARRIVAL AND DEPARTURE | THE GRAMVOÚSA PENINSULA

However you explore the peninsula, it's worth setting out **early** to avoid the crowds who arrive at Balos Bay on boat trips from Kastélli from about 1.30pm. If you got a **taxi** to Kalivianí, you could walk up and get the **boat** back to Kastélli – there are departures between 4pm and 6pm (with a last boat at 7.30pm in July & Aug), though it's worth checking in advance (see p.296) that there will be space.

FALÁSARNA AND AROUND
By bus There are direct services from Haniá (7 daily).
By car To reach Falásarna from Kastélli or the south, head for Platános from where a road descends to the base of the peninsula.

ACCOMMODATION

FALÁSARNA AND AROUND

An increasing number of rooms places are scattered along the road behind Falásarna, many of them very comfortable; unless otherwise specified, all of the following are well signed on, or just off this road. Quite a few people also camp at the back of the beach, either in a couple of small caves or beneath makeshift shelters slung between a few stumpy trees.

Falassarna Beach By the car park, behind Sunset ☎ 28220 41541, ⊕ falassarnabeach.gr. The a/c studios and apartments (sleeping 4), all with sea-view balconies, are probably better value than at neighbouring *Sunset*, though the location and views are less good. Free wi-fi. Studios €45, apartments €65

Golden Sun Slightly inland near the entry to the village ☎ 28220 41485, ⊕ hotelgoldensun.net. Recently built, local-stone block of well-equipped, a/c rooms, studios and apartments (the latter two with cooking facilities), all with balconies or terraces and many with fine views over the coast. The friendly proprietors can also provide food, and there's a garden and a washing machine for guests' use. Rooms €35, studios €45, apartments €70

Kalami Overlooking Big Beach ☎ 28220 41461. Fairly basic a/c place offering rooms and apartments (sleeping 4) with fridge or kitchenette and stunning views from the balconies. Rooms €35, apartments €50

Plakures ☎ 28220 41581, ⊕ plakures.de. The "luxury option", this is the newest and fanciest of the local accommodation with well-appointed balcony rooms and apartments, run by Greek-German proprietors. Facilities include minibar, pool, tennis court, bar and restaurant. Free wi-fi. Breakfast included. €96

Stathis & Anastasia Slightly inland near the entry to the village ☎ 28220 41480, ⊕ anastasiastathis

.com. Immediately behind *Golden Sun*, this is a simple rooms place whose a/c en-suite balcony rooms come with a/c and fridges, and an exceptionally warm welcome. €40

Sunset By the car park ☎ 28220 41204, ⊕ sunset .com.gr. With an enviable location, right above the beach, and a good taverna, the long-established *Sunset* has a lot going for it, though some of its rooms (a/c, with balcony) could do with modernization. They also have very basic seafront apartments and, nearby, luxurious two-storey stone villas overlooking the sea. Free wi-fi. Rooms/apartments €40, villas €180

AROUND THE PENINSULA

Balos Beach Hotel 6km west of Kastélli ☎ 28220 24106, ⊕ balosbeach.gr. An attractive, relatively new hotel in an isolated spot above the sea at the bottom of the peninsula, offering well-equipped balcony studios and apartments (sleeping 4) with fabulous sea views back towards Kastélli. Also has a bar, restaurant, pool and children's pool. Free wi-fi in public areas. Studios €65, apartments €85

Kaliviani Traditional Hotel Kaliviani ☎ 28220 23204, ⊕ kaliviani.com. Wonderful new hotel-restaurant on a raised terrace in the centre of the village. Beautifully appointed a/c rooms come with balcony sea view, fridge, TV and queen-size beds. Free wi-fi. Breakfast available. Taverna daily noon–11pm. €75

Olive Tree Apartments Near Kaliviani ☎ 28220 24336, ⊕ olivetree.gr. Rural option with well-equipped studios and apartments (sleeping 5) with balconies and sea views, ranged around a pool. In the village you'll also find a couple of tavernas and *kafenía*. Free wi-fi. Studios €50, apartments €70

EATING AND DRINKING

FALÁSARNA AND AROUND

There are seasonal drinks stands and beach bars on the busier stretches of beach. For something more substantial to eat, the rooms places immediately above the beaches (*Sunset* and *Falassarna* at the smaller beach, for example) are as good as any – all simple, and somewhat overwhelmed on busy weekends. There's an excellent, if rather pricey minimarket – with all the necessities and more – on the road by the junction to Big Beach. A couple of slightly bigger supermarkets can be found in Plátanos, where there's also fuel and a bank with an ATM.

Mouraki Taverna Plátanos, right at the top of the road before it heads down to Falásarna ☎ 28220 41666. Welcoming, excellent taverna with spectacular views over the coast. Lamb dishes are recommended,

and house specials include stuffed cuttlefish and *kotsi koirino stin ladokola* (oven-baked pork with potatoes). April–Oct daily 9am–midnight.

Orange and Blue Bar Signed from the car park near the Sunset hotel. An excellent spot for a sunset cocktail, with classic and current sounds; often live music at weekends. April–Oct daily 10am–5am.

Panorama Big Beach ☎ 28220 41777. A good taverna serving all the usual Cretan standards. With a nice selection of bottled wines, this is also one of the more reliable places in the area if you're hankering after fresh fish. They have an attractive terrace and a swimming pool bar (open during the day only), which is free for customers. Also some rooms to let. April–Oct daily noon–11pm.

South from Kastélli

There are two routes **south of Kastélli** towards the southwest corner of the island. The **inland route** turns off the north-coast highway at Kaloudhianá, a lovely rural drive up the valley of the Tiflós. The wooded hill country hereabouts is among the greenest parts of Crete, offering the possibility of a stay at the remarkable tourist mountain village of **Miliá**, or for walkers a ravine to explore at **Koutsamatádos**. About halfway across the island you can turn left to continue south towards Paleohóra. The inland route then passes **Élos** and Váthi in the Enneachora, the heart of Crete's chestnut country. From Kefáli, where the two routes meet, you have the option of making this a circular drive back to Kastélli or continuing on to the romantically sited monastery of **Hrissoskalítissa**, and beyond that the idyllic beaches of Elafonísi.

The coast road from Kastélli

The **coast road** southwest of Kastélli, which goes via **Plátanos**, is spectacularly scenic, offering possibilities of access to several coastal settlements before looping round eastwards to join the inland route from Kastélli to the southwest at Kefáli. As you approach Kefáli, magnificent coastal **views** reveal the distant beaches of Elafonísi shimmering mirage-like in a turquoise sea. Around you, olives ripen on the terraced hillsides and the villages seem to cling desperately to the high mountainsides, as if miraculously saved from some calamitous slide to the water, glittering far below.

Sfinári

Some 9km south of Plátanos the road descends towards the sea at the village of **SFINÁRI (Σφηνάρι)** where a turnoff leads to its beachfront extension, a kilometre away. This consists of a quiet pebble beach somewhat spoiled by greenhouses and derelict buildings too close to the water for comfort. It is, however, a very friendly place, with plenty of places to eat by the strand. The southern end of the beach is marginally less cluttered and here a cluster of **tavernas** gather beneath shady tamarisks: they positively encourage **camping** on the beach, and most provide loungers for customers.

Kámbos

Beyond Sfinári the road climbs again for a sinuous 10km to **KÁMBOS (Κάμπος)**. Less developed than its neighbour, there's a **beach** accessible below the village, albeit an hour's hike down a gorge inhabited by colonies of doves. The path, waymarked with yellow and blue dots, sets off from the church by the village square: alternatively there's a steep but driveable track down, apshalted until the last 100m or so. Isolation is the main attraction of the beach, which, close up, is rather stony.

ACCOMMODATION AND EATING | THE COAST ROAD FROM KASTÉLLI

SFINÁRI

Captain Fidias Southern end of waterfront ☎ 28220 41107. The first taverna in line, this is a friendly place where you'll usually see octopus – the house speciality – hanging out to dry on a line by the entrance. All the fish is caught with their own boat and other tasty dishes include *kakaviá* (fish soup). March–Oct daily 9am–midnight.

Sunset Southern end of waterfront ☎ 28220 41627. Good taverna offering fresh fish; stuffed cuttlefish is a house special. April–Oct daily noon–midnight.

Thalami Southern end of waterfront ☎ 28220 41632. With a nice beachfront terrace, this place serves good fish and a few meat dishes. Daily 8am–midnight.

KÁMBOS

Rooms Hartzoulakis Main road ☎ 28220 41445. Rooms with a/c, balcony and fridge above a taverna. On the wall a map details walking trails around this coast, outlining a four-stage route from Kastélli to Paleohóra which avoids the roads followed by the E4. Taverna daily 9am–11pm. €30

Sunset Rooms Main road ☎ 28220 41128, ⊜ info @sunset-crete.gr. Taverna with en-suite rooms with a/c and fridge. Taverna daily 8am–10pm. €27

4

The inland road from Kastélli

The **inland road** south of Kastélli Kissámou passes through some of the most fertile country on the island. Here, lush **woodland** watered by tumbling streams is a haven for a rich variety of flora and fauna and in the sturdy farming villages there are plenty of opportunities to take in the local wildlife, or to do some walking in the oleander- and chestnut-wooded hills and along numerous gorges.

Voulgháro and around

Leaving Kastélli by the Kaloudhianá road which branches right at a fork just east of the town, the village lies only only a couple of kilometres further. Some 3km beyond Kaloudhianá you reach the village of **VOULGHÁRO** (Βουλγάρω) where you could stretch your legs in search of two ancient **churches**: Áyios Yeóryios in the village of **Mákronas** across the valley, and Áyios Nikólaos at **Mourí**, along a track 2km further south. When you reach Mourí, the church lies up a track (signed "Áyios Nikólaos" in Greek) 30m beyond the Venetian church. Follow this for 500m up a rough track to reach another sign indicating the tiny chapel tucked away in an olive grove to the right. The **fresco fragments** at Áyios Nikólaos – especially those of Áyios Pandeleímon and the scenes from the Bible – are extremely fine. Just south of Mourí you could also descend into the Koutsamatádos ravine, making for the village of Koutsamatádos, a **walk** of about 5km.

The Koutsamatádos ravine and around

At **TOPÓLIA**, 3km beyond Voulgháro, the church of Ayía Paraskeví has **frescoes** from the late Byzantine period. Soon afterwards the road passes through a narrow tunnel before emerging above the dramatic **Koutsamatádos ravine** (Φαράγγι Κουτσαματάδος), one of the most imposing on the island. Nearing the middle of the ravine you'll come to a signed stairway cut into the rock on the right, and a muscle-taxing short climb to the **cave of Ayía Sofía**. This is one of the largest caves on Crete and remains found here date its usage back to Neolithic times; it now shelters a small chapel, along with stalactites, stalagmites and its present residents, a colony of bats. Keep an eye out also for the vultures that nest in the surrounding cliffs.

Koutsamatádos

Proceeding along the ravine, you soon reach the hamlet of **KOUTSAMATÁDOS** (Κουτσοματάδος), where a couple of taverna-rooms places make an excellent spot to break the journey. You could stay longer and undertake some of the local hikes, many of which are signed. There is a ten-minute path to the Ayía Sofía cave, for example, as well as a path to Miliá (see opposite), about an hour's climb. You can also head down the gorge (conditions permitting; check first), climb **Koproula**, the highest peak hereabouts, or simply wander in the chestnut woods.

ACCOMMODATION AND EATING   KOUTSAMATÁDOS

Arhondas Just below the main road ☎ 28220 51531. Signs direct you to this place, which has simple, comfortable en-suite rooms in a tranquil spot; the taverna serves excellent food – most of it from the family farm – cooked in a traditional wood-fired oven. Taverna daily 10am–midnight. **€25**

Rooms Taverna Panorama Beside the main road ☎ 28220 51163. Pleasant a/c en-suite rooms with views over the ravine. The taverna is good, too, offering local food – including quite a few vegetarian possibilities. The proprietors can advise on walking routes in the area and there's a track down into the ravine next to the taverna. Taverna March–Oct daily 9am–11pm. **€25**

The Enneachora

South of Koutsomatádos you enter an area known as the **Enneachora** (Ινναχωρίου) – the "Nine Villages". Here – with your own transport – you can turn off (look for the sign to **Miliá**) to follow a beautifully scenic drive through the leafy hills and farming villages on the western flank of the Tiflós valley.

Miliá

A couple of kilometres south of Koutsomatádos, and reached via a signed turn-off, the first village you come to is **Vlátos**. Beyond the *Platania* taverna here (see p.304), a road is signed to **MILIÁ (Μηλιά)**, a remarkable "eco-tourist" village.

The precipitous track, only the first half of which is surfaced, climbs dizzily along the shoulder of Mount Kefáli for 5km offering magnificent **views** over the chestnut- and olive-clad valley below. This eventually arrives at a car park, from where a path leads into a stunningly picturesque hamlet of stone houses, once occupied by farmers and shepherds. The isolation of the village eventually led to its abandonment around a century ago until, in the early 1980s, a relative of a former inhabitant proposed to restore the whole place as a working village, welcoming visitors. Other families who owned ruined houses joined in and a co-operative was formed, backed by EU money. Stonemasons skilled in building traditional dwellings were brought over from the Peloponnese and helped to re-create what you now see: an almost too perfect village with solid stone houses on many levels overlooking a verdant cleft.

You should soon locate the house that serves as the community centre and **bar-taverna** (see p.304). Visitors are welcome to get involved in the farming activities, including planting and sowing as well as chestnut-, olive- and apple-harvesting (Miliá means "apple tree" in Greek), and there are occasionally cookery courses and other activities – you can even help make *raki* at the village's still. Otherwise you can **walk** in the nearby hills – the easier paths are signed – or simply contemplate the natural surroundings; nights up here are truly magical.

Élos and around

A kilometre beyond the turn-off for Vlátos and Miliá there's a turn on the left for Strovlés and Voutás leading to the south coast resort of Paleohóra (p.307). The main route continues southwest past slopes covered with magnificent stands of chestnut, plane and other deciduous trees. Chestnuts are a major local crop and the picturesque village of **ÉLOS** (Έλος), 4km along, lies at the centre of the Enneachora **chestnut-growing** region. Even at the height of summer, this is a wonderfully refreshing place, and it's easy to forget just how high you are here – the mountains to the south rise to about 1200m. Behind the village's *Kastanofolia* taverna (see p.305) there is an impressive old arch, claimed to be a Roman aqueduct (though perhaps more likely Turkish), and just beyond this lies a fourteenth-century **Byzantine chapel**, with fresco fragments including an impressive *Pantokrátor* in the apse; if it's closed, the key should be available from the taverna. The great event in Élos's year is the annual **chestnut festival** in late October.

Perivólia

Some 5km southwest of Élos, a turn on the left indicates a sharp descent to the picturesque hamlet of **PERIVÓLIA** (Περιβόλια), tucked into the folds of a high gorge beneath the northern flank of Mount Áyios Díkeos Ióv (Job the Just). The village is a verdant oasis with charming narrow streets punctuated by simple white-walled dwellings and smallholdings overflowing with vigorously sprouting vegetables. Park any vehicle where you cross a bridge at the foot of the descent and, turning right, continue on foot to the bottom of the village and a fountain, near a bust to one of the noted local *pallikári* (guerrilla fighters) of the nineteenth century, Anagnostis Skalidis.

Perivólia Museum

Near the fountain • 10am–1pm & 5–8pm • €1

The small **museum** was assembled by one of Anagnostis Skalidis' descendants, Zacharia Skalidis. An amiable man who speaks only Greek, he will be delighted to show you around his collection, which includes lots of atmospheric photos from a Crete long gone, as well as old guns, letters and coins.

Kefáli

Just beyond Perivólia you will pass the **turn-off to Elafonísi** (see opposite). Barely 1km beyond this lies another charming Enneachora village, **KEFÁLI** (Κεφάλι), with a wonderful setting perched on a hill looking down the Tiflós valley towards the distant sea. It has a fine fourteenth-century frescoed **church**, Metamórphosis tou Sotirís (Transfiguration of Christ), down a track on the left as you enter the village. Inside, the fine **frescoes** depict the betrayal by Judas (whose face has been gouged) and the lowering of Christ from the cross. There is also some interesting and apparently genuine early graffiti, scratched across the paintings. An Englishman, Francis Lerfordes, has marked his contribution with the date 1553, while Turks later inscribed their blasphemous thoughts along with the crescent symbol.

Váthi

One kilometre south of Kefáli on the Elafonísi road, **VÁTHI** (Βάθη) has two ancient frescoed **churches**: the thirteenth-century Áyios Yeóryios off the central square, and the century-older Mihaíl Arhángelos, just to the south. To reach the former take a track uphill facing the plane tree in the central platía to the left of a drinking fountain. Follow the track uphill for 200m, where it turns into a narrow *kalderími* (ancient footpath) that leads you to the church. Inside, the frescoes are in good condition, with a sensitive portrayal of the Archangel Gabriel and an unusual image of the Virgin and Child in the apse. To see the church of Mihaíl Arhángelos you'll need to locate the village priest, who has the key; try at the *kafenío* near the plane tree. He will conduct you to the southern end of the village to see wonderfully preserved early fourteenth-century **frescoes** depicting the Emperor Constantine and his mother Helena, the Fall of Jericho, Christ entering Jerusalem, and a moving portrayal of the betrayal by Judas.

ACCOMMODATION AND EATING   THE ENNEACHORA

VLATOS

★ **To Metohi Monahoyou** Near the foot of the road to Miliá ☎697 96 81 999. An olive farm selling its organic oil from a small shop near the entrance. The friendly proprietors, mother and daughter, also offer distinctive individually styled rooms in a stone-built house, prepare organic vegetarian meals and can advise on walks in the area. Room only €30, room plus dinner & breakfast €60

Platania Taverna Near the foot of the road to Miliá ☎28220 51406. A woodland path leads to the taverna's terrace, close to the gigantic, thousand-year-old plane tree that gives the place its name. With tables spread out beneath the tree, it's a friendly hideaway serving up good meat and *mezédhes* – the grilled lamb dishes are recommended – and making its money from mammoth wedding feasts. March–Oct daily 9am–midnight.

MILIÁ

★ **Miliá Bar-Taverna** 3km above Vlátos village ☎28210 46774, ⌨milia.gr. Meals served in the taverna, based on traditional Cretan recipes, include excellent soups and dishes such as pork in orange, lamb with rosemary and

a variety of salads and vegetables from the complex's farm. They also serve good Cretan wines. Daily noon–9.30pm; July & Aug closes 10.30pm.

★ **Miliá Eco Village** 3km above Vlátos village ☎28210 46774, ⌨milia.gr. The rustically furnished accommodation varies in size from small "semi-detached" en-suite cottages to houses for four, but all are delightful, furnished with ancient fittings including huge fireplaces (wood provided in winter) and stone ovens. There's hot water and a small bathroom light, but no mains electricity – candles illuminate the rooms and the restaurant in the evening – and the only concession to modernity is a satellite internet connection and phone link. You can simply turn up, but it's wise to reserve; buses from Haniá stop at Vlátos, from where staff will collect you (this must be arranged in advance). Buffet breakfast (included), featuring home-made fruit, cheese and preserves (plus freshly baked bread), is provided in the bar. €75

ÉLOS

Taverna Kamares In the village "square" on the road through ☎28220 61332. The neighbouring *Kastanofolia* tends to grab all the attention, but this is a very friendly alternative for traditional Cretan cooking; the lamb or goat dishes are recommended. Daily 7am–midnight.

Taverna-Rooms Kastanofolia ("Chestnut Den") In the village "square" on the road through ❂ 28220 61258. Shaded by plane, eucalyptus and, of course, chestnut trees, this is a clean and simple place with rooms above a decent taverna. There are ducks in a pool filled by a stream running beside the terrace and, directly over the road, you can stroll along a track that leads a couple of kilometres into the chestnut forests. Taverna daily 7am–midnight. **€35**

KEFÁLI

Taverna-Rooms Panorama Main street, central village ❂ 28220 61198. This aptly named, welcoming taverna has a fantastic view from its terrace and the cooking is reliable. En-suite rooms with fridge are in an attractive stone-built house on the edge of the village, with balconies and roof terrace. Free wi-fi. Taverna daily 8am–10pm. **€35**

Taverna-Rooms Polakis Main street, central village ❂ 28220 61260. Welcoming place with rooms with a/c and fridge above a taverna. Some have a splendid view from their balconies over the Bay of Stomíou. Taverna daily 8am–11pm. **€35**

Elafonísi and around

Some 17km southwest of Kefáli, the tiny uninhabited islet of **Elafonísi** (Ελαφόνησος) lies marooned on the edge of a gloriously scenic turquoise lagoon. It's all too easy to get here, a fact reflected in the huge number of visitors who do so, by daily bus from Haniá, by car, with coach tours, or on a boat from Paleohóra. En route the road passes the much-revered Moní Hrissoskalítissa perched on a rock cliff above the sea.

Moní Hrissoskalítissa (Monastery of the Virgin of the Golden Step)

Daily 8am–8pm • €2 (for the museum); Orthodox faith free

Moní Hrissoskalítissa (Μονή Χρυσοσκαλίτισσας), 10km southwest of Kefáli, is a weathered, white-walled nunnery beautifully sited on a rocky promontory above the waves. Today barely functioning, it has reduced from some two hundred residents to a solitary nun and one monk, whose main task seems to be keeping the place acceptable for tourists. The present church – containing a much-venerated thousand-year-old icon of the Virgin – dates only from the nineteenth century, but this is an ancient foundation: the first church was built in a cave here in the thirteenth century and recent investigations have turned up evidence of a much earlier Minoan settlement (or shrine) as well. A small **museum** has a few icons along with assorted religious paraphernalia. Look out for the ninety steps that lead to the top of the crag around which the place is built: one of them appears golden (*hrissí skála*) to those who are pure in spirit – a fact that the authors of this guide are unable to verify.

Elafonísi Beach

Just over 5km south of Moní Hrissoskalítissa, **Elafonísi Beach** (Παραλία Ελαφόνησος) comes as an exotic shock. The almost tropical waters sheltered by the islet boast white sand tinged pink by coral, aquamarine waters, salt-encrusted rock pools and bright-red starfish. The water is incredibly warm, calm and shallow and the islet itself is a short wade across the sand bar. There are more beaches on its far side (with waves), along with the odd ruined wall, seashells and a monument to Australian sailors shipwrecked here in 1907.

The arrival of crowds has brought lines of sun umbrellas and loungers to the **beach**, but little else in the way of infrastructure (the area is a National Park, so no permanent structures can be erected): there are stalls selling cold drinks and basic food, along with portable toilets and an incongruous phone box. If you're here on a day-trip, the best option is to bring your own picnic.

Walks from Elafonísi

Continuing south from Elafonísi, the E4 **coastal path** to Paleohóra (about 17km away) is reasonably well marked, but it's a tough walk, especially in the early stages, with one hair-raising section above a sheer drop near the hill of Ktista (6km out), which is definitely not for the faint-hearted. Check the route before you set out, and don't venture this way alone, or without plentiful water. You could also hike up a track heading inland to **Sklavopoúla**, 7km away (see p.312), from where paved roads head on towards Paleohóra.

ACCOMMODATION AND EATING   ELAFONÍSI AND AROUND

Due to Elafonísi's National Park status no accommodation is allowed closer than 1km to the beach. The places listed below line the in-road from the north.

Rooms Elafonisi ☎ 28220 61274, ⓦ elafonisi-resort .com. Probably the best choice, with its own taverna and minimarket, and a/c balcony rooms with fridge and sea view. Also some attractive apartments and villas nearby. Closed Nov–March. Taverna April–Oct daily 8am–midnight. **€40**

Glykeria Near Moní Hrissoskalítissa ☎ 28220 61292, ⓦ glykeria.com. Very good taverna on one side of the

road, plus tranquil en-suite rooms with fridge and great balcony sea views on the other. There's also a very nice garden pool. **€50**

Panorama ☎ 28220 61548, ⓦ www.elafonisos-creta .gr. A good taverna with better views than *Elafonisi*, but less appealing en-suite a/c balcony rooms with fridge. Closed Nov–March. Taverna April–Oct daily 8.30am–10.30pm. **€50**

Sélinos

Despite its isolation from the north and centre of the island, the eparchy (province) of Sélinos (Σέλινο), stretching roughly from the village of Flória to the south coast, has played a significant role in the island's history since ancient times. As early as the third century BC several of the communities here were important enough to form a confederation with Górtys (see p.96) and Cyrenaica, in Libya, and under the Romans, cities such as **Lissós**, **Elyrós** and **Syia** (modern Sóuyia) prospered greatly. This distinguished past laid the foundations for the communal pride that created the scores of frescoed **Byzantine churches** here, perhaps the main reason to visit inland Sélinos today. One of the glories of Crete, every village seems to offer at least one example, while some have as many as three or more. We have detailed some wonderful examples in this account, but many more small churches can be found throughout the whole area, particularly if you get off the road into the smaller villages. Few, if any, of them will be open when you arrive – but express an interest at the nearest *kafenío* or to a local passer-by and it rarely takes long to hunt out the priest or someone else with a key.

Flória

FLÓRIA (Φλώρια), some 16km southeast of Kastélli, is divided into two halves. Káto (lower) Flória, straddling the road, and Apáno (upper) Flório above it. The upper village has the church of Áyii Patéres (the Holy Fathers), although here only fresco fragments remain. In the lower village, **Áyios Yeóryios** preserves thirteen panels of fine fifteenth-century frescoes. To reach it, entering from the north end of the village, go down a lane to the right of the second taverna you pass on the right. After about 600m you'll come to a small footbridge over a dry stream bed; cross this and after 50m veer left at a fork to follow the path leading to the church. Near the first taverna (the better of the pair), two war memorials – one German, one Greek – face each other across the road, serving as grim reminders of the terrible atrocities that happened here during World War II.

Kándanos and around

KÁNDANOS (Κάντανος), 9km south of Flória and approached along a verdant valley planted with olives, is the chief village of Sélinos (though it's a great deal smaller than Paleohóra), and makes an appealing, quiet place to stop for coffee or a meal.

Despite an ancient name that goes back to Dorian times and the existence of as many as fifteen Byzantine **churches** in the vicinity (it was the seat of a bishop throughout the Byzantine and Venetian periods), the village buildings are almost entirely new, for the place was razed to the ground by the Germans for its role in the **wartime resistance**. In 1941, after the German army had taken Máleme (see p.265), troops were dispatched urgently along this road to prevent the Allies landing reinforcements at Paleohóra. The resistance fighters of Kándanos determined to stop them, and despite a ferocious pitched battle the Germans could not break through for two crucial days. In retribution the Germans utterly destroyed the village. The original sign erected at the time is today preserved in the museum (currently closed) but a copy stands on a war memorial in the square – in German and Greek it reads: "Here stood Kándanos, destroyed in retribution for the murder of 25 German soldiers, and never to be rebuilt again."

On the outskirts is a waterworks, given to the village by the Germans after the war as an act of reconciliation. Many of the German military who served here have since returned to forge friendships with their erstwhile adversaries.

The Kándanos churches

The village that arose defiantly from the ashes after World War II is today an easy-going place with four Byzantine **churches**. There are good but damaged frescoes at the restored **Mihaíl Arhángelos**, signed to the left up a lane on the northern edge of the village, and in the charming small white chapel of **Áyios Mámas**, signed down a road by the petrol station on the village's main road junction, lying 1km away through the olive groves. **Ayía Ekateríni**, signed off the main street near the central platía, is a beautiful old building with faded fresco fragments. The best of all, though, is **Áyios Ioánnis**, another small white church with superb fresco fragments, signed downhill off the Paleohóra road on the edge of the village, around 1km from the road.

Anisaráki

A short detour from Kándanos climbs a couple of kilometres east to **ANISARÁKI** (Ανισαράκι) where you'll find more fine frescoes in the fifteenth-century churches of **Ayía Ánna** (signed on the left in an olive grove as you enter), with a rare stone iconostasis, **Panayía** and **Ayía Paraskeví** (both signed from the centre). Nearby, in the hamlet of **Koufalotós**, halfway between Kándanos and Anisaráki, the chapel of **Áyios Mihaíl Arhángelos** has fourteenth-century paintings by the Cretan master Ioannis Pagomenos (see p.313). The chapel is located down a track on the right (coming from Anisaráki), and across a stream.

South of Kándanos

Beyond Kándanos the main road south bypasses several more villages with frescoed churches: Áyios Yeóryios, in **Plemenianá**, has paintings dating from the fifteenth century, while **Kakodhíki**, known for its curative springs, has several churches nearby. These include the very ancient chapel of **Mihaíl Arhángelos**, probably early thirteenth-century, beside the modern church of Ayía Triádha, and the hilltop Áyios Isidhóros, with magnificent views and frescoes defaced by the Turks. **Kádhros**, some 9km south of Kándanos, has the churches of Ioánnis Chrysóstomos and the **Panayía** (reached via a downhill path beside a gaily decorated *kafenío*; key from the house near the church) whose fine frescoes are almost complete.

Paleohóra

PALEOHÓRA (Παλαιοχώρα) was known originally as Kastél Selínou – the castle of Sélinos – and for much of its history was no more than that, a castle. Built by the Venetians in 1279, the fort was destroyed by Barbarossa in 1539 and never properly reconstructed even when the small port grew up beneath it. The ruins are still perched

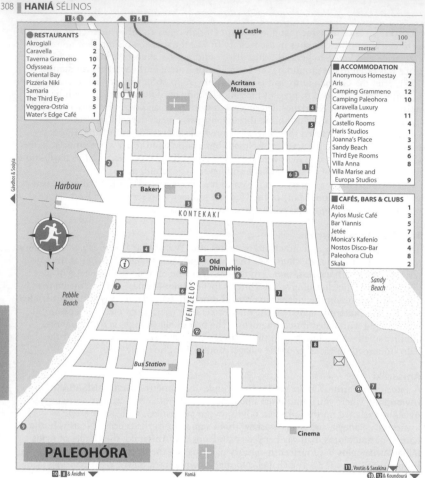

RESTAURANTS
Akrogiali	8
Caravella	2
Taverna Grameno	10
Odysseas	7
Oriental Bay	9
Pizzeria Niki	4
Samaria	6
The Third Eye	3
Veggera-Ostria	5
Water's Edge Café	1

ACCOMMODATION
Anonymous Homestay	7
Aris	2
Camping Grammeno	12
Camping Paleohora	10
Caravella Luxury Apartments	11
Castello Rooms	4
Haris Studios	1
Joanna's Place	3
Sandy Beach	5
Third Eye Rooms	6
Villa Anna	8
Villa Marise and Europa Studios	9

CAFÉS, BARS & CLUBS
Atoli	1
Ayios Music Café	3
Bar Yiannis	5
Jetée	7
Monica's Kafenío	6
Nostos Disco-Bar	4
Paleohora Club	8
Skala	2

PALEOHÓRA

at the bulbous end of the headland now occupied by the settlement of Paleohóra – at its narrowest a bare four blocks across from the harbour on one side to the beach on the other.

Today, the village is rapidly growing into a small town, and can barely cope with the increasing volume of visitors. Even so, Paleohóra retains its enjoyably laidback, end-of-the-line feel, helped no doubt by superb and extensive sands and by the fact that there are no big hotels, and almost all the rooms and restaurants are still owned and run by local families. Warm right through the winter, this out-of-season backwater makes an excellent place to rent an inexpensive apartment long term.

Other than head for the beach, eat and drink, there's not a great deal to see or do here, which of course is a major part of its attraction. However, there are plenty of trips on offer (see p.310), as well as attractive **walks** inland, to charming villages like Ánidhri and Azoyirés (see p.313), or along the coast in either direction.

Paleohóra castle

In town you can check out the **castle**, for the views back over town, or walk right around the end of the promontory to return to the beach on the other side. Neither of

PALEOHÓRA ORIENTATION

The main road from Kándanos leads you into a eucalyptus-lined avenue that becomes Paleohóra's single main street, **Odhós Venizélos**, lined with taverna after café after bar. If you come from the west, on the roads via Voutás or Sarakína, you'll emerge on the road behind the sandy western beach, by the post office. Bisecting the village north to south, **Venizélos** is Paleohóra's vibrant soul, and on summer evenings its central stretch is closed to traffic, brightly illuminated and filled to overflowing as the bar and restaurant tables spill across the pavement and encroach onto the road. From the main street, nothing is further than a five-minute walk away: straight ahead (south) lies the **castle** with a virtually empty marina beyond it; to the left (east) is the aptly named **Pebble Beach**, with its harbour from where boats to Soúyia and Gávdhos depart; to the right (or west) of Venizélos are the broad sands of the fabulous **Sandy Beach**, where you'll find quite a few hotels.

these options is as appealing as it might be, since the fortress itself is little more than a hillock ringed with broken walls, while a new concrete marina and some unsightly harbour buildings dominate the point. Heading up towards the castle you'll see the oldest parts of town, to the south of the harbour.

The beaches

Of the beaches, the western **Sandy Beach** is more impressive: magnificently broad and sandy, lined with tamarisks and supplied with showers, on a bay with excellent easy windsurfing. **Pebble Beach**, facing east, is at first sight a much less attractive proposition. However, this eastern side is far livelier at night, when the beachfront promenade rivals the main street for action and choice of eating; the cafés and restaurants over here have a stunning view of the moon rising over the mountains. The beach is also more sheltered when the wind is blowing, and if you venture far enough north, away from town, you'll even find some sand.

The Acritans Museum

South end of Venizélos opposite the church • Wed–Sun 10am–1pm & 7–9pm • Free

Paleohóra's newest arrival is the rather curious **Acritans Museum**, funded by the EU and dedicated to the understanding of cross-border cultural influences and ethnic mixing in medieval Europe. That may sound a little vague and highfalutin, but the lavishly funded museum has many artefacts from various parts of Europe that are both interesting and beautiful, including musical instruments, saddles and harnesses, jewellery and weaponry.

ARRIVAL AND DEPARTURE PALEOHÓRA

By bus Buses from Haniá (4 daily; 2hr) drop you on Venizélos, towards the northern end of the street.

By boat or ferry Ferries dock on the east side of town, at the bottom of Pebble Beach. There are departures (April–Oct daily 8.30am) to Soúyia (30min) and Ayía Rouméli (1hr 15min): on Mon and Wed these continue to Gávdhos. A smaller boat makes the trip to Elafonísi (May–Oct Mon, Tues, Thurs & Sat 10.30am, returning 4.30pm; €9 one way; 1hr). Confirm times with any of the travel agencies (see p.310), who will have details of

additional departures; Selino Travel, next to the harbour, have constantly updated information. Be aware also that sailings are likely to be cancelled in high winds (frequent on the south coast in summer).

Destinations Elafonísi (April–Oct Mon, Tues, Thurs & Sat 10.30am; 1hr); Gávdhos (April–Oct Mon & Wed 8.30am; 4hr; Tues, Fri & Sun 8.30am via Hóra Sfakíon; 5hr); Hóra Sfakíon (April–Oct daily 8.30am; 3hr); Loutró (April–Oct daily 8.30am; 2hr 45min); Soúyia/Ayía Rouméli (April–Oct daily 8.30am; 45min–1hr 15min).

GETTING AROUND

Taxi There's a taxi office just by the ferry dock, or call ☎ 28230 41128.

Bike rental Nikos (daily 9am–3pm & 6–10pm; ☎ 28230

41536), towards the northern end of Venizélos, has the best mountain bikes, though you can also rent them from the Notos and Sabine travel agencies (see p.310).

INFORMATION AND ACTIVITIES

Tourist information The helpful municipal tourist office (May–Oct Wed–Mon 10am–1pm & 6–9pm; ☎ 28230 41507) is in a cabin fronting Pebble Beach.

Travel agencies Notos Travel (☎ 28230 42110, ⊛ notoscar.com), on Venizélos opposite the old town hall, has a finger in every pie, with a laundry and internet access as well as exchange, car, motorbike and mountain bike rental, tours and more. Sabine Travel (☎ 28230 42105, ⊛ hermescar.gr), virtually next door, also has trips, exchange, and cars, motorbikes and mountain bikes for rent. Selino Travel (☎ 28230 42272, ⊜ selino2@otenet.gr), on Kontekáki just up from the harbour, is a little less frenetic and good for the latest ferry updates.

Tourist train A tourist train tours Paleohóra every summer evening.

Boat trips Local boat trips include dolphin-spotting cruises (though despite claims of 70 percent likelihood, these don't seem to have a very high success rate) plus excursions to Lissós, Elafonísi, Samariá and Gramvoúsa. Contact any travel agent.

Gorge walks There are organized gorge walks of Samariá and Ayía Iríni. It's possible to do these yourself by bus, with a daily service heading for Omalós via Ayía Iríni, daily at 7am throughout the summer. You can then get the boat back from Ayía Rouméli or Soúyia in the late afternoon.

ACCOMMODATION

Finding a **room** is unlikely to be a problem except in August and on summer weekends. Inexpensive places are mostly in the backstreets away from the beach – particularly the street parallel to Pebble Beach and in the narrow lanes towards the castle – but you'll see signs everywhere. The tourist office can also advise.

Anonymous Homestay In a backstreet behind the tourist office ☎ 28230 41509, ⊛ cityofpaleochora.gr. Among the least expensive places in town, and something of a travellers' meeting place. Simple rooms, with use of a communal kitchen, off a charming garden courtyard, and two two-bedroom apartments. A/c (€5). Rooms **€28**, apartments **€50**

⭐ **Aris** On the upper road at the south end of the peninsula, beneath the castle ☎ 28230 41502, ⊛ arishotel.net. Charming, welcoming and peaceful garden hotel with good, en-suite a/c balcony rooms (30 & 31, overlooking the garden, are the ones to go for), most with sea view. Parking on site. Breakfast available. Free wi-fi. **€50**

Camping Grammeno 4km along the coast to the west ☎ 28230 42125 or ☎ 697 92 28 612, ⊛ grammeno camping.gr. Friendly campsite with youthful management, close to the most attractive beach in this direction. Free wi-fi. Two people plus tent (vehicle free) **€16**

Camping Paleohora 2km northeast of the centre, reached along the road behind Pebble Beach ☎ 28230 41120. Attractively sited in an olive grove close to the beach, with plenty of shade. The only drawback here is the bone-hard terrain. Free wi-fi. Two people plus tent (vehicle free) **€15**

Caravella Luxury Apartments Reached via the turn-off for Voutás at the northwest end of town ☎ 28230 41131, ⊛ caravella.gr. On a rise above the resort, these ultramodern a/c apartments have large terrace balconies with stunning views and come with marble floors, lounge (with wood-burning stove) and satellite TV plus a fully equipped kitchen. Free wi-fi. Sleeps up to four. **€88**

⭐ **Castello Rooms** Overlooking the southern end of

Sandy Beach ☎ 28230 41143. Exceptionally friendly place, most of whose simple rooms come with a/c and fridge and have balconies overlooking the beach; a few rooms at the back without view are less expensive (singles available too), and you can still get the views from the terrace taverna. Free wi-fi. **€37**

Haris Studios On the seafront below the east side of the castle ☎ 28230 42438, ⊛ paleochora-holidays .com. A friendly Cretan-Scottish-run place with a/c studios and apartments with balconies and sea views; all are en suite, with cooking facilities. They also have a new block with a pool (which all guests can use). Studios **€45**, apartments **€50**

Joanna's Place South end of the peninsula, beneath east side of the castle ☎ 28230 41801, ⊛ joannas -palaiochora.com. Decent a/c studios with kitchenette and balcony sea view, in a tranquil location. **€60**

Sandy Beach South end of Sandy Beach ☎ 28230 42130, ⊛ sandy-beach.gr. The closest Paleohora comes to chic, with attractive a/c rooms with sea views, equipped with fridge, TV and balcony or terrace. Free wi-fi. Breakfast included. **€60**

Third Eye Rooms Inland from Sandy Beach ☎ 28230 41234. Good value a/c rooms and apartments attached to and directly behind the restaurant of the same name, with fridge and balcony with (some) sea view. Larger family apartments (sleeping 5) come with kitchen. Free wi-fi. Rooms **€20**, apartments **€40**

Villa Anna In a broad side street off Sandy Beach near the post office ☎ 2810 346428, ⊛ villaanna-paleochora .com. Pricey but very pleasant apartments for two to six people – large, nicely furnished, all with kitchen and a/c, and surrounded by lush gardens. Booking recommended. Larger apartments sleep up to six. **€60**

Villa Marise and Europa Studios Sandy Beach, north of the post office ☎28230 83018, ⓦvillamarise.com. Separated by the *Hotel Elman*, these two seafront blocks have a variety of well-equipped, en-suite a/c studios and apartments for up to six people, with direct access to the beach. The more modern *Europa* has a pool for guests. Studios **€50**, apartments **€80**

EATING

There are plenty of **places to eat**, and prices are generally reasonable. The Pebble Beach restaurants tend to be the more touristy, though this does mean that there are several places serving **breakfast**. There are plenty of **cafés** scattered around too, especially on Venizélos and around its junction with Kontekáki, the main cross street, as well as a number of **bakeries** – probably the best is *Bakakis*, near the harbour behind the supermarket.

Akrogiali Pebble Beach. Attractively old-fashioned taverna among the glossier places on Pebble Beach, with good Greek standards. April–Oct daily noon–11pm.

★ **Caravella** Old town seafront, just south of the ferry jetty ☎28230 41131. Paleohóra's best seafood restaurant, with a waterfront terrace. All the fish is caught locally – try the *kathári* (black snapper) – and both cooking and service are excellent, as is their chilled *hyma* (barrelled wine) from the Kastélli Kissámou area; try also their very tasty French-style muscatel dessert wine from the Sélinos village of *Máza*. They also serve some meat, plus a daily selection of *mayireftá* (pre-cooked dishes). April–Nov daily 9am–11.30pm.

★ **Taverna Grameno** 3km west towards Koundourá along the coast road, near Graméno beach ☎28230 41505. Perhaps the area's most authentic Cretan restaurant, this is a friendly garden taverna with a play area for kids, and the cooking is outstanding – take a look in the kitchen for what is seasonal and fresh. April–Oct daily noon–midnight.

Odysseas Pebble Beach ☎28230 41137. Right at the heart of the action, with decent pizza from a wood-fired oven and well-cooked Greek standards. Feb–Oct daily 1pm–midnight.

Oriental Bay Northern end of Pebble Beach ☎28230 41322. With an inviting, tamarisk-shaded terrace fronting the sea, this is one of the nicest places in town for a meal, be it fish or meat (some vegetarian options), often with live guitar accompaniment. Also a decent wine list and excellent juices and breakfasts. April–Oct daily noon–11pm.

Pizzeria Niki Off the south side of Kontekáki ☎28230 41532. An attractive courtyard setting for excellent wood-fired pizzas. May–Oct daily noon–midnight.

Samariá Behind the old Dhimarhio building ☎28230 41572. Friendly new taverna in an atmospheric roofless ruin; in winter a canvas roof is unfurled and they light the fires. The traditional Cretan cuisine is excellent; visit the kitchen to see what's cooking. House specials include *arní tsighariasto* (lamb in olive oil casserole) and *hirinó stámnaki* (pot roasted pork). Daily 6–11pm.

★ **The Third Eye** Inland from Sandy Beach ☎28230 42223, ⓦthethirdeye-paleochora.com. Excellent vegetarian restaurant run by a Greek-New Zealand couple. It's worth putting up with the sometimes brusque service for great food and spices rarely seen on Crete, from curries to *gado-gado* and bean salads, as well as more conventional Greek dishes. The world music background sounds go well with the cuisine, and there are regular concerts of *lyra*, Greek and Asian music in summer. April–Oct daily 8am–3pm & 5.30–11.30pm.

Veggera-Ostria Sandy Beach ☎694 36 31 724. Large, friendly taverna serving well-cooked Greek staples. Thursday is "Cretan night", with traditional music and dancing. April–Oct daily 8pm–midnight.

Water's Edge Café On the seafront below the east side of the castle, at Haris Studios ☎28230 42438. As well as having a lovely sea-view terrace for breakfasts, snacks and drinks, the *Water's Edge* serves dinner on Saturdays (booking recommended); freshly made and excellent. Daily 8am–midnight.

DRINKING, NIGHTLIFE AND ENTERTAINMENT

Paleohóra clings to its village origins, and has no pretensions to be anything other than a tranquil seaside resort with family appeal: if you're looking for all-night discos and raucous bars you've come to the wrong place. Most **bars** keep their volume well down after dark; many of the most popular of these are shoehorned into the area around the Venizélos–Kontekáki junction and down towards the harbour. Nightly showings at the open-air **cinema**, Cine Attikon, tucked away in the northern backstreets, are wonderfully atmospheric; most of their recent-release films are in English and programmes (advertised on billboards outside the cinema and along Venizélos; tickets €6) change daily.

Atoli Southern end of Sandy Beach. Lively café-bar – a good spot to catch the sunset – with pool table and internet, plus occasional live music, traditional and modern. April–Oct daily 9pm–3am.

Ayios Music Café Corner of Venizélos and Kontekáki ⓦagiosbar.gr. Café and central meeting place by day, cocktail bar at night, when there's decent music too. April–Oct daily 7pm–7am.

Bar Yiannis Venizélos. Café/ouzerí with tables spread across the main street (good for people-watching) and whose eponymous proprietor is one of the town's characters. Daily 10am–1am.

Jetée Sandy Beach, right on the sand near the post office. A quiet spot to linger over a sundowner, and often lively later on; occasional "beach party" events in high summer. Free wi-fi. April–Oct daily 8pm–3am.

★ **Monica's Kafenío** Venizélos, slightly north of the old Dhimarhio. Opening at dawn to give the fishermen their morning coffee, this is a plain and simple traditional *kafenío* where the (Greek) coffee is excellent and an ouzo (and other

drinks) comes with a free *meze*. Daily 6am–10.15pm.

Nostos Disco-Bar Pebble Beach. This is the liveliest late-night joint in town, with a chilled club atmosphere and outside courtyard bar. June–Oct daily 6.30pm–5am.

Paleohora Club 1km or so from the north end of Pebble Beach. The one real dance club, far enough from town to be able to make some noise, though still relatively mainstream and restrained. May–Sept daily 11pm–6am.

Skala By the ferry jetty. In the morning this is one of the town's best spots for breakfast; later the drinks get stronger and there's live music on Monday nights. April–Oct daily 24hr.

DIRECTORY

Banks There are several banks with ATMs on Kontekáki west of Venizélos and on Venizélos itself, north of the town hall.

Books and newspapers A well-stocked *períptero* on Venizélos sells foreign newspapers, also available at To Delfíni bookshop on Kontekáki; the latter also has a good selection of books in English, including local walking guides.

Internet Increasingly available at cafés and hotels. The biggest internet café is Coronet (daily 10am–2pm & 4pm–midnight), on Venizélos, and there are also machines at Notos Travel (see p.310).

Laundry At Notos Travel (see p.310), or there's a small launderette a little further north on Venizélos.

Post office On the road behind Sandy Beach (Mon–Fri 7.30am–2pm).

Supermarkets Paleohóra has an extraordinary number of big supermarkets for such a small place, largely thanks to a long-running rivalry between two local family firms. The largest are behind Sandy Beach, but there's a handy one just by the ferry jetty.

Graméno beach

The coastline **west of Paleohóra** is an uneasy mix of tourist development and polytunnel agriculture, rarely very attractive but with a number of worthwhile little coves and beaches along the way. Much the best of the beaches is **Graméno beach** (Γραμμένο), after about 5km, where a small peninsula shelters lagoon-like water and there's a sandy beach with trees for shade. On the landward side of the road here, *Taverna Grameno* (see p.311) is a superb place to eat, and there are a several rooms places nearby.

The Pelekaniotikós valley

With your own transport, you could follow a spectacular, deserted drive along the road which heads **northwest from Paleohóra** and tracks the valley of the River Pelekaniotikós calling at a string of charming Sélinos hamlets. Many of these roads have been recently paved, and there's plenty of excellent, easy driving, though be sure to fill your fuel tank before you set out.

At **Voutás**, 12km northwest of Paleohóra, there is the possibility of a detour to the isolated village of Sklavopoúla and its wonderful frescoed **churches**. Follow the signs towards Sklavopoúla, and 1km before Kítiros the small fourteenth-century church of **Ayía Paraskeví** is worth a stop to see some faded frescoes on its rear wall; one has a remarkably lurid portrayal of hell with devils putting sinners into the flames while others are being crushed by serpents.

Sklavopoúla

Beyond Kítiros, the road climbs among rocky heights for 5km to reach **SKLAVOPOÚLA** (Σκλαβοπούλα) itself, set at an altitude of 640m and one of the remotest communities in the Sélinos, as well as a place with a considerable history. The nineteenth-century English traveller Robert Pashley made it here and identified Sklavopoúla as the site of

THE SKLAVOPOÚLA CHURCHES

As you come in to the village of Sklavopoúla you pass the church of **Áyios Yeóryios**, next to a school playground on the left, with some fine frescoes dating from the thirteenth century. To get the key, go behind the school to the house of Petros, the guardian. Continuing into the village, the other two notable churches – the **Panayía** and **Sotíros Christós** – are reached down a path next to the primitive **kafenío** – not to be missed – on the left. Continue downhill along this path (a **kalderími** – the still-used Turkish name given to ancient tracks and cobbled ways) for 200m or so until you come to the rambling house of Mihailis, the guardian. His welcoming multi-generational family provide a delightful insight into a rural Crete long gone from other parts of the island. You will probably be offered the traditional welcome of sweet bread and a cool drink or even a **raki** before the key emerges. Then Mihailis will lead you to see the churches nearby – the **frescoes** of the Panayía with superb gospel scenes and a portrait of the donor are the more interesting. Although he refuses money for his time, donations are welcome for the churches' upkeep.

Doulópolis, a Dorian city renowned for its military prowess. The village's present name ("Village of the Slavs") may stem from a resettlement of Slavs here by Nikiforas Fokas (see p.334) following his reconquest of Crete from the Saracens in 961. There are seven **churches** (see box above) in the vicinity, all with wall paintings.

Back on the main route, beyond Voutás the road winds northwards through dramatic mountain scenery to join the route that cuts across from the far west to the Paleohóra, a couple of kilometres south of **Stróvles**. Here you can turn right to circle back (or for the direct route towards Haniá), left for the road through the Enneachora (p.302).

4

East of Paleohóra

East of Paleohóra several routes head towards Soúyia, though if you want to follow the **coast** you'll have to do so on foot. Here a driveable dirt road continues beyond the *Camping Paleohora* campsite for a couple of kilometres to Yialaskári Beach, an attractive spot with sunloungers and a seasonal *kantína*. Beyond, the **E4 Pan-European Footpath** traces the shore, passing a succession of grey pebble strips with fewer people clad in fewer clothes the further you venture. This path continues to Lissós (see p.315), a trip of 14km/4hr, and Soúyia (see p.315), 18km/5–6hr – and if you time it right you can return to Paleohóra by boat from Soúyia (currently at 6.20pm in summer). You should carefully check out both the route and the boat times beforehand. The path is waymarked, but it doesn't simply follow the coast all the way, and there are one or two

WALKING TO ÁNIDHRI AND PRODHRÓMI

If you're driving, or want a good circular walk, take the paved road beyond the *Camping Paleohora* campsite, which turns inland, heading towards **Ánidhri**. Some 6km east of Paleohóra, Ánidhri is a particularly beautiful village, with a fourteenth-century church, **Áyios Yeóryios**, which has an unusual double altar and fine **frescoes** depicting the lives of Christ and Áyios Yeóryios by Ioannis Pagomenos (John the Frozen), the most prolific of several painters whose signatures appear frequently around Sélinos.

From Ánidhri, **on foot**, you can follow the verdant Ánidhri Gorge down to the beach at Yialaskári (see above), about an hour below, and from there head back into Paleohóra. There's also a path heading up towards Azoyirés (see p.314), about 90min away. Continuing by road it's another 7km to **Prodhrómi**, from where a track (not very easily spotted on the village's southern edge) winds some 4km down to meet the E4 footpath near the coast. For an easier **alternative walk to Lissós and Soúyia** you could take a taxi this far, halving the total walking distance to around 9km. Beyond Prodhrómi a fine road continues through wild, deserted country, to join the main road west near Teménia.

steep scrambles. Since the most scenic section is through the gorge between Lissós and Soúyia, it might be easier to do it from there.

Azoyirés

Heading north out of Paleohóra on the main road, you'll soon see signs to **AZOYIRÉS** (Αζογυρές), "Paradise Village". The road up to the village is set amid woods of cypress and pine, a lovely drive on good roads. In Azoyirés, head straight for the centre, where there are two **tavernas**. Armed with a **map** from the *Alpha* taverna (see opposite) – the scattered local attractions are relatively easy to find. In addition to those described below there's also a path down to the coast, via Ánidhri.

Azoyirés Museum

Officially Sat & Sun 9am–2pm; when closed enquire at the *Alpha*

The **Azoyirés Museum**, a single-room record of the Turkish occupation, is full of fascinating old stuff, and delightfully located in the valley at the bottom of the village, by the old olive-oil factory and a chapel built into a cliff. A pretty path leads down, above a tree-filled ravine where pine, cypress, olive and maple grow.

The Azoyirés cave

The biggest of several local **caves** is on an easy-to-miss road which (approaching from Paleohóra) sets off left just before the *Alpha* taverna, and winds steeply upwards for nearly 2km (keep climbing and turning where there's any doubt about the way). At the top you'll need to park any transport. From here there's an obvious path leading on – look up and you'll see a cross, some 200m above, which marks your destination. Approaching the cave you may disturb quail; the eerie sounds in the cave itself emanate from more birds, mostly pigeons, amplified by the acoustics. A steep metal stairway and rock-cut steps descend 50m or so to a little shrine lit from above by dim, reflected light. If you have a powerful torch (the *Alpha* will lend you one if not), you can continue a fair way, although there's no proper path.

Teménia

Beyond Azoyirés it's 10km or so to **TEMÉNIA** (Τεμένια) – source of the drinks of that brand name sold throughout western Crete – where there's an interesting **church** and small archeological site as well as the welcoming *Ta Tamenia* **taverna** (see opposite).

Sotíros Christós

The church should be open (enquire at the nearby monastery buildings if not)

Arriving in Teménia from Azoyirés, you come to a road junction on the edge of the village. Turn right downhill along the Rodováni road where soon you'll pass a rebuilt stone chapel atop a low hill to the left and, about 200m further on, a sign on the right to ancient Hyrtakína. Head down this narrow track, and on your right you will soon see the charming drum-domed church of **Sotíros Christós** (Σοτήριος Χριστός), whose entrance has curious stone steps built into the sides of a shallow porch. Inside a number of fine **frescoes** include a stirring image of a mounted Áyios Yeóryios slaying the dragon.

ACCOMMODATION AND EATING	EAST FROM PALEOHÓRA
ÁNIDHRI	83001. The old village school, tastefully converted, makes
Metacom Near Ánidhri (ask at the Kafenío Sto Scolio) ☏ 28230 42188, 🌐 meta-com.de. Comfortable, economical en-suite rooms; they also rent out a whole house, sleeping six. Rooms €40, house per week €500	a good place to pause for a drink or a bite to eat. The cooking is good, with a range of *mezédhes*, and there's an inviting, shady terrace with views; the church is just behind and the footpaths are signed nearby. Daily 9am–11pm; closed Oct.
Kafenío Sto Scolio (The Old School) Ánidhri ☏ 28230	

AZOYIRÉS

Alpha ☎ 28230 41620, ⓦ azogires-alpha.blogspot
.com. Exceptionally friendly and helpful café-taverna and
rooms place where if you so much as stop outside they'll ply
you with maps and information on caves and walks by the
river; they also have economical en-suite balcony rooms
nearby, some with a/c and fridge. Free wi-fi in taverna. €25

TEMÉNIA

Ta Tamenia Taverna Village centre ☎ 28230 51590.
Welcoming taverna serving delicious Cretan traditional
cuisine. Any of the dishes are recommended, including
home-grown lamb and very tasty *loukánika* sausages.
Daily 8am–11pm.

Soúyia and around

The south coast settlement of **SOÚYIA (Σούγια)** is a small village slowly on its way to
becoming a resort. There are no big hotels and no major tour operators, just lots of rooms,
simple restaurants and bars, added to a couple of general stores which double as travel
agencies. A rather unkempt little place – not particularly attractive at first sight – Soúyia
tends to grow on you. Its best feature lies right at the end of the road: an enormous swathe
of bay with sparklingly clean, clear sea and a long, pebbly beach. There's plenty of room to
spread out here – even on summer weekends when it's popular with locals – and you could
camp under the few scraggly trees if you wanted, although you'd be advised to get as far
away from the central beach as possible to be left in peace. Around at the east end of the
bay there's something of a nudist community – known locally as the **Bay of Pigs**.

Lissós

4km west of Soúyia • You can walk (see below) or alternatively book a taxi-boat (about €20 for up to five people) from Soúyia.

The archeological site of **Lissós (Λισσός)** is a great deal more rewarding than anything
you'll see in Soúyia itself and makes a great trip in late afternoon in summer. Originally
a Dorian city, Lissós grew through the Hellenistic and Roman eras and continued to
thrive, along with its neighbours Syia and Elyrós, right up to the Saracen invasion in
the ninth century, when they were all abandoned. These places have little history,
although it is known that they joined together around 300 BC – along with Hyrtakína
in the hills behind, Pikilássos on the inaccessible coast between here and Ayía Rouméli,
and Tarra, at modern Ayía Rouméli – to form the **Confederation of Oreioi**, and were
later joined by Górtys and Cyrenaica (the latter in North Africa). The remains at Lissós
are mostly Classical Greek and Roman.

4

WALKING FROM SOÚYIA TO LISSÓS

The **walk from Soúyia to Lissós**, a little over an hour (3km), is part of the pleasure of a visit to
the ancient site: you set out on the road which heads west, behind the beach, and at the
harbour turn right onto a track leading slightly inland. The route – also the path trodden by
ancient pilgrims – is part of the E4 coastal path, so it's well marked with black and yellow
splodges. It leads up a beautiful echoing gorge, which you follow for about thirty minutes, and
then climb steeply out of towards the coast. After a short level stretch the sea comes into view,
followed almost immediately by Lissós, below you at the back of a delightful little bay with the
chapel of Áyios Kiriákos and the archeological site further inland.

Ideally in summer you'd either walk over early and get the boat to pick you up in the middle
of the day (precarious embarkation), or have them drop you at Lissós's pebble beach late in
the afternoon, leaving time for a look around the site (you'll very likely have it all to yourself
and it's just the place to open a chilled bottle of wine) before the walk back to Soúyia in the
cool of the evening. The path back to Soúyia from the beach is fairly obvious, as it climbs the
steep hill on the east side of the archeological site.

If you're continuing the **walk west towards Paleohóra**, the path is again pretty obvious
(there may be a guard in the hut at the site who can help, but don't rely on it); it's a long
(10km), hot and lonely stretch of coast though, so carry plenty of water and don't try this
alone. The spring (see p.316) should be a reliable place to fill any bottles, even in summer, and
there's a summer beach *kantína* at Yialaskári Beach (see p.313), 3km before Paleohóra.

The site

The most important survival is an **Asklepion**, or temple of healing, built beside a curative spring against the cliffs on the east side of the site. The temple probably dates from the third century BC, although the **mosaic floor** (protected by a broken-down fence) that is its most obvious feature was added later, in the first century AD; it's a poignant ancient relic, however, depicting images of polychrome birds in its central section (including a quail) and elaborate and beautifully crafted geometric patterns on its outer borders. Notice also the marble altar-base that would have supported a statue, and the "snake pit" (or hole to place sacrifices) next to it. On the gentler, western slope of the valley, opposite, are a group of tombs that look like small stone huts, with barrel-vaulted roofs – hardly the best advertisement for the healing temple. You'll also find a small ruined theatre and two thirteenth-century churches, Áyios Kiriákos – with a nearby **spring** – and Panayía, which reused older material from the site.

When you've finished exploring, you can take a refreshing swim at the small pebble **beach**.

Koustoyérako

About 5km northeast of Soúyia, a road cuts off from the main Hanía highway to the villages of Livadás and **KOUSTOYÉRAKO** (**Κουστογέρακο**). The latter is a very ancient village that is still the home of the Paterákis family, famed in the annals of resistance to German occupation. Manoli Paterákis was one of those who took part in the capture of General Kreipe (see p.340). He died some years ago at the age of 73, when he fell while chasing a wild goat through the mountains. Koustoyérako was destroyed during the war for its role in the resistance, but not before the locals had escaped to the mountains.

Today there's a striking modern **war memorial** at the entrance to the village and a simple **taverna**, next to the school and village playground. Further along, you reach the square, with a couple of *kafenía*. Koustoyérako sees an increasing number of **walkers**, with a branch of the E4 path descending from the Omalós plateau. Hiking up is steep and arduous: although Omalós is only some 12km away, the country in between is mountainous, remote and entirely uninhabited.

Áyios Yeóryios

At the top of the village • The church is locked; before setting out ask at the *kafenío* on the square, from where someone should be able to accompany you – upon arrival the key will be retrieved from its hiding-place while you turn your back

The tiny Byzantine chapel **Áyios Yeóryios** (**Άγιος Γεώργιος**) contains some beautiful remains of frescoes, with sixteenth-century graffiti carved into them; the chapel itself may be as early as the tenth century in origin. The inscription inside the door dates from sixteenth-century restorations and records various generations of the Kandanoleon family. The last named is one Maria Theotokopoulos, and from this tenuous connection comes the claim that **El Greco** (Domenico Theotokopoulos) came originally from Koustoyérako. In the graveyard is the tomb of another Kandanoleon, George. One of Crete's great revolutionary leaders, he led the sixteenth-century revolt against Venetian rule (see p.271) and his body was returned to his birthplace following his execution by the Venetians.

The Ayía Iríni Gorge

April–Oct daily 7am–8pm • €2 • The gorge is an easy day-trip from Paleohóra (the 7am Omalós bus passes through Ayía Iríni, and you can get the afternoon ferry back from Soúyia) or Soúyia (again, take the early Hanía bus); you could also get a taxi to the top from either of these places

AYÍA IRÍNI is a very green village, with lots of old chestnut trees. From here you can walk the **Ayía Iríni Gorge** (**Φαράγγι Αγία Ειρήνης**) back to the coast at Soúyia, roughly 12km in all, though the last five are along the road – about a four-hour trek. It's an attractive hike, not too taxing and usually very quiet unless you're unlucky enough to coincide with one of the occasional tours (mainly from Paleohóra). The well-marked route down into the gorge (it's now another branch of the E4 footpath) can be picked up on the south edge of the village; for the first few kilometres it's easy walking, with plenty of water, shade and picnic spots, but it gradually becomes drier, tougher and hotter as you descend. The *Sartzetakis* café-taverna near the gorge entrance (see p.318) is a potential breakfast or lunch stop and, shortly after this, you will pass a warden's hut where you'll need to buy your entrance **ticket**. There's another café, the aptly named *Oasis*, at the bottom end of the gorge; from here, you could summon up a taxi to collect you from Soúyia, or you might well be able to beg a lift from a fellow traveller.

Continuing south by road, you start gradually to descend, looping down to occasional views of the Libyan Sea and, in the last few kilometres, tracing a gorge with Soúyia framed at the far end. Beyond Rodhováni are the remains of ancient **Elyrós**, the most important city in southwest Crete in Roman times and earlier; the site is unexcavated and, although signed from the road, there's very little to see apart from odd chunks of wall.

ARRIVAL AND DEPARTURE

SOÚYIA AND AROUND

By bus There's no bus station: buses drive down the main road and drop passengers on the seafront, then continue west to the harbour. The 7am Haniá bus offers the opportunity to walk either the Ayía Iríni or the Samariá Gorge – it meets the early bus from Paleohóra in Ayía Iríni, and from there one continues to Omalós and the other to Haniá, so you may have to change. Tickets are sold at the *períptero* on the seafront.

Destinations Haniá (2 daily; 7am [noon on Sun] & 6.30pm [after the arrival of the ferry]; 2hr).

By ferry Ferry tickets for Paleohóra, Ayía Rouméli and Gávdhos (the Ayía Rouméli boat continues there on Mon & Wed) are sold from a booth at the harbour, which opens 1hr before each departure. The harbour is right at the western end of the seafront, about a 10min walk from town; the late bus picks up here.

Destinations Ayía Rouméli (April–Oct daily 9.15am); Gávdhos (April–Oct Mon & Wed at 9.15am); Paleohóra (April–Oct daily 6.20pm). More boats are added in season; information on these can be had from the seafront taxi booth.

By taxi or taxi-boat Taxi-boats can be arranged from the Pelican supermarket (see below) or from *Captain George* (☎ 6947 605802). These are handy for getting to isolated beaches along the coast, or ancient Lissós (€20 one way; a reasonable cost split between four or five, especially if you walk one way and get the boat the other). Almost opposite the seafront *Santa Irene* hotel a taxi kiosk (daily 9am–2pm & 5–9pm; ☎ 28230 51403) can arrange taxis to various destinations including the Ayía Iríni gorge (€30 one way), Haniá (€80) and Haniá airport (€95).

INFORMATION

Tourist information Soúyia has virtually no formal tourist infrastructure – boat trips, tours, car rental and the like are arranged through the shops, restaurants or hotels. The seafront taxi booth (see above) is a good source for general and travel information, but the most useful sources of local information are the two minimarkets: Idomeneas, halfway down the main street, and Pelican at the bottom where it meets the seafront.

Internet The seafront *Syva* café-snack bar (April–Oct 24hr; ☎ 28230 51340) has coin-operated internet screens. Free wi-fi is widely available at bars and tavernas along the seafront as well as at most hotels.

Money There is no ATM, though your hotel – or the *Polifimos* taverna (see p.318), providing you eat there – may be willing to give you cash on a credit card.

ACCOMMODATION

Almost every building in Soúyia seems to offer **rooms**. The first options – and some of the best – are off the main road at the top of the hill as it enters town; others, more expensive, are right on the seafront (mostly to the right from the seafront junction); while another cluster of cheaper rooms can be found by turning left along the seafront and left again before the stream. Details of many of the following (and more) can be found on ⓦ sougia.info.

Captain George To the west off the main street ☎ 28230 51133, ✉ g-gentek@otenet.gr. En-suite, a/c balcony rooms with fridge, plus slightly pricier studios and apartments with kitchenette, in a garden setting. Free wi-fi. **€40**

Pension El Greco Down the lane past Captain George ☎ 28230 51186, ✉ elgreco_sougia@yahoo.gr. Upper-floor rooms place with en-suite, a/c rooms, most with balcony and some with fridge and kitchenette. One of several here with a quiet, semi-rural atmosphere. Free wi-fi. €40

Idomeneas Apartments Main road, at the top of the hill ⓣ28230 51540, ⓔidomeneasgeorgiakakis@yahoo.co.uk. Modern a/c studios and spacious apartments with kitchens, TV and balcony. Free wi-fi. Studios €45, apartments €55

Paradisos On the lane by the stream, left and left again at the seafront junction ⓣ28230 51486. Simple a/c en-suite rooms including some family options with kitchenette; a couple of similar places are nearby. Closed Nov–March. €35

Santa Irene On the seafront ⓣ28230 51342, ⓦsanta-irene.gr. For years the fanciest hotel in the village, and still probably the best located, with modern, a/c, en-suite studios and apartments with fridge (some with balcony sea view) around a garden. Free wi-fi. €45

Syia Main street ⓣ28230 51174, ⓦwsyiahotel.gr. Incongruously chic, boutique-style hotel; the most comfortable studios and apartments in town, if not the most beautiful surroundings. Free wi-fi. Breakfast included. €80

Villa Galini Main road, at the top of the hill ⓣ28230 51488, ⓦgalini-sougia.gr. Friendly proprietor offering big, comfortable and modern a/c en-suite rooms and studios all with fridge, balconies and satellite TV – the studios add a kitchenette. Free wi-fi. Rooms €45, studios €50

EATING AND DRINKING

The seafront has most of the **places to eat**, with a few more up the main road. At night, there are a couple of **disco-bars** that sometimes attract a crowd: the first, *Alabama* (daily 11am–small hours), is sited among the trees on the far side of the stream to the east of the village, the other, *Fortuna* (daily 11pm–4am) is at the northern edge of town, on the left as you come in. Other more centrally located **bars** include elegant *Raki* (daily 8pm–small hours) opposite *Rebetika* restaurant, with music after dark.

SOÚYIA

Liviko At the western end of the seafront below the church ⓣ28230 51414. A good bet for traditional Cretan standards as well as grills and fresh fish, often with live music in the evening. Free wi-fi. April–Oct daily 8am–midnight.

Lotos On the seafront, at the corner of the main road ⓣ28230 51191. Coffees and juices, crêpes and snacks by day; drinks and music in the evening. Free wi-fi. April–Oct daily 7am–3am.

Omikron On the seafront east of the main road ⓣ28230 51492. German-run restaurant with a more north European ambience; international menu – including tabbouleh, pastas – as well as various vegetarian choices. April–Sept daily 8am–11pm.

Polifimos Just off the north end of the inroad from Haniá ⓣ28230 51343. Long standing Soúyia favourite run by Yiannis, one of the village's characters. He serves his own wine and the food – fresh fish and meat – is cooked with the taverna's home-grown (and -pressed) olive oil. Tasty dishes include stuffed cuttlefish, marinated pork and *dolmádhes*. April–Oct daily 1pm–midnight.

★ **Rebetiko** Halfway up the main street ⓣ28230 51510. Cretan/Dutch-owned taverna offering well-prepared traditional dishes – including plenty of vegetarian options – on a delightful garden terrace. House specials include *moussaká* and good lamb and chicken dishes made with produce from their own farm; there's also excellent *hyma* (barrelled) wine, both red and white. April–Oct daily 1pm–midnight.

Roxana's Bakery Bottom of the main street opposite the Pelican minimarket ⓣ28230 51362. Great little bakery for breakfast cakes and savouries like *tirópita* and *spanakópita* plus sandwiches and cold drinks to eat in or take away. Daily: July & Aug 24hr; March–June, Sept & Oct 4.30am–midnight.

Santa Irene On the seafront ⓣ28230 51342, ⓦsanta-irene.gr. Attached to the hotel of the same name, this is a top choice for breakfast, juices and snacks. April–Oct daily 8am–1am.

THE AYÍA IRÍNI GORGE

Sartzetakis Café-Taverna Entrance to the Ayía Iríni gorge ⓣ28230 51550. Very welcoming, family-run all-day café-taverna with tables spread under the trees near the gorge entrance. Open for breakfast, it goes on to produce some pretty good cooking later in the day, too. The goat or lamb *stifádho* is recommended, as is their home-made cheese. April–Oct daily 8am–10pm.

Gávdhos

GÁVDHOS (Γαύδος), the southernmost landmass in Europe, is the largest of Crete's offshore islands and the only one with any significant population. Plain and somewhat barren, its attraction lies in an enduring isolation that its inaccessible position has

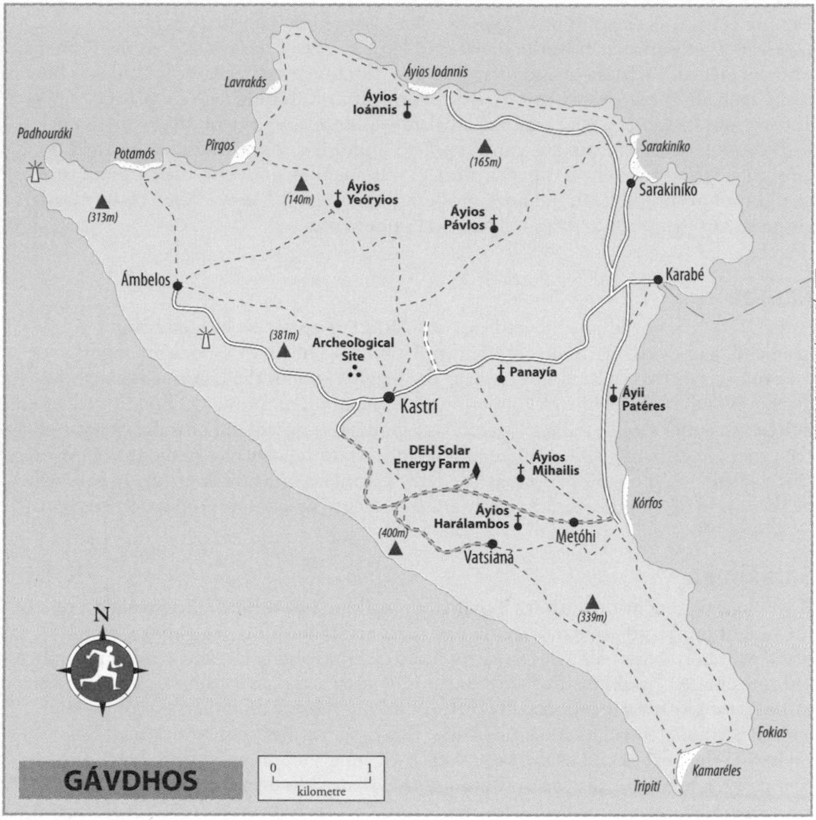
Áyios Ioánnis
Lavrakás
Áyios Ioánnis
Padhouráki
Pírgos
Potamós
(165m)
Sarakiníko
Sarakiníko
(140m)
Áyios Yeóryios
(313m)
Áyios Pávlos
Ámbelos
Karabé
(381m)
Archeological Site
Panayía
Kastrí
Áyii Patéres
DEH Solar Energy Farm
Áyios Mihailis
Kórfos
Áyios Harálambos
(400m)
Metóhi
Vatsianá
(339m)
N
Fokias
GÁVDHOS
0
1
kilometre
Kamaréles
Tripití
Ayia Rouméli, Hóra Sfakíon & Paleohóra
4

helped to preserve. The 50km of rough sea – more than 3000m deep – separating it from the coast of Crete frequently proves too much for the small ferries, which can leave visitors stranded for days when sailings are suspended.

Still in the infancy of tourist development, Gávdhos feels remote, even if thousands of Greek visitors do descend on the place in August. Things are changing rapidly, however, with newly asphalted roads heading out from an enlarged harbour, an electricity plant, and ferries that now carry cars to the island, but for the moment, if all you want is a **beach** and a taverna to grill your fish, this remains the place for you. There's a semi-permanent community of campers and would-be "Robinson Crusoes" resident on the island year-round, swelling to thousands in August – but just six indigenous families. Despite the new power plant, few places on the island have 24hr **electricity** – most rely on candles or part-time generators (which make quite a din after sundown in places like Sarakiníko). **Water**, too, is in relatively short supply, although most rooms on the island now have showers and relatively modern plumbing. Much of the water is not drinkable, so check with locals before drinking from any source you're not sure of.

Brief history

Little is known of the island's early history and although evidence has been found of **Neolithic** and **Minoan** activity, it was most probably not settled until **Classical Greek** times when it was a dependency of Górtys (p.96) and famous for its juniper berries.

Despite Gávdhos's claim to be Calypso's island (visited by Odysseus in Homer's *Odyssey*), it only appears in verifiable record later as a place well known to the **Romans**, who christened it Clauda or Kaudos: the New Testament relates how St Paul was blown past Clauda in the storm which carried him off from Kalí Liménes (see p.110). Throughout its subsequent history the island was notorious as a **pirates'** lair. To deal with this menace the Venetians contemplated building a fortress here as they had done on similar islands elsewhere, but the project was abandoned due to the cost and time it would take to complete. In its more modern history the island was used by dictatorial governments as a place of **exile** for political opponents.

Karabé

As you approach Gávdhos, the harbour at **KARABÉ** (**Καραβέ**) is hidden behind a headland, and the island looks totally uninhabited – only with binoculars might you pick out one or two isolated homes. On the heights behind the harbour squat a few dwellings and a small white church, alongside the modern municipal buildings. For an hour or so either side of the ferry's arrival, Karabé is crowded and chaotic; the rest of the time, there's hardly anyone here at all. In front of the concrete harbour is an open space where everyone mills about as the ferry loads and unloads: somewhere here will be the bus to Sarakiníkos and Áyios Ioánnis, and any other accommodation transport.

Sarakiníko

If you haven't caught the bus, it's a half-hour walk to **SARAKINÍKO** (**Σαρακίνικο**), one of the best of the island's beaches, shaded by scattered tamarisk trees. This is Gávdhos's principal resort, with half a dozen fairly basic tavernas and cafés, and a similar number of rooms places. Even here the broad strip of golden sand has a community of nudist campers settled at each end, usually outnumbering those staying in the rooms. The largely ugly, unplanned architecture aside, this is a beautiful spot, with giant dunes sheltering the eastern end of the beach: each evening the sun goes down behind the island of Crete on the horizon and the Lefká Óri are silhouetted against a crimson sky.

Áyios Ioánnis

A 3km hike to the west of Sarakiníko (or a ten-minute bus ride) brings you to the fine beach of **ÁYIOS IOÁNNIS** (**Άγιος Ιωάννης**). There are high dunes here, and a forest of miniature cedars that provide shade for an army of tents. This is the prime destination for campers, and the summer hangout of a substantial alternative nudist community, despite (or because of) the fact that there are few facilities and little fresh water. The road ends by a **taverna**, *Theofilos* (see p.322), from where the beach itself is ten minutes' walk further west.

Kastrí

KASTRÍ (**Καστρί**), the island "capital", is an hour's walk along a steadily climbing, paved road from Karabé. When you get there it turns out to be a ghostly sort of place with only a handful of dwellings, mangers, stables and barns clustering around the old police station and *dhimarhío*, both rehoused to Karabé (see above), while in the surrounding parched and arid fields older dwellings gradually crumble away to become one with the weathered and fissured rock on which they stand. Most of the time the only sign of life is the odd chicken running for cover or goats foraging in the scrub. To the northwest of the village is a minor (unfenced) archeological site from which some derive proof that the island was settled as far back as Neolithic times. Signs of life are beginning to return, however: some of the dwellings are being refurbished by visitors from Crete, there's an organic farm of sorts, and there's also the incongruously snazzy *Gavdos Princess Apartments* (see p.322).

Ámbelos

Climbing out of Kastrí the track heading west across the island reaches the ridgeline and divides. Close to this junction is the old island school, recently reopened. The right branch leads to the sparse hamlet of **ÁMBELOS** (Άμβελος), 3km north, from where there's a particularly fine view towards North Africa, a sea lane ploughed constantly by enormous supertankers. On the way there you'll pass the impressive nineteenth-century **lighthouse** bombed by the Germans in 1941 and now fully and superbly restored as a **café** and **museum** (9am–9pm; free) depicting images, plans and sketches of other lighthouses throughout Greece. If you can time your visit for early evening, head to the top of the tower – a great place to watch Gávdhos's famed sunsets. A track north from Ámbelos leads to the scenic isolated beaches of **Potamós** – very hard to reach on foot, though you can explore a couple of spectacular ravines behind it – **Pírgos** and, further east, **Lavrakás**; you are totally on your own here, there are no facilities, and you'll need to take along plenty of drinking water.

Vatsianá

Turning left at the junction beyond Kastrí leads, after 3km, to **VATSIANÁ** (Βατσιανά), a three-dwelling hamlet marooned in a rocky, almost lunar landscape. One great surprise in Vatsianá is that it not only has a **café**, but a **museum**, too. The café is the last in Europe before you reach Africa and even more curiously its proprietor is the island's priest, Papás Manolis Bikogiannakis. The museum, a single room of fascinating domestic junk, won't take long to see: the real excitement is that there's something to visit and someone to talk to here at all, in such an inhospitable and desiccated landscape.

From Vatsianá you are in easy walking distance of Kórfos and its beach, to the east. Striking out more adventurously, there's also a path to the southernmost tip of the continent at Tripití, 3km to the south.

Kórfos and around

You can walk pretty much directly down from Vatsianá to **KÓRFOS** (Κόρφος), 2km away, where there's a good (but shadeless) pebbly beach. With a vehicle you'll have to head some way back for the track via Metóhi, or there's a paved road from Karabé. There are two friendly places to stay here (see p.322). There's another accommodation possibility, at **METÓHI** (see p.323), which also has an **open-air performance area** (open to all), that hosts film screenings and live music performances regularly in summer. Beyond these, there's utter rural tranquillity up here. A minibus collects guests from the harbour.

TRIPITÍ, the most southerly point of Europe, can be reached in little over an hour on a well-marked path from Kórfos, or a slightly tougher downhill trek from Vatsianá. The beach here, **Kamaréles**, is pebbly with little shade but the water is brilliantly clear and a snorkeller's paradise, with plenty of aquatic life. When you need a break, you can do what everyone else comes here to do: climb the famous **three-holed rock**, sit in the **giant chair**, and dangle your feet off the edge of a continent.

ARRIVAL AND DEPARTURE   GÁVDHOS

By ferry There are ferries (☺www.anendyk.gr) to Gávdhos from Hóra Sfakíon and from Paleohóra via Soúyia and Ayía Rouméli (see p.290 & p.309). All, however, are   dependent on the weather, which is unpredictable even in high summer; the high-sided, shallow draft *Samariá* cannot handle even moderate winds and seas, while

August is particularly dodgy given the frequency with which the *meltémi* blows. Be aware that you may be stranded on the island longer than you expect, and plan accordingly. Schedules are posted at the harbour in Karabé and at Sarakiníko.

Destinations Hóra Sfakíon (11–19 May Fri & Sat 2.30pm; 20–31 May Wed & Thurs 2pm; June & Sept Tues & Fri 2pm; July & Aug Wed & Thurs 2pm; rest of year check ⓦ www .anendyk.gr; 3hr); Paleohóra via Ayía Rouméli and Soúyia (May–Oct Mon & Wed 2pm; 4hr).

GETTING AROUND

By bus An ancient bus (€2) meets the ferry and makes the trip to Sarakiníko and Áyios Ioánnis beaches, continuing as far as the lighthouse if there's demand, with a return trip from the beaches about 1hr before the ferry departs.

Boat trips There are no organized boat trips on Gávdhos, but if you ask at the *Litsa* taverna in Karabé (see below) you may be able to arrange a boat ride to one of the beaches. If you do rent a boat – particularly to one of the more isolated beaches – make sure to take along sufficient drinking

water and make equally sure the boatman understands when you want to be picked up.

Mopeds and cars Gavdos Travel (☎ 28230 42458, ⓦ gavdos-metoxi.gr; cash only), on the road behind the beach at Sarakiníko, rents cars (around €35–40/day plus petrol) and mopeds (around €15–20/day including petrol).

Bus tours In summer, the island bus runs an afternoon bus tour (€5) starting from Sarakiníko, taking in all the major island sights, including the lighthouse.

ACCOMMODATION AND EATING

Most people still camp out by the beach, so although the **season** is getting longer – July and September are becoming increasingly busy – it is usually possible to turn up on spec and find a bed. Even so, it makes sense to book ahead if you are coming all this way; travel agencies in Paleohóra (see p.310) or Hóra Sfakíon (p.290) can arrange a room. As for **food**, there are several minimarkets, but none is very well stocked – in particular there's little in the way of fresh fruit or vegetables. It makes sense to bring some supplies with you, especially if you plan to camp out.

KARABÉ

Rooms Kalypso On the heights behind the harbour ☎ 28230 41103. Modern rooms with showers; they'll collect you at the harbour if you ring ahead. **€35**

Kantína Immediately above the harbour. This drinks stall offers cold drinks and unexpectedly good food. April–Oct daily 11am–10pm.

Litsa Taverna On the harbour. A pleasant taverna with a lively terrace for watching harbour comings and goings. The food is good; specialities include fresh fish and grilled lamb. April–Oct daily 9am–11pm.

Rooms Tsigonakis Behind the Litsa Taverna ☎ 28230 41104. A/c rooms with and without bath. **€35**

SARAKINÍKO

Nikterida Taverna–Rooms Beachfront ☎ 28230 42120. Good food – including fresh fish – and simple but clean rooms. Their minimarket stocks basic items and essentials. **€35**

Sarakiniko Studios Above the beach to the west ☎ 28230 42182, ⓦ gavdostudios.gr. Recently built en-suite rooms with fridge, and studios with kitchenette; there's also satellite TV in their taverna. They'll collect you from the ferry if you book in advance. **€50**

★ **Vailakakis aka Gerti & Manolis** ☎ 28230 41103, ⓔ gavdosvailakaki@yahoo.com. Friendly, with simple, en-suite a/c rooms (with 24hr power) and rather fancier stone-built houses for four to six people. It also has probably the best food on the beach, with excellent,

good-value seafood caught daily by Manolis himself. Also a minimarket selling essentials and basics. **€40**

ÁYIOS IOÁNNIS

Theofilos ☎ 28230 41418. Excellent, simple food and some new rooms, plus an inexpensive minimarket with supplies for campers. The beach itself is 10min walk further west. Closed Nov–March. Taverna April–Oct daily 9am–10pm. **€35**

KASTRÍ

Gavdos Princess Apartments Beside the road on the way into the village ☎ 28230 41181, ⓦ gavdos-princess .com. Unexpectedly fancy hotel with fully equipped and pricey a/c studios. **€50**

To Steki tis Gogos Beside the road on the way into the village ☎ 28320 41932. This simple taverna offers a range of Sfakian and Greek dishes. April–Oct daily 9am–10pm.

VATSIANÁ

Museum Café Attached to the village museum. The *papás*'s wife, María, serves drinks, postcards and her exquisite *kéik* (cake) or *galaktoboureko* (a lemony egg-custard pudding), which she bakes each morning. May–Sept daily 9am–9pm.

KÓRFOS

Akroyiali On the beach ☎ 28230 42384. Comfortable, a/c rooms with showers; like *Yiorgos & Marias* (see below), this is a very friendly place and will collect guests from the harbour if you ring ahead. Proprietor Yiannis offers guests free tours of the island in his minibus. The taverna serves good food on a seafront terrace. Closed Oct–March. Taverna April–Sept daily 9am–10pm. €30

Yiorgos & Marias On the hill down to the beach ☎ 28230 42166. Spotless en-suite a/c rooms with showers in this friendly, family-run taverna-rooms place. They'll collect you from the harbour if you ring ahead. The taverna serves excellent fish and other local dishes on a terrace overlooking the beach. Closed Oct–March. Taverna April–Sept daily 9am–11pm. €35

METÓHI

Rooms Metoxi 1km or so up the track that crosses the island ☎ 28230 42458, ✉ bikog@in.gr. Isolated, tranquil place offering a/c studios fronting a small pool, plus its own taverna and open-air performance area (see p.321). A minibus collects (booked-in) guests from the harbour. Closed Oct–April. Taverna May–Sept daily 9am–10pm. €35

DIRECTORY

Doctor Kastrí (☎ 28230 42195) – usually an intern opting out of military service.

Money There is no bank or official place to change money on the island: bring sufficient cash with you, remembering that, though life is simple, supplies are relatively expensive, and you may be stuck here longer than expected should ferries be cancelled.

Police There is a police station (☎ 28230 41019) attached to the new *dhimarhío* (town hall) above the harbour at Karabé.

4

Contexts

History

The people of Crete unfortunately make more history than they can consume locally.

Saki

The discovery of the Minoan civilization has tended to overshadow every other aspect of Cretan history; indeed it would be hard for any other period to rival what was, in effect, the first truly European civilization. It was in Crete that the developed societies of the East met influences from the West and North, and here that "Western culture", as synthesized in Classical Greece and Rome, first developed.

Yet this was no accident or freak one-off: Crete's position as a meeting place of East and West, and its strategic setting in the middle of the Mediterranean, has thrust the island to the centre stage of world history more often than seems comfortable. Long before Arthur Evans arrived to unearth Knossós, and for some time after, the island's struggle for freedom, and the Great Powers' inactivity, was the subject of Europe-wide scandal. The battle for the island when the Turks arrived had similarly aroused worldwide interest, and represented at the time a significant change in the balance of power between Islam and Christianity. In fact from Minoan times to World War II, there has rarely been a sustained period when Crete didn't have some role to play in world affairs.

The Stone Age

Crete's first inhabitants, **Neolithic cave dwellers**, apparently reached the island around 7000 BC. They came, most probably, from Asia Minor, or less likely from Syria, Palestine or North Africa, bringing with them the basics of Stone Age culture – tools of wood, stone and bone, crude pottery and simple cloth.

Development over the next three thousand years was almost imperceptibly slow, but gradually, whether through new migrations and influences or internal dynamics, advances were made. Elementary agriculture was practised, with domestic animals and basic crops. **Pottery** (the oldest samples of which were found beneath the palace at Knossós) became more sophisticated, with better-made domestic utensils and clay figurines of humans, animals and, especially, a fat mother goddess or fertility figure. Obsidian imported from the island of Mílos was used too. And though caves continued to be inhabited, simple rectangular huts of mud bricks were also built, with increasing skill and complexity as the era wore on. One of the most important of the Neolithic settlements was at Knossós, where two remarkable dwellings have been revealed below the Central Court, and there is abundant evidence that many other sites of later habitation were used at this time – Mália, Festós, Ayía Triádha, the Haniá area – as were most of the caves that later came to assume religious significance.

6000–2600 BC	2600–2000 BC	2000–1700 BC
Crete's first inhabitants arrive during the Stone Age when habitation starts in caves. Settlements grow at Knossós and elsewhere.	New migration by the "first Minoans" brings more sophisticated culture and settlements: Vasilikí, Móhlos and Mírtos are among the best known.	Evidence of a more formally structured society. First palaces built at most of the famous sites.

The Bronze Age: Minoan Crete

Minoan Crete has been the subject of intense and constant study since its emergence from myth to archeological reality at the beginning of the twentieth century. Yet there is still enormous controversy even over such fundamental details as who the Minoans

THE DISCOVERY OF BRONZE AGE CRETE

So ancient is **Minoan civilization** that even by Classical Greek times it had long disappeared into the mists of mythology and Homeric legend. The story of its rediscovery at the turn of the twentieth century – dominated by two larger-than-life characters in **Heinrich Schliemann** and **Arthur Evans** – is almost as fascinating as that of the Minoans themselves.

HEINRICH SCHLIEMANN

Heinrich Schliemann, a wealthy, self-made, self-educated German, was determined to prove that Homer's stirring tales of prehistoric cities and heroes were true. In the 1870s and 80s, in the face of unremitting hostility from the archeological establishment, he discovered and excavated both Troy and Mycenae, revolutionizing our knowledge of the pre-Classical era. In 1887 he arrived in Crete, made a visit to the site at Knossós, and became convinced that a substantial palace lay waiting to be unearthed. But Crete was still under the subjection of Turkey, and Schliemann never succeeded in getting permission to excavate the site.

ARTHUR EVANS AND KNOSSÓS

Arthur Evans, an independently wealthy British scholar who had been inspired by Schliemann, arrived in Crete for the first time on March 15, 1894. With the assistance of Joseph Hatzidhákis, president of the Cretan Archeological Society, Evans began to negotiate for the purchase of the land at Knossós with its Turkish owners. As the Ottoman Empire crumbled, Evans succeeded in buying the site and excavation began in March, 1900. Within days, evidence of a vast and complex building had been revealed – elegant courtyards with sublime frescoes, pottery, jewellery and tablets bearing an undeciphered ancient script.

Evans was an autocrat whose personal ownership and financing of one of the major sites of antiquity – something that would be unthinkable today – allowed him extraordinary latitude. It was he who named the new civilization **Minoan** after the legendary Cretan king. Far more controversially, he determined that he would not only reveal the palace of Minos but would also restore large parts of it to its original splendour. With the assistance of architects Theodore Fyfe and Piet de Jong, he roofed the Throne Room and reconstructed the grand staircase, replacing the tapered columns with his speculative concrete reconstructions (none of the wooden originals was ever found). Two Swiss artists then began to repaint the reconstructed walls with copies of the frescoes. An almost entirely conjectural upper storey, the Piano Nobile, was added using reinforced concrete and the Central Court was extensively restored as the archeological dig became a building site. Evans argued that he wanted to re-create the "spirit" of the palace structure and decor rather than undertake a literal reconstruction. Few professional archeologists now would defend him, and certainly none would be allowed to carry out such work again, but there can be no doubt that it was the publicity Evans generated that brought Minoan culture to a worldwide audience.

In 1924 Evans donated the Knossós site and the Villa Ariadne, where he lived in style throughout the excavation, to the British School at Athens – it was only in 1952 that it was to become the property of the Greek government. His successor at Knossós was a young English archeologist, John Pendlebury, was killed in the early years of World War II, fighting alongside the Cretans during the German attack on Iráklio in 1941.

c.1700 BC	c.1700–1450 BC	c.1450 BC
Earthquake destroys the palaces.	The Minoan Golden Age. Great palaces at Knossós, Festós, Mália and Zákros; thriving towns at Gourniá and Palékastro.	Final destruction of the palaces.

were and what language they spoke. No written historical records from the time survive (or if they do, they have not yet been deciphered), so almost everything we know is deduced from physical remains, fleshed out somewhat by writings from Classical Greece, almost one thousand years after the destruction of Knossós. Nevertheless it is not hard to forge some kind of consensus from the theories about the Minoans, and this is what is set out below. Fresh discoveries may yet radically change this view.

One of the central arguments is over **dating**. The original system, conceived by Sir Arthur Evans, divided the period into Early, Middle and Late Minoan, with each of these again divided into three sub-periods – a sequence that has become extremely complicated and cumbersome as it has been further qualified and subdivided. Arcane distinctions between the pottery styles of Early Minoan IIa and IIb have no place in a brief history and a simpler system is used here (following the archeologist Nikolaos Platon) of four periods: **Pre-Palatial**, proto-palatial or **First Palace**, neo-palatial or **New Palace**, and **Post-Palatial**. This has the additional advantage of avoiding many of the niceties of exact dating and of uneven development across the island. However, as many archeological texts and guides, as well as numerous museums on the island use the Evans system, the approximate corresponding periods – Early Minoan (E.M.), Middle Minoan (M.M.) and Late Minoan (L.M.) – are given in brackets.

Pre-Palatial: 3000–1900 BC (E.M.–M.M.I.)

Among the more important puzzles of Minoan society is its comparatively **sudden emergence**. During the centuries before 2600 BC, there were important changes on the island, and thereafter very rapid progress in almost every area of life. Villages and towns grew up where previously there had been only isolated settlements, and with them came craft specialists: potters, stonecutters, metalworkers, jewellers and weavers. Many of these new settlements were in the east and south of the island, and there was significant habitation on the coast and near natural harbours for the first time.

It seems safe to assume that these changes were wrought by a new **migration** of people from the east, who brought with them new technologies, methods of agriculture and styles of pottery, but most importantly perhaps, a knowledge of seafaring and trade. The olive and the vine – which need little tending and therefore help free a labour force – began to be produced alongside cereal crops. Copper tools replaced stone ones and were themselves later refined with the introduction of bronze. Art developed rapidly, with characteristic **Vasilikí ware** and other pottery styles, as well as gold jewellery, and stone jars of exceptional quality, based originally on Egyptian styles. Significantly, large quantities of seal stones have been found too, almost certainly the mark of a mercantile people. They were used to sign letters and documents, but especially to seal packets, boxes or doors as proof that they had not been opened: the designs – scorpions or poisonous spiders – were often meant as a further deterrent to robbery.

At the same time new methods of burial appear – tholos and chamber tombs in which riches were buried with the dead. These appear to have been communal, as, probably, was daily life, based perhaps on clan or kinship groupings.

The first palaces: 1900–1700 BC (M.M.I–M.M.II)

Shortly before 1900 BC, the first of the palaces were built, at **Knossós**, **Festós**, **Mália** and **Zákros**. They represent another significant and apparently abrupt change: a shift of

c.1450–1100 BC	c.1100–67 BC
Gradual revival under Mycenaean influence. Earlier sites reoccupied with Kydonia the island's chief city. Eteo-Cretans keep Minoan culture alive at Présos and Karfí. Mycenaean control yields to Dorian.	Island divided into rival groupings, gradually emerging as constantly warring city-states. Dozens of small towns including Láto, Falásarna, Knossós and Górtys.

THE MINOAN ECONOMY

The extent and grandeur of the Minoan palaces themselves in this First Palace era are proof of the island's great prosperity at this time, and the artefacts found within offer further evidence. Advances were made in almost every field of artistic and craft endeavour. From this era came the famous **Kamáres** ware pottery – actually two distinct styles, one eggshell-thin and delicate, the other sturdier with bold-coloured designs. These remarkable works were enabled by the true potter's wheel (as against the turntable) now introduced for the first time, along with a simple form of hieroglyphic writing. Elaborate jewellery, seals and bronzework were also being produced.

Cretan bronze was used throughout the Mediterranean, and its production and distribution were dependent on a wide-ranging **maritime economy**. For though Crete may have produced some copper at this time, it never yielded tin, the nearest significant sources of which were as distant as modern Iran to the east, Central Europe in the north, Italy, Spain, Brittany and even Britain in the west. While some claim that Minoan ships actually sailed as far afield as the Atlantic, it seems more likely that the more exotic goods were obtained through middlemen. Nevertheless, Crete controlled the trade routes in the Mediterranean, importing tin, copper, ivory, gold, silver and precious stones of every kind, exporting timber from its rich cypress forests, olive oil, wine, bronze goods and its fine pottery, especially to Egypt. Minoan colonies or trading posts were established on many Cycladic islands as well as the island of Kíthira off the Peloponnese, Rhodes and the coast of Asia Minor; a fleet of merchant vessels maintained regular trade links between these centres and, above all, with Egypt and the east.

power back to the centre of the island and the emergence of a much more hierarchical, ordered society. The sites of these palaces were also no accident: Festós and Mália both dominate fertile plains, while Zákros had a superbly sited harbour for trade with the east. Knossós, occupying a strategic position above another plain to the south and west of Iráklio, was perhaps originally as much a religious centre as a base of secular power. Certainly at this time religion took on a new importance, with the widespread use of mountain-top peak sanctuaries and caves as **cult centres**. At the same time much larger towns were growing up, especially around the palaces, and in the countryside substantial "villas" appeared. Around 1700 BC, the palaces were destroyed for the first time, probably by earthquake, although raiders from the early Mycenaean Greek mainland may also have seized this opportunity to raid the island while it was temporarily defenceless; this may well account for the wealth of gold and other treasure – much of it obviously Cretan – found in the later royal shaft graves at Mycenae.

The New Palace Period: 1700–1450 BC (M.M.III–L.M.I)

Though the destruction must have been a setback, Minoan culture continued to flourish, and with the palaces reconstructed on a still grander scale the society entered its golden age. It is the new palaces that provide most of our picture of Minoan life and most of what is seen at the great sites – Knossós, Festós, Mália, Zákros – dates from this period.

The **architecture** of the new palaces was of an unprecedented sophistication: complex, multistorey structures in which the use of space and light was as luxurious as the construction materials. Grand stairways, colonnaded porticoes and courtyards, brightly frescoed walls, elaborate plumbing and drainage, and great magazines in which to store the society's accumulation of wealth, were all integral, as were workshops for the technicians and craftsmen, and areas set aside for ritual and worship.

c.300 BC	71 BC	69–67 BC
Cities on south coast form Confederation of Oreoi.	Failed Roman invasion.	Romans invade again and subjugate the island.

Obviously it was only an elite that enjoyed these comforts, but conditions for the ordinary people who kept Minos and his attendants in such style appear to have improved too: towns around the palaces and at sites such as Gourniá and Palékastro were growing as well. (It was Arthur Evans who named Minoan society after the legendary King Minos, but there is little doubt that Minos was in fact the title of a dynasty of priest-kings, a word rather like "Pharaoh").

Very little is known of how the society was organized, or indeed whether it was a single entity ruled from Knossós or simply several city-states with a common cultural heritage. However, in an intriguing reference to Crete in his *Politics*, Aristotle implied that a caste system had operated in the time of Minos. Clearly, though, it was a society in which **religion** played an important part. The great Corridor of the Procession fresco at Knossós depicted an annual delivery of tribute, apparently to a mother goddess; bull-leaping had a religious significance too; and in all the palaces substantial chambers were set aside for ritual purposes. Secular leaders were also religious leaders.

That Minoan society was a very open one is apparent too. There are virtually no **defences**, internal or external, at any Minoan site, and apparently the rulers felt no threat either from within or without, which has led scholars to emphasize a military strength based on sea power. As far as internal dissent goes, it seems safe to assume that the wealth of the island filtered down, to some extent at least, to all its inhabitants: the

CULTURAL ADVANCES IN THE NEW PALACE PERIOD

If the New Palace period was a high point of Minoan power, it also marked the apogee of arts and crafts in the island: again, the bulk of the objects you'll admire in the museums dates from this era. The **frescoes** – startling in their freshness and vitality – are the most famous and obviously visible demonstration of this florescence. But they were just the highly visible tip of an artistic iceberg. It was in intricate small-scale work that the Minoans excelled above all. Naturalistic sculpted figures of humans and animals include the superb ivory bull-leaper, the leopard-head axe and the famous snake goddesses or priestesses, all of them on show in the Iráklio Archeological Museum. The carvings on seal stones of this era are of exceptional delicacy – a skill carried over into beautifully delicate gold jewellery. Examples of stone vessels include the bull's head rhyton from Knossós and the three black vases from Ayía Triádha, which are among the museum's most valuable possessions. And pottery broke out into an enormous variety of new shapes and design motifs, drawing inspiration especially from scenes of nature and marine life.

The other great advance was in writing. A new form of script, **Linear A**, had appeared at the end of the First Palace period, but in the new palaces its use became widespread. Still undeciphered, Linear A must record the original, unknown language of the Minoans: it seems to have been used in written form almost exclusively for administrative records – stock lists, records of transactions and tax payments. Even were it understood, therefore, it seems unlikely that the language would reveal much. The pieces that have survived were never intended as permanent records, and have been found intact only where the clay tablets used were baked solid in the fires that destroyed the palaces. It is probable that a more formal record, an abstract of the annual accounts, was kept on a more valuable but also more perishable material such as imported papyrus (the Minoans had strong trading links with Egypt) or even a paper produced from native date-palm leaves. There is evidence in the Iráklio museum of the use of ink to inscribe text on ceramic drinking cups that lends support to this proposition.

67 BC–395 AD	67 BC	395 AD
Roman rule with Górtys the chief city. Others include Lyttos, Áptera and Knossós. Public works across the island.	Crete merges with the Libyan kingdom of Cyrenaica to form a new province.	Roman Empire splits; Crete falls under Byzantium.

lot of a Minoan peasant may have been little different from that of a Cretan villager as little as fifty years ago.

Externally, **maritime supremacy** was further extended: objects of Cretan manufacture turn up all over the Mediterranean and have even been claimed as far afield as Britain and Scandinavia (amber from the Baltic certainly found its way to Crete). Behind their sea power the Minoans clearly felt safe, and the threat of attack or piracy was further reduced by the network of colonies or close allies throughout the Cycladic islands – Thíra most famously but also at Mílos, Náxos, Páros, Mikonós, Ándhros and Dílos – and in Rhodes, Cyprus, Syria and North Africa. Nevertheless, this appears to have remained a trading empire rather than a military one.

Destruction

Around 1600 BC the island again saw minor earthquake damage, though this was swiftly repaired. But in about 1450 BC came destruction on a calamitous scale: the palaces were smashed and (with the exception of Knossós itself) burned, and smaller settlements across the island were devastated. The cause of this disaster is still the most controversial of all Minoan riddles, and until recently the most convincing theory linked it with the explosion of the volcano of **Thíra** in about 1500 BC – a blast that may have been five times as powerful as that of Krakatoa. The explosion threw up great clouds of black ash and a huge tidal wave, or waves. Coastal settlements would have been directly smashed by the wave, and perhaps further burnt by the overturn of lamps lighted on a day made unnaturally dark by the clouds of ash. Blast, panic and accompanying earth tremors would have contributed to the wreck. And then, as the ash fell, it apparently coated the centre and east of the island in a poisonous blanket under which nothing could grow, or would grow again, for as much as fifty years. Recent surveys by vulcanologists have traced ash from the explosion as far away as Greenland, the Black Sea and Egypt, suggesting that the thousands of tons of ash and pumice thrown into the atmosphere by the blast created a "nuclear winter" across much of Europe and beyond.

Only at Knossós was there any real continuity of habitation, and here it was with **Mycenaean Greeks** in control, bringing with them new styles of art, a greater number of weapons and, above all, keeping records in a form of writing known as **Linear B**, an adaptation of Linear A used to write in an early Greek dialect. In about 1370 BC, Knossós was itself burnt, whether by rebellious Cretans, a new wave of Mycenaeans or perhaps as a result of another natural disaster on a smaller scale.

Such at least is the prevailing theory. But it has its problems – why, for example, should Festós have been burnt when it was safe from waves and blast on the south side of the island? And why should the eruption that vulcanologists dated to 1500 BC have had such a dramatic effect only fifty years later – indeed there are signs that away from the worst effects of the devastation many areas on Crete experienced comparative prosperity after it. As the debate continues, the best that can be said currently is that the volcano theory fits the available evidence better than most of its rivals. But many scholars still claim that the facts are more consistent with destruction by human rather than natural causes.

The main counter-theory assumes an invasion by the Mycenaeans, and points to some evidence that Linear B was in use at Knossós before 1450 BC. But if the Mycenaeans came to conquer, they would have gained nothing by destroying the

395–824	**824–961**	**961**
Crete ruled from Byzantium. Traces of early churches at Górtys, Soúyia and Thrónos.	Arab invasion and rule. Górtys sacked with al-Khandak, later Iráklio, the Arab base.	Liberation by Byzantine general Nikiforas Fokas.

THE RIDDLE OF THE OLIVE BRANCH

The confusion surrounding theories about the end of the New Palace period was dramatically added to in 2005 when Danish vulcanologists working on Thíra discovered an **olive tree branch** buried inside a rock face formed from volcanic debris. The researchers are convinced that the tree was alive when buried in the cataclysmic eruption. The branch's growth rings were intact and using radio-carbon dating the researchers were able to date the tree's death to between 1627 and 1600 BC. If this dating is correct it suggests that the eruption occurred at least 100 years earlier than previously thought. It has also plunged ancient Aegean chronology into confusion. Historians tend to rely on the Egyptian chronology (with its long history, king lists and 365-day years) for setting Minoan dates. Accepted thinking thus far is that Minoan civilization was contemporary with that of the Egyptian New Kingdom (dated c.1550–1050 BC). If the vulcanolgists' new dating is correct and Minoan civilization effectively collapsed c.1600 then this is wildly out of sync. As one Cretan archeologist put it: "We now have absolute chaos as far as giving years to events is concerned and something must give – this is likely to be Egyptian dates which are now out by up to two centuries."

society already flourishing on Crete; nor would they have subsequently left the former population centres deserted for a generation or more.

A third theory attempts to answer these inconsistencies, suggesting that an **internal revolt** by the populace against its rulers (possibly in the wake of the chaos caused by the Thíra eruption) could provide an explanation. This theory would fit the evidence from sites such as Mírtos Pírgos on the south coast, where a villa dominating the site was burned down while the surrounding settlement remained untouched. Needless to say this theory does not find favour with those who see Minoan civilization as a haven of tranquil splendour, but it does fit with the later Greek tradition of a tyrannical Minos oppressing not only his own people but those abroad as well.

Post-Palatial: 1450–1100 BC (L.M.II–L.M.III)

From their bridgehead at Knossós, the Mycenaeans gradually spread their influence across the island as it became habitable again. By the early fourteenth century BC they controlled much of Crete, and some of the earlier sites, including Gourniá, Ayía Triádha, Tílissos and Palékastro, were **reoccupied**. It is a period that is still little known and that was written off by the early Minoan scholars almost entirely. However more recent excavations are revealing that the island remained productive, albeit in a role peripheral to the mainland.

In particular **western Crete** now came into its own, as the area least affected by the volcano. **Kydonia** – the nearest port to the Mycenean heartland –became the chief city of the island, still with a considerable international trade and continuing, in its art and architecture, very much in the Minoan style. But Kydonia lies beneath modern Haniá and has never been (nor is ever likely to be) properly excavated – another reason that far less is known about this period than those that preceded it. In **central Crete** the main change was in retreat from the coasts, a sign of the island's decline in international affairs and trade, and perhaps of an increase in piracy. Even here, however, despite the presence of new influences, much of the art is recognizably Minoan. Most of the famous clay and stone *lárnakes* (sarcophagi) – which were a distinctly new method of burial – date from this final Minoan era.

961–1204	1204	1204–1669
Byzantine rule returns. Small frescoed churches built throughout Crete.	Fourth Crusade. Byzantium sacked; Crete sold to Venice.	Venetian rule. Extensive early building includes churches and monasteries; later, major defence works at Iráklio, Réthymno and Haniá and castles at Frangokástello and on the fortified islets.

More direct evidence of the survival of Crete comes in Homer's account of the **Trojan War**, when he talks of a Cretan contingent taking part under King Idomeneus (according to him, the grandson of Minos). The war and its aftermath – a period of widespread change – also affected Crete. In the north of Greece the Mycenaeans were being overrun by peoples moving down from the Balkans, in particular the **Dorians**. Around 1200 BC the relative peace was disrupted again: many sites were abandoned for the last time, others burnt. Briefly, Mycenaean influence became yet more widespread, as refugees arrived on the island. But by the end of the twelfth century BC, Minoan culture was in terminal decline, and Crete was entering into the period of confusion that engulfed most of the Greek world. Some of the original population of the island, later known as **Eteo-Cretans** (true Cretans), retreated at this time to mountain fastnesses at sites such as Présos and Karfí, where they survived, along with elements of Minoan culture and language, for almost another millennium.

Dorian and Classical Crete

By the end of the twelfth century, the bulk of the island had been taken over by the **Dorians**: there may have been an invasion, but it seems more probable that the process was a gradual one, by settlement. At any event, over the succeeding centuries the Dorians came to dominate the central lowlands, with substantial new cities such as Láto near modern Áyios Nikólaos.

Dorian Crete was not in any real sense a unified society: its cities warred with each other and there may, as well as the Dorians and Eteo-Cretans, have been other cultural groupings in the west, at Kydonia and sites such as Falásarna and Polyrínia. Nevertheless the island saw another minor **artistic renaissance**, with styles now mostly shared with the rest of the Greek world; in the making of tools and weapons, **iron** gradually came to replace bronze.

Much the most important survival of this period, however, is the celebrated **law code** from Górtys. The code (see p.97) was set down around 450 BC, but it reflects laws that had already been in force for hundreds of years: the society described is a strictly hierarchical one, clearly divided into a ruling class, free men, serfs and slaves. For the rulers, life followed a harsh, militaristic regime similar to that of Sparta – the original population, presumably, had been reduced to the level of serfs.

As mainland Greece approached its **Classical Age**, Crete advanced little. It remained a populous island, but one where a multitude of small city-states were constantly vying for power. Towns of this period are characterized by their heavy defences, and most reflected the Górtys laws (Górtys remained among the most powerful of them) in tough oligarchical or aristocratic regimes. At best, Crete was a minor player in Greek affairs, increasingly known as the den of pirates and as a valuable source of mercenaries unrivalled in guerrilla tactics. The island must have retained influence though, for it was still regarded by Classical Athenians as the source of much of their culture, and its strict institutions were admired by many philosophers. In addition, many Cretan shrines and caves show unbroken use from Minoan through to Roman times, and those associated with the birth and early life of Zeus (the Dhiktean and Idean caves especially) were important centres of pilgrimage.

1453	**1541**	**1587**
Fall of Constantinople; renaissance of Byzantine art on Crete.	The artist El Greco (Domenico Theotokópoulos) born in Crete. In 1577 moves to Toledo, Spain where he made his name.	Vitzéntzos Kornáros, Crete's greatest poet and creator of the epic poem *Erotókritos*, born near Sitía.

The multitude of small, independent **city-states** is well illustrated by the Confederation of Oreoi, an accord formed around 300 BC between Élyros, Lissós, Hyrtakina, Tarra, Syia (modern Soúyia) and Pikílassos, six towns in a now barely populated area of the southwest. They were later joined in the Confederation by Górtys and Cyrenaica (in North Africa). Meanwhile Roman power was growing in the Mediterranean, and Crete's strategic position and turbulent reputation drew her inexorably into the struggle.

Conquest by Rome

From the second century BC onwards, **Rome** was drawn into wars in mainland Greece, and the involvement of Cretan troops on one or often both sides became an increasing irritation. The island was also a notorious haven for pirates that frequently preyed upon Roman merchant vessels. Hannibal was staying at Górtys at the time of one Roman attempt to pacify the island, around 188 BC. More than a century passed with only minor interventions, however, before Rome could turn its full attention to Crete – the last important part of the Greek world not under its sway.

In 74 BC Marcus Antonius (father of Mark Antony) attempted an invasion mainly aimed at chastising the pirates, but was heavily defeated by the Kydonians. A fresh attempt was made under **Quintus Metellus** (afterwards called Creticus) in 69 BC. This time a bridgehead was successfully established by exploiting divisions among the Cretans: Metellus was supported in his initial campaign against Kydonia by its rivals at Polyrínia. The tactic of setting Cretan against Cretan served him well, but even so it took almost three years of bitter and brutal warfare before the island was subdued in 67 BC. It was a campaign marked by infighting not only among the Cretans – Górtys was among those to take Metellus's side – but also between Romans, with further forces sent from Rome in an unsuccessful bid to curb Metellus's excesses and his growing power.

With the conquest complete, peace came quickly and was barely disturbed even in the turbulent years of Julius Caesar's rise and fall. Perhaps this was in part because there was little immediate change in local administration, which was simply placed under Roman supervision. At the same time, the end of the civil wars brought much greater prosperity: Crete was combined with Cyrenaica (in North Africa) as a single province whose capital was at **Górtys**, and though there was little contact between the two halves of the province, both were important sources of grain and agricultural produce for Rome.

Through the first and second centuries AD, important public works were undertaken throughout Crete: roads, aqueducts and irrigation systems, important cities at Knossós, Áptera, Lyttos and others, as well as considerable grandeur at Górtys. **Christianity** arrived with St Paul's visit around 60 AD; soon after, he appointed Titus as the island's first bishop to begin the conversion in earnest. Around 250 AD, the Holy Ten – Áyii Dhéka – were martyred at Górtys, probably during the first great persecution of the Christians initiated by the Emperor Decius.

The Byzantine Age

With the split of the Roman Empire at the end of the fourth century, Crete found itself part of the Eastern Empire under **Byzantium**. The island continued to prosper – as the

1645	1669	1669–1898
Turks capture Haniá.	Iráklio surrenders.	Turkish rule. Mosques and fountains constructed in the cities, especially Haniá, Réthymno and Ierápetra, but few public works undertaken elsewhere.

churches that were built everywhere testify – but in international terms it was not important. Byzantine rule, here as everywhere, imposed a stiflingly ordered society, hierarchical and bureaucratic in the extreme. Of the earliest churches only traces survive, in particular of mosaic floors like those at Soúyia or Thrónos, though there are more substantial remains at Górtys, of the basilica of Áyios Títos.

Then in 824 Crete was invaded by a band of **Arabs** under Abu Hafs Omar. Essentially a piratical group who had been driven first from Spain and then Alexandria, they nevertheless managed to keep control of the island for well over a century. There was not much in the way of progress at this time – for its new masters the island was primarily a base from which to raid shipping and launch attacks on the Greek mainland and other islands – but there was a fortress founded at al-Khandak, a site that later developed into Iráklio. At the same time Górtys and other Byzantine cities were sacked and destroyed.

After several failed attempts, the Byzantine general **Nikiforas Fokas** reconquered Crete in 961, following a siege at Khandak in which he catapulted the heads of his Arab prisoners over the walls. For a while the island revived, boosted by an influx of colonists from the mainland and from Constantinople, including a number of aristocratic families (the Arhontopouli) whose power survived throughout the medieval era. By now, however, the entire empire was embattled by Islam and losing out in trade to the Venetians and Genoese. Frescoed churches continued to be built, but most were small and parochial.

Ironically enough it was not Muslims who brought about the final end of Byzantine rule, but Crusaders. The **Fourth Crusade** turned on Constantinople in 1204 (at the instigation of the Venetians), sacking and burning the city. The leader of the Crusade, Prince Boniface of Montferrat, ceded Crete to the Venetians for a nominal sum.

Venetian Crete

Before Venice could claim its new territory, it had to drive out its chief commercial rivals, the **Genoese**, who had taken control in 1206 with considerable local support. By 1210 the island had been secured, though for more than a century thereafter the Genoese pursued their claim, repeatedly siding with local rebels when it looked like there was a chance of establishing a presence on the island.

The Venetians, however, were not going to surrender the prize lightly. Crete for them was a vital resource, both for the control of eastern Mediterranean trade routes that the island's ports commanded, and for the natural wealth of the agricultural land and the timber for shipbuilding. The Venetian system was rapidly and stringently imposed, with Venetian overlords, directly appointed from Venice, administering what were effectively a series of feudal fiefdoms.

It was a system designed to exploit Crete's resources as efficiently as possible, and not surprisingly it stirred up deep resentment from the beginning. There were constant **rebellions** throughout the thirteenth century, led as often as not by one or other of the aristocratic Byzantine families from an earlier wave of colonization. Certainly the wealthy had most to lose: it was their land that was confiscated to be granted to military colonists from Venice (along with the service of the people who lived on it), and their rights and privileges that were taken over by the new overlords. The rebellions

1770	1821	1828
Revolt of Dhaskaloyiannis in Sfakiá; he is defeated and executed at Iráklio.	Greek War of Independence declared. Island repressed by Turkish and Egyptian troops with much bloodshed.	Major battle between Cretans and Turkish forces at Frangokástello fort; more than a thousand killed.

were in general strictly noble affairs, ended by concessions of land or power to their Cretan leaders. But there were more fundamental resentments too. Heavy taxes and demands for feudal service were widely opposed – by the established colonists almost as much as by the natives. And the **Orthodox Church** was replaced by the Roman as the "official" religion, the senior clergy expelled and much Church property seized. Local priests and monasteries that survived helped fuel antagonism: even from this early date the monasteries were becoming known as centres of dissent.

In the mid-fourteenth century, one of the most serious revolts yet saw the Cretans and second-generation Venetian colonists fighting alongside each other, in protest at the low fixed prices for their produce, steep taxes and the continued privileges granted to "real" Venetians. Although on this occasion the revolt was suppressed particularly fiercely, the end result of this and the other rebellions was a gradual relaxation of the regime and integration of the two communities – or at least their leaders. The **Middle Ages** were perhaps the most productive years in Crete's history, with exports of corn, wine, oil and salt, the ports busy with trans-shipment business and the wooded hillsides being stripped for timber.

After 1453, and the final fall of Constantinople, Crete saw a spectacular cultural renaissance as a stream of refugees arrived from the east. **Candia** – as the island and its capital were known to the Venetians – became the centre of Byzantine art and scholarship. From this later period, and the meeting of the traditions of Byzantium and the Italian Renaissance, come the vast majority of the works of art and architecture now associated with the Venetian era. The great icon painter Dhamaskinos studied alongside El Greco in the school of Ayía Ekateríni in Iráklio; the Orthodox monasteries flourished; and in literature the island produced, among others, what is now regarded as its greatest work – the *Erotókritos* (see p.354).

But it was the growing **external threat** that stimulated the most enduring of the Venetian public works – the island defences. Venice's bastions in the mainland Middle East had fallen alongside Constantinople, and in 1573 Cyprus too was taken by the Turks, leaving Crete well and truly in the front line. Large-scale pirate raids had already been common: in 1538 Barbarossa had destroyed Réthymno and almost taken Haniá, and in the 1560s there were further attacks. Across the island, cities were strengthened and the fortified islets defending the seaways were repaired and rebuilt. As the seventeenth century wore on, however, Venice itself was in severe decline: Mediterranean trade was overshadowed by the New World, a business dominated by the Spanish, English and Dutch.

Finally, in 1645 an attack on an Ottoman convoy provided the excuse for an all-out **Turkish assault** on Crete. Haniá fell after a siege that cost forty thousand Turkish lives, and Réthymno rapidly followed. By 1648 the Turks controlled the whole island except **Iráklio** and they settled down to a long siege. For 21 years the city resisted, supplied from the sea and with moral support at least from most of Europe. The end was inevitable, though, and from the Turkish point of view there was no hurry: they controlled the island's produce, they were well supplied, and they enjoyed a fair degree of local support, having relaxed the Venetian rules – for example, they allowed Orthodox bishops back into Crete. By 1669 the city was virtually reduced, and in a final effort the pope managed to persuade the French to send a small army. After a couple of fruitless sorties involving heavy losses, the French withdrew in an argument

1864	**1866**
Elefthérios Venizélos, Cretan revolutionary and statesman, born at Mournies, near Haniá.	Explosion at Arkádhi, a Cretan guerrilla stronghold. Hundreds die in blast and international sympathy for Crete is aroused.

over the command. On September 5, Iráklio surrendered, leaving only the three
fortified islets of Soúdha, Spinalónga and Gramvóusa in Venetian hands, where they
remained until surrendered by treaty in 1715.

Turkish Crete

It is arguable whether the **Turkish occupation** was ever as stringent or arduous as the
Venetian had been, but its reputation is far worse. In part this may simply be that its
memory is more recent, but Turkish rule was complicated too by the religious
differences involved, and by the fact that it survived into the era of resurgent Greek
nationalism and Great Power politics.

If on their arrival the Turks had been welcomed, it was not a long-lived honeymoon.
Once again Crete was divided, now between powerful pashas, and once again it was
regarded merely as a resource to be exploited. The Ottoman Empire was less strictly
ordered than the Venetian, but it demanded no less: rather than attempt to take control
of trade themselves, the Turks simply imposed crippling taxes. There were fewer
colonists than in the Venetian era, and they took far less interest in their conquest so
long as the money continued to come in. Very little was reinvested: outside the cities
there was hardly any building at all, and roads and even defences fell into gradual
disrepair. Imposition of local administration was left to local landlords and the
mercenary **Janissaries** they controlled. At the local level, then, there was a further level
of exploitation as these men too took their cut. Stultified by heavy taxes and tariffs,
slowed by neglect, the island economy stagnated.

One way to avoid the worst of the burden was to become a Muslim and, gradually,
the majority of the Christian population was converted to **Islam** – at least nominally.
Conversion brought with it substantial material advantages in taxation and rights to
own property, and it helped avoid the worst of the repression that inevitably followed
any Christian rebellion. These Greek Muslims were not particularly religious: even
among the Turks on the island, Islamic law seems to have been loosely interpreted, and
many continued to worship as Christians in secret, but the mass apostasies served to
further divide the island. For those who remained openly Christian the burden became
increasingly heavy as there were fewer to bear it. Many took to the mountains, where
Turkish authority barely reached.

As the occupation continued, the Turks strengthened their hold on the cities and the
fertile plains around them, while the mountains became the stronghold of the
Christian *pallikáres*. The first major **rebellion** came in 1770, and inevitably it was
centred in Sfakiá. Under **Dhaskaloyiannis** (see p.284) the Cretans had been drawn into
Great Power politics – drawn in and abandoned, for the promised aid from Russia
never came. With the failure of this struggle, Sfakiá was itself brought under Turkish
control for a while. But a pattern had been set, and the nineteenth century saw an
almost constant struggle for independence.

The War of Independence

At the beginning of the nineteenth century the Ottoman Empire was under severe
pressure on the Greek mainland, and in 1821 full-scale revolution, the **Greek War of
Independence**, broke out. Part of the Turkish response was to call on the pasha of

1883

Nikos Kazantzákis, Crete's most famous writer
and creator of Zorba the Greek, born in Iráklio.

1894

British archeologist Arthur Evans arrives in Crete
and visits the site of Knossós that would later
bring him worldwide fame.

Egypt, **Mehmet Ali**, for assistance: his price was control of Crete. By 1824, in a campaign that even by Cretan standards was brutal on both sides, he had crushed the island's resistance. When in 1832 an independent Greek state was finally established with the support of Britain, France and Russia, Crete was left in the hands of the Egyptians, reverting to Turkish control within ten years.

From now on guerrilla warfare in support of union with Greece – **énosis** – was almost constant, flaring occasionally into wider revolts but mostly taking the form of incessant raids and irritations. The Cretans enjoyed widespread support, not only on the Greek mainland but throughout western Europe, and especially among expatriate Greek communities. But the Greeks alone were no match for the Ottoman armies, and the Great Powers, wary more than anything of each other, consistently failed to intervene. There was a major rising in 1841, bloodily suppressed, and in 1858 another which ended relatively peacefully in the recall of the Turkish governor and some minor concessions to the Christian population.

In 1866 a Cretan Assembly meeting in Sfakiá declared independence and union with Greece, and Egyptian troops were recalled to put down a further wave of revolts bolstered by Greek volunteers. Again the Egyptians proved ruthlessly effective, but this campaign ended in the explosion at **Arkádhi** (see p.191), an act of defiance that aroused Europe-wide sympathy. The Great Powers – Britain above all – still refused to involve themselves, but privately the supply of arms and volunteers to the insurgents was redoubled. From now on some kind of solution seemed inevitable, but even in 1878 the Congress of Berlin left Crete under Turkish dominion, demanding only further reforms in the government. In 1889 and 1896 there were further violent encounters, and in 1897 a Greek force landed to annex the island. Finally, the Great Powers were forced into action, occupying Crete with an international force and dividing the island into areas controlled by the British, French, Russians and Italians.

Independence and union with Greece

The outrage that finally brought about the expulsion of Turkish troops from Crete in 1898 was a minor skirmish in Iráklio (see p.53) that led to the death of the British vice-consul. A **national government** was set up, still nominally under Ottoman suzerainty, with Prince George, younger son of King George of Greece, as high commissioner; under him was a joint Muslim-Christian assembly, part elected, part appointed.

Euphoria at independence was muted, however, for full union with Greece remained the goal of most Cretans. A new leader of this movement rapidly emerged – **Eleftherios Venizélos**. Born at Mourniés, outside Haniá, Venizélos had fought in the earlier independence struggles, and become a member of the Cretan Assembly and minister of justice to Prince George. Politically, however, he had little in common with his new master, and in 1905 he summoned an illegal Revolutionary Assembly at Thériso. Though the attempt to take up arms was summarily crushed, the strength of support for Venizélos was enough to force the resignation of Prince George. In 1908, the Cretan Assembly unilaterally declared *énosis* – much to the embarrassment of the Greek government. For, in the meantime, the "Young Turk" revolution looked set to revitalize the Ottoman Empire, and the Great Powers remained solidly opposed to anything that might upset the delicate balance of power in the Balkans.

1897	**1898**
Great Powers occupy Crete after more uprisings; island divided into British, French, Russian and Italian sectors.	Riot in Iráklion precipitates end of Turkish rule. Independence follows with Prince George acting under Ottoman suzerainty.

The failure of the Greek government to act decisively in favour of Crete was one of the factors that led to the Military League of young officers forcing political reform on the mainland. With their backing, Venizélos became premier of Greece in 1910. In 1912 Greece, Serbia and Bulgaria declared war on the Ottoman Empire, making spectacular advances into Turkish territory. By the peace of 1913, Crete finally and officially became part of the Greek nation.

Though Greece was politically riven by **World War I**, and succeeding decades saw frequent, sometimes violent changes of power between Venizelist and Royalist forces, Crete was little affected. On just one further occasion did the island play a significant role in Greek affairs before the outbreak of war in 1940: in July 1938 there was a popular uprising against the dictator Metaxas and in favour of Venizélos, but it was swiftly put down.

The island was, however, hit hard by the aftermath of the disastrous Greek attempt to conquer Istanbul in pursuit of the "Great Idea" of rebuilding the Byzantine Empire. As part of the peace settlement that followed this military debacle, there was a forced **exchange of populations** in 1923: Muslims were expelled from Greece and Orthodox Christians from Turkey. In Crete many of these "Turks" were in fact Muslim Cretans, descendants of the mass apostasies of the eighteenth century. Nevertheless they left – some thirty thousand in all – and a similar number of Christian refugees from Turkey took their place.

World War II and occupation

In the winter of 1940 Italian troops invaded northern Greece, only to be thrown back across the Albanian border by the Greek army. Mussolini's humiliation, however, only served to draw the Germans into the fight, and although an Allied army was sent to Greece, the **mainland** was rapidly overrun.

The Allied campaign was marked from the start by suspicion, confusion and lack of communication between the two commands. On the Greek side Metaxas had died in January, and his successor as premier committed suicide, leaving a Cretan – **Emanuel Tsouderos** – to organize the retreat of king and government to his native island. They were rapidly followed by thousands of evacuees, including the bulk of the Allied army, a force made up in large part of Australian and New Zealand soldiers. Most of the native Cretan troops, a division of the Greek army, had been wiped out in defence of the mainland.

According to the Allied plan, Crete should by now have been an impregnable fortress. In practice, though, virtually nothing had been done to improve the island defences, there were hardly any serviceable planes or other heavy equipment, and the arriving troops found little in the way of a plan for their deployment.

On May 20, 1941 the **invasion** of the island began, as German troops poured in by glider and parachute. It was at first a horrible slaughter, with the invaders easily picked off as they drifted slowly down. Few of the first wave of parachutists reached the ground alive and many of the gliders crashed, while the main German force was smashed before it ever reached the ground. In the far west, however, beyond the main battle zone, they succeeded in taking the airfield at Máleme. Whether through incompetence (as much of the literature on the Battle of Crete suggests) or breakdown

1898–1913	1905	1908
Independence and emergence of Venizélos who summons a Revolutionary Assembly at Thériso urging full union (*énosis*) with Greece.	The unpopular Prince George resigns.	Crete unilaterally declares *énosis*, which is opposed by the Great Powers.

of communications, no attempt to recapture the field was made until the Germans had had time to defend it and, with a secure landing site, reinforcements and equipment began to pour in. Not long before the battle, the German codes had been cracked, and the Allied commander in Crete, General Freyberg, therefore knew in detail exactly where and how the attacks would come. However, because he was not allowed to divulge secret intelligence findings to his junior officers (who were not cleared to receive them) a fatal misunderstanding by the commander regarding the enemy's intentions contained in the intelligence led him to reduce the forces at Máleme. From now on the battle, which had seemed won, was lost, and the Allied troops, already under constant air attack, found themselves outgunned on land too.

Casualties of the **Battle of Crete** were horrendous on both sides – the cemeteries are reminiscent of the burial grounds of World War I victims in northern France – and the crack German airborne division was effectively wiped out, causing a devastated Hitler to erect the monument to it which still stands outside Haniá (although recently damaged by protesters). No one ever attempted a similar assault again. But once they were established with a secure bridgehead, the Germans advanced rapidly, and a week after the first landings the Allied army was in full retreat across the mountains towards Hóra Sfakíon, from where most were evacuated by ship to Egypt. On May 30, the battle was over, leaving behind several thousand Allied soldiers (and all the Cretans who had fought alongside them) to surrender or take to the mountains.

The resistance

One of the first tasks of **the resistance** was to get these stranded soldiers off the island, and in this they had remarkable success, organizing the fugitives into groups and arranging their collection by ship or submarine from isolated beaches on the south coast. Many were hidden and fed by monks while they waited to escape, most famously at the monastery of Préveli. In this and many other ways the German occupation closely mirrored earlier ones; opposition was constant and reprisals brutal. The north coast and the lowlands were, as in the past, easily and firmly controlled, but the mountains, and Sfakiá above all, remained the haunt of rebel and resistance groups throughout the war.

With the boats that took the battle survivors away from Crete came intelligence officers whose job it was to organize and arm the resistance; throughout the war there were a dozen or so on the island, living in mountain shelters or caves, attempting to organize parachute drops of arms and reporting on troop movements on and around the island. How effective the sporadic efforts of the resistance were in wartime Crete is hard to gauge and it is questionable whether stunts such as the kidnapping of General Kreipe (see box, p.340) brought the end of the war any nearer.

At the end of 1944, the German forces withdrew to a heavily fortified perimeter around Haniá, where they held out for a final seven months before surrendering. In the rest of the island, this left a **power vacuum** that several of the resistance groups rushed to fill. Allied intelligence would no doubt claim that one of the achievements of their agents in Crete was the near-avoidance of the civil war that wracked the rest of Greece. On the mainland the organization of the resistance had been very largely the work of Greek Communists, who emerged at the end of the war as much the best organized and armed group. On Crete, groups in favour with the Allies had been the best armed

1913	1923
Following First Balkan war by Greece and allies against Ottoman Turkey, union of Greece and Crete is formally declared.	Forced exchange of populations between Greece and Turkey following Greek military debacle in the Greco-Turkish war; 30,000 Muslim Cretans expelled.

THE KIDNAP OF GENERAL KREIPE

The Cretan resistance to the Nazi occupation had one spectacular success in 1944 when they kidnapped the German commander **General Kreipe** outside Iráklio, and succeeded in smuggling him over the mountains to the south coast and off the island to Egypt. Among this group were the author Patrick Leigh Fermor and Stanley Moss (whose *Ill Met by Moonlight* describes the incident in detail). The immediate result of this propaganda coup, however, was a terrible vengeance against the Cretan population, in which a string of villages around the Amári valley were destroyed and such menfolk as could be found were slaughtered. Harsh **retribution** against Cretan civilians, indeed, was the standard reaction by the German army to any success the resistance had.

and organized, and certainly in the latter stages of the war, Communist-dominated organizations had been deliberately starved of equipment. There were only a few, minor incidents of violence on the island, and these were swiftly suppressed.

Postwar and modern Crete

In avoiding the civil war, Crete was able to set about **reconstruction** some way in advance of the rest of Greece, and after 1945 it grew to become one of the most prosperous and productive regions of the nation. Politically, postwar Crete was deeply mistrustful of outside control, even from Athens, a situation that persists today. At the local level above all, loyalties are divided along clan and patronage lines rather than party political ones, and leaders are judged on how well they provide for their areas and their followers.

Cretan politicians at the local level (there is no overall island government, only a regional **administration** controlled by appointees from Athens) continue to take an almost universal joy in standing up to central authority. In one famous incident the mayor of Iráklio organized a sit-in at the Archeological Museum to prevent artworks being taken abroad for an exhibition: fifty thousand turned out to support him, and though President Karamanlis ordered his arrest, the national government was eventually forced to back down.

Rivalries within Crete are fierce, too, most notably between Haniá, which was nominated as capital for a short period at the beginning of the century, and Iráklio, the traditional and present capital and nowadays the richer and politically more important city. This factionalism results in all sorts of anomalies and compromises: symptomatic was the rather impractical decision to spread the University of Crete across three campuses, at Iráklio, Réthymno (which has always considered itself the most cultured town in Crete) and the autonomous polytechnic of Haniá.

In **national politics**, the island presents a more unified front as the upholder of the liberal tradition of Venizélos. The 1967 anti-left coup in Athens that brought the junta of the colonels to power was passionately opposed in Crete – one of the few areas of Greece to offer overt resistance to the regime. There followed seven years of repression during which all political activity was banned, the press heavily censored and communists arrested, imprisoned and tortured. In a referendum following the overthrow of the Colonels in 1974, Crete voted heavily against a restoration of the

1941	1944	1945
German invasion of Crete. A fatal blunder allows invaders to take the airport at Máleme and establish a bridgehead.	The island's German commander, Kreipe, is kidnapped by the resistance. The German army carries out brutal reprisals against the islanders.	Liberation. A war-shattered island begins the slow task of reconstruction.

monarchy (the king had been implicated in the coup) and for a republican system. Then, in the succeeding presidential election, support for the right-winger Karamanlis (the winner) was less than half as strong on Crete as it was in the rest of Greece. This has been an abiding pattern: PASOK has consistently polled twice as many Cretan votes as ND.

Into the new millennium

In the late 1980s and early 1990s Crete shared in the Greek and European economic downturn as a split developed between state employees (per capita Greece had two-thirds more than any other EU country) and the conservative Athens government, armed with an austerity programme to cut public expenditure. Strikes and mass protests ended with Néa Dhimokratía's crushing defeat in the general election of October 1993, and the return to power of a **PASOK government**, still led by the ageing and ailing Andreas Papandreou. The austerity programme was halted, but as Papandreou's health deteriorated he reluctantly resigned in January 1996 to be succeeded as leader by the dull technocrat **Kostas Simitis**.

Simitis's period in power was notable for two major events: **taking Greece into the single currency** (the euro replaced the drachma in 2002) and the designation of Athens as the venue for the 2004 Olympic Games. As a result of the latter decision, enormous funds flooded into the country and some of the EU's biggest infrastructure projects got under way, catapulting much of the country's transportation system straight from the nineteenth into the twenty-first century, with new railways, roads and airports such as the one at Sitía in eastern Crete.

Despite winning a further general election victory in 2000 by the narrowest of margins the political tide was turning against PASOK and the government's lack of a majority left it unable to deal decisively with any of the major problems facing the Greek economy. The trade unions wanted to maintain the status quo while the business lobby was convinced that state finances were again about to career out of control. In the latter part of 2003 a stagnant economy and a string of corruption scandals involving PASOK ministers saw a rise in support for **Costas Karamanlis**, the Néa Dhimokratía leader (and nephew and namesake of the 1970s prime minister), who overtook Simitis in the opinion polls for the first time.

Smelling almost certain defeat in the upcoming spring election of 2004, PASOK's power brokers pressured Simitis into stepping aside in favour of foreign minister **Yiorgos (George) Papandreou**, the son of the party's founder. Born in America and educated in Sweden and Britain, the open-minded, innovative and mild-mannered Papandreou gave the party new hope. However, Papandreou's charisma was not enough to destabilize the Néa Dhimokratía bandwagon – in a decisive **electoral victory** ND leader Costas Karamanlis became at 47 Greece's youngest ever prime minister. Despite a nationwide swing to the right, Crete once again stayed loyal to the PASOK cause with the socialist party polling forty percent more votes across the island than its ND rival.

The Karamanlis government proved little more successful than its predecessors in dealing with an ailing economy and rising unemployment. Still, despite industrial action by unions throughout much of 2006 and 2007 opposing labour and pension reforms, in the autumn of 2007 Karamanlis called and won a snap general election.

1960s	1967–74	1986
Tourist boom begins.	Dictatorship of the Colonels. Following their overthrow, in a referendum Crete votes heavily against a restoration of the monarchy.	Greece becomes a full member of the EU.

However, his party gained only a perilously slim two-seat majority over PASOK and it was clearly going to be difficult to impose the government's authority.

And so it proved as the ND administration reeled from one crisis to another. A string of corruption scandals linked to the government rocked the administration and in late 2008 riots broke out across the country, ostensibly against a police shooting, but which flared into a nationwide protest against the effects of the world economic downturn and frustration at the severely limited prospects for young people.

In September 2009, with the government barely clinging to power, Karamanlis called another election. Voters turned out to eject ND and **hand victory to PASOK** and its leader George Papandreou. The electorate seemed more intent on punishing Karamanlis – whose party suffered its worst-ever showing at the polls – than being persuaded by the vague promises offered by Papandreou. With repeated use of buzzwords like "competitiveness", "combating climate change", and "electronic government" Papandreou sought to project a modern image, in contrast to the rather fogeyish outgoing ND administration.

The worst of times

Any chance the new government had of dealing with Greece's ongoing problems was capsized by the financial tsunami of the **government debt crisis** that overwhelmed the country at the end of 2009. Reports that Greece had been using dubious accounting practices to hide the scale of its borrowing triggered panic among overseas investors concerned that the country would be unable to meet its debt obligations. Following numerous revisions of the debt figures, in May 2010 the Greek deficit was again revised upwards to an estimated 15 percent of GDP (against a euro limit of 3 percent), one of the highest in the world. Credit ratings agencies then downgraded Greek government bonds to junk status creating further alarm in financial markets. In order to avert a default by the Greek government, in May 2010 the EU and IMF constructed an urgent €45 billion **rescue package** with a further €65 billion to follow. The price of this funding was a harsh series of austerity measures intended to bring the government's deficit under control. These measures, consisting of public sector workforce cuts and salary reductions plus labour and pension reforms were opposed by large segments of the Greek populace and **a wave of social unrest** swept across the country with strikes and riots occurring in Athens and other cities.

Throughout 2011 Papandreou's government continued to grapple with the crisis, implementing more austerity measures as his popularity plummeted. In November, after failing to enlist the support of the other major parties to form a coalition administration, Papandreou **resigned as prime minister**. The PASOK and Néa Dhimokratía parties agreed to form an emergency government headed by former vice president of the European Central Bank, **Lucas Papademos**, until new elections could be held. In May 2012 the country went to the polls but the outcome was a stalemate in which no party was able to form a government. On June 17 new polls were held with politicians urging electors to vote responsibly to save the country. The ND under its new leader, **Antonis Samaras**, gained the most seats and on June 20 formed a coalition with PASOK under its new leader, Evangelos Venizélos. The new coalition government had a workable majority over the other parties but, worryingly for the future, these

1999	2001	2004
Greece joins eleven other EU states in creating the European Economic and Monetary Union (EMU) and a single currency, the euro.	The drachma is replaced by the euro as Greece's official currency.	Athens stages Olympic Games. Some events held in Crete.

TOURISM: THE ISLAND'S FUTURE?

As falling prices for Crete's major agricultural products – olive oil, raisins and citrus fruits – contribute less to the island's prosperity, a greater dependence on **tourism** has come to the fore. But the age of mass-market tourism is beginning to pall as the attractions of sun, beach and cheap booze along much of the coast attract mainly younger holidaymakers, who tend to move on when prices rise – as they have done as a consequence of the current financial calamity. The fallout from the global economic recession and the country's debt crisis has also taken its toll and tourism is forecast to fall by at least twenty percent over the next few years as a result of this.

Efforts to build a market in **green tourism** are in their infancy, held back by an indifference to environmental concerns by politicians, farmers and a populace that has yet to realize that environmentally organized tourism – for which the island, with its extended season, picturesque landscape and rich variety of flora and fauna is an ideal location – can be enormously profitable. The creation of an autonomous Cretan tourist authority in 2000 with a brief to promote the island should also have been a force for change, but a lack of funding by Athens has left it hamstrung.

The island has faced up to several invaders throughout its history, but the tourist invasion presents it with a new dilemma: to submerge its traditional ways in the pursuit of ever greater numbers or to try to raise the quality of its tourism and at the same time preserve Crete's unique character. The government in Athens has sent conflicting messages in recent years: on the one hand encouraging the Cretan authorities to do more to cater to ramblers, birdwatchers, naturalists and those interested in the island's archeology and history, on the other stating that funds would be available to support the development of conference centres (with golf courses attached), luxury hotels and casinos. The latter policy encouraged a British-led consortium to buy a huge tract of land at the eastern end of the island on Cape Sídheros (see p.157) with plans to build a 7000-room resort complex plus three golf courses and the inevitable conference centre. The then Néa Dhimokratía government firmly backed the project but following national and international protests by environmentalists the Athens Supreme Court finally halted it on ecological grounds in the autumn of 2009. However in 2012 the government accepted a scaled-down version of the plan (with a 2000-room resort) that is to be "fast tracked" under a new law. Other companies continue to carry out surveys related to similar schemes elsewhere. Given the island's serious economic plight, any ventures offering jobs are often keenly supported by local politicians regardless of the consequences. It's to be hoped that the current economic hurricane faced by Crete and Greece will not lay waste to much good work done over previous decades.

included extreme left and neo-Nazi groups opposed to the financial strictures "imposed by foreigners".

As we went to press at the end of 2012 Greece remains mired in recession while fresh austerity measures are applied to secure further **bail-outs** from the EU and IMF, without which the government would be unable to pay pensions and public-sector salaries. The future is hard to predict and many experts are convinced that Greece will have to leave the euro zone and devalue if it is to save itself from ruin. But exiting the euro zone is by no means risk-free and would leave its banking system in chaos with no access to foreign lending. As one economist put it "Whatever happens, it's going to be a wild and bumpy ride".

2008	2009–12	2012
Crete is badly hit by the worldwide recession.	Greek government debt crisis and a possible default threatens the stability of the world's monetary system. Crete shares in severe austerity measures to cut the nation's deficit.	Reopening of the Iráklio Archeological Museum, following a six-year closure for reconstruction.

Crete in myth

Crete is intimately associated with much of ancient Greek mythology, and in particular with Zeus, who was not only brought up on the island, but according to some ancient Cretans was buried here as well. The Dhiktean Cave, a gash on the face of Mount Dhíkti, which soars above the Lasíthi plateau, has most claims to be the birthplace of the greatest god in the Greek pantheon, and symbolizes the potent influence of Minoan Crete on the land to the north.

The birth of Zeus

According to the earliest accounts of the myth, **Zeus** was the third generation of rulers of the gods. The original ruler, Uranus, was overthrown by his youngest son Kronos. In order to prevent such a fate overtaking him, too, Kronos ate his first five children at birth. When she was bearing the sixth child, his wife, Rhea, took refuge in a Cretan cavern (a site much argued over, but most commonly assigned to the Dhiktean Cave; see p.138). Here Zeus was born, and in his place Rhea presented Kronos with a rock wrapped in blankets, which he duly devoured. Zeus was brought up secretly in the cave, his cries drowned by the **Kouretes**, who kept up a noisy dance with continuous clashing of shields and spears outside. The Kouretes, believed by Cretans to be the sons of the Earth Mother, were especially revered on the island as the inventors of beekeeping and honey as well as the hunting bow, and an inscription found at Palékastro suggests that they may well have a Minoan origin. The baby fed on milk from a mountain goat-nymph, Amalthea, one of whose horns he later made into a miraculous gift that a wish would fill with whatever was desired (hence the horn of plenty).

Having grown to manhood on Crete, Zeus declared war on Kronos and the Titans, a struggle that lasted ten years. Eventually, however, Zeus emerged as supreme ruler of the gods on **Mount Olympus**, and Kronos was banished to the Underworld. This myth has a precedent in Hittite texts of the second millennium BC that themselves had taken it over from the earlier Hurrians, a people who had settled in Syria and northern Mesopotamia. The Minoans passed it on to the Greeks.

The origin of the Cretans

The sexual prowess of Zeus led him into a bewildering number of affairs, one of which led to his best-known return to the island of his birth – with Europa – and the founding of the Cretan race. **Europa** was a princess, the daughter of King Phoenix (after whom Phoenicia was named), and Zeus lusted after her mightily. Approaching the shore of Phoenicia, Zeus saw her gathering flowers, and came to her in the guise of a **white bull**. Fascinated by the creature's docility Europa climbed onto its back, at which he leapt into the sea and carried her off across the sea to Crete. They landed at Mátala, travelled to Górtys (where one version has it Zeus ravished her beneath a plane tree that has never lost its leaves since) and were married at the Dhiktean Cave. One of the presents Zeus gave to his bride was **Talos**, a bronze giant who strode round the island hurling boulders at approaching strangers. Jason and the Argonauts were greeted by a hail of stones from Talos when they approached Crete. Aided by their companion, the sorceress Medea, they brought about the giant's fall by piercing a vein on his ankle – his single vulnerable spot – thus allowing the *ichor*, a divine fluid that served as blood, to drain from his body.

Minos and the Minotaur

The Zeus of the Europa tale, taking the form of a **bull**, is almost certainly mixed up with earlier, native Cretan gods. The sun god of Crete also took the form of a bull, and the animal is a recurrent motif in the island's mythology.

In the story of **Minos**, a bull once again has a prominent role. Europa bore Zeus three sons – Minos, Rhadamanthys and Sarpedon – before eventually being abandoned. Later she married the king of Crete, Asterios, who adopted her children. Upon reaching manhood the three brothers quarrelled for the love of a beautiful boy named Miletos (a reflection of the mores and customs of the time). When Miletos chose Sarpedon, an enraged Minos drove him from the island. However, before boarding a ship to Asia Minor, Miletos killed King Asterios. Legend associates both Miletos and Sarpedon – who joined him in Asia Minor – with the founding of Miletus (see p.134), later an important city in Greek and Roman times.

With Sarpedon removed, Minos claimed the throne and settled upon Rhadamanthys a third of Asterios' dominions. Rhadamanthys became renowned as a law-maker, appears in some tales as ruler at Festós, and every ninth year visited Zeus's cave on Mount Dhíkti to bring back a new set of laws. So great was Rhadamanthys's fame as a lawgiver that Homer tells of how Zeus appointed him one of the three judges of the dead along with Minos and Aeachus.

Minos, meanwhile, was another ruler driven by lustful passions. He liaised with a succession of lovers including the Minoan goddess **Britomartis**, whom he chased relentlessly around the island for nine months until she threw herself into the sea off the end of the Rodhopoú peninsula to escape his attentions. Rescued from drowning by the net of a fisherman, she became known as Diktynna ("of the net"), and a great temple to her was erected on the site (see p.268). Minos's wife and queen, **Pasiphae**, incensed by her rakish husband's infidelities, put a spell on the king: whenever he lay with another woman he discharged not seed but a swarm of poisonous serpents, scorpions and insects that devoured the woman's vitals. News of his affliction (which bears a striking resemblance to venereal disease) apparently got around, and one of his bedmates Prokris, daughter of the Athenian king Erechtheus, insisted that he should take a prophylactic draught before their tryst which apparently prevented her invasion by serpents and scorpions.

Earlier, when he had gained the throne of his father, Minos prayed to Poseidon (or perhaps his father Zeus) to send a bull from the sea that he could offer as a sacrifice, thus signifying the god's recognition of the justice of his claim to the throne. When the radiant bull emerged from the sea, Minos was so taken by its beauty that he determined to keep it, sacrificing in its place another from his herds. Punishment for such hubris was inevitable, and in this case the gods chose to inflame Minos's wife, Pasiphae (a moon goddess in her own right – again the bull symbolizes the sun), with intense desire for the animal. She had the brilliant inventor and craftsman **Daedalus** construct her an artificial cow, in which she hid and induced the bull to couple with her: the result was the **Minotaur**, a beast half man and half bull (probably human with a bull's head). To hide his shame, Minos had Daedalus construct the **labyrinth** in which to imprison the monster.

Theseus and Ariadne

The myth goes on to relate how Minos waged war on Athens after Androgeous, one of his sons by Pasiphae, had gone off to that city and won every event in the Panathenaic games, only to be slain on the orders of the outraged Athenian king, Aegeus. Part of the settlement demanded by the victorious Minos was that an annual tribute of seven young men and women be provided as sport or sacrifice for the imprisoned Minotaur. The third time the tribute was due, **Theseus**, the son of King Aegeus, resolved to end the slaughter and himself went as one of the victims. In Crete he met Minos's daughter

THE DEATH OF ZEUS

The postscript to these Greek myths concerns **Zeus's death**. According to the Cretans, and reflecting the older Minoan idea of a fertility god who annually died and was reborn, Zeus was buried beneath Mount Yioúhtas near Knossós, in whose outline his recumbent profile can still be seen from the palace site. It was a purely local claim, however, and clashed with the northern Greek concept of Zeus as an immortal and all-powerful sky-god. The northern Greeks regarded the islanders' belief in a dying Zeus as blasphemy, and their contempt for the Cretan heresy gave rise to the saying "all Cretans are liars".

Ariadne, who fell in love with him and resolved to help him in his task. At the instigation of the sympathetic Daedalus, she provided Theseus with a ball of thread that he could unwind and, if he succeeded in killing the Minotaur, follow to find his way out of the labyrinth.

At first everything went to plan, and Theseus killed the beast and escaped from the island with Ariadne and the others. On the way home though, things were less successful. Ariadne was abandoned on a beach in Náxos (where she was later found by the god Dionysos and carried off to Olympus). Approaching Athens, Theseus forgot to change his black sails for white – the pre-arranged signal that his mission had succeeded. Thinking his son dead, King Aegeus threw himself into the sea and drowned.

Back on Crete, Minos imprisoned Daedalus in his own labyrinth, furious at Ariadne's desertion and his part in it, and at the failure of the maze. Locked up with Daedalus was his son, **Ikarus**. They escaped by making wings of feathers – from birds devoured by the Minotaur – held together with wax. Daedalus finally reached Sicily and the protection of King Kokalos: Ikarus, though, flew too close to the sun, the wax melted and he plunged to his death in the sea. Still set on revenge, Minos tracked Daedalus down by setting a puzzle so fiendishly difficult that only he could have solved it: a large reward was promised to the first person who could pass a thread through a triton shell. When Minos eventually arrived in Sicily he posed the problem to Kokalos who said it would be easy. He then consulted secretly with Daedalus who drilled the shell at its point and tied a thread to the leg of an ant that was sent into the shell. When the insect emerged through the hole, Kokalos took the shell to show Minos. Now certain that Daedalus was hidden in the palace, Minos demanded that Kokalos hand him over. Kokalos appeared to agree to the request and offered Minos hospitality in the palace. There Minos met an undignified end when he was scalded to death in his bath by the daughters of the king, urged on by Daedalus.

Wildlife

Although the south coast of Crete is closer to Libya than it is to Athens, the island's wildlife owes much more to mainland Greece than it does to Africa. This is because Crete lies at the end of the long range of drowned limestone mountains called the Hellenic arc which make up most of the Balkan peninsula, and you need to go a long way south into the Sahara before you again find mountains as high as the Cretan ones. Crete, then, has northern Mediterranean fauna and flora across a range of habitats.

Islands tend to be short on wildlife because of their isolation from the main bulk of species on the mainland. Not so Crete – it's rich in flora and fauna, and provides the full range of Mediterranean habitats. In fact, there are over two thousand species of **plants** in Crete, of which over 180 are endemic to the island, making up nearly a third of the Greek flora, and about as many as in the whole of Britain. With the wealth of plant life come far more **insects** than you get further north. The survival of Cretan wildlife in all its richness and diversity has been facilitated by the fact that agriculture remains fairly "undeveloped". Although the pressures are mounting, in the form of widespread use of chemicals, increased water abstraction, road construction and tourist development. You won't find many birds or wildflowers among the hectares of polytunnels around Timbáki, but you will in the mountains where such methods remain uneconomic.

The only feature really lacking, as elsewhere in Greece, is **trees**. The Minoan civilization was a seafaring one, so as early as the Bronze Age there was a high demand for timber for shipbuilding. Some of the lower hills were perhaps deforested four thousand years ago, a process completed by the Venetians. Today, native forests exist only in remote uplands and gorges.

Crete's chief drawback, at least if you hope to combine nature with the rest of the island's sights and life, is the pattern of its **climate**. Because it's so far south, the summers are long and dry, and that period equates to our northern winters, when many plants shut down or die, with a corresponding decline in activity from all other wildlife. Trying to see wildflowers or birds in lowland Crete in August is a bit like going out for a nature ramble in Britain or Massachusetts in January.

Habitats

Rarely in Europe do you find such a wide range of habitats so tightly packed, or real "wilderness" areas so close to modern towns and resorts, as in Crete. Broadly speaking, you can divide the island into four major **habitats**: the coast; cultivated land; low hillsides less than 1000m; and mountains above 1000m. Crete is the only Greek island that is mountainous enough to have all four of these habitats.

Along the coast, sandy beaches and low rocky cliffs are the norm. Marshy river deltas or estuaries are rare (simply because Crete is a dry country and there aren't many rivers) but where you can find them, these wetland habitats are among the best places to look for birds.

Cultivated land is very variable in its wildlife interest, though look out for small market gardens – *perivólia* – often found on the edges of towns and villages, which are particularly good for small birds. Small hayfields can be a colourful mass of annual flowers and attendant insects in spring and early summer.

Low hillsides up to 1000m comprise much of Crete. Scrubby hillsides, loosely grazed by goats and sometimes sheep, are the most typical Mediterranean habitat, extremely rich in flowers, insects and reptiles. Botanically, they divide into two distinct types: the first is *phrígana*, and consists of scattered scrubby bushes, always on limestone, especially rich in aromatic herbs and wildflowers. You can often find *phrígana* by looking for beehives: Cretan beekeepers know where to find the thyme and rosemary that gives the local honey its wonderful flavour. The other hillside habitat is maquis, a dense, very prickly scrub with scattered trees. Of these two hillside habitats, *phrígana* is better for flowers, maquis for birds.

Mountains over 1000m are surprisingly common: three separate ranges go over 2000m, and they are responsible for much of the climate, creating rain and retaining it as snow for a large part of the year. The small upland plateaux amongst the mountains – Omalós or Lasíthi most famously – are a very special feature, with their own distinctive flora and fauna. Although the Cretan mountains don't as a rule have the exciting mammals of the mainland, they are very good for large and spectacular birds of prey.

Flowers

What you will see, obviously, depends on where and when you go. The best time is **spring**, which is heralded as early as January when the almond tree flowers, its petals falling like snow and carpeting the streets of small mountain villages. The season seriously gets under way in mid-February, however, in the southeast corner of the island, is at its peak during March over most of the lowlands (but continues well into April), and in the mountains comes later, starting in late April and going on through to June. In **early summer**, the spring anemones, orchids and rockroses are replaced by plants like broom and chrysanthemum; this ranges from mid-April in southern Crete to late July in the high mountains though these timings can vary – exceptionally by as much as a month.

Things are pretty much burnt out over all the lowlands from July through to the end of September, though there are still some flowers in the mountains. Once the hot summer is over, blooming starts all over again. Some of the **autumn-flowering** species, such as cyclamens and autumn crocus, flower from October in the mountains into December in the south. And by then you might as well stay on for the first of the spring bulbs in January.

Year-round, the best insurance policy is to be prepared to move up and down the hills until you find flowers – from the beginning of March to the end of June you are almost guaranteed to find classic displays somewhere on the island, and you'll see the less spectacular but still worthwhile autumn-flowering species from October to early December. If you have to go in July, August or September, then be prepared to see a restricted range, and also to go high up the mountains. The four habitats all have their own flowers, though some, of course, overlap.

Flower species

On the **coast** you might find the spectacular **yellow horned poppy** growing on shingled banks, and **sea stocks** and **Virginia stocks** growing amongst the rocks behind the beach. Sand dunes are rare but sometimes there is a flat grazed area behind the beach; these are often good for **orchids**. In the autumn, look for the very large white flowers of the **sea daffodil**, as well as **autumn crocuses** on the banks behind the shore.

The trees and shrubs on **low hillsides** are varied and beautiful, with colourful brooms flowering in early summer, preceded by bushy **rockroses** – *Cistaceae* – which are a mass of pink or white flowers in spring. Dotted amongst the shrubs is the occasional tree; the **non-deciduous plane tree** is an endemic variety, and the **Judas tree** flowers on bare wood in spring, making a blaze of pink against green hillsides that stands out for miles. Lower than the shrubs are the **aromatic herbs** – sage, rosemary, thyme and lavender – with perhaps some spiny species of **Euphorbia**. Because Crete is dry and hot for much of the year, you also get a high proportion of **xerophytes** – plants that are adapted to drought by having fleshy leaves and thick skins.

Below the herbs is the ground layer; peer around the edges and between the shrubs and you'll find a wealth of **orchids, anemones, grape hyacinths, irises**, and perhaps **fritillaries** if you're lucky. The orchids are extraordinary; some kinds – the *Ophrys* species – have especially fascinating and unusual flowers.

Once spring is over, these plants give way to the early summer flowering of the brooms and aromatic herbs, as well as a final fling from the annuals that sense the coming of the heat and their own death. When the heat of the summer is over, the autumn bulbs appear, with species of **crocus** and their relatives, the **colchicums** and the **sternbergias**, and finally the **autumn cyclamens** through into early December.

Mountains are good to visit later in the year. The rocky mountain **gorges** are considered to be the elite environments for plants, and house the greatest biodiversity; this is because most gorges are generally left ungrazed and undisturbed and it's often easy to find at least ten Cretan endemics without too much difficulty. The gorges are the home of many familiar garden rock plants, such as the **aubretias, saxifrages** and **alyssums**, as well as **dwarf bellflowers** and **anemones**. Look for dwarf **tulips** in fields on the upland plateaux in spring. The mountains are also the place to see the remaining Greek native pine **forests**, and in the woodland glades you will find **gentians, cyclamens** and **violets**. Above 1500m or so the forests begin to thin out, and in these upland meadows glorious **crocuses** flower almost before the snow has melted in spring – a very fine form of *Crocus seiberi* is a particularly early one. Autumn-flowering species of crocus and cyclamen should reward a visit later in the year.

Birds

More than 330 species of **birds** have been reported in Crete to date. Greece has a good range of Mediterranean species plus a few very rare ones such as the **Eleanora's falcon** and the **Ruppell's warbler**, which have their European breeding strongholds in Greece, particularly on Crete. The great thing about birdwatching in Crete is that, if you pick your time right, you can see both resident and migratory species. Crete is on one of the main fly-past routes for species that have wintered in East Africa, but breed in eastern and northern Europe. They migrate every spring up the Nile valley, and then move across the eastern Mediterranean, often in huge numbers. This happens from mid-March to mid-May, depending on the species, the weather, and where you are. The return migration in autumn is less spectacular because it is less concentrated in time, but still worth watching out for.

On the outskirts of towns and in the fields there are some colourful residents. Small predatory birds such as **woodchat shrikes, blackeared wheatears, kestrels** and migrating **red-footed falcons** can be seen perched on telegraph wires. The dramatic pink, black and white **hoopoe** and the striking yellow and black **golden oriole** are sometimes to be found in woodland and olive groves, and **Scops owls** (Europe's smallest owl) can often be heard calling around towns at night. They monotonously repeat a single "poo", sometimes in mournful vocal duets.

Look closely at the **swifts** and **swallows**, and you will find a few species not found in northern Europe: **crag martins** replace house martins in the **mountain gorges**, for example, and you may see the large **alpine swift**, which has a white belly. The **Sardinian warbler** dominates the rough scrubby **hillsides** – the male with a glossy black cap and an obvious red eye. These hillsides are also the home of the **chukar**, a species of partridge similar to the red-legged partridge found in Britain.

Wetlands and **coastal lagoons** are excellent for bird-spotting, especially at spring and autumn migration, although this habitat is hard to find. There's a wide variety of **herons** and **egrets**, as well as smaller waders such as the rare **avocet** and **marsh sandpiper** and **black-winged stilt**, which has ridiculously long pink legs. **Marsh harriers** are common too, drifting over the reedbeds on characteristic raised wings. Scrubby woodland around coastal wetlands is a good place to see migrating smaller birds such as **warblers, wagtails** and the like.

The mountains hold some of the most exciting birds in Crete. Smaller birds like the **blue rock thrush**, **cirl bunting** and **alpine chough** are common, and there is a good chance of seeing large and dramatic birds of prey. The **buzzards** and smaller eagles are confusingly similar, but there are also **golden eagles**, **Bonelli's eagles** and **vultures**. One very rare species of vulture, the **lammergeier** (or bearded vulture), is currently on the dramatically endangered list although it used to be more common in Crete than anywhere else in Europe; you may be lucky enough to spot one of the island's twenty-five remaining birds (only four breeding pairs) soaring above the Lasíthi or Omalós plateaux. It's a huge bird, with a wingspan of nearly 3m, and with narrower wings and a longer wedge-shaped tail than the other vulture you are likely to see, the **griffon vulture**.

Mammals

Cretan **mammals** are elusive, generally nocturnal, and very hard to see. Islands tend to have fewer species than the mainland and in this Crete is no exception, with about half the species that you could expect to see on mainland Greece. Even such common animals as the red squirrel and fox have never made it across the water, nor will you find large exciting mammals like wolves or lynxes in the mountains, as you might (rarely) on the mainland.

However, there are some compensations. Islands often have their own endemic species, and one in Crete is the **Cretan spiny mouse**, which is found nowhere else; if you happen to be on a rocky hillside at dusk you may see this largish mouse with very big ears and a spiny back fossicking around. The other compensation in Crete is the ancestral **wild goat** or *kri-kri*; a small population still exists in the White Mountains around the Samariá Gorge, and also on some offshore islands – but you'll be lucky if you see one outside the zoos. Apart from those, Crete has fourteen bat species, as well as **weasels**, **badgers**, **hares**, **hedgehogs**, **field mice**, **shrews** and **beech martens**.

One recent addition to the zoological record was the rediscovery in 1996 of the **Cretan wildcat** (see p.212), long thought to be either extinct or a folktale. Only a single specimen has ever been captured alive and the population status of the animal is still unknown.

There are several marine mammals that can occasionally be seen in offshore waters. The critically endangered and extremely rare **Mediterranean monk seal** breeds in a few sea caves around the island. The deep waters off the south coast of Haniá have recently become well known for a resident population of **sperm whales**. **Dolphins** – which so delighted the Minoans – can be seen all round the island but you'll be most likely to see them while on a boat or ferry.

Reptiles and amphibians

The hot, rocky terrain of Crete suits **reptiles** well, with plenty of sun to bask in and plenty of rocks to hide under, but the island's isolation has severely restricted the number of species occurring: fewer than a third of those that are found on the mainland. Identification is therefore rather easy. If you sit and watch a dry stone wall almost anywhere in the western half of the island you're bound to see the small local wall lizard, **Erhard's wall lizard**. A rustle in the rocks by the side of the road might be an **ocellated skink** – a bit like a lizard, but with a thicker body and a stubbier neck. In the bushes of the maquis and *phrígana* you may see the **Balkan green lizard**, a truly splendid bright-green animal up to 50cm long, most of which is tail – usually seen as it runs frantically on its hind legs from one bush to another.

At night, **geckoes** replace the lizards. Geckoes are small (less than 10cm), have big eyes and round adhesive pads on their toes that enable them to walk upside down on the ceiling. Sometimes they come into houses – in which case welcome them, for they will keep down the mosquitoes and other biting insects. Crete has three out of four European species. The island is also one of only a handful of places where the **chameleon** occurs in Europe, although it is extremely rare, and there are only a couple of known specimens; this may (or may not) be attributed to its camouflage skills. It lives in bushes and low trees, and hunts by day; its colour is greenish but obviously variable.

Tortoises, sadly, don't occur in Crete, but the stripe-necked **terrapin** does. Look out for these in any freshwater habitat – Lake Kournás and the Ayía bird sanctuary for example, or even in the cistern at the Zákros palace. There are also **sea turtles** in the Mediterranean: you might be lucky and see one while you're swimming or on a boat, since they sometimes bask on the surface of the water. The one you're most likely to see is the **loggerhead turtle**, which can grow up to 1m long. Crete has important breeding populations on beaches to the west of Haniá, around Mátala, and the largest (more than 350 nests) at Réthymno, but tourism and the development associated with it are threatening their future. Each year, many turtles are injured by motorboats, their nests are destroyed by bikes and jeeps ridden on the beaches, and the newly hatched young die entangled in deckchairs and umbrellas left out at night on the sand. The turtles are easily frightened by noise and lights too, which makes them uneasy cohabitants with freelance campers and discos.

The Greek government has passed **laws** designed to protect the loggerheads, and the Sea Turtle Protection Society of Greece now operates an ambitious conservation programme, but local economic interests tend to prefer a beach full of bodies to a sea full of turtles.

The final group of reptiles are the **snakes**, represented by four species, only one of which is poisonous – the **cat snake**. Even this is back-fanged and therefore extremely unlikely to be able to bite anything as big as a human, so you can relax a bit when strolling round the hillsides; most snakes are very timid and easily frightened anyway. One species worth looking out for is the beautiful **leopard snake**, which is grey with red blotches edged in black. It's fond of basking on the sides of roads and paths.

Only three species of **amphibian** occur in Crete. The **green toad** is smaller than the common toad, with an obvious marbled green and grey back. The **marsh frog** is a large frog, greenish but variable in colour, and very noisy in spring. And **tree frogs** are small, live in trees, and call very loudly at night.

Insects

There are around a million different species of insects in the world, and even in Crete there are probably a few hundred which have yet to be scientifically described or labelled. About a third of all insect species are beetles, and these are very obvious wherever you go. You might see one of the dung beetles rolling a ball of dung along a path like the mythological Sisyphus. If you have time to look closely at bushes and small trees, you might be rewarded with a stick insect or a **praying mantis**, creatures that are rarely seen because of their excellent camouflage.

The **grasshopper** and **cricket** family are well represented, and most patches of grass will hold a few. Grasshoppers produce their chirping noise by rubbing a wing against a leg, but crickets do it by rubbing both wings together. **Cicadas**, which most people think of as a night-calling grasshopper, aren't actually related at all – they're more of a large leaf-hopper. Their continuous whirring call is one of the characteristic sounds of the Mediterranean night, and is produced by the rapid vibration of two membranes, called tymbals, on either side of their body.

Perhaps the most obvious insects are the **butterflies**. Any time from spring through most of summer is good for butterfly-spotting, and there's a second flight of adults of many species in the autumn. Dramatic varieties in Crete include two species of **swallowtail**, easily identified by their large size, yellow and black colouring, and long spurs at the back of the hind wings. **Cleopatras** are large, brilliant yellow butterflies, related to the brimstone of northern Europe, but bigger and more colourful. Look out also for **Cretan Argus** – chocolate brown in colour and only found in the Psilorítis and Dhíkti mountain ranges, it is now thought to be increasingly threatened by human activity.

by Pete Raine and Stephen Roberts

Books

From Homer on, Crete has inspired an exceptionally wide range of literature, and in Nikos Kazantzákis the island has also produced one truly world-class author. Sadly, some of it is out of print (o/p), but many of the more popular titles below are widely available in Crete – although local editions tend to be shabby, and imported ones expensive. By contrast with the proliferation of ancient history, there is no book in English devoted to modern Cretan history, though there's a good general account included in Hopkins's book on the island (see below).

The more specialist titles might be more easily found at a dedicated travel bookstore or a Greek-interest bookshop: in the UK, try the Hellenic Book Service, in Kentish Town, London (☎020 7267 9499, ⊛hellenicbookservice.com). On Crete, Planet International Bookstore, Hándhakos 73, Iráklio (☎2810 289605, ✉ritio@otenet.gr), is an excellent source. If you phone or email them, they will post books out to you immediately, trusting you to pay later.

Books marked with the ★ symbol are particularly recommended.

ARCHEOLOGY AND ANCIENT HISTORY

Gerald Cadogan *Palaces of Minoan Crete*. Complete guide to all the major sites, with much more history and general information than the name implies.

John Chadwick *Linear B and related scripts*. A short version of *The Decipherment of Linear B*, in which the whole fascinating story is graphically told by Chadwick who collaborated with Ventris, the English architect who made the crucial breakthrough. The same author's *Mycenaean World* vividly describes the society revealed by the tablets.

Leonard Cottrell *The Bull of Minos*. Breathless and somewhat dated account of the discoveries of Schliemann and Evans (see p.326); easy reading.

Costis Davaras *Guide to Cretan Antiquities*. A fascinating guide by the distinguished archeologist to the antiquities of Crete (from the ancient through to the Turkish eras). Cross-referenced in dictionary form, it has authoritative articles on all the major sites as well as subjects as diverse as Minoan razors and toilet articles, the disappearance of Cretan forests and the career of Venizélos. Widely available at museums on the island.

★ **Arthur Evans** *The Palace of Minos* (o/p). The seminal work, still worth a look if you can find it.

Reynold Higgins *Minoan and Mycenaean Art*. Solid introduction to the subject with plenty of illustrations.

★ **J. Alexander Macgillivray** *Minotaur: Sir Arthur Evans and the Archaeology of the Minoan Myth*. Outstanding book by a Crete-based archeologist, which demonstrates how Evans fitted the evidence found at Knossós to his own preconception of the Minoans as peaceful, literate and aesthetic second-millennium BC Victorians. A superb read.

Paola Pugsley *The Blue Guide*. An excellent, detailed guide to the churches, archeological sites and museums across the island. However, some directions to remoter sights occasionally lack clarity.

★ **J.D.S. Pendlebury** *The Archaeology of Crete* (o/p). Still the most comprehensive handbook, detailing virtually every archeological site on the island. Pendlebury's *Handbook to the Palace of Minos* remains an excellent guide to the Knossós site by someone who – as curator after Evans's retirement – knew it inside out. A local edition has been reprinted in Crete.

Nikos Psilakis *Monasteries and Byzantine Memories of Crete* (locally published). Readable and well illustrated.

Peter Warren *The Aegean Civilizations* (o/p). A very good and concise introduction to Minoan and Mycenean Crete by one of the leading modern experts; good illustrations, but in need of a new edition.

R.F. Willetts *Everyday Life in Ancient Crete* (o/p). An interesting survey of Minoan daily life as lived in the towns, villages and farms as well as the palaces.

MODERN HISTORY AND ARCHITECTURE

Michele Buonsanti & Alberta Galla *Candia Veneziana – Venetian Itineraries Through Crete*. Useful guide to the under-documented wealth of monuments surviving from La Serenissima's four and a half centuries of hegemony over the island. Widely available from bookshops on Crete.

Richard Clogg *A Concise History of Greece*. A rigorously historical account of Greek history from its emergence from Ottoman rule to the present day, covering the wider aspects of Crete's struggle for independence and union with Greece.

★ **Adam Hopkins** *Crete, Its Past, Present and People* (o/p). Excellent general introduction to Cretan history and society with lots of interesting detail on topics as diverse as the Battle of Crete, daily life and diet, the arrival of mass tourism and medicinal wild herbs.

★ **John Julius Norwich** *Byzantium: the Early Centuries; Byzantium: the Apogee; Byzantium: Decline and Fall; A History of Venice; The Middle Sea*. The three volumes of Norwich's history of the Byzantine Empire are terrific narrative accounts, and much can be gleaned from them about Crete in this period. *History of Venice* relates the fascinating story of the rise and fall of the power that ruled Crete for four and a half centuries while *Middle Sea* charts three thousand years of Mediterranean history allowing the island's past to be seen in its wider geographical context.

★ **James Pettifer** *The Greeks: the Land and People since the War* (o/p). Excellent (if now somewhat dated) introduction to contemporary Greece. Pettifer roams the country and charts the state of the nation's politics, food, family life, religion, tourism and all points in between. Only passing references to Crete, however.

★ **Oliver Rackham & Jennifer Moody** *The Making of the Cretan Landscape*. An enthralling botanical and anthropological study of the Cretans in their environment, from antiquity to the present day, with sections devoted to the island's geological formation, vegetation, people and settlements.

WORLD WAR II

★ **Antony Beevor** *Crete: The Battle and the Resistance*. Relatively short study of the Battle of Crete, with colourful insights into the characters involved. Beevor dissects recent evidence to conclude that defeat was at least in part due to Cretan commander General Freyburg's fatal misinterpretation of an Ultra coded message leading him to divert troops away from the Máleme invasion site, critically weakening the Allied defences.

Alan Clark *The Fall of Crete*. Racy and sensational – but very readable – military history by the late maverick English politician. Detailed on the battles, and more critical of the command than you might expect from a former cabinet minister.

★ **Lew Lind** *Flowers of Rethymnon* (Efstathiadis, widely available on the island). A gripping personal account of his part in the Battle of Crete and subsequent escape by a 19-year-old Australian soldier. The carnage of the battle is rivetingly described and shining through the grim horror of it all comes the unflinching bravery of the Cretan villagers who put themselves in mortal danger of German reprisals by helping servicemen trapped on Crete – such as Lind – escape to Egypt.

W. Stanley Moss *Ill Met by Moonlight*. An account of the capture of General Kreipe by one of the participants, largely taken from his diaries of the time. Good *Boys' Own*-style adventure. Moss also translated Baron von der Heydte's *Daedalus Returned* (o/p), which gives something of the other side of the story.

★ **George Psychoundakis** *The Cretan Runner*. Account of the invasion and resistance by a Cretan participant; Psychoundakis (who died in 2006) was a guide and message-runner for all the leading English-speaking protagonists. Great, although not much appreciated by many of his compatriots who tend to dismiss him as an English lackey.

Tony Simpson *The Battle for Crete, 1941* (o/p). A very different way of looking at the subject, putting the campaign into an international context and relying heavily on oral history for details of the combat. Uncompromisingly critical of the command, and far more interesting than straight military history.

Evelyn Waugh *Officers and Gentlemen; Diaries*. Both include accounts of the Battle of Crete, and particularly of the horrors of the flight and evacuation.

TRAVEL WRITING

Edward Lear *The Cretan Journal*. Diary of Lear's trip to Crete in 1864, illustrated with his sketches and water-colours. He didn't enjoy himself much.

★ **David MacNeil Doren** *Winds of Crete*. An American and his Swedish wife find enlightenment on Crete in the early 1970s and before the arrival of mass tourism. An amusing and well-observed travelogue documenting many of the island's customs and curiosities in addition to some hair-raising brushes with Cretan physicians. Widely available at bookshops on the island.

★ **Henry Miller** *The Colossus of Maroussi*. Miller's idiosyncratic account of his travels in Greece on the eve of World War II includes a trip to Crete, where diarrhoea, biting flies and Festós palace all get bit-parts in the epic.

★ **Robert Pashley** *Travels in Crete* (o/p). The original nineteenth-century British traveller, full of erudite observations, interesting anecdotes and outrageous attitudes.

Dilys Powell *The Villa Ariadne*. The story of the British in Crete, from Arthur Evans to Paddy Leigh Fermor, through the villa at Knossós that saw all of them. Good at bringing the excitement of the early archeological work to life, but rather syrupy in style.

Pandelis Prevelakis *Tale of a Town* (Doric Publications, Athens). English translation of a native's description of life and times in Réthymno during the first quarter of the twentieth century.

J.E. Hilary Skinner *Roughing It in Crete* (1868; o/p). Great title for this account of another Englishman's adventures, this time with a band of rebels. Interesting on the less glamorous side of the independence struggle, since he spent the whole time searching for food or dodging Turkish patrols.

Christopher Somerville *The Golden Step*. Inspired by an epic (and extreme) long-distance gorge and mountain race from end to end of the island, Somerville set out to hike the same route, much of it along the loosely waymarked Pan-European E4 Footpath. Colourful descriptions of scrapes, scrambles and encounters en route make for an entertaining, perceptive and occasionally poignant tale.

★ **Capt. T.A.B. Spratt** *Travels and Researches in Crete*. Another nineteenth-century Briton who caught the Cretan bug while surveying the island's coastline, and left behind this account of its natural history, geology and archeology.

★ **Patricia Storace** *Dinner with Persephone*. Although not specifically about Crete, this is one of the best books ever written on the Greeks by a foreign author. Storace, an American poet, learned the language and went to live with, and travel among, the Hellenes for a year, delving deep into the psyche of this superficially attractive, but fiendishly complex people. Ideal holiday reading – you'll never look at the Greeks in the same light again.

Peter Trudgill *In Sfakiá*. In the 1970s British student Trudgill travelled to Crete, ending up in Hóra Sfakíon. It was the start of a thirty-year love affair during which time the author – now a Greek sociolinguist – has returned annually to the coastal village. An astute and often witty portrait of rugged Sfakiá's customs, legends, history and its equally rugged people.

FICTION

Victoria Hislop *The Island*. The former leper colony of Spinalónga forms the backdrop to this novel about a young woman discovering her Cretan roots. A potentially good story is marred by the cloying and derivative manner of its telling.

Homer *The Iliad* and *The Odyssey*. The first concerns itself, semi-factually, with the Trojan War; the second recounts the hero Odysseus's long journey home, via Crete and seemingly every other corner of the Mediterranean. Homer's accounts were in some ways responsible for the "rediscovery" of Minoan Crete in the nineteenth century, so it seems appropriate to read them here.

★ **Nikos Kazantzákis** *Zorba the Greek*; *Freedom and Death*; *Report to Greco*. Something by the great Cretan novelist and man of letters is essential reading. Forget the film that distorted the story's essentials: *Zorba the Greek* is a wonderful read on Crete that provides the backdrop to the adventures of one of the most irresistible characters of modern fiction. *Freedom and Death* is, if anything, even better.

Ioannis Kondylakis *Patouchas*. The story of a Cretan shepherd on a journey of self-discovery; a wonderfully observed and humorous fictional sketch of Turkish Crete in the nineteenth century by a little-known Cretan author. Widely available on the island.

Vitzentzos Kornaros (trans. Theodore Stefanides) *Erotokritos*. A beautifully produced English translation of the massive sixteenth-century Cretan epic poem.

★ **Mary Renault** *The King Must Die*; *The Bull from the Sea*. Stirring accounts of the Theseus legend and Minoan Crete for those who like their history in fictionalized form.

WILDLIFE AND GEOLOGY

Michael Chinerey *Collins Guide to the Insects of Britain and Western Europe*. This doesn't specifically include Greece (there's no comprehensive guide to Greek insects) but it gives a good general background and identification to the main families of insects that you're likely to see.

Stephanie Coghlan *Birdwatching in Crete* (Snails Pace Publishing, UK; order direct by email: ✉coghlansm @aol.com). Slim book detailing the best birdwatching sites throughout the island and what you may see there, with checklists. No pictures for identification though, so you'll need a guide too.

Charalampos G. Fassoulas *Field Guide to the Geology of Crete*. Excellent introduction to Crete's fascinating geology, explaining the island's geological evolution, paleography and paleontology. Superb colour photos and details of where to find many of the most interesting sites. Widely available at bookshops on the island.

Rob Gibbons *Travellers' Nature Guides: Greece*. Good general guide to the ecology, flora and fauna of Greece with a section devoted to Crete.

★ **Mullarney, Svensson, Zetterstrom & Grant** *Bird Guide to the Birds of Britain and Europe*. Outstanding guide to European birds covering most species you're likely to find in Crete. Superbly illustrated, it's a more recently published alternative to the Peterson et al volume (below).

★ **Anthony Huxley & William Taylor** *Flowers of Greece* (o/p). The best book for identifying flowers in Crete.

Peterson, Mountfort & Hollom *Field Guide to the Birds of Britain and Europe*. There's no complete guide to Cretan birds; this is one of the best general tomes – ageing but excellent.

George Sfikas *Wild Flowers of Crete*. Comprehensive

illustrated guide to the island's flora. Widely available at bookshops on the island.

Paul Whalley *The Mitchell Beazley Pocket Guide to* *Butterflies* (published in the US as *Butterflies*). A useful identification guide.

HIKING AND TRAVEL GUIDES

Anavasi *Crete Hiking Maps*. Excellent 1:25.000 scale hikers' map series with maps dedicated to the Lefká Óri, Samariá and Sfakiá, as well as the Psilorítis range and the area around Zákros; more maps are planned. Widely available at bookshops on Crete and from the website.

Bruce & Naomi Caughey *Crete off the Beaten Track*. Details a large number of walks throughout the island; available in bookstores in major towns.

Lance Chilton *Ten Walks in the Plakiás Area; Six Walks in the Georgioupolis Area* (ⓦ marengowalks.com). Well-described rambles and treks ranging from half an hour to half a day in these two scenic areas, by an experienced guide. *More Challenging Walks in the Plakiás Area* is a more recent addition. Walk updates are available on the website.

Freytag & Berndt *Crete Hiking Map*. Booklet and map pack in German, Greek and English describing twenty walks all over the island ranging from a couple of hours to full-day treks; the accompanying large-scale 1:50,000 map is admirably clear. Widely available from bookshops on the island.

★ **Jonnie Godfrey & Elizabeth Karslake** *Landscapes of Eastern/Western Crete (7th edition)*. Full of hiking and touring suggestions.

Alan Hall *Western Crete – 45 Walks in Kissamos and Sélinos*. A useful book with plenty of background detail, covering the extreme west of Crete and detailing more than forty walks of between 5km and 20km, with the majority shorter than 10km.

Loraine Wilson *Crete: The White Mountains*. Thorough guide, written by an experienced trekker, to fifty-plus hikes in the Lefká Óri. Walks range between 3km and 20km, and routes can be linked for extended treks over several days.

FOOD AND DRINK

★ **Miles Lambert-Gócs** *The Wines of Greece*. Comprehensive survey of the emerging wines of Greece with plenty of fascinating historical detail; a chapter is devoted to Cretan wines. Now in need of an update.

Konstantinos Lazarakis *The Wines of Greece*. More up to date than the Lambert-Gócs work (above), this is a comprehensive survey of the rapidly changing Greek wine world detailing what's new and where to find the rising stars.

★ **Maria and Nikos Psilakis** *Cretan Cooking*. Highly recommended guide to the Cretan kitchen – if only these dishes were generally available in the island's tavernas. The authors have gathered recipes from all parts of the island and interspersed with them illustrations not only of the food but of rural life past and present. Widely available on the island.

Language

So many Cretans have been compelled by poverty and other circumstances to work abroad, especially in the English-speaking world, that you'll find someone who speaks some English in almost every village. Add to that the thousands attending language schools or working in the tourist industry – English is the lingua franca of the north coast – and it's easy to see how so many visitors come back having learnt only half a dozen words between them. You can certainly get by this way, even in quite out-of-the-way places, but it isn't very satisfying.

Greek is not an easy language for English-speakers, but it is a beautiful one, and even a brief acquaintance will give you some idea of the debt western European languages owe to it. And the willingness to say even a few words will transform your status from that of *touristas* to the honourable one of *kséno*, a word which can mean stranger, traveller and guest all rolled into one.

Alphabet and grammar

On top of the usual difficulties of learning a new language, Greek presents the added problem of an entirely separate **alphabet**. Despite initial appearances, this is in practice fairly easily mastered and is a skill that will help enormously if you are going to get around independently (see box, p.362). In addition, certain combinations of letters have unexpected results. This book's transliteration system should help you make intelligible noises but you have to remember that the correct **stress** – marked in the book with an accent – is absolutely crucial. With the right sounds but the wrong stress people will either fail to understand you, or else understand something quite different from what you intended.

Greek **grammar** is more complicated still: nouns are divided into three genders, all with different case endings in the singular and in the plural, and all adjectives and articles have to agree with these in gender, number and case. (All adjectives are cited in the neuter form in the following lists.) Verbs are even worse. To begin with at least, the best thing is simply to say what you know the way you know it, and never mind the niceties. If you worry about your mistakes, you'll never say anything.

Useful words and phrases

TALKING TO PEOPLE

Hello	Yá sas/yá sou (polite/ informal) or Hérete	I (don't) understand	(Dhen) katalavéno
		Speak slower, please	Parakaló, miláte pió sigá
How are you?	Ti kánis/ti kánete?		
I'm fine	Kalá íme	How do you say it in Greek?	Pos léyete sta Eliniká?
And you?	Ke esís?		
What's your name?	Pos se léne?	I don't know	Dhen kséro
My name is…	Me léne…	Let's go	Páme
Yes	né	See you tomorrow	Tha se dho ávrio
Certainly	málista	See you soon	Kalí andhámosi
No	óhi	Good morning	Kalí méra
Please	parakaló	Good evening	Kalí spéra
OK, agreed	endáksi	Goodnight	Kalí níkhta
Thank you (very much)	Efharistó (polí)	Goodbye	Adhío

| Excuse me, do you speak English? | Parakaló, mípos miláte angliká? | Please help me | Parakaló, na me voithíste |
| | | Sorry/excuse me | Signómi |

QUESTIONS

To ask a question, it's simplest to start with *parakaló*, then name the thing you want in an interrogative tone.

May I have a kilo of oranges?	Parakaló, éna kiló portokália?	why?	yatí?
where?	pou?	at what time...?	ti óra ?
how?	pos?	what is/which is...?	ti íne/pió íne..?
how many?	póssi/pósses?	How much (does it cost)?	póso káni?
how much?	póso?	What time does it open/close?	Tí óra aníyi/ klíni?
when?	póte?		

ESSENTIALS

today	símera	big/small	megálo/ mikró
tomorrow	ávrio	cheap/expensive	ftinó/akrivó
more	perisótero	hot/cold	zestó/krío
less	ligótero	with/without	mazí/horís
a little	lígo	quickly/slowly	grígora/sigá
a lot	polí	Mr/Mrs/Miss	Kírios/Kiría/Dhespinís

OTHER NEEDS

to eat/drink	trógo/píno	bank	trápeza
bakery	foúrnos, psomádhiko	money	leftá/hrímata
pharmacy	farmakío	toilet	toualéta
post office	tahidhromío	police	astinomía
stamps	gramatósima	doctor	iatrós
petrol station	venzinádhiko	hospital	nosokomío

ACCOMMODATION

hotel	ksenodhohío	for one/two/three nights	ya mía/dhío/trís vradhiés
a room	éna dhomátio	with a double bed	me megálo kreváti
We'd like a room for two	Parakaló, éna dhomátio ya dhío átoma	with a shower	me doús
		hot water	zestó neró
for one/two/three people	ya éna/dhío/tría átoma	cold water	krío neró
		Can I see it?	Boró na to dho?

GREEK'S GREEK

There are numerous words and phrases that you will hear constantly, even if you rarely have the chance to use them. These are a few of the most common.

Éla!	Come (literally), but also Speak to me! You don't say! etc.
Oríste?	What can I do for you?
Bros!	Standard phone response
Ti néa?	What's new?
Ti yínete?	What's going on (here)?
Étsi k'étsi	So-so
Ópa!	Whoops! Watch it!
Po-po-po!	Expression of dismay or concern, like French "O la la!"
Pedhí mou	My boy/girl, sonny, friend, etc.
Maláka(s)	Literally "wanker", but often used (don't try it!) as an informal address
Sigá sigá	Take your time, slow down
Kaló taxídhi	Bon voyage

| Can we camp here? | Boróume na váloume ti skiní edhó? | tent | skiní |
| campsite | kamping/kataskínosi | youth hostel | ksenodhohío neótitos |

ON THE MOVE

airplane	aeropláno	I'm going to...	Páo sto...
bus	leoforío	I want to get off at...	Thélo na katévo sto...
car	aftokínito	Can you show me the	Parakaló, o dhrómos ya ?
motorbike, moped	mihanáki, papáki	road to...?	
taxi	taksí	Where is the bakery?	Parakaló, o foúrnos?
ship	plío/vapóri/karávi	near	kondá
bicycle	podhílato	far	makriá
hitching	otostóp	left	aristerá
on foot	me ta pódhia	right	dheksiá
trail	monopáti	straight ahead	katefthía
bus station	praktorío leoforíon	a ticket to...	éna isistírio ya...
bus stop	stási	a return ticket	éna isistírio me epistrofí
harbour	limáni	beach	paralía
What time does it leave?	Ti óra févyi?	cave	spiliá
What time does it arrive?	Ti óra ftháni?	centre (of town)	kéndro
How many kilometres?	Pósa hiliómetra?	church	eklissía
How many hours?	Pósses óres?	sea	thálassa
Where are you going?	Pou pas?	village	horió

NUMBERS

1	énas/éna/mía	40	saránda
2	dhío	50	penínda
3	trís/tría	60	eksínda
4	tésseres/téssera	70	evdhomínda
5	pénde	80	ogdhónda
6	éksi	90	enenínda
7	eftá	100	ekató
8	okhtó	150	ekatón penínda
9	ennéa	200	dhiakóssies/ia
10	dhéka	500	pendakóssies/ia
11	éndheka	1000	hílies/ia
12	dhódheka	2000	dhío hiliádhes
13	dhekatrís	1,000,000	éna ekatomírio
14	dhekatésseres	first	próto
20	íkosi	second	dhéftero
21	íkosi éna	third	tríto
30	triánda		

TIME AND DAYS OF THE WEEK

Monday	Dheftéra	What time is it?	Ti óra íne?
Tuesday	Tríti	One/two/three o'clock	Mía/dhío/trís óra/óres
Wednesday	Tetárti	Twenty to four	Tésseres pará íkosi
Thursday	Pémpti	Five past seven	Eftá ke pénde
Friday	Paraskeví	Half past eleven	Éndheka ke misí
Saturday	Sávato	half-hour	misí óra
Sunday	Kiriakí	quarter-hour	éna tétarto

MONTHS AND SEASONAL TERMS

You may see Katharévoussa, or hybrid, forms of the months written on timetables or street signs; these are the spoken forms.

January	Yennáris	August	Ávgoustos
February	Fleváris	September	Septémvris
March	Mártis	October	Októvrios
April	Aprílis	November	Noémvris
May	Maïos	December	Dhekémvris
June	Ioúnios	summer schedule	Therinó dhromolóyio
July	Ioúlios	winter schedule	Himerinó dhromolóyio

Food and drink

BASICS

aláti	salt	paximádhia	twice-baked Cretan rusks softened with water and used in *dákos* or served with *mezédhes*
avgá	eggs		
boútero	butter		
fayitó	food		
(horís) ládhi	(without) oil	pipéri	pepper
hortofágos	vegetarian	piroúni	fork
kalambokísio	corn	potíri	glass
katálogo/lísta	menu	psári(a)	fish
koutáli	spoon	psomí	bread
kréas	meat	siskalísio psomi	rye bread
ládhi, eleóladho	olive oil	sídi	vinegar
lahaniká	vegetables	skórdho	garlic
lemóni	lemon	thalassiná	seafood
olikís aleseos	whole-grain/meal	thimárisio	thyme honey; highly prized on Crete
o logariasmós	the bill		
mahyéri	knife	tirí	cheese
méli	honey	yiaoúrti	yoghurt
neró	water	záhari	sugar

COOKING TERMS

Iliókafto	sun-dried	sto foúrno	baked
makaronádha	spaghetti-/pasta-based dish	tiganitó	pan-fried
psitó	roasted	tis óras	grilled/fried to order
skáras	grilled	yemistá	stuffed (squid, vegetables, etc)
sti soúvla	spit-roasted		

STARTERS, SALADS AND MEZÉDHES

angourodomáta saláta	cucumber and tomato salad	fáva	purée of split peas with onion
avgolémono	egg and lemon soup	horiátiki (salatá)	Greek salad (with olives, féta, etc)
bouréki, bourekákia	courgette/zucchini, potato and cheese pie	kalitsoúnia	pies filled with *mizíthra* cheese
dákos	barley rusks soaked in oil and tomato, often sprinkled with cheese and oregano	keftédhes	meatballs
		kolokythakeftedhes	courgette balls (fried)
		kolokythákia tiganitá	courgette/zucchini slices fried in batter
dolmádhes/dolmadhákia	stuffed vine leaves/small vine leaves	kolokithoánthi yemistá	stuffed courgette/zucchini flowers, a delicious Cretan speciality
domatosaláta	tomato salad		
eliés	olives	láhano-karóto saláta	cabbage and carrot salad
fasoládha	bean soup	maroúli saláta	lettuce salad

THE MINOAN DIET

Like today's islanders, the Minoans ate the wild plants and herbs that grow in the hills and mountains (known by modern Cretans as *hórta*) as well as a variety of grains and pulses. Lovers of **seafood**, they also fished the seas around the island's coast for many of the varieties familiar to modern diners in the island's tavernas: *tsipoúra*, *sargós* and *fangrí* (types of bream) plus *safriós* (mackerel), *okhtapódhi* (octopus) and *ahinosalata* (sea urchins' eggs). Remains found at many Minoan sites indicate that lobster, crab, oyster, whelks and mussels were also highly regarded.

The Minoans' favourite **meats** (again as today) were sheep and goat and the Cretan passion for *tsalingária* or *cochlí* (snails) was just as strong three and a half thousand years ago. Duck and partridge were also eaten, although chicken (and their eggs) were unknown in Minoan times. The **olive** was introduced in the Neolithic period and the great *píthoi* oil containers found in the Minoan palaces testify to the importance of oil at all levels of society. The Minoans were probably just as choosy about their olive oil as islanders today and each region – as now – was no doubt renowned for its subtle differences in taste and quality.

Almonds, figs, pears, plums and pomegranates were the Minoans' preferred **fruits** and their **bread** – cooked on flat dishes using flour with little gluten (raising agent) – would be instantly recognizable to a modern Cretan as the flat *píta*, today a staple throughout Greece. Honey was the main source of sugar in Minoan times and no doubt *thimárisio* (thyme honey) was as popular then as now. The Minoans were also enthusiastic **wine** drinkers: a four-thousand-year-old winepress discovered at Vathýpetro (see p.73), at the centre of a still-working vineyard, has a fair claim to being the oldest in the world.

melitzanosaláta	aubergine/eggplant dip	**taramósalata**	fish roe pâté
melitzánes tiganités	aubergine/eggplant slices fried in batter	**tsalingária, cochlí**	snails
		tyrópita/tyropitákia	cheese pies/small cheese pies
saganáki	fried cheese		
soúpa	soup	**tzatzíki**	yoghurt and cucumber dip
spanakópita /spanakopitakia	spinach pies/small spinach pies		
		yígandes	white haricot beans

VEGETABLES

angináres	artichokes	**ladhéra**	vegetables stewed/ baked in oil
angoúri	cucumber		
bámies	okra	**melitzána**	aubergine/eggplant
briám	ratatouille of courgettes, potatoes, onions, tomato	**papoutsákia**	stuffed aubergine/ eggplant
		patátes	potatoes
domátes	tomatoes	**patátes limonátes**	potatoes baked with lemon and oil
fakés	lentils		
fasolákia	string beans	**piperiés**	peppers
hórta	greens (usually wild)	**radhíkia**	wild chicory
imám bayaldí	stuffed, oven-baked aubergine/eggplant	**rízi/piláfi**	rice (usually with *sáltsa* – sauce)
kolokithákia	courgette/zucchini	**saláta**	salad
koukiá	broad beans	**spanáki**	spinach
kremídhia	onions	**yemistés**	stuffed vegetables

MEAT AND POULTRY

agrimí stifádo	braised goat with shallots	**hirinó**	pork
arnáki me rízi	ragout of lamb with rice	**katsikáki**	kid (goat)
arní	lamb	**keftédhes**	meatballs
apákia	smoked pork loin	**kléftiko**	meat, potatoes and veg cooked together in a pot or foil; a Cretan
biftéki	hamburger		
brizóla	pork or beef chop		

	speciality traditionally carried to bandits in hiding	patsás	tripe soup, often served at Easter
kókoras krasáto	coq au vin	pastítsio	macaroni baked with meat liver
kokorétsi	liver/offal kebab	sikóti	liver
kotópoulo	chicken	souvláki	chunks of seasoned meat or fish skewered and chargrilled
kounéli	rabbit		
loukánika	spicy sausages	stifádho	meat stew with tomato and onion
moskhári	veal or yearling beef		
moussaká	aubergine/eggplant, potato and mince pie	tsalingária	garden snails
		tsoutsoukákia	meatballs in tomato sauce
païdhákia	lamb chops	vodhinó	beef
papoutsáki	meat-stuffed version of *imám bayaldí* (see "Vegetables" above)	yíros	doner kebab; sliced, spit-roasted seasoned lamb
		yiouvétsi	meat casserole with pasta

FISH AND SEAFOOD

ahini	sea urchins; briny orange roe eaten as *ahinosálata*	marídhes	whitebait
		melanoúri	saddled bream
astakós	lobster	mýdhia	mussels
barbóunia	red mullet	okhtapódhi	octopus
fangrí	sea bream	sardhélles	sardines
garídhes	prawns	sargós	white bream
gávros	anchovy	sinagrídha	dentex
glóssa	sole	skáros	parrotfish
gópa	bogue	skorpína	scorpion fish
kakaviá	bouillabaisse-style fish stew	skoumbrí	mackerel
		soupiá	cuttlefish
kalamária/kalamarákia	squid/baby squid	strídhia	oysters
kathári	black snapper	tónnos	tuna
koliós	mackerel	tsipoúra	sea bream
lavráki	sea bass	xifías	swordfish

DESSERTS, FRUIT AND NUTS

baklavá	honey and nut pastry	loukoúmia	Turkish delight; rosewater-flavoured jelly cubes dusted with powdered sugar
banána	banana		
bougátsa	creamy cheese pie sprinkled with sugar and cinnamon; a tasty Cretan speciality		
		míla	apples
fistíkia	pistachio nuts	milopita/milopitákia	apple pies
fráoules	strawberries	pagotó	ice cream
galaktobóureko	custard-cream filo pie	pastéli	sesame and honey bar
halvás	sesame-based sweetmeat	pepóni	melon
karidhópita	walnut cake	portokália	oranges
karpoúzi	watermelon	rizógalo	rice pudding
kataïfi	"angel hair" pastry filled with nuts and/or almonds	rodhákino	peach
		síka	(dried) figs
		stafília	grapes
kéik	cake	yaoúrti	yoghurt; superb in Crete and often served with honey as a dessert
kerásia	cherries		
loukoumádhes	dough fritters served hot with honey or cinnamon		

THE GREEK ALPHABET: TRANSLITERATION

Set out below is the Greek alphabet, the system of transliteration used in this book and a brief aid to pronunciation.

Greek	Transliteration	Pronounced
Α, α	a	a as in father
Β, β	v	b as in vet
Γ, γ	y/g	y as in yes when before an e or i; when before consonants or a, o or ou it's a breathy, throaty g as in gasp
Δ, δ	dh	th as in then
Ε, ε	e	e as in get
Ζ, ζ	z	z sound
Η, η	i	ee sound as in feet
Θ, θ	th	th as in theme
Ι, ι	i	i as in bit
Κ, κ	k	k sound K, k
Λ, λ	l	l sound
Μ, μ	m	m sound
Ν, ν	n	n sound
Ξ, ξ	ks	ks sound
Ο, ο	o	o as in toad
Π, π	p	p sound
Ρ, ρ	r	rolled r sound
Σ, σ, ς	s	s sound
Τ, τ	t	t sound
Υ, υ	i	ee, indistinguishable from g
Φ, φ	f	f sound
Χ, χ	h	harsh h sound, like ch in loch
Ψ, ψ	ps	ps as in lips
Ω, ω	o	o as in toad, indistinguishable from o

Combinations and diphthongs

ΑΙ, αι	e	e as in get
ΑΥ, αυ	av/af	av or af depending on following consonant
ΕΙ, ει	i	ee, exactly like g
ΟΙ, οι	i	ee, identical again
ΕΥ, ευ	ev/ef	ev or ef depending on following consonant
ΟΥ, ου	ou	ou as in tourist
ΓΓ, γγ	ng	ng as in angie
ΤΚ, γκ	g/ng	g as in goat at the beginning of a word, ng in the middle
ΜΠ, μπ	b	b at the beginning of a word, mb in the middle
ΝΤ, ντ	d/nd	d at the beginning of a word, nd in the middle
ΤΣ, τσ	ts	ts as in hits
ΣΙ, σι	sh	sh as in shame
ΤΖ, τζ	ts	j as in jam

Note: An umlaut on a letter indicates that the two vowels are pronounced separately; for example Αόös is Ah-oh-s, rather than A-ooos.

CHEESE

anthótiros	soft, full-fat unsalted cheese, similar to mizíthra	kasséri	semi-hard sheep's milk cheese
graviéra	gruyère-type hard cheese	kefalotíri	salty, hard sheep's or goat's milk cheese

ladhotíri	hard cheese matured in oil	mizíthra	sweet or savoury ricotta-style goat's or sheep's milk cheese
manoúri	mild, soft sheep's milk cheese		

DRINKS

bíra	beer	limonádha	lemonade
boukáli	bottle	neró metalikó	mineral water
frappé	cold instant coffee shaken with condensed milk until it gets a frothy head, served with ice; a Greek institution	oúzo	distilled grape spirit; the national drink of Greece
		portokaládha	orangeade
		potíri	glass
		stiniyássas!	Cheers!
gála	milk	tónik	tonic water
gálakakáo	chocolate milk	tsáï	tea
gazóza	generic fizzy drink	tsikoudhia/ráki	highly popular grappa-style firewater; the vast majority of islanders make their own which is of course "the best in Crete"
hýma (krasí)	wine from the barrel		
kafé	coffee		
koniák	brandy		
krasí	wine		
áspro	white		
mávro/kókkino	red	tsípouro	spirit; similar to oúzo
rosé/kokkinéli	rosé	yiásou!/yiámas	Cheers!/Good health!

Glossary

acropolis ancient, fortified hilltop

agora market and meeting place of an ancient city

amphora tall, narrow-necked jar for oil or wine

áno upper, as in upper town or village; eg Áno Zákros

apse curved recess at the altar end of a church

Archaic period Late Iron Age, from around 750 BC to the start of the Classical period in the fifth century BC

arsenali arsenals – a term used rather loosely for many Venetian defensive and harbour works

asklepion sanctuary dedicated to Asklepios, the Greek god of healing, where the sick sought cures for their ailments

atrium central altar-court of a Roman house

áyios/ayía/áyii saint or holy (m/f/pl), common place-name prefix (abbrev. Ag. or Ay.): Áyios Nikólaos is St Nicholas; Ayía Triádha is the Holy Trinity

basilica colonnaded "hall-type" church

Byzantine empire created by the division of the Roman Empire in 395 AD, this was the eastern half, ruled from Byzantium or Constantinople (modern Istanbul). There are many Byzantine churches of the fifth to the twelfth century on Crete, and Byzantine art flourished again after the fall of Constantinople in 1453, under Venetian rule, when many artists and scholars fled to the island

central court paved area at the heart of a Minoan palace

Classical period from the end of the Persian Wars in the fifth century BC to the unification of Greece under Philip II of Macedon (338 BC)

dhimarhío town hall (modern usage)

dhomátia rooms for rent in private houses

Dorian civilization that overran the Mycenaeans from the north around 1100 BC, and became their successor throughout much of southern Greece, including Crete

eparhía Greek Orthodox diocese, also the smallest subdivision of a modern province

Eteo-Cretan literally true Cretan, the Eteo-Cretans are believed to have been remnants of the Minoan people who kept a degree of their language and culture alive in isolated centres in eastern Crete as late as the third century BC

Geometric period Post-Mycenaean Iron Age, named for the style of its pottery: beginnings are in the early eleventh century BC with the arrival of Dorian peoples – by the eighth, with the development of representational styles, it becomes known as the Archaic period

Hellenistic period the last and most unified Greek empire, created by Philip II and Alexander the Great in the fourth century BC, finally collapsing with the fall of Corinth to the Romans in 146 BC

hóra main town of a region; literally it means "the place"

iconostasis screen between the nave of a church and the altar, often covered in icons

ipnákos Greek version of the siesta, which is widely practised in Crete, especially during the hot summer months. It usually lasts from around 1.30pm to 5.30pm. Many stores and businesses close during these hours

janissary member of the Turkish Imperial Guard: in Crete under the Turks a much-feared mercenary force, often forcibly recruited from the local population

kafenío coffeehouse/café: in a small village the centre of communal life and probably the bus stop, too

kaïki a caïque, or medium-sized boat, traditionally wooden. Now used for just about any coast-hopping or excursion boat

kámbos fertile agricultural plateau, usually near the mouth of a river

kapetánios widely used term of honour for a man of local power – originally for guerrilla leaders who earned the title through acts of particular bravado

kástro medieval castle or any fortified hill

káto lower, as in lower town or village; eg Káto Zákros

kernos ancient cult vessel or altar with a number of receptacles for offerings

krater large, two-handled wine bowl

lárnakes Minoan clay coffins

lustral basin a small sunken chamber in Minoan palaces reached by steps; perhaps actually some kind of bath but more likely for purely ritual purification

megaron principal hall of a Mycenaean palace

meltémi north wind that blows across the Aegean in summer (can be vicious in Crete). Its force is gauged by what it knocks over – "tableweather", "chairweather", etc

Minoan Crete's great Bronze Age civilization which dominated the Aegean from about 2500 to 1400 BC

moní monastery or convent

Mycenaean mainland civilization centred on Mycenae c.1700–1100 BC: probably responsible for the destruction of Minoan civilization. Mycenaean influence pervaded Crete in the late and post-Minoan periods

Neolithic the earliest era of settlement in Crete, characterized by the use of stone tools and weapons together with basic agriculture

néos, néa, néo new

nomós modern Greek province: Crete is divided into four

odeion small amphitheatre used for performances or meetings

paleós, paleá, paleó old

pallikári Literally "brave man": in Crete a guerrilla fighter, particularly in the struggle for independence from the Turks, also a general term for a tough young man

Panayía the Virgin Mary

paniyíri festival or feast, the local celebration of a holy day

Pantokrátor literally "The Almighty", a stern figure of Christ or God the Father frescoed or in mosaic in the dome of many Byzantine churches

paralía seafront promenade

peak sanctuary mountain-top shrine, often in or associated with a cave, sometimes in continuous use from Neolithic through to Roman times

períptero street kiosk

peristyle colonnade or area surrounded by colonnade, used especially of Minoan halls or courtyards

píthos (pl. píthoi) Large ceramic jar for storing oil, grain etc, very common in the Minoan palaces and used in almost identical form in modern Cretan homes

platía square or plaza. "Kentrikí Platía" means the main square

propilea portico or entrance to an ancient building

rhyton vessel, often horn-shaped, for pouring libations or offerings

stele upright stone slab or column, usually inscribed

stoa colonnaded walkway in Classical-era marketplace

theatral area open area found in most of the Minoan palaces with seat-like steps around; may have been a type of theatre or ritual area

tholos conical or beehive-shaped building, especially a Minoan or Mycenaean tomb

Acronyms

ANEK Anonimí Navtikí Evería Krítis (Shipping Company of Crete Ltd), which runs most ferries between Pireás and Crete, plus many to Italy.

ELTA The postal service.

EOS Greek Mountaineering Federation, based in Athens with branches in Haniá and Iráklio.

EOT Ellinikós Organismós Tourismoú, the National Tourist Organization.

KKE The Communist Party, unreconstructed.

KTEL National syndicate of bus companies. The term is also used to refer to bus stations.

ND Néa Dhimokratía, the Conservative party led by Antonis Samaras. Following a narrow election victory in June 2012, ND is the largest party in the current coalition government.

OSE Railway corporation.

OTE Telephone company.

PASOK Socialist party (Pan-Hellenic Socialist Movement) currently led by Evangelos Venizélos and the governing party for most of the last thirty years; finished in a humiliating third place in the elections of June 2012 and agreed to join a coalition administration with ND.

SYRIZA A radical left-wing rainbow coalition (Coalition of the Radical Left) including Maoist, Trotskyist and Green elements that narrowly lost the June 2012 election to ND; now the official opposition party.

XA (Hrisí Avgí or "Golden Dawn") Ultra-nationalist neo-Nazi party; when this guide went to press, the fifth largest party in the Greek parliament with 21 seats.

Small print and index

A ROUGH GUIDE TO ROUGH GUIDES

Published in 1982, the first Rough Guide – to Greece – was a student scheme that became a publishing phenomenon. Mark Ellingham, a recent graduate in English from Bristol University, had been travelling in Greece the previous summer and couldn't find the right guidebook. With a small group of friends he wrote his own guide, combining a highly contemporary, journalistic style with a thoroughly practical approach to travellers' needs.

The immediate success of the book spawned a series that rapidly covered dozens of destinations. And, in addition to impecunious backpackers, Rough Guides soon acquired a much broader readership that relished the guides' wit and inquisitiveness as much as their enthusiastic, critical approach and value-for-money ethos.

These days, Rough Guides include recommendations from budget to luxury and cover more than 200 destinations around the globe, as well as producing an ever-growing range of eBooks and apps.

Visit **roughguides.com** to see our latest publications.

Rough Guide credits

Editor: Samantha Cook
Layout: Anita Singh, Pradeep Thapliyal, Ankur Guha
Cartography: Deshpal Dabas
Picture editor: Marta Bescos
Proofreader: Karen Parker
Managing editor: Monica Woods
Assistant editor: Jalpreen Kaur Chhatwal
Production: Charlotte Cade
Cover design: Nicole Newman, Anita Singh

Editorial assistant: Olivia Rawes
Senior pre-press designer: Dan May
Design director: Scott Stickland
Travel publisher: Joanna Kirby
Digital travel publisher: Peter Buckley
Operations coordinator: Helen Blount
Publishing director (Travel): Clare Currie
Commercial manager: Gino Magnotta
Managing director: John Duhigg

Publishing information

This ninth edition published June 2013 by
Rough Guides Ltd,
80 Strand, London WC2R 0RL
11, Community Centre, Panchsheel Park,
New Delhi 110017, India
Distributed by the Penguin Group
Penguin Books Ltd,
80 Strand, London WC2R 0RL
Penguin Group (USA)
375 Hudson Street, NY 10014, USA
Penguin Group (Australia)
250 Camberwell Road, Camberwell,
Victoria 3124, Australia
Penguin Group (NZ)
67 Apollo Drive, Mairangi Bay, Auckland 1310,
New Zealand
Penguin Group (South Africa)
Block D, Rosebank Office Park, 181 Jan Smuts Avenue,
Parktown North, Gauteng, South Africa 2193
Rough Guides is represented in Canada by Tourmaline
Editions Inc. 662 King Street West, Suite 304, Toronto,
Ontario M5V 1M7
Printed in Malaysia by Vivar Printing Sdn Bhd

© John Fisher and Geoff Garvey, 2013
Maps © Rough Guides
No part of this book may be reproduced in any form
without permission from the publisher except for the
quotation of brief passages in reviews.
376pp includes index
A catalogue record for this book is available from the
British Library
ISBN: 978-1-40936-645-4
The publishers and authors have done their best to
ensure the accuracy and currency of all the information
in **The Rough Guide to Crete**, however, they can accept
no responsibility for any loss, injury, or inconvenience
sustained by any traveller as a result of information or
advice contained in the guide.
1 3 5 7 9 8 6 4 2

MIX
Paper from
responsible sources
FSC™ C018179

Help us update

We've gone to a lot of effort to ensure that the ninth
edition of **The Rough Guide to Crete** is accurate and up-
to-date. However, things change – places get "discovered",
opening hours are notoriously fickle, restaurants and
rooms raise prices or lower standards. If you feel we've got
it wrong or left something out, we'd like to know, and if
you can remember the address, the price, the hours, the
phone number, so much the better.

Please send your comments with the subject line
"**Rough Guide Crete Update**" to ✉ mail@uk.roughguides
.com. We'll credit all contributions and send a copy of the
next edition (or any other Rough Guide if you prefer) for
the very best emails.
Find more travel information, connect with fellow
travellers and plan your trip on Ⓦ roughguides.com

ABOUT THE AUTHORS

John Fisher was one of the authors of the first ever Rough Guide
– to Greece – and has been inextricably linked with the series ever
since, much of the time stuck in the office. Now living in London
with his wife, Adrienne, and two sons, he is a freelance writer, editor
and dispute mediator.

Geoff Garvey first came to Crete as a student of ancient history
and progressed from his study of the Minoans to develop a great
affection both for the island and its people. When away from Crete
he lives in a Spanish mountain village and is co-author of the *Rough
Guide to Andalucia.*

Acknowledgements

We are especially grateful for help on this ninth edition to publisher Nikos Karellis in Iráklio and to Professor Costis Davaras, J. Alexander (Sandy) MacGillivray and Joseph and Maria Shaw for archeological advice; thanks also to Stephen Roberts at the Natural History Museum of Crete. Special thanks as well to photographer Bastian Parschau for helping out with photos of Iráklio's impressive new archeological museum. We were also greatly assisted by Dora Georga, Alexandros Konstantinou and Kyriaki Boulasidou at the Greek National Tourist Office in London. Last, but by no means least, a big "thank you" to our editor Sam Cook who steered this edition through the inevitable storms and squalls to bring it safely into port.

John would like to thank all those who helped along the way, including Eleni Vardaki in Plakiás, Yiannis and Aspasia Katsikalakis in Palékastro, Paul, Renata and Eric at Sitia Bay, Mary Daftsidou in Eloúnda, Ioanna Sergiou in Mílatos, Yiannis and Katerina Hatzidakis in Xerókambos, Anita Pridmore and Mark Cardnell in Handhrás, Lucia Jongbloed and Xenia Samartsidi in Áyios Nikólaos, Faye Papaioannou and Nikos Sfakianakis in Hersónisos, Marina Theodoraki in Iráklio, Eva Koumartzi in Ayía Pelayía and Gloria Sivell at Cachet Travel. And as always, special thanks to A and the two Js for ruining their holidays.

Geoff would like to thank Heracles Papadakis in Spíli, Yiannis Lougiakis, Carline Harber and Eftechi Botonakis in Paleohóra, Manolis and Yiorgos Sergentakis in Kastelli Kissámou, Lucy Andonaki in Balí, Vangelis and Yiorgos Androulakakis in Loutró, Irene Michaelaki, Stavros Badoyiannis, Irene Valiraki, Ioanna Koutsoudaki and Nikos Stavroulakis in Haniá, Froso Bora in Réthymno, Gerti Vailakaki on Gávdhos, Yiorgos Saridakis, Chryssy Karelli and Yiorgos Margaritakis in Iráklio, Chrisostomos Orfanoudakis in Mármara, Gabi and Theo Schmitz-Koukounarakis in Frangokástello, Josef Schemberger in Omalós, Andonis Georgedakis in Áyios Ioánnis and Petros Marinakis at the Fournés Botanical Park. Yet another very special "efharistó para poli" must also go to Stelios Manousakas, Johanne Gaudreau and Maria Manousakas down on the farm in Argiroúpolis – here's to bumper avocado harvests in the years to come. And finally a wholehearted "dank je wel, schat" to Han for helping out yet again along Crete's highways and byways.

Readers' updates

Thanks to all the readers who have taken the time to write in with comments and suggestions (and apologies if we've inadvertently omitted or misspelt anyone's name):

Viv Aitken, Gail Baker, Angie Barker, Samantha Barton, Michael Berry, Lara Bianciardi, Yiannis Bikakis, Chris and Pat Biles, Patricia Bisset, Claire Brown, Peter Bullock, Leonora Charles, Eleni Christonaki, Mike Coleman, Frieja Current, Bob Dent, Igor Fabjan, Paul Fletcher, E.R.Francis, Edna Gallagher, Tom Gallagher, Patrick Hammett, Jane Henchley, Nigel Hicks, Catherine Higgins, Beth Hope-Cleverly, Bob Hutchinson, Lucia Jongbloed, Nick Keating, Fotis Kokotos, Kyrstyn Kralovec, David Lanfear, Linda Lashford, John Mooney, John Morgan, Patrick J Morriss, Marco Moutzanakis, Marie and Dennis Murphy, Hank Murrow,John Newstead, Jane Northcote, Antonis Paspalakis, Dave Patton, Christine Petersen, Margarita Poultidis, Anna Price, Stuart and Julia Raeburn, Ian Randall, Chris and Sheila Riley, Peter Robinson, Michael Russell, Carol Shepherd, Toby Simpson, Amalia Siskou, Martin Smith, Jasper, Joel and Claudia Stanley, Hanna Stephenson, Christine Sutton, Robert Thornberry, Hans van der Schaaf, Maurice Waite, Mike Warburton, Paul and Carrie Winstanley, Sue Wood.

Photo credits

Index

Maps are marked in **grey**

Map symbols

The symbols below are used on maps throughout the book

⊠	Post office	♜	Castle	//	Pass	♣	Tree
ⓘ	Information office	∴	Archeological site	♖	Mosque	⊕♩	Church (town/regional)
P	Parking	⌒	Cave	✡	Synagogue	▮	Building
⛽	Fuel station	⩗	Gorge	⛪	Monastery/convent	◯	Stadium
♦	Point of interest	▲	Mountain peak	⊠	Gate	⬚	Park/forest
@	Internet access	⩘	Mountain range	�	Lighthouse	▢	Beach
≍	Bridge	زليزان	Cliff	✈	Airport		
⊤	Fountain	/١١	Hill	★	Bus/taxi stop		

Listings key

■	Accommodation
●	Restaurant/café
■	Bar/club
●	Shop

ALIANTHOS
car & bike rental

ALIANTHOS welcomes you to sunny and beautiful **Crete**, an island of unique and unforgettable experiences. Our company offers high quality rent a car and rent a bike services, low prices and special internet offers.

Alianthos is a family company, founded in Plakias in 1980 with just 10 cars. Today, thanks to our great service, we are one of the largest car and bike hire companies in Crete, with a fleet of more than 800 new cars and bikes, and offices at airports and resorts across the island.

☎ +30 28320 31851 🄴 info@alianthos-group.com
Ⓦ www.alianthos-group.com